THE OXFORD

SPORTS HISTORY

THE OXFORD HANDBOOK OF

SPORTS

HISTORY

Edited by

ROBERT EDELMAN

and

WAYNE WILSON

OXFORD

UNIVERSITY PRESS

OXFORD
UNIVERSITY PRESS

Oxford University Press is a department of the University of Oxford. It furthers
the University's objective of excellence in research, scholarship, and education
by publishing worldwide. Oxford is a registered trade mark of Oxford University
Press in the UK and certain other countries.

Published in the United States of America by Oxford University Press
198 Madison Avenue, New York, NY 10016, United States of America.

Library of Congress Cataloging-in-Publication Data
Names: Edelman, Robert, 1945– author. | Wilson, Wayne, author.
Title: The Oxford handbook of sports history /
edited by Robert Edelman and Wayne Wilson.
Description: New York, NY : Oxford University Press, [2017] |
Includes bibliographical references and index.
Identifiers: LCCN 2016033956 | ISBN 9780199858910 (hardcover) |
ISBN 9780197520956 (paperback) | ISBN 9780199984749 (online resource)
Subjects: LCSH: Sports—History. | Sports—Social aspects.
Classification: LCC GV571 .O95 2017 |
DDC 796—dc23 LC record available at
https://lccn.loc.gov/2016033956

Contents

PART VI. NEW GLOBALIZATIONS AND THEIR DISCONTENTS

PART VII. RECONSIDERING ESTABLISHED CATEGORIES AND CONTEMPLATING NEW ONES

PART VIII. EMERGING AREAS OF INTEREST

Contributors

Robert K. Barney is professor emeritus of sport studies and the founding director of the International Centre for Olympic Studies at Western University in London, Canada. His thirty-five years of Olympic historical research and publication has resulted in over 150 pieces of literature: reviews, articles, chapters in books, and books, the best known of which is the coauthored seminal monograph, *Selling the Five Rings: The International Olympic Committee and the Rise of Olympic Commercialism.*

Douglas Booth is professor of sport studies and dean of the School of Physical Education at the University of Otago, New Zealand. He is the author of *The Race Game* (1998), *Australian Beach Cultures* (2001), and *The Field* (2005). Douglas serves on the editorial boards of *Rethinking History* and the *Journal of Sport History* and is an executive member of the Australian Society for Sport History.

Mauricio Borrero is associate professor of history at St. John's University in New York City. He is the author of *Hungry Moscow: Scarcity and Urban Society in the Russian Civil War* (2003) and several articles on sport and society in the Soviet Union. He is currently at work on an international biography of Lev Yashin, the legendary goalkeeper of Dinamo Moscow and the USSR national football team.

Susan Brownell is professor of anthropology at the University of Missouri–St. Louis. She is the author of *Training the Body for China: Sports in the Moral Order of the People's Republic* and *Beijing's Games: What the Olympics Mean to China*. She is editor of *The 1904 Anthropology Days and Olympic Games: Sport, Race, and American Imperialism* and coeditor (with William Kelly) of *The Olympics in East Asia: Nationalism, Regionalism, and Globalism on the Center Stage of World Sports*. She coedited (with Richard Giulianotti) the special issue of the *British Journal of Sociology* on "Olympic and World Sport: Making Transnational Society?"

Jacob J. Bustad teaches in the Department of Kinesiology at Towson University, as part of the sport management faculty. He has published research centered on urbanization, sport, and physical activity, specifically focusing on sport and urban development in Baltimore, Maryland. His research and teaching interests also include sport and globalization, as well as urban governance and physical activity opportunity.

John Carvalho is associate professor of journalism and directs the journalism program in the School of Communication and Journalism at Auburn University. He is the author of *Frick*: Baseball's Third Commissioner.*

Pascal Charitas is associate professor of sport sciences and techniques at the Research Center on the Sport and the Movement Laboratory of the University of Paris Ouest Nanterre La Défense. He is the author of several articles and essays, including "Imperialisms in the Olympics of the Colonization in the Postcolonization: Africa into the International Olympic Committee, 1910–1965" (*International Journal of the History of Sport*) and "Imperialism in the Olympics, 1910–1965: British and French Empires to the International Olympic Committee" (*Journal of Olympic History*).

Laurent Dubois is professor of romance studies at Duke University. He is the author of *Soccer Empire: The World Cup and the Future of France* and writes about soccer at his blog Soccer Politics.

Brenda Elsey is associate professor of history at Hofstra University. She is the author of *Citizens and Sportsmen: Fútbol and Politics in Twentieth-Century Chile*. Her work has appeared in the *Journal of Social History*, *The International Journal of the History of Sport*, and *Radical History Review*. Her current research examines the history of women's sport, gender, and sexuality in Latin America.

Michael T. Friedman teaches in the Department of Kinesiology at the University of Maryland, College Park. He is currently working on his first book, *Mallparks: The Social Construction of Contemporary Cathedrals of Consumption*. He has published articles in the *Sociology of Sport Journal*, *Journal of Sport History*, and the *Journal of Urban Affairs*.

Angela Gleason is assistant director of the Center for Language Study at Yale University, where she also teaches in the history department. Her research focuses on legal and social aspects of leisure in medieval Europe, which she has contributed to books and journals.

Richard Gruneau is professor of communication at Simon Fraser University. His books include *Class, Sports and Social Development*; *Hockey Night in Canada: Sport Identities and Cultural Politics* (with David Whitson); and *The Missing News: Filters and Blind Spots in Canada's Press* (with Robert Hackett). His edited or coedited books include *Popular Cultures and Political Practices*; *Artificial Ice: Hockey, Commerce and Culture* (with David Whitson); and *Mega-Events and Globalization: Capital and Spectacle in a Changing World Order* (with John Horne).

Amit Gupta is an associate professor at the US Air Force Air War College, Maxwell Air Force Base, Alabama. His most recent book is *Global Security Watch—India*.

Sayuri Guthrie-Shimizu is Dunlevie Family Professor of History at Rice University. She is a specialist on the history of United States–Asian relations. Her most recent book is *Transpacific Field of Dreams: How Baseball Linked the United States and Japan in War and Peace*.

Douglas Hartmann is professor of sociology at the University of Minnesota. He is the author, most recently, of *Midnight Basketball: Race, Sports, and Neoliberal Social*

Policy. Hartmann is also publisher and editor (with Christopher Uggen) of The Society Pages.org.

John Hoberman is professor of Germanic studies at the University of Texas at Austin. His books include *Sport and Political Ideology* and *The Olympic Crisis: Sport, Politics, and the Moral Order*.

Mike Huggins is emeritus professor of cultural history at the University of Cumbria. He has published over one hundred books, chapters, and peer-reviewed articles on the history of sport, leisure, and education and is currently writing a monograph on the cultural history of British horse racing in the long eighteenth century.

Thomas M. Hunt is associate professor in the Department of Kinesiology and Health Education at the University of Texas at Austin, where he also holds an appointment as assistant director for academic affairs at the H. J. Lutcher Stark Center for Physical Culture and Sports. With research interests that include sport law, history, and international relations, he has published articles in, among others, *The Journal of Sport History, The International Journal of the History of Sport*, and *Olympika: The Journal of Olympic Studies*. He is the author of the book *Drug Games: The International Olympic Committee and the Politics of Doping, 1960–2008*.

Erik N. Jensen is an associate professor of history at Miami University in Oxford, Ohio. His first book, *Body by Weimar: Athletes, Gender, and German Modernity*, explores the role of sports in shaping social and cultural ideals after the First World War. He is currently finishing a textbook on the Weimar Republic and working on a deep biography of the tennis player and pioneering journalist Paula von Reznicek, whose fraught identity and increasing marginalization reflected the twentieth-century Germany through which she lived.

Amy Koehlinger is an associate professor at Oregon State University. She is the author of *The New Nuns: Racial Justice and Religious Reform in the 1960s*. She is currently completing a manuscript for Princeton University Press, *Rosaries and Rope Burns: Boxing, Manhood, and American Culture*.

Donald G. Kyle is a professor of history at the University of Texas at Arlington and the author of *Sport and Spectacle in the Ancient World* (2nd ed., 2015) and various other publications on ancient sport.

Boria Majumdar is senior research fellow at the University of Central Lancashire and adjunct professor at Monash University, Australia. His books include *Twenty-Two Yards to Freedom: A Social History of Indian Cricket* and *Olympics: The India Story*.

David McDonald is the Alice D. Mortenson/Petrovich Distinguished Professor of Russian History at the University of Wisconsin–Madison. A specialist on the history of late imperial Russia, McDonald also served as a senior administrator in the UW–Madison's athletic department. He has written on American intercollegiate athletics.

Andrew McFarland is associate professor of history at Indiana University Kokomo and researches sport and physical education's introduction to Spain. His publications include "The Importance of Reception: Explaining Sport's Success in Early Twentieth-Century Spain" and "Building a Mass Activity: Fandom, Class, and Early Spanish Football." He organized and edited the special issue "Sport, the Body, and Mass Culture in Twentieth-Century Spain" for the journal *Sport in Society* and is working on his first book *Regeneration through Sport: Sport, Football, and Cultural Modernization in Spain, 1890–1920*.

Mike O'Mahony is a reader in history of art at the University of Bristol. His books include *Sport in the USSR: Physical Culture—Visual Culture*; *Olympic Visions: Images of the Games in History*; and *The Visual in Sport* (coedited with Mike Huggins). He is currently completing a book on *Photography and Sport*.

Gary Osmond is senior lecturer in sport history in the School of Human Movement and Nutrition Sciences at the University of Queensland. He is also the coauthor of *Black and Proud: The Story of an Iconic AFL Photo* (with Matthew Klugman) and coeditor of *Sport History in the Digital Era* (with Murray G. Phillips).

Dilwyn Porter is professor emeritus of sports history and culture at De Montfort University, Leicester and currently visiting professor in history at Newman University, Birmingham. He coedited *Sport and National Identity in the Post-War World* with Adrian Smith and has published articles and reviews relating to this theme in *History, The International Journal of the History of Sport, National Identities*, and *Sport in History*.

Alon K. Raab is a retired professor of religious studies at the University of California Davis whose work includes articles and essays about sport and society. He coedited *The Global Game: Writers on Soccer* (with John Turnbull and Thom Satterlee) and *Soccer in the Middle East* (with Issam Khalidi). He has been a lifelong football player and cyclist since his Jerusalem childhood.

Rob Ruck is a professor of sport history at the University of Pittsburgh. He is the author of *Raceball: How the Major Leagues Colonized the Black and Latin Game*; *Rooney: A Sporting Life* (with Maggie Patterson and Michael Weber); *The Tropic of Baseball: Baseball in the Dominican Republic*; and *Sandlot Seasons: Sport in Black Pittsburgh*. His documentary work includes *The Republic of Baseball: Dominican Giants of the American Game* and *Kings on the Hill: Baseball's Forgotten Men*.

Lewis H. Siegelbaum is the Jack and Margaret Sweet Professor of History at Michigan State University. He is the author of books on the Stakhanovite movement of the 1930s, the Soviet state and society in the 1920s, and the award-winning *Cars for Comrades*. He coauthored with Jim von Geldern the award-winning website "Seventeen Moments in Soviet History," an online sourcebook used extensively to teach Soviet history, and with Leslie Page Moch *Broad Is My Native Land: Repertoires and Regimes of Migration in Russia's Twentieth Century*.

Sasu Siegelbaum is a social media specialist at CNN's short video documentary project Great Big Story in New York City. He has published "Putting the Work Back into Newswork: Searching for the Sources of Normative Failure," in *Journalism Studies*.

Matthew Taylor is professor of history at the International Centre for Sports History and Culture at De Montfort University, UK. His books include *The Association Game: A History of British Football*; *The Leaguers: The Making of Professional Football in England, 1900–1939*; and *Moving with the Ball: The Migration of Professional Footballers* (with Pierre Lanfranchi). He is also coeditor of Peter Lang's "Sport, History and Culture" book series.

Wray Vamplew is emeritus professor of sports history at the University of Stirling and visiting research professor in exercise and sport science at Manchester Metropolitan University. He is past editor of *The Journal of Sport History* and *The International Journal of the History of Sport* and is now general editor of the *Bloomsbury Cultural History of Sport*. He is writing a world economic history of sport.

Patricia Vertinsky is a Distinguished University Scholar and professor of kinesiology at the University of British Columbia. She is a social and cultural historian working across the fields of women's and gender history with a special interest in physical culture, physical education, and modern dance. She is author of, among others, *The Eternally Wounded Woman: Doctors, Women and Exercise in the Late 19th Century*; coeditor of *Physical Culture, Power and the Body* with Jennifer Hargreaves; *Disciplining Bodies in the Gymnasium: Memory, Monument and Modernism* with Sherry Mckay; and, most recently, *The Female Tradition in Physical Education: Women First Reconsidered* with David Kirk.

Stephen R. Wenn is professor of kinesiology and physical education at Wilfrid Laurier University in Canada. A former president of the North American Society for Sport History, Wenn's research interests lie in the area of Olympic commercialism. He is a coauthor of *Selling the Five Rings: The International Olympic Committee and the Rise of Olympic Commercialism* (rev. ed., 2004) and lead author of *Tarnished Rings: The International Olympic Committee and the Salt Lake City Bid Scandal*.

Daniel Widener teaches modern American history, with a focus on expressive culture and political radicalism. He began his educational career at the Echo Park-Silverlake Peoples' Childcare Center before taking degrees at Berkeley and New York University. He is the author of *Black Arts West: Culture and Struggle in Postwar Los Angeles*. He is a supporter of Tottenham Hotspur and currently manages Red Star San Diego in the San Diego County Soccer League.

Christopher Young is professor of modern and medieval German languages and associate dean of arts and humanities at the University of Cambridge, where he is also a Fellow of Pembroke College. He has written and edited over a dozen books in the fields of sports history and German literature, language, and culture. He is coeditor of the University of California Press's "Sport in World History" series, and his *The 1972 Munich Olympics and the Making of Modern Germany* (with Kay Schiller) won the book prizes of the North American and British Societies of Sports History.

INTRODUCTION

ROBERT EDELMAN AND WAYNE WILSON

NOT long ago, a British historian observing the changing landscape of academic inquiry remarked to a colleague, "Sport, it would seem, is the new film." His remark was apt. These days no leading university would omit the cinema from its offerings, and the study of sport is rapidly approaching a similar status. Our handbook proposes to examine the present state of this burgeoning field and point to what still remains to be done. Today, sport's grandest events are watched by billions of viewers, while billions of dollars are generated by its globalization and commercialization. Sport occupies an enormous part of the content on the Internet and other forms of media. Inevitably, sport has attracted the attention of scholars who increasingly have found it to be a subject that can help us answer the big questions facing historians of all sorts. Once a domain of unadorned empiricism, sport history today mobilizes complex and sophisticated social and cultural theories to derive a vast range of meanings. The grand old categories of class, race, gender, nation, and religion can all be used to understand sport, and in turn sport can give us new understandings of those same categories.

The emergence of sport history is the culmination of more than a half century of disparate developments. As early as 1951, John Rickards Betts completed a pioneering doctoral dissertation at Columbia University titled "Organized Sport in Industrial America."[1] Betts, who became a member of the history faculty at Boston College, continued to research and write about sport in the 1950s and 1960s, but he was one of very few Anglophone historians to do so. Unencumbered by the intellectual inhibitions of traditional historians, physical educators took the lead in organizing the International Committee for the History of Physical Education and Sport in 1967. This step was followed six years later by the establishment of the North American Society for Sport History (NASSH), a scholarly association made up of physical educators and historians. In 1974, it launched the *Journal of Sport History*. NASSH was also a model for the development of subsequent associations, including the British Society of Sport History, the Australian Society for Sports History, the International Committee for the History of Physical Education and Sport, and the European Committee for Sport History. The growing academic interest in sport was not limited to history, as sport subfields took root in several other disciplines in the social sciences and humanities. This interdisciplinary interest led to the establishment of numerous scholarly societies in the next two decades. The International Committee for the Sociology of Sport, the International Society of Sport Psychology, the International Association for the Philosophy of Sport, and the Sport Literature Association were among the most notable such groups.

Concurrent with the growth of these sometimes insular scholarly societies were much broader intellectual developments, as a wide variety of thinkers began advocating a more comprehensive examination of the human experience. Dismayed by the dismissal of popular culture in general and sport in particular, by the New Left and particularly the Frankfurt School, a later generation of thinkers sought a more nuanced and optimistic understanding of the reception of mass culture by very various audiences. Instead of diversion from the weighty matters of life, they sought to stress the possibilities for resistance and agency to be found in play and entertainment. At the University of Birmingham during the 1970s, Stuart Hall, Raymond Williams, and their colleagues, inspired by Antonio Gramsci's concept of cultural hegemony, devoted intelligent and rigorous attention to television, film, sport, and many other human activities once dismissed as "not serious."[2] In creating the new field of cultural studies, these scholars established the intellectual and political preconditions for sport studies to flourish. Such well-established historians as Eric Hobsbawm, Richard Holt, and Tony Mason began exploring the role of sport in the development of mass culture and class consciousness.[3] In North America, Elliot Gorn, Jules Tygiel, Steven Riess, and Randy Roberts turned their talents to sporting matters.[4] The literary scholar John Hoberman published a rich and intelligent work on sport and political ideology.[5] Allen Guttmann, of Amherst College, wrote *From Ritual to Record*, a seminal work that analyzed the transformation of sport from a premodern to modern phenomenon.[6] The anthropologically trained John MacAloon produced an intellectual and political biography of Pierre de Coubertin, founder of the modern Olympics, that we now can see was light years ahead of its time.[7] We have come a long way since 1938, when the great Dutch historian Johan Huizinga produced *Homo Ludens,* his pioneering study of the play impulse throughout history.[8]

At much the same time in France, Michel Foucault was elaborating an approach to historical knowledge that placed the human body at the center of scholarly concerns and deployed a concept of power that was particularly helpful to understanding how relations of domination and subordination were constituted and expressed in sport.[9] His fellow theorist Pierre Bourdieu pointed to the importance of the habits and practices surrounding the body and argued that the body could express much that the mind and speech could not.[10] Deploying the concept of cultural capital, he called for mobilizing a rigorous, historically informed sociology to study a wide range of cultural forms, sport included. Along with sex and dance, sport is the most corporeal of human activities. By the 1990s, these and many other thinkers in turn helped precipitate what has come to be called the "cultural turn" in the historical profession. In subsequent decades senior historians who had established reputations in more traditional subfields came to examine sport with rigor and nuance.[11] They in turn inspired young researchers and graduate students in history to study sport as their career path.[12]

These shifts have changed scholars' older notions of what is important. Topics that were once deemed marginal—murder mysteries, musical comedies, soap operas, and sport, to name a few—have today assumed new significance. In the process, popular culture in general and sport in particular have become the subjects of an explosion of thoroughly serious, rigorous research and writing, filled with all manner of compelling implications. At the same time, historians of sport came to realize the importance of addressing their work to the larger profession. Sport was no longer treated as an autonomous realm—an escape from a so-called real world. It touches the most significant elements of the human condition. Sport has been a gender factory—a site where men made themselves into men and where women fought and overcame the consequences of that historically constructed "male bastion." Sport is the terrain over which struggles between social classes, religions, and nation-states have been ardently and at times dangerously contested. It is, to paraphrase Clifford Geertz, the place we tell ourselves stories about ourselves.[13] Whether it is Bourdieu's "cultural capital" or Huizinga's "play," sport is, has been, and will continue to be one of the great engines of culture creation.

While these changes were taking place in the academy, there were other processes going on in the larger world. Since the 1980s, we have been experiencing yet another wave of a globalization process that has had several previous iterations in the course of world history. Sport has now come to occupy an increasingly large portion of the world's cultural, economic, and political space. Such organizations as soccer's international federation (FIFA) and the International Olympic Committee (IOC) boast more members than the United Nations and offer a platform to large and small nations alike that is unrivaled by any other cultural or political body. The production, communication, and consumption of sport through myriad and increasingly complex interrelationships across transnational corporations, federations, and forms of media have allowed recent so-called mega-events to balloon to cumulative audiences in excess of 40 billion. High-performance athletes enjoy greater mobility and visibility, and conglomerates have more vested interests in supporters, stadia, clubs, franchises, and international markets than at any other point in the history of sport. So-called mega-events that last for weeks and are transmitted all over the world are more "mega" and costly than ever. Both the 2014 Olympic Winter Games in Sochi and the 2014 men's soccer World Cup in Brazil were simultaneously dripping in political implication and commercial exploitation. The women's soccer World Cup and the new and hard-fought gender equality of the Olympic Games have generated profound rethinking of what is femininity and, in their wake, masculinity. The historic dominance of men in sport, a product of the nineteenth century, is now challenged by the useful if fluid concept of metrosexuality.

As sport itself has gone increasingly global, so has its study. International scholarly sport societies have grown and matured. All publish journals and organize annual conferences. Many colleges and universities offer courses on a wide range of sporting topics. Graduate students now choose sporting topics for dissertations and succeed in finding gainful employment. There are even chairs of sport history at major universities. Today, the leading university presses have all published books on this subject. Networks of researchers have formed with only a tenuous relationship to the established sport studies associations. The 2010 Sport in Modern Europe Project was one such example of a European-based network, led by academics from departments of history, sociology, literature, and business in several countries. The Cold War International History Project's multiyear, multisite research program on Cold War sport is another example of broadly international cooperation to tackle an important element of transnational history.

Sport, for us and for most historians, is a form of competition featuring physical performance, pursued in accordance with written rules and administered by formal organizations. Rather than focus on recreational physical activities, or the German gymnastics tradition, sport's main competitor as a form of bodily culture, we are primarily concerned with organized spectator sport.

We believe sport occupies a profoundly useful place within the larger historical profession. Joseph Nye's concepts of soft and hard power have been extremely useful to scholars, but which of them best describes sport?[14] Because sport is liminal, it constitutes and expresses its meanings not only through institutions and printed sources but in the spaces between them—in families, neighborhoods, courtyards, street corners, the criminal world, parks, pubs, kitchens, cafes, schools, schoolyards, and places of worship. If sport has been one part of a popular culture that seeks to impress and convince, it can be seen as a form of soft power, but the links among sport, physical fitness, and military preparedness make it an especially hard form of soft power. At the same time, the question of fitness is one element of the military world that does not directly involve weapons and destruction, making sport a softer form of hard power.

A great deal of energy has gone into studying how sport reflects the strengths of competing political and economic systems, but sport can just as easily mask their weaknesses. Indeed, sport can do both at the same time. For scholars seeking to make sense of the *big* issues of history, sport then turns out to be what the British journalist Simon Kuper has called a "slippery tool."[15] Due to its competitive nature, sport is unlike such well-studied cultural activities as ballet, theater, music, literature, movies, art, and design. It is unscripted, unpredictable drama that feeds off deep personal and collective loyalties and fascinations. It produces easily measured results from which governments and their citizens draw rapid conclusions. Yet, for the historian intrigued by the fabric and weave of societies rather than grand moral master narratives, these can be tricky calibrations. Sport is not a shortcut that obviates the need for meaningful contextualization and rigorous research.

While sport history is primarily focused on the modern period and the rise of sport is usually associated with the coming of modernity, we offer three chapters explicitly about premodern sport and several others that touch on premodern antecedents to modern sport. First and foremost, this is a historical handbook and not a work of anthropology. It is, therefore, largely but not entirely limited by the existence of written sources and documents. Accordingly, the premodern chapters are concerned with those activities in Europe, North America, and Asia that played roles in the development of modern sport. Africa, which commands one of our chapters, offers the clearest contrast of the anthropological with more conventional historiography. Relevant documents were produced by the colonial powers who sought to portray indigenous populations as "peoples without history" before the coming of the "white man" and his often uncivilized imposition of the civilizing mission.

Because it is impossible to provide full coverage of every sport and country, we have chosen to take a more thematic approach. Still, geography is important. The section on the familiar modernization narrative provides coverage of Great Britain and North America and examines the most popular forms of sport. Other geographic regions are addressed separately, covering an even wider range of sports and their precursors. We look at the many directions of transnational acculturation and seek to reveal the diffusion of sport to and from all parts of the planet.

Sport history remains a developing field that has only recently begun to occupy a significant space in the larger profession. For decades the great bulk of research and writing on our subject has been concerned with Europe and North America and focused on the sporting activities of men who consciously and unconsciously created a masculinity factory from which women were excluded. As is the case throughout the discipline, that emphasis is changing. We have endeavored in this work to examine a broad range of regions in what was once called the developing world. Much less work presently exists on Asia, Africa, and Latin America. Yet, that situation too is now changing as younger scholars all over the world have taken up the subject of sport as their area of specialization to which they plan to devote their careers.

THEORIZING SPORT HISTORY

For too long, historical writing on sport was dominated by an unadorned empiricism that had long ago been deemed insufficient by most researchers. Numbers of home runs and goals were surely interesting, but what did they tell us about the grand questions and great debates confronted by practitioners? Historians these days are guided by a great variety of theories that help us choose our topics, structure our narratives, and derive our meanings. For these reasons, scholars from sociology and cultural studies discuss the contributions their disciplines have made and can make to the understanding of sport. We also asked a historian of international politics to pose two questions: What can historians expect and demand from historians of sport in order to include sporting matters in their larger accounts, and what must sport historians do to be taken seriously by the rest of the discipline?

PREMODERN SPORT

Sport is a modern set of practices closely tied to the rapid evolution of capitalism and the growth of cities. The Industrial Revolution had its roots in the revamping of agriculture and the exploitation of colonial people and goods from empires. Nevertheless, physical contests of all sorts had existed for centuries prior to the coming of modernity, and we cannot ignore them. Those who have argued ancient Greece was the cradle of democracy and civilization also see it as a matching cradle of sport. The practice and organization of physical contests were highly developed and well organized in the Greek and Roman empires. From the Olympic Games to the spectacles of gladiatorial combat, the ancient world has often been seen as the first site of sporting activity. In both places sport became a form of popular culture through which citizens were created. The fit athlete and the fit warrior became central figures in the projection and maintenance of empire.

By the nineteenth century, philo-Hellenism became a driving force in the creation of the modern Olympics. The founder of the modern version of the Olympic Games, Baron Pierre de Coubertin, claimed to be reviving the games of ancient Greece, but he also used the Greek example to gain support in Germany and other countries for his movement. One must then ask if this highly male, elitist, and positive interpretation of these ancient societies was connected to only one of many possible interpretations of the classical world. If ancient Greece, in particular, was the cradle of civilization, what sort of civilization was it, and what role did sport play in its creation and reproduction?

It has been said that medieval sport is still awaiting its H. A. Harris, the author of one of the definitive texts on ancient Greek sport. Nevertheless, there is a body of literature on medieval sport, albeit one that relies heavily on British and western European sources from the later Middle Ages. Many sports of the period such as wrestling, archery, and water tilting had martial origins. One study of the sporting pursuits of thirteenth-century English peasants noted that nearly half were "war-related." People at both ends of the social spectrum pursued sport, while religious leaders attempted to exert varying degrees of control over these bodily and often violent pastimes. The tournament, in which noblemen engaged in jousts and melees, is the best-known form of medieval sport, but less violent activities such as forms of tennis also took root. One of the differences between medieval and modern sport is the increased degree to which contemporary sport seeks to minimize violence, injury, and death and thus be less warlike. Sport, as Norbert Elias wrote, is part of the "civilizing process," but battles on the playing field are mimetic and not real despite the militarized language that often surrounds them.[16]

The early modern period witnessed the rise of several activities that adopted some of the defining characteristics of modern sport. This process occurred in only some sports and advanced at different rates in different countries. Cricket, horse racing, and golf, to cite three examples of sports that eventually became global, developed written rules, formed clubs, recorded results, and consciously sought to attract spectators in the premodern period. The growth of premodern sport took place in the context of efforts—of varying success—by church and state to control and direct leisure pursuits and in particular to harness the violence associated with some of them.

Modern Sport

Historians no longer believe that the origins of capitalism and industrialization were the exclusive products of late-eighteenth and early-nineteenth-century British genius. Nevertheless, the United Kingdom was the cradle of certain modern sports, most notably soccer/football. Over a century, these claims were expanded, and a master narrative of sport's creation and growth developed. Today, this version of history is thought to have roughly the same validity as the claim that "jazz came up the river from New Orleans." Nevertheless, it is worth repeating to establish an understanding of what might be called the first wave of sport history.

With the first stages of the agrarian and industrial revolutions late in the eighteenth century, a burgeoning and expansive middle class elite emerged. These newly wealthy men had not gained their power and status from the traditional sources of military service and landed wealth. Instead, they sat in offices and "made" money. Sport then became a way to demonstrate their otherwise ambiguous strength and manliness. At the same time, the higher rungs of the British middle class sought to send their sons to the ancient institutions of secondary education known as the "public schools." Today, the names Eton, Harrow, Rugby, and many others can be called global brands, but in the late eighteenth century these were unruly places. Headmasters, most notably but not exclusively Thomas Arnold of Rugby, came to introduce sport into the curriculum in order to provide a release for otherwise violent and sexual adolescent energy. In the process, they sought to create the future leaders of the nation and empire. This experiment was a huge success. Sporting activity then spread to elite British universities.

In the second half of the nineteenth century, rules were codified for various sports. By the 1880s and 1890s, many sporting activities had spread virally to the various laboring classes who had moved into the newly expanding cities and had achieved greater leisure time and expendable income through decades of political struggle. With mass audiences, sport subsequently became organized and commercialized. A crucial role in these processes was played by technological breakthroughs in transportation, most notably the railroad, which allowed athletes and fans to travel greater distances to games and events. The telegraph permitted the instantaneous reporting of sports events to places far away from where the contests were taking place. In the process, sport became national rather than simply local. All of this was said to have taken place outside the purview of the state. Yet such a view overlooks the close ties of sport to the military and to empire. Sport may not have been war, but many elites have mistakenly and tragically thought so.

In light of the strong criticism modernization theory has endured in recent years, one may well ask which parts of the old modernizing narrative are still seen as true. The rise of industry and the rise of modern sport have been closely tied to each other. Accordingly, these profound changes led to the emergence of a class of sporting entrepreneurs who found new sources of profit in what had been games and pastimes. Were Britain and the United States the only centers of sporting activity, or was the path to sport repeated elsewhere? How did sport constitute and express the demands and aspirations of the industrial age? Were the often conflicting roles of social classes the same elsewhere as those described in the standard "British model" of modern sport's emergence? Again, was sport's growth truly independent from the state, and did governments play similarly limited roles elsewhere?

The urban centers that arose all over the world in the nineteenth century contained the necessary conditions for the rise of modern sport. Large numbers of spectators, transportation systems, communications systems, media companies, and technological expertise could only be found in cities. Although sport developed at different times in different parts of the world, the central role of the city has been consistent. Historians have examined not only the effect of the city on sport but the impact of sport on cities. The first wave of sport historiography produced several works on sport and urbanization during the Industrial Revolution. Writers addressed the relationship between sport and class identity, ethnic identity, associativity, and assimilation. Later works, incorporating research from sociology, urban studies, architectural history, and geography, have opened new avenues of inquiry by examining evolving concepts of space.

Advances in the technology of communication both drove and supported the growth of modern sport. Mass-market newspapers, powered by the telegraph and later the telephone, were able to supply readers with quick and detailed information about sporting events. These publications and the multiple discourses they produced intensified the appetite of the sporting public for more and bigger spectacles. At the same time, the power of sporting accounts drew readers to the press and improved readership and advertising revenues. By the 1920s, the mass press was joined by radio and newsreels to expand and excite the audience for sport. The impact of these new and older media on the citizenry has been the subject of a rich and ongoing debate.

Empires have played fundamental roles in the diffusion of sports. Scholars have examined the impact of colonializing nations with their administrators carrying balls, bats, and rule books from their elite institutions of higher learning. Yet others have stressed the role of existing indigenous cultures and pastimes. Did modern sport trample traditional games and force locals into a single oppressive and controlling mode of civilization? Were those local populations able to use and change sports in ways that allowed them to resist the authority of their colonial masters? Much of this work takes C. L. R. James's classic study of Trinidadian cricket as a conceptual starting point.[17] Yet one must also ask how the sports of formal colonial empires run by administrators and soldiers differed from the informal commercial empires established by expatriate businessmen, managers, engineers, workers, engineers, and sailors. Finally, what kinds of states emerged in the developing world after the initial period of diffusion and the later collapse of colonialism? Did these new governments deploy sport in ways that enhanced their authority, or did sport remain one form of popular culture that supported continued resistance to authority?

Patterns of Diffusion

How did certain sports spread from the places of their creation to other parts of the world? How in less than three centuries did we get from a situation in which the rules of games varied from village to village to the opening matches of men's soccer World Cups when the entire planet gazed upon one single place and everyone knew how the game would be played? The diffusion of sport is not simply a process of cultural flow from Europe and North America. It has been a complex, multidirectional phenomenon. The diffusion of three of many possible sports illustrates differing patterns of dispersal and shifting balances of political and financial power within world sport. There are also sports of equal importance that have, however, not generated the wealth of serious, theoretically informed academic literature. Track and field (athletics), basketball, Asian martial arts, cycling, volleyball, wrestling, ice hockey, skiing, and even gymnastics have yet to inspire the massive body of work one fully expects to appear in the future.

New Globalizations
and Their Discontents

Originating in the nineteenth century, the modern Olympic Games are the world's premier sports event. Because of their magnitude and public visibility, the Olympics have provided a stage on which most of the major developments and conflicts of modern sport have played out for more than one hundred years. The International Olympic Committee, which drew its early inspiration from the gentlemen amateurs of Victorian Britain, has confronted the major issues of the twentieth century—nationalism, professionalism, and commercialism, not to mention war and peace. Initially, banning female participation, the Olympics became one of the principle arenas where women struggled for inclusion. Scholarly interest has been piqued by the widespread perception, encouraged by the IOC, that Olympic sport is a "movement" capable of inspiring social and political transformations. Along with a politically conservative version of internationalism, Olympism maintained a politically liberal belief in the possibility of social improvement. In practice, commitment to these ideals was combined with continuing cooperation with some of the world's vilest regimes. Accordingly, historians have been eager to analyze this grandiose, idealistic framing of the Olympics, frequently offering critical alternative readings of the Games and their meanings. In the course of the most recent wave of globalization, the Olympics have transformed from a festival of nominal amateurs to an extravaganza of openly professional athletes competing on a world stage promoted by global marketing and sponsorship campaigns.

As a result, a high-stakes cauldron of competition has emerged that offers great monetary rewards for the most visible and elite performers. Although doping in sport is often framed as a contemporary issue driven by athletes' desires to win riches, athletes, ancient and modern, have long sought to supplement their normal diets with foods, drinks, or drugs to improve sport performance. Accounts of nineteenth-century sport doping abound. The IOC discussed the problem as early as the 1930s. In the post–World War II period, the use of performance-enhancing drugs grew throughout the world. In 1968 the IOC introduced drug testing, and most other major sports organizations eventually followed. Efforts at doping control in the late twentieth century were carried out by disparate organizations with almost no coordination among them. A series of international doping scandals in the 1990s culminated in the creation of the World Anti-Doping Agency, which sought to impose a single anti-doping regime on world sport. The history of doping and anti-doping efforts raises fundamental questions about how different societies view the nature of sport, competition, fair play, as well as the health and rights of athletes. In an environment in which the hormonal, structural, and genetic manipulation of athletes are all possible, doping squarely raises the question of what it means to be human.

Reconsidering Old Categories and Contemplating New Ones

The long-established historical categories of class, gender, race, religion, and nation have guided historians for decades, but how useful are each of these analytical tools for the understanding of sport? They can still provide ways to explain behaviors, choices, and identities. At the same time, the history of sport may require other historians to modify their understandings of the ways these categories work and what they can and cannot explain. In recent years, the historical profession has taken a variety of "turns." Moving on from the "cultural turn," scholars have taken things one step further and have devoted attention to the role of emotions. Although many studies make use of the emotional to make sense of sport, the literature on this topic is still thin, but two new approaches have been influenced by the psychological. Sport is watched by both spectators and participants. It is inescapably visual. Following this logic, the scholarly study of sport has taken an explicitly visual turn. Art historians, photographers, film makers, television producers, and webmasters have turned increasing attention to sport, and, in the process, they have produced sources of use to the historian. At the same time, sport historians have turned more and more to using visual sources in both teaching and research.

Despite noteworthy exceptions such as Allen Guttmann's *The Erotic in Sport* and Thomas Scanlon's *Eros and Greek Athletics*, sexuality in sport has received less attention than the related topics of gender roles and sex-based discrimination.[18] The connection between sport and sexuality, however, has spanned the history of sport from the homosocial bonding of Greek athletics to the contemporary eroticization of soccer player David Beckham and countless other athletes. The relationship between sport and sexuality has been the subject of considerable conjecture. Victorian public school headmaster Edward Thing maintained that sports would keep public school boys from masturbating. Freud claimed that sport was a means of sexual sublimation. And, as any viewer of Hollywood boxing movies knows, corner men believe that sex weakens the legs. Sexuality is integral to sport. Athletic bodies typically reflect prevailing notions of sexual attractiveness. In this way, body culture is closely linked to the emotional turn in the historical profession.

In 2012, a multiyear research project on sport in the Cold War sent out a call for papers, and scores of proposals came in from all over the world. Nearly half of them were from graduate students and early-career professionals. The topic's strong resonance with young historians demonstrates two things. First, researchers in our field have come to produce first-rate scholarship of sufficient quality to attract others to follow their path. Second, we are on the verge of greater growth with a new, younger cohort who have chosen sport history as their field of specialization. Our hope is that this handbook will inspire others to take up the proverbial torch or grab the baton from the previous runner. Sport is, indeed, the new film, and that is a very good thing indeed.

Notes

1. John Rickards Betts, "Organized Sport in Industrial America" (PhD diss., Columbia University, 1951).
2. Stuart Hall, *Encoding and Decoding in the Television Discourse* (Birmingham, UK: Centre for Cultural Studies, University of Birmingham, 1973); *Resistance Through Rituals: Youth Subcultures in Post-War Britain* (London: Hutchinson, 1976); Raymond Williams, *Television: Technology and Cultural Form* (New York: Schocken Books, 1975).
3. Eric Hobsbawm, *Nations and Nationalism Since 1780: Programme, Myth, Reality* (New York: Cambridge University Press, 1990); Richard Holt, *Sport and the British: A Modern History* (New York: Oxford University Press, 1989); Tony Mason, *Sport in Britain: A Social History* (New York: Cambridge University Press, 1989).
4. Elliot Gorn, *The Manly Art: Bare-Knuckle Prize Fighting in America* (Ithaca, NY: Cornell University Press, 1986); Jules Tygiel, *Baseball's Great Experiment: Jackie Robinson and His Legacy* (New York: Oxford University Press, 1983); Steven Reiss, *City Games: The Evolution of American Urban Society and the Rise of Sports* (Urbana–Champaigne: University of Illinois Press, 1991); Randy Roberts, *Jack Dempsey: The Manassa Mauler* (Baton Rouge: Louisiana State University Press, 1979).
5. John Hoberman, *Sport and Political Ideology* (Austin: University of Texas Press, 1984).
6. Allen Guttmann, *From Ritual to Record: The Nature of Modern Sport* (New York: Columbia University Press, 1978).
7. John J. MacAloon, *This Great Symbol: Pierre de Coubertin and the Origins of the Modern Olympic Games* (Chicago: University of Chicago Press, 1981).
8. John Huizinga, *Homo Ludens* (Haarlem, The Netherlands: Tjeenk Willink, 1938).
9. Michel Foucault, *Discipline and Punish: The Birth of Prison* (New York: Pantheon Books, 1977).

10. Pierre Bourdieu, *Outline of a Theory of Practice* (New York: Cambridge University Press, 1977).
11. Robert Edelman, *Serious Fun: A History of Spectator Sports in the USSR* (New York: Oxford University Press, 1993); Kay Schiller and Christopher Young, *The 1972 Munich Olympics and the Making of Modern Germany* (Berkeley: University of California Press, 2010).
12. Amy Bass, *Not the Triumph but the Struggle: The 1968 Olympics and the Making of the Black Athlete* (Minneapolis: University of Minnesota Press, 2002); Sandra S. Collins, *The 1940 Tokyo Games: The Missing Olympics: Japan, the Asian Olympics and the Olympic Movement* (London: Routledge, 2007); Barbara Keys, *Globalizing Sport: National Rivalry and International Community in the 1930s* (Cambridge, MA: Harvard University Press, 2006).
13. Clifford Geertz, "Deep Play: Notes of the Balinese Cockfight," in *The Interpretation of Cultures* (New York: Basic Books, 1973), 421–453.
14. Joseph Nye, *Bound to Lead: The Changing Nature of American Power* (New York: Basic Books, 1990).
15. Simon Kuper, *Ajax, the Dutch, the War: Football in Europe during the Second World War* (London: Orion, 2003).
16. Norbert Elias and Eric Dunning, *The Quest for Excitement: Sport and Leisure in the Civilizing Process* (Oxford: Berg, 1986), 43.
17. C. L. R. James, *Beyond a Boundary* (Durham, NC: Duke University Press, 2013).
18. Allen Guttmann, *The Erotic in Sports* (New York: Columbia University Press, 1996); Thomas F. Scanlon, *Eros and Greek Athletics* (New York: Oxford University Press, 2002).

PART I

THEORIZING SPORT HISTORY

CHAPTER 1

···

SPORT AND SOCIAL THEORY

···

DOUGLAS HARTMANN

WITH a few notable exceptions and setting aside a passing comment here or there, neither classical nor contemporary social theorists have had a great deal to say about sport.
Nevertheless, social theory has a great deal to offer the systematic academic study of
sport, historically oriented and otherwise. The purpose of this chapter is to provide a
brief, schematic overview of some of the conceptual resources available in classical and
contemporary social theory for sport history and scholarship.

The chapter begins by identifying key concepts and orienting frameworks from the
traditional sociological canon, drawing in particular from the classic theoretical trinity
of Karl Marx, Max Weber, and Émile Durkheim, as well as the symbolic interactionist school represented by Georg Simmel, George Herbert Mead, and Erving Goffman.
All of these works have relevance and utility for sport scholarship. An explicit, self-
conscious engagement with the general social theoretical orientation that unifies them
can help readers better understand both the historical origins and development of sport,
as well as its particular status and function in the modern world. Three distinctive overarching characteristics are highlighted: a constructivist orientation, a contextualizing
impulse, and the need for a critical/systemic perspective. The final section draws out
some of these broader characteristics and their analytical implications by summarizing
the contributions of certain social theorists who have been most specific, systematic,
and self-conscious about situating sport in the context of broad theoretical interests and
questions—Norbert Elias, Pierre Bourdieu, and C. L. R James among them.

This general approach and admittedly idiosyncratic collection of thinkers is not
meant to be systematic or comprehensive. It is not, for example, intended to survey that
vast and impressive body of theoretical work on sport that has been engaged in the last
fifteen or twenty years. Nor is this a chapter about how various social theories and theorists have been appropriated, deployed, and reworked in the context of sport research
and writing over the years. Rather, it is a basic, conceptual overview of the value and
utility of a social-theoretical framing approach to sport history. It is, in short, intended
to be conceptual rather than genealogical, illustrative of the fundamental, multifaceted
relationships between sport and society in modern history.

THEORETICAL RESOURCES IN
THE SOCIOLOGICAL CANON

Classical social theory is, for sociologists at least, still delineated and defined by the research and writing of three founding scholars, the so-called holy trinity of Marx, Weber, and Durkheim. Each of these theorists and their followers have their own orientation to history. Each has produced his own set of terms and organizing concepts for analyzing social life, and each has inspired particular lines of research and thought. At the risk of oversimplification, the core insights and contributions of each can be captured by a central organizing term: capitalism for Marx, rationality and/or rationalization for Weber, and social solidarity for Durkheim.

Marx's description of capitalism and all the analytic concepts that go along with it (labor, value, profit, class, exploitation, stratification, alienation, ideology, and false consciousness, just to name a few) are, of course, well-known analytic tools all across the academy. They have been used to explain the historical emergence of modernity; the development of its complex, stratified, and unequal societies; and a diverse array of human experiences therein. Sport scholarship has been no different. When the field took shape in the 1960s and 1970s, the theoretical resources inspired by and developed in the Marxist tradition were prominent and influential. Studies of the emergence of a market-based, for-profit system of sport provision and consumption (both participatory and spectator forms) were most apparent, along with works that analyzed the exploitation of professional (and other) athletes and their "labor" by the owners, administrators, and leaders of the sporting world. Most famously, the idea of sport as some kind of opiate of the masses—an institutionalized, cultural practice functioning to distract spectators and consumers from seeing the systemic sources of their own stratification—traces its lineage from Marx's notions of ideology, consent, and control.

Recognizing the Marxist roots of sports history and scholarship is not just a matter of tracing an intellectual lineage. Such theoretical engagements can make it easier for sport scholars to identify the assumptions and anticipate the directions, implications, and potential conclusions of work in this tradition or other approaches deriving from it. An example would be research into unequal access to sport as a participatory form in contemporary societies. Much of this work is focused on class and derives directly (if not always self-consciously) from the Marxist emphasis on the inequities generated by market-based, capitalist economies. Studies that attend to other social forms and the inequalities associated with them—probably most notably gender and race—also adopt and adapt many of the general Marxist concepts of inequality and systemic social stratification. Valuable in itself, such theoretical awareness can also help connect sport history and research to intellectual developments and innovations in other, related fields.

Weber, a German sociologist and best known for *The Protestant Ethic and the Spirit of Capitalism*, is obviously indebted to Marx but shifted from a materialist analysis of capitalism to a more cultural critique of the rationalization and bureaucratization of modern life. The focus and result was an emphasis on how different institutional realms of social life (or "spheres") functioned in society, the ethos they required of their adherents, and the more existential questions of meaning and purpose to which they gave rise. These insights are expressed most famously in his notion of the iron cage. The cultural trap Weber described was not capitalism per se but the world wrought by capitalism, a world marked by incessant complexity, activity, and striving that has become entirely detached from any meaning or moral purpose, most of all the religious ethics that originally gave it purchase.

Weber's ideas and writings about rationalization in the modern world may not be as familiar to sport scholars as Marx's critique of capitalism, but they are actually fairly deeply embedded, even taken for granted, in much of the historical and theoretical work on the evolution of modern sporting systems and their role in society. Steven Overman's *The Protestant Ethic and the Spirit of Sport* is obviously in this vein, but Allen Guttmann's classic *From Ritual to Record* may be a better and certainly more influential work within the sport canon itself. At a basic level, Guttmann charts an essentially Weberian institutional history of the emergence and development of sport as a distinctive social sphere or set of practices, one in which sport as a social form becomes more and more regulated, rule-oriented, disciplined, and differentiated as time goes on. In addition, Guttmann suggests a much broader shift and transformation in sport's meaning, purpose, and function in the modern world from one of communal rites to physical excellence and record-setting for its own, spectacular if essentially unjustifiable, purpose. Such Weberian framings have also given rise to the larger, more general concept of sportization. Here it is worth noting that Weber's critique of meaning and purpose in modern life—or the lack thereof—yields perhaps the single most famous sport reference in all of classical social theory: "the pursuit of wealth, stripped of its religious and ethical meaning, tends to become associated with purely mundane passions, which often actually give it the character of sport."

Like Weber, the French sociologist Durkheim can and should be understood to begin from Marx's critique of capitalism. However, Durkheim's interest and analysis was less on the inequalities produced by modern economies and more on how the increasingly complex division of labor that they required challenge and change traditional forms of social solidarity and moral order. Durkheimian notions of solidarity, morality, and order may be less well known or frequently referenced among contemporary sport scholars, but they actually resonate quite well with those interested in the broad mobilization and collective impacts of sport spectatorship and consumption in terms of community-building and collective identification. Indeed, the concept of collective effervescence put forward in Durkheim's masterwork *The Elementary Forms of the Religious Life* inevitably leads first-year sociology graduate students to speculate about mass sporting practices. Such ideas about the role of sport in creating, perpetuating, as well as contesting social solidarity is exemplified in the work of sport specialists such as John MacAloon or Susan Brownell on Olympic rituals, symbols, and ceremonies, both of whom trace their

Durkheimian roots through the leading midcentury American anthropologist Victor Turner's work on ritual and community.

Several other important lines of research and thought in sport history and scholarship chart a direct lineage to Durkheim as well. One of Durkheim's immediate followers, Roger Caillois, produced the first serious, sociological response to Johan Huizinga's foundational *Homo Ludens*. In contrast to Huizinga's philosophical treatise, Caillois's interest was in the socially differentiated meaning, status, and function of sport, play, and leisure in the modern world. Additionally, there is the notion of *habitus*, perhaps the most well-known and influential theoretical concept to come out of studies of sport, athletics, and the body. While this is obviously not the place for an extensive discussion of this formative notion, made famous by Bourdieu, it should be noted that the term itself was originally introduced by Marcel Mauss, Durkheim's nephew, student, and collaborator. Mauss introduced the notion of techniques or "habits" of the body as a way to call attention to the distinctive ways in which people from different nations used their bodies in walking, swimming, or marching. He sought to make a larger argument about the power of the collective in shaping individual activity and behavior.

This brings us, in many ways, to symbolic interactionism. One of the conceits of many sociological theorists and thinkers is that all of social theory and sociological conceptualization can be traced back to the Marx–Weber–Durkheim triad. This yields certain blind spots and misunderstandings, chief among them an absence of attention to social interaction (particularly at the face-to-face or "micro" level) and the minimization of the symbolic significance and cultural meaning endowed in and reproduced through all human interactions and relationships. In sociological theory at least, this orientation is typically called "symbolic interactionism" and can be traced from the work of Simmel in Germany and Mead in the United States to that of the mid-twentieth-century iconoclast Canadian American Goffman.

With their emphasis on culture, symbols, and representations, as well as the making of meanings in and through institutions and social interactions, the ideas that social theorists typically associate with symbolic interactionism often appear in sport scholarship under the headings of communication and consumption, mass media, or cultural studies. However, these foundations and connections are not always explicit or self-conscious. A better exemplar would be Gary Alan Fine's ethnographic study of little league baseball. With his attention to peer group interaction and how it produces a subculture of its own, Fine's work highlights both the interactive and the symbolic dimensions of this tradition. It should also be noted that the earliest and most probing social theoretical treatments of "play" in social interaction and human life can be found in symbolic interactionism. In scattered but extensive discussions, Simmel, Mead, and Goffman's formulations all help shape how sport scholars can think about the larger cultural meaning, status, and function of sport and its experiential significance with respect to how people actually engage and understand ostensibly playful forms of social activity and interaction.

Distinctive Characteristics of
a Social Theory Orientation

As useful as each of these different thinkers and schools of theory may be, what is arguably more important are the overarching but taken-for-granted insights and assumptions they hold in common. There are at least three larger, more general characteristics of what might be called the social theoretical worldview or "sociological imagination" that merit attention: its constructivist orientation, its contextualizing impulse, and the need for a critical perspective.

The constructivist orientation shared by social theorists, whatever their other intellectual interests and analytic proclivities, is that nothing about social life and human history is given, universal, or invariable. In other words, almost everything we know and think, not to mention all the ways we organize and interact, are social constructions. They are the product of social actions and historical forces that are not always visible and usually well beyond the comprehension and control of individual actors. This perspective and orientation may be obvious for some. Many historians speak of a historical imagination as well. But recognizing sport as a social construction, as something that has been produced by human activity, reminds that the basic facts, institutions, and practices of the sporting world were not given or inevitable but have a history of their own. They can and do change over time. Extending from this, classic social theory suggests sport history is thoroughly bound up with the history of modernity itself. This emphasis on the human-made structure and function of sport also, almost invariably, raises historical questions about how the sports world became the way it is. What forces or actors were the historical drivers? Whose interests has it served; who benefited as well as who did not? In other words, this constructivist orientation leads into both the critical and the contextualizing impulses that also define a social theoretical orientation to history and social life.

A second core characteristic of social theoretical thought is the impulse to contextualize—to situate any group, social practice, or cultural form in the broader social environment within which it took shape and assumed its particular meaning and function. The view that human history and social life are not a series of disconnected, discrete parts but a whole system helps makes manifest the historical forces and social structures often forgotten or ignored. In sport studies, for example, this might mean explaining the rise of any particular sporting practice (or sport more generally) as owing not only to qualities of a sport itself but as a result of the rise of leisure time and extra income or even the emergence of cities and mass populations, the building of urban infrastructure, the emergence of mass media, commodification, and consumer society itself. Sport scholars should not see sport, its history, and its impact in the world as a self-contained, isolated institution or set of practices. Instead, the sport scholar must situate sport in the broader social and historical context of which it is part and parcel. This contextualizing orientation reminds us of the necessary, if multifaceted, relationship between sport and society. If we are truly to understand sport, we cannot think about sport as if it were in a vacuum but instead must understand its place and role in society and history more broadly and generally.

The third distinguishing characteristic and contribution of a fully formed social theoretical approach involves a critical orientation. When it comes to critical theory and sociology, many historians and other academicians think of social inequalities and the activist push for social change—the belief that the goal of social writing and research is not just to analyze the world but also to engage the world and bring about change. However, there is a broader and more important analytic point about a critical theoretical orientation that is often lost in this framing. A critical-theoretical perspective also provides a degree of distance and a standard of evaluation that allows social and historical research to go beyond mere descriptive empiricism and dig deeper into both meanings and causes. More specifically, having a more or less fully formed critical orientation to the world provides standards and criteria against which to analyze and evaluate history and an awareness of the mechanisms, processes, and forces that have made the historical world and continue to shape and maintain the social status quo as we know it today.

In its earliest manifestations, critical analytic frameworks were mostly focused on the inequalities and injustices associated with class and economics, especially those generated by market-based, capitalist systems of exchange. Critical theory was, in other words, all about class—economic-based exploitation, oppression, and social stratification. Indeed, throughout much of the twentieth century the phrase "critical theory" was essentially synonymous with Marxism itself, the term having been invented by such German social theorists as Max Horkheimer and Theodor Adorno (members of the Frankfurt School) who had fled Germany for the United States where Marxist thought was about as popular as fascism. Yet the basic, generic tenets of critical theory—the need for a systemic framework and an independent analytic standpoint—have been expanded and reworked in the second half of the twentieth century with the rise of feminist theory, queer theory, postcolonial theory, subaltern studies, critical race theory, and intersectional (race–class–gender) analyses. Such analytic orientations have been attuned not only to a wider array of social forms but also stem from broader, more culturally oriented visions of worldview, meaning and purpose, efficiency and rationality. In terms of social differences and inequalities, the shift, both in the sporting world and in terms of the sporting world's role in society, has been from class and economics to other social forms and forces, perhaps most notably gender and race due to the influence of the rise of feminist studies, critical race theory, and cultural studies more generally.

These grand, orienting assumptions about context, critique, and construction can be difficult to grasp or engage in the abstract. They are illustrated and usefully applied by several members of that small but exclusive set of social theorists who have been among the most explicit and self-conscious about sport as social form and historical force. It is an exercise that both illustrates these general social theoretical principles and extends our understandings of the complicated, multifaceted relationships between sport and society and, by extension, the role of sport in history.

APPLICATIONS, ILLUSTRATIONS, AND EXTENSIONS

The well-known sport research and writing of Elias is probably most useful in terms of illustrating and operationalizing ideas about social construction and contextualization in sport scholarship. In his historical essays about sporting practices like fox hunting and more abstract orienting essays, Elias offers a very specific argument about the emergence and development of modern social life (the civilizing process, as he calls it) and the place of sport therein. At one level, Elias's work provides a constructivist framework for both recognizing the distinctive characteristics of the institutionalized set of practices and activities we call sport as well as for thinking about how that institution took shape and developed. Even more, Elias provides a broad, sociological context for—and explicit argument about—sport's larger role and function in the modern world. I am referring here particularly to his argument, most famously represented in the collected volume he did with Eric Dunning about sport filling an institutional role and function in the modern, "civilized" world by providing a place for excitement—leisure, recreation, and function marked by physical activity and intensive emotional engagement and release. Elias's emphasis on the experiential and emotional dimensions of sporting practices also undergirds and foreshadows recent work on bodily practices developed by scholars such as Pierre Bourdieu, Michel Foucault, and Judith Butler.

With notions like "field," "practice," and the aforementioned "habitus," the eminent French sociologist Bourdieu did more than any one scholar or theorist to bring terminology and imagery from the sporting world into social theory and social scientific practice. Bourdieu also has a quite specific and refined vision of the emergence, development, structure, and functioning of sport in the modern world. In fact, his is probably the best example and realization of a fully formed social theoretical approach to sport in the social theory cannon.

Bourdieu's approach to sport is grounded in a Marxist-materialist perspective on processes of social distinction, stratification, and control in modern societies and how sport is implicated therein. His empirical work on sport starts from a Weberian analysis of the emergence of sport as a distinctive institutional arena and focuses mainly on how different sporting practices—and the meaning and significance attributed to such practices—mark and distinguish social groups (Durkheim's solidarity and division of labor), thus reinforcing their power and position in society (or lack thereof). Bourdieu's emphasis is not on mass, nationalist sport but on the way in which different groups or classes participate in different sporting forms—for example, the working classes tend to participate in sports such as boxing or soccer while those in the upper classes tend to play golf or tennis. Drawing on the symbolic interactionist tradition, Bourdieu highlights the more experiential and micro-level processes in and through which various sporting practices cultivate and inculcate distinctive worldviews and orientations.

Although illustrative of all the distinctive characteristics of a social theoretical approach, it is important to realize that Bourdieu and his work tend toward a very specific understanding of the relationships between sport and society, one where sport plays an essentially conservative, reproductive role in social life, reflecting larger historical forces rather than driving them, reinforcing rather than challenging existing societal arrangements. For instance, Bourdieu generally adopted the traditional leftist line that the investment of the working classes in sporting practices, particularly in the consumption of sporting spectacles through spectatorship and fandom, distracts them away from the difficult and fundamentally unjust conditions of their labor and lives. Bourdieu comes to these conclusions for a number of empirical and historical reasons—his understanding of the original form and function of athletic pursuits for boys and young men in elite English public schools, for example, as well as the rigid class structure of French society (his capital empirical case) and its particular sporting scene. Whatever the reasons, these formulations allow relatively little independent space or impact for sport as a social force in its own right.

An important variation on this view of sport as essentially reproductive and reflective can be found in the work of anthropologist Clifford Geertz. Though not always included on the list of social theorists with a particular interest or expertise in sport, Geertz's famous article on cockfighting in Bali as "deep play" adds a crucial dimension to our understanding of the more cultural aspects of sport in its relation to society, especially as a mass form. In this now-classic paper, Geertz describes popular cultural forms and practices such as those associated with the sport as "texts" that social analysts might read over the shoulders of their subjects. Geertz's point is that if social analysts and cultural critics can properly "read"—that is, situate, analyze and contextualize—these texts, we have a powerful window onto the ideas and meanings that constitute the lifeworlds and worldviews of human subjects in specific contexts and communities. Geertz's argument about the importance and impact of cultural practices went still further and endowed such cultural forms with an important and relatively autonomous role or function in social life.

Geertz explained the meaning and significance of the cockfight in Bali by showing how the betting around the fights mirrored and thus reinforced the social kinship structure of local tribes and communities. People in Bali bet for particular animals and trainers, in other words, in order to demonstrate their communal ties and commitments to kin. On the surface, nothing specific or concrete *changed* in winning and losing. However, at a deeper level, according to Geertz, something important *happened*: social networks were put on display and enacted. In this performance, community and kinship ties were confirmed and re-established. The Balinese may not have wanted or been able to explain their fascination with cocks and cockfighting as a reflection of their social structure, but it provided a dramatic, engaging cultural space for them to experience and live out their communal connections. Thus the cockfight was, in Geertz's memorable formulation, both a model *of* and a model *for* social solidarities and alliances.

Geertz's framing of the cockfight as a cultural performance suggests that the social and historical dynamics played out in sporting forms do not just reflect the larger, more general forces of history and society; they actually serve as an experiential platform that consolidates and ensures the reproduction of existing social ties. In fact, according to Geertz, sporting practices and performances like cockfights in Bali are all the more powerful as social forces because their participants are so deeply engaged in them and yet so unwilling or unable to articulate exactly why they are so engaged or what is actually going on. Thus these social effects are achieved even as participants think nothing particularly important or social is going on. Here Geertz connects a Durkheimian interest in social solidarity with the symbolic interactionist focus on interaction and symbolic meaning. Semiotic anthropologist Roland Barthes's famous discussion of the performativity among professional wrestlers offers another, even more self-conscious and strategic variation on this approach.

Whether in Bourdieu's straight social reproduction model or Geertz's more nuanced cultural approach, these different approaches to thinking about the role of sport in social life can make it difficult to envision the irreducible, relatively independent roles that sport can play in people's lives, in society, and in history. In sport studies, one line of research and writing that has pursued the relative independence and causal impact of sport is work that conceives of sport as a "contested terrain." This approach was derived largely in dialogue with the writing of Italian cultural Marxist Antonio Gramsci (though typically through the work of his interpreters, scholars such as Raymond Williams, Stuart Hall, Paul Willis, and the whole Birmingham School of Cultural Studies). Unlike Geertz, this work starts from the assumption that society is not a naturally harmonious, well-integrated place but instead is fraught with inequality, stratification, conflict, and struggle. In contrast to Bourdieu, it sees cultural venues like sport as arenas in and through which these social forces collide and struggle. The social dynamics that are played out, in the contested terrain frame, are not social order and stability but the struggle for order, the quest for control and power—not hegemony but the *struggle for* hegemony. Sport is best understood as an institutional arena where popular consciousness is constructed and contested, often without the participants being fully aware of the social processes in which they are so clearly implicated. In the sport context, this emphasis brings us to C.L.R. James and his magisterial, autobiographical rumination on cricket in the colonial context, *Beyond a Boundary*.

Formulated as a critique of colonialism, James starts from the presupposition that the modern world has been organized by race, both as a principle for the unequal distribution of resources and power as well as a mode for thinking about culture more generally. Squarely within the critical theoretical tradition, he further insists that these arrangements are neither just nor inevitable—and that the task of the analyst is to identify, understand, explain, and deconstruct the often unseen or misunderstood social processes and cultural beliefs that maintain existing racial formations and inequalities. And, for James, sport, specifically cricket, was a preeminent site for recognition, contestation, and change on a large social scale.

Several things about sport are important and unique as a force for contestation and change in James's vision. One is the disproportionate involvement, access, and success that otherwise marginalized and disempowered groups often have in sport, at least in the Western context. Another is the widespread popularity of sport and the tremendous passion people bring to the practice both as participants and spectators. These characteristics—especially in combination with sport's own dramatic qualities—means that the social dynamics of the sporting world take on meaning and significance far "beyond the boundaries" of the sporting world itself. Much of this impact relies on the consciousness and agency of athletes, many of whom James saw as more socially aware than most American sport scholars would imagine. Almost all of this holds, at least in theory, for a variety of popular cultural forms; however, James was convinced that there was something even more specific and unique about sport (or really cricket) that made it such an important and distinctive social force. It is what I have called the "moral structure" of the game itself—the ideals of meritocracy, competition, fair play, respect for the rules, loyalty, teamwork, and mutual respect embedded in athletic contests themselves. This moral structure of cricket and Western sport more generally was marked for James both by formal rules and structural equality as well as by a deep and intuitive sense of fairness and self-discipline that all participating individuals were required to have and hold to in order to make the competitive system work.

This summary framing may resemble Geertz's depiction of culture as a "model of and model for" formation. Yet, where Geertz's conception of modeling was essentially conservative and reproductive—reinforcing things as they were—James's "model" served as an ethical standard to hold up against the status quo. It was a moral ideal that stood outside of the social world as it was and thus revealed and put demands upon those who held it. As sport sociologist Mike Messner, who has applied this model to struggles for gender equity in sport, has summarized: "[T]he game provided a context in which the contradiction of racism and colonial domination were revealed for all to see."

In a post–civil rights, postcolonial era—where racism, prejudice, and discrimination still appear rampant both in sport and through sport *and* where so much of the scholarship aims to unpack the complicated ways in which sports images, ideologies, and identities function to maintain existing racial hierarchies—it can be easy to be cynical or skeptical about the accuracy and utility of the abstract, universalistic norms and values James believed were inculcated in sport. Indeed, they sound like the self-righteous rhetoric so often trumpeted by conservative or self-congratulatory sports elites, what the Olympic historian John Hoberman once derisively dismissed as the movement's "universal amoralism." The key point about James's work is the way in which he endowed sport with an autonomy and relative independence as a social force, drawing analytic attention to the broader social impacts and implications of these struggles and the social contestation and change that can occur through sport, not just in it.

THE USE, VALUE,
AND LARGER IMPLICATIONS
OF THEORETICAL ENGAGEMENT

This overview of some of the basic conceptual resources available for sport history in the social theory canon has been admittedly, even intentionally, schematic and idiosyncratic. In fact, many of the concepts, analytic insights, and broader theoretical orientations outlined here have been elaborated, extended, and applied more extensively, and perhaps more eloquently, in more recent sport research and writing. Once again, the goal here is not to be comprehensive but rather to be conceptual, suggestive of some of the theoretical resources that are useful and valuable for doing sport history.

Such an exercise has a number of potential benefits for the sport historian and social analyst. By referencing or signposting some of these classic concepts and frameworks, one can minimize or even eliminate the need to reinvent the conceptual toolkit with every study, paper, or book project. In addition, a working awareness of the core works and concepts of the social theory cannon can help sport scholars better anticipate the directions, implications, potential problems, and probable conclusions of certain approaches if and when they are applied to sport. These uses are important since denizens of commentators and large secondary literatures have taken shape around each of these well-established bodies of social theory. Further, a more self-conscious and systematic engagement with social theory can also help better situate sport history and research in the context of broader intellectual currents and more general scholarly debates. This latter point is somewhat larger and more substantive than it may first appear.

Throughout, I have argued and tried to show that a more theoretically engaged and informed sport scholarship can contribute to a better, fuller understanding of sport—its emergence and historical development, its relationships with society, and the ways in which it is implicated in the history and evolution of modern social life itself. This "grandiose" framing is obviously intended to contribute to a better, more sophisticated sport scholarship and history, but it has another, arguably more important implication as well. I am thinking here of those historians, social scientists, and cultural critics who normally do not pay much attention to sport. Indeed, I suggest here by way of conclusion that a more theoretically engaged and informed sport scholarship is essential for bringing sport history and scholarship from the margins of the academy closer to the center of history and its aligned academic fields, disciplines, and departments. A more theoretically sophisticated sport studies will, I believe, cultivate new attention to and awareness of the power, complexity, and impact of sport as a social phenomenon and force among that large contingent of scholars who have not previously seen it as such. What is to be gained from demonstrating and explicating sport's larger social status and historical significance is not just an appreciation of sport but a bigger, broader conception of history and social life, one that more fully attends to the power of play, popular practices, and symbolic meanings in modern life. Sport scholarship is obviously still far from such ambitious interventions and goals; however, there should be little doubt that a more deliberate engagement with social theory is a key part of making this project a reality.

Bibliography

Barthes, Roland. *Mythologies*. London: Paladin, 1972. First published 1957.

Birrell, Susan, and Cheryl L. Cole, eds. *Women, Sport, and Culture*. Champaign, IL: Human Kinetics, 1994.

Bourdieu, Pierre. "Program for a Sociology of Sport." *Sociology of Sport Journal* 5 (1988): 153–161.

Caillois, Roger. *Man, Play, and Games*. New York: Shocken Books, 1979.

Elias, Norbert. "The Genesis of Sport as a Sociological Problem." In *Quest for Excitement*, edited by Norbert Elias and Eric Dunning, 126–149. Oxford: Blackwell, 1986b.

Guttmann, Allen. *From Ritual to Record: The Nature of Modern Sports*. New York: Columbia University Press, 1978.

Hall, Stuart. "Gramsci's Relevance for the Study of Race and Ethnicity." In *Stuart Hall: Critical Dialogues in Cultural Studies*, edited by David Morley and Kuan-Hsing, 411–440. London: Routledge, 1996.

Hargreaves, John. "Sport, Culture, and Ideology." In *Theorizing Sport: An Introduction,* edited by Jennifer Hargreaves, 30–61. London: Routledge, 1982.

Hartmann, Douglas. "Community." In *Berkshire Encyclopedia of World Sport*, edited by David Levinson and Karen Christensen, 359–365. Great Barrington, MA: Berkshire, 2005.

Hartmann, Douglas. "Rethinking the Relationships between Sport and Race in American Culture: Golden Ghettos and Contested Terrain." *Sociology of Sport Journal* 17 (2000): 229–253.

Hartmann, Douglas. "What Can We Learn From Sport If We Take Sport Seriously as a Racial Force? Lessons from C. L. R. James's *Beyond a Boundary*." *Ethnic and Racial Studies* 26.3 (2003): 451–483.

Hoberman, John. *The Olympic Crisis: Sport, Politics, and the Moral Order*. New Rochelle, NY: Aristide D. Caratzas, 1986.

Huizinga, Johan. *Homo Ludens: A Study of the Play Element in Culture*. Boston: Beacon Press, 1950.

James, C. L. R. *Beyond a Boundary*. Durham, NC: Duke University Press, 1983. First published 1963.

Lipsitz, George. "The Struggle for Hegemony." *Journal of American History* 75.1 (1988): 146–150.

MacAloon, John J. "Olympic Games and the Theory of Spectacle in Modern Societies." In *Rite, Drama, Festival, Spectacle: Rehearsals Toward a Theory of Cultural Performance*, 241–280. Philadelphia: Institute for the Study of Human Issues Press, 1984.

MacAloon, John J. *This Great Symbol: Pierre de Coubertin and the Origins of the Modern Olympic Games*. Chicago: University of Chicago Press, 1981.

Mauss, Marcell. "Body Techniques." In *Sociology and Psychology: Essays*, 95–123. London: Routledge and Kegan Paul, 1979. First published 1950.

Messner, Michael. *Power at Play: Sports and the Problem of Masculinity*. Boston: Beacon Press, 1992.

Morgan, William J. "Hegemony Theory, Social Domination, and Sport: The MacAloon and Hargreaves-Tomlinson Debate Revisited." *Sociology of Sport Journal* 11 (1994): 309–329.

Overman, Steven J. *The Protestant Ethic and the Spirit of Sport: How Calvinism and Capitalism Shaped America's Games.* Macon, GA: Mercer University Press, 2011.

Szymanski, Stefan. "A Theory of the Evolution of Modern Sport." *Journal of Sport History* 35.1 (2008): 1–32.

Turner, Bryan. *The Body and Society: Explorations in Social Theory.* 3rd ed. London: SAGE, 2008.

Weber, Max. *The Protestant Ethic and the Spirit of Capitalism.* New York: Charles Scribner's Sons, 1958. First published 1905.

Williams, Raymond. "Base and Superstructure in Marxist Cultural Theory." In *Problems in Materialism and Culture*, 31–49. New York: Verso, 1980.

Willis, Paul. "Women in Sport in Ideology." In *Sport, Culture, and Ideology*, edited by Jennifer Hargreaves, 117–135. London: Routledge and Kegan Paul, 1982.

CHAPTER 2

∙∙∙

SPORT AND POLITICAL DOCTRINE IN A POST-IDEOLOGICAL AGE

∙∙∙

JOHN HOBERMAN

FOLLOWING the fall of the Soviet Union, East Germany, and the other Communist dictatorships of eastern Europe, there was good reason to ask what these momentous events had done to the status and *raison d'être* of political ideology in a post-Communist world. Examining the role of political ideology in the politically charged world of international sports was one way to test the proposition that the "end of ideology" had finally arrived. "The collapse of Eastern European Communism and its vaunted sports systems," I wrote in 1993, "raises the question of whether the familiar left–right bipolar model of the ideological spectrum is still relevant to political life in general or to international sport in particular."[1] In retrospect, what strikes me about this passage is the confident assumption that "the familiar left–right bipolar model of the ideological spectrum" had been an important dimension of international sport. While it is not surprising that, as the author of *Sport and Political Ideology*, I saw political ideology as an animating force in the pre-1989 sports-political universe, an examination of the sports politics of the past two decades presents an opportunity to define the actual roles political ideologies have played in sports politics both before and after the transition to a post-Communist world. Political ideologies are real in that they exist as official doctrines that are imbued with varying degrees of authority. Such doctrines can exert a profound influence on a political culture, and the more dictatorial or totalitarian the regime, the more such doctrines will be applied to various social venues, including sport. What we want to know is the degree to which national governments have translated official ideological positions into actual sports policies during and after the Cold War. A retrospective look back also affords an opportunity to compare the sports-political doctrines of the Cold War period with those that have been formulated by national governments in the absence of the ideological polarization that marked the political standoff between the capitalist democracies and the Soviet system. Which if any of these political doctrines simply disappeared along with the Soviet empire, and which if any have survived?

Sport and Political Ideology (1984) prioritizes the study of official sports doctrine over the governmental policies regarding sport that conformed to official doctrine to one degree or another. The second part of this chapter describes what some may regard as a "post-ideological," namely, post–Cold War political world in which governments around the world offer political rationales for the instrumental use of sport for a variety of reasons. This chapter argues that there is a political doctrine governing the professed or actual use of sport by national governments that is so widespread and so fundamental that it persists independent of the traditional left–right political ideologies. These policies and their goals turn out to be quite uniform across the globe. Both wealthy and less developed countries pursue, or at least pay lip service to, sportive-nationalist objectives that range from the pursuit of Olympic glory to combatting juvenile delinquency. Government officials in poor countries often articulate these goals without having the resources (or the resolve) to achieve them.

There is a modern sports-functional orthodoxy that government officials everywhere feel they must adhere to: elite success plus public benefits. Richard Pringle has identified this orthodoxy with the sociological paradigm known as "functionalism," and that concept fits the evidence. Functionalism "is typically regarded as a meta-theory that views society as an organized system of inter-related structures that function to produce social integration and stability. Sport, under a functionalist regime of truth, is believed to help society by contributing to 'personal growth and the preservation of social order at all levels of social organization.' Functionalist discourses see the strengthening of the structures of sport at both grass roots and elite levels resulting in a more cohesive society."[2] It is readily apparent that this functionalist discourse of sport is a state-sanctioned ideology that promotes the value of sport as a resource for implementing various forms of social engineering.

In the last analysis, all of these objectives are undertaken under the rubric of an expansive concept of national security that comprises both international stature and internal national conditions and development. At the same time, Richard Pringle and others have pointed out that the conventional sports-functional orthodoxy is supported by no credible evidence whatsoever, at which point two things happen: the topic of ideology (socially sanctioned fantasies about causes and effects) reasserts itself, and it becomes necessary to look at the interest groups that profit (financially and/or emotionally) from the promotion of sportive nationalism. The sports-functional orthodoxy is, therefore, both a sincere (if probably mistaken) faith on the part of some officials in sport's beneficial social effects or an official justification for self-serving policies by government and sports officials—or both at the same time. We can call all of this a sports-functional ideology that is itself a consequence of sportive nationalism. This sports-functional ideology is currently an unchallenged international dogma, a global consensus about the importance of a nation's being internationally competitive and using sport to achieve other national goals that include various forms of social development.

Because totalitarian regimes are the most determined and effective promoters of political ideologies that aim to penetrate every aspect of life and national policy, our examination of the ideological uses of sport should first describe the ideas and policies of the Nazi and Soviet regimes. To what extent do a dictatorship's ideological declarations correspond to the policies it actually carries out? And can these policies, perhaps, express contrary ideological values even as the policy serves the political objectives of the regime? For example, one might argue that the Nazi regime's willingness to stage the 1936 Berlin Games both confirmed and violated Nazi ideological norms. The Berlin Olympiad offended Nazi purists and violated Hitler's political instincts by allowing interracial competitions between blacks and whites. A principled hostility to internationalism is implicit in fascist ideology, which extols the cult of the nation, the glorification of war, and the doctrine of race.

Doctrinaire Nazis were deeply offended by sporting contacts with "primitive" races and by competing against Negro athletes, in particular. In 1932 the virulently racist *Völkischer Beobachter* demanded racial segregation in Olympic sport: "Negroes have no place at an Olympiad . . . unfortunately, one finds today that the free man must often compete against unfree blacks, against Negroes, for the victory wreath. This is an unparalleled disgrace and degradation, and the ancient Greeks would turn in their graves if they knew what modern men have made out of their holy National Games. . . . The next Olympic Games will take place in 1936 in Berlin. Hopefully, the men who are responsible in this regard will know what their duty is. The blacks must be excluded. We expect nothing less."[3] In 1940, during a conversation with Albert Speer, his minister of armaments, Hitler himself endorsed the segregationist position on interracial athletic competitions. "People whose antecedents came from the jungle were primitive, their physiques were stronger than those of civilized whites. They represented unfair competition and hence must be excluded from future games."[4]

Yet the racist argument against staging the Berlin Games did not prevail. In March 1933 Hitler and propaganda minister Goebbels were persuaded to turn this Olympiad into a national mission that would demonstrate Germany's greatness on a world stage. One version of this pro-Olympiad argument cleverly made athletic competition into a test of racial strength. Writing in 1941, Carl Diem, a Nazi fellow-traveler and a principal organizer of the Berlin Olympiad, rationalized a racially integrationist sports policy by emphasizing the Nazi value of sheer self-assertion against other peoples and races. "There are many," he noted, "who, consciously or unconsciously, believe that their race should avoid engaging in physical competition with more primitive races." This, Diem argued, is precisely the wrong policy since the "masterful position of the superior race" will last only as long as Europe is willing to compete against the best athletes in the world, regardless of their race.[5] Diem's argument was, in effect, that, for this occasion, acting out Nazi racial megalomania required the kind of multiracial cosmopolitan venue Nazi ideologues despised.

The Nazi regime's quandary about whether to stage its Olympiad thus resulted from competing ideological claims that could be made to serve the regime's various political goals. The racist ideology that would exclude blacks was not, in fact, entirely suppressed, since the regime was prepared to cancel these Games at the last moment in the event the United States decided not to participate.[6] But the presence of, and competition against, the United States, the possibility of Negro victories notwithstanding, trumped the requirements of racial ideology, regardless of whether this decision disappointed the ideological purists. This conflict between Nazi distaste for competition against "primitive races" and the regime's decision to make these multiracial Games an important instrument of foreign policy caused considerable confusion in the Ministry for Popular Enlightenment and Propaganda, which had no choice but to improvise in response to policy decisions coming from the top of the political hierarchy.[7] At the same time, staging the Games had an ideological significance beyond achieving the foreign policy objective of enhancing Germany's stature among the nations. Olympic sport embodied a visible dynamism of movement and force that expressed in dramatic form the narcissistic and aggressive elements of the Nazi ethos that are a significant part of Nazi ideology.[8] The Olympic medals won by German athletes put the inherent dynamism of high-performance sport in the service of the Nazi regime.

The "Nazi Olympics" of 1936 were, therefore, compatible with Nazi ideology in this and in other respects. First, idealizing athletes could be presented as an expression of biological racism. A physically healthy person, Hitler says in *Mein Kampf*, is always to be preferred to a brainy weakling; the Nazi sport ideology that idealized the statuesque bodies and racially pure athletic competitions of the ancient Greeks translated Hitler's preference for robust male bodies into racial ideology.[9] Second, an Olympiad lends itself to being converted into spectacle, and the Nazis were the masters of the spectacle genre at this time. How many Olympic spectators are aware that important elements of Olympic spectacle, such as the torch relay and Hitler's invitation to "the youth of the world," were invented by the creators of the 1936 Games?

The great dictatorships of the twentieth century marked the high point of "the left–right bipolar model" of political ideology. To a greater extent than democratic governments, authoritarian regimes promulgate distinctive and intrusive political anthropologies. These doctrines are formulas for producing the exemplary citizens of a regimented social order. The two great authoritarian political ideologies thus prescribed contrasting "conceptions of what human beings are, what their capacities are, and what sort of social order best serves their needs."[10] The Communist and fascist approaches to sports," Robert Edelman notes, "are by no means subsumable under some broader 'totalitarian' category. Sports in the USSR were to be organized bureaucratically and rationally with the concrete goal of supporting the efficiency of production. Fascism, by contrast, embraced a wide range of irrational appeals, and its approach to sports similarly stressed the joy, ecstasy, aggressiveness, and (for them) virility of athletic competition."[11] A sport could have an ideological signature: "Track and field, a sport of specialists, could be seen as the sporting correlate of the newly empowered [Soviet] technical specialists" of the 1930s.[12] Hitler praised boxing above other sports as a celebration of raw aggression. In short, a sportive style could have ideological content for those who were willing or able or instructed by political leaders to see it.

Both totalitarian regimes achieved great Olympic success. Nazi Germany finished far ahead of the United States in the medal count at the Berlin Games. At every Olympiad from its debut in 1952 until 2000, the Soviet Union (and then Russia) finished either first or second in the Olympic medal count. But it was not the intensified role of political ideology in the dictatorial regimes of Hitler and Stalin that produced athletic success. As an historian of Italian soccer has pointed out: "It would be naïve . . . to make a direct link between fascist ideology and practice and the winning of a lot of football matches." For the fact is that Italian success in soccer both preceded and followed Mussolini's reign. As this author points out: "Fascism was good for Italian football, and football was good for fascism."[13]

But that does not mean that fascism produced better football than another type of political regime might have done. One could point to similar correlations between Stalinism and weightlifting, the Nordic welfare state and skiing, or American democracy and basketball. These are only a few of the illusory causes and effects that tempt us to believe in the power of an ideology to produce superior athletes. The most persuasive of these illusions are generated by the sports triumphs of dictatorial regimes that trumpet their athletic ambitions to the world. The tendency of many people to "identify with the aggressor" persuades them to see correlation as causation when dictators flaunt their powers and their harsh demands for athletic victory. Less forceful governmental policies to promote success in international sport do not call forth the fascination with power that promotes fantasies about causal relationships between political force and the athletic performances they seem to make possible.

The reigning ideologically inspired athletic stereotype of the politically charged competition between capitalist and Communist "systems" was that of the Soviet athlete as a robotic and insensate creature. The Western understanding of Soviet sport was "dominated by the image of a state-sponsored, medal-producing assembly line."[14] This factory-like operation for the production of athletes embodied the collectivism that was a fundamental ideological requirement of the Soviet model. In 1955 the president of the International Olympic Committee, the American business tycoon Avery Brundage, declared that "Russia is building the greatest mass army of athletes the world has ever known." "By American standards," he said, the Soviet sports program "is harsh and severe. It is both Spartan and puritanical. Most of the spirit of fun seems to have been bled from it, and it thrives on regimentation and fierce national pride."[15] "Their athletes are deadly serious," an American sportswriter commented in 1954.[16] Communist athletes who were sullen automatons were living indictments of the political ideology that had spawned them.

Citizens of the United States who absorbed these images of "Communist" athletes did not see American athletes as ideologically motivated performers. What they did see amidst the ideological polemics of the Cold War were elite athletes who had been enlisted as patriotic political proxies in the competition between the United States and the USSR. The high-jump duels between the American John Thomas and his Soviet rival Valery Brumel during the early 1960s were emblematic of this symbolic struggle. When Thomas died in January 2013, *The New York Times* looked back on an era "when sport was often another arena for ideological struggle."[17]

Even as such a verbal formula dramatizes Cold War political tensions, it also conveys a sense of unreality that haunts the ideological polemics that enlisted athletes as reluctant political foils. Sport is properly designated "*another* region for ideological struggle," as opposed to the more dangerous arena in which Khrushchev and Kennedy were rattling their nuclear sabers. As Thomas and Brumel competed against each other around the world, "massive political overlays" covered them like a quilt, as the *Times* put it, making them apolitical actors engaged in what many imagined to be a political ritual. The description of their jumping duels as "theater" confirms that interpreting their performances as political acts required a willing suspension of disbelief. It took an act of the imagination to transform these physical performances into symbols of a nation's political efficiency or superiority.

American politicians of both major parties published reflections on the sports politics of the Cold War that indicate little interest in engaging in ideological arguments with Soviet ideas or politicians. Senator Robert F. Kennedy, for example, saw sportive supremacy as a strategy for breaking the political deadlock between the United States and the Soviets. Olympic medals were also a form of strategic propaganda that could refute Soviet claims about the decline of the West: "[I]n this day of international stalemates," Kennedy wrote in 1964 in *Sports Illustrated*, "nations use the scoreboard of sports as a visible measuring stick to prove their superiority over the 'soft and decadent' democratic way of life. It is thus in our national interest that we regain our Olympic superiority—that we once again give the world visible proof of our inner strength and vitality." One theme is political stature: "Part of a nation's prestige in the cold war," he wrote, "is won in the Olympic Games. In this quadrennial conflict the U.S. skidded steadily for 16 years. The record is there for all the world to see—and to note as proof of a decline in our once-acknowledged national energy."[18]

The second and related theme is a quasi-biological notion of national "vitality" and "energy." Four years earlier, President John F. Kennedy had declared that "the knowledge that the physical well-being of the citizen is an important foundation for the vigor and vitality of all the activities of the nation, is as old as Western civilization itself." More explicitly than his brother Robert, President Kennedy warned against "the softness on the part of the individual citizens [that] can help to strip and destroy the vitality of a nation."[19] "Physical vigor," he said in 1962," was the key to "insuring the continued flourishing of our civilization."[20] In 1974 President Gerald R. Ford wrote that "competitive athletics" played a crucial role in maintaining "our competitive spirit in this country, the thing that made us great, the guts of the free-enterprise system." He also promoted the propaganda value of sportive excellence: "I don't know of a better advertisement for a nation's good health than a healthy athletic representation."[21]

This bipartisan rhetoric has two related concerns: the health status of the national organism and the nation's global athletic reputation. The core fantasy expressed here is that the biological health of the population will eventually manifest itself as national strength in political, economic, and athletic competitions. Almost none of these verbal formulas refer specifically to a Soviet threat or Communist ideology; the exception is Robert Kennedy's reference to "the 'soft and decadent' democratic way of life"—an oblique response to the Soviet propaganda cliché he has quoted. Cliché or not, however, all of these politicians express a concern about American "softness," a metaphor that signifies both physical decline and a loss of national willpower. All of these hortatory essays appeared in *Sports Illustrated*, the most widely circulated sports publication in the United States, then and now.

These calls to improve the health of the population and the medal counts at the Olympic Games are ideological in that they faithfully reproduce an ideology of national vitality that was formulated in Victorian England during the second half of the nineteenth century. President Kennedy quotes in 1962 from a speech the former Prime Minister Disraeli delivered on June 24, 1877: "The health of the people is really the foundation upon which all their happiness and all their powers as a State depend."[22] The more famous and earthier quotation in this vein appeared in 1861 in Herbert Spencer's essay on "Physical Education": "the first requisite to success in life is 'to be a good animal'; and to be a nation of good animals is the first condition to national prosperity." Writing decades before the modern Olympic movement made sportive nationalism a familiar part of the global political landscape, Spencer notes without much alarm that Victorian England took greater interest in the production of a racehorse than "a modern athlete."

At the same time, Spencer seems to have intuited the future role of the athlete as a representative of national energy on the international stage along with men whose physical performances take a more tangible form. The result of "a war often turns on the strength and hardiness of soldiers," while "the contests of commerce are in part determined by the bodily endurance of producers." It is at this point that Spencer articulates that concern about national vitality American presidents would articulate a century later; "Thus far we have found no reason to fear trials of strength with other races in either of these fields. But there are not wanting signs that our powers will presently be taxed to the uttermost. The competition of modern life is so keen, that few can bear the required application without injury." An important task of the modern state is thus to make English children mentally and physically tough enough to cope with the "excessive wear and tear" to which the modern struggle for existence will subject them.[23]

Other Victorian commentators made a direct connection between sportive prowess and national power. The Reverend J. E. C. Welldon, headmaster of Harrow School from 1881 to 1895, wrote that: "In the history of the British Empire it is written that England has owed her sovereignty to her sports." In his treatise on *Our Public Schools. Their Influence on English History*, J. G. C. Minchin wrote in 1901 that "there is assuredly nothing more splendidly Greek than the Eton eight in training for Henley. Such thews and sinews must give the hegemony of the world to the country that can produce such athletes."[24] As early as 1868 the *Times* of London had described the University Boat Race as a demonstration of "that instinct which urges every Englishman to be as good as his neighbor, and which keeps up the whole nation at least on a par with other nations."[25]

These commentaries make it clear that the fundamental premise (or illusion) of sportive nationalism—namely, that elite athletes embody and express an essential competitive instinct that serves the national security—was alive and well during the Victorian period. What is more, the origin of its "ideological" component is a fantasy about the collective biological energy of the nation. Social-psychological thinking (or fantasies) about the "role-model" effects of elite athletes are a post-Victorian development that still coexist with vaguely biological ideas about the health and athletic prowess of the body politic. Consider, for example, the young Russian nationalists who marched through the streets of Moscow in November 2011 chanting slogans that included "Sport! Health! Nationalism!"—a formula that sums up the sports-nationalist doctrine of Cold War American presidents as well as that of the Victorian inventors of this "ideology" from whom American politicians and others have inherited this extremely influential version of sportive nationalism.[26]

In retrospect, as we observe totalitarian and nontotalitarian sports cultures, it becomes clear that governments large and small, and across the political spectrum, have employed *raison d'état* as the spoken or unspoken justification for promoting success in international sport. The sportive nationalism that originates in shared fantasies about a linkage between the production of high-performance athletes and national viability constitutes the fundamental sports ideology of the twentieth and twenty-first centuries. A remarkable sense of urgency about the importance of athletic respectability in the eyes of the world has produced a set of sports policies that can be called *generic* in that they serve state-sponsored objectives that most nations have pursued irrespective of their political ideologies.

While the megalomania of the totalitarian dictatorships attracted massive attention to their use of sport for *raisons d'état,* many nonauthoritarian governments have both accepted and proclaimed the generic doctrine of sportive nationalism that regards international competitiveness as nothing less than a matter of national security. This is the only way to explain the almost ubiquitous emotional and financial investments in this form of national prestige. The perceived psychological lift for a nation that achieves sportive supremacy can seem both real and fantastical. For example, the Soviet performance at the 1952 Helsinki Olympic Games came close to matching that of the United States and had a Sputnik-like effect on morale five years before the USSR launched mankind's first artificial satellite into Earth's orbit: "The very idea that that their nation could perform as well as the United States in any field of human endeavor had great resonance with the Soviet public."[27] In a similar vein, "when Brazil in 1970 won the Football World Cup, there was a strong feeling within the country that their way of life was equal to or even better than the first world countries and they felt that their country had become recognized in international society."[28] Spain's 2010 World Cup soccer victory in South Africa stimulated fantasies of a sudden boost to a national economy whose disastrous condition still persists. The alleged murder scandal involving the South African Paralympic champion Oscar Pistorius that erupted in February 2013 exposed once again the fragility of such euphoric national experiences, which are "united around a temporary emotion associated with winning, or even around a personality, rather than a set of values, principles or ideals."[29]

State-sponsored sports initiatives of various kinds express a "post-ideological" doctrine (or ideology) of sheer utilitarianism that includes sport's (socially useful) inspirational impact on the nation as a whole as well as the pursuit of international prestige. Like the pig whose every body part must be put to profitable use, governmental agencies regard sport as a multifaceted resource that must not be allowed to go to waste. Sports England, which aims at creating a "community sports system," declares that "The value of sport to local government extends beyond sport for sports sake." The claimed benefits include health, community safety, employment, and economic growth. The Australian Sports Commission is a statutory agency of the Australian Government; the Australian Institute of Sport is Australia's premier sports training institute. Russia has a Ministry of Sport. The Norwegian Ministry of Culture has a "Strategy for R & D in Sports," even as Norwegian sports officials struggle to balance their purportedly high ethical standards vis-à-vis doping against the mandate to win medals.[30] High Performance Sport New Zealand is a subsidiary of Sport New Zealand, the Crown agency that oversees the sports establishment. Atypically among the wealthier nations, in 1978 the United States Congress delegated responsibility for elite sport to the United States Olympic Committee, a nongovernmental body. The United States Anti-Doping Agency (USADA) is a "nongovernmental" body that is recognized (and largely funded) by the US Congress as "the official anti-doping agency for Olympic, Pan American and Paralympic sport in the United States." This makes USADA a curious hybrid among the agencies around the world that bear responsibility for the integrity of a nation's elite sports. Note that every government with the resources to invest in international sports prestige thereby creates an internal conflict between the requirements of national ambitions to win medals and the pressure to promote or tolerate doping. In some countries, while one governmental agency is charged with developing high-performance athletes, another may be assigned the task of reducing the national medal count by catching the dopers the first agency produces, assuming of course the anti-doping agency has the resources to do so.

The utilitarian ideology of sport, and its implicit (and often vague) invocations of national security and social well-being, has also been embraced in word or deed by many small countries, some of which cannot afford to compete at the elite level. Like the governments of Zambia and Namibia, the government of Jamaica, a small and poor country that still manages to produce world-class sprinters, has appealed for private investment in sport. Wealthy Brunei sponsors the Brunei Gold Project to win medals in regional competitions; physical fitness underlies "national development." The government of Malta invests in sports to create "a sports Economy that will result in quality jobs." Sport in Ireland is "an investment in the health and well-being of the country." The government of Fiji promotes sport as "nation building." The government of the Azores sees sport as having "raised the Azores to prominence" in the wider world. The determination on the part of micro-states to engage in this global contest on a micro-scale conveys a sense of urgency that derives from a concept of national security whose "ideology" is a doctrine of perpetual competition and slavish obedience to the performance principle. Less competitive civilizational ideals have been discounted in this world of unending global struggle.

This sportive nationalist ideology now coexists with an authoritative anti-doping ideology promulgated by the World Anti-Doping Agency (WADA). The basis of this doctrine is the World Anti-Doping Code that entered into force on January 1, 2004; a revised version of the code took effect on January 1, 2009. It is important to note that WADA's inability to prevail against the doping epidemic in global sport has not up to this point reduced the authority of its anti-doping ideology. On the contrary, WADA's prohibition-ist ideology directed against doping has become increasingly influential even as its lead-ership has become increasingly pessimistic over the past couple of years and has even proclaimed that the global "war" against doping cannot be won. The WADA doctrine and sportive nationalism thus coexist as the predominant, and fundamentally incom-patible, sports ideologies of the early twenty-first century.

Do we, therefore, inhabit a "post-ideological" era in which the traditional left–right divide has actually disappeared? In fact, the global anti-doping doctrine continued to demonstrate some ideological differentiation along the left–right spectrum in Germany during the 1980s and 1990s. The election of "Green" Party members to the Bundestag (the Parliament) during the 1980s revived the West German neo-Marxist critique of high-performance sport that appeared in the late 1960s and early 1970s. This critical perspective attacked dangerous training regimens, biochemical manipulation of ath-letes, exploitation of child athletes, and the unwholesome determination to disregard human limits. The Greens' critique of elite sport found its place within a more compre-hensive attack on technological interventions into the human organism such as genetic engineering.[31]

This ideological conflict over the proper roles and values of high-performance sport between German conservatives and the Social Democrats and Greens in the German Parliament reasserted itself many years later. Following the 2012 London Olympic Games, it was revealed that the Interior Ministry had assigned Olympic medal quotas to German sports federations and had stipulated that funding levels would reflect perfor-mance levels in international competitions. In partnership with the German Olympic Sports Association, the Interior Ministry refused to make public its internal delibera-tions about what amounted to mandated "performance goals" (*Zielvereinbarungen*). This episode signaled that the federal government's postwar national security ideology regarding Germany's international sports achievements was still intact. In 1989, while serving as Chancellor Helmut Kohl's interior minister, Manfred Kanther (a conserva-tive) had famously declared that high-performance sport was a "national priority" (*ein nationales Anliegen*). A generation after Kanther's pronouncement, Germany's "func-tional" approach to sports policy continued under another conservative chancellor; and, once again, what appeared to be a politically conservative attachment to sportive nation-alism was challenged by left-of-center German parliamentarians. This fundamental left–right ideological conflict over the proper roles and limitations of sportive national-ism could intensify as sports doping scandals continue to erupt around the world.

The attenuation of left–right ideological conflict regarding doping has been succeeded by a more subtle competition between national anti-doping programs. Given the global hegemony of WADA orthodoxy, a new criterion of national superiority is anti-doping fervor and the willingness of governments to enforce anti-doping measures even at the cost of disqualifying their best athletes. Dionne L. Koller has argued that this develop-ment resulted from growing public awareness of doping: "It was out of this climate that there emerged a new paradigm for sport in the late 1990s. While the private sector was delivering athletes who were winning, they were no longer enhancing national prestige because of the cloud of doping. The United States Government, therefore, recalculated its interest to reflect that it is no longer in the national interest to simply have athletes who are successful in international athletic competition. It must do so with the moral authority that the United States does not cheat."[32] Koller argues convincingly that the global anti-doping campaign has changed the symbolic politics of sport, in that doping positives can cancel out at least some of the national prestige that is conventionally associated with victorious athletes. This suggests that the perceived efficacy of a nation's anti-doping efforts now represents a secondary (if unofficial) form of international competition. The integrity of drug-testing thus becomes an important dimension of the WADA-enforced anti-doping ideology that is now a global doctrine. Koller calls anti-doping regulation "a more evolved manifestation of sportive nationalism. Accordingly, it is no longer winning medals in Olympic Movement competition that provides international prestige. The medals must be won with moral authority."[33]

This important observation must be evaluated in the larger context of the ongoing contest between traditional sportive nationalism and the anti-doping bureaucracy that attempts to contain its pharmacological excesses. While anti-doping regulation can indeed be seen as "a more evolved manifestation of sportive nationalism," its prestige and impact on sportive nationalism should not be overestimated. For it is not quite the case that Olympic "medals must be won with moral authority." It would be more accurate to say that they must be won without the medalists testing positive for doping drugs. By now it is widely understood that a significant number of doped athletes continue to win medals without being detected. The result is that these medal-winning performances exist in a kind of purgatorial state. The urine samples of Olympic athletes are now frozen and stored for a period of eight years, so that the improved testing methods of the future may reveal doping that cannot be detected today. A growing cynicism about elite sport in general—and extraordinary athletic performances in particular—now pervades the global sporting public. A series of doping mega-scandals, ranging in time from Ben Johnson's Olympic disgrace in 1988 to the spectacular fall of Lance Armstrong twenty-five years later, have taken a toll on the prestige value of international sporting triumphs.

National governments have demonstrated varying degrees of commitment to the "secondary" competition (and ideology) of doping control. In the United States, the Office of National Drug Control Policy, established in 1989, partly funds the USADA and has publicly opposed doping in sports. The US government played a leading role in the establishment of WADA. At the same time, the US Department of Justice has taken legal action against confirmed or suspected American dopers such as Barry Bonds, Marion Jones, Roger Clemens, and Lance Armstrong. In February 2004, then-US Attorney General John Ashcroft went on television to announce indictments in the BALCO doping conspiracy case. "The government, as a prosecutorial and reform vehicle, entered the steroids era with zeal and optimism: Finally, baseball and its players had to answer to a more powerful body, one that it could not simply lie to and laugh at."[34]

Sportive nationalism in the age of anti-doping morality, as noted earlier, creates a perpetual tension between government-sponsored programs to win international medals and (in some countries) government-sponsored anti-doping agencies charged with detecting their own doped athletes. Adherence to the WADA Code amounts to a form of global political correctness. In 2010, for example, Swiss Sport Minister Ueli Maurer mentioned the anti-doping mandate in the context of virtuous Swiss internationalism: "It's clear that Switzerland is obliged to do something to fight corruption as we have lots of international federations with headquarters in Switzerland and we want to set an example in solving this problem."[35] In the same year, Indian Sports Minister M. S. Gill described his message to Indian athletes: "It is true that we do want lots of medals in the Commonwealth Games. But even if we get one, we want that medal with honour. . . . We have to kill the abuse of dope."[36] The potential for farce regarding such commitments was evident in 2012 when Alexander Lukashenko, the authoritarian head of state of Belarus, declared: "We need to criminalize the use of doping."[37] This statement came three days after Lukashenko lambasted the country's "complete failure" at the 2012 London Olympic Games. A week earlier the Belarussian president castigated the national soccer team following a 4–0 loss at home to the world and European champions from Spain. "I've never seen such a disgrace for our nation," he said. "Our team, excuse my language, just shit themselves. They came out on the pitch with their legs and arms shaking."[38] Dictators who bully their sports officials and athletes are not likely to subscribe to the anti-doping ethos, but they feel, nonetheless, that they are obliged to pledge allegiance to the anti-doping ideology.

Russian President Vladimir Putin has employed the same strategy of demanding drug-free sport and international sporting success simultaneously. The Russian Anti-Doping Agency was created in January 2008 by the Federal Agency for Physical Culture and Sport in compliance with the WADA Code and the 2005 UNESCO International Convention Against Doping in Sport. In 2009 and 2012, Putin called for crackdowns on doping.[39] The Russian Parliament passed anti-doping laws in 2011.[40] Russian sports federations have announced and enforced doping bans against a number of their athletes. But this ostensible compliance with international anti-doping norms coexists with a degree of cynicism about doping controls. In 2010 President Dmitry Medvedev stated: "We must get rid of this image, which our country seems to have picked up. We need to evaluate the situation and take all necessary measures, including the adoption of new laws." He added that doping scandals "are a well-known means of settling scores and an element of global sporting competition. We must know how to defend ourselves and not turn the other cheek."[41] Here the politics of doping is regarded, all too realistically, as a matter of image management and political maneuvering. But even as these sobering realities are addressed, public fealty to the WADA Code and its ideology of sporting virtue must be performed if not sincerely embraced.

Behind the façade of governmental anti-doping pronouncements, government officials and national federations often tolerate the bending or ignoring of anti-doping rules. The Brazilian swimming federation in 2011 accepted the alibis of four swimmers who had tested positive for a banned substance.[42] The superstar among this group was selected as Brazil's Athlete of the Year despite this suspicious finding.[43] In

2010 the National Anti-Doping Commission of Slovenia refused to accept a finding by the International Cycling Union (UCI) that its blood passport procedure indicated Slovenia's best road cyclist had doped.[44] In 2011 the Russian Cycling Federation refused to ban a rider who had tested positive for a banned diuretic, thereby contesting a ruling from the UCI.[45] In 2010 an Indian weightlifter was reprieved by an Anti-Doping Disciplinary panel after testing positive for an abnormal testosterone level; the panel accepted his argument that the testosterone was a medically indicated treatment for "infertility."[46] In 2011 Spanish Prime Minister Zapatero declared that the Spanish cycling star Alberto Contador was innocent of a doping charge that had been upheld by WADA, the UCI, and the Court of Arbitration for Sport in Lausanne.[47] Nor was this the only time a head of state had chosen sportive nationalism over anti-doping ideology.

This survey of the ideological dimension of international sports politics has shown that the classic left–right spectrum has lost most of its relevance as an interpretive framework following the end of the Cold War. That once-familiar ideological spectrum has been replaced by two competing ideologies that exist in a state of tension with each other. The first is a "functionalist" doctrine that treats sport as a multifaceted national resource that includes the self-assertive doctrine of sportive nationalism. The second is the global anti-doping doctrine that WADA promulgates and attempts to enforce with its limited resources.

For sports bureaucrats, the ideological content of sportive nationalism, which includes social development at home and national self-assertion abroad, is both an inspiration and an instrument. Sports administrators and politicians convince themselves and others that the production of elite athletes provides the nation with socially useful role models and dynamic representatives on the global stage. Given the ancient primacy of physical combat as a metaphor of political struggle, modern imaginations can easily transform athletic demonstrations of physical superiority into powerful symbols of national vitality and a people's determination to survive. At the same time, sports bureaucrats enlist the appeals of sportive nationalism to promote sportive nationalist projects that provide them with both career benefits and public recognition. Inspiring ideas commingle with self-serving motives. In this sense, any sports "ideology" that functions in the real world today will alternately inspire pride or shame in those who understand its composite nature.

The ideological character of both of the contending doctrines—sportive nationalism and anti-doping—is evident in their essentially aspirational status. Sportive nationalism has thrived around the world in the absence of any empirical evidence that it confers at home the social benefits it is supposed to produce or the international stature it is supposed to create abroad.[48] (Let the Olympic triumphs of the former East Germany stand as a lesson to us all.) Anti-doping doctrine expresses a set of values that are constantly being debated as doping scandals proliferate. An attractive ideology, in the last analysis, is not a verifiable claim. It is at its core a hypothesis whose charisma conceals its nonrational origin, its initial leap of faith into a claim about truth.

Notes

1. John Hoberman, "Sport and Ideology in the Post-Communist Age," in *The Changing Politics of Sport*, ed. Lincoln Allison (Manchester, UK and New York: Manchester University Press, 1993), 15.

2. Richard Pringle, "Examining the Justifications for Government Investment in High Performance Sport: A Critical Review Essay," *Annals of Leisure Research* 4 (2001): 63.

3. Arnd Krüger, *Die olympischen Spiele 1936 und die Weltmeinung* (Berlin, München, Frankfurt: Verlag Bartels & Wernitz, 1972), 172.

4. Albert Speer, *Inside the Third Reich* (New York: Avon Books, 1971), 114.

5. Carl Diem, "Weltspiele?" in *Olympische Flamme: Das Buch vom Sport*, vol. I (Berlin: Deutscher Archiv-Verlag, 1942), 245.

6. Arnd Krüger, "Germany: The Propaganda Machine," in *The Nazi Olympics: Sport, Politics, and Appeasement in the 1930s*, eds. Arnd Krüger and William Murray (Urbana and Chicago: University of Illinois Press, 2003), 26.

7. Krüger, "Germany," 24.

8. John Hoberman, *The Olympic Crisis: Sport, Politics, and the Moral Order* (New Rochelle, NY: Aristide D. Caratzas, 1986), 105.

9. *Nationalsozialistiche Leibeserziehung*, ed. Hajo Bernett (Schondorf bei Stuttgart: Verlag Karl Hofmann, 1966), 21.

10. Hoberman, *Sport and Political Ideology*, 2.

11. Robert Edelman, *Serious Fun: A History of Spectator Sports in the USSR* (New York: Oxford University Press, 1993), 10.

12. Edelman, *Serious Fun*, 76.

13. John Foot, *Winning at All Costs: A Scandalous History of Italian Soccer* (New York: Nation Books, 2007), 440, 33.

14. Edelman, *Serious Fun*, 243.

15. Avery Brundage, "I Must Admit—Russian Athletes Are Great!" *Saturday Evening Post* (April 30, 1955).

16. Don Canham, "Russia Will Win the 1956 Olympics," *Sports Illustrated* (October 25, 1954).

17. "John Thomas Dies at 71; Set Standard in the High Jump," *The New York Times* (January 22, 2013).

18. Robert F. Kennedy, "A Bold Proposal for American Sport," *Sports Illustrated* (July 27, 1964): 13.

19. President-Elect John F. Kennedy, "The Soft American," *Sports Illustrated* (December 26, 1960): 15, 16.

20. President John F. Kennedy, "The Vigor We Need," *Sports Illustrated* (July 16, 1962): 14.

21. Gerald R. Ford, "In Defense of the Competitive Urge," *Sports Illustrated* (July 8, 1974): 16.

22. Kennedy, "The Vigor We Need," 12.

23. Herbert Spencer, "Physical Education," in *Essays on Education and Kindred Subjects* (London: Dent, 1911), 116–152.

24. J. A. Mangan, *The Games Ethic and Imperialism* (New York: Viking, 1986), 36, 48.

25. Bruce Haley, *The Healthy Body and Victorian Culture* (Cambridge, MA and London: Harvard University Press, 1978), 170.

26. "Russian Nationalism May Be Biggest Threat to Putin's Power, Experts Warn," *The Guardian* (November 9, 2011).

27. Edelman, *Serious Fun*, 123.

28. Chien-Yu Lin, Ping-Chao Lee, and Hui-Fang, "Theorizing the Role of Sport in State-Politics," *International Journal of Sport and Exercise Science* 1 (2008): 26.
29. "Oscar Pistorius's Rise and Fall Reflects the State of South Africa," *The Guardian* (February 19, 2013).
30. Dag Vidar Hanstad, "Toppidrettens dilemma," *Aftenposten* (January 13, 2013).
31. See John Hoberman, *Mortal Engines: The Science of Performance and the Dehumanization of Sport* (New York: Free Press, 1992), 239–252.
32. Dionne L. Koller, "From Medals to Morality: Sportive Nationalism and the Problem of Doping in Sports," *Marquette Sports Law Review* 19 (2008): 112.
33. Koller, "From Medals," 116.
34. Howard Bryant, "Swing and Miss," *ESPN: The Magazine* (July 18, 2012). http://espn.go.com/mlb/story/_/id/8132551/the-failed-prosecution-roger-clemens-just-one-man-espn-magazine.
35. "Sport Minister to Lead Corruption Fight," swissinfo.ch (November 23, 2010). http://www.swissinfo.ch/eng/sport/Swiss_vow_to_lead_sport_corruption_fight.html?cid=28858632.
36. *The Times of India* (September 8, 2010). http://articles.timesofindia.indiatimes.com/2010-09-08/india/28254333_1_national-games-commonwealth-games-ioa.
37. http://news.belta.by/en/news/president?id=697298.
38. "Olympics-Uncompromising Lukashenko blasts Belarus Games failure," *Reuters* (October 26, 2012). http://mobile.reuters.com/article/olympicsNews/idUSL3E8LQ6TM20121026.
39. "Putin Calls for Crackdown on Sports Doping," *UPI* (February 24, 2009). http://www.upi.com/Top_News/2009/02/24/Putin-calls-for-crackdown-on-sports-doping/UPI-65461235487570/; http://india.nydailynews.com/business/b772be64fb258a0710d-e453d274e93ee/putin-seeks-fight-against-doping-sports-gambling.
40. "Russia Toughens Anti-doping Regulations," Prokeraia.com (June 8, 2011). http://www.prokerala.com/news/articles/a227013.html.
41. http://en.rian.ru/russia/20100326/158320973.html; http://www.themoscowtimes.com/news/article/medvedev-seethes-as-flag-rises-in-sochi/402698.html.
42. "Swim Body Wants Brazil Doping Action Fast," *The Sydney Morning Herald* (July 5, 2011). http://news.smh.com.au/breaking-news-sport/swim-body-wants-brazil-doping-action-fast-20110705-1gzj9.html.
43. http://www.gazetaesportiva.net/noticia/2011/12/natacao/melhor-do-ano-cielo-chora-ao-recordar-doping-antes-do-mundial.html.
44. "Cyclist Valjavec Cleared of Doping Charges," *STA* [Slovenia] (July 29). http://www.sta.si/en/vest.php?s=a&id=1539082.
45. "UCI Appeals Kolobnev Case to CAS," *VeloNews* (January 5, 2012). http://velonews.competitor.com/2011/12/news/uci-appeals-kolobnev-case-to-cas_199013.
46. "Panel Absolves Sharma," *The Hindu* (September 22, 2010). http://www.thehindu.com/sport/other-sports/article740747.ece.
47. "WADA President: 'No choice but to Appeal' Contador case Following Zapatero Comments," *Cycling News* (February 8, 2012). http://www.cyclingnews.com/news/wada-president-no-choice-but-to-appeal-contador-case-following-zapatero-comments.
48. See, for example, Richard Pringle, "Examining the Justifications for Government Investment in High Performance Sport: A Critical Review Essay," *Annals of Leisure Research* 4 (2001): 58–75.

BIBLIOGRAPHY

Edelman, Robert. *Serious Fun: A History of Spectator Sports in the USSR*. New York: Oxford University Press, 1993.

Hoberman, John. "Sport and Ideology in the Post-Communist Age." In *The Changing Politics of Sport*, edited by Lincoln Allison, 15–36. Manchester, UK and New York: Manchester University Press, 1993.

Hoberman, John. *Sport and Political Ideology*. Austin: University of Texas Press, 1984.

Koller, Dionne L. "From Medals to Morality: Sportive Nationalism and the Problem of Doping in Sports." *Marquette Sports Law Review* 19 (2008): 91–124.

Pringle, Richard. "Examining the Justifications for Government Investment in High Performance Sport: A Critical Review Essay." *Annals of Leisure Research* 4 (2001): 58–75.

CHAPTER 3

THE "SOMATIC/LINGUISTIC TURN" AND HISTORIES OF EXERCISE AND SPORT

RICHARD GRUNEAU

WHILE there has always been an interest in bodies in Western social thought, a widespread concern for the *social* and *historical* analysis of human bodies did not develop until the late 1980s. In historiography, over the next twenty or so years, the body suddenly seemed to be on nearly everyone's agenda, leading the prolific British historian Roy Porter to declare in 2001 that the body had become "the historiographical dish of the day."[1] What Porter observed in Western historiography has been equally true in most other disciplines in the humanities and social sciences, although perhaps not to the same degree in sport history. The human body is the object of particularly intense manipulation and scrutiny in sport, but, with a few significant exceptions, the body has never quite reached the same importance in sport history as in Western historiography more generally.

It would be far too ambitious in a single book chapter to attempt a history of the early twenty-first century fascination with all things corporeal. The "turn to the body" in Western social thought has been shaped by a complex array of social, economic, political, and cultural factors, as well as a diversity of intellectual traditions in different countries. These factors and traditions are also at play in the more focused historical literature on bodies in sport and related forms of training or exercise, and they are further complicated by a very distinctive set of subdisciplinary traditions. Rather than attempt a superficial unraveling of this complexity, I have opted for much narrower strategy. This chapter focuses on the work of Pierre Bourdieu and Michel Foucault, explaining their respective approaches to the study of the body and highlighting their influences on historical writing on physical exercise and sport from the 1970s to the present day. It would be equally valuable to develop another line of analysis centered on important traditions in German social thought, beginning with implications for the study of sporting bodies in Karl Marx's analysis of machines and moving through Max Weber's analysis of rationalization, Norbert Elias's discussion of the civilizing process, or Max Horkheimer and Theodor Adorno's discussions of the dialectic of enlightenment and the rise of modern "industries" of culture. However, I focus on Bourdieu and Foucault for two key reasons: first, their work, and Foucault's in particular, has had an extraordinary influence on the late twentieth century turn to the body; and second, the structuralist underpinning of their work provides connections to a parallel, and highly influential, "linguistic turn" in contemporary historiography where bodily history has come to be understood as an effect of discourse and power.

Structuralism, Habitus, and Bodily Practice: From Althusser to Bourdieu

There was intense debate in French intellectual life after the Second World War about relationships between human subjectivity and the structures that constituted social and cultural life. The French existentialist philosopher Jean Paul Sartre was on one side of the debate. The anthropologist Claude Lévi-Strauss was on the other. Sartre insisted that human beings are what they *make* themselves, and he championed a view that emphasized the importance of subjectivity and moral judgment. Lévi-Strauss rejected Sartre's vision of human agency and subjectivity and countered with an attempt to "decenter" the Cartesian subject from what he perceived as its privileged, and undeserved, place in Western philosophy. The structuralist sensibility championed by Lévi-Strauss was built on the idea that both subjectivity and corporeal practice could be understood as roughly analogous to how the deep structures of language create the possibility for different utterances to become meaningful speech. But, at the same time, the active speaker was being "spoken by," or embedded into, the symbolic order. This line of argument greatly influenced a younger generation of theorists, including Michel Foucault and Pierre Bourdieu, who became interested in the role of the body in the production and reproduction of societal logics of difference, power, and social organization.

Bourdieu was influenced along these lines by his studies with the prominent Marxist philosopher Louis Althusser, despite his considerable reservations about his teacher's Communist Party affiliation. For example, Althusser's influence is evident in Bourdieu's discussion of embodied subjectivity in his 1972 book *Outline of a Theory of Practice*, which draws on field research conducted in Algeria between 1958 and 1962. Bourdieu noted that women among the Kabyle people maintained posture that was downward looking, suggesting modesty, in contrast to the upright stances of men. In addition to posture, the freedom and visibility of men in public spaces, and restriction of females to more enclosed spaces in the home, could be seen in the shapes of the bodies of Kabylian men and women. The look and practices of male or female bodies expressed a "durably installed generative principle of regulated improvisations." Borrowing an idea from an essay written in 1934 by Marcel Mauss, Bourdieu referred to this generative principle as a "habitus," which "produces practices which tend to reproduce the regularities immanent in the objective conditions of the production of their generative principle while adjusting to the demands inscribed as objective potentialities in situation, as defined by the cognitive and motivating structures making up the habitus."[2]

For Bourdieu, the behaviors of any acting subject operate within a cultural/cognitive frame that literally becomes materialized unconsciously in the tissues of body. Taking certain positions or postures has the effect of "reinforcing the feelings they represent."[3] Bourdieu does not mean that memory and subjectivity are simply passive reflections of an otherwise constituted social and cultural/linguistic order. Rather, habitus is *generative* of regulated improvisations and structured "like language" insofar as it "regulates the range of possible practices without actually selecting specific practices, just as linguistic forms may limit individual utterances without in any way determining which of the infinite number of possible sentences or combinations of words are actually spoken at any given moment."[4] But this is done without the conscious knowledge of subjects, whose bodies and perceptions are set in motion by the generative principles of the sociocultural symbolic order.

Bourdieu wrote several papers during the 1970s and 1980s specifically devoted to outlining how sport "as a field of practice" would necessarily involve considerations of the body. Bourdieu suggests that the social production of sport *as a distinctive field of practice* in Western societies has been characterized by three structuring principles: autonomization, rationalization, and philosophical/political/moral justification. *Autonomization* refers to the institutional separation and disembedding of sporting practices from other logics of practice in social life, such as folk rituals, economics, and politics. *Rationalization* refers to the increasing emphasis on predictability and calculation in the development of rules and in the creation of self-administering governing organizations, as well as in the areas of training technique and tactics. *Philosophical/political/moral justification* refers to the structuring discourses that develop within sport in respect to such things as producing a dominant social definition of sport; establishing the legitimate meaning, purpose, and ethical principles of sporting practice; and producing an accompanying set of "definitions of the legitimate body and the legitimate uses of the body."[5]

Bourdieu insists that that historical emergence of sport as "its own object" did not occur as a reflection of broader economic or technological development, urbanization, or industrialization, although these processes were important. Nor did sport develop in any evolutionary way. Rather, the production of sport as an "objective" field of practice occurred within a broader "field of struggles," between social classes and "fractions of the dominant classes" over the uses of time and differing conceptions of morality and between men and women over respective visions of manliness and femininity. These struggles are inseparable from understanding the production of differentiated "dispositions" that are one dimension of a *"particular relation to the body"* that is " part of the system of tastes and preferences associated with a class habitus."[6] Class habitus, in Bourdieu's view, with its accompanying understandings of taste and morality, and relationships to different forms of "capital" (e.g., economic and cultural), becomes manifest in bodily practice, influencing everything from deportment to an appreciation of some techniques and styles of play over others (e.g., working-class males' appreciation of strength and toughness over an appreciation of artistry and technical sophistication among fractions of the dominant classes). These dispositions, bodily relations, and practices play a role in reproducing the dominant logic of the sporting field, as well as class and gender relations more broadly, in social life as a whole.

Like Althusser, Bourdieu is often viewed as a structuralist theorist accused of being more interested in synchronic rather than historical analysis and with a formal or systemic focus on how particular logics of inequality and domination are reproduced in and through the body. There is a measure of truth to this accusation, and that is why Bourdieu's work has generally been of greater interest to sociologists and cultural studies theorists than to historians. Still, Bourdieu's concept of habitus has been increasingly influential in historical analysis, especially in respect to the analysis of changes in habitus over time. More notably, Bourdieu's categories of autonomization, rationalization, and philosophical/moral legitimation (to which I would add the category of "aestheticizing") are historical in intent, and there has been greater recognition in recent years of the historical dimensions of Bourdieu's work. My own early work on social class and the institutional "structuring" of Canadian sport in the nineteenth and twentieth centuries took some of its inspiration from Bourdieu,[7] although other writers with an interest in sport history have followed Bourdieu's methods and ideas more closely and in more detail. One very interesting recent example is John Bale's use of Bourdieu's ideas about differing forms of capital (e.g., economic, cultural, bodily, and social capital) to develop a highly contextualized discussion of the biography of the legendary English runner Roger Bannister.[8]

Still, the most significant historical analyst in this tradition is Jacques Defrance, who studied with Bourdieu and wrote a dissertation in the mid-1980s on the making of French sport between 1770 and 1914.[9] In a recent essay Defrance notes how his newer historical work on the genesis of the "sport field" in France from 1895 to 1955 continues to be influenced by three methodological "rules" drawn from Bourdieu: analyzing the structuring of the field of sport within the broader "field of power;" mapping the "objective structures" of relations between "the positions occupied by agents or institutions" who compete to define "the legitimate form of specific activity within the field;" and analyzing the habitus of the agents, including the "different systems of dispositions they have acquired by internalizing a determinate type of economic and social conditions, and which find in a definite trajectory within the field under consideration a more or less favorable opportunity to become self-actualized."[10]

MICHEL FOUCAULT AND
THE HISTORICIZED BODY

Louis Althusser was also one of Michel Foucault's teachers, and there are suggestions in Foucault's work of Althusser's concern for the role of embodied subjectivity in the reproduction of dominant social relations. However, Foucault's graduate supervisor was the philosopher Georges Canguilhem, a trained physician interested in ethics, histories of epistemology, and medical discourses of normality. Foucault was also interested in German phenomenology and studied with the French phenomenological philosopher Maurice Merleau Ponty. In the midst of the ongoing debate in postwar France about relations between structures and subjectivity Merleau Ponty had largely taken the subjectivist side, arguing for a theory of embodiment where "the theory of the body is already a theory of perception . . . we shall need to reawaken our experience of the world as it appears to us in so far as we are in the world through our body."[11]

However, Foucault was initially less interested in the body than in the kinds of questions about epistemology of interest to Canguilhem. When Foucault did turn to the body, he embraced the structuralist rejection of subjectivity as an inherent condition of human life as well as any idea of "experience of the world" as a pathway to understanding. Additionally, and in contrast to both Althusser and Bourdieu, Foucault took a much more self-consciously historical approach to the relationship of bodies and subjectivities to power, arguing for a "history of bodies" and "the manner in which what is most material and most vital in them has been invested." [12]

Foucault's work has been variously described as structuralist and poststructuralist in orientation, although Foucault defiantly resisted attempts to label his work using either category. Lévi-Strauss had argued that we understand the meaning of words only in their relations to other words, and, like language, cultural meanings are a product of relations between differentiated elements in a system, made possible by an underlying set of generative principles. He especially focused on the significance of fundamental binaries in culture, such as light/dark, male/female, culture/nature, or raw/cooked. However, by the late 1960s, a poststructuralist movement led by Jacques Derrida and others rejected structuralism's obsession with binary oppositions and criticized the idea that language could be understood as a system of differences that was tied to deep structuring codes.[13] Instead, poststructuralism promoted the idea that language was an inherently unstable affair that produced a plurality of texts, "an endless play of signifiers which can never be nailed down to a single center or essence, or meaning."[14]

Foucault was never very interested in the structuralist analysis of cultural binaries. However, his earliest work accepts the possibility of an underlying generative logic beneath surface appearances that makes discourse meaningful and allows for it to cohere in a systematic way. That is one reason why he chose the metaphor of archeology when referring to his preferred approach to the study of history. Foucault envisioned archeology as a method that excavates the past in search of "épistèmes" and "discursive formations"—rule-governed systems of thought that operate paradigmatically to define the conceptual possibilities that determine what can be thought, and how it can be thought, in a given domain and period. His work through much of the 1960s can be regarded as a series of intellectual "excavations" of differing discursive formations governing how people spoke from the seventeenth through the nineteenth centuries about such things as madness and science.

However, Foucault grew to believe that his archeological method was too focused on excavating and describing the formation of discursive fields and making comparisons with other fields. What was needed was an additional method that could explain *how* the transition from one epistemic way of thinking to another occurred, shifting the frame of reference from a focus on the generative paradigmatic character of discourse to interactions between discourse and physical practice. In a lecture in 1971, Foucault introduced the idea of a "genealogical" approach to history that paid greater attention to the body.[15] Borrowing from Friedrich Nietzsche, Foucault turned to genealogy to reference the idea of "disruption" and "descent" as opposed to the more static idea of origins: "The search for descent is not the erecting of foundations: on the contrary, it disturbs what was previously considered immobile; it fragments what was thought unified; it shows the heterogeneity of what was imagined consistent with itself."[16] These remarks about fragmentation and heterogeneity reveal further movement toward a poststructuralist sensibility that had already become apparent in Foucault's work in the late 1960s. In Nietzsche, Foucault also found a philosopher who made a point of emphasizing differences in physicality between social types, for example, between the disciplined repression embodied in priestly asceticism and the allegedly "powerful physicality" of "knightly-aristocratic peoples."[17] Foucault went on to argue: "the body is the inscribed surface of events" and genealogy, "as an analysis of descent, is thus situated within the articulation of the body and history.... Genealogy ... seeks to re-establish the various systems of subjection ... [and] the hazardous play of dominations."[18]

Foucault acknowledged the existence of considerable historical writing on the body in respect to such things as "the attacks of germs or viruses," as well as the extent to which "historical processes were involved in what might seem to be the purely biological base of existence," or the place that should be given "in the history of society to biological 'events' such as the circulation of bacilli, or the extension of the life-span."[19] However, as Roger Cooter suggests, what made Foucault's turn to the body so distinct, and so powerful, was its "non-essentialist politically invested" view of the body that "undermined how historians had previously conceived it." In Foucault's work, "it was not 'body history' that came to excite interest, but the notion of a historicized body."[20]

FOUCAULT'S GENEALOGY OF BODILY DISCIPLINE AND THE EMERGENCE OF BIOPOWER

In his 1975 book *Discipline and Punish*, Foucault argued that violence in European medieval life was normalized and sustained symbolically by a metaphorical attachment between the understanding of individual bodies and collective bodies. Priests, monarchs, and local leaders promoted an organic conception of the world complete with complex hierarchies, interdependencies, and distinctions between rulers and the ruled as part of the natural order of things. In this context, social disruptions, which were frequent, could be interpreted as a symbolic violation, a kind of mutilation, of the body of the monarch himself or herself and, indirectly perhaps, even of Christ. For that reason, public mutilation and bodily humiliation by inquisitors or royal torturers seemed a necessary response. However, with the advent of the European Enlightenments in the eighteenth century, the gradual spread of the liberal values of universal liberty and equality, and the formation of the liberal state, the idea of the "social body" began to emerge as the dominant sign of social solidarity in Western life. It was the body of society that now needed protection. This protection was increasingly understood "in a quasi-medical sense. In the place of rituals that served to restore the corporal integrity of the monarch, remedies and therapeutic devices are employed such as the segregation of the sick, the monitoring of contagions, the exclusions of delinquents."[21]

So, for Foucault, by the nineteenth century we witness the consequences of modernity in a shift in the understanding of relations between the individual body, the social body, and the body politic and of strategies and tactics of the administration of individual bodies. The body of the sovereign as a sign of social authority was challenged by an emergent belief in the need to defend the integrity of the social body—now seen to be comprised by the idea of "society" in the abstract—and the preferred method of social administration shifted from violent punishment to discipline and surveillance. The age of inquisitors, torturers, and dungeons passed over into an era of new regulatory organizations that operated first and foremost through the deployment of panoptic surveillance, bodily and emotional discipline, and the production of new standards of normality: the prison, the poor house, the asylum, the factory, the hospital, and the school.

While Foucault does not discuss gymnasiums or other sports venues, it is a short step to add these emerging sites and spaces of disciplinary power to the list. Foucault does trace one important tradition of physical exercise in Europe back to early monasteries and the bodily practices of Christian monks. The monastic approach to exercise disciplined the body by subjecting it to a regime of austere religious practices designed to promote revelation and the achievement of salvation. However, in the development of European societies, Foucault argues that exercise in the form of military drills or physical training in schools became an attempt to impose complex activities on bodies in order to control them. Thus Foucault clearly envisaged gymnasia and other sports venues as disciplinary sites and spaces along with other modern disciplinary sites and spaces such as schools, barracks, hospitals, poor houses, factories, and asylums. Through the deployment of categories, classifications, regulations, instruction, and surveillance in these sites and spaces, potentially unruly bodies were rendered "docile." In this process, individuals learned to become responsible for their own normalization and developed new understandings of their identities, thereby enhancing the "health" of the social body.

Foucault does not see these developments of knowledge and administration as something that emerged in the service of direct class or state interests. On the contrary, he argues that power in the emerging forms of corporeal management has a capillary form, flowing through the social body without any direct connection to sovereign might. Furthermore, in a roughly similar way to Bourdieu's conception of habitus as "generative" of improvisations, Foucault emphasizes that power is not inherently negative. Rather, power is productive. It makes things happen, including generation of its own oppositions. Still, in *Discipline and Punish* the productive side of power mostly takes a back seat to describing the effectiveness of discipline, surveillance, and knowledge in the making of docility. Disciplinary power sets new conditions for an accompanying form of willful agency associated with the internalization of bodily discipline. The ultimate goal is a situation where people *choose* to become managed. It is in this sense that disciplinary organizations were instrumental in making the exercise of power in Europe more normative than overtly coercive.

To develop these ideas further, Foucault turned in the late 1970s to the concepts of biopower and governmentality. By the term *biopower* he means to reference the modern emphasis on the administration of biological life in Europe. From the history of Catholicism through the expansion of the modern state system and emerging capitalist economy, Foucault argues that European societies underwent an accelerating process of regulating phenomena such as birth, death, sickness, disease, health, and sexual relations. Modernity became a project centered on the microphysics of power involved in the administration of life itself. Biopower is meant to reference the emergence of new regimes and technologies devoted initially to classifying, mapping, calculating, and recording people's lives, as well as to producing domesticated bodies and optimizing somatic capacities through disciplinary organizations. At the risk of considerable simplification, *governmentality* can be viewed as the mode or regime of administration involved in the management of biopower. In other words, biopower can be seen to operate historically through processes, practices, organizations, and technologies of governmentality.[22] But this does not happen in any orderly or determined way. In the same way that geneology is meant to view "descent" as a complex and often fractured process, governmentality operates across a variety of institutions, binding some together, creating disruptions, and driving others apart.

In lectures given shortly before his death in 1984, Foucault suggested that the primary goal of his life's work was to "sketch out a history of the different ways in our culture that humans develop knowledge about themselves: economics, biology, psychiatry, medicine, and penology" and "to analyze these so-called sciences as very specific 'truth games' related to specific techniques that human beings use to understand themselves." To provide context for this statement, he outlined a typology of four interrelated technologies: technologies of production, technologies of sign systems, technologies of power, and technologies of the self. In a move that suggests a greater allowance of human agency than in some of his earlier work, he suggests that the latter set of technologies "permit individuals" to effect "a certain number of operations on their own bodies and souls, thoughts, conduct, and way of being, so as to transform themselves in order to attain a certain state of happiness, purity, wisdom, perfection, or immortality."[23] Foucault emphasizes that these technologies "hardly ever function separately," and each technology involves practical reason applied to the body.

Bodily training figures more strongly in Foucault than in the work of any other postwar social theorist or historian. So it is not surprising that his writing has had a major impact on historians interested in health, physical exercise, or sports, as well as on the specific disciplines and sciences that have analyzed and organized such activities.

Geneviève Rail and Jean Harvey point out that much of the earliest research in France on physical exercise and bodily discipline, influenced by Foucault, tended to focus on excavations and critiques of discursive formations, although this work blended relatively seamlessly with later analyses that were more influenced by Foucault's arguments in *Discipline and Punish*.[24] However, Georges Vigarello's definitive book *Le corps redressé*, which examines normalization discourses in eighteenth-century French and Swiss orthopedic and hygienic gymnastics, is the most exhaustive early historical work to draw heavily on Foucault's ideas.[25] Roughly translated as "the straightened up body," Vigarello's book analyzes the way that discourses and practices promoting "uprightness" and the growth in physical and moral "strength" of children were expressions of disciplinary power. As Vigarello explains: "for the strength of the child to grow, both the child's power and the constraint exerted on him had to increase."[26]

From the late 1980s through the turn of the twenty-first century, so many English-speaking writers began to draw on Foucault's ideas in their work on exercise and sport history that is impossible to note them all. John Hargreaves's use of Foucault's conception of disciplinary power in a critique of the knowledge discourses and bodily practices in British physical education is a significant early example, along with Harvey and Sparks's later work on nineteenth-century gymnastics in France.[27] In addition, Foucault's influence is evident in Patricia Vertinsky's early work on gendered bodily practices in disciplines focused on sport and exercise.[28] Foucauldian ideas, in addition to Bourdieu's conception of habitus, continue to be present in Vertinsky's more recent historical analyses of gendered practices, spaces and bodies in medicine, physical education, and dance, as well as the sites where bodily techniques are taught, rehearsed, and reproduced.[29] A similar fusion of ideas from Bourdieu and Foucault are found in several of the historical essays included in a recent edited collection on the body by Vertinsky and Jennifer Hargreaves.[30] Other important examples include David Kirk's analysis of "schooling bodies" in the Australian and English educational systems between 1880 and 1950[31] and Susan Brownell's ethnohistorical work on the nature of "body culture" in China between 1970 and 1995.[32] Finally, a number of Foucault's ideas, along with ideas by Bourdieu, Max Weber, Norbert Elias, and several others, are fruitfully woven into an eclectic mix in the recent work of Henning Eichberg, a pioneering figure in the emergence of historical "body culture" studies in the late twentieth century.[33]

BEYOND BOURDIEU AND FOUCAULT: BIOCOMMERCE, BIOPOLITICS, AND THE RETURN TO EMBODIMENT

Bourdieu and Foucault both wrote extensively, engaging many different subjects, and the thinking of both writers evolved over the course of their careers. Bourdieu always remained closer to Marxism than Foucault, although the Marxian influences in

Foucault's work are often understated and misunderstood. Similarly, while Bourdieu's work developed greater range and flexibility over the course of his career, he retained a consistent emphasis on the unconscious willingness of the subjugated to reproduce the power of the dominant and especially of the dominant classes. He also felt compelled to intervene extensively in French politics. Foucault's philosophical and political underpinnings arguably shifted further, giving his work a more chameleon-like quality than Bourdieu's. Domination was always a central theme in Foucault's work, and he maintained a consistent critique of the humanistic idea of self-constitution, but, late in life, he opened up to more optimistic understandings of the development of the self, an autonomous ethics of self-care, and even to the possibility that "bodies and pleasure" might somehow escape the deployments of certain epistemic discourses.

Today both Bourdieu and Foucault are among the most widely cited writers in contemporary social thought. Both writers, and Foucault in particular, *anticipated* the "turn to the body" that that was beginning to occur in Western social thought, and both contributed significantly to that turn. Furthermore, the work of both writers has been interpreted and reinterpreted over the past forty years in conjunction with massive changes in cultural attitudes to the human body associated with the changing nature of consumer cultures in Northern nations, and the transformation of the economies and technologies of capitalist societies toward more flexible forms of accumulation. One of the significant cultural dimensions of the late twentieth century was the growth of industries and technologies associated with the pursuit of pleasure, identity, and self-knowledge through the body, as well as the uses of the body as forms of physical capital: examples include fitness, tattoos, diets, piercing, body building, cosmetic surgery, organ transplants, as well as drugs for disease prevention, strength, longevity, and sexual enhancement. Some of these changes led to countering movements concerned with the environmentalism and cultivation of more meaningful or spiritual body experiences, through such things as yoga or tai chi.[34] But the key aspect of these changes was the integration of positive health discourses into an emerging digital world where information on every aspect of human life could be monitored and where advertising widely promoted products that linked the development of the self to the goal of being healthy, the apparent joys brought by good health, and the ways of achieving it.

This emerging world of biocommerce and biopolitics created an insatiable hunger for explanatory frameworks that focused on corporeality. It was in this context that Bourdieu and Foucault emerged as leading historian/theorists in the late twentieth century, not only because their work emphasized bodily practices but also because it provided compelling standpoints from which to apprehend the present. Concepts such as habitus, fields of practice, discursive formation, surveillance, discipline, technologies of the self, biopower, and governmentality seemed literally to come alive in the late twentieth century. There were certainly other historically oriented writers whose concepts and theories provided relevant understandings of the present, but Foucault's language and concepts, in particular, seemed perfectly suited to the times.

Foucault also found a receptive audience among many late-twentieth-century feminists, whereas Bourdieu's work was *initially* less influential here because of the strong emphasis on social class habitus throughout his work. Bourdieu's later work on *La Domination Masculine* attracted greater attention from feminist theorists.[35] Early post-war feminists had demonstrated early on how the priority given to mind over bodies in Western social thought had relegated women to the domain of nature based on biological processes such as menstruation and childbirth. Similarly, "second wave" feminism had revealed how patriarchy was manifest in legal and public policies designed to control women's bodies, through such things as access to property, birth control, or abortion, as well as in idealized conceptions of women's bodies. Foucault's focus on how human bodies are produced by discursive practices and technologies of power both challenged and added to feminist criticism by shattering the idea of the body having any fixed essence, thereby opening the door to new challenges to the sex/gender binary that had so long been a foundational principle in postwar feminist theory. These ideas also generated intense debate among feminist theorists: about whether Foucault's view of power inevitably reduced social agents to docile bodies, with equally docile subjectivities; whether Foucault's apparent antihumanism fit with the more traditional goals of feminist politics; or whether his work promoted an excessively discursive view of the production of gendered bodies that downplayed the lived experiences of female embodiment.[36]

One of the longstanding criticisms of Foucault's historical work is his tendency to offer histories that are overly suggestive and not able to meet acceptable tests of credibility. Many critics have also argued that Foucault viewed power in an overly abstract fashion and, despite his own involvement in the politics of prison reform and sexual preference, that he was too unwilling to indicate theoretically how some forms of power may be more noxious than others. Another commonly voiced criticism is that Foucault's critique of the self-constituting subject cannot be squared with the conception of the self-constituting subject that emerges in his later ethical writings.[37] But, for me, one of the most troubling aspects of Foucault's intellectual legacy is the way in which it was so readily incorporated into an excessively linguistic/discursive approach to the study of history and society. Foucault's turn to the body, with its poststructuralist and Neitzchean emphases on disruptions and heterogeneity, and on the productive nature of discourse, power, and knowledge, was moved increasingly away from a materialist anchorage in favor of closer association with a parallel linguistic/postmodern turn that was occurring simultaneously in Western social thought. In its most extreme poststructuralist iterations—particularly when read through Derrida's deconstructionist legacy—the linguistic/postmodern turn in late-twentieth-century historiography championed a view that was so far removed from any realist epistemology that history and society could only be understood as a series of representations, fraught with tensions and deferrals of meaning. Here the challenge for critical analysis turned on the need to point to the constant effort of cultural construction involved in producing accepted truths, as well as the constant tendency of those truths to break apart and reveal their internal inconsistencies and "aporias." The materiality of bodies came to be seen almost exclusively as an effect of discourses that had no discernable social origin.

The debates surrounding this hyper-constructivist approach to history and society are now well rehearsed, and it is not my intention to engage them again here. By the turn of the twenty-first century, despite some useful invocations against scientism, positivism, the quest for universals, and other forms of modernist pretension, the poststructuralist jump into an anti-essentialist world of discursive construction was widely challenged. Not the least of these problems, as Michel Rolph-Trouillot has suggested, is that while radical constructivism "can give many examples of how narratives are produced, it cannot give a full account of the production of any single narrative."[38] Furthermore, there is no necessary reason why Foucault should be read through the lens of linguistic poststructuralists, such as Derrida. Both Foucault and Bourdieu would recognize, with Derrida, that there is no "body," only *bodies*. Both would agree that discourse is important in history, that what people often know as the truth is a product of discourse, and that bodies are historically and culturally produced. But Bourdieu's work is anchored strongly in the belief that tests of credibility can be found external to the discursive realm, and when Foucault lays claim to a post-Kantian critical tradition in some of his later work, he is making the case that his own discourse is coherent and stable enough able to throw analytic light on the "truth games" of modern science and other discursive formations.

One response to these epistemological challenges for writers interested in the history of exercise and sports has been a return to questions of "lived" material experience and interpretive understanding. I see this as partly rooted in a desire in contemporary historiography to return to a more solid grounding—if not to a new kind of essentialism, at least to a recognition of the visceral reality of meaningful life, including time, space, and memory, as experienced through living minds and bodies in the present and in the past. It is precisely this concern that has underwritten a resurgent epistemological realism and re-evaluation of materialism in recent years as well as a renewed interest in the phenomenology of embodiment. Nick Crossley's work on "technique," which examines embodiment by revisiting the work of Marcel Mauss, is one example of a return to social and materialist analysis.[39] In a second case, the trend has seen a move, as it were, from Foucault back to Merleau Ponty or to Heidegger, or in many instances, rereading Foucault, or even Bourdieu, through the lens of a reworked phenomenological perspective. In the analysis of sport and exercise, for example, we can see this renewed interest in embodiment in several works that have relevance for historical analysis; such as some of P. David Howe's work, which fuses ideas from Bourdieu, Foucault, and Merleau Ponty, and, more recently, in Kath Woodward's attempt to analyze sport after London in 2012 by drawing on some of Heidegger's ideas about being and time. [40]

These works, in comparison and contrast to some of the others that I have discussed earlier in this chapter, suggest, as Chris Shilling argues, that "the body" will continue to be one of the most contested concepts in contemporary social sciences and historiography, providing the material substance for an "intellectual battleground" where the claims of philosophical standpoints associated with poststructuralism and postmodernism, phenomenology, feminism, and Marxism, among others, fight it out.[41] There was arguably a time when researchers interested in the history of sport, bodily training, or physical culture found themselves on the periphery of broader issues and debates in contemporary social theory and historiography. Now, in conjunction with the turn to the body in late-twentieth-century Western social thought, the study of sport and physical culture has moved into the center of the action.

NOTES

1. Roy Porter, "History of the Body Reconsidered," in *New Perspectives on Historical Writing*, ed. Peter Burke (Cambridge, UK: Polity Press, 2001), 236.
2. Pierre Bourdieu, *Outline of a Theory of Practice* (1972; repr., London: Cambridge University Press, 1977), 78.
3. Pierre Bourdieu, "Program for a Sociology of Sport," *Sociology of Sport Journal* 5 (1988): 181.
4. George Steinmetz, "Bourdieu, Historicity and Historical Sociology," *Cultural Sociology* 5.1 (2011): 51.
5. Pierre Bourdieu, "Sport and Social Class," *Social Science Information* 17.6 (1978): 826.
6. Bourdieu, "Sport and Social Class," 833.
7. Richard Gruneau, *Class, Sports and Social Development* (Amherst: University of Massachussets Press, 1983).
8. John Bale, "Amateurism, Capital and Roger Bannister," *Sport in History* 26.3 (2006): 484–501.
9. Jacques Defrance, "*L'Excellence Corporelle: La Formation des Activités physique et sportives moderne, 1770–1914*" (Rennes, France: Presses Universitaire de Rennes, 1987).
10. Jacques Defrance, "The Making of a Field with Weak Autonomy: The Case of the Sports Field in France, 1895–1955," in *Bourdieu and Historical Analysis*, ed. Philip S. Gorski (Durham, NC: Duke University Press, 2013). Kindle edition, 4273.
11. Merleau Ponty, cited in Richard Askay, "Heidegger, the Body and the French Philosophers," *Continental Philosophy Review* 32 (1999): 30.
12. Michel Foucault, *The History of Sexuality*, trans. R. Hurley (New York: Penguin Books, 1978), 151–152.
13. Jacques Derrida, "Structure, Sign and Play in the Discourse of the Human Sciences," in *Writing and Difference*, trans. Alan Bass (1967; repr., London: Routledge and Kegan Paul, 1978).
14. Terry Eagleton, *Literary Theory: An Introduction* (Minneapolis: University of Minnesota Press, 1983), 158.
15. Michel Foucault, "Nietzsche, Genealogy, History," in *The Foucault Reader: An Introduction to Foucault's Thought*, ed. P. Rabinow (London: Penguin, 1991), 76.
16. Foucault, "Nietzsche, Genealogy, History," 82.
17. John Hoberman, *Sport and Political Ideology* (Austin: University of Texas Press, 1984), 90.
18. Foucault, "Nietzsche, Genealogy, History," 83.
19. Michel Foucault, *Discipline and Punish: The Birth of the Prison* (New York: Random House, 1977), 25.
20. Roger Cooter, "The Turn of the Body: History and the Politics of the Corporeal," *ARBOR Ciencia Pensamiento y Cultura* 186.743 (2010): 393.
21. Michel Foucault, *Power/Knowledge: Selected Interviews, 1972–1977* (New York: Random House, 1981), 55.

22. Michel Foucault, "Governmentality," in *The Foucault Effect—Studies in Governmentality*, eds. Graham Burchell, Colin Gordon, and Peter Miller (Chicago: University of Chicago Press, 1991), 102–103.
23. Michel Foucault, "Lectures at Vermont University in October 1982," in *Technologies of the Self*, ed. L. H. Martin, H. Gutman, and P. H. Hutton (Amherst: University of Massachusetts Press, 1988), 16.
24. Geneviève Rail and Jean Harvey, "Body at Work: Michel Foucault and the Sociology of Sport," *Sociology of Sport Journal* 12 (1995): 164–179.
25. Georges Vigarello, *Le corps redressé* (Paris: Editions universitaires, 1978).
26. Vigarello, *Le corps redressé*, 161.
27. John Hargreaves, *Sport, Power and Culture: A Social and Historical Analysis of Popular Sports in Britain* (Cambridge, UK: Polity Press, 1987); Jean Harvey and Robert Sparks, "The Politics of the Body in the Context of Modernity," *Quest* 43 (1991): 164–189.
28. Patricia Vertinsky, *The Eternally Wounded Woman: Women, Doctors and Exercise in the Late Nineteenth Century* (Manchester, UK: Manchester University Press, 1990).
29. Patricia Vertinsky and John Bale, eds., *Sites of Sport: Space, Place and Experience* (London: Routledge, 2004); Patricia Vertinsky and Sherry McKay, *Disciplining Bodies in the Gymnasium: Memory, Monument and Modernism* (New York: Routledge, 2004).
30. Patricia Vertinsky and Jennifer Hargreaves, eds., *Physical Culture, Power and the Body* (New York: Routledge, 2007).
31. David Kirk, *Schooling Bodies: School Practices and Public Discourse, 1880–1950* (London: Leicester University Press, 1998).
32. Susan Brownell, *Training the Body for China: Sports in the Moral Order of the People's Republic* (Chicago: University of Chicago Press, 1995).
33. Henning Eichberg, *Body Cultures: Essays on Sport, Space and Identity*, ed. John Bale and Chris Philo (New York: Routledge, 1998).
34. Chris Shilling, "Sociology and the Body: Classical Traditions and New Agendas," *Sociological Review* 55 (2007): 1–17.
35. *La Domination Masculine* (Paris: Seuil, 2002).
36. Alexandra Howson, *Embodying Gender* (Thousand Oaks, CA: SAGE, 2005).
37. Jürgen Habermas, "Taking Aim at the Heart of the Present," in *Foucault: A Critical Reader*, ed. David Couzens Hoy (Cambridge, UK: Blackwell, 1986).
38. Michel-Rolph Trouillot, *Silencing the Past: Power and the Production of History* (Boston: Beacon Press, 1995), 13.
39. For example, see Nick Crossley, "Researching Embodiment by Way of Body Techniques," *The Sociological Review* 55 (2007): 80–94.
40. P. David Howe, "Habitus, Barriers and the (Ab)use of the Science of Interval Training in the 1950s," *Sport in History* 26.2 (2006): 325–344; Kath Woodward, *Sporting Times* (London: Palgrave Pivot, 2013).
41. Shilling, "Sociology and the Body," 9.

Bibliography

Besnier, Niko, and Susan Brownell. "Sport, Modernity and the Body." *Annual Review of Anthropology* 41 (2012): 443–449.
Eichberg, Henning. *Body Cultures: Essays on Sport, Space and Identity*. London: Routledge, 1998.

Markula, Pirkko. "Sport and the Body." In *Blackwell Encyclopedia of Sociology*, edited by George Ritzer. Malden, MA: Blackwell, 2007. Blackwell Reference Online, accessed September 8, 2015, http://www.blackwellreference.com/public/tocnode?id=g9781405124331_chunk_g978140512433125_ss1-224#citation.

Mauss, Marcel. "Techniques of the Body." In *Zone 6: Incorporations*, edited by Jonathan Crary and Sanford Kwinter, 455–477. New York: Zone Books, 1992. Originally published as "Les Techniques du corps," *Journal de Psychologie* 32.3–4 (1934).

Park, Roberta. "A Decade of the Body: Research and Writing about the History of Health, Fitness, Exercise and Sport, 1983–1993." *Journal of Sport History* 21.1 (1994): 59–82.

Shilling, Chris. *The Body and Social Theory*. 2nd ed. Thousand Oaks, CA: SAGE, 2012.

Vigarello, Georges. "The Life of the Body in 'Discipline and Punish.'" *Sociology of Sport Journal* 12 (1995): 158–163.

CHAPTER 4

....

SPORT HISTORY AND THE
HISTORICAL PROFESSION

....

DAVID McDONALD

ACADEMIC historians of modern sport occupy a curious position within their profession. Although they study one of the most pervasive features in the modern world—attested by the global audiences for the World Cup or the Olympics—sport historians occupy the margins of "mainstream" historical scholarship. Certainly, they share many of the trappings that one associates with any disciplinary subfield—journals, professional associations, debates running a gamut of themes, methods, and interpretations, many of which—gender, class, race, imperialism, and others—are treated in these volumes.

To be sure, sport has occasionally drawn the attention of nonspecialist scholars. Norbert Elias and Jan Huizinga saw fit to reflect on the role of sport, while Huizinga discussed the "ludic spirit," in human society.[1] Conversely, some specialists in the history of sport have become important references for historians of society and culture. Richard Holt's and Tony Mason's studies on sport's role in modern British society or J. A. Mangan's works on sport and the Victorian middle classes have become standard references in social histories of modern Britain. Similarly, Pamela Grundy's *Learning to Win* has gained wide acceptance among historians of the United States.[2] More recently, sport has appeared as a special theme in more general historical journals.[3]

These examples, however, stand as proverbial exceptions to the rule in the profession at large. More often, with the exceptions of studies addressing gender and race, sport rarely gains *entrée* into the broader profession. Textbooks on modern European history seldom incorporate sport in their treatments of mass culture, beyond obligatory reference to Hitler's Berlin Olympic Games in 1936 or Joe Louis and Jack Robinson as symbolic figures in the American civil rights movement. Elsewhere, general studies of American higher education pay little regard to the impact of the quasi-professional athletics programs that, as much as anything, have long distinguished American universities from their counterparts abroad. Instead, mainstream historical scholarship emphasizes other areas of mass culture—the production and consumption of nationalism or cultural and material commodities—as forces shaping or reflecting notions of gender/sexuality, class, and new identities in modern society.

This curious neglect of sport and the relative rarity of sport historians in the academy cast into sharp relief the disparity between general historical scholarship and sport's undeniable global impact. This neglect becomes all the more paradoxical given sport's sheer omnipresence as an object of mass participation, consumption, and, as important, experience for more than a century. Historians who have traditionally paid more attention to film, print culture, or popular music and entertainments would find in the study of sport a powerful lens on the central processes they have identified as the shapers of modern society and identities.

Perhaps most notably, the history of sport appears to have made little impact on the discussions of "modernity" that have occupied such a prominent place in the discipline over the last quarter-century and more. Thus a recent *American Historical Review* forum addressing modernity and its application in several realms of historiography failed even to mention spectator sport as one of its defining attributes.[4] However elusive modernity's precise definition, scholars have reached a rough consensus about its origins or expression in the processes earlier embraced by optimistic modernization theorists: accelerating rates of industrialization, urbanization, and social transformation; the tightening interconnectedness of the global economy; and the emergence of the nation-state, with its technologies and ideologies of broad social mobilization and discipline that vastly expanded older ambits for the exercise of power. These forces created spaces, socioeconomic relationships, and modes of discourse that made possible the imagining of new types of community to supplant the confessional, agrarian, and ostensibly traditional hierarchies of the "premodern" orders. Histories of the era have followed the effects of these changes in their established areas of inquiry: political thought and institutions, the emergence of new social formations and political parties, high and low culture. More generally, they have documented the ways in which these forces destabilized norms associated with agrarian economies and orders of privilege. These changes produced doubt or alienation, complicated identities, and saw the continuous reinvention of tradition and of the self.

Historians have also agreed that the making of the modern went hand-in-hand with a broad transformative program, conscious and not, expressed in the parallel extension of social control over the new societies and their imperial dominions. It fostered the democratization promised by modernization theorists but also totalitarian colossi driven by their own vision of the modernity they claimed to build. At the same time, these transformations gave rise to movements—from trade unionism to anticolonialism—that pressed their own visions of the modern. In science the uncertainties of quantum theory undermined the Newtonian edifice. In philosophy, Nietzsche and Freud overturned an older positivist consensus, much as Cubism, constructivism, or the twelve-tone scale transformed the arts. "Modernity's" sheer variability has persistently defied historians' attempt to render it coherent.

Inevitably, the history of modern sport mirrors the complexity and ambiguities that have modulated each of these processes. At the same time, sport's boundedness—its set matches, rules, times and spaces, or binarized narratives of "us" and "them," winning and losing—affords a clear view of sites and vectors of interaction so difficult to define in studying consumption of culture or the direction of capital flows. If that bounded-ness makes sport seem cloistered, it also gives a surprisingly clear perspective on the embedding and social internalization of the "modern." As a realm of practice, experience, and performance, mass spectator sport has played an unappreciated part in the experience of the modern for millions of consumers worldwide and as such merits fuller incorporation into our larger narratives of the period. One could well argue that large sections of the world's population—largely male until the last twenty years—learned, through these experiences and the emotions, conflicts, and bonds they elicited how to *be* modern.

The mass spectator sports that emerged in the second half of the nineteenth century have left modernity's imprint in the form of the grand stadiums that stand as local or national landmarks in cities the world over. The earliest of these appeared in the late nineteenth and early twentieth centuries—Hampden Park in Glasgow, Wembley Stadium, or Boston's Fenway Park—and served as models for such subsequent entrants as Maracana in Rio de Janeiro and Beijing's "Bird's Nest." Over the century and more since their construction, they have also spawned miniature replicas in the playing fields and schoolyards of virtually every community on the planet, where millions of children emulate their local or global sporting heroes in physical education classes and on school, village, or club teams.

These huge structures, accommodating crowds exceeding 100,000, provide a visible dividing line between modernity and what went before. As sites, they represent dense points of convergence for the forces and processes that created this modernity. Their size and construction demonstrate the mobilizational capacities of industrial capitalism, able to assemble the funds and the labor to build them. The clubs that played their matches in these stadiums depended on audiences of urbanites, the descendants of peasants or immigrants, with the disposable means and leisure time to attend these spectacles.[5] These crowds arrived at these stadiums on new forms of mass transit to watch "their" side against competitors from other neighborhoods or cities. These "fans" formed their own sort of civic associations, their members sporting their side's colors. Specialized sports pages attracted readers for countless newspapers and magazines, while advertisers hawked their wares in stadiums and the press alike, seeking association with these teams and their star performers.

These stadiums and the teams they hosted anchored identities grounded in the new neighborhoods and institutions of urban life, giving compelling expression to the shared experience and values of these new communities. Social and cultural historians could learn much about the formation, performance, and variability of urban identities through the study of sporting crowds, which have long demonstrated seemingly dissonant loyalties in different settings. In league matches, their allegiances might reflect such ties as location, workplace, confessional allegiance, class, or ethnicity. Yet these local loyalties could dissolve in the equally powerful appeal of national belonging. The latter became a fixture in association football with the inception of the Scotland–England rivalry in 1872, a mere nine years after the codification of the game's rules. These contests saw the most bitter local adversaries—for instance, Glasgow's sectarian Rangers and Celtic supporters—become ardent fellow patriots celebrating national triumph. Likewise, the modern Olympics, conceived as a celebration of a sort of "pure" athletic achievement on the model of an imagined classical Greece, quickly became an arena for the glorification of national accomplishment.

Stadiums served as settings where communities could see and feel themselves embodied and actively assert their shared identity. Stadium terraces became proprietorial territory for supporters staking out "our" space *versus* "theirs." Recurrent instances of "hooliganism" and violence associated with the claiming of space—in stadiums or adjoining pubs and squares—have become a virtually universal phenomenon in national and international sports. The Heysel disaster of 1985 represents merely the bloodiest of the conflicts bred by the "modern" identities and venues of modern sport. Space also divided supporters' communities also divided along lines of social or economic status. The traditional genteel seating areas in stadiums dominated by standing crowds have become catered "luxury" suites for the privileged, perched above the mortals exposed to the elements and the dubious fare of stadium vendors.

Just as striking, however, is the relentless proliferation of these new modes of performance and consumption and the intensity of the meaning with which populations—or the states that rule them—invest in them the world over. As David Goldblatt has documented at length, association football led the way in a well-documented spread across Europe and around the world during the late nineteenth and twentieth centuries.[6] The Olympic Games soon followed, along with such varied entertainments as prize-fighting, cricket, rugby—union and league—baseball, and ice hockey. The World Cup and the Olympic Games have become truly global phenomena viewed by hundreds of thousands of on-site spectators but also by billions of others on ubiquitous television sets or computer terminals in every imaginable setting.

This new cultural sphere also showcased a new sort of notable, the "star," who gained status, wealth, and fame for excelling at disciplines that have long struck many as arcane or childish. These figures arose as cognate types to new models of celebrity in the more widely studied forms of mass entertainment. Alongside Sarah Bernhardt and Rudolph Valentino, sporting heroes enjoyed the adulation of their own admirers. They acquired fame or notoriety that could transcend class or ethnic belonging, like boxing's Jack Johnson or football's Diego Maradona.

Like their counterparts in entertainment, and unlike both groups' predecessors, these figures came to enjoy a social status that provoked dismay among traditional and newer commercial elites, an ironic reprise of the bemusement that had greeted the latter's own arrival a century earlier. Many deplored the professionalization of what they regarded as an avocation, while for others the new celebrities' visibility—and often their conduct—flouted norms of racial or social deference.[7] By the post-1945 era, such stars as Pele or Muhammad Ali were the most widely recognized figures in the world. During the same period, new heroes appeared from once-marginalized groups, including former colonial subjects, African Americans, and women. These new notables ultimately gained acceptance, even esteem, among their erstwhile "betters," earning titles, marrying into families that would once have rejected them, and finding themselves courted by political leaders.

Reflecting and burnishing the "images" of these modern stars were the proliferating media of the modern era: mass advertising, sport journalism, newsreels and broadcasts.[8] New genres of literature also appeared, such as the sporting analogues of Horatio Alger stories; by the mid-twentieth century, these stories had also found a place in film. They recounted fictional athletes' overcoming such obstacles as prejudice or foul play to earn redemption and learn the moral of lives well lived and games well played. Sport preached its own moral code, modeled on formal legal norms, which became the rules culture that distinguishes modern competition. Sportswriters even developed a normative aesthetic that still informs contemporary reportage of football, cricket, and baseball, stressing the artistry of play as an indispensable complement of a competition's outcome. Like so much of modernity, these genres proved adaptable to an impressive variety of social and political contexts, finding a place in "liberal" Europe and America, as well as socialist, fascist, nationalist, or imperial orders. In each *milieu*, stories used sport and competition to frame morality tales grounded in the aspirational *mores* of the host society. Reflecting the strength of the genre, and the familiarity of sport as experience and myth, there also emerged a harshly critical counternarrative that saw in sport a microcosm of abuses and exploitation abroad in modern society as a whole.

Like the industrial economy that gave it a framework, a clientele, and working-class athletes, sport reflected modernity's impact.[9] New technologies, sites, and scales of production replaced the seasonality and flexibility of agrarian production with the factory shifts and regulated workdays engendered a new temporality that also shaped modern sport. Although weather still played a part in determining the optimal "season" for various sports, competitive seasons became ever more fixed, assuming their own unvarying rhythms, that replaced in many ways the seasons of the agrarian year. In Britain, Saturday matches became a regular possibility with the curtailment of the workweek by the late nineteenth century, while the Sabbath often gave way to new demand for leisure and consumption. Artificial lighting effaced the difference between night and day in scheduling matches, as it had on the factory floor. Similarly, playing times and their measurement became standardized in most field games and boxing. (Interestingly, devotees of cricket and baseball celebrate the *un*measured times in these sports.)

Finally, sport has long embraced the peculiar historicism that marks modernity, inventing its own traditions, as Eric Hobsbawm noted.[10] Baseball historians argue over Abner Doubleday's claims to have created the sport, while historical research yields ever newer accounts of the "first" game in the sport. Football has its own version of these disputes, tracing the game's origins variously to ancient China or Renaissance Italy, among other places. Each team has its own lovingly kept history, periodized as "eras" personified in a star player or coach. Individual fans have their own versions of events, resting on interpretations of cause and context, which often lead to fiercer controversies than those engaged at academic conferences or on the pages of scholarly journals. Teams and sports also maintain detailed chronicles of record performances and cumulative performance tallies as quantified measures of historical trajectories. This sense of historicity extends to arenas and stadiums, whose "histories" invariably allude to the Coliseum or the hippodromes of the classical world. These narratives provide a usable past that binds supporter communities at the club and national level, much as nationalists imagine their present and future through their own reading of the past.

Even such a compressed survey of modern sport and its social or cultural byproducts reminds one of the power and ubiquity of this complex phenomenon as a defining attribute of modernity. In failing to take adequate note of this area, historians have neglected not only concrete evidence of modernity's progress but also one of the chief elements in the lived experience of millions of men, and far fewer women, in every quarter of the world. If sport as industry generates untold revenues as a commercial operation, it also constitutes a site onto which beholders map their aspirations, antipathies, morality, or identities.

At the same time, sport offers them a concrete area in which they can see clear and decisive competition under a regime of rules, imparting in turn a sense of control or clear norms that confirm or contest their own understanding of the rules and competitions that uncontrollably buffet their own daily lives. These experiences have produced a rich record of press reports, official and popular histories, visual and sound imagery, biographies, and memoirs. More than in other forms of modern mass culture, sport often records the "reception" of its offerings in the form of cheers, songs, memorabilia, or visually recorded performances—by players and crowds—in addition to more conventional documentary sources. Surely, these experiences form a critical part of the social existence historians seek to reconstruct.

Sport and the "Liberal Project"

If the history of mass spectator sport provides concrete insight into change associated with modernity, it also limns the overarching processes that framed that change, especially the pursuit of thoroughgoing transformation that one might term the "liberal project."[11] This endeavor sprang from various sources, particularly the prospect of power and wealth that the British example seemed to promise by the mid-nineteenth century. Viewing Britain's progress through their own historicizing perspectives, statesmen in even the most conservative monarchies—such as Prussia's Friedrich List or Russia's Ser'gei Witte—saw the manifold benefits offered by a properly managed industrial economy. Presiding over professionalizing bureaucracies, supported by the emerging social sciences, and armed with ever more detailed information about their populations and economies, these statesmen shared a strong conviction in the state's ability to guide development. They and their allies in civil society believed that state power could catalyze the creation of a better society, while cultivating the active support of modern citizens and subjects. They understood the reach of the state's and society's interest as extending to the interior life of their population in ways undreamed of by even the most ambitious proponents of the eighteenth-century *Polizeistaat*.

In addition to the exploitative relationships that impressed socialist and many conservative commentators at the time, these efforts to modernize sought to domesticate or civilize European and imperial subjects through the inculcation of "values" that came from participating in the hegemonic culture: literacy, prosperity and a better life within one's class, and an appreciation for higher goods, such as membership in a great nation or empire, or an appreciation for high culture. In terms of these transformative goals, sport instructed its practitioners in the benefits of competition as a test of one's merit while inculcating a respect for rules and fostering the development of healthy minds and bodies. In liberal Europe, where civil associations played such a large part in these processes, the effort sought to recast the working classes in the image of their betters in the entrepreneurial and manufacturing classes.

This "project" comprised twinned paths of assertion, one directed "inward" at inhabitants of the home country and the other abroad in the colonies of the Global South. At home, this meant the conversion of the new working classes to the virtues associated with the industrial order that had spurred the *bourgeois'* success. Thus, in addition to fostering the development of industry and trade, governments sought to improve society through investment in infrastructure, transportation, legal reform, the expansion of state-sponsored education, more inclusive governance, and the foundations of what became the welfare state.

The "civilizing mission" in the European colonies of Africa and Asia—prosecuted by officials, clerics, and traders alike—projected the ameliorative program across the seas, valorizing visible difference and self-consciously introducing into these societies the benefits of a superior European civilization, which, from this viewpoint, replaced sensuality with restraint, arbitrariness with law, passion with reason, and benightedness with enlightenment. The aftereffects of these original impulses still continue to shape the world in the persisting class and political conflicts that divide societies, as well as the enduring legacies of the colonial era across the Third World.

The career of modern sport lends strong support to prevalent narratives of social discipline, hegemonic advance, colonization, global homogenization, or neoliberalism encountered in the works of such scholars as Michel Foucault or James Scott, as well as theorists of postcolonialism or neo-imperialism. Certainly, abundant evidence suggests the globalization and corporatization of sport that critics see in other areas of the global economy. The Olympics and the World Cup have become huge commercial ventures that enrich a small *pléiade* of "content providers," marketers of consumer goods, and, not least, local *compradores* who often achieve great personal profit while leaving their compatriots to assume the considerable expenses of staging them.

The same economic forces have seen the creation of an international workforce of athletes sold and traded among a small coterie of elite leagues and associations in Europe and North America. The stars of present-day European football come from as far away as Africa, South America, and East Asia, while broader trends of global migration have seen the appearance of African-descended players on the national sides of such traditional colonial countries as Britain or France and also such noncolonizing states as Poland. North America's National Hockey League, once overwhelmingly Canadian, now includes dozens of players from Scandinavia and eastern Europe.

Indeed, much as one might trace modernity's advance in the ramifying of stadiums and sport complexes, sport's global spread provides an excellent guide to the circulatory system of imperialism in its "hard" and "soft" forms. Historians of association football have long known the role of British expatriates as exporters of the sport to continental Europe and South America. Other Englishmen introduced cricket to their colonial subjects in "settler" colonies, the Caribbean and South Asia. Indeed, contemporary "test" matches and the Commonwealth Games emblematize the persisting ties of empire. By a similar process, American baseball became popular in the Hispanophone Caribbean and parts of South America. It also sank roots in Japan, whose subjects took it to their own Taiwanese and Korean colonies. Thus the domestic and international careers of international sport echo the broader integrative economic and cultural impulses that have driven industrial economies since the early nineteenth century.

This dissemination of sport bore a transformative mission to reshape subjects and citizens as participants in modernity. As manufacturers and political leaders have long understood, mass-spectator sport can instill compelling affiliations that transcend older identities and "local" loyalties. Scholars of immigration, first to North America and later to the erstwhile metropole states in post-1945 Europe, have appreciated the integrative power of sports for arrivals in new societies. In the United States, baseball's emergence as the "national pastime" gave generations of immigrants a means to absorb American culture and strengthen their identification with their new home. Baseball, boxing, American football, and basketball also served as avenues of social mobility for these immigrants' children but also, more slowly and controversially, as a means by which such black athletes as Jesse Owens could become national heroes in the Jim Crow United States.

For their part, histories of nationalism, the dominant discourse of in/exclusion for much of the past 150 years, have often neglected the symbolic power of sport, with the exception of such conspicuous instances as the Berlin Olympic Games or socialist Spartakiads. Equally often, they overlook sport as a powerful experiential mediator through which aspirations of small groups of intellectuals came to be embraced and inscribed with meaning, both by large populations and their rulers.

Similarly, beginning with the interwar appearance of the antiliberal transformative regimes that took root in the Soviet Union, Germany, Italy, and much of the postcolonial world, international competition has assumed a metaphorical significance as a test of a given system and its vision of the brave new world in the making. Leni Riefenstahl's [in]famous *Triumph of the Will* remains the best-known artifact of this use of sport. The Communist states of the Warsaw Pact dedicated large amounts of resources from straitened economies to the selection and training of generations of athletes in the Olympic disciplines. Their competitive success ostensibly proved the superiority of the political order. These efforts included the development of kinesiological science and a pharmacopeia of performance-enhancing compounds administered to athletes with little consideration for their welfare. While historians of sport and journalists have chronicled these developments, the field at large has troubled itself too little with how such pursuits acquired such meaning and significance for participants and spectators, as well as the totalizing understanding of the state's instrumentality that inspired these measures.

International competition provided spectators and participants a concrete setting that reinforced broader narratives about competition as the way of the world and the test of true worth. The first missionaries of sport, largely from the new middling classes, imagined that competition would cultivate the virtues they saw as the reason for their own success. Thomas Hughes's *Tom Brown's Schooldays* (1857) stands as the *Ur*-text for the promulgation of these values through sport. "Muscular Christianity" and the promotion of a "healthy mind in a healthy body" proselytized abstinence, self-discipline, and hard work as tools for success and advancement accessible to all regardless of birth.

Competition itself became a powerful and concrete illustration of the social Darwinist principles that drove so much *Belle époque* discourse and easily transmuted into the essentializing racism of the time. At the same time, fair play, modesty in victory and defeat, adherence to the rules and spirit of the game, and competition for its own sake propagated "gentlemanly" conduct while providing a moralizing framework for explaining competition's inevitable win–loss outcome. In the British colonies particularly, the introduction of sport constituted the exportation of a certain vision of "Englishness" as a model for elite males in South Asia and Africa.

More broadly, these ideologies also offered societies new definitions of an idealized masculinity, represented by real and fictional paragons exemplifying the distinguishing attributes of a national or political type. Explicitly and implicitly, these modes of thought created new ways to marginalize or subordinate femininity's supposed domesticity and passivity. They also brought issues of racial and ethnic difference into play, often subverting elite norms. If many of these themes have figured increasingly prominently in general histories, they have elicited little interest among historians of the emotions, culture, or other attributes of modernity.

THE TENACITY OF PARTICULARISM

Still, if the history of professional, spectator, global sport substantiates theories of social discipline, colonization, globalization, and other forms of hegemony, it also brings into view the complexity and ambiguities stemming from the transformative impulses that informed its development and spread. As in other modes of transfer, the intended objects of domestication encountered the new games in their own dense social and experiential contexts. Whatever the intentions and aspirations informing the "civilizing mission," the urban working classes and colonials alike read these new games from their own perspective—through a "revaluation of values," to filch Nietzsche's phrase—making them their own in ways unanticipated by their original sponsors. These revaluations ran parallel to currents of resistance and accommodation flowing through other spaces of the encounter between the *Kulturträger* and their putative objects. Stadiums and sports became their own spaces of contestation and accommodation along the shear-lines long known to social history: class, region/nation, race, gender, and metropolis/colonial periphery, to name only the most prominent.

The history and persistence of these appropriations challenges the apparent irresistibility of the totalizing processes that have preoccupied historians since Marx's *German Ideology*. In fact, the practice and consumption of mass-spectator sport demonstrate the tenacity of particularity. If the globalization of football or ice hockey, for example, seem to reflect the relentless concentration of international markets on one hand, the intensity of national sentiment apparent at any World Cup, or the passionate support of individual sides in national leagues, on the other suggest limits to the reach of the transformative endeavor. As a result, the picture presented by modern mass-spectator sports looks highly sedimented, inscribed with varying meanings and morals according to the origin and circumstances of the participant.

One of the earliest episodes of such contestation arose in the late nineteenth century with the challenge of professionalism to the earliest proponents of organized, public competition. The demand for skilled athletes and the growing popularity of spectatorship as a leisure pastime soon created a market for players who would help "our" side win. Middle-class convention held, to the contrary, that exclusive devotion of one's time and talents to athletics perverted the spirit of competition and contravened the balance of the well-rounded gentleman.

These arguments yielded to the popularity of and demand for the rising "stars" of the new sports among the urban working—and immigrant—classes, as with baseball or association football, who made these sports their own. In response, international elite society strove to uphold amateurism in such areas as the modern Olympics or American intercollegiate athletics, as well as in "gentleman's" games like golf, tennis, or rugby union, directed by "old boys." Even these sacrosanct areas proved unable to withstand the wave of professionalization. The last holdout, American university sport, has become a compelling example of the conflicting imperatives involved in defending an amateurism seen by many as anachronistic or hypocritical in an environment that materially rewards the very sort of specialization decried by its original codifiers.

The process by which even these self-declared bastions of amateurism eventually accepted professionalization during the twentieth century offers historians an interesting and complex example of the conflicts in values and worldviews produced by the modernizing project. The same applies *a fortiori*, to the evolution of distinctive cultures, often masculine and defiantly local or class-based, among the consumers of these modern sports. The formation of urban and/or class identity or consciousness arguably owed as much to the experience of sharing in ritual chants and songs or mass processions to and from stadiums for matches as it did to the workplace. Sport served as escape from work, offering membership in a group to which one belonged by choice rather than economic necessity, while reinforcing the culture and status bred by new economic statuses and relationships.

As Lewis and Sasu Siegelbaum note in their contribution to this volume, professional athletes followed other working-class occupations in seeking a greater share of the proceeds generated by their labors and the revenues they produced. Rejecting elite arguments about amateurism, they sought recognition as workers in their own right, demanding better salaries and working conditions and resorting to work-action when they decided the occasion demanded.

In addition to professionalism, the appropriation of sport by the objects of the ameliorative project injected competition with a decidedly different ethos than that propagated by the original apostles. For many spectators, sporting success became an end in itself, inspiring a fierce partisanship that still bemuses the uninitiated, certainly a far cry from the "sportsmanship" envisioned by Victorians. The emphasis on competitive success—with its potential financial returns—also brought changes in attitudes to rules. If their inventors relied on a sense of honor and respect for laws to govern the playing of games, later generations of players tested the rules' limits, not unlike their counterparts in business, to enhance their competitive edge. "Body-line" bowling in cricket, baseball's "spitter," and "flopping" in soccer or basketball invert the relationship between rules and outcome in ways unimagined by the James Naismiths or de Coubertins of the founders' era. Such shifts in attitudes offer potential insight into larger discussions about the career of the "rule of law" as a humanizing or civilizing process, addressing as it does the problem of reception of these programs.

The rooting of sport in the heart of popular culture has had other effects better studied by historians of race/ethnicity and gender. The categoricity of competition forced racists to contemplate the possibility of superior achievement by the offspring of former slaves. Such realizations contributed to the imposition of the "color bar" in American sport; it only disappeared entirely in the late 1960s. Ironically, however, the restrictions of Jim Crow ensured that white Americans tended most often to encounter African American achievement in a sporting arena whose popularity burgeoned throughout the period.

Sport's role as a marker of inclusion in modern societies inevitably extended to women, as newsreels celebrated the accomplishments of Gertrude Ederle or "Babe" Didrickson. The relationship between sport and status has also found reflection in the continuing efforts of female athletes to gain recognition as legitimate competitors in their own right, whether the inclusion of the marathon as a women's event in the Olympics, its prominent place in the American "Title IX" laws, or the recurrent cases of women from largely Muslim societies seeking to participate in competition. More recently, sport has served as a forum for the discussion of sexuality and gender belonging, in cases involving the putative sex of such competitors, whether the female East European competitors of the Cold War or South African sprinter Caster Semenya. As historians of gender and race appreciate, these broader controversies have found concentrated expression in sport.

Popular sport culture has also turned the stadium into a venue for political expression and interaction, especially given the crowd's role as a literal *vox populi*, often in defiance of organizers' or rulers' intentions. The leaders of liberal democracies, feeling obliged to be seen at showcase events, receive catcalls as often as cheers when introduced. In more authoritarian and repressive orders, stadiums and their vicinities as gathering points have represented rare instances of a genuinely public sphere, largely free from the restraint and coercion in other areas of sanctioned organized activities. These spaces and the interactions within them have begun to draw the interest of sport historians; their mainstream colleagues interested in relations between authoritarian/totalitarian states and their societies would also benefit from appreciating their uniqueness. The history of international sport is studded with such resonant instances as the "riots" in Czechoslovakia following their team's defeat of the Soviet team at the world ice-hockey championships in 1969 or, more recently, the wearing of green clothing by Iranian fans and footballers during the disturbances of 2009.

Similar tensions and ambiguities characterized the "imperial" side of sport's world-wide expansion, a problem that has received attention from such well-known commentators as C. L. R. James. As elsewhere in the history of sport, Britain and its colonies present the paradigmatic case, as games and sports established there found homes throughout the empire. In these realms as well, the local appropriation of sport serves as a vivid mirror of interactions that historians have documented in the realms of politics or culture.

As historians of sport have shown, different societies adopted their "own" games. Cricket took root across much of the empire, outside of central and northern Africa. Both forms of rugby, though, flourished in the white settler colonies in Africa and the anitpodes. Soccer, on the other hand, found strong support chiefly in Africa, except among white South Africans. Since postwar decolonization, much of erstwhile French Africa has also embraced association football.

Not infrequently, competitions pitted teams from the metropolis and the population, giving spectators from both sides a chance to visualize their larger relationships. In colonial times, locals could test themselves against their purportedly superior British rulers. After decolonization, the same competitions, often with other former colonies, served as vessels for envisioning the new nations. Thus, as with players and sports the world over, athletes and fans in former colonies pride themselves on specific "styles" that they see as distinguishing them from one another, but particularly from the English. Alternatively, repeated defeats in "their" sports can provoke morose reflection about England's decline. More recently, the development of such competitions as the "20/20" professional cricket league in India suggests new contours in postcolonial relationships and legacies, with British professionals finding employment on sides and in a league underwritten by a new generation of Indian entrepreneurs.

Sport also left a colonial legacy in propagating class and racial divisions that outlived British rule. The power of the reaction produced by Nelson Mandela's appearance at 1995 Rugby Union World Cup final, clad in the uniform of the South African Springboks—national representatives of a traditionally "white" sport—testifies to the power and concreteness of sport as a forum for popular discourse about societal issues and identities. Thus, even as the institutional and financial frameworks of spectator sport have become increasingly concentrated and global in scope, consumers experience the product in their own contexts, investing it with their own meaning and value. As with the working classes in metropolitan societies, the experience of sport and the setting of the stadium are often underappreciated as media for the expression and reinforcement of larger collective identities, rendered concrete and compelling by the circumstances of competition.

Conclusion

In the past half-century, mass-spectator sport has become a pervasive feature of an increasingly global culture, rivaling and complementing such other forms as movies, television, or music. Statistical indicators from television ratings to worker productivity during major sporting events attest to its significance in the lived and felt experience of billions of people the world over. For more than a century, sport has acted as a medium for the spread of multinational capitalism and international migration, the focal point of identities, a boundary of in- and exclusion, the buttress of political orders, and a commodity for consumption, able to serve as a universal point of reference for largely male populations from all corners of the globe. Critics have decried its universal attraction as a modern version of "bread and circuses" that distracts the oppressed from their exploitation. Its champions laud the virtues it teaches—discipline, teamwork, adherence to rules, and mutual respect.

Like other mass phenomena associated with modernity, sport did not spring up overnight. Its current practices and its popularity stem from deep historical roots that are bound up with the other forces—economic, demographic, political, and cultural—that created the modernity in all of its manifestations. Yet, unlike the areas of modernity that have commanded scholars' attention, the history of sport has long been consigned to the sidelines. As much as its critics would like sport to disappear or to return to some "pure" or less conspicuous state, historians have to take seriously a phenomenon of such magnitude and reach. It serves as an inextricable ingredient in the shaping of class and national loyalties; the assimilation and socialization of broad populations to urban, colonial, or modern life; and a still vital set of institutions, practices, and modes of consumption that shape the lifeworlds and aspirations of broad sections of global society. Failure to take account of its importance means depriving oneself of an important lens on the central questions that have preoccupied our profession since the dawn of the "new" social history and through the profusion of "turns" that have succeeded it. The fact of modern sport and the intensity of the responses elicited by "games" in modern life demand their inclusion in our histories.

Notes

1. Norbert Elias and Eric Dunning, *The Quest for Excitement: Sport and Leisure in the Civilizing Process* (London: Oxford University Press, 1985); Johan Huizinga, *Homo Ludens: A Study*

of the Play-Element in Culture, trans. R. C. F. Hull (London: Routledge and Kegan Paul, 1949).

2. Pamela Grundy, *Learning to Win: Sports, Education and Society in Twentieth-Century North Carolina* (Chapel Hill: University of North Carolina Press, 2001).

3. For example, the French historical journal *Clio: histoire, femmes et sociétés* 23 (2006): *Le genre du sport.* See also *Journal of Contemporary History* 38.3 (2003): *Sport and Politics,* and *Ethnologie francaise* 41.4 (2011): *La diffusion du sport,* which features articles by prominent historians of sport, despite its disciplinary affiliation. For an excellent discussion on the historiography of American sport, see Amy Bass, "State of the Field: Sports History after the Cultural Turn," Journal of American History, vol. 101, no. 1 (June 2014): 148-172, with comments from Lisa Alexander, Adrian Burgos, Susan Cahn, Nathan Daniel, Randy Roberts, and Rob Ruck, concluding with Bass's response: 173-197.

4. "AHR Roundtable: Historians and the Question of 'Modernity,'" *American Historical Review* 116.3 (2011): 631–751. For an excellent discussion on the historiography of American sport, see Amy Bass, "State of the Field: Sports History after the Cultural Turn," *Journal of American History,* vol. 101, no. 1 (June 2014): 148–172, with comments from Lisa Alexander, Adrian Burgos, Susan Cahn, Nathan Daniel, Randy Roberts, and Rob Ruck, concluding with Bass's response: 173–197.

5. Wray Vamplew's contribution to this collection provides a detailed analysis of the modern city as the setting for mass spectator sport.

6. David Goldblatt, *The Ball Is Round: A Global History of Soccer,* 2nd ed. (New York: Riverhead Books, 2008).

7. Interestingly, Huizinga's celebration of play as a central element in culture did *not* extend to modern professional sport, in which "the spirit of the professional is no longer the true play-spirit; it is lacking in spontaneity and carelessness." *Homo Ludens,* 197.

8. Michael Oriard gives a magisterial account of this process in American media in *King Football: Sport and Spectacle in the Golden Age of Radio and Newsreels, Movies and Magazines, the Weekly and the Daily Press* (Chapel Hill: University of North Carolina Press, 2001).

9. Allen Guttmann has written extensively on the "modernization" of sport, most notably in *From Ritual to Record: The Nature of Modern Sports* (New York: Columbia University Press, 1978). See also Wray Vamplew's discussion of industry and sport in this volume.

10. Eric Hobsbawm, "Mass-Producing Traditions: Europe, 1870–1914," in *The Invention of Tradition,* ed. Eric Hobsbawm and Terence Ranger (Cambridge, UK: Cambridge University Press, 1983), 300–301.

11. Vamplew's article discusses the same project in a different context.

BIBLIOGRAPHY

Burgos, Adrain. *Playing America's Game: Baseball, Latinos, and the Color Line.* Berkeley: University of California Press, 2007.

Cahn, Susan K. *Coming on Strong: Gender and Sexuality in Women's Sport, 1900–1960.* New York: Free Press, 1994.

Collins, Tony. "Review Article: Work, Rest and Play: Recent Trends in the History of Sport and Leisure." *Journal of Contemporary History* 42.2 (2007): 397–410.

Edelman, Robert. *Spartak Moscow: A History of the People's Team in the Workers' State.* Ithaca, NY: Cornell University Press, 2009.

Eisenberg, C. "Die Entdeckung des Sports durch die modern Geschichtswissenschaft." *Historical Social Research* 27.2–3 (2002): 4–21.

Elias, Norbert, and Eric Dunning. *The Quest for Excitement: Sport and Leisure in the Civilizing Process.* London: Oxford University Press, 1985.

Goldblatt, David. *The Ball Is Round: A Global History of Soccer.* New York: Riverhead Books, 2008.

Grundy, Pamela. *Learning to Win: Sports, Education, and Social Change in Twentieth-Century North Carolina.* Chapel Hill: University of North Carolina Press, 2001.

Guttmann, Allen. *From Ritual to Record.* New York: Columbia University Press, 1978.

Holt, Richard. *Sport and the British: A Modern History.* Oxford Studies in Social History. New York: Oxford University Press, 1989.

Oriard, Michael. *King Football: Sport and Spectacle in the Golden Age of Radio and Newsreels, Movies and Magazines, the Weekly and the Daily Press.* Chapel Hill: University of North Carolina Press, 2001.

PART II

PREMODERN SPORT

....

CHAPTER 5

ANCIENT GREEK
AND ROMAN SPORT

....

DONALD G. KYLE

ALLEN Guttmann's *Ritual to Record*, published in 1978, energized sport history by examining whether ancient and modern sport are fundamentally different in their practices and natures. That debate continues because definitions of "sport" are various and capacious, and because sources for ancient and modern sport differ. Modern sport historians can access abundant and constantly growing evidence, from print to media to stadiums, but the material and textual evidence for ancient sport (e.g., poetry, papyri, inscriptions, pottery, art, burials, ruins) is limited and distant. Also, both ancient and modern sport are "moving targets." Modern sport is changing in terms of new events, science, and participation, and our understanding of ancient sport is being changed by revisionism, new approaches, and discoveries. To demonstrate the growth and sophistication of ancient sport historical studies, this chapter surveys traditions, major trends, and recent debates and discoveries.

THE HISTORIOGRAPHY OF ANCIENT SPORT

....

Ancient sport has been studied intermittently since the Renaissance but traditionally as a minor topic within classical studies. It appealed to an antiquarian interest in procedures, techniques, and puzzles—how Greeks threw the discus or scored the pentathlon or how Romans classified gladiators, regulated seating, or produced chariot races.

The traditional approach, focusing on sport at Olympia and spectacles at Rome, asserted an idealistic, amateurist, moralistic scenario of early athletic glory and tragic decline. After aristocratic Homeric funeral games, Greek sport supposedly peaked with amateur Panhellenic Games in the sixth century, but soon corruptive lower-class professionalism brought a long social and moral decline. Fourth-century and Hellenistic sport became mere "spectacles," and by Roman times despots pandered to the mob's "bloodlust" at decadent arena combats.

Growth and Revisionism (c. 1975–2000)

Critical studies of ancient sport grew in the 1970s as idealism about modern sport waned. Harris innovatively includes Greek sport under Rome and Roman and Byzantine chariot racing but omits other Roman entertainments.[1] Pleket notes that ancient sport studies were hindered by antiquarianism, classicist rise and fall patterns, and anachronistic amateurism.[2] He argues that upper-class athletic participation, and the aristocratic ethos of sport (stressing glory, toil, and endurance), continued into postclassical times. Finley and Pleket realistically acknowledge problems, profits, and political abuses at ancient Olympia.[3]

In the 1980s and 1990s, North Americans built upon European scholarship from revisionist and interpretive perspectives. Poliakoff shows that Greek combat sports were quite brutal and that earlier cultures had similar events.[4] Attacking the Olympist "myth," Young argues that Greek athletes were never amateurs and that the lower classes competed at Olympia from the beginning.[5] The debate about the status of athletes ignited by Young is still ongoing (see later discussion). Promoting a social historical approach, Golden suggests that Greek sport involved a "discourse of difference" among groups involved in or excluded from competition.[6]

Going beyond the Panhellenic Games, Kyle examines the social and civic significance of athletics in the city-state of Athens.[7] Neils's edited works elaborate upon aspects of Athens' Panathenaic festival, and Goldhill and Osborne apply the innovative concept of "performance culture" to Athens.[8] Studying Sparta, Kennell and Christesen revise the history of education and sport in that famous state.[9]

Turning to Rome, historians in the 1990s, forgoing traditional sensationalistic, condemnatory approaches, began reinterpreting the Roman arena. Wiedemann perceptively explains the relationship between violent games, Roman identity, and imperial sovereignty.[10] More interpretive approaches followed.[11] Interpreting gladiatorial combats as human sacrifices, Futrell examines the spread of amphitheatral architecture in the northern Empire in terms of imperial power and cultural Romanization.[12] Investigating the combats, death, and disposal of victims, Kyle presents gladiators as professional performers whose preparations, combats, and rewards had "sporting" aspects.[13] Highlighting performances, Beacham clarifies the stagecraft and politics of spectacles in the Early Empire.[14]

Recent Ancient Sport History: Balance and Sophistication

In the new millennium, ancient sport history became broader and more nuanced. Greek athletes were no longer amateur gentlemen, nor were Roman gladiators berserk butchers doomed to certain death. Sport now is studied as socially and culturally signifi-cant; revisionists are reexamining and rethinking existing sources and studies; new evi-dence is being discovered; and scholars are using broader chronological, geographical, social, comparative, and interpretive approaches.

Ancient sport historians now are acutely aware of interpretive issues (e.g., genre, lacu-nae, interpolation, intertextuality, representation, perception) in reading literary works and even official documents. Realizing that authors who commented positively or neg-atively on sport were engaged in cultural discourses and constructions of identity, we no longer take at face value the testimony of oft-cited sources. New Historicism now encourages deeper thought about the meanings—the communications, constructions, discourses, social tensions, contestations, and negotiations—of our literary and mate-rial evidence and thus of sport and spectacle.

BROADER SCOPES OF PLACE AND TIME

Traditional studies focused overly on centers and heights—on Archaic and Classical Panhellenic Games, and on spectacles in Rome and Italy in the Late Republic and Early Empire, but there were Greeks and Romans (and others) all over the Mediterranean world. As modern historians study postcolonial, transnational, and world history, ancient sport scholars are taking a more "Mediterranean studies" approach to cultural interactions and connections between peoples on the fringes and centers in home-lands.[15] The Greek and Hellenistic states and the Roman Empire were not homogeneous or static in culture or sport; there were general patterns, regional variations, ongoing sporting discourses, and reciprocal acculturation via trade networks, colonies, and conquests.

The traditional periodization of ancient sport emphasizing "classical" ages privi-leged political history, moral criteria, and "classicist" or biological models (rise and fall, growth, and decline). Traditional dates and termini are now challenged. The Olympics seem not to have begun in the canonical year of 776 BCE[16] (see later discussion), Constantine did not ban gladiatorial combats, and Christian emperors probably did not end athletic contests (e.g., the Olympics c. 393 CE) by specific edicts. Recent periodiza-tions recognize long-term patterns, continuities, transitions, and cultural discourse before and after "classical" ages, notably in the Bronze Age, the Greek age of coloniza-tion, the Hellenistic age, the rise of Rome, and the centuries of Greco-Roman sport and spectacle in the Roman Empire.

Questioning Olympocentrism, Eurocentrism, and the "exceptionalism" of Greece and Rome, we now embrace inclusive and comparative approaches to sport and compe-tition from the Neo-Assyrian and Aztec Empires to Spanish bullfights.[17]

Broader perspectives inspire new paradigms. Discussing sport from the Near East to the Roman Empire, Kyle suggests that Greek athletic contests and Roman spectacles were not incompatible but rather formed a spectrum of public performances. Greek athletics contested before large audiences had spectacular aspects, and Roman enter-tainments of the circus and arena entailed competition, rules, and rewards. Similarly, Potter presents both Greek and Roman events as public "entertainments" involving pro-ducers, performers, and audiences.[18]

Social History

Following Golden, social history and the sociology of sport are increasingly applied to ancient sport.[19] Laments about moral decline and professionalism have yielded to debates about social classes, access, prizes and rewards, and mobility in Greek sport (see later discussion). We have moved from retelling tales of individual stars at temporary, artificial gatherings at Olympia to look at athletics "at home" in the social contexts of local games and facilities. Interest also has increased in nonelite, fringe, or marginal "others" in Greek sport (e.g., females, slaves, hired drivers, functionaries, trainers, arti-sans, merchants), as well as the social status and treatment of various humble but often popular performers in Roman spectacles.

Spectatorship

We now go beyond the performers to study the viewing audiences, to "spectacology" and the social psychology of mass spectatorship.[20] Greek and Roman spectators were engaged, knowledgeable, and empowered "active" viewers who appreciated good per-formances, producers, and officials. Although the facilities differed, Greek and Roman spectators shared the attraction of physical performances and the appreciation of skill, courage, and endurance. They felt passion, partisanship, and the emotional thrills of suspense and unpredictable results. Excited by their watching (and by being watched), they socialized and were socialized by attending.

Sport and Culture

Cultural "turns" (rhetorical, linguistic, visual, somatic, etc.) have made ancient sport studies more analytical, interpretive, and theoretical. An eclectic and useful approach, "performance culture" sees sports and spectacles as "cultural performances" (in "per-formance cultures"); both the performance and performer communicated cultural vir-tues and values, from the Greek adulation of athletes to the Roman stigmatization of gladiators.[21]

IDENTITY: ETHNICITY, COMMUNITY, STATUS

Ancient sport and spectacle were central to the cultural or ethnic identity and self-representation of different individuals, families, and groups (e.g., elites, genders). Greekness and Romanness—in culture and in citizenship—were prized and privileged, so Greeks and Romans broadcast their ethnicity (their community membership) by attending, staging, and spreading games and facilities over vast areas (see later discussion on Macedonia and Asia Minor). Just as Greeks constructed, (re)presented, and displayed their ethnic legitimacy by practicing and watching athletics, crowds at Roman spectacles shared Roman values and proudly defined themselves by contrast with the degraded or slave performers in spectacles.

ANCIENT BODIES

Increasing ("somatological") attention is being paid to the images and meanings of ancient bodies as symbolic, communicative cultural "texts." Performers' bodies created immediate, visual, subjective, emotional impressions based on cultural norms and ideals of gender, beauty, and social worth. Scanlon's work on Greek athletic training, eroticism, and females sets the Greek body in the context of education and socialization, and modern sport sociological theories (e.g., hegemony, functionalism) have offered insights on the treatment (e.g., diet, medical care, or abuse), disciplining, and display of bodies as conditioning to assist (or challenge) social order.[22]

ORIGINS AND GREEKS

Greek athletic exceptionalism, hailing Greeks as the inventors of sport because of some unique agonistic spirit, is no longer sacrosanct. Challenging earlier theories about the (Greek) origin of sport in cults or funeral games, Sansone asserts a single universal nature and origin for both ancient and modern sport in the "ritual sacrifice of physical energy."[23] Paleolithic hunting practices endured, became stylized, and took on new communicative functions as sport. Sansone's explanations of some features of Greek sport (e.g., nudity, oil, crowns) may not persuade all, but his thesis remains stimulating.

Greek sport became distinctive for its prizes, nudity, and facilities, but the emergence of Greek sport was not *ex nihilo*. Works now suggest widespread pre-Greek sport, from combat sports (e.g., boxing, wrestling) to bull sports, in the Bronze Age Mediterranean world. The contexts apparently were spectacular performances at court—from New Kingdom Egypt and Minoan Knossos (with bull sports as elite male, but not female, sporting initiations) to the Hittite and Neo-Assyrian empires—but the events, skills, and competitive spirit cannot be denied.

Moreover, sport discourses of difference and adaptations started early. Minoan bull sports had ties to early Egyptian and Mesopotamian bull imagery, and, in turn, Minoanizing paintings of bull sports have been found in the delta of New Kingdom Egypt. The Mycenaean Greeks, who on their own may have only known chariots and performing boxers, adapted rather than invented other events.

Hittite and Egyptian contests arguably influenced Homer, who sets the funeral games of *Iliad* 23 in the Late Bronze Age; but Homer's "world" now is generally down-dated to the Early Iron Age (ninth to eighth century BCE), and his sport is that of an age in transition from aristocratic warriors to city-states and open athletic festivals.

ARCHAIC AND CLASSICAL GREECE

The Archaic Age (c. 750–500), especially the sixth century, was the formative age of Greek sport with city-state (*polis*) formation, colonization, the adoption of money, and other socioeconomic changes. When Archaic Greeks founded new colonies as independent city-states from the Black Sea to Sicily, they took their games with them, and soon they returned to watch or compete at Olympia and other sites. Interactions between dispersed Greeks and the Greek mainland raise interesting questions of ethnicity and status display as groups used sport for propaganda and legitimization. Like modern expansion franchises, new city-states abroad established local games to display their ethnic legitimacy, resources, and status, and they competed for prestige as homes of victors, festivals, and patrons of sport. Sophisticated and broad, Hornblower and Morgan's volume uses Pindar and other sources to show that athletic prestige was sought by individuals, families, and communities all over the Greek Mediterranean.[24] Essays on regions prominent in Pindar (e.g., Argos, Corinth, Aegina, Thessaly) discuss the influence of local patronage, the regional dimensions of victory odes, and Pindar's adaptation of local myth-historical imagery. The work also covers Western colonial elites, the tyrants of Sicily, and Greek sport in Hellenistic Egypt and the Roman Empire.

Applying New Historicism to Pindar, Nicholson examines the poetics of representation and omission as victors and poets attempted to re-create realities for personal and political ends. Elites and tyrants displayed their wealth and status by personal athletic competition or indirectly via equestrian events in which hired or slave drivers risked injury but the owners claimed the victories. Nicholson argues that socioeconomic changes brought challenges by nonelite citizens in Archaic and Classical Greece, moving anxious aristocrats to minimize the contributions of hired charioteers and jockeys, and paid trainers, in their victory commemorations (odes, dedications, vases).

OLYMPIA

The most prestigious ancient games took place in the festival of Zeus at Olympia, and information on the events, rules, program, and so on is readily available.[25] Archaeology, however, suggests that major games at Olympia arose not in 776 but probably around 700[26]; and Christesen's important work on the Olympic victor lists shows that victors' names and details are unreliable until the sixth century.[27] Moreover, scholars have demythologized ancient Olympia (and other famous games) by noting excessive violence, ethnic and gender chauvinism, corruption, commercialization, and political propaganda.

Olympia was a sanctuary, but it was within, and was administered by, the independent state of Elis, and while the Eleans managed the games well, there sometimes was bias and interference. Also, despite modern illusions, the famous Olympic truce only mandated safe passage for visitors; it did not stop all wars in Greece or even at Olympia.[28]

THE *PERIODOS*

In the first half of the sixth century, a coordinated cycle of four games (later called the *periodos* or "circuit") developed at neutral "interstate" sanctuaries at Olympia, Delphi, Isthmia, and Nemea. These four are usually termed "crown" (stephanitic) games because they only offered wreath prizes, in contrast with local material prize (chrematitic) games.

Archaeology at the sites of the *periodos* has revealed the significance of settings and spectatorship in ancient sport. For example, Nemea has provided new information about the facilities and operation of Greek games. A later fourth-century stadium, with seating arrangements for some 40,000 people, has a vaulted entrance tunnel (complete with graffiti) leading from a "locker room" (*apodyterion*) to the track with its starting line and mechanism (*hysplex*).[29] Even great games in neutral sanctuaries, however, were not simply "sport for the sake of sport."[30] Contests were produced by ambitious, politicized states,[31] and war cut short Nemea's athletic history.[32]

LOCAL OR CIVIC GAMES

The "crown" games provided grand stages for the most talented (and wealthiest) competitors, but those games and those competitors were not the norm. The Olympics, held only every four years and involving perhaps 200 to 250 elite athletes, show us only part of the Greek athletic world, not the part experienced by most Greeks. [33] "Greece" included several hundred independent states, and, due to distance and expense, the average athlete or spectator probably did not regularly attend the great Panhellenic festivals but instead went to games closer to home. Appreciating the rich variety and vitality of Greek athletics, and attempting athletic social history, involves looking beyond the *periodos* to local or civic contests. Many states built facilities and staged local sporting festivals, which are far more relevant and revealing for Greeks in their social and civic contexts.[34]

ATHENS AND SPARTA

The sixth-century athletic explosion enhanced the importance of exercise and sport in the social life, topography, economies, and politics of Greek city-states.

Sparta remains famous for its physical training of males (and females; see later discussion), but the evidential challenges of looking past the Spartan "mirage" are daunting.[35] Spartans have been seen as isolationists obsessed only with militarism, but chariot racing and athletics were prevalent within Sparta.[36] Studies of ancient education always highlight Sparta, but Ducat suggests that Sparta's mandatory male training (*agoge*) was not so unusual.[37] Kennell reconstructs early forms of Spartan physical training but down-dates some notoriously excessive practices to later eras.[38]

Athens, whose democracy and empire expanded its sport to spectacular lengths, offers abundant evidence for the staging of games, local variations, and athletes in society.[39] Interest continues in Athens' Panathenaic festival and its contests, prizes, procession, and other elements.[40]

Athens is a main focus of a major debate about "democratization" (access and social mobility) in Greek sport, involving issues of class, financial resources, patronage, meritocracy, ideology, and education. Fisher disagreeing with Pritchard's exclusivist arguments about athletic education, expands his own argument for nonelite access to athletics via team events.[41] The debate continues with Christesen asserting broad access and "mass sport," and Pritchard reiterating his position that athletics remained elitist.[42]

GYMNASIA AND TRAINING

Gymnasia arose in the sixth century as public facilities for nude exercise and athletic training, but they also became centers for male social and erotic interaction and also for the education and socialization of youths in preparation for citizenship. Gymnastic nudity was a symbolic costume, a social marker of freedom, elite male status, and Greekness. Social historians discuss issues of nudity, class, age groups, sexuality, and education in the gymnasia as places of becoming, longing, and belonging. Scanlon examines the role of eroticism in Greek sport, religion, education, and gender formation, and he explains that nude physical education (*gymnike paideia*) constructively incorporated erotically charged (pederastic) relationships in which teenage youths followed the example of mature males.[43]

'The relationship between athletics and warfare in Greece has been debated. Early athletic training was of practical military value only indirectly, but later the gymnasium training of cadets (*epheboi*) took on more military and educational elements, which continued in Hellenistic and Roman times.[44]

GENDER

Interest in Greek female sport and Roman female gladiators is understandable, but both were relatively minor phenomena that left limited evidence. Spartan female physical education was rigorous but eugenic and exceptional. Greek girls' initiation rites with dances or running, as at Brauron, seem widespread, but such activities ended with marriage. Scholars still disagree about the participants and significance of the races for virgins in the festival of Hera at Olympia. Mature women were banned from watching the male Olympics, and accounts of heroines who supposedly challenged sexism in sport by defying the ban and watching male athletics (Kallipateira) or by winning chariot races *in absentia* at Olympia (Kyniska) have been both defended and doubted.[45] Ironically, female equestrian sport expanded in Hellenistic times (see later discussion), and female sport became more fully athletic under Rome.[46]

MACEDONIA AND HELLENISTIC SPORT AND SPECTACLE

Recent interests in transitional ages and ethnic discourse have scholars revising views of later Greek sport as in decline. Rather, postclassical history offers an exciting opportunity for studying the dispersion of Greek sport and spectacle. Like earlier Greek colonization, Macedonian and Hellenistic imperial phenomena demonstrate the value of sport and spectacle for ethnic and political agendas.

King Philip II (359–336 BCE) of Macedonia publicized his Olympic equestrian victories as propaganda for ethnic legitimization while he conquered Greece, but he also patronized Olympia and other sites of games. Contrary to ancient claims that Philip's son, Alexander the Great, disliked sport, that famous conqueror staged athletic contests during his campaigns, and he spread Greeks, cities, sport, and facilities widely over formerly non-Greek lands from Egypt to Asia Minor.[47]

The Hellenistic world (323–331 BCE) knew sporting discourse among Greece, the Near East, and Rome. Near Eastern traditions of spectacular entertainment at royal palaces were compounded with Greco-Macedonian sporting customs. With a concerted sport and propaganda policy, the Ptolemaic kings of Egypt created new athletic festivals (e.g., the Ptolemaia), subsidized "Egyptian" or "Alexandrian" athletes at major competitions,[48] built facilities at home to house ephebic education and to encourage a "gymnasium class," and patronized Olympia with benefactions. When Ptolemaic (and other Hellenistic) royals competed in the Olympic and Panathenaic games, like earlier colonists, they were "on display"—not as Macedonian upstarts but as wealthy legitimate Greeks.

Significantly, Ptolemaic females were prominent at court and in equestrian competitions. Discovered in 2001, a papyrus with poems by Posidippus of Pella, third-century poet to Ptolemies I and II, includes eighteen victory epigrams (the *Hippika*) for equestrian wins at Olympia, Athens, and elsewhere by male and female members (and associates) of the royal court. The poems dramatically confirm the aspirations and self-representation of Hellenistic rulers on the edges of the Greek world.[49]

In transitional times and liminal areas, Hellenistic Greeks adapted to lavish public processions and performances staged for—and by—male and female royalty. Moreover, Hellenistic spectacles, including displays of exotic animals as symbols of territorial domains, were soon imported by Roman leaders (see later discussion) as Rome expanded into a wider world of sport and spectacle. Finally, the Hellenistic era also saw an expansion of "crown" or "Iso-" (equal to) major athletic festivals, a trend that continued into the Roman Empire (see later discussion).

ROMAN SPECTACLES

Rome has attracted much attention recently, mainly for its arena spectacles (gladiatorial and beast combats) and its circus events (mainly chariot races), but also for its acceptance and patronage of Greek sport in Rome itself and in Rome's eastern provinces. Scholars challenge the image of Romans as sadistically obsessed with deadly mass spectacles and as too brutish to appreciate Greek athletics. Certainly there were differences at Rome: performers seldom were free volunteers, combats with men and animals were dangerous and often fatal, and Roman purpose-built facilities became far more monumental. Also, Roman games, associated with the emperors and the emperor cult, developed a more efficiently centralized administrative system than the Greeks had earlier. Yet, like Greek games, Roman spectacles had rules, prizes, talented performers, chances of fame, and appreciative audiences. Accordingly, historians increasingly accept the spectacles as Rome's "sport."

FROM REPUBLIC TO EMPIRE

As the Roman Republic grew, it combined native festivals (*ludi*) with the inclination to nonparticipatory sport spectatorship of the nearby Etruscans and with Hellenistic customs of processions and animal shows. Chariot races were the earliest and longest enduring Roman spectacle, but in 264 BCE a wealthy family staged the first recorded gladiatorial combat as a funerary show (*munus*), and in 168 Fulvius Flaccus presented both an animal show (*venatio*) and a display of Greek athletes at Rome. Both gladiatorial and beast events escalated dramatically as the Republic conquered more territories, while Greek sport grew more popular later under the empire.

In the Late Republic, ambitious politicians expanded the traditional festival games, and military leaders such as Sulla, Pompey, and Caesar staged lavish shows in association with military triumphs and funerals.[50] Following the Near Eastern tradition of "royal hunts," professional hunters killed exotic animals in arenas to demonstrate Rome's control over threats and territories,[51] and sensational combats between trained gladiators (see later discussion) appealed to the militaristic Romans. Ultimately the popularity and political value of such shows became so great that Augustus took control of such entertainments.[52]

At its height in the early third century CE, the eclectic entertainment system of the Roman Empire, incorporating the sporting entertainment traditions and tastes of various regions and peoples, was well managed and socially and politically beneficial. Despite Juvenal's famous phrase "bread and circuses" (*panem et circenses* 10.78–81), Roman emperors did not simply manipulate debased, impotent masses. Seating arrangements reflected the hierarchy of Rome, but the emperor and his people interacted at the games. The ideology of spectacles included the expectations and involvement of the crowds and obligations—from generosity to decorum—of the emperors.[53]

Spectacular Facilities

Before amphitheaters emerged in the Late Republic, the earliest Roman spectacles took place in the Roman Forum or the Circus Maximus (Rome's chariot-racing venue). Rome's facilities started out modestly but exploded in size and number in the Late Republic and Early empire.

Humphrey's authoritative study of circuses throughout the empire explains the history and organization of the races and the evolution, design, and operation of circuses.[54] Cameron's works remain essential on Roman and Byzantine charioteers and on the circus "factions" (i.e., the organizers who produced races and the fan groupings distinguished as "colors").[55]

Stadiums for Greek contests (and Greek hippodromes for horse and chariot races) were more common in Greece and the Roman East, and characteristically Roman amphitheaters—more than 250 of them—were more common in the West, but local adaptations and mixed-use facilities arose throughout the empire.[56]

Welch's major study locates the amphitheater's origin in early wooden facilities in the Roman Forum, and she associates the development of arenas with the army and military discipline.[57] As well as her profound articles on mythologically staged executions (*fatale charades*), mass spectatorship, and more, Coleman has provided a translation and commentary on Martial's poems on the inauguration of the Flavian Amphitheater or "Colosseum" in 80 CE.[58]

GLADIATORS AS ENTERTAINERS AND CULTURAL PERFORMERS

Building on Ville's magisterial work, scholars have applied sociological and psychological models to gladiators.[59] They read gladiatorial combats as cultural performances in which lowly gladiators recalled early Roman foes (e.g., Samnites, Gauls) but demonstrated Roman skills and virtues (e.g., masculinity, courage, acceptance of death). Romans were conflicted and had ambivalent feelings about gladiators because of that discordance between their debased status and their military discipline.

Investigating the arena's allure for spectators, Fagan looks comparatively at violent public shows in ancient and later eras through the lens of social psychology. Seating arrangements in amphitheaters and preconceived notions about the performers reinforced the attraction of gladiatorial "sports spectaculars."[60] Experiencing emotions, excitement, identification, or animosity, spectators also felt empowered by participating in determining whether defeated gladiators should be spared.

Inscribed epitaphs and records of outcomes reveal the careers and self-representation of gladiators. Their combats were not mass slaughters but rather staged duels between skilled, well-matched professionals, with sporting elements including referees and rules or conventions. Gladiators were such valuable entertainers that emperors established categories and price lists for them.

After early reluctance, the Greek East embraced arena combats. Gladiators in the Greek East applied Greek athletic terms and iconography to their combats, elite Greeks demonstrated their "Romanization" by supporting arena spectacles, and cities often adapted their theaters and stadiums for Roman blood sports.

GLADIATOR BURIALS

Archaeological finds in the Greek East and Great Britain clarify much about gladiators' lives and combats. Second-century CE gladiator burials were discovered in 1993 at Ephesus,[61] a Greek city in Asia Minor. Analysis of the bones of sixty-eight skeletons of mostly robust twenty- to thirty-year-old males revealed the gladiators' living conditions, largely vegetarian diet, injuries, and prospects of survival. That there were few multiple injuries indicates that paired opponents fought face-to-face combats without excess hacking and bludgeoning. Healed skull injuries confirm that combats were not necessarily "to the death." Some gladiators were spared, medical care aided the recovery of some, and some later fought again and died. Defeated and not released fighters accepted a deathblow to the heart via the neck or shoulder blade. Mortally wounded fighters were finished off with a hammer blow to the skull. The combats were undeniably dangerous, but the burials suggest rites and respect; gravestones bore epitaphs and reliefs of proud gladiators.

In 2010 another gladiator graveyard was discovered, this one of the first to fourth century CE, at York (Roman Eboracum). It yielded eighty skeletons of robust men, most of whom were violently decapitated. Some burials involved ritual meals, but no epitaphs were found. Intriguing elements include the burial of skeletons with their skulls anatomically displaced—possibly as a regional ritual variation—a carnivore bite mark on one skull, and the asymmetry of arm lengths from sword training.[62]

These graveyards confirm the "ambivalent" status of gladiators. Although stigmatized, they normally were not doomed to fight "to the death," and, if killed, they could receive decent or even honorific burials with memorialization.

GREEK SPORT AT ROME: ACCEPTANCE AND GROWTH

Just as Romanization in the Greek East included acceptance of arena spectacles, Hellenization for Romans included endorsing and encouraging Greek athletics within Rome's broad entertainment policy of assimilation and patronage. The old notion that Rome rejected Greek sport came from facile acceptance of a few isolated intellectual criticisms.

Newby's art historical study clarifies that, after some cultural adjustments (e.g., to nudity) in the Later Republic and Early empire, Greek sport became part of the festivals, art, and social life of Rome.[63] Emperors (e.g., Augustus, Nero, Domitian) fostered Greek sport with athletic festivals and a stadium at Rome, the headquarters of the international guild of star athletes moved to Rome, and public facilities, especially the imperial baths, made Greek-style exercise more appealing and convenient for Romans. While Greek sport never rivaled Roman games in the West, athletic mosaics and copies of Greek sculptures in baths, villas, and public spaces show that athletics influenced Roman life and recreation.

THE ROMAN EAST: MORE GREEK GAMES AND CULTURAL DISCOURSE

Scholars have revealed a wider and thriving later world of Greek sport in Greece and the Roman East, especially in Asia Minor. From Hellenistic times Greeks in the East continued to found new local and Iso-periodic games, and facilities (gymnasia, stadiums, baths) flourished because agonistic festivals and ephebic education remained central to the self-representation of cities and individuals as ethnically Greek.

Sophisticated cultural studies by van Nijf and others show that Eastern Greeks (and Greekish folk from fringe areas) wanted to claim, retain, or display Greek ethnicity and elite status though sport.[64] Cities, elite patrons, aspiring athletes, and fathers of sons wanted to identify themselves with classical athletic culture through ephebic education, competition, masculine self-display, facilities, festivals, art, and literature.

König's major study applies critical theoretical studies of rhetoric, representation, and bodily display to claims about athletics in inscriptions, art, and literary works, which also offered contestations and indications of alternative opinions or rival claims to identity and status.[65] He analyzes texts (e.g., Lucian, Philostratus) that reveal athletics as a locus of conflicted elite self-identification and broader cultural controversies about education, bodies, civic virtue, and Greek traditions. He shows that constructions of the history of sport in Classical Greece in literature of the Imperial era were fashioned by the authors' concerns about nostalgia, Panhellenic legacies, self-representation, or professional rivalries.

Philhellenic Patronage of Greek Sport: Hadrian, Athletes, and Olympia

Imperial support for Greek athletic festivals reflects a positive relationship between Roman authorities and provincial urban elites. By sanctioning networks of numerous festivals and supervising athletic pensions and professional guilds, Rome's imperial administration and the emperor cult provided institutionalization and regularity for both Greek and Roman games in the empire's Greco-Roman entertainment system.[66]

A major discovery in 2003, a lengthy inscription at Alexandria Troas (in modern Turkey), contains Emperor Hadrian's instructions in 134 CE to representatives of guilds of athletes and actors for the operation of performances.[67] Hadrian responds to petitions about the display and provision of athletic prizes, pensions, and the flogging of athletes. He also decrees a detailed reordering of the calendar and sequence of numerous crown games, starting with Olympia, over a four-year period. Hadrian clearly wanted to resolve existing disputes with professional performers, to restore order (e.g., concerning skimming of prize money, starting dates of pensions, punishments, etc.), and to address problems with the expansion, status, and scheduling of games.

As Hadrian's inscription indicates, Scanlon appropriately rejected the old notion that Rome oppressed and corrupted Olympia, a notion based on the decline scenario and over citation of Nero's visit of 66–67 CE.[68] Placing the games in a broader context, Scanlon shows continuity, growth, and welcome patronage and prosperity as Olympia adapted constructively to Roman rule. Olympic victories remained supremely honorific, and the "ecumenical" Olympics drew competitors and spectators from a wider

Greco-Roman world. The site reached its physical peak in the second century CE through Roman patronage (e.g., Herodes Atticus's fountain house), and recent archaeology suggests the games endured into late Roman times.

CONCLUSION

As suggested, the modernism debate continues because both modern sport and our understanding of ancient sport are changing. We are reading ancient sources in new ways, and new discoveries, especially inscriptions, make us rethink earlier assumptions. Although traditionally associated with Greek athletics, recent modern sport increasingly resembles the inclusive and spectacular entertainment system of the Roman Empire.

Despite critics and abuses, ancient sport and spectacle were significant and beneficial for recreation and entertainment; for providing a sense of identity, community, and pride; and for communicating, reinforcing, and sometimes challenging social orders and cultural traditions throughout ancient states and empires.

NOTES

1. H. A. Harris, *Sport in Greece and Rome* (Ithaca, NY: Cornell University Press, 1972).
2. H. W. Plecket, "Games, Prizes, Athletes, and Ideology. Some Aspects of the History of Sport in the Greco-Roman World," in *Greek Athletics*, ed. J. König, 145–174.
3. M. I. Finley and H. W. Pleket, *The Olympic Games: The First Thousand Years* (New York: Viking Press, 1976).
4. M. B. Poliakoff, *Combat Sports in the Ancient World* (New Haven, CT: Yale University Press, 1987).
5. D. C. Young, *The Olympic Myth of Greek Amateur Athletics* (Chicago: Ares, 1984).
6. Golden, *Sport and Society*.
7. D. G. Kyle, *Athletics in Ancient Athens* (Leiden: E J. Brill, 1987).
8. J. Neils, ed. *Goddess and Polis: The Panathenaic Festival in Ancient Athens* (Princeton, NJ: Princeton University Press, 1992); ed., *Worshipping Athena: Panathenaia and Parthenon* (Madison: University of Wisconsin Press, 1996); S. Goldhill and R. Osborne, eds., *Performance Culture and Athenian Democracy* (Cambridge, UK: Cambridge University Press, 1999).
9. N. M. Kennell, *The Gymnasium of Virtue: Education and Culture in Ancient Sparta* (Chapel Hill: University of North Carolina Press, 1995); P. Christesen, "Athletics in Sparta in the Classical Period," *Classical Antiquity* 31.2 (2012a): 193–255.
10. T. Wiedemann, *Emperors and Gladiators* (London: Routledge, 1992).
11. For example, C. A. Barton, *Sorrows of the Ancient Romans. The Gladiator and the Monster* (Princeton, NJ: Princeton University Press, 1993); P. Plass, *The Game of Death in Ancient Rome: Arena Sport and Political Suicide* (Madison: University of Wisconsin Press, 1995).
12. A. Futrell, *Blood in the Arena: The Spectacle of Roman Power* (Austin: University of Texas Press, 1997).

13. D. G. Kyle, *Spectacles of Death in Ancient Rome* (London: Routledge, 1998).

14. R. C. Beacham, *Spectacle Entertainments of Early Imperial Rome* (New Haven, CT: Yale University Press, 1999).

15. For example, Z. Papakonstantinou, ed., *Sport in the Cultures of the Ancient World: New Perspectives* (London: Routledge, 2010); Hornblower and Morgan, eds., *Pindar's Poetry.*

16. P. Christesen, *Olympic Victor Lists.*

17. D. G. Kyle, *Sport and Spectacle in the Ancient World* (Malden, MA: Blackwell, 2007); G. G. Fagan, "*The Lure of the Arena*": Social Psychology and the Crowd at the Roman Games (Cambridge, UK: Cambridge University Press, 2011); N. Fisher and H. van Wees, eds., *Competition in the Ancient World* (Swansea: Classical Press of Wales, 2011).

18. D. Potter, *The Victor's Crown: A History of Ancient Sport from Homer to Byzantium* (Oxford: Oxford University Press, 2012).

19. Golden, *Sport and Society*; Christesen, *Sport and Democracy.*

20. Fagan, "*The Lure of the Arena.*"

21. Goldhill and Osborne, eds., *Performance Culture*; M. Carter, "Gladiators and Monomachoi: Attitudes to a Roman 'CulturalPerformance,'" in *Sport in the Cultures*, ed. Z. Papakonstantinou, 298–322. Also see B. Bergmann and C. Kondoleon, eds., *The Art of Ancient Spectacle* (New Haven CT: Yale University Press, 1999) on reading the art and "language" of ancient spectacle.

22. T. F. Scanlon, *Eros and Greek Athletics* (Oxford: Oxford University Press, 2002); König, *Athletics and Literature*, 97–157; Christesen, *Sport and Democracy.*

23. Sansone, *Greek Athletics and the Genesis of Sport*, 37.

24. Hornblower and Morgan, eds., *Pindar's Poetry.*

25. Lee, *Program and Schedule*; N. B. Crowther, *Athletika: Studies on the Olympic Games and Greek Athletics* (Hildesheim, Germany: Weidmann, 2004); S. G. Miller, *Ancient Greek Athletics* (New Haven, CT: Yale University Press, 2004); N. Spivey, *The Olympics: A History* (Oxford: Oxford University Press, 2004); D. C. Young, *A Brief History of the Olympic Games* (London: Blackwell, 2004); J. Swaddling, *The Ancient Olympic Games*, 2nd ed. (Austin: University of Texas Press, 2008).

26. U. Sinn, *Olympia: Cult, Sport and Ancient Festival*, trans. T. Thornton (Princeton, NJ: Princeton University Press, 2000), 7–14.

27. Christesen, *Olympic Victor Lists.*

28. Kyle, *Sport and Spectacle*, 127–130.

29. Miller, *Ancient Greek Athletics*, 38–45; Miller, ed., *Nemea: A Guide to the Site and Museum* (Athens: Archaeological Receipts Fund, Directorate of Publications, 2004c), 198–208.

30. Miller, *Ancient Greek Athletics*, 216–225.

31. On "spatial politics," see M. Scott, *Delphi and Olympia: The Spatial Politics of Panhellenism in the Archaic and Classical Periods* (Cambridge, UK: Cambridge University Press, 2010).

32. Miller, ed., *Nemea*, 61–64.

33. Crowther, *Athletika*, 171–179.

34. Miller, *Ancient Greek Athletics*, 129–145; P. Valavanis, *Games and Sanctuaries in Ancient Greece: Olympia, Delphi, Isthmia, Nemea, Athens* (Los Angeles: J. Paul Getty Museum, 2004), 336–397; Kyle, *Sport and Spectacle*, 148–197.

35. Kennell, *Gymnasium of Virtue*, 5–27.

36. S. Hodkinson, "An Agonistic Culture? Athletic Competition in Archaic and Classical Spartan Society," in *Sparta: New Perspectives*, ed. S. Hodkinson and A. Powell (London: Duckworth, 1999), 147–187; Christesen, "Athletics in Sparta."

37. J. Ducat, *Spartan Education,* trans. E. Stafford, P.-J. Shaw, and A. Powell (Swansea: Classical Press of Wales, 2006), 179–222.

38. Kennell, *Gymnasium of Virtue.*

39. Kyle, *Athletics in Ancient Athens.*

40. Neils, ed., *Goddess and Polis;* ed., *Worshipping Athena;* J. L. Shear, "Prizes from Athens: The List of Panathenaic Prizes and the Sacred Oil," *Zeitschrift für Papyrologie und Epigraphik* 142 (2003): 87–105.

41. N. Fisher, "Competitive Delights: The Social Effects of the Expanded Programme of Contests in Post-Kleisthenic Athens," in *Competition in the Ancient World,* ed. N. Fisher and H. van Wees, 175–219; D. Pritchard, "Athletics, Education and Participation in Classical Athens," in *Sport and Festival in the Ancient Greek World,* ed. D. J. Phillips and D. Pritchard (Swansea: Classical Press of Wales, 2003), 293–349; "Sport, War and Democracy in Classical Athens," in *Sport in the Cultures,* ed. Z. Papakonstantinou, 64–97.

42. Christesen, *Sport and Democracy,* 153–178; D. Pritchard, *Sport, Democracy and War in Classical Athens* (Cambridge, UK: Cambridge University Press, 2013), 34–83.

43. Scanlon, *Eros and Greek Athletics.*

44. Poliakoff, *Combat Sports,* 94–103; Golden, *Sport and Society,* 23–28; D. Pritchard, "Sport, War and Democracy in Classical Athens," in *Sport in the Cultures,* ed. Z. Papakonstantinou, 64–97; Z. Newby, *Greek Athletics in the Roman World: Victory and Virtue* (Oxford: Oxford University Press, 2005), 168–201.

45. On females, Scanlon, *Eros and Greek Athletics,* 98–174, is essential, but also see S. Pomeroy, *Spartan Women* (Oxford: Oxford University Press, 2002); D. G. Kyle, "'The Only Woman in All Greece': Kyniska, Agesilaus, Alcibiades and Olympia," *Journal of Sport History* 30 (2003): 183–203; *Sport and Spectacle,* 217–228; and T. F. Scanlon, "The Heraia at Olympia Revisited," *Nikephoros* 21 (2008): 159–196.

46. On female gladiators as trained combatants but largely as novelties, see K. M. Coleman, "*Missio* at Halicarnassus," *Harvard Studies in Classical Philology* 100 (2000): 487–500.

47. W. L. Adams, "Other People's Games: The Olympics, Macedonia and Greek Athletics," *Journal of Sport History* 30 (2003): 205–217.

48. S. Remijsen, "Challenged by Egyptians: Greek Sports in the Third Century BC," in *Sport in the Cultures,* ed. Z. Papakonstantinou, 98–123.

49. Remijsen, "Challenged by Egyptians."

50. Beacham, *Spectacle Entertainments,* 45–91.

51. R. Dunkle, *Gladiators: Violence and Spectacle in Ancient Rome* (Harlow, UK: Pearson/ Longman, 2008), 207–244.

52. See Beacham, *Spectacle Entertainments,* 92–154, on the politics and stagecraft of Augustus.

53. Wiedemann, *Emperors and Gladiators,* 165–183.

54. J. Humphrey, *Roman Circuses: Arenas for Chariot Racing* (Berkeley: University of California Press, 1986).

55. A. Cameron, *Circus Factions: Blues and Greens at Rome and Byzantium* (Oxford: Clarendon Press, 1976); *Porphyrius—The Charioteer* (Oxford: Clarendon Press, 1973).

56. H. Dodge, "Amusing the Masses: Buildings for Entertainment and Leisure in the Roman World," in *Life, Death, and Entertainment in the Roman Empire,* 2nd ed., ed. D. Potter and D. Mattingly (Ann Arbor: University of Michigan Press, 2010), 205–255.

57. K. E. Welch, *The Roman Amphitheatre: From Its Origins to the Colosseum* (Cambridge, UK: Cambridge University Press, 2007).

58. K. M. Coleman, *Martial: Liber Spectaculorum* (Oxford: Oxford University Press, 2006). Also useful on amphitheaters and their games are D. L. Bomgardner, *The Story of the Roman Amphitheatre* (London: Routledge, 2000); A. Gabucci, ed. *The Colosseum*, trans. M. Becker (Los Angeles: J. Paul Getty Museum, 2001); Dunkle, *Gladiators*, 245–287; and T. Wilmott, ed., *Roman Amphitheatres and Spectacula: A 21st-Century Perspective* (Oxford: Archaeopress, 2009).
59. G. Ville, *La Gladiature en Occident des origines à la morte de Domitien*, ed. P. Veyne (Rome: Ecole française de Rome, 1981).
60. Fagan, "*The Lure of the Arena*," 209–229.
61. F. Kanz and K. Grosschmidt, "Dying in the Arena: The Osseous Evidence from Ephesian Gladiators," in *Roman Amphitheatres and Spectacula*, ed. T. Wilmott, 211–220.
62. "Gladiators: A Cemetery of Secrets," York Archaeological Trust (2011), http://www.yorkarchaeology.co.uk/headless-romans/index.htm.
63. Newby, *Greek Athletics in the Roman World*, see also König, *Athletics and Literature*, 205–253.
64. O. van Nijf, "Athletics, Festivals and Greek Identity in the Roman East," in *Greek Athletics*, ed. J. König, 175–197; Pleket, "Games, Prizes"; Newby, *Greek Athletics in the Roman World*, 141–201, 229–271.
65. König, *Athletics and Literature*.
66. H. W. Pleket, "Roman Emperors and Greek Athletics," *Nikephoros* 23 (2010b): 175–203.
67. W. J. Slater, "Hadrian's Letters to the Athletes and Dionysiac Artists concerning Arrangements for the 'Circuit' of Games," *Journal of Roman Archaeology* 21 (2008): 610–620.
68. Scanlon, *Eros and Greek Athletics*, 40–63.

BIBLIOGRAPHY

Adams, W. L. "Other People's Games: The Olympics, Macedonia and Greek Athletics." *Journal of Sport History* 30 (2003): 205–217.
Barton, C. A. *Sorrows of the Ancient Romans. The Gladiator and the Monster*. Princeton, NJ: Princeton University Press, 1993.
Beacham, R. C. *Spectacle Entertainments of Early Imperial Rome*. New Haven, CT: Yale University Press, 1999.
Bergmann, B., and C. Kondoleon, eds. *The Art of Ancient Spectacle*. New Haven CT: Yale University Press, 1999.
Bomgardner, D. L. *The Story of the Roman Amphitheatre*. London: Routledge, 2000.
Cameron, A. *Circus Factions: Blues and Greens at Rome and Byzantium*. Oxford: Clarendon Press, 1976.
Cameron, A. *Porphyrius—The Charioteer*. Oxford: Clarendon Press, 1973.
Carter, M. "Gladiatorial Ranking and the *SC de Pretiis Gladiatorum Minuendis* (*CIL* II 6278 = *ILS* 5163)." *Phoenix* 57 (2003): 83–114.
Carter, M. "Gladiators and Monomachoi: Attitudes to a Roman 'Cultural Performance.'" In *Sport in the Cultures of the Ancient World: New Perspectives*, edited by Z. Papakonstantinou, 298–322. New York: Routledge, 2010.
Christesen, P. "Athletics in Sparta in the Classical Period." *Classical Antiquity* 31.2 (2012a): 193–255.

Christesen, P. *Olympic Victor Lists and Ancient Greek History*. Cambridge, UK: Cambridge University Press, 2007.

Christesen, P. *Sport and Democracy in the Ancient and Modern Worlds*. Cambridge, UK: Cambridge University Press, 2012b.

Coleman, K. M. "Fatal Charades: Roman Executions Staged as Mythological Enactments." *Journal of Roman Studies* 130 (1990): 44–73.

Coleman, K. M. *Martial: Liber Spectaculorum*. Oxford: Oxford University Press, 2006.

Coleman, K. M. "*Missio* at Halicarnassus." *Harvard Studies in Classical Philology* 100 (2000): 487–500.

Crowther, N. B. *Athletika: Studies on the Olympic Games and Greek Athletics*. Hildesheim, Germany: Weidmann, 2004.

Decker, W. *Sports and Games of Ancient Egypt*. Translated by A. Guttmann. New Haven, CT: Yale University Press, 1992.

Dodge, H. "Amusing the Masses: Buildings for Entertainment and Leisure in the Roman World." In *Life, Death, and Entertainment in the Roman Empire*, 2nd ed., edited by D. Potter and D. Mattingly, 205–255. Ann Arbor: University of Michigan Press, 2010.

Ducat, J. *Spartan Education*. Translated by E. Stafford, P.-J. Shaw, and A. Powell. Swansea: Classical Press of Wales, 2006.

Dunkle, R. *Gladiators: Violence and Spectacle in Ancient Rome*. Harlow, UK: Pearson/Longman, 2008.

Egan, R. "How the Pentathlon Was Won: Two Pragmatic Models and the Evidence of Philostratus." *Phoenix* 61 (2007): 39–54.

Fagan, G. G. *"The Lure of the Arena": Social Psychology and the Crowd at the Roman Games*. Cambridge, UK: Cambridge University Press, 2011.

Finley, M. I., and H. W. Pleket. *The Olympic Games: The First Thousand Years*. New York: Viking Press, 1976.

Fisher, N. "Competitive Delights: The Social Effects of the Expanded Programme of Contests in Post-Kleisthenic Athens." In *Competition in the Ancient World*, edited by N. Fisher and H. van Wees, 175–219. Swansea: Classical Press of Wales, 2011.

Fisher, N. "Gymnasia and the Democratic Values of Leisure." In *Greek Athletics*, edited by J. König, 66–86. Edinburgh, UK: Edinburgh University Press, 2010.

Fisher, N., and H. van Wees, eds. *Competition in the Ancient World*. Swansea: Classical Press of Wales, 2011.

Futrell, A. *Blood in the Arena: The Spectacle of Roman Power*. Austin: University of Texas Press, 1997.

Gabucci, A., ed. *The Colosseum*. Translated by M. Becker. Los Angeles: J. Paul Getty Museum, 2001.

Gardiner, E. N. *Athletics of the Ancient World*. Oxford: Clarendon Press, 1930.

"Gladiators: A Cemetery of Secrets." York Archaeological Trust, 2011. http://www.yorkarchaeology.co.uk/headless-romans/index.htm.

Golden, M. *Greek Sport and Social Status*. Austin: University of Texas Press, 2008.

Golden, M. *Sport and Society in Ancient Greece*. Cambridge, UK: Cambridge University Press, 1998.

Goldhill, S., and R. Osborne, eds. *Performance Culture and Athenian Democracy*. Cambridge, UK: Cambridge University Press, 1999.

Guttmann, A. *From Ritual to Record: The Nature of Modern Sports*. New York: Columbia University Press, 1978.

Harris, H. A. *Sport in Greece and Rome*. Ithaca, NY: Cornell University Press, 1972.

Hodkinson, S. "An Agonistic Culture? Athletic Competition in Archaic and Classical Spartan Society." In *Sparta: New Perspectives*, edited by S. Hodkinson and A. Powell, 147–187. London: Duckworth, 1999.

Hodkinson, S., and A. Powell, eds. *Sparta: New Perspectives*. London: Duckworth, 1999.

Hopkins, K., and M. Beard. *The Colosseum*. Cambridge, MA: Harvard University Press, 2005.

Hornblower, S., and C. Morgan, eds. *Pindar's Poetry, Patrons, and Festivals: From Archaic Greece to the Roman Empire*. Oxford: Oxford University Press, 2007.

Humphrey, J. *Roman Circuses: Arenas for Chariot Racing*. Berkeley: University of California Press, 1986.

Junkelmann, M. "*Familia Gladiatoria*: The Heroes of the Amphitheatre." In *Gladiators and Caesars: The Power of Spectacle in Ancient Rome*, edited by E. Köhne and C. Ewigleben, 31–74. Berkeley: University of California Press, 2000.

Kanz, F., and K. Grosschmidt. "Dying in the Arena: The Osseous Evidence from Ephesian Gladiators." In *Roman Amphitheatres and Spectacula: A 21st-Century Perspective*, edited by T. Wilmott, 211–220. Oxford: Archaeopress, 2009.

Kennell, N. M. *The Gymnasium of Virtue: Education and Culture in Ancient Sparta*. Chapel Hill: University of North Carolina Press, 1995.

Köhne, E., and C. Ewigleben, eds. *Gladiators and Caesars: The Power of Spectacle in Ancient Rome*. Berkeley: University of California Press, 2000.

König, J. *Athletics and Literature in the Roman Empire*. Cambridge, UK: Cambridge University Press, 2005.

König, J., ed. *Greek Athletics*. Edinburgh, UK: Edinburgh University Press, 2010.

Kyle, D. G. *Athletics in Ancient Athens*. Leiden: E J. Brill, 1987.

Kyle, D. G. *Spectacles of Death in Ancient Rome*. London: Routledge, 1998.

Kyle, D. G. *Sport and Spectacle in the Ancient World*. Malden, MA: Blackwell, 2007.

Lee, H. M. *The Program and Schedule of the Ancient Olympic Games*. Hildesheim, Germany: Weidmann, 2001.

Miller, S. G. *Ancient Greek Athletics*. New Haven, CT: Yale University Press, 2004.

Miller, S. G. *Arete: Greek Sports from Ancient Sources*. 3rd ed. Berkeley: University of California Press, 2004b.

Neils, J., ed. *Goddess and Polis: The Panathenaic Festival in Ancient Athens*. Princeton, NJ: Princeton University Press, 1992.

Newby, Z. *Greek Athletics in the Roman World: Victory and Virtue*. Oxford: Oxford University Press, 2005.

Nicholson, N. *Athletics and Aristocracy in Archaic and Classical Greece*. Cambridge, UK: Cambridge University Press, 2005.

Papakonstantinou, Z., ed. *Sport in the Cultures of the Ancient World: New Perspectives*. London: Routledge, 2010.

Phillips, D. J., and D. Pritchard, eds. *Sport and Festival in the Ancient Greek World*. Swansea: Classical Press of Wales, 2003.

Plass, P. *The Game of Death in Ancient Rome: Arena Sport and Political Suicide*. Madison: University of Wisconsin Press, 1995.

Pleket, H. W. "Roman Emperors and Greek Athletics." *Nikephoros* 23 (2010): 175–203.

Poliakoff, M. B. *Combat Sports in the Ancient World*. New Haven, CT: Yale University Press, 1987.

Pomeroy, S. *Spartan Women*. Oxford: Oxford University Press, 2002.

Potter, D. *The Victor's Crown: A History of Ancient Sport from Homer to Byzantium.* Oxford: Oxford University Press, 2012.

Potter, D., and D. Mattingly, eds. *Life, Death, and Entertainment in the Roman Empire.* 2nd ed. Ann Arbor: University of Michigan Press, 2010.

Pritchard, D. *Sport, Democracy and War in Classical Athens.* Cambridge, UK: Cambridge University Press, 2013.

Pritchard, D. "Sport, War and Democracy in Classical Athens." In *Sport in the Cultures of the Ancient World: New Perspectives,* edited by Z. Papakonstantinou, 64–97. London: Routledge, 2010.

Remijsen, S. "Challenged by Egyptians: Greek Sports in the Third Century BC." In *Sport in the Cultures of the Ancient World: New Perspectives,* edited by Z. Papakonstantinou, 98–123. London: Routledge, 2010.

Robert, L. *Les gladiatures dans l'orient Grec.* Amsterdam: A.M. Hakkert, 1971.

Sansone, D. *Greek Athletics and the Genesis of Sport.* Berkeley: University of California Press, 1988.

Scanlon, T. F. *Eros and Greek Athletics.* Oxford: Oxford University Press, 2002.

Scott, M. *Delphi and Olympia: The Spatial Politics of Panhellenism in the Archaic and Classical Periods.* Cambridge, UK: Cambridge University Press, 2010.

Shear, J. L. "Prizes from Athens: The List of Panathenaic Prizes and the Sacred Oil." *Zeitschrift für Papyrologie und Epigraphik* 142 (2003): 87–105.

Sinn, U. *Olympia: Cult, Sport and Ancient Festival.* Translated by T. Thornton. Princeton, NJ: Princeton University Press, 2000.

Swaddling. J. *The Ancient Olympic Games.* 2nd ed. Austin: University of Texas Press, 2008.

Thuillier, J.-P. *Les jeux athlétiques dans la civilization étrusque.* Rome: BEFAR, 1985.

Valavanis, P. *Games and Sanctuaries in Ancient Greece: Olympia, Delphi, Isthmia, Nemea, Athens.* Los Angeles: J. Paul Getty Museum, 2004.

van Nijf, O. "Athletics, Festivals and Greek Identity in the Roman East." In *Greek Athletics,* edited by J. König, 175–197. Edinburgh, UK: Edinburgh University Press, 2010.

Ville, G. *La Gladiature en Occident des origines à la morte de Domitien* Edited by P. Veyne. Rome: Ecole française de Rome, 1981.

Welch, K. E. *The Roman Amphitheatre: From Its Origins to the Colosseum.* Cambridge, UK: Cambridge University Press, 2007.

Wiedemann, T. *Emperors and Gladiators.* London: Routledge, 1992.

Wilmott, T., ed. *Roman Amphitheatres and Spectacula: A 21st-Century Perspective.* Oxford: Archaeopress, 2009.

Young, D. C. *A Brief History of the Olympic Games.* London: Blackwell, 2004.

Young, D. C. *The Olympic Myth of Greek Amateur Athletics.* Chicago: Ares, 1984.

CHAPTER 6

....

MEDIEVAL SPORT

....

ANGELA GLEASON

WHEN sports historians probe the medieval period, they immediately are faced with the obstacles and limitations of the source material. Few research pathways into the medieval sources have been cut for sports history. Sports historians who are not also medievalists must confront linguistic and paleographic challenges they seldom face in other historical periods. Beyond problems of access is a profound reticence. The majority of sources from the Middle Ages survives in Latin and is directly or indirectly a product of the Church. While it is inaccurate to say that the medieval Church disapproved of all sports and games, it *is* accurate to say that the medieval sources are generally silent on whatever approval the Church held. As such, much of the evidence for medieval sports and games exists in the margins, in sources and societies outside of the standard medieval frame. This evidence, which survives in sources written in Old Norse, Old Irish, and Middle Welsh, is often out of the reach of the sports historian who is not also a medievalist. References to medieval sports are often needles in haystacks and reveal themselves only through painstaking and linguistically specialized research. As will be seen, assembling a picture of sports in the Middle Ages is an exercise in nut gathering.[1]

Challenging and unappealing as it may be for sports historians to plumb the Middle Ages for evidence, sports history has been equally unappealing to medieval historians. The reasons for such an aversion have less to do with occupational hazards and more to do with disciplinary orthodoxy. Medieval historians have tended to be a thematically stuffy bunch. Interest in sports, pastimes, and what America's first medievalist, Charles Homer Haskins, called "the lighter side of life" is relatively new. In Haskins own time, the early twentieth century, sports history of the Middle Ages amounted to a few antiquarian compendia and a small collection of thematic examinations of social pastimes. These studies were usually geographically specific—for example, greater London, central France—and primarily associated with war or the pomp and pageantry of the medieval tournament. Haskins' treatment of the subject, published in the 1929 *Speculum* article "The Latin Literature of Sport," was in fact part of a new age in historical scholarship.

Wider and deeper research in medieval sports began as the result of a deliberate disciplinary turn toward social and cultural history that began in the early twentieth century but was to come into itself in the second half of the century, more specifically the last quarter. Sports history was one of several social and cultural topics to garner such attention, helped along by the emergent and increasingly popular fields of gender, sexuality, and queer studies, as well as expanding fields of the history of children, family, and private life. While this turn toward historical "others" swelled and advanced the field of sports history in general, sports history of the Middle Ages simply would not exist without it.

A difficulty in presenting an overview of any medieval theme, including sports history, is avoiding a tendency toward generalization. The Middle Ages started with the decline and subsequent collapse of the Roman Empire. Recovery and renewal was accomplished in different ways and at different rates and times across the medieval map. It is problematic to render anything as typically medieval; little can be said that is representative of what it may mean to be medieval. This is especially true of social and cultural history. Perhaps the only generalization that can be made about medieval sports and pastimes is that they were site-specific. There has also been a strong tendency in sports history for the Middle Ages to let any and all evidence suffice. As a consequence, sports historians have tended to inflate and overreach in sporting categories and particulars, while medieval historians have simply shied away.

THE MIDDLE AGES

It can be said that the Middle Ages are where sports went to die. Popularly, and to a certain degree what the sources reveal, this is true. Conventional theories of the origins of sports often suggest that sports appeared with the Greeks, were transformed into spectacles with the Romans, and then summarily disappeared with the Middle Ages, not to be seen again until the Industrial Age. Outside of the lopsidedly robust scholarship and debate concerning the tournament, medieval historians, when they have been interested in sports at all, have done little to dispute this. From a superficial glimpse at history, it is indeed tempting to assume a slow and steady chronological decline of sports interest, starting with the apex of the athletic contests of ancient Greece, continuing through the arguably ambivalent attitudes of Rome, and ending with the stultifying and cheerless Middle Ages. If this is true (and it is not), it is a problem of the scholarship. While life for those who lived in the Middle Ages was challenging and uncertain, there is ample evidence that sports, games, and entertainment were a way to both celebrate life and make it bearable.

The breakdown of the Roman Empire, beginning in earnest in the late fourth century and complete by the end of the fifth, brought massive social and political collapse on a scale and pace the world has rarely seen. Nearly every corner of the Western world contracted as one of history's largest empires dried inward from its edges. Starting here, the timeline of the Middle Ages (c. 500–1500) can be neatly summarized as a few centuries of social and political upheaval, followed by a few centuries of religious reorganization and reform, followed by a final few centuries of political solidification and artistic and intellectual blossoming. The medieval hallmarks of war, famine, pestilence, and plunder are found in every stage, as are steady advances in agriculture, technology, medicine, and scholarship. While a timeline is useful to demonstrate a trajectory of progress, the way the Middle Ages in fact played out was to be different in every given time for every given place. The Middle Ages are a puzzle that looks like a period only in retrospect.

The onset of the of the early Middle Ages is popularly known as the Dark Ages, evoking the bleakness that followed the failure of centralized government and the light, typically embodied by religion and learning, that disappeared with it. In the collective imagination Goths, Vikings, and Huns prowled the Dark Ages, wreaking havoc and ruin. While there was plenty of both, the Dark Ages were not entirely devoid of recreation and fun, and the sports and spectacles of the Roman Empire did not disappear immediately or completely. Gladiatorial bouts and chariot racing continued sporadically and intermittently well into the Middle Ages, usually until the substantial sums necessary to arrange them dried up or local activities replaced them. When this happened, Roman spectacles generally gave way to the indigenous pastimes, pursuits, and entertainments of every local corner.

In this early medieval period, much of the best evidence for sports and pastimes comes from Europe's margins, namely, the vernacular sources and societies of England, Ireland, Wales, and Scandinavia. Anglo-Saxon, Irish, Welsh, and Norse sources, respectively, offer a wealth of information on the entertainments, pastimes, and sports of the time. It is in fact difficult to find a saga text, legal tract, or poem in these vernaculars that does not reveal at least a brief glimpse into what entertained their respective societies. Anglo-Saxon epics such as *Beowulf* describe horse races; Norse sagas regale the athletic and seafaring feats of their heroes; Irish legal treatises define penalties and reparations for injuries in ball games; and Welsh panegyrics celebrate the skills and accomplishments of their patrons in everything from hawking to archery to board games. What is perhaps most exciting about these sources for the sports historian is that they generally leave no one out. Taken as a corpus, they reveal a wide engagement with sport and recreation, prompting sociological, anthropological, and philosophical implications beyond a simple historical frame.

Here, a caution must be given. While vernacular evidence for sports and pastimes of the early medieval period is abundant, it is not always easy to find. *Beowulf* and a small assortment of other well-known early medieval texts are the exceptions that prove the rule. Translations of the vernacular sources, when they exist, are most often outdated and found in obscure and highly specialized philological journals such as *Studia Hibernica, Scandinavica,* and *Zeitschrift für Celtische Philologie.* To compound the problem, many of the vernacular sources, particularly the sagas and legal texts, were first translated in the nationalistic fervor that characterized the late nineteenth century. Many translations are unreliable, with linguistic, historical, and contextual errors that can mislead the modern researcher. Reexamination and new translations of the sources offer exciting opportunities for future research. Setting aside this caution, there is much to be said and learned about sports and pastimes of the early medieval period, and medieval vernaculars are the places to look.

Following on the heels of the Dark Ages, the advent of feudalism is another popular but problematic interpretation of the Middle Ages. While the historical model of feudalism is now widely disputed, even obsolete, it continues to loom over most discussions of the period. In basic terms, feudalism, thought to have taken root in the tenth century, describes a social and political system that brought about reliable agricultural production by a large and powerless peasant class for a small and powerful ruling class. The small ruling class, the political and religious elite, produced the surviving sources, so we know the least about the greatest numbers in the latter half of the medieval period. The history of sports in this period, and in contrast to the earlier period, is largely the history of the activities and amusements of the upper classes—hunting, hawking, hounding, coursing, and fishing—and the staged combat of the tournament.[2]

Common to the sports and amusements of the ruling class was the horse. It is difficult to escape the assumption, largely the assumption of feudalism itself, that if one did not have a horse in the Middle Ages, one did not have much, including fun.[3] This was true, but only for the ruling class. Also common to these activities is violence and bloodshed, reaffirming to a modern audience just how medieval the medieval period was. Hunting and other so called "blood sports," however, were activities that were equally performative. While the activities were no doubt enjoyed by those fortunate enough to participate, they were also events that allowed the ruling classes to perform and affirm important social and political roles. Hawking was the particular reserve of emperors and kings. Perhaps the greatest sportsman of the medieval world was the prodigiously talented Holy Roman Emperor Frederick II (†1250). Deemed *stupor mundi* by his contemporaries and regarded by Nietzsche as the *first European*, Frederick II was an avid hawker who authored the first comprehensive book on falconry, perhaps the first essentially medieval sport, having been brought to Europe from the East in the fifth century by the invading Alans and Huns.

Rather famously, it has been remarked that the favorite sport of the Middle Ages was war.[4] The statement is attractive but misleading. While war and especially the threat of war in the Middle Ages was constant, its historical reputation has exceeded its practice. In reality, there was not as much war as preparation for war. A more accurate reformulation of the statement might be that preparation is practice, practice is competition, and competition is sport. Until the establishment of sports history as a comparative field in the late twentieth century, the medieval hallmarks of upper-class sports (i.e., jousting, mock combat, and blood sports) were generally agreed upon as military training. With new eyes, modern sports historians (and some medievalists) have suggested that we see these and other pursuits not as military training but simply as entertainment. The military class in the medieval period generally did nothing but train for war or fight in it. The tournament, as staged in its traditional form, offered little to prepare one for actual war and would likely have set any forms of real training back.

The tournament was the favorite sport of the Middle Ages, though it was hardly a singular affair. Predictably, while the medieval tournament was found in nearly every corner of Europe, it was at the same time variable with local characteristics. Unlike the rest of sports history for the medieval period, there is a surfeit of evidence for the medieval tournament, especially the tournament as staged in England and France. This is the result of both an abundance of contemporary material, namely, sources written by the societies that staged the tournaments, as well as a proliferation of later literature and scholarship by a wide range of scholars, including medievalists, art historians, archaeologists, and philologists. In fact, historical interest in the medieval tournament began as early as the Renaissance. Several books of tournament histories appeared in the late fifteenth and early sixteenth centuries. These books, a few of which often include sumptuous illustrations, were compiled mainly by antiquarians and chroniclers with a vested interest in reviving the events. Their pages offer a wealth of detail for the modern historian.[5]

Tournaments in the Middle Ages arose out of local festivals. As such, they came in all shapes and sizes and with local flavor. By the end of the Middle Ages, they were organized, publicized, and politicized on a grand scale across the medieval world, but each tournament remained infused with habits and customs peculiar to its own region and society. By the later Middle Ages chivalric codes had also given rise to a class of professional knights. Those who were most successful and popular, perhaps the only medieval equivalent to today's sports stars, followed the money and fame of the tournament circuit. Those with political backing and social favor were able to accumulate property and goods to ensure a comfortable life after their competitive days were over. Praise poems, elegiacs, and other tributes survive to confirm the popularity and fame of the celebrities of the age.

The tournament was finally a market and a social mixer. Large audiences of men and women, some of whom had traveled considerable distances, gathered to take advantage of the many social and economic opportunities the tournament provided. Marriages were conducted, livestock and land were bought and sold, and, similar to the opportunists who line the outskirts of modern sporting events, merchants and vendors followed tournaments from town to town to push their wares on passersby. Judging from court records, tournaments also attracted their share of crime. The bustle of the occasion concealed swindlers, thieves, and a variety of illegal and violent acts. The aspects and auspices of the medieval tournaments, therefore, affected medieval society in a variety of ways, regardless of how few could experience the events themselves. The social reach of the tournaments provides an array of medieval source material to investigate. The sources demonstrate how deeply and broadly societies of the Middle Ages experienced the tournaments.

A peasant's daily life in the late medieval period was not as far removed from the daily life of a nineteenth-century farmer as may be thought. Life was dominated by agriculture and was carried out according to well-established social and seasonal cycles and rhythms. Long summer days and nights afforded predictable occasions of free time indulged in with many of the activities we recognize today. Swimming, wrestling, and racing were common among all ages and both genders, while organized ball games of various types can be found in every medieval society and culture.[6] Ball games in fact frustrated the ruling classes throughout the later Middle Ages. English kings were especially intolerant of these games. By the fourteenth century no fewer than thirty bans had been placed by English kings on ball games such as football, handball, and hurling. Bans were prompted both for the public disorder ball games caused—including the drinking and fighting generally associated with them—and for the wasted time and industry of the players, which could be better spent in the fields or in training for war.

The best sources for the entertainments and pastimes of the later medieval peasantry are political and legal. Eyre rolls—case records of common pleas from twelfth- to fourteenth-century English circuit courts—are rich sources for the various complications and mischiefs occasioned by sporting events. Much of the royal distaste for ball games can be justified, or at least better understood, by an examination of the eyre rolls. Similarly, coroners' rolls—records of inquests into deaths—relate evidence of casualties for almost every sport and pastime imaginable in the Middle Ages. Deaths while swimming, skating, hunting, riding, boating, fishing, racing, throwing, and cheering highlight the list, as well as a particularly unfortunate accident in a board game.[7]

Despite the rather divided nature of later medieval societies and the sources that describe them, there is ample evidence for how medieval men and women sported. While the tournament and other amusements of the ruling class dominate the sources, the less spectacular but more common sports and pastimes of the peasantry did not go unnoticed. Examined closely and in concert, the diverse and wide-ranging sources of the Middle Ages confirm, perhaps surprisingly to a modern audience, that all classes, ages, and genders sported, competed, and played.

MODERN HISTORIOGRAPHY

The first modern efforts to document medieval sports and recreation appeared in the early nineteenth century. Joseph Strutt's *The Sports and Pastimes of the People of England* is one of the earliest compendias. Published in 1801, the volume is comprehensive in aim and specific in detail, best evidenced by the book's full title, *The Sports and Pastimes of the People of England; From the Earliest Period, including the Rural and Domestic Recreations, May Games, Mummeries, Pageants, Processions and Pompous Spectacles.* Strutt, an accomplished antiquarian, artist, and engraver, published *Sports and Pastimes* quickly on the heels of his best-known work, *Dresses and Habits of the English People.* The success of the two publications was immediate, and each underwent multiple printings. A generation later, two works broadly similar to Strutt's and certainly borrowing from their successes, were published in London in 1832; Henry Alken's *The National Sports of Great Britain*, notable for its illustrations and plates, and Jehoshaphat Aspin's *Ancient Customs, Sports and Pastimes of the English.* Like their precursor, the two volumes offer a wealth of detail for sports of their contemporary period.

A half-century after the works of Alken and Aspin, scholarly studies and publications began to appear on medieval sports history on the European continent.[8] By the last quarter of the nineteenth century, several seminal works were published, including Julius Binz's *Die Liebesübungen des Mittelalters* (1880) and J. J. Jusserand's *Les sports et jeux d'exercise dans l'ancienne France* (1901). An early historian of sport, Jusserand lectured on the subject at the Sorbonne and published numerous articles detailing medieval sport in *Revue des deux mondes*. These works and others both broadened and deepened the study of sport with new historical approaches beyond the prior cataloging quality of compendia. These new approaches, emerging when modern sports themselves were taking shape, were also expressly nationalistic. The history and heritage of individual sports and pastimes were now examined through national lenses, with the aim of incorporating sports and games into the bloodline of a particular society or nation. As with other cultural commodities such as language, literature, music, and dance, historians (as well as antiquarians, archaeologists, philologists, etc.) sought early prototypes for current sports and recreations in the Middle Ages.[9]

Social and cultural history blossomed throughout the first half of the twentieth century. Prominent medievalists such as Charles Homer Haskins and Johan Huizinga were joined by several others publishing on such quotidian subjects as *The Medieval English Village* (George Gordon Coulton, 1926); *Life and Work in Medieval Europe* (Prosper Boissonade, 1927); and *Life on the English Manor* (H. S. Bennett, 1937). While the study of sports history in the medieval period did not attract a comprehensive treatise, several important books and articles on specific sports or sporting histories appeared that are still relevant today. D. H. Madden's 1924 study, *A Chapter of Medieval History: The Fathers of the Literature of Field Sport and Horses,* was the first of its kind for the origins of polo and other equestrian sports. In 1933 the German scholar Albrecht Wettwer published *Englischer Sport im 14. Jahrhundert*, while Henry L. Savage, lecturer in English at Princeton, contributed "Hunting in the Middle Ages" to *Speculum*. Slightly earlier, in 1929, the Harvard Chaucerian F. P. Magoun scoured Middle English sources to present a picture of early English football in "Football in Medieval England and in Medieval English Literature." His treatment of the subject, one that combined his historical and linguistic expertise, remains a research model for what is needed even today in the field of medieval sports history. A decade later Magoun published an expanded version of his research in his 1938 volume *A History of Football: From the Beginnings to 1871*. In 1939, Johan Huizinga revolutionized cultural history with his *Homo Ludens*, a remarkable work combining elements of the history, philosophy, and sociology of play to conclude that play, and thus sport, is a primary and necessary aspect of culture. The impact of the work was profound, immediately shaping the emergent fields of cultural and sports history.

Between Huizinga's *Homo Ludens* and the relative explosion of sports history that began in the 1980s, research and publication on medieval sports faded. While important advances and theories in social history continued to reshape subjects associated with medieval sports and pastimes, the fertile methods, innovations and ideas of the previous generation of medievalists ceased. In their stead, however, a multidisciplinary group of scholars ushered the field ahead. Beginning in the mid-1950s, several contributions added to the overall development of sports history, while touching lightly on medieval themes. Kinesiologist and educator Marvin Eyler published his physical education doctoral dissertation *Origins of Some Modern Sports* in 1956. In 1960 Carl Diem, a German Olympic committee member and administrator who was perhaps best known for his controversial cooperation with the Nazis, published *Weltgeschichte des Sports und der Leibeserziehung*. More closely in line with his medieval forebears, in 1962 the American philologist Urban T. Holmes issued *Daily Living in the Twelfth Century*.

The prolific research, debate, and publication of the next three decades (1970s–1990s) would legitimize and affirm sports history as a viable and acknowledged field of scholarship. While medieval sports history would continue to struggle with problems of specialization (as it does today), this overwhelming sea change propelled an increasing number of scholars, medievalists and otherwise, to examine sports and pastimes of the Middle Ages. First and foremost, the pivotal publication of the 1970s was Allen Guttmann's *From Ritual to Record: The Nature of Modern Sports*. Like Huizinga, Guttmann theorized that sport was fundamental to society. Unlike Huizinga, Guttmann claimed that modern sports were fundamentally different from the sports and play of all other periods and, by extension, so too is modern society. Rounding out the decade, the prolific French medievalist Jacques LeGoff joined the growing focus on how societies spend time with *Time, Work and Culture in the Middle Ages* (1980). And in 1981 Allen Guttmann began an important conversation on the spectator in premodern sports with "Sports Spectators from Antiquity to the Renaissance." (*Journal of Sport History* 8.2, 1981).

Until the 1980s, sports history of the Middle Ages was a small but steadily growing collection of special topics, issues, and essays. If the field of medieval sports history now exists, it was the creation of a single man—John Marshall Carter. Starting in earnest in the 1980s, at the same time as scholars in other periods of sports history, Carter began a prodigious effort to research, document, and describe sports in the Middle Ages. The sum of his work, which spans three decades and covers nine centuries, is foundational to the field. His work in the 1980s was accompanied by a small group of specialized treatments of individual sports or social groups, for example, M. L. Howell and R. A. Howell's "The Role of Women in the Tournament in the Middle Ages" (1980); Jim Bradbury's *The Medieval Archer* (1985); and Richard Hoffman's "Fishing for Sport in Medieval Europe: New Evidence" in *Speculum* (1985). Curiously, two nearly contemporaneous attempts at categorizing medieval sports by type (e.g., "sitting" or "standing" games) were made in the mid-1980s, namely, Teresa McLean's discussion in *The English at Play in the Middle Ages* (1984) and Helmut Nickel's "Games and Pastimes" in *Dictionary of the Middle Ages*, edited by Joseph Strayer (1986). Rounding out the 1980s were several important contributions to the study of the medieval tournament. In 1986 Juliet Barker published *The Tournament in England*, followed closely by her collaboration with Richard Barber and Robert Liddiard, *Tournaments: Jousts, Chivalry and Pageants in the Middle Ages* (1989). Finally, the 1980s saw Heiner Gillmeister begin his exhaustive investigation on medieval tennis and other ball games.

Slightly later than its historical counterparts, the field of medieval sports history experienced a surge of scholarship in the 1990s and 2000s. In 1992, Carter collaborated with the German sports scholar Arnd Krüger to issue *Ritual and Record: Sports Records and Quantification in Pre-Modern Societies,* at least in part a response to Guttmann. In 1999, Richard Mandell offered *Sport: A Cultural History,* and 2000 saw the release of Norbert Elias's seminal work, *The Civilizing Process,* which sparked several journal contributions on sports-related themes. Shortly after the millennium, several volumes on the tournament appeared, including Alan Baker's *The Knight: A Portrait of Europe's Warrior Elite* (2003), Andrea Hopkins' *Tournaments and Jousts: Training for War in Medieval Times* (2004), Richard Barker's *The Reign of Chivalry* (2005), Emma Griffin's *Blood Sport: Hunting in Britain since 1066* (2007), and John McLelland's comprehensive *Body and Mind: Sport in Europe from the Roman Empire to the Renaissance* (2007). Rounding out the contemporary period, several journal articles take on new themes, including Robert Delete's "Catholic Perspectives on Sports: From Medieval to Modern Times" (in *Sport, Ethics and Philosophy,* 2013) and John McLelland's "The Accidental Sports Tourist: Travelling and Spectating in Medieval and Renaissance Europe" (in *Journal of Tourism History,* 2013).

Future Research

With the meteoric rise of sports history in the past three decades, the future of medieval sports history should be secure. Rather unfortunately, it is not. In 2004, Carter summarized the situation: "Since 1987, sports history has seemingly become a viable discipline with sports history courses in colleges and universities, international conferences and organizations on the subject, and dissertations in droves on varied and interesting topics. The same cannot be said for the study of medieval sports history."[10] Many of the reasons for this have already been outlined. Headlining the list is the difficulty of the source material and a general reluctance (unavailability?) of medieval historians to explore the topic. The very same reasons, however, confirm that the field is ripe with potential. To move forward, much more research and collaboration needs to done. The history of medieval sports is currently the focus of only a handful of researchers. We hope that the potential of the field can be broadened and made attractive to a new generation of scholars.

Indeed, sports historians who want large, open fields of opportunity should look first to the Middle Ages. There is much to be examined and reexamined and much that is new. First and foremost, considerably more research is needed by historians familiar with medieval vernaculars. There is a large corpus of medieval vernacular source material that is either untranslated or poorly translated. Recent and ongoing examination and translation has brought critical light to bear on the social history of medieval Scandinavia, England, Ireland, Scotland, and Wales.[11] Early medieval saga texts and legal sources are especially rich with descriptions of sporting contests and their participants.

At the same time, the sports history of the Middle Ages should not be confined only to sports historians or medievalists. Extant archaeological evidence for sports in the

Middle Ages is as problematic as the written sources. Much like their philologist counterparts, archaeologists of the late nineteenth and early twentieth centuries were often
untrained amateurs and frequently overzealous in their efforts. Anyone who has examined their reports knows how ready these archaeologists were to identify scraps of metal
as horse trappings and bits of wood or glass as gaming pieces. Advances in archaeology
in the past two decades have vastly improved the ability to date and contextualize artifacts and sites. A reassessment and exploration of archaeological evidence promises new
pathways for understanding sports and entertainment in the medieval period.

Finally, there is a dearth of comparative work. With very few exceptions, sports and
pastimes were local in the Middle Ages. That they were local does not mean that they
were unrelated. Individual sports in specific regions have been resurrected with impressive detail and clarity (e.g., F. P. Magoun's early work on English football and Heiner
Gillmeister's recent work on German tennis). Few efforts, however, have been made to
compare these sports across the medieval world. Questions jump from the page. Stick
and ball games can be found in nearly every place and time in the Middle Ages: Is there a
definitive or even meaningful relationship between them? Do Irish hurling and Basque
pelota share a common ancestor? If so, what is that ancestor, and how does it relate to
their respective social and political histories? How does the medieval spectator in any
given society change over time, and what do changes and differences across societies tell
us? Assembling and then comparing the vast and varied evidence for medieval sports
offers a rich vein for a wide variety of specialties and disciplines.

NOTES

1. Evidence for sports might be found in obscure legal texts regarding inadvertent injury or in
   satirical poetry where games of chance are common metaphors for the precariousness of life.
2. For medieval surveys of feudalism, see, for example, Marc Bloch, *Feudal Society*, trans. L. A.
   Manyon (Chicago: University of Chicago Press, 1961); J. R. Strayer, *Feudalism* (Princeton,
   NJ: Van Nostrand, 1965); Susan Reynolds, *Fiefs and Vassals: The Medieval Evidence
   Reinterpreted* (Oxford: Oxford University Press, 1994).
3. Like feudalism, this is disputed and a rich vein for future research. See, for example, Richard
   Mandell, *Sport: A Cultural History* (Bloomington, IN: iUniverse, 1999), 101–112; Lynn White
   Jr., *Medieval Technology and Social Change* (Oxford: Clarendon Press, 1962).
4. Charles Homer Haskins, "The Latin Literature of Sport," *Spectrum* 2.3 (1927): 238. In this
   important article, Haskins also distinguishes between sport and spectacle in the classical
   period, attributing the former to Greece and the latter to the Rome.
5. For the history of tournaments, see, for example, F. H. Cripps-Day, *The History of the
   Tournament* (London: B. Quaritch, 1918); Josef Fleckenstein, ed., *Das Ritterliche Turnier
   im Mittelalter: Beitrage zu einer vergleichenden Formen- und Verhaltensgeschichte des
   Rittertums* (Göttingen: Vandenhoeck & Ruprecht, 1985); Juliet Barker, *The Tournament in
   England 1100–1400* (Woodbridge, UK: Boydell Press, 1986); Richard Barber Juliet Barker,
   and Robert Liddiard *Tournaments; Jousts, Chivalry and Pageants in the Middle Ages*
   (Woodbridge, UK: Boydell Press, 1989).
6. For example, handball, football, quoits, tennis, hurling, shinty.

7. See, for example, Charles Gross, *Select Cases from the Coroners' Rolls, A. D. 1265–1413, with a Brief Account of the History of the Office of Coroner* (London: Seldon Society, 1896); H. F. Hunnisett, "The Medieval Coroners' Rolls," *The American Journal of Legal History* 3.2 (1959): 95–124; J. G. Jenkins, ed., *Calendar of the Roll of the Justices on Eyre, 1227* (Bedford, UK: N.p., 1945). For a discussion in association with sport, see John Marshall Carter, *Sports and Pastimes of the Middle Ages* (Lanham, MD: University Press of America, 1988), 22–25.

8. As well as the American physical fitness pioneer Fred Eugene Leonard. See his "The Transition from Medieval to Modern Times—Chapters in the History of Physical Training," *American Physical Education Review* 10.4 (1905): 189–202.

9. For example, the nascent Gaelic Athletic Association pointed to eleventh-century Irish legal texts to grant "ancient" status to hurling and gaelic football.

10. J. M. Carter, "The Study of Medieval Sports, Games, and Pastimes: A Fifteen-Year Reflection, 1988–2003," *Sport History Review* 35 (2004):, 163.

11. See, for example, works by medievalists William Ian Miller, Robin Chapman-Stacey, Fergus Kelly.

BIBLIOGRAPHY

Barber, Richard, Juliet R. V. Barker, and Robert Liddiard. *Tournaments: Jousts, Chivalry and Pageants in the Middle Ages*. Woodbridge, UK: Boydell Press, 1989.

Barker, Juliet R. V. *The Tournament in England, 1100–1400*. Woodbridge, UK: Boydell Press, 1986.

Carter, John Marshall. *Medieval Games: Sports and Recreations in Feudal Society*. New York: Greenwood, 1992.

Carter, John Marshall. *Sports and Pastimes of the Middle Ages*. Lanham, MD: University Press of America, 1988.

Carter, John Marshall, and Arnd Krüger. *Ritual and Record: Sports Records and Quantification in Pre-Modern Societies*. Vol. 30. New York: Greenwood, 1992.

Gillmeister, Heiner. *Tennis: A Cultural History*. London: Continuum, 1998.

Griffin, Emma. *Blood Sport: Hunting in Britain since 1066*. New Haven, CT: Yale University Press, 2007.

Guttmann, Allen. *From Ritual to Record: The Nature of Modern Sports*. New York: Columbia University Press, 2004.

Guttmann, Allen. "Sports Spectators from Antiquity to the Renaissance." *Journal of Sport History* 8.2 (1981): 5–27.

Huizinga, Johan. *Homo Ludens: A Study of the Play-Element in Culture*. Boston: Beacon Press, 1967.

Magoun, F. P. "Football in Medieval England and Medieval English Literature." *The American Historical Review* 35.1 (1929): 33–45.

Magoun, F. P. *The History of Football: From the Beginnings to 1871*. Bochun, Germany: N.p., 1938.

Mandell, Richard D. *Sport: A Cultural History*. Bloomington, IN: iUniverse, 1999.

McClelland, John. *Body and Mind: Sport in Europe from the Roman Empire to the Renaissance*. New York: Routledge, 2007.

Strutt, Joseph. *The Sports and Pastimes of the People of England . . . from the Earliest Period to the Present Time*. London: Tegg, 1841.

CHAPTER 7

....

EARLY MODERN SPORT

....

MIKE HUGGINS

THE "early modern" has always suffered problems of periodization. Its beginnings over-lap with the Late Middle Ages, when "sport" and athletic exercise were moving away from military training. It encompasses the Renaissance, Reformation, and Counter-Reformation and the scientific shifts of the Age of Enlightenment, movements that were diverse chronologically, geographically, culturally, and intellectually. Some historians link its beginnings to block-printing, the beginning of the Tudor period, or the redis-covery of America in the late fifteenth century; others trace it to the early sixteenth cen-tury and the Reformation. Its end dates are equally problematic. The French Revolution is sometimes used, as are the nebulous beginnings of the Industrial Revolution.

Its sporting source material is likewise challenging: simultaneously rich yet also frag-mentary and patchy with many silences and biases. Sport was rarely a main focus of dis-cussion. Even so, different discourses indicate that sporting and other leisure activities, in complex cultural combinations, were becoming more apparent across the period. Such sources reflected the intellectual interests of the male leisured elite, helping to legitimate their leisure time and practices.

The new medium of print reflected and helped to shape new forms of sporting life-style, disseminating rules, playing skills, and expected behavior patterns. Recreational guidebooks and manuals focused on the sports popular with their dominant readership. This was usually in sports with military connections such as wrestling or swordsman-ship, horse riding, archery, or swimming. During the Renaissance educators, surgeons, and military theorists all stressed sporting leisure was necessary and utilitarian, ben-eficial psychologically, and vital for battle training, guiding appropriate social behav-ior and *healthy* exercise. Moral discourses stressed moderation, not excess. Pedagogic discourses and educational programs written for courtiers, university students, and children stressed the importance of recreational physical exercise to develop strength, suppleness, physical appearance, or mental and moral well-being and to gain status and respect.

Renaissance humanists such as Castiglione looked back to the classical past and stressed the hygienic values of exercise to improve the capacity to study. Medical discourse stressed the positive, psychological health-preserving roles of moderate sporting exercise to keep genteel bodies in balance. Juristic literature, especially from Italy and Spain, debated the economic relationship between profits and gambling games, adding to the published moral, religious, and political debates about sport. Sport increasingly appeared in fiction. Rabelais's *Gargantua* (1534), for example, made 218 mentions of sports and games, and sport assumed literal and metaphorical centrality in popular works of literature such as Shakespeare's histories. Diaries, autobiographies, memoirs, journals, and other personal documents show that some rulers and many of the elite enthusiastically enjoyed playing or watching physical sports, seeing them as legitimate outlets for their physical energies. The diaries and chronicles of P. H Mair (1517–1579), an Augsburg official and sports fan, for example, reveal fascinating data on fencing and the rules, prizes, participants, winners, expenses, and dates of various competitive target shooting events in German cities.[1]

If sources for elite (learned) culture are good, sources for the study of popular (often illiterate) culture are more scattered. The boundaries between work and leisure activities were drawn differently in different regions and at different times in ways that are not yet clear. The multifaceted and fragmented micro-cultures that made up commoners ("the lower sort") and their recreational experiences and ideological sporting involvements were rarely worthy of notice unless deemed problematic. Even in 1801 when the antiquarian Joseph Strutt wrote on English sport, he concentrated on the rural exercises practiced by persons of rank. However, he also covered those more generally practiced alongside pastimes enjoyed in towns and domestically.[2]

From the late seventeenth century, competitive sport events, prize money, and results were more widely publicized. This was first through pamphlets, broadsides, woodcuts, posters, or copperplate engravings and then by weekly newspapers. These appeared first in mainland Europe and then in Britain, where there were twelve London newspapers and twenty-four provincial papers by the 1720s. This new coverage stimulated interest and aided sport's growth.

Can we use the word "sport" for these various callisthenic, competitive, or recreational physically participative games, activities, and pleasurably enjoyable sporting recreations, often associated with refreshment and regeneration in terms of mind, body, or soul?[3] Specialists in modern sport usually think not, making technical distinctions between "play," "game," "contest," and "sport." Historians of early modern sports, recognizing sport's complex, multilayered contemporary status and functional and political roles in exercising and disciplining people and individuals, have been happier to use the term to explore the extent to which such "sport" developed across Europe in its various physical, material, and ideological entities. Cultural historians have variously utilized early modern concepts of "recreation," "sport," "refreshment," "diversion," or "exercise" in order to do so.

Social consciousness was elusive, with varied, fluid, and complex social identities, driven by context. It was linked to wealth and income, administrative power, and prestige, and to deferential hierarchies such as order and degree, not to modern notions of "social class." Most recreation was undertaken with people of similar status. Early modern society's perceptions, descriptions, and representations of economic function and societal position indicate a sense more of "sorts" of people. They lived in highly differentiated communities that were far from uniform, rigid, or unchanging in their patterns of inequality. Marks of gentility separated perhaps 4 or 5 percent of the population from the common people. The experiences and relationships formed around sport were important for the predominantly male political and ruling elite, the "gentlemen," the small numbers of tight-knit nobility, plus land-owning gentry, leading churchmen, and very wealthy, socially prominent urban bourgeoisie, with their honor code. Enthusiasm for sport was widespread even in the sixteenth century in the courts of France, England, Spain, Italy, Germany, and elsewhere. And open-air public sporting events attracted participants and spectators of all sorts, even if social contexts and structures of power that included wealth, age, and marital status shaped culture and sporting experiences.

The Moral, Religious, and Political Battleground of Sport

Early modern sport has to be set in its moral, religious, and political context. Both ecclesiastical and civil authorities periodically attempted to exert some discipline, control, and direction over popular sports, festivities, and "carnival" activities that only just contained potentially dangerous countermoralities. Mendicant preachers preached against sport even in Renaissance Italy, but Puritanism, in its multiple manifestations across the larger cities of Europe, Britain, and America, found it most problematical. Reformist and radical Puritans were austere, sincere, purposeful, militant, zealous, egalitarian, and moralist, wanting to assertively repress all nonspiritual forms of recreation. They were suspicious of sport's frivolity, pleasure, occasional violence, passionate feelings, and cruelty and its links to gambling, self-destructive indulgence, and "mere idleness" rather than proper purpose. A pleasure-loving, sinful people needed to be policed and purified to create a holy, "saved" community. Sunday was for worship, quiet contemplation, good works, and reflective spirituality, not skittles or wrestling.

Puritanism probably retarded rather than furthered modern sport, though it effected some reformation of manners amongst the "middling sort." Puritans showed little opposition to callisthenic-style healthy exercises, despite occasional offensives against traditional rural pastimes. Some commended, in moderation, "innocent" amusements and "honest" and "sober" recreations such as archery, shooting, running, and wrestling or hunting, hawking, and wild-fowling, though with limited enthusiasm, agonizing over their moral appropriateness. In colonial America, such activities had instrumental functions. There was limited concern for animal suffering, despite Biblical support for the belief that animals should not suffer unnecessarily. As Keith Thomas has noted, in early modern England "exploitation [of animals], not stewardship, was the dominant theme."[4] In the later eighteenth century evangelical Methodism began preaching against the cruelty of more plebeian sports such as throwing sticks at cocks, bull-baiting, and bull-running, alongside the gambling and prostitution found on racecourses, and this marked a further shift in Nonconformist attitudes. Tory squires, uninterested in Enlightenment philosophies, continued to enjoy hunting, fishing, and shooting unmolested. Many simply regarded Puritans as "killjoys" and moved away from religious ideas, emphasizing individual consciousness and choice.

The state already played a role in sports debate. In the fifteenth century, state proclamations were more likely to condemn Sunday sports such as bowling or bull-baiting only as unlawful distractions from important military exercises. In Tudor England, urban authorities sought to compel men to develop their military skills. Coroners' reports between 1500 and 1576 indicate that at least fifty-six English individuals died in the context of archery practice.[5] In European Catholic cities in the sixteenth century, sports such as tournaments, target shooting, fencing, or horse racing took place on Sundays. Protestant rulers were less convinced. In Britain, growing Puritan power in some counties meant that ritual festivities and sports were faced with increasing opposition. This produced a royal reaction, a "cultural counter-offensive."[6] In *The King's Declaration of Sports* (1617), James I attempted to distinguish between lawful and unlawful sports. He stressed moderate "lawful recreation" for his "good people," emphasizing the need for military preparedness and promoting games and sports on Sundays and holy days, though condemning interference with religious services. Charles I took a similar stand though he banned Sunday bull- and bear-baiting, wrestling, and bowling. Sport became increasingly ambivalent, a focus of moral discourse and contestation concerning its salutary and harmful societal characteristics, especially if done to excess.[7] Robert Dover's Cotswold Games, valorized in *Annalia Dubrensia* (1636), supported Charles in celebrating poetry and sport as communal competitions but made concessions to Puritanism by renouncing gambling. The Cromwellian period saw edicts against all Sunday sports activities, represented as popish and disreputable, a view critiqued in Isaac Walton's *Compleat Angler* (1653). In 1654 a Protectorate Ordinance banned cockfighting because fights disturbed the peace and were "commonly accompanied with Gaming, Drinking, Swearing, Quarreling, and other dissolute Practices, to the Dishonor of God."[8] Puritan controversialist Philip Stubbes made exaggerated complaint of the Sabbath being used for "bowling, tennis playing; in bear-baiting, cock-fighting, hawking, hunting and such like . . . wicked and ungodly pastimes and vain pleasures of the flesh."[9] Horse racing was banned lest it provided a pretext for plotting, and other gambling sports almost disappeared until Charles II on his return reaffirmed the place of sport and play.

THE CHARACTERISTICS OF EARLY MODERN SPORT

In an often insightful, scholarly, and impressively wide-ranging study, Allen Guttmann provided a highly influential categorizing, systematizing typology. He suggested that the formal-structural characteristics of early modern sports were very different from modern sport. The latter had seven key characteristics: secularism, equality, specialization, bureaucratization, rationalization, quantification, and obsession with records. Modern sport, he argued, stemmed from the intellectual revolution associated with the "Enlightenment" alongside industrial capitalism and Protestantism.[10]

Most important, Guttmann accepted that all these characteristics appeared, if sometimes sporadically, in earlier periods, including the early modern. His point was that by comparison "the characteristics of modern sports interact systematically."[11] In other words, they fitted together. In premodern times examples were more isolated, not widespread. Not all scholars noted this critical caveat. This led some to represent early modern sports in oversimplistic, essentially *negative* ways, implying that they entirely lacked such attributes, a view exacerbated since Guttmann had sometimes contrasted modern sport with "primitive," "preliterate," "ancient," or "traditional" sports. Such binary divisions made differences stark. They were convenient but potentially misleading. And there is still debate about how far back we can push "modernity," however defined.

Like Guttmann, Henning Eichberg seemed to imply that sport's emergence was part of broader processes of modernization.[12] Sociologists have also linked the rise of modern sport to what Norbert Elias called the "civilising process," in which people began to internalize values that reduced the levels of expressive interpersonal violence, and Michel Foucault called the rise of "discipline."

Another important debate has concerned the extent of fundamental discontinuity, or how much the "great divide" between early modern and industrial society was a distinct phase of rupture rather than an evolutionary continuum. More recent research suggests that by 1700 Britain was already deemed a modernizing society and becoming more secular, individualistic, and economically successful.[13] It was beginning to quantify its sport and create sporting records, although even the later early nineteenth century sporting changes accompanied large elements of continuity.

Guttmann's model attracted some criticism.[14] Scholars of the early modern period were quick to respond, with a collection of essays edited by John Marshall Carter and Arnd Kruger on early sports records and quantification.[15] Recent work on the Renaissance has likewise challenged Guttmann's work.[16] Most specialists now agree that from the late fifteenth century onward distinctive, situationally specific forms of physical culture were being elaborated in Europe. John McClelland has argued for a distinct period of "Renaissance" sport lasting until the late seventeenth century and suggested that, even by the sixteenth century, "the athletic activities that were amply practiced . . . were not the formless, unproblematic, ritually dominated, violent folk or noble games that most sports historiography described. They displayed organization, purposeful motivation, structure, rules, professionalism, i.e. many of the characteristics of sport today. They just did so in a way that now seems unfamiliar."[17]

In England, likewise, argued Kruger, "many elements of modern sports [had] been there a long time" before the Industrial Revolution.[18] Cultural historian Peter Burke suggested something like modern leisure first emerged in the late fifteenth century as an analogous word, "pastime," came into use. This led, in the sixteenth through the eighteenth century, to a broader European "leisure system," well predating the Industrial Revolution, albeit with multiple and uneven paths of change.[19] More recently, Behringer has conceptualized the early modern period as "a distinct epoch in the history of sport," due to the high levels of institutionalization and standardization sport underwent in many western European countries. He sees the Renaissance era as witnessing the sportification of tournaments, military exercises, and popular games, followed by the emergence of important new sports, increasingly associated with "modern" characteristics.[20] Increasingly, the early modern period is being presented as an independent era in the history of sport and also as the formative, anticipatory period of modern sport. Alan Tomlinson and Christopher Young, for example, follow Behringer in suggesting that modern sports emerged from developments in the early modern era, rather than from industrialization.[21]

As just one example of modern sport's characteristics, sporting rules, in the early modern period, were clearly developing institutional forms but were never uniform even within countries. Even without any national sporting authorities, printed rules and instructions were widely disseminated though books, court culture, peripatetic university students and staff, and elite transnational tourism. Rules offered orderly instructions and advice for playing, written down in printed, itemized, or numerical form, and reflected the social and worldviews of the rule-makers. Even in the late fifteenth century, for example, jousting rules had certain commonalities, as Joachim Ruhl has noted in comparisons between those of Francesco Sforza Visconti (1465) and John Tiptoft (1466) or the tournament regulations of Heilebron (1485).[22]

Italians between 1450 and 1650 produced various scoring systems for jousting and rules and tactics for tennis, as well as fencing, team ball sports, horsemanship, and even gymnastics. The Italian priest Antonio Scaino provided his readers with regulations for *calcio* (a goal-scoring game using a kicked or batted ball), *pallacorda* (indoor tennis), and *pallone* (handball/rackets) in 1555.[23] Florentine count Giovanni Bardi (1534–1612) further codified *calcio* in 1580, providing advice for foreigners on roles, rule specialization, and quantification.[24] In France various rulebooks for *jeu de paume* began appearing in the later sixteenth century, and quite detailed rules for indoor tennis with stringed racquets were provided by a tennis professional Forbet l'Aisne in 1599, by which time many Parisian courts were separate commercial units. Over time rules slowly became more complex. By 1655, for example, there were eighty-three rules for pall-mall, a precursor to croquet.

The need for formation and development of rules was given a further boost by betting, since betting on head-to-head results needed common features. By the mid-eighteenth century, written rules relating to betting often formed part of the contractual "articles of agreement" common to most stake-money contests, aimed at removing ambiguities. Contracts tried to regularize the times, places, playing practices, and amounts staked. Whilst initially specific to the individual match, over time repetition and usage helped further standardization. Gamblers might wish the odds to be twisted in their favor, so rules attempted to create "fair play" for the contest. Sports like dueling had provided an informal means of achieving justice and defending honor. If equality was a manifestation of the modern, then the language of "fair play," the notion of equity, a measured spirit of fairness, was being increasingly taken up by wider society from the late sixteenth century onward. [25] Thereafter it was increasingly applied to sport, along with another key sporting idea, often applied to cock-fighting or horse racing—that of competitors being "properly" or "fairly matched" so that gentlemen could be sure of "fair" battles and "excellent sport." Alongside this went "fair gaming" and avoidance of betting disputes, so rules often set up means of arbitration in order to arrive at more reliable, agreed, unbiased verdicts.

In horse racing, the twenty rules laid down by Charles II for the running of the Newmarket Town Plate in 1665 and rules of racing for a course at Newton Heath, Lancashire, laid out in 1678 by the local lord of the manor, both focus largely on betting aspects, as do other local rules of the period. Cockfighting rules first appeared in print in Cheny's *Racing Calendar* for 1743, but they were clearly of earlier origin, and its rules increasingly traveled. In South Carolina in 1768, cockfights "adhered to the rules of cocking in England." The first printed (thirteen) rules of golf were issued by the Gentlemen Golfers of Leith in 1744, for a competition usually played on Saturdays, instituted when the city presented them with a silver club as a prize, with the winner made captain for the year. A newly founded coastal golf club at St. Andrews, the Society of St. Andrews Golfers, specified that they related to the game as played on St. Andrews links but otherwise copied these rules almost verbatim for their own silver club competition. But in all sports, while there might be overlap, there was rarely wider agreement across regions. In hare-coursing, "Laws of the Leash" were laid down by Thomas Howard, Fourth Duke of Norfolk, in the sixteenth century to govern competitive matches between two hounds and were often drawn on thereafter, but as late as 1828 it was common to find that "the principle upon which courses are decided vary in different countries and over different grounds."[26]

Cricket had been played for a century under various generally understood but unwritten rules before they were written down in the articles of agreement for a match in 1727 between teams organized by the Second Duke of Richmond and Mr. Alan Broderick, heir to Viscount Middleton, which specified time, place, stakes, numbers on each side, and how to settle disputes. A published version of the rules in 1744 by the "Cricket Club," which played at the Artillery Ground in London, showed that the game had taken on many of its permanent features such as the length of the pitch, size of the wickets, and forms of dismissal. These cricket "laws," as they were symbolically labeled, were clearly intended to be more universally applied. Boxing rules were written down by pugilist-turned-boxing-promoter Jack Broughton in August 1743 to control the conduct of fights on stage in his London amphitheater, where he had introduced more social exclusivity to further encourage upper-class attendance. As such rules spread, they contributed to future national standardization and to the emergence of national and sometimes international sporting culture.

Alongside such factors as rule development or the growth of sports architecture, the growing institutionalization of sport can be seen in many other dimensions, from the still relatively small production of and international trade in sporting goods and equipment to the many specialized teachers of sporting skills, coaches, trainers, referees, judges, and groundsmen (another manifestation of the modern) and the growth of early forms of sports reporting and advertisement. And though many sports had their roots in religious festivals, Sundays, and other holy days, popular sports were often held then merely because this was traditionally time free from work.

Associativity

Until recently, relatively little attention has been paid to concepts of associativity, despite Johan Huizinga's early emphasis on the links between the play and associational elements of culture, and this provides a complementary way of looking at the period to that of Guttmann.[27] Early modern sport was institutionally connected to associational forms such as courts, municipal governments, academies, and universities, since participants often gained social capital through playing sports together. In courts, for example, royal ball games and riding and shooting contests fostered socialization and smoothed the negotiations of diplomacy. Hunting helped cement social relationships, and gifts of rabbit, venison, boar meat, fish, or fowl were highly prized. As the eighteenth-century private packs of fox hounds hunted more regularly, they attracted followers, although in a social context where roles, performances, and relationships were tacit but very clear. Highly formalized and regulated team games such as the Florentine *calcio*, played during Lent by two well-advertised named teams of twenty-seven men (gentlemen, *signori* and princes) dressed in colored silk, helped build associational bonds.

In towns, an early example of sporting associativity was provided by the societies associated with military training, such as fencing clubs or the archer and crossbow guilds of Flanders, popular in society and encouraged by the dukes of Burgundy. There was as much or more stress on associational life as sport, and their annual meals strengthened their unity through commensality. These guilds were an important part of regional festive networks, holding competitions across the low countries and northern Germany. They could last weeks and involve hundreds of fully armed competitors. The shift to handguns saw similar shooting confraternities, such as the Guild of St. George in London. Such societies and clubs wrote their own rules and ensured members followed them. Brotherhoods, fraternities, corporations, and clubs practicing elements of equality in organization and in sport were common in much of Europe in the sixteenth and seventeenth centuries.

From the late seventeenth century onward, it was a new form of associativity, the voluntary associations and clubs formed by the elite and upper middling groups, that slowly aided the construction of sporting culture. Indeed, Stefan Szymanski locates the origin of English sports, for example, in eighteenth-century associativity, not in nineteenth-century industrialization.[28] British historiography on club formation has tended to underemphasize the eighteenth-century growth of sports associativity, partly through using inappropriate modern notions of the sports "club." Staying at taverns and inns, town or country houses, or hunting lodges for annual race weeks, or for hunting, cockfights, or coursing, for example, was common and fostered shared sporting interest. Such association was informal, seasonal, or short-lived and left little historical trace. The few *formal* eighteenth-century "clubs" doing more "modern" sports were largely but not entirely organized by the better, not the middling, sort. Unlike the French nobility who spent their time at court, the British nobility divided their time between country estates, county towns for assize attendances, and the metropolis so had more opportunity for different sporting involvements. London, with its dynamic economy, stimulated sport's growth. In cricket, popular in London, surrounding towns, and the rural south, there are teasing references to club formation from early in the eighteenth century. A team from the Punch Club Society were playing by 1718; the Duke of Duke of Richmond had "his club" in 1728; by 1744 the "Cricket Club" played at the Artillery Ground; the Star and Garter Club had the Prince of Wales; and in the 1750s the famous Hambledon Club was formed. The Marylebone Cricket Club emerged in 1787 out of White's Conduit Club, a meeting place for aristocratic players and supporters of the game, and issued its first set of cricket rules in 1788.

In horse racing, though historians have conventionally dated the formation of the Jockey Club to circa 1750 at London's Star and Garter Club, there are several references to a Jockey Club with meetings in William's Coffee and Chocolate House in St. James in the 1730s. As early as 1729, the Jockey Club, which consisted "of several noblemen and gentlemen," was invited "to meet one day next week at Hackwood, the Duke of Bolton's seat in Hampshire, to consider of methods of the better keeping of their respective strings of horses at Newmarket."[29] The Maryland Jockey Club, founded in Annapolis in 1743, a club dedicated to horse racing and the oldest known sports club in America, presumably emulated the English model, and similar clubs developed in South Carolina, Virginia, and New York around the same time.

Coursing clubs only emerged toward the end of the eighteenth century. Swaffham Coursing Club in Norfolk was formed by George Walpole, Third Lord Orford, in 1776, initially with twenty-six members, each naming their greyhounds after a different alphabet letter. Ashdown Park Club was founded by Lord Craven in 1780 and Yorkshire's Malton Club in 1781, initially with twenty members.

Sometimes associativity formed round a club but more commonly around an occasion at a particular place. During the Renaissance, the evidence of decoration, paintings, maps, and guides all show that specialist areas for sporting play had been created in and around major cities. There were tiltyards for jousting; central, nearly rectangular Italian public squares; more irregular playing spaces alongside rivers or outside the walls; churchyards, racecourses, training areas, and shooting ranges. Specialist sporting architecture was also being created—indoor riding arenas, temporary bull rings in Spain, bear- and bull-baiting arenas in London ball courts, cockpits, bowling greens, inns, and taverns—while it has been argued that sports buildings erected specifically for ball games at this period "represented a genuine innovation."[30] There were game parks, chases, and forests in the countryside, which required high-maintenance and expensive game management, and kennels and stables at country houses and hunting lodges.

Access to such space marked out and maintained the hierarchy sustaining social and gender order, as enclosure put pressure on common land.

CHANGE AND CONTINUITY

Elite court sport changed over time. Tennis was the dominant indoor elite game in the seventeenth century, spreading right across Europe and especially popular in France, but by the early eighteenth century it was starting to seem too strenuous. *Calcio* remained popular in Florence through the seventeenth century, but thereafter the elite participated less and events were held more irregularly. Other activities such as dressage, epee fencing, and military exercise were also becoming minority pursuits. In part this may have been due to increasing reluctance by gentlemen to subject themselves to physical danger or perhaps simply to changes in fashion.

Certainly hunting continued for those with forest available. There were substantial elements of continuity in hunting across *ancien régime* France, Britain, and elsewhere, at least until the French Revolution took land away. Hunting provided a *rite de passage* into elite culture and offered pleasure, mental stimulation, exercise, or relaxation depending on the activity; close links to nature, dogs, and horses; and sacrificial and ritual elements, as well as food for the table. At the same time there were changes. Some are relatively easy to explain, others less so. For example, as deer in Britain became hunted out and stocks more difficult to maintain, there was a decline in deer hunting and a shift toward fox hunting, formerly a more functional plebeian pastime. Propertied society was often devoted to falconry until the late seventeenth century but then declined in Britain, though not in Holland and Germany, from some combination perhaps of loss of social cache, increased costs, a shortage of hawks, gentlemen's shift to use of sporting guns, or competing sports.

By the eighteenth century, less strenuous sports such as cricket, horse racing, and golf became increasingly popular in Britain. They offered entertaining, enjoyable open-air opportunities for socialization and for social and political rivalries to be enacted peacefully. For much of the early modern period, golf remained largely a sport for lowland Scottish nobility and gentry, though by the mid-eighteenth century bankers, physicians, merchants, and others from the urban elite of Edinburgh were also playing. Cricket's heartland was largely around London and in areas of pasture, cloth-making, and dairying in the southeast, but it was becoming a major sport by the mid-eighteenth century and spreading north.

Activities such as horse racing, cockfighting, hunting, and hare-coursing were all sports where greater wealth and access to greater expertise, either personal or bought in, could help one assert hierarchical position, gain reputation, or win substantial sums of money without putting oneself in any personal danger. Gambling on animals took away the personal risks associated with jousting, a duel, or warfare but still entailed powerful vocabularies of emotion and sentiment: the thrill of risking one's money, the exhilaration of a win, and the despair of a loss, especially when "deep play" was involved. Towns such as Chester, York, Salisbury, and Lanark were already organizing race meetings in the later sixteenth century. James I established Newmarket as a hunting and racing retreat, and Charles I made it Britain's turf center, making racing socially popular. By the eighteenth century many towns in Scotland, England, and America were raising funding to encourage greater attendance of the "better sort."

Elite sporting life changed fastest in Britain, largely because of the eighteenth-century consumer revolution and commercialization of material life. Sport offered extensive opportunities to make money. The better sort was becoming rapidly wealthier, variously through mercantile, industrial, military, or overseas investments, stock-market speculation, or income from agricultural and mineral holdings. Investment was risky but potentially highly profitable. Unsurprisingly, betting soon developed a competitive market economy on a smaller scale. For some of the better off, betting, like emergent capitalism, demonstrated competitive skills, ruthlessness, self-interest, chauvinism, confidence in judgment, and enjoyment of risk. Gambling became a symbol of excessive consumption, wealth, and time for leisure. Sporting events like horse racing, pugilism, and cricket were among the first leisure activities to encourage such betting. This in turn helped change these sports into more specialized, complex commercial enterprises. Poorer working men were increasingly paid to act as jockeys, pugilists, or cricketers to help win the bets of the better sort.

Magisterial social control over lower order games such as football or bowls might be exercised when longbow practice at butts was still taken seriously in some but not all English towns in the early 1500s, but these games expanded again as archery declined by the 1560s; whether this was from bow supply problems, alternative sports, opposition to its Sunday use, longer working hours, poorer diets, or the shift to handguns (all contemporary explanations) is unclear. Continental town organizations shifted to handguns even earlier.

Popular sport continued to have substantial regional and national differences, which often remained part of communal or festive culture: hurling in Cornwall, cnapen in Wales, shinty in the Scottish highlands. Activities such as football, foot-racing, various ball sports, hunting, throwing stones or quoits, wresting, or boxing might well be found in various forms across Europe.[31]

The impact of social control was clearly sometimes a factor in change, a view strongly stressed by some historians. [32] In Picardy popular culture was largely suppressed by an absolutist state and reformed Catholic Church between 1600 and 1789. In Britain in the later 1700s, in many market towns, magistrates were intent on improving public order, reducing uninhibited behavior and damage to property, and facilitating commercial trade and street passage. They tried, often with much success, to suppress town center sports formerly central to popular culture, such as bull- and bear-baiting, annual street football matches, or throwing at cocks. In many towns these disappeared; in others they moved to the outskirts.

Combat sports brought together the rich and poor to watch. In early-eighteenth-century London, wrestling fell from favor and was replaced by more commercial forms of sword, staff, and cudgel fighting displayed in amphitheaters. As elite tastes changed, leisure entrepreneurs like Broughton increasingly foregrounded working-class pugilists, encouraging elite patronage and betting. Cockfighting was a cross-class sport across England through the seventeenth century and beyond, but by the later eighteenth century it remained popular largely in northern England. Owners gained vicarious self-validation and gambling thrills, while large, mostly male crowds of mature age and across the social scale usually paid "pit money" for entrance, with prices varying with distance from the pit.

Conclusion

There is much we still do not know about early modern sport and exercise. We know little about the "middling sorts of people" and their affinities and behavior in sporting terms. There are difficulties in defining their membership and identity, even in terms of wealth distribution, local office-holding, and material culture. In England, outside London, for example, there was little concept of a middling group before 1700, and it then spread only slowly to the major towns. Women's sport likewise largely remains an unknown quantity. As when sport reflected martial skills, elite women's role was still often that of spectator. However, aristocratic women could take part in tennis, and female monarchs and their companions often rode with little apparent difficulty. Queen Elizabeth I, for example, reputedly enjoyed coursing and rode out deer hunting with a few friends. She also was a noted archer. Noble women took up falconry too, using merlins flown at snipe and larks. For plebeian women, festivals, times of carnival, with their inversions of the power structure, and commercial sport sometimes offered opportunities for them to participate. Currently our knowledge is largely confined to the later eighteenth century.[33] We still lack a comprehensive study of the sporting life and culture of the various social groups, contextualized in terms of social, economic, political, and urban developments. Different societies moved in different ways and in different trajectories to take up more consistently *some* of the major characteristics of modern sport, which might be praised or reviled in different contexts. It is already clear, however, that recreational and competitive physical pursuits were ubiquitous amongst all social groups and in all countries despite minority opposition. Sport was a key part of cultural life, and the early modern period played a crucial role in its growth.

Notes

1. Kasuhiko Kusodo, "PH Mair (1517–79): A Sports Chronicler in Germany," in *Sport and Culture in Early Modern Europe*, ed. John McClelland and Brian Nerrilees Toronto: CRRS Publications, 2009), 339–355.

2. See Joseph Strutt, *Sports and Pastimes of the People of England* (London: Methuen, 1801). For a perceptive critical review, see Agata Mackow, *Joseph Strutt as a Writer on the History and Folklore of Sports* (Poznan, Poland: Wydawcy, 2008).

3. Elaine McKay, "'For Refreshment and Preservinge Health': The Definition and Function of Recreation in Early Modern England," *Historical Research* 81.211 (February 2008): 52–74.

4. See Keith Thomas, *Man and the Natural World: Changing Attitudes in England, 1500–1800* (London: Allen Lane, 1983), 25.

5. Simon Gunn, "Archery Practice in Early Tudor England," *Past and Present* 209 (2011): 53–81.

6. David Underdown, *Revel, Riot, and Rebellion: Popular Politics and Culture in England, 1603–1660* (Oxford: Clarendon Press, 1985). See also Dennis Brailsford, "Puritanism and Sport in Seventeenth Century England," *Stadion* 1.2 (1975): 316–330; Nicholas McDowell, "The Stigmatizing of Puritans as Jews in Jacobean England: Ben Jonson, Francis Bacon and the Book of Sports Controversy," *Renaissance Studies* 19.3 (2005): 348–363.

7. Gregory M. Colon-Semenza, *Sport, Politics, and Literature in the English Renaissance* (Newark: University of Delaware Press, 2003).

8. March 31, 1654, "An Ordinance for Prohibiting Cock-Matches," in *Acts and Ordinances of the Interregnum, 1642–1660* (London: H.M. Stationery Office, 1911; British History Online), 831.

9. Philip Stubbes, *The Anatomie of Abuses* (London: N.p., 1583), sigs L2 to L4V.

10. Allen Guttmann, *From Ritual to Record: The Nature of Modern Sports* (New York, Columbia University Press, 1978); *Sports: The First Five Millennia* (Amherst: University of Massachusetts Press, 2004), 4–5.

11. Guttmann, *From Ritual to Record*, 172.

12. Susan Brownell, "Thinking Dangerously: The Person and His Ideas," in *Body Cultures: Essays on Sport, Space and Identity*, ed. Henning Eichberg (London: Routledge, 1998), 22–46, esp. 28–29.

13. Alan Houston and Steve Pincus, eds., *A Nation Transformed; England After the Restoration* (Cambridge, UK: Cambridge University Press, 2001).

14. *Sports History Review* 32.2 (2001) contains critiques by Doug Booth, Susan Brownell, Colin Howell, and Gerd von der Lippe and a critique and "laconic reply" by Guttmann. See also Richard Guilianotti, *Sport: A Critical Sociology* (Cambridge, UK: Polity Press, 2005), 22–25.

15. John Marshall Carter and Arnd Kruger, eds., *Ritual and Record: Sports Records and Quantification in Pre-Industrial Societies* (Westport, CT: Greenwood Press, 1990).

16. John McClelland, *Body and Mind: Sport in Europe from the Roman Empire to the Renaissance* (Abingdon, UK: Routledge, 2007).

17. McClelland, *Body and Mind*, 132.

18. Arnd Kruger, "Which Associativity? A German Answer to Szymanski's Theory of the Evolution of Modern Sport," *Journal of Sport History* 35.1 (2008): 40.

19. Peter Burke, "The Invention of Leisure in Early Modern Europe," *Past and Present* 146 (1995): 149.

20. Wolfgang Behringer, "Arena and Pall Mall: Sport in the Early Modern Period," *German History* 27.3 (2009): 331, 357.

21. Behringer, "Arena and Pall Mall." Alan Tomlinson and Christopher Young, "Towards a New History of European Sport," *European Review* 19 (2011): 487–507.

22. Joachim K. Rühl, "Regulations for the Joust in Fifteenth-Century Europe: Francesco Sforza Visconti (1465) and John Tiptoft (1466)," *International Journal for the History of Sport* 18 (2001): 193–208. Joachim Ruhl, "A Treasure Trove: One of the Four Originals of the Tournament Regulations of Heilbronn, 1485," in *Sport and Culture*, 145–182.
23. Antonio Scaino, *Trattato del giuoco della palla* (Venice: Quattro Venti, 2000).
24. Giovanni Bardi, *Discorso sopra il giuoco del calcio Fiorentino* (Florence: Giunti, 1580). See William Heywood, *Patio and Ponte: An Account of the Sports of Central Italy from the Age of Dante to the XXth Century* (New York: Hacker Art Books, 1969).
25. Mark Fortier, *The Culture of Equity in Early Modern England* (Aldershot, UK: Ashgate, 2005).
26. Thomas Goodlake, *The Coursers' Manual or Stud Book* (Liverpool, UK: Whittaker, 1828), xx.
27. Johan Huizinga, *Homo Ludens: A Study of the Play-Element in Culture* (Boston Beacon Press, 1944).
28. Stefan Szymanski, "A Theory of the Evolution of Modern Sport," *Journal of Sport History* 35 (2008): 4.
29. *Daily Advertiser* (London), Wednesday, March 10, 1731; *Daily Post* (London), Saturday, August 2, 1729.
30. Berenger, "Arena and Pall Mall," 339.
31. See, for example, Mike Huggins, "Sporting Life in the Rural Margins of Late Eighteenth Century England: The World of Robert Anderson, 'the Cumberland Bard,'" *Eighteenth Century Studies* 45.2 (2012): 189–205.
32. R. W. Malcolmson, *Popular Recreation in English Society, 1700–1850* (Cambridge, UK: Cambridge University Press, 1973); Emma Griffin, *England's Revelry: A History of Popular Sports and Pastimes 1660–1830* (Oxford: Oxford University Press, 2005).
33. Catriona M. Parratt, *"More Than Mere Amusement": Working-Class Women's Leisure in England, 1750–1914* (Boston: Northeastern University Press, 2001); Nancy L. Struna, "Gender and Sporting Practice in Early America, 1750–1810," *Journal of Sport History* 18.1 (1991): 10–30.

BIBLIOGRAPHY

Arcangeli, Alessandro. *Recreation in the Renaissance: Attitudes Towards Leisure and Pastimes in European Culture, c. 1425–1675*. Basingstoke, UK: Palgrave Macmillan, 2003.
Behringer, Wolfgang. "Arena and Pall Mall: Sport in the Early Modern Period." *German History* 27.3 (2009): 331–357.
Burke, Peter. "The Invention of Leisure in Early Modern Europe." *Past and Present* 146 (1995): 136–150.
Carter, John Marshall, and Arnd Kruger, eds. *Ritual and Record: Sports Records and Quantification in Pre-Industrial Societies*. Westport, CT: Greenwood Press, 1990.
Griffin, Emma. *England's Revelry: A History of Popular Sports and Pastimes 1660–1830*. Oxford: Oxford University Press, 2005.
Mafany, Joan-Lluis. "Debate: The Invention of Leisure in Early Modern Europe." *Past and Present* 156 (1997): 174–219.
Malcolmson, R. W. *Popular Recreation in English Society, 1700–1850*. Cambridge, UK: Cambridge University Press, 1973.

McClelland, John, and Brian Nerrilees, eds. *Sport and Culture in Early Modern Europe.* Toronto: CRRS Publications, 2009.

Struna, Nancy L. "Gender and Sporting Practice in Early America, 1750–1810." *Journal of Sport History* 18.1 (1991): 10–30.

Underdown, David. *Start of Play.* London: Penguin, 2000.

PART III

THE BIRTH AND ESTABLISHMENT OF MODERN SPORT, 1820-1940

CHAPTER 8

···

INDUSTRIALIZATION
AND SPORT

···

WRAY VAMPLEW

THE first generation of historians who looked at sport in Britain believed that the Industrial Revolution actually had a negative impact on sporting activity.[1] The violent human and animal sports of rural Britain, the ploughing matches and hedge-laying contests that demonstrated agricultural skills, and the mob football matches played over extensive areas of land were all seen as incompatible with industrial society, industrial location, or industrial work patterns. They felt that the demands of industrialists for a disciplined workforce capable of working long and regular hours throughout the year undermined the leisure calendar of the agrarian economy in which bursts of intense activity at planting, harvesting, or shearing time were interspersed with long periods of irregular work. Not only did industry reduce the amount of leisure time available, but industrialists joined with religious evangelicals, political economists, and other middle-class reformers to attempt to change workers' attitudes to both work and leisure. Sobriety, thrift, order, and hard work were all part of a new morality of respectability that they intended to impose on the working class. Encouragement and exhortation were strengthened by legislation at the national level to outlaw many blood sports and ban Sunday entertainments and at the urban level to prohibit street football. The early nineteenth century thus came to be regarded as a leisure wasteland.

However, the growing interest in sports history and the consequent detailed examination of the early industrialization period has shown that many traditional sports continued to be played into the later nineteenth century and that there was apparently no leisure vacuum to be filled.[2] Indeed, Adrian Harvey's intensive study of eighteenth- and nineteenth-century newspapers and sporting periodicals, particularly *Bell's Life* and the *Sporting Magazine*, led him to suggest that during the first half of the nineteenth century a commercial sporting culture developed to serve a mass public. He also argues that there was a major expansion in sporting activity in Manchester, the cotton capital of Britain.[3] In other words, there was a chronological coincidence between industrialization and the expansion of sporting activity.

The conventional view now, as shown by the following comments from outside Britain and outside sports history, is that modern sport originated in the nineteenth century as a direct consequence of Britain's industrialization. European scholars Jean-François Bourg and Jean-Jacques Gouguet claim "modern sport was born in England at the time of the industrial revolution"; Paris-based historian Raymond Thomas maintains that "sport was born in nineteenth century England and diffused into France and Europe"; and sociologist Daniel Bloyce takes it as a matter of fact that "the majority of sports played across the globe were essentially "modernised" in England."[4]

However, there is a danger that the pendulum has swung too far. The role of industrialization as a driver of modern sport is too often taken as a chronological correlation without the causal relationship being fully specified. It is hard to see how early industrialization could have impacted positively on sport. Possibly the mindset that encouraged venture capitalists to risk investment in industry was of the same ilk that persuaded wealthy gamblers to promote sport as a means to wager.[5] The version of team sports that emanated from the public schools may have emphasized qualities of use for the industrialist—teamwork, obeying orders, and discipline—but this should not be exaggerated. Such sport encompassed the idea of chivalry (fair play) rather than that of industrial capitalism, and, as can be seen from Sir Henry Newbolt's famous poem *Vitai Lamparda*, sport taught the virtues of war, not commerce. No evidence has yet been discovered of industrialists actively promoting sport until the last third of the nineteenth century. The real contribution of industrialization to the development of sport lay in the increased incomes and leisure time that productivity brought. And, despite some precursors in particular trades, this was a product of the late rather than even the mid-nineteenth century and certainly not before then.[6]

Even if a link between industrialization and sport can be identified, we must consider another historical revision that disposes of the idea that there was an industrial *revolution* in Britain. Instead, it has been recognized that the process of industrialization was a drawn-out one that accelerated significantly only with the widespread application of steam power in the second quarter of the nineteenth century. The first factories were little more than a bringing together of handicraft workers under one roof. Even when power was adopted for mechanization, it was limited to areas where water flow was fast. The cotton works on the hillsides of Lancashire had neither a significant influence on national economic production nor any real impact on leisure patterns of workers generally or even in the county itself. Nationally, even by the mid-nineteenth century, 5.5 million of the 7.25 million industrial workers were employed in nonmechanized industry and agriculture was still the largest employment sector.[7] Only when steam became the driving force for mass production did factories become less geographically determined and did industry *begin* to change the environment in which sport took place as increased urbanization, concomitant upon industrialization, began to lessen the open space available.

The major impact of industrialization on sport came in its later stages as the widespread application of steam power vastly increased productivity, thus enabling employers to concede to demands to lessen the working week for their labor force and to pay them higher wages. This had two major consequences for sport. First, it helped create a mass market for spectator sport by setting Saturday afternoons aside free of work and thus providing a time slot into which gate-money sport could fit. Second, for those who preferred to be active rather than watch others play, the increase in disposable income allowed the purchase of bicycles and other sporting equipment. By this time too, in both Britain and America, the middle-class attitude toward sport had changed; they now accepted that, if appropriately controlled, sport could be a force for good in creating healthier citizens, rejuvenating labor, and building character.[8]

Hence the impact of British industrialization on sport was in the later decades of the nineteenth century. But did modern sport then spread from Britain to the rest of the world? A recent research project on European sport history has led Alan Tomlinson and Christopher Young to claim "the widely held belief that Britain gave sport to the world is in need of urgent revision."[9] It is argued that, although Britain incubated many athletic pursuits, others had no connection with Britain and were a product of the diverse movement cultures extant in Europe. A few examples will suffice. Despite British upper-class holidaymakers, the development of winter sports owes more to making a living in the frozen Scandinavian landscape; cycling was a continental sport that traveled to Britain, and the multistage cycle race was a non-British innovation. In addition, handball, although basing some of its rules on football, was an invisible sport in Britain's gymnasia. In all Tomlinson and Young address twenty-two significant sports and suggest that only six or seven can be considered as having uniquely British origins.

The authors identified four clusters of sport development within Europe alone: not just the British but also German, Soviet, and Scandinavian versions. The British version is characterized by an absence of state intervention, a reliance on private organizations, and a domination by an anticommercial ethos through the ideology of amateurism. The German cluster originated in nineteenth-century militarized forms of physical culture and was marked by an emphasis on the collective, the individual body in harmony with the body politic, and a noncompetitive ethos. Scandinavia had a variant on the German with an equal focus on improving national spirit and defense in the nineteenth century but placed greater emphasis on individual movement, bodily harmony, and aesthetics. Additionally, its notion of *idrott* proposed a recreational outdoor physical development in harmony with nature. In the Soviet/eastern European cluster, which emerged in the twentieth century, sport was an extension of the state apparatus both in spheres of mass display and the cultivation of elite athletes. Whether any of these clusters were associated with industrialization remains to be researched. In America, British sports immigrated with the colonists and prizefighting and horse racing vied for precedence as early spectator sports. Yet the sport that emerged as America's national one in the late nineteenth century was baseball, which had British origins but no popularity in its homeland. The later developments of American football and basketball were clearly innovations from within the United States.[10]

GUTTMANN AND
THE MODERNIZATION OF SPORT

British economic historian Neil Tranter suggested that "as a general rule, the more industrial and commercial the economy the greater the extent of organised sport and the earlier its inception" and according to two American cultural historians "organised sports . . . are a creature of modernity, a trademark of advanced industrial societies."[11] Modernity depicts the shift of a society from underdeveloped to developed, part of which is the emergence of new activities, including sport, but sport of a certain type with specific characteristics.

In his seminal work *From Ritual to Record* first published in 1978, Allen Guttmann has argued that there are seven such structural characteristics.[12] First, modern sport was secular with no religious reasons for participation. Second, it was expected to demonstrate equality: theoretically everyone should have an opportunity to compete, and the conditions of competition should be the same for all contestants. Third, it introduced the idea of specialization: everyone who wanted to could join in folk football, a sport in which there were no sharply defined roles, but the emphasis on achievement in modern sport brought in specialization both within a sport and between sports. Fourth was rationalization, in particular the development of rules that in primitive societies were often considered "divine instructions"—God-given rituals, not to be tampered with by mere humans. In contrast, nonsecular modern sports were invented with their own written rules. Even more rationalization came via the development of coaching and sports science. Guttmann's fifth feature was bureaucratization. Almost every major modern sport has a national and international organization that developed extensive bureaucracies to establish universal rules for the sport and oversee their implementation. These were not required when there were no written rules. Sixth was quantification, by which modern sports transform every athletic feat into statistics. Following on from quantification is Guttmann's seventh point, the modern emphasis on records. Like many models, Guttmann's was an ideal-type postulation that may never have all its conditions fully satisfied. However, it has stood the test of time, if not in its entirety then as a basis on which others have built.

Whilst acknowledging the intellectual ingenuity, influence, and longevity of Guttmann's model, Tomlinson and Young criticize his misuse and misrepresentation of Weberian concepts.[13] Primarily whereas Guttmann claimed that his seven characteristics were replicated in modern society and were derived "from the fundamental Weberian notion of the difference between the ascribed status of traditional society and the achieved status of a modern one," Tomlinson and Young maintain that "nowhere did Weber state that modern societies were essentially based upon achieved status." They also argue that, in his discussion of rationalization, while Guttmann correctly identified a logical relationship between means and ends as being Weberian, this was only one aspect of Weber's complex explanation of social action. Yet here one has to query whether Guttmann is being critiqued not for his ideas but for invoking Weber as an influence on his thinking.

Tomlinson and Young also believe that Guttmann has stuck too rigidly to his original ideal-type model and refused to revise it in the light of new research findings, though they do acknowledge that he has integrated some of the critical perspectives into his work. There may be a semantic issue here: the critics may want to see a revisiting and reconstruction of the model, whereas Guttmann might see integration and minor amendment as enough. Tomlinson and Young are right that, while Guttmann concedes that he should have examined Renaissance sport as part of his model, he did not do so when the opportunity arose, both in the reissue of *From Ritual to Record* in 2004 or in his new book of that year, *Sports: The First Five Millennia*. John Carter and Arnd Krüger argue that both quantification and a mania for records had precursors in medieval Europe and even earlier.[14] Other critics, on the basis of their own research into sport in New York and British horse racing, have suggested that the model requires more input on press publicity, marketing, commercialization, and professionalization.[15]

Moreover, Tomlinson and Young follow Wolfgang Behringer in suggesting that modern sports emerged from developments in the early modern era rather than as a byproduct of industrialization.[16] They argue that many modern traits are evident from as early as 1450. Sport became increasingly institutionalized by the creation and codification of rules, the building of dedicated sport spaces, a European-wide trade in sports equipment, and the emergence of a professional class of athletes, coaches, and officials. They also note that from the Renaissance onward the sportification of military exercises and the rise of spectator sports as popular entertainment are observable. What is not clear is whether the examples discovered are precursors rather than initiators, atypical rather than commonplace, and further research is needed before full support can be given to their view that "the weight of current evidence indicates that the threshold for the beginnings of modern sport—at least in some social classes in some regions—could be moved back before 1800."[17] What can be argued is that some of the preconditions for the emergence of modern sport originated before widespread industrialization but that its actual takeoff required further stimuli. Guttmann himself saw preconditions emerging before industrialization as he views modern sport as a (long-delayed?) byproduct of the scientific revolution of the European enlightenment. Szymanski too sees the European enlightenment as a starting point, as the roots of modern sport can be seen in the new forms of associativity created at that time, specifically the club, which is the fundamental unit of modern sport and less so of earlier forms of sport.[18]

INDUSTRIALIZATION, URBANIZATION, AND THE COMMERCIALIZATION OF SPORT

In examining the development of sport, it is important to differentiate the interrelated but semi-independent concepts of industrialization, urbanization, and commercialization. Industrialization contributed to the commercialization of sport, but many aspects of sport were commercialized long before industrialization. Cricket, pedestrianism (professional athletics), prizefighting, rowing, and especially horse racing had "a long history of mass spectating, profit-seeking promoters, paid performers, stake-money contests and gambling."[19] However, although some spectators paid to watch from grandstands or to be close to the action, generally much of the commercialization of the time was associated with sidelines of the sport—beer and food stalls, itinerant entertainers, and so on—rather than with the sport itself. Indeed, Harvey's study of commercialization in British sport before 1850 uses a wide definition that includes not just gate money but also participants' meals purchased as a condition of entry, competitors' direct entry fees, spectators' refreshments, and additional associated entertainments such as balls and theatrical shows.

Mass spectator sport did exist before the end of the nineteenth century, though it was intermittent, often annual at best. Harvey's claims for widespread mass spectator sport by the 1840s is undermined by an inability to present any systematic figures for sports crowd attendance. He does produce a table representing attendances of over a thousand on an annual basis for the 1840s, but as this averaged less than forty-five such crowds a year, it is scarcely evidence of sufficient effective demand for these to be more than sporadic occurrences.[20] The market was not yet ready for regularly scheduled sports events. As I have stated elsewhere, "it was not until the economic benefits of industrialization filtered down to the mass of the population that a large and regular paying clientele could be relied upon for sports events."[21] Moreover, mass markets for sport required not only spending power and time in which to spend it but also a concentration of population *and* ease of access to the venues. This came with urbanization and the development of intertown but especially intratown transportation. Earlier urbanization did not fulfill the latter requirement. The "walking cities" of early America were not big enough to promote commercialized sport, but later those towns that were sufficiently large enough required intra-urban transport for demand to become fully effective.[22] Later, in all countries industrialization and associated urbanization created the conditions in which organized, commercial, gate-money sport could flourish.

It is also important to distinguish the influence of industrialization from that of urbanization. Without urbanization, there would have been no sporting consumer culture whereby recreation was transformed into entertainment and became a commodity for sale. First, the early factories were not the large buildings associated with water-powered and steam-powered machinery but merely places that gathered together handcraft workers. Second, although much urbanization was a consequence of industrialization either directly (manufacturing centers) or indirectly (ports and distribution centers), other forces were at work, such as population growth, immigration, and agricultural change, not all of which can be totally attributed to the coming of industry.

Sport as an Industry

Sport can be regarded (and measured) as an industry in its own right in several ways: as spectator gate-money events, as a driver of demand for sports apparel and equipment, and as an employer of labor. However, sport is a special industry for, although much of it follows normal business axioms, some aspects are unusual. Much conventional economic activity occurs *within* sport, including sports-related occupations such as groundsmen and equipment manufacturers, as well as the less sports-specific jobs of publicists and salespersons, all of which help to get the game underway. There is also the normal revenue-seeking activity associated *with* sport, such as the landlord who put on a cricket match to get a drinking clientele among the spectators. However, in team sports there may be unusual economic behavior. Competing firms in the normal economy do not need to collaborate to make a product, unlike rival football teams. Moreover, the ultimate aim of those running the football firms may be to maximize utility (the winning of matches and trophies) rather than to earn profit; so, whereas a conventional business would be concerned with controlling the margin between outlay and revenue, the utility seeker would be willing to spend on players—sometimes at the risk of insolvency—to try and produce a winning team.[23]

Stephen Hardy's model, still not superseded, postulates a tripartite view of the sport commodity, "which can exist in isolation but which reach full expression in combination."[24] The components are the game form itself, which becomes a commodity once spectators are prepared to pay to watch it; services ancillary to the game form, such as the stadiums to hold the paying public and the media that advertise the events; and the equipment required to participate in the sport. Here a difference in the markets can be distinguished: in the era when gate money was the prime source of revenue, the game commodity relied on a local market whereas the market for equipment and apparel, though initially supplied by local craftspersons, more quickly became a national one.

At least three traditional sports—pugilism, cricket, and horse racing—demonstrated their popularity across Britain by attracting large crowds in the early nineteenth century, but these had been irregular events. As they were scheduled more frequently for the paying customer, their nature changed. This included both product improvement—that is, a sporting competition is modified to attract larger audiences but that does not change the essence of the sport—and product development, which can drastically alter the nature of a sport and the way in which it is played. Cricket introduced the county championship to give an edge to previously friendly fixtures; bare-fisted prize fights to exhaustion gave way to gloved, time-limited contests; and in horse racing the development of sprints for two-year-olds replaced the traditional long-distance races for older, staying animals. These traditional sports were joined by newer ones, particularly football. Here major football leagues were established in both England and Scotland to provide weekly competitive fixtures in place of ad hoc friendly matches and cup competitions from which teams might make an early departure. In the United States the growing popularity of baseball led some clubs to seize the commercial opportunity to charge admission fees and eventually pay their players. By 1876 America had a national league, a decade ahead of English football. Its key elements of a league structure, territorial franchises, annual championship tournaments, revenue sharing, and the reserve clause shaped the nature of American team sports for over a century.[25]

In Britain the abandonment of punitive taxes on newspapers, the emergence of a reading public in commercial proportions, and advances in transport, telegraph, and printing technology all contributed to the development of a media industry with which sport could have a symbiotic relationship. Specialized sporting magazines such as the *Sporting Magazine* (1792), *Bell's Life in London and Sporting Chronicle* (1820), and *Life in London and Sporting Guide* (1824) existed in Britain beginning in the late eighteenth century, but they were expensive, catered to a select market, and were London-based. They were joined in the 1860s by a cheaper product, also produced in the capital but aimed at a clerical and artisan market, with an emphasis on horse-racing news. These included *Sporting Life* (1859), *Sporting Gazette* (1862), *Sporting Opinion* (1864), *Sportsman* (1865), and *Sporting Times* (1865). New titles were promoted in the provinces in the 1870s, including the Manchester-based *Sporting Chronicle* (1871) and the *Athletic News* (1875), which concentrated on football, rugby, cricket, athletics, and cycling. The next decade saw the publication of Saturday-night football special editions giving the afternoon's results.[26] All of this was in addition to the gradual intrusion of sport into the daily press. In America the first major sports weeklies were the rural-oriented *American Turf Register and Sporting Magazine* (1829), which focused on horse racing, and the *Spirit of the Times* (1831), which promoted angling and horse racing but also covered cricket, rowing, and yachting. As in Britain, the market was a limited, class-based one. The first sports weekly aimed at a wider audience was the *Sporting News* in 1886, and a decade later the importance of sport in American life was acknowledged when the *New York World* published the first newspaper sports section, an innovation quickly taken up by most major papers.[27]

Equipment manufacturers were more concerned with the participant market than the spectator one. Supplying equipment was a "profitable experience for many companies" though many small enterprises went to the wall as mass-production technology undermined the craftsman.[28] By 1914 there were in Britain alone some 350,000 golf club members and between 300,000 to 500,000 amateur soccer players, all requiring equipment of various kinds.[29] The extent of the ancillary industry that this generated can be seen in the advertisements in the various golf and football annuals of the time. In the United States the 1895 Sears, Roebuck catalogue had over eighty pages devoted to sporting goods.

The role of agency must not be forgotten. Three categories of entrepreneur can be identified. First were the conventional businessmen seeking profits. These included men such as A. G. Spalding in America, who opened his first store in Chicago in 1876 but by 1899 had extended his company backward into manufacturing, where he employed 3,500 workers producing bicycles, boats, uniforms, baseball bats, and other sporting equipment and horizontally into marketing, where he sold his sporting goods to some 20,000 retailers.[30] Football ground designer Archibald Leitch was the architect and engineer responsible for at least forty-six individual stands and pavilions in Britain between 1899 and 1939 from which he gained "considerable rewards."[31] His designs became the best practice of twentieth-century football, and millions of spectators watched from his stands protected by his patented crush barriers.

Second were those promoting sport who hoped perhaps to cover their costs but were not profit-maximizers. Here the founders of the Football League in England and the boards of the constituent clubs can be considered. In a way, these can be compared to the early gamblers who promoted sport as a means to other ends. The new men, however, were looking for psychic income rather than economic rewards from gate revenue or gambling; they invested for civic pride rather than their pocketbooks. Such nonprofit maximizing behavior can be found in other sports: county cricket clubs were dependent on the distribution of revenue from matches involving the national team to keep themselves afloat, and horse racing existed only because owners were prepared to treat it as a hobby rather than a business.[32] Football, golf, and some other sporting clubs adopted limited liability company status usually to protect the finances of their members rather than as a move to pay them dividends.[33] They did not define themselves as profit-seeking enterprises, unlike perhaps in the United States where team owners may have seen their franchises in a different light, a subject area where more research is needed.

Third were political promoters of sport. In Britain in the late nineteenth century, the development of golf courses and recreational parks by local authorities was part of a wider movement in which the health and welfare of the electorates were served by the provision of municipally owned transport and utility companies. American cities, too, used publicly owned land for parks and municipal golf.[34] Here participatory sport was encouraged, rather than spectatorship.

What apparently disappeared is the promotion of sport by the professionals themselves. In the 1840s, various cricketing elevens toured Britain playing matches for a share of the gate, which was distributed, not always equally, between the players. By the late nineteenth century this could be seen only in such exhibitions as the footballing "Zulus" and the like for charity matches.[35] The authorities of the various sports were now in full control, and self-help professionalism was frowned upon. There was one major exception in Britain, the Professional Golfers' Association (formed in 1902), which by 1913 had played a major role in establishing an incipient tour by organizing tournaments at the national, regional, and local level and actively seeking sponsorship for them.[36] In the United States, the ill-fated Players' League lasted just one baseball season before being crushed by the financial power and political acumen of the rival capitalist-owned leagues.[37]

Paid players existed before industrialization. Harvey has shown that sports laborers learned early that they could make money from sport not only from winning prizes but also by securing a patron, providing tuition and exhibitions, and selling instruction books, portraits, and memorabilia. These early professionals did not rely on gate money but on their patron's gambling proclivity for employment. Those who wished to be full-time (or thereabouts) professionals had to be prepared to travel, which was not that easy in the prerailway era, as the disposable income levels for most of the populace were too low for regular attendance at sports events. Hence jockeys plied their trade on regional racing circuits, riding at different meetings lasting a day or two at the most, and the various professional cricket elevens toured the countryside playing local sides. Prizefights were one-off, infrequent events with the combatants needing time to recover from their brutal exertions. It is likely that some jockeys, pedestrians, and pugilists developed as sportsmen out of their servant tasks of messengers and bodyguards, while cricketers found employment as estate workers because of their bowling skills.

Once team sports developed with competitive leagues, the professionals found that, unlike workers in the normal economy, they lost the freedom to change their employer. To prevent wealthier clubs from garnering all the best playing talent and dominating an unbalanced competition, restrictions were often placed on the mobility of professional players. Cricketers either had to be born in the county they represented or have resided there for two years before they could be selected. In soccer, after their initial decision to join a club, players were no longer free to select their employers as that first club had an exclusive right to their services. At the end of each season, clubs would produce a list of players whose services they wished to retain and a second list of those it wished to transfer (for a fee) to other clubs. Players could not insist on being transferred even if another club was willing to pay a transfer fee, and if a player refused to be transferred, his career could be over. Baseball in America established a similar "reserve" clause. In addition to this restraint of trade policy in the labor market, the English football authorities imposed a maximum wage so that players were unable to earn their economic rent and received less than they would in a free labor market.

Industrial Sport

Industrial workplace sport is an underresearched topic, but we know that in nineteenth-century Britain several philanthropic employers, including chocolate makers Cadbury and Rowntree, the chemist Boot, and soap manufacturer Lever, provided sports facilities for their workers, and this seems to have spread across a range of industries in the twentieth century.[38] Pilkingtons organized a cricket team for its glassworkers in the 1860s, but most others seem to have developed during the last quarter of the century.[39] The early motive appears to have been altruism, perhaps a sharing of the views of many religious and temperance reformers who offered sport as a countermeasure to unrespectable behavior by the lower classes; in their case, however, this included not just violence and drunken behavior but also trade union activities. Some industrialists also began to see the provision of sport as a positive move to aid productivity in their businesses, not so much by keeping workers fit but as part of wide band of welfare facilities that might encourage workforce loyalty and reduce labor turnover. Later, as unionism grew in influence, workers began to seek such extra benefits as part of their labor contract. One aspect of these industrial teams that merits attention is that they offered sport to both men and women.

It was not just in factory industry that this occurred. In London by the 1890s, many of the banks, railway companies, insurance firms, and utility providers were offering sporting facilities to their employees, including grounds, clubhouses, boating houses, and rifle ranges.[40] Nor was this confined to Britain. Across the Atlantic, works teams also expanded. Some companies appear to have done it for prestige, with the aim of giving pride to supporters by producing teams that could win local championships. The soccer team sponsored by the Farr Alpaca Mill in Holyoke, Massachusetts, did not lose a league game for five years, a record assisted by a policy of hiring workers because of their athletic abilities.[41]

Such developments, while always a minority among employers, were found in all modernizing economies. In Australia, for example, trades football emerged in Melbourne after legislation in 1896 granted Wednesday half-day holidays. Here two distinct motivations can be found. Frederick Cato, chairman of Moran & Cato, a suburban grocery chain, saw properly administered and organized sport as maintaining moral discipline, whereas Francis Clapp, the American-born managing director of the Melbourne Tramways and Omnibus Company, seized it as an opportunity to dilute the effectiveness of attempts to unionize his labor force.[42]

CONCLUSION

A microcosm of what happened nationally in Britain may be seen in the experience of football in one English county. A folk football match between the inhabitants of the Leicestershire agricultural villages of Medbourne and Hallaton was first played around 1796 but was still an annual Easter Monday occurrence at the end of the nineteenth century (and beyond). It was a sporting event suitable for an agrarian economy, played once a year when there was time to spare from work and utilizing the natural environment by being played entirely across open countryside, with steeply sloping ground and a number of obstacles—hedges, fences, and ponds obstructing the mile between the two respective goals.[43] There was an oral tradition that determined that the "ball" (a barrel filled with nine pints of ale) was not directed into the opponent's territory but was to be carried to one's own goal and that the match did not end until one set of villagers had brought two barrels home. Other than that, there were no rules on the number of players or their gender, no requirements for the teams to be of equal size, and no team colors to be worn.

This can be contrasted with the contemporaneous football matches being played every second week during the season at Filbert Street, home of Leicester Fosse F.C., just 13 miles away. The ground was surrounded by houses, and the pitch itself was in a defined area of about 7,000 square meters. The club had been formed in 1884 by old boys from Wyggeston School and for several years had a nomadic existence involving mainly friendly matches before moving to Filbert Street stadium in 1891, when it joined the Midland League. After finishing second in that competition, the club was elected to the National Football League in 1894. As Leicester became an important center for the manufacture of hosiery, textiles, and footwear and, toward the end of the century, also engineering, its population had risen from 68,000 in 1861 to 217,000 by 1901. This provided the base for a regular football crowd with an average attendance of around six thousand even in the lower reaches of the league. This gate money paid the wages of the fully professional male playing staff, only eleven of whom were allowed to participate in any match. On the pitch, their uniforms of royal blue shirts and stockings with white shorts were easily distinguishable from their opponents who, by regulation of the football authorities, had to wear different colors. The players, unlike those involved in the rough and tumble at Hallaton, had specialized roles, some offensive, some defensive. Games lasted just ninety minutes with teams changing ends at halftime to ensure equal use of any prevailing weather or terrain conditions. A bureaucratic structure in the form of the league, the rules that it imposed on the team, the specialization of playing roles, and the efforts to ensure equality—none of them visible at Hallaton—are all features of Guttmann's "modern" sport. Nevertheless, despite a century between their origins, the two forms of football coexisted, a prime example of historical continuity and change in sport.

NOTES

1. See, for example, Robert Malcolmson, *Popular Recreations in English Society 1770–1850* (Cambridge, UK: Cambridge University Press, 1975); and Hugh Cunningham, *Leisure in the Industrial Revolution* (London: Croom Helm, 1980).

2. Tony Collins, John Martin, and Wray Vamplew, eds., *Encyclopedia of British Traditional Rural Sports* (Abingdon, UK: Routledge, 2005).

3. Adrian Harvey, *The Beginnings of a Commercial Sporting Culture in Britain, 1793–1850* (Aldershot, UK: Ashgate, 2004).

4. Jean-François Bourg and Jean-Jacques Gouguet, *Economie du Sport* (Paris: La Découverte, 2005), 4; Raymond Thomas, *Histoire du Sport* (Paris: Presses Universitaires de France, 1991), 58. Both translated and cited in Stefan Szymanski, "A Theory of the Evolution of Modern Sport," *Journal of Sport History* 35.1 (2008): 3; Daniel Bloyce, "So That's Your Way of Playing Rounders, Isn't It?" *Sporting Traditions* 22.1 (2005): 94.

5. Allen Guttmann, *From Ritual to Record: The Nature of Modern Sports* (New York: Columbia University Press, 1978; 2004), 59–60.

6. Wray Vamplew, *Pay Up and Play the Game* (Cambridge, UK: Cambridge University Press, 2004), 44–50.

7. Vamplew, *Pay Up*, 42, 48.

8. Richard Holt, "The Amateur Body and the Middle-Class Man: Work, Health and Style in Victorian Britain," *Sport in History* 26.3 (2006): 352–369; Steven Riess, *Sport in Industrial America 1850–1920* (Wheeling, IL: Harlan Davidson, 1995), 5.

9. Alan Tomlinson and Christopher Young, "Towards a New History of European Sport," *European Review* 19 (2011): 487–507.

10. Wray Vamplew, "The Development of Team Sports Before 1914," in *Handbook on the Economics of Sport*, ed. Wladimir Andreff and Stefan Szymanski (Cheltenham, UK: Edward Elgar, 2006), 435–439.

11. Neil Tranter, *Sport, Economy and Society in Britain 1750–1914* (Cambridge, UK: Cambridge University Press, 1998), 29; Elliott J. Gorn and Warren Goldstein, *A Brief History of American Sports* (New York: Hill & Wang, 1993), 111.

12. Guttmann, *From Ritual to Record*, 15–55.

13. Alan Tomlinson and Christopher Young, "Sport in History: Challenging the *Communis Opinio*," *Journal of Sport History* 37 (2010): 5–17.

14. John M. Carter and Arnd Krüger, eds., *Ritual and Record: Sports Records and Quantification in Pre-Modern Societies* (New York: Greenwood Press, 1990).

15. Melvin L. Adelman, *A Sporting Time: New York City and the Rise of Modern Athletics 1820–70* (Urbana: University of Illinois Press, 1986); Wray Vamplew and Joyce Kay, "A Modern Sport? 'From Ritual to Record' in British Horseracing," *Ludica* 9 (2003): 125–139.

16. Wolfgang Behringer, "Arena and Pall Mall: Sport in the Early Modern Period," *German History* 27 (2009): 331–357. See also the papers at the Sport in Early Modern Culture conference held at the German Historical Institute, London, November 17–19, 2011.

17. Tomlinson and Young, "Towards a New History," 10.

18. Szymanski, "Evolution of Modern Sport," 1–32. It should also be noted that participant and spectatorship may have required different environments for their development.

19. Tranter, *Sport, Economy and Society*, 14–15.

20. Harvey, *Commercial Sporting Culture*, 175.

21. Vamplew, *Pay Up*, 281.

22. Riess, *Sport in Industrial America*, 12.

23. For a discussion of this, see Wray Vamplew, "Economic Approaches To Sports [and Cultural] History," in *Cultural Histories and Cultural Politics*, ed. Christiane Eisenberg and Andreas Gestrich (Berlin: Arbeitskreis Deutsche Englandforschung, 2012).

24. Stephen Hardy, "Entrepreneurs, Organizations and the Sport Marketplace: Subjects in Search of Historians," *Journal of Sport History* 13 (1986): 17–19.

25. Steven W. Pope, *Patriotic Games* (New York: Oxford University Press, 1997), 59.

26. Steve Tate, "James Catton, 'Tityrus' of *The Athletic News* (1890 to 1936): A Biographical Study," *Sport in History* 25.1 (2005): 98–115; Tony Mason, "Sporting News, 1860–1914," in *The Press in English Society from the Seventeenth to Nineteenth Centuries*, ed. Michael Harris and Alan J. Lee (Cranbury, NJ: Associated University Presses, 1986), 168–186.

27. Riess, *Sport in Industrial America*, 31–32; Pope, *Patriotic Games*, 7.

28. Tranter, *Sport, Economy and Society*, 77.

29. Wray Vamplew, "Sharing Space: Inclusion, Exclusion and Accommodation at the British Golf Club before 1914," *Sport and Social Issues* 34 (2010): 359; Vamplew, *Pay Up*, 52.

30. Peter Levine, *A. G. Spalding and the Rise of Baseball* (New York: Oxford University Press, 1985).

31. Simon Inglis, *Engineering Archie* (London: English Heritage, 2005), 10, 58.

32. Vamplew, *Pay Up*.

33. John Lowerson, "Joint Stock Companies, Capital Formation and Suburban Leisure in England, 1880–1914," in *The Economic History of Leisure: Papers Presented at the Eighth International Economic History Congress, Budapest 1982*, ed. Wray Vamplew (Adelaide, UK: Flinders University, 1982), 67; Wray Vamplew, "Concepts of Capital: An Approach Shot to the History of the British Golf Club before 1914," *Journal of Sport History* 39 (2012): 299–331.

34. Wray Vamplew, "Sharing Space," 370–371; George B. Kirsch, "Municipal Golf Courses in the United States: 1895 to 1930," *Journal of Sport History* (2005): 23–44. Riess (*Sport in Industrial America*, 9–10) sees a major promotional role in America for professional politicians and close associates whose connections provided sports entrepreneurs with protection, inside information, and preferential treatment. But this was profit-seeking, not civic, boosterism.

35. Wray Vamplew and Joyce Kay, "Beyond Altruism: British Football and Charity 1877–1914," *Soccer and Society* 11 (2010): 181–197.

36. Wray Vamplew, "Exploited Labour or Successful Workingmen: Golf Professionals and Professional Golfers in Britain Before 1914," *Economic History Review* 61 (2008): 54–79.
37. Riess, *Sport in Industrial America*, 160–161.
38. Roger Munting, "The Games Ethic and Industrial Capitalism before 1914: The Provision of Company Sports," *Sport in History* 23.1 (2003): 45–63.
39. Theo C. Barker, *The Glassmakers* (London: Weidenfeld & Nicolson, 1977), 93.
40. Michael Heller, "Sport, Bureaucracies and London Clerks 1880–1939," *International Journal of the History of Sport* 25.5 (2008): 582.
41. Brian D Bunk, "The Rise and Fall of Professional Soccer in Holyoke Massachusetts, USA," *Sport in History* 31.3 (2011): 286–287.
42. Peter Burke, "Trades Football in Melbourne 1896–1909: From Middle-Class Leisure to Working-Class Sport," *Sporting Traditions* 19.1 (2002): 1–15.
43. Hugh Hornby, *Uppies and Downies: The Extraordinary Football Games of Britain* (London: English Heritage, 2008), 154–163.

BIBLIOGRAPHY

Adelman, Melvin L. *A Sporting Time: New York City and the Rise of Modern Athletics 1820–70.* Urbana: University of Illinois Press, 1986.

Cunningham, Hugh. *Leisure in the Industrial Revolution.* London: Croom Helm, 1980.

Gorn, Elliott J., and Warren Goldstein. *A Brief History of American Sports.* New York: Hill & Wang, 1993.

Guttmann, Allen. *From Ritual to Record: The Nature of Modern Sports.* New York: Columbia University Press, 2004.

Hardy, Stephen. "Entrepreneurs, Organizations and the Sport Marketplace: Subjects in Search of Historians." *Journal of Sport History* 13 (1986): 14–33.

Harvey, Adrian. *The Beginnings of a Commercial Sporting Culture in Britain, 1793–1850.* Aldershot, UK: Ashgate, 2004.

Harvey, Adrian. *Football: The First Hundred Years.* Abingdon, UK: Routledge, 2005.

Holt, Richard. "The Amateur Body and the Middle-Class Man: Work, Health and Style in Victorian Britain." *Sport in History* 26 (2006): 352–369.

Levine, Peter. *A. G. Spalding and the Rise of Baseball.* New York: Oxford University Press, 1985.

Malcolmson, Robert. *Popular Recreations in English Society 1770–1850.* Cambridge, UK: Cambridge University Press, 1975.

Munting, Roger. "The Games Ethic and Industrial Capitalism before 1914: The Provision of Company Sports." *Sport in History* 23 (2003): 45–63.

Riess, Steven A. *Sport in Industrial America.* Wheeling, IL: Harlan Davidson, 1995.

Tranter, Neil. *Sport, Economy and Society in Britain 1750–1914.* Cambridge, UK: Cambridge University Press, 1998.

Vamplew, Wray. *Pay Up and Play the Game.* Cambridge, UK: Cambridge University Press, 2004.

CHAPTER 9

....

SPORT AND URBANIZATION

....

MICHAEL T. FRIEDMAN AND JACOB J. BUSTAD

"THE evolution of the city, more than any other single factor, influenced the development of organized sport and recreational athletic pastimes in America."[1] The process
of urbanization provided the essential infrastructure for the development of modern
sport in both the United States and Europe. Despite paeans to the virtues of rural life,
only the city offered the critical mass of potential participants, spectators, and media
outlets that enabled modern sport to emerge during the nineteenth century as both a
structured activity and a viable commercial enterprise. However, the city has been much
more than the "setting" for the development of sport but also "an organic environment
whose changing elements shaped and were shaped by sport."[2]

This dialectical relationship is evident within more than the structures of modern
sport, as sport has substantially impacted the development of the city and urban life.
With rapid urban growth overwhelming existing infrastructure, creating anxiety about
sedentary lifestyles, raising public health concerns and causing fear about public morality and civic cohesion, sport and public recreation were mobilized against these urban
ailments. As part of this response, sport and recreation were incorporated gradually
into the urban fabric through the development of major metropolitan parks, facilities
for spectator sports, small parks, playgrounds, and recreation as an important city service. Sport and recreation have also been utilized for their significant symbolic value
(although their economic value has been less than expected) as cities have used major
events, professional teams, and state-of-the-art facilities to convey status, build civic
cohesion, and promote tourism.

In analyzing the development of modern sport, discussions of urbanization are often
paired with industrialization.[3] Indeed, both processes have historically existed in a symbiotic relationship. Cities have enabled industrialization through providing efficiencies
of scale and markets for goods, while growing industries created economic opportunities that attracted migrants and accelerated urbanization. As the impacts of industrialization on the development of modern sport are discussed elsewhere in this collection,
this chapter focuses on the specific processes of urbanization within the industrial city.

The levels of urban development were different in North America and Europe in 1800, but similar urbanization processes during the nineteenth and twentieth centuries raised similar challenges in both contexts. North American cities generally developed from small, trade-oriented towns that were built on a receding frontier beginning in the seventeenth century, while many major European cities had much deeper historical legacies. However, as industrialization proceeded apace during the nineteenth and twentieth centuries, many remnants of past urban development in Europe (e.g., Paris's slums or Copenhagen's military ramparts) were transformed in response to the needs of the modern city.[4] These transformations raised fears of "exacerbating potentially disastrous breakdowns of physical health, personal morality, social stability, and cultural quality."[5] Sport and physical activity were considered among the solutions.

In this chapter, we analyze the dialectical impact between modern sport and urbanization. First, we discuss early scholarship, which presents sport as the product of urbanization, whether as a reaction to the social ills of urban life or through the opportunities created by and in the urban environment. As this unidirectional perspective has been superseded by scholarship recognizing the city's more complex interaction with sport, we examine the city–sport relationship in two time periods: 1800 to 1870 and 1870 to 1940. We discuss the emergence of modern sport within the industrializing city, the impacts of sport on the urban form, and the associations between ideas of urban citizenship and physical activity and sport. In the conclusion, we identify some of the themes in the continued dynamic relationship between cities in sport since World War II.

Sport as a Product of Urban Life

Frederic Paxson was one of the first historians to examine sport as a serious topic. Building upon Frederick Jackson Turner's 1893 thesis regarding the closing of the American frontier, Paxson argued sport had replaced the frontier as the country's safety valve by providing "a partial substitute for pioneer life" and enabling the "continued bearable existence under increasing pressure generated in industrial society." Recognizing "city congestion stimulated the need [for sport] at this immediate moment" while providing numerous examples that identified the city as the locus of sport participation, spectatorship, innovation, and organization, Paxson refused to credit urbanization as a factor in the development of modern sport writing, "without the cities the transition must any way have occurred." [6]

Paxson's positioning of sport as a reaction to the negatives of urban life dominated scholarship examining the relationship between sport and urbanization over the next half-century. Betts challenged the anti-urban view by stating, "industrialization and urbanization ... were more fundamentally responsible for the changes and developments in sports [between 1850 and 1900] than any other cause."[7] As the city was the center for manufacturing, a magnet for immigration with large populations, Betts argued that modern American sport developed as both a product of and reaction to urbanization, with cities providing critical masses of participants, spectators, mass media, and reform organizations advocating sports to address social problems. This "urban paradigm"—the view that sport is a product of urban life—dominated sport historiography until it was challenged in the 1980s by work examining the impacts of sport upon the processes of city-building.[8] Adelman argued the urban paradigm was limited by examining "'urban' in the context of 'site' rather than 'process'; hence, the city emerges merely as the setting for the transformation of sport."[9] The urban paradigm oversimplified the city–sport relationship by reducing sport to a function of urban growth and denying space's active role in structuring (and being structured by) social relations.

SPORT AS A PRODUCT AND PRODUCER OF URBAN LIFE

Moving beyond the older urban paradigm, the work pioneered by Hardy, Adelman, and Riess has sought to understand how sport and urbanization have transformed one another. In *How Boston Played*, Hardy asked, "how were sport and recreation a part of the particular process of city-building in Boston?"[10] Adelman's *A Sporting Time* examined the modernization of sport within New York City by focusing on the "relationship between urban change and sport change."[11] In *City Games*, Riess considered the relationship between urbanization and sport from a "dual perspective" that examined the intertwined processes of sport development and urban development.

Urbanization and Sport, 1800–1870

Between 1800 and 1870, cities in North America and Europe transformed into mature, capitalist-oriented industrial manufacturing centers. The emergence of modern sport in this era is not coincidental as Adelman argued the emergence of capitalism and its evolving production system "required a new division of urban space based solely on the criteria of economic utility and value.[12] Following these criteria, public spaces that previously had multiple and undefined uses were developed for specific residential, commercial, and industrial use.[13] These rapid spatial changes were accompanied by significant social challenges for foreign immigrants (in the case of the United States) and rural migrants (in both the United States and Europe), many of whom were young, unaccompanied males requiring integration into urban life. The rapid pace of change also raised concerns about public health and morality as population density, slum conditions, pollution, and the loss of open spaces were associated with sedentary lifestyles, epidemics, and a vibrant tavern culture.

If "sport would be made to pay its way"[14] within the modernizing city, traditional recreational activities were restructured to provide tangible social and economic value. Baseball's early development between 1845 and 1860 in New York was driven by middle-class men, who played to improve physical health, engage in "respectable" forms of leisure and sociability, and demonstrate self-control and masculinity.[15] The commercialization of sports such as boxing, baseball, and harness racing in the United States was also an urban phenomenon. Cities, which provided a critical mass of potential spectators, a media involved in sport promotion, and entrepreneurs recognizing growing public interest, were central to the commercialization of sport.

Within cities, taverns were important sites for the development of commercialized sport and a central element within a working-class urban culture that included billiard parlors, gambling halls, volunteer fire companies, dance parlors, and brothels. Urban reformers believed these activities and industrial work created cities that were increasingly unhealthy, immoral, and dangerous. To redirect urban residents away from "immoral" amusements and improve urban health, reformers advocated participation in vigorous, structured, and organized sports activities. Reformers also advocated for the creation of such natural spaces as parks which would provide pastoral tranquility into industrializing cities.[16] Reformers also considered sport an important tool for the integration of migrants and diverse ethnicities into a unified urban culture.

Urbanization and Sport, 1870–1940

As urbanization between 1800 and 1870 provided the context enabling the development of modern sport, a more interactive relationship between sport and urbanization existed between 1870 and 1940. Referring to urbanization in the United States, Riess described the primary differences between the cities of the two time periods as increased physical size and population, an economy based on industry rather than trade, and, most importantly, highly specialized land uses with distinct commercial, residential, and industrial zones.[17]

As in the previous period, urbanization continued to shape sport due to the city's concentration of potential athletes, spectators, and media. Sport's impact upon urban life grew as stadiums, arenas, public parks, playgrounds, and gymnasiums were integrated into the urban fabric and public policy. This period included the beginning of public funding of spectator stadiums for prestige and economic purposes, the development of "natural" spaces to improve public health and the provision of public recreation programs toward integrating migrants into urban culture and improving public morality.

The City and the Development of Commercialized Sport

The commercialization of sport accelerated within the industrialized city, with increasing numbers of urban residents consuming recreation, social reformers using sport to integrate the children of (im)migrants into urban culture, and the media industry using sport to increase circulation. Although only a few sports facilities for spectator sport were developed before the mid-nineteenth century, numerous arenas, gymnasiums, stadiums, and racetracks were built later.[18] Urban reformers, municipal governments, and institutions developed formal recreation and physical education programs for children that later produced many professional athletes. With sports as an important source of content, cities also featured intense competition between newspapers for circulation and the emergence of radio and movies.

Most of the commercial sports facilities built between 1870 and 1940 were privately financed and located within major cities. In the United States, outdoor stadiums and horse tracks were often built on the urban periphery, where land was "relatively inexpensive and where the neighborhood was either underdeveloped or middle class."[19] These locations were close to mass transit, which, by the early twentieth century, was affordable to all but the poorest urban dwellers. In Great Britain, football clubs were neighborhood-based with grounds located in close proximity to the club's working-class supporters and transportation links.[20] Continental Europe offered another model as stadiums were designed for multiple purposes, often featuring running tracks and such other sports facilities as gymnasiums and tennis courts located in close proximity.

"Participation and success in professional sport were functions of class, ethnicity, size, and urban space,"[21] with boxers and baseball players disproportionately born in major cities through 1940. Although baseball's rural mythology suggested that boys in small towns and farms had more room to practice and play, urban youth enjoyed a higher quality of competition and access to better coaching. Urban reformers unintentionally abetted this process by providing facilities for sport and sponsoring organized competitions.

The media were important to the early development of commercial sport. In this later period, however, sport conversely featured prominently as part of an intense competition for readership. Oriard suggests that this struggle was a prominent part of the emergence of American football, as newspapers spectacularized the sport by devoting increasing amounts of coverage toward promoting and analyzing the games and surrounding events.[22] To attract readers, newspapers established separate sports sections and prominently featured sports content within extra editions. Bale describes the British media's similarly important role in the growth of soccer with widely circulated sports newspapers, and "by the 1890s, few towns of any size in England were without their 'football special,' published for Saturday evening reading."[23]

The Impact of Commercialized Sport on Urban Form, Cohesion, and Image

As the commercialization of sport intensified, civic leaders recognized its potential to project positive images of their cities to external audiences and diverse local constituencies. In the United States, direct public investment in spectator sports began during the 1920s as municipal governments sought to encourage economic development. In Europe, sporting facilities were occasionally part of the public provision of social services. Everywhere sports teams and events became focal points for urban identity, promotion, and communal cohesion, with teams used to project "sophisticated and progressive" images of urban development. Events were utilized to attract tourism and favorable media coverage.

Although the earliest baseball stadiums were spartan and utilitarian, the privately financed concrete-and-steel stadiums of the early twentieth century were built with ornate designs that promoted and celebrated their cities, as team owners were often involved with dominant political machines and recognized the advantages of their facilities for serving political ends.[24] With the largest capacities of any semipublic space within urban areas, stadiums hosted a variety of events beyond sports, including papal masses, revival meetings, public celebrations, and music concerts. Although entrepreneurs envisioned large profits from locating businesses, such as restaurants, taverns, and souvenirs in close proximity to stadiums, the overall impacts on local neighborhoods were much less than anticipated. Riess suggests stadiums in general had "relatively little impact on sites that were previously underdeveloped, other than to publicize them and promote confidence in future growth."[25]

The economic impacts of sports facilities may have fallen short of expectations, but teams and stadiums often became focal points for civic cohesion. In this regard, the Brooklyn Dodgers were "a cultural totem, a tangible symbol of the community and its values" for many residents of Brooklyn[26] with the team's 1957 relocation remaining to this day a traumatic incident for the borough. Similarly, Hardy recognized that athletes, such as John L. Sullivan, Jack Johnson, and Francis Ouimet, served as focal points for collective identification within Boston.[27]

SPORT AND URBAN CITIZENSHIP

As the process of urbanization transformed the city, sport became an important element in efforts to promote physical fitness, bodily health, and urban citizenship. For reform-minded individuals and groups, it was a potentially useful "tool" in their efforts to cultivate urban citizens with appropriate moral attributes and civic attitudes. However, at the same time broader forces and elites were shaping the development of commercial sport and public recreation policies. The urban "masses" were themselves practicing and shaping sport forms through their own involvement.

The British context evinces a distinct relationship between both domestic and foreign populations and sport during urbanization. English sporting practices retained characteristics of traditional activities while encountering other cultures from locations throughout the empire.[28] However, even as traditional games transformed into modern sports, British sporting practices were essentially male and marked by stratified social class structures dividing the aristocracy from the working class. These institutionalized class divisions reflected and perpetuated differences in sporting activity, both within Great Britain and among colonial populations.

Immigration, Migration, and Urban Sport

While the early-twentieth-century Reform Movement in the United States may represent the most prominent advocates linking sport and physical activity with notions of citizenship, the ideologies and values of Jacksonian America (1830s) contributed to the contouring of sport along nationalist ideals. There was a concerted effort to link sport with the development of proper citizens. This endeavor focused on developing forms of urban community and citizenship, which were often made complex by the continual arrival of foreign immigrants with their own preferences and sporting practices.

Experiences of immigration and assimilation into American (sporting) culture varied with differences based on the cultural similarities and dissimilarities between (im) migrant groups and the dominant Anglo-Saxon culture as well as the generational changes within ethnic communities. For English and Scottish immigrants, their traditional sport cultures often "dissipated" as they quickly adopted familiar "nativist" American sporting forms. Alternatively, German immigrants tended to preserve their traditional activities through *Turnverein*, which were social clubs promoting the German tradition of gymnastics. Riess highlighted that these cultural differences often were generational with many immigrants attempting to maintain their native cultures, while their children recognized American sport forms as an opportunity to "prove they were real Americans and not greenhorns."[29]

Describing Boston at the end of the nineteenth century, Hardy suggested different ethnic and class groups used sport for specific social goals.[30] Similar to other cities, Bostonians configured sport toward promoting forms of social inclusion within ethnic communities and advancing certain forms of leisure as alternatives to illegal, unhealthy, and socially detrimental practices, such as gambling and drinking. Social elites created sporting spaces for their own and for public use as they specified particular activities for these spaces. In doing so, elites sought to reproduce their own class position and define proper social practices for all groups.

In Great Britain, sport similarly defined urban citizenship in this period as British elites recognized the necessity for the working class to engage in "productive" social activities. With British and imperial sporting practices predicated on social standing, urban elites shared their sport developed in boarding schools and universities with the working masses in order to achieve productive and assimilatory goals. As the processes of industrialization made previous activities incongruent with changing patterns of life and work, the traditional games of feudal culture were replaced by "modern" sports more appropriate for urban life.

Notions of urban citizenship promoted through national sport cultures were thus integral in the emergence of *sporting nationalisms*. Cronin and Mayall describe sport and physical activity as primary venues for the construction of group and individual identities along axes of difference (e.g., national identity, ethnicity, racial formations, gender, and sexuality).[31] Throughout the late nineteenth and early twentieth centuries, urban sport forms allowed immigrant populations to modify their cultural difference and assimilate into dominant American culture and thus make claims for citizenship. However, urban sport also functioned to exclude individuals and groups based on these same differences. Jewish immigrants into New York City around 1900 found that sport was used both to challenge and to reinforce the cultural and social exclusion of Jews.[32] As immigrant groups were often perceived as racial threats, in both biological and cultural terms, sport was expected to assimilate immigrants into dominant cultural institutions and practices while paradoxically promoting social exclusion through ethnically segregated practices.

While foreign immigration to America's cities was a prominent characteristic of US urbanization, migration of domestic rural populations was a challenge in both the United States and Europe. The Great Migration of African Americans from the rural South to the industrial cities of the northern, midwestern, and western United States featured the relocation of more than one million citizens between 1910 and the mid-1930s.[33] While the urban sporting experiences of these migrants were similar to those of foreign immigrants, they also evinced distinct forms of exclusion and discrimination based in the racial logics of early-twentieth-century American society.[34] In any case, expanding and culturally diverse urban populations presented numerous challenges as problems of cultural assimilation were matched with concerns regarding health and morality. Just as sport helped assimilate diverse populations, it was also recognized as a solution to these problems.

Physical Activity, Health, and Urban Citizenship

The Reform Movement of the late nineteenth and early twentieth centuries impacted not only the American political arena but also the physical lives and experiences of many urban denizens. The movement centered on progressive ideas of educating the "masses" into becoming an appropriate American public with each individual possessing particular characteristics and values of citizenship. Similar ideas existed within British and European settings as the development of particular forms of physical activity were important elements in the emergence of a specific type of urban *governance* over populations and individuals.

Davis suggests the Reform Movement's original concerns about education allowed issues of moral and physical health to be easily incorporated, as it was "a logical step from kindergartens to campaigns for public playgrounds."[35] Health reformers emphasized the dual role of sports as both a physiological and a spiritual educational tool. They recognized the potential of sport and physical activity to encourage character, fitness, and integrity. This view positioned "play" as a waste of otherwise productive time due to its unstructured and unsupervised nature.[36] Individual reformers and reform-oriented institutions sought to influence the development of urban sport and physical cultures. They did so by creating spaces to promote specific forms of "play." These efforts included the work of Jane Addams (whose Hull House organization organized the first public playground in Chicago in 1893), Luther Gulick, and G. Stanley Hall. These three reformers held differing political and social views, but all were concerned with establishing spaces for mental, physical, and moral education, especially in the increasingly congested and unregulated spaces of the growing city.

The development of public parks and open, green spaces also involved the concerns for public hygiene, health, and well-being, often tied to ideas of citizenship. Gagen explains that the formation and maintenance of these "everyday spaces of physical culture" are primary markers of reformers' efforts to assert social control and regulate populations.[37] While these efforts were progressive insofar as the physical spaces of playgrounds and parks were accompanied by an understanding of their "public" nature, the activities within the spaces were highly circumscribed.[38] As the City Beautiful Movement of the early twentieth century spread, public parks became important elements of urban policy.

The movement toward designing public urban spaces for physical activity and sport were matched by efforts to design appropriate citizen-producing programs and activities. Already fueled by health concerns regarding growing urban populations, the promotion and evaluation of physical fitness increased further after World War I. Cultural linkages between physical fitness and citizenship—including and emphasizing military action—were entrenched within reinvigorated forms of nationalism in United States and Europe.[39] American urban residents were subjected to new standards regarding the ways individuals and groups were or were not deemed physically "fit" for citizenship. Numerous programs were instituted to cultivate forms of physical and moral certitude. Park examines the ways in which scientific evidence was utilized to justify social policy initiatives at the federal, state, and municipal levels that promoted healthy lifestyles through physical fitness.[40]

Conclusion

The development of modern sport is inseparable from urbanization. Cities provided the concentrations of participants, audiences, media, and affluence that were all essential ingredients for modern sports to evolve. While the urban environment may be the crucible in which modern sport was forged, that development redounded upon the city. As the process of urbanization transformed people's lives, sport and recreation helped to improve urban life through public parks, playgrounds, recreation centers, and facilities for spectator sports. Sport helped to integrate the millions of migrants moving into cities from rural area and/or other countries by providing focal points for the development of a collective urban identity.

Since 1940, the relationship between urbanization and sport has evolved in different directions. The trends of suburbanization, deindustrialization, and disinvestment that have redefined urban areas since World War II have led to the relocation of professional sports franchises to suburbs, the evolution of downtown areas with easy highway access, and the emergence of very different kinds of cities in the American South and West.[41] The relationship between local governments and sports teams has changed with increased expectation that new sports facilities should receive public financing, with teams and events becoming more important to urban boosters as they have attempted to demonstrate the growing importance or continuing relevance of their cities.[42] More recently, increased public investments in sports facilities and events have coincided with decreased investments in public recreation and the closure or privatization of facilities.

Today, the global urban population is over 50 percent (and rising), and more than 70 percent of Americans and Europeans live within cities and their surrounding suburbs. While sport has evolved into a high-profile, multimedia global product, it is still tightly enmeshed with the processes of urbanization. The city remains a center for spectatorship as large audiences attend games and broader communities continue to support their teams. Games and events are transmitted through the media to global audiences. Involvement in physical activity through programs focused on youth, adult, and senior bodily health and well-being has grown. New sporting forms, such as skateboarding and its commercialized forms, have emerged from and make use of the urban context. Given this continuing symbiotic relationship, examining the role of urbanization in the development of sport remains an important and ongoing undertaking.

Notes

1. Steven Riess, *City Games: The Evolution of American Urban Society and the Rise of Sports* (Urbana: University of Illinois Press, 1989), 1.

2. Riess, *City Games*, 2; Melvin Adelman, *A Sporting Time: New York City and the Rise of Modern Athletics, 1820–70* (Urbana: University of Illinois Press, 1986).

3. John Betts, "Technological Revolution and the Rise of Sports, 1850-1900," *Mississippi Valley Historical Review* 40 (1953), 231-256; Benjamin Rader, *American Sports: From the Age of Folk Games to the Age of Televised Sports*, 5th edition (Upper Saddle River, NJ: Prentice Hall, 2014).

4. Jim Toft, "The Copenhagen Idraetsparken: From Democratic Institution to Private Enterprise," in *The Stadium and the City*, ed. John Bale and Olof Moen (Keele, UK: Keele University Press, 1995), 59-80.

5. Andrew Lees, "Urban Development in European and American Discourse in the Nineteenth and Early Twentieth Centuries," *OAH Magazine of History* 5(3), 38.

6. Frederic Paxson, "Rise of Sport," *Mississippi Valley Historical Review* 4.2 (1917): 143–168.

7. Betts, "Technological Revolution and Rise of Sports, 1850–1900," 231.

8. Stephen Hardy, "Sport in Urbanizing America," *Journal of Urban History* 23.6 (1997): 675–708.

9. Adelman, *Sporting Time*, 7.

10. Stephen Hardy, *How Boston Played: Sport, Recreation, and Community, 1865–1915* (Boston: Northeastern University Press, 1982), 17.

11. Adelman, *Sporting Time*, 1.

12. Adelman, *Sporting Time*, 7.

13. John Bale, *Sport, Space, and the City* (Caldwell, NJ: Blackburn Press, 2001).

14. John Bale, *Landscapes of Modern Sport* (Leicester, UK: Leicester University Press, 1994), 28.

15. Warren Goldstein, Playing for Keeps: A History of Early Baseball (Ithaca, NY: Cornell University Press,1989), 4.

16. Mark Dyreson, "Nature by Design: Modern American Ideas About Sport, Energy, Evolution, and Republics, 1865-1920," *Journal of Sport History* 26 (1999), 461.

17. Riess, *City Games*.

18. Xavier Pujadas, "Sport, Space and the Social Construction of the Modern City: The Urban Impact of Sports Involvement in Barcelona (1870–1923)," *The International Journal of the History of Sport* 29.14 (2012): 1963–1980; Riess, *City Games*.

19. Riess, *City Games*, 220.

20. Bale, *Sport, Space, and the City*.

21. Riess, *City Games*, 86.

22. Michael Oriard, *Reading Football: How the Popular Press Created an American Spectacle* (Chapel Hill: University of North Carolina Press, 1993).

23. John Bale, *Sport and Place: A Geography of Sport in England, Scotland and Wales* (London: C. Hurst & Company, 1982), 25.

24. Neil Sullivan, *The Diamond in the Bronx: Yankee Stadium and the Politics of New York* (New York, Oxford University Press, 2001).

25. Riess, *City Games*, 6.

26. Neil Sullivan, *The Dodgers Move West* (New York: Oxford University Press, 1987), 18.

27. Hardy, *How Boston Played*.

28. Dennis Brailsford, *British Sport: A Social History* (Cambridge, England: Lutterworth, 1992).

29. Riess, *Sport in Industrial America*, 83.

30. Hardy, *How Boston Played*.

31. Michael Cronin and David Mayall, eds., *Sporting Nationalisms: Ethnicity, Immigration and Assimilation* (London: Frank Cass, 1998).

32. Peter Levine, *Ellis Island to Ebbets Field: Sport and the American Jewish Experience* (New York: Oxford University Press, 1992).

33. Davarian Baldwin, *Chicago's New Negroes: Modernity, the Great Migration, and Black Urban Life* (Chapel Hill: University of North Carolina Press, 2007); James Gregory, *The Southern Diaspora: How the Great Migrations of Black and White Southerners Transformed America* (Chapel Hill: University of North Carolina Press, 2005).

34. David Wiggins, "From Plantation to Playing Field: Historical Writings on the Black Athlete in American Sport," *Research Quarterly* 57 (1986): 101–116.

35. Allen Davis, *Spearheads for Reform: The Social Settlements and the Progressive Movement, 1890–1914* (New Brunswick, NJ: Rutgers University Press, 1984), 60.

36. Riess, *City Games.*

37. Elizabeth Gagen, "Making American Flesh: Physicality and Nationhood in Early Twentieth-Century Physical Education Reform," *Cultural Geographies* 11 (2004): 417–442.

38. Gagen, "Making American Flesh"; Dyreson, "Nature by Design," 447–469.

39. Steven Pope, "An Army of Athletes: Playing Fields, Battlefields, and the American Military Sporting Experience, 1880–1920," *Journal of Military History* 59.3 (1995): 435–456.

40. Roberta Park, "Setting the Scene—Bridging the Gap between Knowledge and Practice: When Americans Really Built Programmes to Foster Healthy Lifestyles, 1918–1940," *The International Journal of the History of Sport* 25 (2008): 1427–1452.

41. Michael Lomax, "Stadiums, Boosters, Politicians and Major League Baseball's Reluctance to Expand: An Exploration of Post-Second World War US Trends," *The International Journal of the History of Sport* 25 (2008): 1511–1528; Riess, *City Games;* Maureen Smith, "From 'the Finest Ballpark in America' to 'the Jewel of the Waterfront': The Construction of San Francisco's Major League Baseball Stadiums," *The International Journal of the History of Sport* 25 (2008): 1529–1546.

42. George Lipsitz, "Sports Stadia and Urban Development: A Tale of Three Cities," *Journal of Sport and Social Issues* 8.2 (1984): 1–18; Glen Gendzel, "Competitive Boosterism: How Milwaukee Lost the Braves," *Business History Review* 69.4 (1995): 530–566; Peter Richmond, *Ballpark: Camden Yards and the Building of an American Dream* (New York: Simon & Schuster, 1993); Phillip Suchma, "If They Built It? Stadium Dreams and Rustbelt Realities in Cleveland," *The International Journal of the History of Sport* 25 (2008): 1547–1564.

BIBLIOGRAPHY

Adelman, Melvin. *A Sporting Time: New York City and the Rise of Modern Athletics, 1820–70.* Urbana: University of Illinois Press, 1986.

Baldwin, Davarian. *Chicago's New Negroes: Modernity, the Great Migration, and Black Urban Life.* Chapel Hill: University of North Carolina Press, 2007.

Bale, John. *Sport, Space, and the City.* Caldwell, NJ: Blackburn Press, 2001.

Betts, John. *America's Sporting Heritage: 1850–1950.* Reading, MA: Addison-Wesley, 1974.

Brailsford, Dennis. *British Sport: A Social History.* Cambridge, England: Lutterworth, 1992.

Cavallo, Dominick. *Muscles and Morals: Organized Playgrounds and Urban Reform, 1880–1920.* Philadelphia: University of Pennsylvania Press, 1981.

Cranz, Galen. *The Politics of Park Design: A History of Urban Parks in America.* Cambridge, MA: MIT Press, 1982.

Cronin, Michael, and David Mayall, eds. *Sporting Nationalisms: Ethnicity, Immigration and Assimilation.* London: Frank Cass, 1998.

Davis, Allen. *Spearheads for Reform: The Social Settlements and the Progressive Movement, 1890–1914.* New Brunswick, NJ: Rutgers University Press, 1985.

Dyreson, Mark. "The Emergence of Consumer Culture and the Transformation of Physical Culture: American Sport in the 1920s." *Journal of Sport History* 16.3 (1989): 261–281.

Gems, Gerald. *The Athletic Crusade: Sport and American Cultural Imperialism.* Lincoln: University of Nebraska Press, 2006.

Gershman, Michael. *Diamonds: The Evolution of the Ballpark from Elysian Fields to Camden Yards.* Boston: Houghton Mifflin, 1993.

Goldstein, Warren. *Playing for Keeps: A History of Early Baseball.* Ithaca, NY: Cornell University Press, 1989.

Gorn, Elliott. *The Manly Art: Bare-Knuckle Prize Fighting in America.* Ithaca, NY: Cornell University Press, 1986.

Gregory, James. *The Southern Diaspora: How the Great Migrations of Black and White Southerners Transformed America.* Chapel Hill: University of North Carolina Press, 2005.

Hardy, Stephen. *How Boston Played: Sport, Recreation, and Community, 1865–1915.* Boston, MA: Northeastern University Press.

Levine, Peter. *Ellis Island to Ebbets Field: Sport and the American Jewish Experience.* New York: Oxford University Press, 1992.

Lipsitz, George. "Sports Stadia and Urban Development: A Tale of Three Cities." *Journal of Sport and Social Issues* 8.2 (1984): 1–18.

Lomax, Michael. "Stadiums, Boosters, Politicians and Major League Baseball's Reluctance to Expand: An Exploration of Post-Second World War US Trends." *The International Journal of the History of Sport* 25 (2008): 1511–1528.

Oriard, Michael. *Reading Football: How the Popular Press Created an American Spectacle.* Chapel Hill: University of North Carolina Press, 1993.

Park, Roberta. "Setting the Scene—Bridging the Gap between Knowledge and Practice: When Americans Really Built Programmes to Foster Healthy Lifestyles, 1918–1940." *The International Journal of the History of Sport* 25 (2008): 1427–1452.

Pope, Steven. "An Army of Athletes: Playing Fields, Battlefields, and the American Military Sporting Experience, 1880–1920." *Journal of Military History* 59.3 (1995): 435–456.

Pujadas, Xavier. "Sport, Space and the Social Construction of the Modern City: The Urban Impact of Sports Involvement in Barcelona (1870–1923)." *The International Journal of the History of Sport* 29.14 (2012): 1963–1980.

Rader, Benjamin. *American Sports: From the Age of Folk Games to the Age of Televised Sports.* 5th ed. Upper Saddle River, NJ: Prentice Hall, 2004.

Richmond, Peter. *Ballpark: Camden Yards and the Building of an American Dream.* New York: Simon & Schuster, 1993.

Riess, Steven. *City Games: The Evolution of American Urban Society and the Rise of Sports.* Urbana: University of Illinois Press, 1989.

Riess, Steven. *Sport in Industrial America, 1850–1920.* Wheeling, IL: Harlan Davidson, 1995.

Riess, Steven. *Touching Base: Professional Baseball and American Culture in the Progressive Era.* Rev. ed. Urbana: University of Illinois Press, 1999.

Smith, Maureen. "From 'the Finest Ballpark in America' to 'the Jewel of the Waterfront': The Construction of San Francisco's Major League Baseball Stadiums." *The International Journal of the History of Sport* 25 (2008): 1529–1546.

Somers, Dale. *The Rise of Sports in New Orleans, 1850–1900.* Baton Rouge: Louisiana State University Press, 1972.

Suchma, Phillip. "If They Built It? Stadium Dreams and Rustbelt Realities in Cleveland." *The International Journal of the History of Sport* 25 (2008): 1547–1564.

Sullivan, Neil. *The Diamond in the Bronx: Yankee Stadium and the Politics of New York.* New York: Oxford University Press, 2001.

Sullivan, Neil. *The Dodgers Move West.* New York: Oxford University Press, 1987.

Toft, Jim. "The Copenhagen Idraetsparken: From Democratic Institution to Private Enterprise." In *The Stadium and the City,* edited by John Bale and Olof Moen, 59–80. Keele, UK: Keele University Press, 1995.

Trumpbour, Robert. *The New Cathedrals: Politics and Media in the History of Stadium Construction.* Syracuse, NY: Syracuse University Press, 2007.

Wiggins, David. "From Plantation to Playing Field: Historical Writings on the Black Athlete in American Sport." *Research Quarterly* 57 (1986): 101–116.

CHAPTER 10

....

COMMUNICATIONS
AND JOURNALISM

....

JOHN CARVALHO

URBANIZATION, industrialization, and changing cultural norms concerning religion, recreation, and the body have interacted for more than two hundred years to shape modern sport. Mass media have played an integral role in that process. The emerging media of the nineteenth century profoundly influenced the growth of sport and in turn were influenced by the very changes they had helped create in sport.

Before the Industrial Revolution, the organization, consumption, and documentation of organized sports were primarily pursuits of the upper classes. Among the first mentions of sports in news-related publications were reports of Charles II and his court observing a wrestling match in 1681 and a cockfight in 1683—both described in *The Loyal Protestant*, a court journal. For the middle and lower classes, energy and time were directed toward more pressing concerns of daily survival, within a rugged and more rural society without the technological advances that would emerge. Participation in sports was also discouraged by Puritan religious values that considered sports a morally destructive distraction from matters of hard work and religious devotion. Even so, the *Boston Gazette* reported on a boxing match in 1733—one of the first mentions of a sporting event in a colonial newspaper.

Soon after, publications devoted to sports began appearing in England and the United States. It is not surprising that these journals were aimed at the upper classes. The first publication dealing with sports only was the English Jockey Club's *Racing Calendar*. It was started in 1751 to inform club members about upcoming races and included information on racing rules. This is an example of one of the first important functions of early sports publications: to help in the codifying of rules within sports.

The first acknowledged sports periodical to a more general audience was *The Sporting Magazine*, published in England beginning in 1793 by John Wheble. The magazine resembled today's aggregated sports news Web sites. Its content was mainly provided by readers who attended sporting events of the time, not Wheble, who added accounts reprinted from local newspapers. To extend the comparison, Wheble also allowed his contributors to debate each other on sports content within their pages, much like comments posted on Web sites. Despite the title, Wheble also included news of crime, sometimes graphic, in his attempts to draw readers.

At this point, newspapers in England began devoting a section specifically to sports—an innovation that would not happen in the United States for several decades. The *Morning Herald* introduced its sports section in 1818, with the *Globe* following a year later. Even the conservative *London Times* was publishing a sports page by 1829.

A popular and recognized sports journalist of the era was Pierce Egan, who first gained fame among sports fans with his multi-volume book *Boxiana*, an authoritative guide to boxing that was published in the 1810s and 1820s. Eventually Egan, who published a *Life in London* periodical, yielded to the demands of sports enthusiasts and renamed his journal *Pierce Egan's Life in London and Sporting Guide* in 1824. His journal was actually preceded by *Bell's Life in London* (1822), which included sports among the lively pursuits chronicled in its pages, but Egan's magazine is noteworthy for its publisher's higher profile within sport. Both journals were written by gentlemen for an upper-class audience, many of whom were seeking information to help them in betting on horse races and prizefights. In 1827, Egan's publication merged with *Bell's*, and it continued publishing until the mid-1880s. Egan turned his attention back to other writing pursuits and published *Pierce Egan's Book of Sports and Mirror of Life* in 1832.

In the United States, *American Turf Register and Sporting Magazine* (1829) is credited as being the first American sporting magazine. Not surprising given the title, the magazine mainly covered horse racing and horse breeding, though topics also included fishing and hunting. As in Great Britain, in the United States coverage reflected the continued influence of the upper classes on sports content, as these represented their favored pursuits.

The first successful sports publication, however, was William T. Porter's *Spirit of the Times* (1831), which was patterned after Egan's *Life in London*—covering sports, entertainment, and literature. As John Rickards Betts has noted, Porter was careful to avoid political controversy, however, considering it a threat to circulation and profitability. The sports covered by the *Spirit* included cricket, foot racing, yachting, and, later, baseball. Its most popular writer was Henry William Herbert, who, under the pseudonym of Frank Forester, was the first popular sports magazine writer in the United States. Herbert used the pseudonym to protect his greater aspirations as a novelist, but sports writing turned out to be a more successful vocation. He published articles and popular books on hunting, fishing, and horse racing. Porter purchased the *American Turf Register* in 1839, and his *Spirit* enjoyed success until the 1860s.

The first sports magazine in France imported the English word directly into its title: *Le Sport*. Established in 1854 by Eugene Chapuis, its subtitle identified it as *journal des gens du monde*. The phrase *gens du monde* has the connotation of identifying the fashionable "people of the world" (*gens du monde*). The magazine reflected that in its coverage of such sports as horse racing, hunting, shooting, yachting, dog racing, and even chess.

As the century progressed, several forces interacted to create the setting for increased interest in sports and sports journalism. The dominant historical narrative regarding this growth was first articulated in a pioneering 1953 *American Quarterly* article by John Betts, who documented the interrelationship among industrialization, technological innovation, urbanization, education, and the rise of sport in the nineteenth and early twentieth centuries. Building on Betts's foundation, other writers such as Michael Oriard, Robert McChesney, and Tony Mason have enhanced the analysis by examining the role of culture, ideology, and consumerism in the developing relationship between media and sport.

In the mid-nineteenth century, spurred by the popularity of "Penny Press" newspapers in urban areas and commitments to public education that promoted both reading and physical fitness, literacy filtered down through the middle classes. Sports journalism was one beneficiary of the trend. Economic forces unleashed by the Industrial Revolution also enhanced the symbiosis between sports, media, and culture, as sports provided not only a means for athletes and promoters to earn money but also promotional and human resource–related opportunities for industries, teaching values like teamwork and hard work. As work conditions improved, the increase in leisure time allowed for greater attention to sport, whether spectator or participant. Crucial to this equation was the rise of the industrialized cities of the mid-eighteenth century—which caused the audiences for both sport and media to grow.

Middle class–supported spectator sports, more than upper class–supported participant sports, benefited from the rise of the city, mainly because of a lack of opportunities to exercise in the crowded cities. Indeed, while progressives throughout the ensuing decades would promote the ideal of sports competition for developing character and health, at this point participant sports were still reserved mainly for the upper-class members who had the leisure time available for such pursuits. Enthusiasts from the lower economic classes would mainly watch and read about it, though as the century progressed, they too began to take advantage of the exercise opportunities. As these migrating city residents left behind the traditional ties to family, sports team loyalty emerged as one force uniting the residents of cities, promoted by newspapers that found this an advantageous narrative.

In the 1840s, activist publishers such as Horace Greeley of the *New York Tribune* faced an internal ethical debate. They expressed skepticism toward such sports as boxing and a general concern about the sports mania they saw permeating their cultures but could not ignore the potential profits from running sports news. As a result, many newspapers would criticize America's sports obsession on their editorial pages, even as their sportswriters covered championship fights and horse races. By contrast, publishers such as James Gordon Bennett of the *New York Herald* grasped the potential of sports for building audiences early on, unapologetically highlighting such sports as boxing, trotting, and thoroughbred horse racing.

Such was the relationship between sport and media that Henry Chadwick, a reporter for the *New York Clipper* sports magazine, is called the "father of baseball." The title recognizes his role in helping to codify and promote the new sport. Besides the basic rules and organization, Chadwick helped in the development of a scorecard system that still serves as the foundation for the sport today. He later wrote for *The New York Times* and *Tribune* before joining the *Herald* as its baseball writer in 1862.

He also wrote a popular book, *The Game of Baseball: How to Learn It, How to Play It, and How to Teach It*, which was published in 1868. In his writings to promote the game to a younger audience, Chadwick reflected the "brains versus brawn" debate that has endured within most sports. He advocated smart, controlled play marked by singles and strategic base running as opposed to the home run and brash play of more emotional players. Chadwick reflected a familiar theme of sports books in the nineteenth century: the focus on younger readers and the use of sports to educate them on life principles.

New technologies such as the telegraph also increased interest in sports. Before the telegraph, publications could cover only local events in a timely manner, relying on the mail or other newspapers to bring delayed information on distant events. Within ten years of the telegraph's introduction, Bennett's newspaper was using the emergent technology to develop a constantly updated narrative on a championship boxing match between Yankee Sullivan and Tom Hyer. Enterprising newspapers also used the telegraph to provide sports fans with developments on distant sporting events, updating baseball scores on bulletin boards outside their offices as crowds of fans awaited the results. Some newspaper offices enhanced the experience for fans by providing visual depictions of game developments on large bulletin boards. One newspaper even recruited local armed forces members to reenact the game, based on information gathered over the wires. Some poolrooms and saloons even installed telegraph receiving sets, the better to keep their patrons (mainly sports bettors) updated on results. The laying of the Atlantic cable in 1866 allowed news of international athletic contests to be transmitted with equivalent speed.

Improvements in transportation, particularly railroads, also helped make sports more popular. Whether transporting fans to distant sporting events, athletes to events in urban centers, or even well-known horses on "barnstorming tours," the steam locomotive (and, to a lesser degree, the steamship) benefitted from and contributed to rising sports interest. Media accounts of transportation wonders and their role in sporting events increased interest in the events themselves.

Perhaps the most aggressive and successful promoter of sports content in the mid-1800s was the *National Police Gazette*. The *Gazette* had been founded in 1845 by George Wilkes, who turned his attention to his own version of *Spirit of the Times* after purchasing it from Porter in 1856. Richard Kyle Fox bought the *Gazette* in 1877, and under his leadership it became the widest selling sports magazine in the country. His lurid tales of crime and adulterous affairs caused many vendors to refuse to sell the publication, and he was constantly in trouble with censoring government agencies. But his emphasis on sports, particularly boxing, in addition to his successful marketing to such male-dominated gathering places as barbershops and bars, pushed his nationwide circulation to as much as 400,000 when an important prize fight was featured.

Betts traced the emergence of mass-circulation sports magazines like *Sporting Life* and *Sporting News* in the United States during this period. They, like Fox's publication, used sports news to build a readership that was mostly male, in contrast to magazines popular with females, such as *Godey's Picture Book*. Specific magazines devoted to sports like baseball, hunting, and even cycling thrived during this period. Popular titles included the outdoor magazine *Outing*, which wrote about camping and travel, and *Wheelman*, one of several magazines to capitalize on the cycling craze of the late nineteenth century. From the period just after the Civil War until the 1880s, it was these magazines more than newspapers that fueled interest in sports and saw their circulation benefit.

Cycling magazines were just as popular in France in the 1880s. The most popular titles were *Le Sport Velocipedique*, *Le Velosman*, and *Le Monde Cycliste*. General-interest magazines were also popular during this period, including *Les Revue des Sports*, founded in 1876; *La Gazette des Sports*, founded in 1888; *L'Echo des Sports* (1890); and *L'Almanach des Sports* (1899).

In Great Britain, daily sports publications emerged mid-century to challenge the monopoly that *Bell's Life in London* enjoyed with the sporting public. These included *Sporting Life*, which started publishing in 1859 and quickly grew to a circulation of a quarter-million. It was joined by the *Sportsman* in 1865 and the *Sporting Chronicle* in 1871. Priced at a penny, these journals enjoyed popularity with the masses and reflected the growing interest in timely sporting journalism among the middle class.

This growing emphasis on the middle-class audience was also reflected in the Austrian weekly *Allgemeine Sportzeitung*, founded in 1878. Its publisher, Viktor Silberer, directed his staff to write so that even the "cook's assistant" could understand it, setting it apart from the upper-class publications that had preceded it.

Professional sports emerged and became more organized in the late eighteenth century. Baseball club owners in the United States formed the National League in 1876. In Great Britain, an athlete-like cricketer W. G. Grace, though technically an amateur, could gain financial success through appearance fees and "expenses," even earning bonuses for reaching high performance standards. As sports and culture engaged in the "amateur versus professional" debate, sports publications provided a setting, but their involvement in the debate often straddled both sides, as they sought to preserve their audience and access to athletes.

Misgivings about the excesses of professional sports (as related to both the concept of financial gain and media reports of off-the-field behavior of athletes) could not diminish the enthusiasm toward sports that swept the United States and Europe in the late 1800s. Proponents in journals claimed that sports could provide participants with both physical fitness and an enhanced understanding of teamwork. Both were upheld as key values within the complex bureaucracy of industry that was developing. To newspaper publishers, however, it would be spectator sports that generated reader attention.

In Great Britain, the *Daily Mail* prominently featured sports from its founding in 1896. The *Daily Herald* also provided its readers with sports news (except for betting-related information). Only the *Times*, with its more conservative tone, withstood the pressure to respond to the clamor for sports news. But the other newspapers' emphasis on sports, particularly in Sunday editions, began to cut into the daily sports journals' circulations. Pressure also came from sports newspapers such as the *Referee* (1877), the *Umpire* (1884), and the *Sunday Chronicle* (1886), which ran larger editions crammed with information from Saturday football matches, horse races, and prizefights. Popular sports dailies were also established in France (*Le Velo*, 1891) and Germany (*Sport um Wort*, 1899).

Newspaper publishers in the United States, particularly in New York City, also took note of these trends and began to incorporate sports into their own circulation-building strategies. Charles Dana (*New York Sun*), Joseph Pulitzer (*New York World*), and William Randolph Hearst (*New York Journal*) were among the most aggressive. Dana's *Sun* took the lead in providing extra space for accounts of horse races and prizefights. For Hearst and Pulitzer in particular, sport became another front along which they waged their "yellow journalism" wars. The sensationalism of yellow journalism's news reporting adapted well to sports.

The innovations of the period can be seen even in today's modern sports section. Instead of dropping sports articles throughout, the New York newspapers gathered them together on one or two pages (as had been done in Great Britain for decades), as many as three or four pages on a Sunday. The section often was identified with a banner, whether sports-related artwork or a large-type list of the newspapers' best-known sportswriters. These sportswriters emerged as distinct staffs on newspapers that previously had assigned the articles across all staff members. Now, the newspapers could promote the expert sports journalists on their staffs, as aggressive reporting was presented within a lively writing style that came to distinguish sports writing from so-called "hard news" journalism.

This aggressive reporting provided both depth and breadth to sports event coverage. On the day after a heavily promoted event, the newspapers would run several articles, some written by "expert" athletes and coaches. In the days leading up to the event, they would run almost daily updates to enhance interest in the event and then use that interest to sell newspapers. Thus promoters were able to see their events reported, even when there was no actual event to report.

These innovations included increasing use of illustrations and photographs, as technology improved. Before photographs became feasible, woodcuts of illustrations provided powerful, and often fictitiously whimsical, images of athletes and sports moments. The Eastman Kodak camera, introduced in 1888, allowed newspapers and magazines to abandon woodcut illustrations in favor of photographic halftones. Although early-action photos lacked clear resolution, large photos of athletes and sports settings created reader interest while developing the concept of the athlete as celebrity. Before the turn of the century, the technology had been adapted toward the creation of "moving pictures." Brief clips of boxing matches and other examples of athletic movement were popular in the early days of film. By 1910, movie producers were filming the World Series and paying $500 for the rights to show highlights.

At this point, businesses began to see the promotional benefits of sponsoring sports teams and events. Bovril, the British company that produced the popular beef bullion–type extract, sponsored the Nottingham Forest soccer club in 1896. The Tour de France bicycle race was organized and sponsored in 1903 by the French sports magazine *L'Auto* (which was later renamed *L'Equipe*). By the 1920s, newspapers themselves joined in promoting sporting events; the *Chicago Tribune* and *New York Daily News* started sponsoring the Golden Gloves amateur boxing tournament.

In Japan, newspapers not only promoted baseball within their pages but also helped establish the first professional baseball teams. Baseball had been introduced to Japan late in the nineteenth century and caught on among the upper class, who were adopting Western fashion. The *Yomiuri Shimbun* newspaper organized a symposium in September 1911 to promote baseball in schools. The newspaper's owner, Matsutaro Shariki, helped to put together a tour of US baseball stars, including Babe Ruth and Lou Gehrig, in 1934. The *Shimbun* was one of four newspapers to sponsor teams in the Japan Professional League when it was organized in 1936.

But journalism's contribution to sport was not limited to promotion. The muckraking spirit of the late nineteenth century turned its attention to college football, particularly a rash of injuries and even deaths. As a result, President Theodore Roosevelt intervened with a highly publicized meeting in 1905 to reform college football, resulting in changes to the rules and equipment to make the sport safer. Subsequent research challenges the notion of Roosevelt revolutionizing college football to make it safer—documented injuries and deaths did not immediately decrease—but the episode reinforced the power of the press to influence the very institutions it covered.

World War I caused sport to receive less attention—on both the field and in newspaper pages. Many top athletes answered the call to serve in their nations' armed forces, and readers followed them with their attention. The war also slowed development of the latest emergent technology—wireless radio. Guglielmo Marconi's invention had been used to report on international yacht races for the Associated Press in 1899. But as the Great War began, governments appropriated the technology for war efforts.

As the world recovered from the horror of the conflict and sought distraction, sport contributed to the energy that fueled the Jazz Age. As both Bruce Evensen and Mark Dyreson have written, the struggle for the soul of sport was intense, as combating perspectives argued both for the economic pragmatism of professional sports and the more romanticized view of amateur sport played for its own sake. Sportswriters in newspapers and magazines reported on and participated in the debate while protecting their own industry's interests.

The age was hungry for heroes and celebrities, and newspaper sports sections and sports magazines complied. Sports stars such as Babe Ruth, Suzanne Lenglen, Jack Dempsey, and Bobby Jones grew to iconic status in a culture that elevated a new kind of hero. Advertising and public relations emerged as professions that promoted products and causes, and the athletes themselves learned the value of using the sports page to promote themselves. Ruth in particular coopted the loyalty of sportswriters to build a larger-than-life persona.

Although boxer Jack Dempsey did not share Ruth's natural skill in building a narrative for the media, he benefitted from the work of his manager, Doc Kearns, and promoter Tex Rickard. Rickard in particular was able to promote Dempsey's few-and-far-between heavyweight title defenses in a manner that fueled public interest. Their efforts were able to create compelling narratives, in which Dempsey portrayed the smaller scrapper (typically weighing in at less than 200 pounds) who emerged from the rowdy American West. They were instrumental in changing boxing from an illegal, immoral circus of violence into a more acceptable spectator sport.

The professional versus amateur athlete debate intensified. Traditional upper-class amateur sports advocates argued for the pure "sports for sports' sake," even as professional sports such as baseball and boxing drew widespread interest. But by the twentieth century, the debate was turning more in favor of professional sports. At the turn of the century, baseball began to provide a means for poorer athletes to experience the upward mobility that had been promised to all as the result of hard work. Their stories of success were popular among readers who were finding the same upward mobility denied to them.

By the 1920s, athletes in other sports were beginning to see the potential earnings from sport, even in tennis and golf. In those sports, traditional authorities had been the strongest advocates for the amateur ideal of play for its own sake and were able to enforce this ideal through their authority over national tournaments. Tennis players and golfers had to resort to exhibition tours to make money off their talents, forfeiting the privilege of playing in tournaments. Newspapers took no side in the professional versus amateur debate (except when it threatened their favorite athletes and sports). Their aggressive coverage of all sports created a welcome setting for the expansion of professionalism.

The emergence of the Olympics as a nationalistic sporting phenomenon was promoted on sports pages. To many, despite pleas for international harmony at the games, the Olympics represented a form of sanctioned war. Newspapers found that they could increase interest and thus sales by playing off nationalistic fervor in these and other international competitions (tennis's Davis Cup, for example).

The newspapers themselves benefitted financially from all of these trends. By promoting sporting events and heroes within their pages, newspapers saw their circulation increase as they devoted more pages to sports. "There is no single classification of news that sells more papers than sports," said W. P. Beazell, managing editor of the *New York World*, in 1929. Indeed, the sportswriters themselves were as recognizable on the sports page as the athletes they wrote about were on the field. Writers like Grantland Rice, W. O. McGeehan, Ring Lardner, and Paul Gallico created a "Golden Age of Sportswriting" as well. Newspapers in France, Paris in particular, were just as sport-intensive. According to one scholar, the newspaper *Paris-Soir* employed as many as 139 sports correspondents in the 1920s.

Amidst all of the social upheaval, the role of women in sports journalism remained marginal, even as female sports icons such as tennis player Suzanne Lenglen and Olympian Babe Didrickson Zaharias grew in popularity. Female sports journalists like Margaret Goss of the *New York Tribune* were rare and usually were consigned to covering women's sports or giving a stereotypically female response to male-focused sports situations, much as had been the case for decades.

Such was the interest in sport that newspapers often ran columns under the byline of well-known sports stars. Most of the articles were ghostwritten by newspaper staff members, frequently without any input by the athlete. For example, Ford Frick, who would later serve fourteen years as baseball commissioner, was Babe Ruth's ghostwriter during Frick's days with the *New York Journal*. Sports fans did not seem to dwell on the level of involvement by the athlete represented in the byline.

Athletes like Bill Tilden wrote their own columns. Before ascending to his top ranking in tennis, Tilden had been a journalist in his hometown of Philadelphia. He frequently came under sanction by the US Lawn Tennis Association (USLTA) for his critical comments, while earning an estimated $25,000 a year for his writing. The disputes resulted in the USLTA passing a rule that would be used to declare Tilden a professional because he benefitted financially (though indirectly) from his tennis playing. The outcry over losing Tilden for the Davis Cup led the USLTA to rescind the rule one year later.

Sports interest in the 1920s also benefited from the introduction of wireless radio, freed from its wartime shackles. This technology brought a new aspect to sports media: the ability to bring the audience the immediacy of the game itself, with all of its dramatic moments. In addition, as broadcasters introduced interviews into their programming, sports fans were able to hear their sports heroes' voices, connecting the two even more closely. Both features made fans feel closer to the actual experience of attending the game.

The first sporting event broadcast live on the radio was a boxing match in Pittsburgh in 1921. That same year, two radio stations in New York City broadcast live a heavyweight championship boxing match between Jack Dempsey and Georges Carpentier. Most homes did not have radio sets, so almost 300,000 boxing fans paid to hear the match on radio sets in theaters, barns, and hotel ballrooms.

The first live broadcast of baseball's World Series occurred in 1923. Some team owners and newspaper publishers feared that the new medium would lessen interest in both game attendance and printed sports sections. As a result, the first regular season broadcast of a game in New York City did not happen until 1931. The fears were unfounded; dramatic announcing by pioneers such as Graham McNamee drew crowds to the actual events. Daily sports wrap-ups by commentators such as Frick (who also worked in radio before his baseball administration career) were also popular among audiences.

The introduction of radio also spurred the development of a new income model. Originally, radio manufacturers also bought stations and produced content as a means to sell radio sets. The radios sold so well and so quickly, however, that another income model would be needed for the long term. Thus radio turned to free content, including sports, with paid advertising as a dominant source of income for media outlets.

Sports broadcasting in Great Britain evolved more slowly because of the power of the Press Association, which complained in 1923 that "broadcasting of racing and football results and similar matter would certainly seriously interfere with the sale of newspapers." By 1927 the BBC was covering such events as Wimbledon, the British Amateur golf tournament, and the England–Wales Rugby Union Invitational. Football league team owners were also reluctant to allow their games to be broadcast, fearing the impact on attendance. Individual cricket leagues had contractual agreements with the General Press Agency regarding access for journalists and photographers covering the sport, to the exclusion of radio. It was not until 1935 that cricket games were broadcast over the BBC in their entirety, with full-season coverage soon following.

By the late 1920s, newspaper publishers were increasingly concerned that the sports section was creating ethical problems for journalism, even as the profession itself was enhancing its stature through the development of codes of ethics, college degree programs in journalism, and professional associations. Owing perhaps to its yellow journalism roots, the sports section had developed a reputation for unruly behavior. Newspaper sports staff members, paid the low salaries of the period, were alleged to have accepted payoffs from sports promoters to promote events within their sports pages. Sports section pages often bypassed the managing editor and copy desk entirely, being sent directly to the composing room, which eliminated an important quality-control step. At the same time, newspaper publishers could not ignore the contribution of sports to the bottom line and thus the hazard of minimizing a form of content that drew in so many readers.

In both 1923 and 1927, the American Society of Newspaper Editors accepted committee reports on how to "rein in" these rogue sports journalists and increase their professionalism without eliminating sports coverage altogether. Among the recommendations adopted at the meetings were to increase the pay of sportswriters; decrease the number of pages for sports sections, even given its circulation benefits; and promote participation sports as much as spectator sports.

The twin threats of economic depression and then political upheaval signaled an end to the Jazz Age. Even the onset of worldwide economic depression could not quench the enthusiasm for sport, as it provided a welcome distraction from the difficult times. While this was not a time for growth or expansion in sport, it was not a period of decline either. For example, newspapers ran fewer pages but still assigned a consistent proportion of pages to sports news.

In 1938, Leni Reifenstahl's documentary of the 1936 Berlin Olympics, *Olympia*, demonstrated how film could be a powerful sports medium. The film also generated controversy for its connection to Nazi propaganda, though Reifenstahl claimed that she worked independently of the party and government. While her film's powerful images highlighted the strength and grace of the athletes, some felt the connection to the myth of Aryan superiority was apparent. Nevertheless, the film has been celebrated for its powerful images—particularly of the American track and field champion Jesse Owens.

As the clouds of war began to loom, preliminary forays into televised sports showed promise. In Great Britain, the BBC overcame print press obstinacy and resistance from its own radio sports operation and began broadcasting cricket games on television. The first telecast, on June 28, 1938, featured the Lord's Test between England and Australia. It was so much of a success that three more tests were scheduled for broadcast in 1939.

The first television broadcast of a sports event in the United States happened on May 17, 1939, when NBC's experimental station broadcast a college baseball game between Columbia and Princeton. The broadcast was limited to a single, low-resolution camera situated on a platform down the third-base line. As a result, the ball was difficult to follow, the players were hard to distinguish, and game action resulted in a jerky image from a camera that had difficulty following the action. By the time of the first major league baseball game broadcast, on August 26 of the same year, a second camera had been added, and even over those few months the clarity of the image had improved.

But developments such as these, and their accompanying societal upheaval, would be delayed by World War II, much as World War I delayed the development of wireless radio. No one could foresee how television would so explosively illustrate the synergy between sports, media, and culture. But the foundation had been laid for more than a century, so the phenomenon would hardly be considered new.

BIBLIOGRAPHY

Beck, Daniel, and Louis Bosshart. "Sports and Media." *Communication Research Trends* 22.4 (2003): 3–27.

Betts, John Rickards. "Sporting Journalism in Nineteenth-Century America." *American Quarterly* 5.1 (1953): 39–56.

Dyreson, Mark. "The Emergence of Consumer Culture and the Transformation of Physical Culture: American Sport in the 1920s." *Journal of Sport History* 16 (1989): 261–281.

Evensen, Bruce. "'Cave Man' Meets 'Student Champion': Sports Page Storytelling for a Nervous Generation During America's Jazz Age." *Journalism Quarterly* 70.4 (1993): 767–779.

Mason, Tony. *Sport in Britain.* London: Faber & Faber, 1988.

McChesney, Robert W. "Media Made Sport: A History of Sports Coverage in the United States." In *Media, Sports and Society,* edited by Lawrence Wenner, 49–69. Newbury Park, CA: SAGE, 1988.

Oriard, Michael. *Reading Football: How the Popular Press Created an American Spectacle.* Chapel Hill: University of North Carolina Press, 1998.

CHAPTER 11

··

DIFFUSION AND EMPIRE

··

LAURENT DUBOIS

SPORT is an ideal vehicle for studying empire. It embodies and illuminates all of the many contradictions of imperial practice. It is simultaneously an ideal form for the embodied transmission of the values of colonial powers and a prominent site for the expression of anticolonial desires. It is never quite what it seems: for at the very moment that the colonized demonstrate their mastery of the sports they have been told to master, they seem to threaten the very structure their apprenticeship was meant to consolidate. Precisely because it represents a widely shared and highly codified form of play, sport can allow for the punctuated expression of community or individual distinctiveness. The narratives, symbols, and events surrounding sporting events are always ripe for infusion with political meaning and thus sites of potential rupture and instability.

At the same time, it is impossible to write a history of sport without taking into account the routes of its diffusion. Especially during the nineteenth and twentieth centuries, those routes have been profoundly shaped by imperial geography. To be sure, sport has never respected political boundaries. Yet, it is striking the extent to which the geography of sport and the geography of empire have overlapped and shaped one another. Perhaps the most extreme case of this is cricket. "From the remnants of wickets and bats," notes Allen Guttmann, "future archaeologists of material culture will be able to reconstruct the boundaries of the British Empire." At the other end of the spectrum is football, a sport that spread with stunning rapidity both through and outside imperial boundaries. Even in the case of football, however, the merchant and military routes of the combined formal and informal British Empire were central in the diffusion of the sport, notably in Latin America, during the late nineteenth century. The case of baseball, in turn, offers another set of complexities: though it developed largely in parallel in societies such as the United States, Canada, Cuba, and Japan, over the course of the twentieth century it has become dominated by the US league, though Japan has remained an exception.[1]

This chapter seeks to grapple with the contradictory ways in which sport and empire have intersected in various historical and geographical contexts. I take as my central examples the parallel if contrasting histories of cricket, football, and baseball, which allow for exploration both of the well-trodden story of sport in the British Empire and of the story of French and US empires. The focus is on the period from 1880 to 1940, though some of the broader implications and trajectories of sport and empire are also considered. This is necessarily a very partial history, with a few geographical examples taken to illustrate and explore a broader set of processes. The aim is ultimately to reflect on the complex and contradictory dynamics of diffusion, paying attention both to forms of hegemony exercised by colonial powers and to the agency and visions of the colonized who decided, in a striking array of places and societies, to begin playing a small number of global sports.

Sport, Pierre de Coubertin—the founder of the modern Olympic games—wrote in 1912, could play "a role in colonization—an intelligent and effective role." The "races" that Europeans had "attempted to dominate and direct," Coubertin went on, were not "rebellious against sport." Indeed, "athletic instinct is born on its own among primitive peoples, as long as they have a good physical equilibrium and normal conditions of existence." But colonial powers other than the English, he lamented, had neither "sought" nor even "accepted" opportunities to compare "their athletic exploits to those of the natives." They had done so out of a misguided worry that "a victory—even just for laughs, or play—of the dominated race over the dominant one would have dangerous implications and risk being exploited by local opinion as an encouragement for rebellion." Coubertin found this worry ridiculous: "If an Annamite mandarin or a Malagasy noble wins a race, will the power of France in Hué or Tananarive really be challenged?" On the contrary, he argued, the example of the English colonies showed that athletic participation in fact smoothed and even strengthened imperial control. When an "indigenous team" won at polo—a game, he noted, that might have "Tibetan origins" but that had gained popularity in India only thanks to "British officers"—they did not see it as a blow against imperial power. Instead, the "yoke" under which they lived became "much lighter and more tolerable." "The native is doubly proud: of his personal success first, and then of the confidence offered him."[2]

Coubertin, however, thought that sport could do even more in the service of colonization. To be sure, there were approaches to be avoided: if sport took on "a too martial appearance" or certain forms of "regimentation," it could indeed help to "prepare a future rebellion." "It's obvious that, in the Far East, the propagation of jiu-jitsu is not desirable from the perspective of European domination." But this could be avoided, and instead sport could be used to as a "vigorous instrument of disciplinization." For both colonial administrators (whom Coubertin noted were in danger of falling prey both to "alcoholism" and "carnal" pleasures) and the "natives" they commanded, sport "engenders all kinds of good qualities," encouraging "cleanliness," "good hygiene," "order," and—Coubertin used the English word here—"self-control." "Won't it be better for the natives to be in possession of such qualities, and won't they will be easier to control than they would be otherwise?" "Most of all," Coubertin continued, "they will have fun." From sport, natives would gain "an interest in existence," and as they pursued "culture" and "personal perfection" through games, they would also gain "a little patriotism."[3]

Coubertin was concerned about the potential symbolism surrounding sport and warned that administrators should avoid making athletic events into "official spectacles." "The national flag, the presence of authorities, speeches, uniforms" all had the potential to backfire. For if the "natives" won a game in such conditions, their victory might "diminish the authority of the governors." It would not be the victory in itself, he explained, but the fact that it took place in the presence of officialdom that would make it so. As such, sport could serve colonialism best when it was not "an instrument of governance, but rather an institution alongside it."[4]

Coubertin's essay managed to capture many of the contradictions surrounding the project of using sport in support of colonization. On the one hand, boosters of sport like Coubertin believed profoundly that it was an ideal mechanism for communicating, and literally embodying, "Western" ideals they hoped to transmit to the colonized. On the other hand, there was an obvious problem—one that reflected more broadly the ambiguities of colonial governance. If the colonized became *too* good at the games, and began winning, it might threaten the structure of hierarchy upon which colonial governance depended. Furthermore, teams could all too easily become rallying symbols for communities seeking sites and events through which to protest and perform alternatives to colonial rule. This happened in different European empires during the early twentieth century, notably in Algeria and French West and Central Africa.

How should scholars find a balance between an appreciation for the power of hegemony and an acknowledgement of the agency of the colonized? In a thoughtful treatment of the question, Allan Guttmann sought to find a middle ground between various approaches. One part of the analysis, he notes, has to be an understanding of the ways in which "intrinsic" aspects of a sport make it a candidate for "adoption by one group of a sport popular among another." "It is reasonably certain that whiffleball will never replace soccer football as the world's most widely played game," he notes with a wink. In other cases, geography limits access to a particular sport—"Fiji islanders are unlikely to become bobsledders," he notes (an unlikelihood that forms the basis for the comedy *Cool Runnings*, released in 1993, about the Jamaican bobsled team), and "very few Uzbeks own surfboards." Nevertheless, Guttmann insists, in the study of "ludic diffusion," "intrinsic properties alone cannot determine a sport's popularity."[5]

The key, Guttmann argues, is to "distinguish among aspects of power," "avoid facile assumptions of unidirectionality," and "remind ourselves that the motivations involved in the diffusion of sports have been diverse." Direct and conscious political motivations did spur on the diffusion of sport in certain contexts. "In British India and elsewhere," Guttmann notes, "there were many occasions when colonizers forced modern sports upon the colonized, quite intentionally, as part of a program of political domination." And yet such occasions were only part of a larger fabric of exchange and need always to be placed within a broader context. If Guttmann urges caution with regard to an overemphasis on politically driven diffusion, he is also unconvinced by economic models that attempt to correlate the power of a given nation or region with its capacity to diffuse its sport. Though admitting that economic explanations are part of the story, he urges scholars to avoid forms of analytical determinism that do not hold up in the face of the evidence provided by sport history.[6]

Ultimately, Guttmann concludes that the application of a Gramscian approach best suits the analysis of sport and empire and that "cultural hegemony" describes the phenomenon more aptly than "cultural imperialism." That is because this approach "stresses the fact" that "cultural interaction is something more complex than the domination by the totally powerful by the totally powerless." Sport is "contested terrain in theory as well as practice," he notes. "Culturally dominated groups have often had sports imposed upon them; they have also—perhaps just as often—forced their unwelcome way into sports from which the dominant group desire to exclude them."[7]

In an introduction to a rich volume of essays on sport and empire, J. A. Mangnan comes to a similar conclusion. Sport has to be understand as an "area of negotiation." In writing history of its diffusion, he suggests, the "trick is to weave a complex pattern while not losing individual threads." Analysis needs always to be aware of "the possible disparities between ideological assertion, intention and realization."[8]

At first view, the history of cricket in the British Empire might seem the most obvious case of successful and concerted diffusion of a sport as a mechanism of colonial control, but cricket's diffusion in India was not a matter of centralized policy. Rather, it was the result of the initiative of local administrators. In the early 1890s Lord Harris, governor of Bombay, oversaw "the construction of cricket grounds and the organization of native teams." He was a believer, announcing in one birthday speech that his audience should love cricket, "for it is more free from anything sordid, anything dishonourable, than any game in the world." In 1892, he created a tournament between British and Parsee residents of the town, and in time it expanded to include other local teams. He even went so far as to invite one Indian side to lunch during a match, an act "considered by many to be a reckless act of excessive goodwill." He imagined cricket as a force that could unite the diverse population of India, an idea pursued later by Lord Bradbourne who, as governor of Bombay in the 1930s, urged the creation of teams that brought together Hindu and Muslim players.[9]

As Richard Cashman has written, there is a long tradition of writers emphasizing the "power of cricket and its assorted ideology to indoctrinate colonial subjects." This goes back to the late nineteenth century, in which the Indian Prince Ranjitsinhji described cricket as "amongst the most powerful links which keep our Empire together" or Lord Harris, who claimed the game had "done more to consolidate our Empire than any other influence." Many twentieth-century scholars have frequently offered the same analysis while flipping from celebration to condemnation, interpreting sport as an effective tool of imperial control and ideological indoctrination. Yet at least since C. L. R. James' *Beyond a Boundary*, such unidirectional interpretations have been critiqued as too simple and ultimately indeed as problematically patronizing for the way in which they ultimately exclude the colonial subjects who played the games from the frame of analysis. As Richard Cashman notes, the study of sport in fact forces us to ask a series of intricate questions:

> Where does the promoting hand of the colonial master stop and where does the adapting and assimilating indigenous tradition start? . . . How far can the colonial

acceptance of cricket be seen as superior colonial salesmanship or a successful exercise of social control using the highly developed and subtle ideology of games and colonialism? Or was it that many colonial subjects chose to pursue a game, because of the ideology, or even in spite of it, because it suited them to take up cricket for their own reasons? Or was the ideology of colonialism the starting point for the adoption of cricket but once the game was launched other factors came to bear which lead to its spread and consolidation?[10]

Football offers up a similarly complex landscape. In both the French and British empires, it was repeatedly deployed by colonial administrators and missionaries in schools and other settings as a way of transmitting European values of discipline and respect for the rules. A French sergeant who had served in the French colony of Togo wrote in 1937 that sport was a powerful tool of "social discipline" that could turn Africans into "tomorrow's agricultural laborers and artisans," as well as encouraging loyalty to the colonial regime. In 1951, a French magazine article argued that sport was an ideal method for pressuring Africans to shed their "primitive mentality." On the field, colonial subjects in the thrall of their traditional religious worldviews would "learn that, through patient and methodical training, they will get better results than using a fetish." "Forced to respect the rules of the game," the African athlete would learn to think rationally, accepting that "injustice and chance are not the powerful masters he once assumed, and that in the end it is the best who wins." And in Algeria, colonial administrators also celebrated the virtues of sport as a way of creating understanding and links between colonized and colonizer. Through sports, the board of one soccer club in Oran, declared in 1935, "we learn to know each other better, to love one another, to be brothers."[11]

Yet it quickly became clear in France's African and North African colonies that football could just as easily trouble colonial rule as buttress it. It was an extremely popular game and rapidly escaped the walls of schools and missions to become a focus of community, notably in the continent's rapidly expanding urban areas and among the migrants to the cities that colonial administrators saw as a particularly worrisome group. By 1943 there were 184 sports clubs in French West Africa—55 in Senegal alone—and though the French regime subsidized many such clubs in the hopes that they would draw people away from "purely political" activity, many clubs became hubs—symbolic and otherwise—of community mobilization and at times anticolonial activism.[12]

Algeria offers a particularly powerful example of the political possibilities of football. The founding of "Muslim" football clubs—whose uniforms and flags sported green and white colors and whose matches became ideal sites for activists seeking to mobilize nationalist sentiment—posed a serious problem for colonial officials. Even though only some clubs became explicitly politicized, the very fact that regular matches pitched "Muslim" teams against those composed of European settlers created a constant and repetitive possibility for conflict, community identification, and ultimately consciousness-raising. Football became a pivotal political tool during the war of independence in Algeria, when a series of high-profile professional footballers from the colony playing in France, including two who were tapped to play on the World Cup team in 1958, disappeared and created an insurgent Algerian national team that toured the world, carrying the nationalist flag and anthem with them.[13]

But football also has a peculiarity, which is that while it circulated through imperial boundaries it also spilled outside of them with great rapidity. Indeed, football is probably the sport that spread the fastest and most indiscriminately across the globe. Between the late nineteenth century and World War II, it went from being a game largely contained to the British Isles into a global phenomenon, with footholds on every continent.

A big part of this story, however, remains about empire—not in its formal but in its informal form. In comparing the difference between the diffusion of cricket and the diffusion of football, Guttmann argues that the particular global configuration of empire at a particular moment can shape the way a game circulates. The popularity of cricket, he notes, "remains limited, for the most part, to what was once the British empire." Although he admits that one reason may be "the greater complexity of its rules," Guttmann instead leans toward an "extrinsic" explanation. Cricket's diffusion, he argues, "occurred at a time when it was by no means clear that Great Britain was destined to emerge victorious from the imperial wars of the eighteenth and nineteenth centuries." By the late nineteenth century, however, "Victorian Britain had become a truly hegemonic power," its influence spreading far beyond the boundaries of its own empire. "Manchester's economic—and cultural—influence extended far beyond the limits of London's political control. And Manchester's favorite sport was soccer football." In Latin America, for instance, the economic presence of British firms—notably in railroad and shipping industries—along with British communities in most large cities was the initial vector for the introduction of football in Brazil, Argentina, and throughout the continent.[14]

Baseball offers another intriguing example of diffusion. Like cricket, as a sport it is relatively contained to a certain geographical area: all of North America, a portion of the Caribbean (Cuba, Puerto Rico, and the Dominican Republic, all former Spanish colonies), and Japan. Though it has been tempting for scholars to see this feature as proof of its spread through US Empire, the history there is also a bit more complex. In fact, as recent scholarship has shown, baseball really developed in parallel in places like Cuba, Canada, the United States, and Mexico.

The story of Caribbean baseball illustrates this well. "Although the United States invaded Caribbean basin countries on more than a score of occasions in the early twentieth century, it was not chiefly responsible for spreading baseball throughout the region," writes historian Rob Ruck. "Cubans, not U.S. Marines, brought baseball to the Dominican Republic, Venezuela, Puerto Rico, and the Yucatán." It was internal forms of migration in the Caribbean basin rather than US Empire that was the key to the story of the diffusion of baseball. That is one reason that Haiti, occupied by the United States from 1915 to 1934, never adopted the sport, sticking with football until the present day as its major athletic focus.[15]

Baseball did initially come to Cuba from the United States, but it did so via returning and immigrants and exiles. During the late nineteenth century, a time of steady conflict over Spanish rule in Cuba, there was increasing travel back and forth between the country and the United States. In the context of growing anti-Spanish sentiment, baseball was embraced—along with other North American cultural forms—as an expression of an alternative form of social activity and community. Informal networks of teams developed in the provinces, played during the periods between sugar-cane harvests, and brought together people of many different social classes. One writer described the game in 1899 as a "rehearsal for democracy." The Spanish colonial regime understood the threat and had regulated the names of teams. As would be the case a few decades later in Algeria, the names and symbols surrounding teams often veil nationalistic or anticolonial messages, and some became focal points for political organizing. One team in Havana adopted the name "Yara," but the Spanish authorities were concerned this was a reference to the famous "Grito de Yara," a proclamation that had incited anticolonial revolt in 1868. "Another club," writes Ruck, "drew their wrath for calling itself Anacoana, after the Taina Indian chieftain who died opposing the Spanish conquest of Hispaniola" in the sixteenth century. When, in 1895, a war for independence began in Cuba, the Spanish banned the game throughout the island, considering it politically subversive. As Lou Perez has shown, these actions only deepened the link between baseball and ideas of national liberation in the Cuban political imagination.[16]

Cubans helped to spread baseball elsewhere in the Caribbean, where it took root in Puerto Rico and the Dominican Republic. US economic and political power ultimately did play a clearer role later, in what Ruck bluntly but accurately calls the "colonization" of baseball both internally, vis-à-vis the Negro leagues in the United States, and externally with regard to the Caribbean and Mexican leagues. All of these were ultimately brought under the umbrella of Major League Baseball despite some resistance. This took shape through direct incorporation of players—but not, importantly, of managers or clubs themselves—in the case of the Negro leagues, or, in the case of the Caribbean and Mexican leagues, through a process of marginalization that has left Puerto Rico and the Dominican Republic essentially as feeder sites for Major League Baseball. Cuba, of course, because of its revolution, has remained outside the circuits of US control. And Japan successfully has maintained its own league system in parallel with that of the United States.[17]

Diffusion, of course, is only one part of the story. There is much to be analyzed and explored about why particular sports ultimately take root in communities and also find themselves ripe for institutionalization on regional and ultimately international levels. Here, too, football stands out for the ways in which its global institutions, particularly Fédération Internationale de Football Associatio (FIFA), represent a remarkable condensation of economic, political, and cultural power whose exercise (along with various forms of corruption that go with it) is today seemingly inexorably on the rise. But all of these newer forms of institutionalization, capitalization, and media concentration are built upon the foundations of the earlier phase of diffusion of the late nineteenth century. Whether those who carried football, cricket, and baseball during that era would recognize much about today's sport, and the spectacle and discourse that surrounds it, is not so certain.

These stories are, of course, just a partial reflection of the much later and complex history of the diffusion of sport. But they allow us to see some of the broad outlines of the forms of diffusion that have shaped the global athletic landscape. If both formal and informal empire were often critical to the routes of diffusion of certain sports, the ultimate geography of athletic practice depended deeply on the particular contexts that shaped why individuals and communities adopted the sports to which they were exposed. In many cases, there was an undeniable attraction to the idea of adopting a colonial sport and ultimately beating the colonized at their own game. But there were also many other reasons: the pleasures of the games, the freshness of new forms of conviviality and community, the respite and possibilities offered by sporting activity. In the nineteenth and early twentieth century, as today, questions of power—economic and institutional—always shaped the terrain of sport, and yet that terrain always offered up surprises and unpredictable outcomes, as it will certainly continue to do.

NOTES

1. Allen Guttmann, *Games and Empires: Modern Sports and Cultural Imperialism* (New York: Columbia University Press, 1994), 18.
2. Pierre De Coubertin, *Essais De Psychologie Sportive* (Paris: Librarie Payot, 1913), 234–236.
3. De Coubertin, *Essais*, 237, 240.
4. De Coubertin, *Essais*, 239.
5. Guttmann, *Games and Empires*, 171–172.
6. Guttmann, *Games and Empires*, 174–175.
7. Guttmann, *Games and Empires*, 178–179.
8. J. A. Mangan, ed., *The Cultural Bond: Sport, Empire, Society* (London: Frank Cass, 1992), 7.
9. Guttmann, *Games and Empires*, 33–34.
10. Richard Cashman, "Cricket and Colonialism: Colonial Hegemony or Indigenous Subversion?," in *Pleasure, Profit and Proselytism: British Culture at Home and Abroad, 1700–1914*, ed. J. A. Mangan (London: Frank Cass, 1988), 258–261.
11. Laurent Dubois, *Soccer Empire: The World Cup and the Future of France* (Berkeley: University of California Press, 2010), 33–34.
12. Dubois, *Soccer Empire*, 34–35.
13. I tell this story in detail in Dubois, *Soccer*, chapter 8.
14. Guttmann, *Games and Empires*, 40.
15. Rob Ruck, *Raceball: How the Major Leagues Colonized the Black and Latin Game* (Boston: Beacon Press, 2011), 17.
16. Ruck, *Raceball*, 4–7; Louis A. Pérez, *On Becoming Cuban: Identity, Nationality, and Culture* (Chapel Hill: University of North Carolina Press, 2008).
17. Ruck, *Raceball*.

BIBLIOGRAPHY

Cashman, Richard. "Cricket and Colonialism: Colonial Hegemony or Indigenous Subversion?" In *Pleasure, Profit and Proselytism: British Culture at Home and Abroad, 1700–1914*, edited by J. A. Mangan, 258–272. London: Frank Cass, 1988.
De Coubertin, Pierre. *Essais de Psychologie Sportive*. Paris: Librarie Payot, 1913.

Dubois, Laurent. *Soccer Empire: The World Cup and the Future of France*. Berkeley: University of California Press, 2010.

Guttmann, Allen. *Games and Empires: Modern Sports and Cultural Imperialism*. New York: Columbia University Press, 1994.

Mangan, J. A., ed. *The Cultural Bond: Sport, Empire, Society*. London: Frank Cass, 1992.

Ruck, Rob. *Raceball: How the Major Leagues Colonized the Black and Latin Game*. Boston: Beacon Press, 2011.

PART IV

PATTERNS OF
DIFFUSION

CHAPTER 12

··

THE GLOBAL SPREAD
OF FOOTBALL

··

MATTHEW TAYLOR

It is commonplace to refer to association football as the global game or the world's game. It differs from other sports in that it made a significant impression in every continent and in most regions and nations. It has not become the most popular game, or the designated "national" sport, everywhere, but the scope of its geographical dissemination, and the depth of its cultural impact, remains extraordinary and unique. For historians seeking to explain football's route from a pastime of the British elite to a worldwide passion, peculiarities and exceptions complicate the search for consistent patterns. Detailed research at the local level has led to an increasingly nuanced picture of the multiple directions in which the game and its values traveled between and across borders and cultures. New perspectives and angles, focused on recipients as much as diffusers, on exchange as well as dissemination, and on transnational connections alongside international ones, have helped to update a historiography characterized by a reliance on rigid national frameworks and a tendency to overplay the role of the British.

The first problem one faces in examining the global spread of football relates to terminology. The most common word used to describe the process, "diffusion," has never completely satisfied scholars. It has been criticized for implying a natural, linear process that obscures the complexities and conflicts that were fundamental to sport's spatial expansion. "Diffusion," it has been argued, fails to grasp the intentions of those, often in leadership positions, who might have wanted to expand or, conversely, constrain a sport's popularity.[1] In addition, it fails to account for opposition and resistance to the spread of sporting codes and for their translation and domestication in local contexts.[2] With its suggestion of a smooth and uncomplicated journey across territories and cultures, the notion of "diffusion" seems insufficient to deal with the bumps and barriers that football faced and the twisted routes that it actually took. References to the "export" and "import" of football, though fine as neutral descriptors, are similarly unsatisfactory as explanatory concepts. Notions of cultural transfer, exchange, or circulation seem to offer a step forward from simplistic unidirectional models of diffusion.[3] Considering the global spread of football in terms of the flow of people, information, and objects in different directions allows us to think beyond notions of "sending" and "receiving" nations and to highlight the specific interactions and sets of relationships that shaped dissemination in particular contexts.

Thinking beyond "diffusion" might also allow us to consider the dispersal of football as a longer term process than it is normally perceived. If we look past assumed moments of transfer, beyond the first games and clubs, their founders, players, and patrons, we can begin to examine the permanence of these initial trajectories and patterns and the extent to which they were built upon, modified, or absorbed by other influences. We can assess the importance of subsequent contacts, exchanges, and interactions—of traveling teams, coaches, players, and the movement of ideas and values in different directions. It allows us, in other words, to explore not just how and why football was "passed" from one region and culture to another but the way in which the game developed in motion and over time and the degree to which it became rooted in different parts of the world in the context of both local and transnational influences.

The game of football traveled with the movement of people. Migration, both short and long term, was essential to its dissemination, with those in peripatetic occupations playing a key role. Football spread both spatially and across social groups, but identifying models or common patterns is fraught with difficulties. Its initial journey though the regions and nations of Britain was particularly complex. Ex-public school and university men were prominent in the codification of the association game in the 1860s, but popular versions of football were also extant in Sheffield, Edinburgh, Nottingham, and elsewhere. It was not uncommon for sons of the local elite to return home from school and form a team, as occurred in both Darwen and Turton in Lancashire, or for former public schoolboys who wanted to continue to play in adulthood to do likewise. Schoolteachers were especially important disseminators. Teacher training colleges spewed out hordes of young men eager to set up football clubs wherever they went and to share their enthusiasm for the game with their pupils.[4] The "institutions of order"— the church and the military as well as schools—were key to the growth of football, especially in Scotland and Ireland. The Ayr, Hamilton, and Kilmarnock Academies spawned prominent football teams during the late 1860s and early 1870s; Queen's Park in Glasgow and Hibernian in Edinburgh emerged respectively from Protestant and Catholic young men's associations, though the backbone of the former was actually a group of middle-class migrants from the Highland counties; and many clubs in the west of Scotland, such as Third Lanark, had military connections. Elsewhere, as with the dissemination of the game to the industrial regions of Dunbartonshire and Lanarkshire, industrial patrons such as Alexander Wylie and the Bairds of Gartsherrie were instrumental in sanctioning and sponsoring football, though they often wielded little control over its subsequent trajectory.[5] The spread of football to and across Ireland was similarly multifaceted. It came to Dublin via students at Trinity College who had played at English public schools, but in the north the game arrived through the region's cultural and socioeconomic connections with Scotland. The first game in Belfast, between Scottish teams Caledonians and Queen's Park, was organized in 1878 by a clothes-shop manager who had witnessed soccer while on his honeymoon in Scotland. The earliest Belfast teams tended to consist of Scottish migrants or to have Scottish connections.[6]

Even when we can identify a point of transmission, explaining why football took hold in some places but not in others is a more demanding proposition. Contemporaries were puzzled by the inconsistencies in the spread of Britain's main football codes. Their distribution, the *Times* remarked in 1880, was "sporadic and curious. The seed of the one or the other game has, for no visible reason, settled in some districts and been wholly driven out in others."[7] It may be that cultural and physical boundaries were a factor. In Yorkshire, soccer was popular in the Sheffield area but struggled to spread north to the textiles towns of Bradford, Halifax, Huddersfield, and Leeds, where rugby remained the dominant code for many years. Similar cultural boundaries seem to have separated a soccer-playing north Wales, with social and cultural links to the northwest of England, from the rugby-playing south. In the sparsely populated Irish county of Donegal, the Blue Stack mountains represented a crucial dividing line between the northeast and east, where association football was the dominant sport, and the south and southwest, where Gaelic football became more popular. Here, in contrast to other parts of Ireland, there was little military influence in the growth of soccer. More important were the connections with clubs in nearby Derry City, the cultural links and the continual traffic of people in both directions from the county's ports to Scotland, and the resilience of individual administrators and pockets of supporters in the face of aggressive competition from the self-proclaimed "national" code.[8]

As founders of the modern game, the British were undoubtedly its most important international disseminators. They were to be found almost everywhere in the late nineteenth and early twentieth centuries, not just in the territories of the empire but also along the circuits of international trade and finance. Particular occupational groups—often itinerant in nature—were to the fore in Britain's sporting diaspora. Mention is often made of the sailors and soldiers who carried footballs in their kitbags and knapsacks, but the mobile agents of British commerce and education were probably most important of all in the global spread of the game. In Bilbao, British mining engineers are said to have first played football in 1893; in Russia, it was Lancastrian factory manager Harry Charnock who introduced it to his textile workforce; and in Montevideo, a teacher at the English High School, William Leslie Poole, is credited with founding the first club and football league.[9] British expatriate communities offered a suitable environment for the fomentation of the game. Sons educated back in Europe frequently returned with a passion for football, which they shared within, and sometimes beyond, their elite circle. One celebrated example was Charles Miller, born in São Paulo to a Scottish father and Brazilian mother, who introduced the game to the cricket-playing members of the local athletic club in 1894. Miller had learned football during his school years in Southampton, and returning home with two footballs and a knowledge and passion for the game, he promoted and organized matches between British émigrés working in the gas, railway, and banking industries.

The British influence on the emergence of football in continental Europe was substantial, but it was not always direct. Sport in general, and football especially, was one element of a broader mood of Anglophilia that was manifest among sections of the middle-class urban elite. In the late nineteenth century, students and teachers, as well as doctors, lawyers, engineers, and technicians, businessmen and bankers, often traveled to and from Britain, or spent time there, regularly coming into contact with British people, culture, and values. For them, Britain was not an archaic nation but one associated with technological advancement, social and economic transformation, and, above all, modernity. To speak English, and to follow British leisure pursuits, was a symbol of cosmopolitan sophistication. Football, along with other British sports, was highly fashionable. As a Basque observer noted at the beginning of the twentieth century, the game chimed with "a modern and open-minded tendency directed at upper and middle class people with 'advanced' and cultivated ideas."[10] This explains why so many clubs, regardless of nationality, adopted English names—Go Ahead Eagles and Be Quick in Holland; Grasshoppers and Young Boys in Switzerland; AC Milan and Genoa rather than Milano or Genova in Italy—or initially chose, like the White Rovers club of Paris, to speak exclusively in English while playing.

In the creation of football clubs across Europe, connections and associations with Britain were frequently more important than the British themselves. The game traveled via the transnational networks of education, industry, and commerce, with many of the continent's clubs the product of cross-national alliances and cosmopolitan perspectives. The French banker Henry Monnier, for example, studied in Switzerland and England before setting up Sporting Club de Nîmes in 1901 on his return to the family firm. Schooled in Switzerland, Walter Bensemann founded football clubs in Karlsruhe, Strasbourg, and Basle before moving to Britain as a schoolmaster in 1901 and then, after the First World War, becoming a prominent sports journalist in Germany. Schools and technical institutes in Switzerland often operated as a connecting point between Britain and southern Europe and a contact zone in the dissemination of football.[11] Exiled Englishmen and Scotsmen were among the first footballers in Barcelona, but it was a Swiss accountant, Hans Gamper, who founded the city's premier club, FC Barcelona, in 1899. In a city with a sizable foreign community, the game was embraced for its international flavor, bringing the Catalan industrial middle class "into accord with the cultural activities of the rest of Europe."[12] In port cities, with their mix of nationalities, football was often framed in an international context. The doctor James Spensley became the key figure at the British-only Genoa Cricket and Football Club at the turn of the century, but he opened up the club's membership to Italians, Austrians, and Swiss. In Naples, the two main teams included three Britons—a shipping executive, department store manager, and engineer—alongside a multinational cast of Belgians, Germans, Swiss, an Egyptian, and Italians, including the Scarfoglio brothers, who had been educated in Switzerland.[13]

Football moved first to those parts of Europe most closely connected with Britain economically and culturally, with education representing a particularly important link. Denmark, Belgium, and Switzerland, and then the Netherlands, the Scandinavian countries, France, and Germany were the earliest to take up the game; the central European territories came next, with Italy and Spain "comparatively tardy" in embracing it.[14] In many cases, it spread as part of wider cross-cultural networks based on trade, education, and technology and characterized by the mobility of people and the transfer of ideas. In Belgium, the Catholic schools were a suitable transnational contact zone, where the sporting interests of English and Irish students merged with the experiences of local students and teachers, one of whom, Pater Germain Hermans, having kept goal on a Jesuit school team in Croydon, carried the game—and a copy of the Football Association rule book—with him to posts across Belgium. Pim Mulier, who had studied at an English boarding school, helped to found Holland's first soccer club, Haarlemse FC, in 1879, as well as its first sports newspaper and national federation. He was part of a larger educational diaspora "that saw English-educated Dutchmen set up sports clubs all across the Netherlands" during the 1870s.[15] Itinerant scholars were similarly instrumental in the foundation of Denmark's earliest football club, København Boldklub, in 1876.

Searching for national "founders" and for singular moments and locations of "transfer" simplifies the complexities of football's movement from place to place. The game often arrived in one territory via different sources and multiple routes. Traveling students were one point of entry into the Netherlands, for example, but in the eastern provinces football came via Lancashire workers at the spinning mills in Enschede. It expanded, socially and geographically, with working-class teams mushrooming in the early twentieth century alongside the elite middle-class sporting clubs and organized football closely tracing the growth of the Dutch railway network. Football was being played by British embassy staff and English-educated Swedes in Stockholm, by Scottish workers in Gothenburg, and by locals youths at a training camp organized by Robert Carrick in Gävle, all at around the same time in the early 1880s.[16] In France, football came via British students and expatriates in Paris and the Channel ports and through British and Swiss connections in Mediterranean ports like Marseille and Séte. Thereafter, it spread to industrialized areas, such as Lens and Lille in the north, and sketched a similar path as the spread of the railway and the electrical and technical industries. But it made few inroads in much of central France or in big cities like Bordeaux and Toulouse in the southwest, where it was rugby rather than soccer that developed through the English presence in the wine and shipping trades. The case of France demonstrates the awkwardness of national categories, given that football spread to towns, cities, and regions rather than nations per se, and traveled via transport and commercial networks that crossed national boundaries. In the north, the Flanders Lions competed with Belgian, Dutch, English, and German teams in preference to those in southern France, whereas the sporting network of clubs in Marseilles before 1914 incorporated regular fixtures with opponents from Barcelona and Geneva but not Paris.[17]

There is increasing evidence that Western patterns and influences were not replicated in football's dissemination to eastern parts of Europe. A British connection can normally be identified, but this was not always the only, and rarely the most significant, stimulus. In Bulgaria, for example, British seamen did play the game along the Black Sea coast, but football had already begun to emerge from two different sources: wealthy students returning home having picked up the game in the schools of Constantinople and imported Swiss educators who brought football with them in the 1890s. Here, as in many other cases, football's origins in the territory are best described as polygenetic, with Bulgarian football developing in subsequent decades "in a complex post-colonial mode," taking in multiple influences from Turkey, Austro-Hungary, Russia, and Britain, among other countries.[18] The situation was more complex still in Poland, a territory divided between the Austro-Hungarian, German, and Russian empires before 1918. Here football progressed slowly and unevenly, influenced by the emergence of a number of interlocking transnational networks. In Galicia, under Habsburg rule, there were fewer restrictions on the organization of sport than in cities such as Warsaw and Lodz, under Russian control, and German-dominated Poznan. Here, in cities such as Krakow and Lwow, the first matches were played and the first clubs formed, between 1903 and 1906. Most of these clubs quickly became integrated into the sporting networks of the Habsburg Empire and, by extension, the football culture of central Europe more widely. Cracovia and Wisla Krakow joined the Austrian Football Association in 1910 and regularly competed against Austrian, Hungarian, and Czech teams. At Cracovia, club president and journalist Stanislaw Kopernicki hired the club's first professional foreign trainer in 1911, a Czech named František Koželuh, who introduced a new playing style, based on short ground passing; originating in Scotland and dominant in Vienna, this soon became known in Poland as the "Krakow style."[19]

In addition, evidence from eastern Europe should encourage scholars of football's diffusion to look more seriously at cross-national flows and networks and to question the criticality ascribed to modernization. While British migrants had some influence at an early stage in parts of Bulgaria and Poland, this was much less important than connections with the networks of central Europe and Adriatic football and later links with France as a hub for sporting internationalism and a magnet for the importation of local players as professionals. The success of football in the predominantly rural Galicia, meanwhile, rather than in industrialized Warsaw or Silesia, demonstrates that in Poland sport "did not follow simple patterns of modernization." Indeed, it was often traditional and nonmodern sections of the population, such as east European Jews, who favored football (often for practical reasons) rather than gymnastics and took the lead in promoting the game. Here, as in other parts of the continent, many of football's disseminators were members of migrant or transnational communities, and the game's arrival via "multiple and twisted routes" complicates linear patterns of diffusion.[20]

Recent work on football in Latin America also points toward more complex and nuanced lines of early development than are normally acknowledged. Most English-speaking scholars have, perhaps not surprisingly, taken Britain and its so-called informal empire as the starting point for understanding football's origins in this part of the world. Football, it is argued, came to South America "on the wide-ranging tentacles of British capitalism"[21] as part of what has been called the "trading ecumene" (as opposed to the "colonial ecumene" through which cricket and rugby flourished), transmitted along with technological and industrial expertise and through business interactions.[22] A clear link is made in this literature between British commercial and cultural penetration of the continent, with local emulation of the British the key to cultural transfer and dissemination. Here, as in Europe, British schools were crucial incubators of the game: the first clubs were formed in Buenos Aires, and this is where the early administrators, such as the Scot Alexander Watson Hutton, were based. Railway workers were also active, providing the initial base for clubs such as the influential Central Uruguayan Railway Cricket Club (later renamed Peñarol) and Rosario Central and Excelsior in Argentina. Patterns of diffusion are regarded as fairly consistent. Once the game was "delivered," so to speak, it then supposedly spread via three stages: first to British émigrés; then on to the local elites who played with, and copied, their British counterparts; and finally down the social hierarchy to the mass of the local population. From "British origins" and "English lessons," the usual narrative is then of the rapid "creolization" and popularization of football and its appropriation as a central component of national cultural identity.[23]

Accounts that quickly pass over periods of early British influence to focus on the game's nationalization in each country have done little to challenge these accepted narratives. But the limitations of British-centered interpretations have become increasingly discussed by Latin American specialists.[24] First, it is clear that immigrant communities other than the British influenced football's development and growth. A Dutch PE teacher, William Paats, introduced football to Paraguay and helped found the first club, Olympia; and German clubs were prominent in both Uruguay and Mexico.[25] In São Paulo, an immigrant from Hamburg, Hans Nobiling, played a key role, and cosmopolitan teams, such as Sport Club Internacional (founded in 1899 by a group of young Brazilian, German, French, Portuguese, and English men) were common. Anglo-Brazilians and Brazilians such as Oscar Cox and António Casemiro Da Costa, who had met at college in Lausanne, were instrumental in connecting the embryonic football cultures of Rio de Janeiro and São Paulo in 1901. Elsewhere, particularly outside Argentina and Uruguay, clubs and associations often had multinational origins. Sporting Football Club in Medellín, Colombia, for instance, was founded in 1912 by two Swiss merchants, Juan Henizger and Jorge Herzig; it was not until much later that they were joined by an Englishman, Harold C. Maynham, in the local administration of the sport. Much of the focus on British impact is explained by the skewed reliance on examples from Argentina and Uruguay and, to a lesser extent, Brazil, where British cultural influence was at its strongest. Argentina in particular has been described by historians as an honorary British dominion with a powerful and prominent "Anglo-Argentine filament" in Buenos Aires especially, boasting numerous schools, hotels, churches, and newspapers alongside sports clubs.[26] But it was not typical of Latin America in this respect, particularly the Andean countries that have yet to be fully researched.

Second, there was a crucial cross-cultural dimension to the game's introduction in Latin America. In Chile, for instance, where organized football began among British immigrants working in banking and mining, football soon became representative of a complex amalgam of racial, national, and international relationships and rivalries. In the port of Valparaíso, the earliest footballers emphasized their Anglo-Saxon roots and saw in football an activity that reflected the modernizing, cosmopolitan, and "European" character of the city. As in parts of Europe, references to Englishness and "English spirit" became a shorthand for cosmopolitan sophistication, and the decision by clubs in Valparaíso to compose their rule books, constitutions, and even club songs in English should be seen in this context. The sportsmen of rival Santiago, by contrast, celebrated through football the *mestizo* character of city and nation, portraying the racial mixing of Native Americans and Europeans in positive terms and connecting it to a more "authentic" version of Chilean identity.[27] Continued interactions between Latin American and European football cultures in the early decades of the twentieth century also complicate the notion of discrete "British" and "national" stages of development. The role of touring teams, and the later influence of coaches and administrators, from Europe were undoubtedly important in enhancing interest in the game and influencing how the locals played, but there was surely more reciprocity in these encounters than is normally acknowledged. The tourists learned lessons too, about the game itself but also about how it might be promoted to increase public enthusiasm back home. The impact of touring Argentinian, Brazilian, and Uruguayan club and national teams in Europe during the 1920s, and of large numbers of imported players at French, Spanish, and Italian clubs in the 1930s, was in certain respects a continuation of this two-directional, "mutual" influence between European and Latin American football.[28]

Colonial and trading links were crucial factors in the pattern of football's diffusion in Africa and Asia. In the former, the timing and manner of the game's arrival was obviously dependent upon the influence of European colonizers. In general, football spread more quickly and smoothly to British colonies than to French, Belgian, Portuguese, and German ones, largely due to the British "mania" for sport and their belief in its beneficial moral properties.[29] It arrived in the late nineteenth century through the main port cities and expanded into the interior via the railways, Western-style schools, and the colonial military. It made its earliest mark where Europeans settled first. In the Cape and Natal colonies, various codes of football were played among soldiers and colonial officials from the 1860s, with the first clubs and football associations arriving in the 1880s. The whites-only South African Football Association, founded in 1892, was the first national governing body in Africa and became the first member of FIFA on the continent in 1910. French settlers in Oran, Algeria, set up a football club in the 1890s, while in Tunis, the Racing Club was founded in 1906. Football reached Nigeria via the ports of Calabar in the east and Lagos in the west. In Calabar, it was first played in 1902 at the prestigious Hope Waddell Training Institution, an elite Presbyterian mission that produced a third of Nigeria's teachers up to the 1930s and whose graduates were influential in popularizing the game more widely. A British commercial agent, Frederick Mulford, was the key figure in Lagos, organizing matches between Europeans but also inviting Nigerian teams to play and coaching football in local schools.[30] But in Africa, as in other continents, football spread sideways from place to place, not just outward from Europeans to locals. African intermediaries—civil servants, interpreters, soldiers, policemen, traders, and railway and port workers—were instrumental in spreading the game into the interior, especially in French West Africa. In Bobo Dioulasso (now part of Burkina Faso), workers from Mali, Togo, Benin, and the Gold Coast helped to develop the first organized teams in the 1930s and 1940s. Expatriate colonial officials from West Africa and Gabon were similarly crucial in the formation of the first black clubs in parts of Benin, Cameroon, and in Brazzaville, then the capital of French Equatorial Africa.[31]

If similar vectors and mechanisms of transmission occurred throughout the globe, it was the relationship between local circumstances and regional, imperial, or global contexts that invariably determined whether or not football took root. In both British and Portuguese India, churches and educational institutions were important agents in popularizing the game, and football could be used to "discipline" and "improve" the Indian elite.[32] However, the colonial influence "was only a small part of the story" of football's rise to social and cultural prominence in places like Bengal and Goa.[33] In the former, the game had emerged by the 1930s as a powerful vehicle for local energies and communal identification. Indian teams such as Mohammedan Sporting dominated competition, meaning that explanations of football's significance by this time "required no focus on the British at all."[34] Many of the social agencies that helped popularize football in all parts of the world—missionary schools, religious organizations, and the press—were equally important in Korea. Matches and the formation of clubs have been dated to the late nineteenth century and 1900s, but, significantly, football became "woven into the fabric of Korean nationalism" under Japanese rule from 1910. Its main rival, baseball, was considered a sport more appropriate to the propertied classes and was largely confined to the south, where the Japanese influence was greater. Football also became an important vehicle for interregional identity, particularly through the rivalry between Pyongyang and Gyungsung (Seoul), which gained a sharper edge with the inauguration of a championship between the two cities in 1929. For the people of Pyongyang, in particular, football was a means of demonstrating their successful modernization and of differentiating themselves from, and resisting the centralizing power of, Gyungsung.[35]

The places and contexts in which football failed to take hold illuminate particularly brightly the dynamics of its global circulation. Few historians have taken seriously the notion that certain sports failed in certain places because they did not suit local temperament or taste. The idea of a "typical" stop–start, modular approach to cultural forms in North America, reflected in games such as baseball and gridiron football, which sat uneasily with the unfolding narrative flow of soccer, has, like many similar theories, limited historical grounding.[36] More likely, context and timing was the key. Throughout the settler colonies of the English-speaking world, from at least the 1850s onward, "football" games, in a generic sense, were fairly regularly played. Different versions of football were being practiced, developed, and codified across these territories, with debates about rules and regulations rarely taking place in national isolation. The development of football codes should be viewed, in this sense, as "an interlinked and interdependent international phenomenon, involving the exchange of ideas and sporting practices that transcended national boundaries."[37] Soccer was part of this transnational process of cultural interaction. The game rarely arrived in its colonial setting as a fully formed, packaged product ready to be passed on and bought into by locals: rather, it was often "present at its own arrival," in the Australian case, for example, in the form of pre-existing traditions of small-sided and rule-bound games.[38]

The relationship between domestic and external influences was crucial to football's ensuing fortunes. In various parts of New Zealand, a number of codes coexisted during the 1870s. The turning point was the 1875 tour by a rugby team from Auckland, helping to ignite interprovincial rivalries in the south, which were then successfully molded into a sense of national identity when an English representative rugby team visited in 1888. Contests between representative soccer teams within New Zealand were, by contrast, infrequent, and few teams from Britain visited Australia or New Zealand in an attempt to challenge rugby's status as the dominant football code.[39] In Tasmania, similarly, the ascendancy of the Victorian version of the game in the 1880s resulted from a particular set of circumstances in which the missionary efforts of clubs such as Melbourne's Hotham FC eventually prevailed over the local and distant advocates of the "British" codes of football.[40] In such cases, the subsequent marginalization of association football was neither as inevitable nor as clear-cut as is often presented in official, nation-based narratives. Moreover, if soccer retreated into the background in many parts of the Anglophone world as other codes and sports came to the fore in the last decades of the nineteenth century, it continued to flourish in certain localities, such as Newcastle in New South Wales and Fall River in Massachusetts, buoyed by fresh waves of immigration and by continued contacts with officials, players, and supporters of the game in Europe and South America.[41]

The growth of FIFA, the world governing body, and its World Cup competition both reflected and stimulated the global spread of football. Founded in 1904 by representatives from seven European associations and clubs, FIFA had grown to embrace twenty-four associations by 1914, including non-European members such as South Africa, Argentina, Chile, and the United States, and had risen to fifty-one national associations by 1938. If it continued to be dominated by a European–South American axis up to and beyond 1945, projecting the national, imperial, and gender hegemonies common in most international networks, the inclusion of a scattering of associations from Africa, Asia, and Central America in the 1920s and 1930s offered "some evidence," at least, "that FIFA regarded itself as a world organization."[42] Regular international conferences, congresses, and competitions helped to facilitate the further spread of football and foster interactions and connections across regions and continents. Neither the Olympic Games football tournament nor the World Cup was anything approaching a global event until much later in the twentieth century. In Amsterdam in 1928, for instance, only Egypt and the United States (among seventeen entrants) were from outside Europe and Latin America; these two nations were joined by China and Japan (of sixteen in total) in 1936 in Berlin. Nor were they merely neutral contact zones—"middle grounds of accommodation, compromise, and amalgamation"—divorced from wider relationships of power and economic influence. Football was a sport, after all, structured around competition and contestation, and thus it would have been surprising if the game's burgeoning international bodies and competitions had not become "sites of assertion, rivalry, and contention."[43] The rift between FIFA and its South American associations provoked by the decision to order Peru to replay its quarter-final victory against Austria during the 1936 Olympics was a case in point, demonstrating that tensions and fissures were ever-present during events designed to promote football and celebrate its universal appeal.

Nonetheless, international competitions and meetings were about making connections as well as unmaking and refusing them.[44] They often provided the opportunity for association, contact, and exchange and for the establishment of a transnational community of players, officials, and journalists bound together by shared interests and objectives—a development that is sometimes ignored if we focus too much on insulated national histories and trajectories. National footballing styles and traditions were constructed within these larger systems of circulation; "worlds in motion" in which "nothing ... stays fixed quite where we imagined it was supposed to be."[45] Identities and rivalries emerged along, and in response to, the complex and uneven routes that football took. As a cultural practice, it was continually formed and reformed as it moved across long distances. The twentieth-century football world, as historians are increasingly recognizing, was made in, and through, travel.

Notes

1. Tony Collins, "Le peur de la pénalité chez le joueur de rugby: histoire et diffusion du sport," *Ethnologie française* 4 (2011): 593–600.
2. Lloyd Hill, "Football as Code: The Social Diffusion of 'Soccer' in South Africa," *Soccer & Society* 11.1–2 (2010): 14.
3. Maarten van Bottenburg, "Beyond Diffusion: Sport and Its Remaking in Cross-Cultural Contexts," *Journal of Sport History* 37.1 (2010): 41–53.
4. Colm Kerrigan, *Teachers and Football: Schoolboy Association Football in England, 1885–1915* (Abingdon, UK: Routledge, 2005), 151.
5. Matthew L. McDowell, *A Cultural History of Association Football in Scotland, 1865–1902* (Lewiston, NY: Edwin Mellen, 2013), chapters 2, 5, and 6.
6. Matthew Taylor, *The Association Game: A History of British Football* (London: Longman, 2008), 38.
7. Cited in David Russell, "'Sporadic and Curious': The Emergence of Rugby and Soccer Zones in Yorkshire and Lancashire, c. 1860–1914," *International Journal of the History of Sport* 5.2 (1988): 192.
8. Conor Curran, "The Development of Gaelic Football and Soccer Zones in County Donegal, 1884–1934," *Sport in History* 32.3 (2012): 426–452.
9. Tony Mason, "Some Englishmen and Scotsmen Abroad: The Spread of World Football," in *Off the Ball: The Football World Cup*, ed. Alan Tomlinson and Garry Whannell (London: Pluto Press, 1986), 68–69.
10. Quoted in John Walton, "Football and Basque Identity: Real Sociedad of San Sebastián, 1909–1932," *Memoria y Civilización* 2 (1999): 261–289.
11. Pierre Lanfranchi and Matthew Taylor, *Moving with the Ball: The Migration of Professional Footballers* (Oxford: Berg, 2001), 23–24, 29.
12. Andrew McFarland, "Founders, Foundations and Early Identities: Football's Early Growth in Barcelona," *Soccer & Society* 14.1 (2013): 97.
13. Lanfranchi and Taylor, *Moving with the Ball*, 29.
14. Bill Murray, *The World's Game: A History of Soccer* (Urbana: University of Illinois Press, 1998), 23.

15. David Goldblatt, *The Ball Is Round: A Global History of Football* (London: Viking, 2006), 121–122.

16. Alan Bairner, "Sweden and the World Cup: Soccer and Swedishness," in *Hosts and Champions: Soccer Cultures, National Identities and the USA World Cup*, ed. John Sugden and Alan Tomlinson (Aldershot, UK: Arena, 1994), 199.

17. Pierre Lanfranchi, "Exporting Football: Notes on the Development of Football in Europe," in *Game Without Frontiers; Football, Identity and Modernity*, ed. Richard Giulianotti and John Williams (Aldershot, UK: Arena, 1994), 28.

18. Alan Tomlinson and Christopher Young, "Towards a New History of European Sport," *European Review* 19.4 (2011): 500–501.

19. Anke Hilbrenner and Britta Lenz, "Looking at European Sports from an Eastern European Perspective: Football in the Multi-Ethnic Polish Territories," *European Review* 19.4 (2011): 595–610.

20. Hilbrenner and Lenz, "Looking at European Sports," 602.

21. Lincoln Allison, "Association Football and the Urban Ethos," in *Manchester and São Paulo: Problems of Rapid Urban Growth*, ed. John D. Wirth and Robert L. Jones (Stanford, CA: Stanford University Press, 1978), 218.

22. Richard Giulianotti and Roland Robertson, *Globalization and Football* (London: SAGE, 2009), 8.

23. Tony Mason, *Passion of the People? Football in South America* (London: Verso, 1995); Rory Miller, "Introduction: Studying Football in the Americas," in *Football in the Americas: Fútbol, Futebol and Soccer*, ed. Rory Miller and Liz Crolley (London: Institute for the Study of the Americas, 2007).

24. Matthew Brown, "The Origins of Association Football in the Andes (1862–1916)," paper presented at the Football 150 conference, National Football Museum, Manchester, UK, September 2013.

25. Pierre Lanfranchi et al., *100 Years of Football: The FIFA Centennial Book* (London: Weidenfeld & Nicolson, 2004), 47.

26. James Belich, *Replenishing the Earth: The Settler Revolution and the Rise of the Anglo-World, 1783–1939* (Oxford: Oxford University Press, 2009), 537.

27. Brenda Elsey, *Citizens and Sportsmen: Fútbol and Politics in Twentieth-Century Chile* (Austin: University of Texas Press, 2011), 23–24.

28. David Wood and Louise Johnson, "Presentation," in *Special Issue: Sporting Cultures: Hispanic Perspectives in Sport, Text and the Body*, ed. David Wood and P. Louis Johnson, *International Journal of the History of Sport* 22.2 (2005): 137.

29. Allen Guttmann, *Games and Empires: Modern Sports and Cultural Imperialism* (New York: Colombia University Press, 1994), 68, 63–64.

30. Peter Alegi, *African Soccerscapes: How a Continent Changed the World's Game* (London: C. Hurst, 2010), 2–13.

31. Alegi, *African Soccerscapes*, 16–17.

32. James Mills, "Football in Goa: Sport, Politics and the Portuguese in India," in *Soccer in South Asia: Empire, Nation, Diaspora*, ed. Paul Dimeo and James Mills (London: Frank Cass, 2001), 75–88; Paul Dimeo, "Football and Politics in Bengal: Colonialism, Nationalism, Communalism," in *Soccer in South Asia*, 57–74.

33. James Mills and Paul Dimeo, "Introduction: Empire, Nation and Diaspora," in *Soccer in South Asia*, 6.

34. Dimeo, "Football and Politics in Bengal," 71.

35. Jong Sung Lee, "Football in North and South Korea c. 1910–2002: Diffusion and Development" (unpublished PhD diss., De Montfort University, 2012), 29–71; quote on 29.

36. Robert W. Rydell and Ron Kroes, *Buffalo Bill in Bologna: The Americanization of the World, 1869–1922* (Chicago: University of Chicago Press, 2005), 169.

37. Tony Collins, "Unexceptional Exceptionalism: The Origins of American Football in a Transnational Context," *Journal of Global History* 8.2 (2013): 211.

38. Ian Syson, "The 'Chimera' of Origins: Association Football in Australia before 1880," *International Journal of the History of Sport* 30.5 (2013): 465.

39. Nick Gouth, "Loss of Identity: New Zealand Soccer, Its Foundations and its Legacies," *Soccer & Society* 7.2–3 (2006): 187–207.

40. Syson, "Chimera of Origins," 455–459.

41. Roy Hay, "'Our Wicked Foreign Game': Why has Association Football (Soccer) Not Become the Main Code of Football in Australia?," *Soccer & Society* 7.2–3 (2006): 168; Matthew Taylor, "Transatlantic Football: Rethinking the Transfer of Football from Europe to the USA, c. 1880–1930s," *Ethnologie française* 4 (2011): 645–654.

42. Emily S. Rosenberg, "Transnational Currents in a Shrinking World," in *A World Connecting, 1870–1945* (Cambridge, MA: Harvard University Press, 2012), 833; Paul Dietschy, "Making Football Global? FIFA, Europe, and the Non-European Football World, 1912–74," *Journal of Global History* 8.2 (2013): 287.

43. Daniel T. Rodgers, "Cultures in Motion: An Introduction," in *Cultures in Motion*, ed. David T. Rodgers, Bhavani Raman, and Halmut Reimitz (Princeton, NJ: Princeton University Press, 2013), 14.

44. Pierre-Yves Saunier, *Transnational History* (Basingstoke, UK: Palgrave Macmillan, 2013), 40.

45. Rodgers, "Cultures in Motion," 2–3.

BIBLIOGRAPHY

Brown, Matthew. *From Frontiers to Football: An Alternative History of Latin America since 1800.* London: Reaktion, 2014.

Dietschy, Paul. *Histoire du football.* Paris: Librairie Académique Perrin, 2010.

Giuliannotti, Richard, and Roland Robertson. *Globalization and Football.* London: SAGE, 2009.

Goldblatt, David. *The Ball Is Round: A Global History of Football.* London: Viking, 2006.

Guttmann, Allen. *Games and Empires: Modern Sports and Cultural Imperialism.* New York: Columbia University Press, 1994.

Koller, Christian, and Fabian Brändle. *Goal! A Cultural and Social History of Modern Football.* Washington, DC: Catholic University of America Press, 2015.

Lanfranchi, Pierre, and Matthew Taylor. *Moving with the Ball: The Migration of Professional Footballers.* Oxford: Berg, 2001.

Murray, Bill. *The World's Game: A History of Soccer.* Urbana: University of Illinois Press, 1998.

Rosenberg, Emily S., ed. *A World Connecting, 1870–1945.* Cambridge, MA: Harvard University Press, 2012.

CHAPTER 13

··

BASEBALL'S GLOBAL
DIFFUSION

··

ROB RUCK

SETTING out from Chicago in the fall of 1888, baseball magnate A. G. Spalding circumnavigated the globe, staging baseball exhibitions along a 32,000-mile journey. After barnstorming by rail to San Francisco, his entourage of professional ballplayers steamed across the Pacific to play in New Zealand and Australia. These baseball tourists performed next in Ceylon and in the shadow of Egypt's Pyramids. After stops in Italy and Paris, they concluded the foreign portion of their travels with a dozen games in Great Britain, including one at the Lord's Cricket Ground of the Marlyebone Cricket Club.

Returning to the United States six months later, Spalding feted his players at Delmonico's restaurant in Manhattan. Proclaiming his pride in establishing "our national game throughout the world," Spalding assured his audience that Australia and England would soon adopt baseball. Mark Twain, following Spalding to the podium, declared that nothing embodied America more than its favorite sport. The Spalding tour, he asserted, had "carried the American name to the outermost parts of the earth, and covered it with glory every time."[1]

But both Spalding and Twain's claims were wildly inflated. Though baseball would become the United States' national pastime by century's end and Spalding American sport's most powerful figure, the game's diffusion abroad was episodic and fairly limited. British sport had already preempted most global playing fields, and baseball never challenged its grip. Moreover, the brand of baseball Spalding's party conveyed was irredeemably stamped with his nation's racial prejudices, damaging its chances of forging sporting ties in much of the world. When baseball did take hold outside the United States, its success had little to do with the imperial pretensions of men like Spalding. Instead, the sport's viability reflected the degree to which Cubans, Japanese, Dominicans, and other nationalities made baseball their own game. Even now, long after Spalding's world tour, baseball lags far behind football, cricket, rugby, and basketball as a global sport. Though Spalding considered himself the emissary for a sport born and bred in the United States, and struggled mightily to establish its indigenous *bona fides*, his beliefs regarding baseball's pedigree were a fiction. Baseball had its origins in English folk games, not in Cooperstown. Nor did it spring forth fully formed on North American soil like Athena from Zeus's head. Still, Spalding sought to proclaim its American roots and, more important, profit from its overseas expansion. In time, his successors would benefit from baseball's global diffusion but never as easily nor as profitably as Spalding anticipated.

Early baseball historians shared Spalding and Twain's myopia, writing as if Major League Baseball (MLB) and the United States were all that mattered. But studies addressing baseball's evolution elsewhere in the world have revised earlier interpretations by tracing the sport's transnational connections in a less MLB-centric manner.[2] Baseball's global evolution has entered its fourth century, with global capitalism ever more in command, but the international game is not simply the American version transported across national boundaries. Nor has baseball around the world been completely commodified along the American model. The ranks of those holding on to baseball as play or a cultural tenet are robust. Moreover, people in the Caribbean basin and the baseball-playing parts of Asia have often rejected much of the American recreational ideology that accompanied the game when they first encountered it. They continue to find baseball a means to forge cohesive identities defined by nationality.

Albert Goodwill Spalding, who came of age during baseball's post–Civil War transition to commercial play, internalized the Gilded Age's approach to questions of race and power. A leading player in the 1870s, Spalding owned the Chicago White Sox by the time he was thirty-two. He also built the most successful sporting goods company in the country, selling more bats, ball, uniforms, and gloves than any other firm. His *Spalding Base Ball Guide* circulated both domestically and abroad. Not satisfied with dominating the national market, Spalding sought international markets.[3]

Spalding joined baseball's earliest Atlantic crossing, accompanying British-born cricket player Harry Wright and his Cincinnati Red Stockings to England in 1874. Spalding both played and served as Wright's chief assistant in baseball's first effort to crack a foreign market. The trip's limited impact did not dissuade Spalding from launching a bolder undertaking in 1888. Realistic about the likelihood of turning an immediate profit from his 1888 tour, Spalding said, "I do so more for the purpose of extending my sporting goods business to that quarter of the globe and creating a market for goods there." In addition, the tour would bathe him in the limelight as a patriot, who would, Thomas Zeiler argued, spread American notions of "free enterprise, progress, racial hierarchy, cultural virtue, and exceptional national greatness."[4] Spalding's undertaking came during the nation's precipitous, postbellum, economic ascent. European nations were planting the flag in Africa and Asia, and the United States, while eschewing formal colonial projects, joined the scramble for foreign markets. Anticipating a growing overseas US presence, Spalding believed that foreigners would take to baseball as readily as they had to other American products, absorbing American values while buying his sporting goods. Adrian Burgos contends that Spalding and other reformers "believed that baseball should follow the U.S. flag as the nation embarked on its imperial and colonial projects in the Caribbean and Pacific."[5]

Although early historians might have agreed with Spalding's agenda, few foreigners bought either baseball's ideological baggage or the implements of play Spalding wished to export. American baseball encountered enormous difficulty in sparking interest among Australians, Italians, the French, and Egyptians. Nor were the British eager to adopt the sport. Baseball's timing was off and its connections weak. The British, who were already exporting their games, had beaten baseball to the punch, and they, not the Americans, had the imperial connections to establish a global sporting presence. Spalding, however, was confident that America's game would prevail, and his tour underscored the United States' place in the Western world. But it stumbled. In Hawai'i, prohibitions against Sunday play prevented the tourists from staging a game while in Pago Pago, their next stop; they were afraid to go ashore because of skirmishes among Samoan and foreign factions. They finally played outside the United States in New Zealand, but few took notice.

Undeterred by an underwhelming reception in New Zealand, Spalding headed for Australia. British sport, however, had preceded baseball and was already entrenched. This would be the case in most of the world where the British imperial presence dwarfed that of the United States.

The US economy, more focused on domestic markets, would not match Britain's impact abroad until World War I. As Stefan Symanksi and Andrew Zimbalist point out, Great Britain then led all nations in global manufacturing exports. Their goods, carried on British ships, financed by British firms, and often sold by British citizens, required an extensive expatriate infrastructure. In addition, Britain annually stationed far more troops abroad than did the United States.[6]

These expatiate, soldiers, and fellow travelers brought along their bats and balls, entertaining themselves and teaching the sport to the students at schools where some taught. Meanwhile, visitors and students to Britain returned home with a zeal for football, cricket, and rugby. Football, already making inroads on the European continent in the 1860s and 1870s, was spreading throughout South America and Asia. Meanwhile, British professionals and amateurs toured the world, every bit as fervent as Spalding in believing their sport capable of spreading national values. But they were much more successful in spreading the gospel of sport because their tours were part of ongoing athletic contact with local sportsmen who were appropriating football as their own. A few baseball exhibitions could not dislodge these British games. Nor did baseball resonate in the public consciousness as powerfully as an international test match in which national honor was part of the stakes.

The after-effects of Spalding's tour were limited. Despite a few short-lived leagues in Australia and England, baseball did not take root in British athletic soil. Spalding proclaimed that baseball would undoubtedly become a fixture in New Zealand and had great potential to take hold in England and Ireland. He dismissed Ceylon, India, and Egypt, however, as too tropical and backward to accept the game. With bravado, he concluded: "I unhesitatingly pronounce baseball peer of [cricket and rugby], and expect to see it become the universal athletic sport of the world."[7]

Spalding did not explain why baseball was thriving in the Caribbean, also a tropical clime and one that this unabashed proponent of the white man's burden considered backward. He did not appreciate or did not care that his tour projected an image of baseball that had no place for players or fans of color. It did not include a single African American or Afro-Caribbean player, although it did feature Clarence Duval.

An African American minstrel, Duval had worked as Spalding's Chicago club's mascot. During the tour, the tiny but talented Duval entertained spectators by performing routines redolent of plantation life. Cap Anson, who captained the White Sox, belittled Duval as "a no account nigger." A vocal advocate of baseball's segregation, Anson reviled black players. His infamous threat, "Get that Nigger off the field!" came to symbolize baseball's rejection of black players; his refusal to play with African Americans lent momentum to their ouster.[8]

African Americans, especially in the North, played baseball after the Civil War, and a score took part in professional leagues. But they were driven from the so-called major leagues amidst a rising racial reaction in which the gains won during Reconstruction were reversed. Organized baseball, as the National and American Leagues and their farm system of minor leagues became known, would remain off-limits to African Americans and darker-skinned players until 1947.

MLB's racial divide limited its global appeal. But that did not stop the sport from gaining purchase in and around the Caribbean, where it was played and watched by people of various colors. While American advocates of the game spoke of it as a vehicle for democracy and development, reality belied such rhetoric. Nevertheless, the game's future as a global game free of racial restrictions was already on display in Havana, Cuba, where the best ballplayers of all nations and colors competed with and against each other. For Cubans, baseball realized the vision offered by the architect of their independence struggle, José Martí, that of a nation for all. Though a Spanish colony, Cuba's economy and infrastructure became tied to the United States during the late nineteenth century. Meanwhile, Spanish efforts to subdue insurgents seeking independence caused many Cubans to take refuge in the United States. They joined thousands of their compatriots already studying and working there at a time when baseball's popularity was rising. Returning students formed Cuba's first teams in the late 1860s. A league commenced play in 1878.

For many Cubans, the United States represented a fresh, democratic vision of their future, and they embraced baseball as part of this model. They evangelized for what historian Louis A. Pérez Jr. called "a paradigm of progress."[9] Before long, Cubans made baseball their own game. Unlike the United States, that meant integrated play. Slavery had been abolished in Cuba in 1886, and Afro-Cubans were in the vanguard of independence ranks. Cuban baseball quickly reached critical mass, and more than two hundred teams, mostly self-organized, noncommercial ventures, were on the field by the 1890s.

With Spanish authorities suppressing independence efforts, Cubans looked at baseball, in contrast to bullfighting, as a sport in which all distinctions of class, race, and even gender, could be set aside, one where mobility and freedom prevailed. Baseball was, author Benjamin de Cespedes said in 1899, "a rehearsal for democracy." Spain, unwilling to allow these rehearsals to take place, frequently banned the game and prevented teams from adopting names suggesting resistance to colonial rule. Colonial authorities knew that rebels had ties to baseball and used the sport to advance their cause. Émigrés in Key West and Caracas staged games to raise money and rally support; on the island, players and former players picked up arms and became leaders in independence ranks. The more the Spanish denounced baseball, the more they elevated its political profile. "Baseball," Pérez argues, became "identified with the cause of *Cuba Libre*, fully integrated into the mystique and the metaphysics of national liberation."[10] Playing baseball had become an act of defiance to Spanish rule.

Though US occupation forces advanced their own racial agenda in Cuba after Spain relinquished its grip, a racially inclusive brand of baseball won out. That had implications beyond Cuba, which became global baseball's most important arena. By World War I, Havana was the baseball world's hub, the center of a network of Atlantic cities where baseball had penetrated. As far north as New York City, as far south as Caracas, and by ship and rail to Mexico City, this sporting world included a have-glove, will-travel motley crew of Cubans, Latin Americans, and US citizens of different colors. This was global baseball, not the racially exclusionary major league game where only whites and those able to pass for white could play.

Given its proximity to the United States, Cuba offered North American ballplayers and clubs the chance to generate income during their off-season. The lure of financial gain soothed major league teams' racial anxieties about playing with darker-skinned players. While Cuban teams traveled to Key West and beyond, North American clubs visited the island. By then, a number of lighter-skinned Latinos played for major and minor league clubs in the States; their darker-skinned countrymen came north to play for Negro League teams.

US corporations monopolized Cuba's sugar industry and controlled the island's infrastructure, but Cubans, not North Americans, directed their nascent baseball industry and set the terms of engagement. Cubans negotiated from strength because they had cultivated the market, owned the venues, and promoted the games. Nor did they worry about losing their fans to MLB; distance, national autonomy, and the limited range of media protected the island game. Also, because Cuban professional baseball took place mostly during the major league off-season, teams did not face competition for players.[11]

Ballplayers and owners alike in the early twentieth century needed to make a living in the off-season, and Havana became a pleasant, remunerative alternative to working stateside. Ballplayers made money doing what they did best in a city known as the Paris of the Caribbean. Ballplayers—especially black ones—stormed the island, arriving on steamers from Key West. Spalding, who overcame his racial prejudices and sold baseball gear in Cuba before the 1898 conflict, began publishing his *Spalding Base Ball Guide* in Spanish in 1906 with rules, photos, and narratives of the game's development in the Caribbean. Cuba quickly became baseball's—and Spalding's—best foreign market.

A cohort of Cuban promoters crafted relations with North America. Their ties were especially strong to the burgeoning network of black teams that gave rise to the Negro National League in 1920. For black ballplayers, Cuba was a place to play for good pay with fewer racial restrictions. Cuban teams began barnstorming the United States during the summer, and African American ballplayers arrived on the island each winter, part of a sporting cross-fertilization that brought the best of black and Latino baseball together. Victories over North American teams and the feats of Cubans against major leaguers became part of the island's political mythology. Some became idols whose stories were told and retold, refined and embellished as they were passed down from one generation to the next. Baseball, with its level playing field, was an arena where Cubans could compete with the United States and win.

Major league teams lost more frequently than they won in Cuba before World War I, prompting American League president Ban Johnson to ban intact league teams from barnstorming there. "We want no makeshift club calling themselves the Athletics to go to Cuba to be beaten by colored teams," he explained.[12] Defeat at the hands of integrated Cuban clubs was not meant to be part of the white man's burden.

But these off-season paydays kept Negro League, MLB, and independent teams coming to Cuba until World War I interrupted the trans-Atlantic sporting trade. Almost every Negro Leaguer and many a major leaguer elected to the Hall of Fame played or managed there. For several decades, Cuba was an alternative baseball universe with its own set of social and racial mores where a diverse and talented collection of ballplayers appeared together.[13]

Baseball, which had galvanized resistance to Spain, infusing it with a vision of a democratic egalitarian future, now tied Cuba to a larger Atlantic world. As Cuban baseball spread abroad, it carried its multiracial make-up with it. In contrast, the United States, despite its frequent occupation of Caribbean basin countries, played only an ancillary role in spreading baseball throughout the region. Cubans, not the US Marines, brought baseball to the Dominican Republic, Venezuela, Puerto Rico, and Mexico's Yucatan Peninsula. Pedro Julio Santana, an early chronicler of baseball in the Dominican Republic, reflected on Cuba's role in bringing baseball to his country. "It is much the same as that which happened with Christianity," Santana mused. "Jesus could be compared to the North Americans, but the apostles were the ones that spread the faith, and the apostles of baseball were the Cubans. They went out into the world to preach the gospel of baseball."[14]

Because Cubans, not North Americans, initiated baseball in the region, it was racially integrated. Race was never a bar to Dominicans, Venezuelans, or Puerto Ricans. Baseball among Cuba's disciples also took on a nationalistic cast. Dominicans and Venezuelans did not see themselves as playing the US game or even the Cuban game but the Dominican or Venezuelan game. They, like Cubans, appropriated baseball as their own.

Because most of the baseball-playing Caribbean was occupied at one time or another by the US military, baseball often reflected political overtones. During their 1916–1924 US occupation, some Dominicans—like Cubans before them—played baseball against foreign troops while others took up arms against them. Juan Bosch, who became the country's first democratically elected president after dictator Rafael Trujillo's assassination in 1961, watched these contests as a boy. Remembering the games seventy years later and through his own ideological filter, he observed that "These games manifested a form of the peoples' distaste of the occupation. They were a repudiation of it. And when a Dominican player would do something great, the people would shout their hurrahs. The game was seen as to go beat the North Americans." The top team from Santiago, Dominican Republic, even adopted the name *Las Aguilas* in solidarity with Nicaraguan rebel leader Agosto Cesar Sandino, who was known as the Eagle (*El Aguila*) of the Chipote Mountains.[15]

As long as the color line prevailed in MLB, Cuba remained the epicenter of both winter and Caribbean baseball. Cubans set the standard for play. Fans in other countries listened to Cuban games on the radio and were elated when their players proved good enough to play there. Dominican amateur baseball modeled itself after the Cuban game, not that of the United States, and Dominicans adopted Cuban baseball metaphors and expressions. Cuba's winter leagues attracted scores of white and black ballplayers each season. During the summer, Cubans and a small number of other light-skinned Caribeños played in the United States' major and minor leagues. African American and Afro-Caribbean players, for their part, circulated between winter play in the islands and the Negro Leagues in the summer. As long as the Caribbean's professional circuits stuck to winter play, there was no conflict with either league over players.

There was, however, conflict with Mexico, which played a summer season and began signing top Negro Leaguers during World War II. After the war, Mexican baseball's leader, Jorge Pasquel, decided to contest both Cuban and MLB. His considerable corporate wealth made the Mexican League more than an annoyance. Bringing together scores of Cuban and Negro Leaguers and adding expatiate major leaguers to the mix in 1946, he posed the most serious threat MLB has ever faced from beyond US borders. His timing was impeccable, coming during Jackie Robinson's first season in the Brooklyn Dodgers organization.[16]

In 1946, Pasquel challenged MLB's monopoly over its players. Though MLB would win this fight and the Caribbean lose control of its own leagues and players as a result, the conflict allowed major leaguers of all races and nationalities to take steps toward gaining power over their working lives. Cuba had a better and deeper pool of players, but Mexico possessed more economic heft and population. After buying a Mexican League franchise in 1940, Jorge Pasquel funded the league's expansion as a summer circuit and went after players from the Negro Leagues. More than sixty Negro Leaguers and scores of top Cuban ballplayers, accustomed to going wherever salaries were the highest, began playing in Mexico. After World War II, Pasquel not only signed Negro Leaguers but major leaguers; he wanted his league to rival MLB.

His assault came as Jackie Robinson's signing reverberated through MLB and hundreds of ballplayers returned from the war. With a glut of players on the market and the specter of Negro Leaguers seeking their jobs, major league ballplayers were no longer in great demand. Owners took advantage of market dynamics and offered meager contracts. The players, lacking a union and the right to free agency, had little recourse. That gave Pasquel an opening. He offered contracts that staggered the players and signed Cuban, Negro League, and eighteen major leaguers for the 1946 summer season.

With major leaguers defecting to Mexico, integration likely, and union organizing by players underway, the owners vowed to crush Pasquel before he shattered their monopoly over players. Major league owners did not consider forging collaborative relationships with a foreign owner, making him a partner rather than treating him like a pariah. Their vision of global baseball was one where they maintained total control. But over half of the men who played in the Mexican League that summer were foreigners. MLB announced that any major leaguers who went to Mexico would be suspended for five years; it subsequently banned eighteen men from playing for any club under its jurisdiction.

"Those who manipulate the baseball monopoly in the United States," Pasquel retorted, "are alarmed because they are paying their players slave wages. We are paying them exactly what they are worth and this is why they are coming to Mexico." Baseball once again reflected global politics. *New York Times* writer Milton Bracker underscored Mexico's enthusiasm for defying MLB. "In fact it has even been said that not since the historic oil expropriation of March, 1938 has any circumstance so delighted the Mexican national ego as that of 'Saint Jorge' tilting with the 'dragon' of American baseball."[17]

Although MLB made concessions in order to prevent more players from abandoning their clubs for better paychecks in Mexico, it threatened to suspend any ballplayer under its jurisdiction who played with or against any of the blacklisted players. This secondary boycott affected hundreds of ballplayers and cast a pall over barnstorming and Caribbean league play. Although aimed at white major leaguers, it threatened African American and Latin ballplayers too. Top African American and Latin players made a good living by playing in Mexico in the summer of 1946 and in Cuba during the winter; some made more money than many major leaguers. MLB's grip over players would weaken considerably if this Mexican–Cuban nexus thrived. But the secondary boycott meant that aspiring major leaguers jeopardized their careers by playing in a league with blackballed players. This included Cubans playing in Cuba. MLB had never intervened so directly in the affairs of a foreign league.

"Since baseball has turned its back on us here," Cuban national director of sports Luis Orlando Rodriguez warned, "there seems to be no alternative but for us to form a Latin American federation of baseball and compete as best we can against the American monopoly." After a score of Cubans were banned, Rodriguez called the majors a "commercial, imperialistic monopoly."[18]

Two competing leagues played in Cuba during the 1946–1947, one abiding by MLB dictates and the other challenging them. Meanwhile, MLB's impending reintegration meant that the color line no longer foreclosed the possibility to play major league ball in the United States. With the Mexican League losing money and Pasquel's commitment to it weakening, Cuban rhetoric about MLB's imperial policies softened. Not willing to incur additional suspensions and endanger its ties with MLB when the latter was likely to accept darker-skinned players, the Cuban League reached an agreement with the major leagues in 1947 that surrendered its autonomy.

The pact regulated the flow of players between MLB and the Cuban League, essentially making the latter a minor league for player development. MLB, not the Cuban

League, determined player eligibility and could prevent players under contract from playing in Cuba. The emphasis in Cuban baseball became preparing players to do well in the United States.

The few Caribbean leagues outside MLB's orbit did not last long. After Cuban baseball reached agreements with MLB, leagues in Puerto Rico, Panama, Venezuela, and the Dominican Republic normalized relations *á la* the Cuban model. These leagues played during the winter; their best players sought to sign with major league organizations.[19]

Mexico was the outlier. But Pasquel could not make his Mexican League economically viable. After sustaining large financial losses for a few seasons, he grew bored with his venture. When Pasquel left baseball for good following the 1948 season, the Mexican League capitulated. It no longer sought US players. Mexico continued to play a summer season but, unlike most of the Caribbean, did not become an appendage to MLB. Instead, the Mexican League and MLB reached an agreement in 1950 to respect each other's contracts. If a major league team wanted to sign a native player under contract to a Mexican team, it was required to pay that ball club to do so. Because of these additional costs, few major league teams sought Mexican players, slowing the flow of Mexicans to the majors and bolstering the Mexican League. Elsewhere in the region, because professional baseball was played during the winter, aspiring pros could sign contracts with both a major league and a winter league team.

Caribbean baseball's center of gravity moved northward to the United States. As a consequence, the sport's role and meaning in the Caribbean changed. What happened at the Ebbets Field or Forbes Field became more important than island play. This global shift in power relations took place during an era in which MLB was also aggressively consolidating its control of the game at all levels stateside.

Cuba, still the pearl of the baseball Antilles, was back in the orbit of the US game, but not for long. The Havana Sugar Kings played in the International League, the top minor league circuit during the 1950s, but after Fidel Castro came to power, the International League removed the franchise from Cuba. Cuban baseball became a noncommercial, state-supported venture often used as a tool of statecraft. While featuring strong leagues and players, it has had an uneasy relation with MLB ever since. Although Cuban and major leagues have played exhibition games, dozens of Cuban players have defected to sign major-league contracts. Others have played in the Mexican League but maintained Cuban citizenship and continue to represent their nation in international play. Cuba, while long dominating the *Mundiales*, the World Amateur Baseball Championships, has won Olympic and Pan Am medals. But as more Cubans leave to play abroad, a normalization of relations may soon be on global baseball's agenda.

Since integration, the number of Latinos in MLB has steadily increased. In the past decade, about one-fourth of all major leaguers and over 40 percent of all minor leaguers are Latino. The Dominican Republic alone accounts for over a tenth of all major leaguers and a third of minor leaguers. Many spent time at academies in the Dominican Republic where each major league organization maintains a full-time facility. Another half-dozen teams operate academies in Venezuela. Each houses and trains forty to fifty young players. These youths, who became eligible to sign contracts the summer they turned seventeen, compete to rise through the professional ranks. Latinos, who have outperformed other demographic groups in MLB statistically for over a decade, have become the new face of baseball. Between salaries, signing bonuses, and the academies, MLB injects $1 billion a year to the region.

THE PACIFIC RIM

Baseball has also gained purchase in the Pacific where a few communities took ownership of the sport and came to think of it as their own game. Baseball's appropriation has been most apparent in Japan, whose professional league is the world's second most powerful circuit. Due to distance, culture, and a sizable economy, Japanese baseball has forged more of a win–win relationship with MLB than the Caribbean.[20]

During the 1870s, Japan's government hired a number of Americans—the *oyatoi*—to implement state-inspired modernization programs. With education ministry backing, several integrated baseball into the physical education curriculum at a time when education was being made available to all children. At the same time, Japanese students attracted to baseball during their studies in the United States returned to take positions in government and the private sector. A few formed ball clubs, including the country's first private team, the Shinbashi Athletic Club, in 1878. These athletic clubs, along with high school and college teams, birthed an enduring baseball infrastructure. They played each other as well as teams of US sailors and Americans living in the Yokohama foreign settlement. The most notable of these Japanese teams, Ichiko, adopted what has been described as a *samurai* style of play in which players trained relentlessly as they disciplined their minds and bodies to sport. That quintessentially Japanese approach to the sport has characterized Japanese baseball ever since. When Ichiko defeated the Yokohama A.C. (a team of American expatiates who had initially refused to play them), many hailed the victories as affirmation of the nation. In addition to challenging teams made up of Caucasians residing in Japan, university squads toured the United States during the early twentieth century.

Japanese baseball soon lost its insularity as clubs from the United States and Japan began crisscrossing the Pacific. A score of collegiate squads and a handful of professional teams toured the Pacific, playing in Japan, in the Philippines, and on the US Pacific Coast before World War I. A 1913–1914 tour by teams fashioned from American and National League stars and led by New York Giants manager John McGraw and Chicago White Sox owner Charles Comiskey captured the most attention. It showcased the still-wide technical gap between American and Japanese play and pushed the latter to further develop their training and technique.

But Japanese baseball did not orient itself toward MLB in the United States. Instead, Japan became the hub of a trans-Pacific baseball world that operated independently of baseball in the United States. Just as Cuban *emigres* spread baseball around the Caribbean, Japanese settlers and government officials brought the game to Taiwan,

Southern Manchuria, and Korea. For the most part, baseball was meant to offer recreation for these Japanese and their sons in industrial leagues and the schools. Administrators believed that baseball, part of the overseas curriculum, would encourage students to maintain their Japanese identity.[21]

But the game spread to indigenous populations and sometimes took on political overtones, especially if a Japanese club played a Korean team. Sayuri Guthrie Shimizu describes how Japanese occupiers in Taiwan considered baseball and Western sport as the means to make Taiwanese men physically fit and better able to serve in the Japanese military. They also saw baseball as building fraternal bonds between the colonizers and the colonized.

In Korea, Japanese efforts to promote baseball were complemented by American missionaries who saw baseball as a way to convey muscular Christianity to converts and Korean students who had picked up the game during their studies in Japan. But Japan's annexation of Korea marginalized US influence, and baseball developed with a Japanese orientation and segregated play. Japanese students and industrial workers played in Japanese-only leagues, while Koreans competed on Korean teams. Koreans also bought their sporting goods from Japan.

Baseball traveled along with Japanese settlers to Hawai'i, California, Canada, and Brazil. Shimizu-Guthrie contends that the sport was so evocative of Japanese cultural meaning that it forged links to Japan while easing adaption to new surroundings.

Although World War I interrupted trans-Pacific baseball tours, they resumed afterwards. Negro Leaguers traveled to Japan while Lou Gehrig, Mickey Cochrane, and Lefty Grove led a star-studded squad there. In 1934, Japan hosted a group that featured the most popular ballplayer in the world, Babe Ruth. Nearing the end of his career, Ruth was showered with adulation. The exhibitions surpassed all others at the gate, and the first Japanese professional league formed afterward, beginning play in 1936.

Unlike MLB, where franchises were mostly owned by sporting entrepreneurs, Nippon Professional Baseball Association clubs were owned by railway companies and newspapers. The teams were designed to generate revenue by increasing riders and readers, as well as customers for the department stores and recreational facilities the companies owned. Just as MLB and Negro League clubs in the United States added Latinos to their rosters, these Japanese teams fielded the sons of the Japanese diaspora to Hawai'i, the Pacific, and the United States.[22]

By the late 1930s, professional and independent baseball had taken hold in three regions of the world: the United States and parts of Canada, the Caribbean basin, and the Pacific. While Cuba was the epicenter of Caribbean play, Japan was the center of gravity for the Pacific. World War II interrupted the efforts of those capitalizing on their ball-playing abilities and halted the amateur competitions that had begun to bring together national squads in the World Amateur Championships. These global connections resumed soon afterward.

After the war, Mexico and the Caribbean leagues resolved their differences with MLB, mostly on the latter's terms, while Japanese baseball regained its footing during the postwar Allied occupation. Japanese baseball operated with the sanction of the Supreme

Commander for the Allied Powers, which approved of the game's resurrection and saw it as a means of advancing the democratic and ideological goals of the occupation. In that regard, the United States had a more direct—if temporary—influence over Japanese baseball than it did in the Caribbean. According to Shimizu, a "new national iconography of peace, democracy, and freedom" emerged, in which the "rhetoric of baseball as America's and Japan's shared pastime and cultural connective tissue was strategically circulated" by both sides. Baseball offered a template for the "New Japan" as a "metaphor for democracy and American-style consumer culture and a symbol of a new partnership between the two nations." In 1949, the Japanese goodwill tour of San Francisco Seals of the Pacific Coast League was touted as evidence of the now-allied nations' mutual interests at a time of Cold War.[23]

Baseball's grip on Japan's sporting culture tightened at the scholastic, semiprofessional, and professional levels. The latter had little to fear from MLB, which was interested in neither its fans or its players. The possibility of MLB generating revenue from Japan did not yet extend beyond barnstorming; hence there was little potential conflict. Instead, Japanese baseball's ties with the nation's corporations advanced their mutual interests.

In the 1950s, squads of major leaguers resumed their post-season tours of Japan, generating revenues for both the visitors and their hosts. Other than these trans-Pacific tours and the presence of a few former major leaguers in Japanese baseball, the two nations' baseball systems operated independently of each other with no conflict over fans, players, or broadcast rights. Masanori Murakami pitched for the San Francisco Giants in the 1960s, but no Japanese player followed him to the United States until the 1990s when Hideo Nomo joined the Los Angeles Dodgers. Since then, more than forty Japanese players have debuted in the US major leagues. Some, especially Ichiro Suzuki and Hideki Matsui, have starred in the United States, just as they had in Japan.

The number of Japanese major leaguers has been limited by the player transfer agreement between the two nations' professional leagues. If a Japanese player and his team agree that the player can be "posted," the MLB squad submitting the highest bid to the player's Japanese club wins the right to negotiate with that player to sign a contract. If a contract is reached, the Japanese club keeps the bid. That makes Japanese players more expensive as major league clubs are required to pay both a salary and a posting fee. Japanese players who sign with major league teams before signing with a Japanese professional team are cheaper options.

Baseball also revived after World War II in Taiwan, Korea, and the Philippines. Taiwanese teams dominated Little League championships in the United States, winning seventeen of its international tournaments between 1969 and 1996. Some of the players on those squads played professionally in Japan, Korea, and their own island's Chinese Professional Baseball League. A few have joined major league teams in the United States, as have players from Korea.

Despite professional baseball's sway in regions where the game is popular, the sport's nonprofessional arena persists. The Little League World Series, reflecting youth baseball's appeal, brings eight teams from the United States and eight from other nations together for a championship series each summer. Olympic baseball has a longer but less consistent record. Played sporadically as an exhibition or demonstration sport at Olympic competitions since 1904, baseball gained official medal status at the 1992 Barcelona Games, only to lose it after the 2008 games for what International Olympic Committee president Jacques Rogge said was its lack of universality. When the international baseball federation tried to regain its status in a joint bid with women's softball, the committee restored wrestling instead. MLB's unwillingness to free up its players during the professional season in the United States as well as the league's belated efforts to confront the use of performance-enhancing drugs undermined baseball's chances.

Prior to the 1984 Los Angeles Games, Olympic baseball usually meant one-game exhibitions in which a US squad played the host nation. Though 100,000 spectators reportedly watched the 1956 Melbourne exhibition preceding the track and field competition, the sport could not claim a widespread global audience. During the five competitions for which a medal was at stake, beginning in 1992, Cuba won three times.

But while baseball was unable to retain its status as an Olympic sport, the World Baseball Classic has gained purchase. The Classic has been contested three times since 2006, with Japan winning in 2006 and 2009 and the Dominican Republic in 2013. The success of these sixteen-team tournaments (twenty-eight nations attempted to qualify) reflected MLB's desire to expand markets and hence its willingness to interrupt spring training so that many of its players from several nations were able to compete. The Classic has drawn well at the gate and reached a large international television audience, though it pales in comparison with the World Cups in soccer or rugby. Nevertheless, professional leagues in different countries seek to profit from a degree of global exposure the Olympics did not achieve. The 2017 Classic might prove to be the best gauge of baseball's capacity to reach more of a global audience in the immediate future.

Alan Klein, analyzing MLB efforts to extend its commercial reach, asks whether "it will do so as a twentieth-century colonialist or as a twenty-first-century decentered global enterprise." He describes the efforts of teams and their global division, MLB International, to find talent, sell merchandise, and gain broadcast revenues around the world, as well as their less commercial, long-term attempts to introduce the game in South Africa and other baseball hinterlands. MLB, he notes, already markets apparel made in Vietnam, Cambodia, and Bangladesh by Korean and Taiwanese manufacturers.[24] On some levels, it is thoroughly globalized. Spalding's vision persists long after his 1888 circumnavigation.

NOTES

1. Mark Lamster, *Spalding's World Tour: The Epic Adventure that Took Baseball Around the Glove—And Made it America's Game* (New York: Public Affairs Press, 2006).
2. Alan Klein and Robert Whiting were among the first to offer perspectives that recentered baseball's story on another society and considered the sport's transnational evolution. See also Rob Ruck, The Tropic of Baseball: Baseball in the Dominican Republic (University of Nebraska Press: 1999, second edition) and Raceball: How the Major Leagues Colonized the Black and Latin Game (Beacon Press: 2011); Adrian Burgos, Playing America's Game: Baseball, Latinos, and the Color Line (University of California Press: 2007) and Cuban Star: How One

Negro-League Owner Changed the Face of Baseball (Hill & Wang: 2011); Sayuri Guthrie Shimizu, *Transpacific Field of Dreams: How Baseball Linked the United States in Peace and War* (Chapel Hill: University of North Carolina Press, 2012).

3. Thomas Zeiler, *Ambassadors in Pinstripes: The Spalding World Tour and the Birth of the American Empire* (Lanham, MD: Rowman & Littlefield, 2006).

4. Lamster, *Spalding's World Tour*, 35; Zeiler, *Ambassadors*, x–xi.

5. Adrian Burgos Jr., "Baseball Should Follow the Flag: Latinos, the Color Line, and Major League Baseball's Globalization Strategies," paper presented at the Conference of Globalization and Sport in Historical Context, University of California, San Diego, March 2005.

6. Stefan Symanksi and Andrew Zimbalist, *National Pastime: How Americans Play Baseball and the Rest of the World Plays Soccer* (Washington, DC: Brookings Institution Press, 2006).

7. Lamster, *Spalding's World Tour*, 252.

8. Lamster, *Spalding's World Tour*, 66–68; Zeiler, *Ambassadors*, 47–50.

9. Louis A. Pérez Jr., "Between Baseball and Bullfighting: The Quest for Nationality in Cuba, 1868–1898," *The Journal of American History* 81.2 (1994): 500.

10. Perez, "Between Baseball," 9.

11. In addition to Perez, "Between Baseball," and Burgos, "Baseball Should Follow," Roberto González-Echevarría offers an account of Cuban baseball anchored in Cuba that goes well beyond analyses that treat the Latin game simply as an appendage of MLB and the United States in *The Pride of Havana: A History of Cuban Baseball* (Oxford: Oxford University Press, 1999).

12. Adrian Burgos Jr., *Playing America's Game* 90.

13. Until Robert Peterson (*Only the Ball Was White: A History of Legendary Black Players and All-Black Professional Teams* [New York: Prentice-Hall, 1970]); Donn Rogosin; Neil Lanctot (*Negro League Baseball: The Rise and Ruin of Black Institution* [Philadelphia: University of Pennsylvania Press, 2004]), and others who began studying the Negro leagues, baseball's historiography largely ignored Latin ball.

14. Pedro Julio Santana, interview, June 25, 1988, Santo Domingo, D.R.

15. Juan Bosch, interview, June 18, 1988, Santo Domingo, D.R.

16. Mexican baseball has begun to receive some attention, notably from John Virtue.

17. Milton Bracker, "Ruth's Visit Stirs Interest of Fans: Bambino Is Due in Mexico City Today— He Will 'Observe' and Also Enjoy Himself Interest Still Great A Curious Atmosphere," *The New York Times*, May 16, 1946, p. 32.

18. Luis Orlando Rodriguez Cuban Criticizes Chandler's Stand: Says Baseball Commissioner Opposes Agreement With Latin-American Group Excludes Cuban League Cites Players During War, *The New York Times*, December 13, 1946, p. 31.

19. Studies Cuban baseball since the 1959 Revolution include Milton Jamail, *Full Count: Inside Cuban Baseball* (Carbondale: Southern Illinois University Press, 2000); Peter Bjarkman, *A History of Cuban Baseball: 1864–2006* (Jefferson, NC: McFarland, 2007); and Mark Rucker, *Smoke: The Romance and Lore of Cuban Baseball* (Kingston, NY: Total/Sports Illustrated, 1999).

20. Robert Whiting's formidable trio of books about Japanese baseball, *The Chrysanthemum and the Bat* (New York: Avon, 1983); *The Meaning of Ichiro* (New York: Warner, 2004); and *You Gotta Have Wa* (New York: Macmillan, 1989), have recently been complemented by Shimizu, *Transpacific Field of Dreams*.

21. Shimizu, *Transpacific Field of Dreams*, traces the emergence of Japan as the epicenter of Asian baseball.

22. Alan Klein, *Growing the Game: The Globalization of Major League Baseball* (New Haven, CT: Yale University Press, 2006), and Guthrie-Shimizu, *Transpacific Field of Dreams*.

23. Shimizu, *Transpacific Field of Dreams*, 198–199.
24. Klein, *Growing the Game*.

BIBLIOGRAPHY

Bjarkman, Peter C. *A History of Cuban Baseball: 1864–2006*. Jefferson, NC: McFarland, 2007.

Burgos, Adrian Jr. "Baseball Should Follow the Flag: Latinos, the Color Line, and Major League Baseball's Globalization Strategies." Paper presented at the Conference of Globalization and Sport in Historical Context, University of California, San Diego, March 2005.

Burgos, Adrian Jr. *Cuban Star: How One Negro-League Owner Changed the Face of Baseball*. New York: Hill & Wang, 2011.

Burgos, Adrian Jr. *Playing America's Game: Baseball, Latinos, and the Color Line*. Berkeley: University of California Press, 2007.

Burk, Robert F. *Much More Than a Game: Players, Owners, and American Baseball Since1921*. Chapel Hill: University of North Carolina Press, 2001.

Burk, Robert F. *Never Just a Game: Players, Owners, and American Baseball to 1920*. Chapel Hill: University of North Carolina Press, 1994.

González-Echevarría, Roberto. *The Pride of Havana: A History of Cuban Baseball*. Oxford: Oxford University Press, 1999.

Jamail, Milton H. *Full Count: Inside Cuban Baseball*. Carbondale: Southern Illinois University Press, 2000.

Jamail, Milton H. *Venezuelan Bust, Baseball Boom: Andres Reiner and Scouting on the New Frontier*. Lincoln: University of Nebraska Press, 2008.

Kirsch, George. *The Creation of American Team Sports: Baseball & Cricket, 1838–72*. Urbana: University of Illinois Press, 1989.

Klein, Alan. *Baseball on the Border: A Tale of Two Laredos*. Princeton, NJ: Princeton University Press, 1997.

Klein, Alan. *Growing the Game: Globalization and Major League Baseball*. New Haven, CT: Yale University Press, 2006.

Klein, Alan. *Sugarball: The American Game, The Dominican Dream*. New Haven, CT: Yale University Press, 1991.

Lamster, Mark. *Spalding's World Tour: The Epic Adventure that Took Baseball around the Globe—And Made It America's Game*. New York: Public Affairs Press, 2006.

Lanctot, Neil. *Negro League Baseball: The Rise and Ruin of Black Institution*. Philadelphia: University of Pennsylvania Press, 2004.

Pérez, Louis A. Jr. "Between Baseball and Bullfighting: The Quest for Nationality in Cuba, 1868–1898." *The Journal of American History* 81.2 (1994): 493–517.

Peterson, Robert. *Only the Ball Was White: A History of Legendary Black Players and All-Black Professional Teams*. New York: Prentice-Hall, 1970.

Pettavino, Paula, and Geralyn Pye. *Sport in Cuba: Diamond in the Rough*. Pittsburgh: University of Pittsburgh Press, 1994.

Ruck, Rob. *Raceball: How the Major Leagues Colonized the Black and Latin Game* Boston: Beacon Press, 2011.

Ruck, Rob. *The Tropic of Baseball: Baseball in the Dominican Republic*. 2nd ed. Lincoln: University of Nebraska Press, 1999.

Rucker, Mark. *Smoke: The Romance and Lore of Cuban Baseball.* Kingston, NY: Total/Sports Illustrated, 1999.

Sayuri, Guthrie Shimizu. *Transpacific Field of Dreams: How Baseball Linked the United States in Peace and War.* Chapel Hill: University of North Carolina Press, 2012.

Symanksi, Stefan, and Andrew Zimbalist. *National Pastime: How Americans Play Baseball and the Rest of the World Plays Soccer.* Washington, DC: Brookings Institution Press, 2006.

Thorn, John. *Baseball in the Garden of Eden: The Secret History of the Early Game.* New York: Simon & Schuster, 2011.

Whiting, Robert. *The Chrysanthemum and the Bat.* New York: Avon, 1983.

Whiting, Robert. *The Meaning of Ichiro.* New York: Warner, 2004.

Whiting, Robert. *You Gotta Have Wa.* New York: Macmillan, 1989.

Zeiler, Thomas. *Ambassadors in Pinstripes: The Spalding World Tour and the Birth of the American Empire.* Lanham, MD: Rowman & Littlefield, 2006.

CHAPTER 14

....

CRICKET: THE INDIANIZATION OF AN IMPERIAL GAME

....

AMIT GUPTA

In the past twenty years, the center of power in international cricket has shifted away from the Western nations to the non-Western nations and the Board of Control for Cricket in India (BCCI) has emerged as the hegemon in the multinational game that was born in England but has been appropriated by India. The BCCI now controls over 80 percent of the advertising revenue in the game, and the Indian cricket team has replaced England and Australia as the team that brings financial rewards to any cricket tournament or national tour.[1] With this transformation we have seen the game enter the realm of modern commercialized and commodified sports. This chapter discusses the recent history of the changing power structure in world cricket, a transformation that represents a significant departure from the early history of cricket.

BACKGROUND

....

Cricket was a semi-amateur game whose decision-making process was dominated by the white nations of the British Empire. Several factors contributed to the game's semi-amateur status: until 1962 it maintained an amateur–professional divide in England, the birthplace of the game; cricket had a role in maintaining the status of British imperialism through the exercise of soft power; it was restrictive in its decision-making process; and, unlike other international sports, cricket at the highest levels sought to exclude nations from the most prestigious form of competition in the game—something that a truly commercial and capitalist enterprise would never condone.

Thus cricket was a game with its own internal class system where the amateur, even though a "shamateur"[2] in actual practice because many were paid under the table or through bogus jobs, were considered the elite and given status and special privileges while the professionals were looked down upon. Consequently, Keith A. P. Sandiford argues that class distinctions were "so rigidly preserved by the Victorians that professionals and amateurs used different facilities, dressed in different pavilions, used different gates, travelled in different compartments on trains, and, generally speaking, maintained a discreet distance."[3]

In addition to maintaining class distinctions, cricket helped perpetuate the myth of British Empire. As Mike Cronin and Richard Holt write, "Cricket was not only England's 'best loved game', it was also 'more than a game.' It was held to embody a style of behavior and system of values that were distinctively English."[4] From a British self-image perspective, cricket was viewed as providing English sportsmen who had a sense of fair play and leadership "to look after natives for their own good."[5] Thus Hilary Beckles and Michael Manley explain how the game took root in the Caribbean as part of the British imperial enterprise while Ramachandra Guha and Ashis Nandy have examined the reasons why the game gained popularity in India, which, by the early twenty-first century, dominated the game.

More important perhaps, the game became the embodiment of Englishness across the British Empire and formed a formidable weapon of British soft power in incorporating other nations into the British fold. Brian Stoddart makes the point more persuasively when he points out that British hard power—military force and repression—was only one part of the toolkit used by London to maintain the empire. The English language, culture, and sports were also a large part of the socialization of various nations into the British Empire: "But perhaps the most neglected agency in the process of cultural transfer from Britain to her colonial empire is that which involved sports and games. Through sport were transferred dominant British beliefs as to social behaviour, standards, relations, and conformity, all of which persisted beyond the end of the formal empire, and with considerable consequences for the postcolonial order."[6]

The game was initially exported to colonies like the United States, Canada, Australia, and South Africa (and there were even cricket clubs in countries like Mexico), and by 1909 the Imperial Cricket Council (which became the International Cricket Conference in 1965 and the International Cricket Council [ICC] in 1989) had been set up with the Maryleborne Cricket Club, the Australian Board of Control for International Cricket, and the South African Cricket Association as the original members. By 1926, New Zealand and the West Indies had joined the council, although at that time cricket in the West Indies was dominated by the expatriate white population—it was only in the 1960s, with Frank Worrell, that the West Indies gained its first black captain.

When the ICC was dominated by the Western nations, there was little emphasis on broadening the international fan base of the game or of making it into a truly professional sport. The old ICC was very reluctant to increase the number of Test-playing nations in the world (and in fact did not seek to promote the game in the non-Commonwealth nations) or for that matter to treat a country such as New Zealand as a bona fide Test-playing nation. (Tests are the highest level of the game, played between nation-states.) In the 1950s, England was to restrict New Zealand to three-day Test matches while Australia, through the 1950s and 1960s, did not bother to play its trans-Tasman Sea neighbor in Tests.

A Western-dominated ICC set the rules of the game, decided on event location (the first three cricket World Cups were held in England), and determined who was to be allowed to participate in Test cricket. Countries like Bangladesh, Zimbabwe (Rhodesia until 1980), and Sri Lanka were kept out of the Test-playing fold with Sri Lanka only being allowed to join in the 1980s, while Bangladesh and Zimbabwe became Test-playing nations in the 1990s. Nor was there an attempt until the 1980s to develop a set of Associate nations that played cricket and that could one day aspire to Test status. Most damaging, perhaps, was, as Melville shows, the fact that the game of cricket was allowed to lose its standing in the United States, which would have been a huge commercial market when the game was finally commercialized in the late twentieth century.

Last, the traditional authorities of the game did not make it financially attractive for cricketers to make it a long-term and full-time profession. Cricketers were so poorly paid that they often had to retire when in their twenties to try to earn a living wage. Test players made low wages, with Australian cricketers seeing their wages rise from AUD$20 a Test match to AUD$200 a game from 1970 to 1975.[7] Not surprisingly, cricketers put their own businesses and professions ahead of the game they loved to play and sought early retirement or limited their appearances in the national side.

The first real blow for player power and wage equality came in the form of Kerry Packer's World Series Cricket tournament in 1977 that poached Test players from all the cricket-playing nations except India (which strong-armed potential defectors Sunil Gavaskar and Bishen Singh Bedi) and set up an alternative first class competition to that of the traditional cricketing establishment. Packer's World Series Cricket was truly innovative: it brought in day–night games that were played under floodlights, thus permitting office-goers to enjoy the game; it brought colored clothing and multiple camera angles to make the telecast of the game more appealing; and, most important, it increased the wages of players and gave them real power in a game that had for long been dominated by administrators.

After two seasons, establishment cricket was able to buy off Packer by awarding his television station the rights to broadcast cricket in Australia, and the game was returned to the hands of the national boards. Yet the game had changed fundamentally, as the players were now willing to challenge national authority and risk bans and social ostracism in order to gain financial benefits. This was especially the case in the 1980s as the apartheid sporting establishment of South Africa sought to bring in rebel cricket tours to break its sporting isolation.

Apartheid South Africa's cricket team played its last Test series in 1970 against Australia. After that, thanks to the antiapartheid protests in both England (1970) and Australia (1971), the proposed South African tours of those countries were canceled (earlier the 1968–1969 tour of South Africa by England was cancelled because the South African government refused the nonwhite cricketer Basil D'Oliveira permission to come as part of the English team to South Africa).[8] By 1972, therefore, South African cricket had been banned from competing internationally and the government of South Africa itself faced increasing global pressure because of its racist policies.

In the 1980s, the South African cricket authorities sought to break out of the cricketing isolationism that international sanctions had imposed on them. Spearheaded by the former captain, Ali Bacher, the South African authorities organized a series of rebel cricket tours to the country by offering very attractive salaries to unofficial teams from Sri Lanka, England, Australia, and the West Indies. Despite international and Commonwealth-level bans against sporting links with South Africa, the rebel cricketers opted to go and face both international and domestic sanctions. The severity of these sanctions varied, as Peter May has written, with England and Australia issuing three-year bans and actually welcoming players back into the Test sides, Sri Lanka and the West Indies giving players lifelong bans, and Caribbean countries vilifying players to politicians and the general public.

The Rise of India, the Changing of the Guard, and the Advent of Technology

Two major changes took place that reshaped power relations within international cricket and moved it from being a semi-amateur game to one modeled on other international sports: the changing of the guard in the ICC and the advent of modern communications technology.

In the 1980s, bowing to pressure from the non-Western nations, the ICC elevated Sri Lanka to full Test-playing status, and then, in the 1990s, Zimbabwe and Bangladesh became the ninth and tenth Test-playing nations. This changed the voting politics of the ICC as the non-Western nations became the majority; it also coincided with the rise of India and the advent of global communications technology.

India: The Hub of Global Cricket

India's emergence as the principal financial backer of international cricket resulted from a combination of global and local factors. Despite the popularity of cricket in post-independent India, it was not a favored venue for international teams to visit, and India, in fact, did not play many international Tests from the 1940s to the 1970s. It played only forty-seven Tests in the 1950s and forty-nine in the 1960s. Thus the international careers of the Indian cricketers of that era were limited to a few appearances on the Test match stage. Mansur Ali Khan Patuadi, India's first modern Test captain, was in fact to retire from the game at the age of twenty-nine to pursue business interests. Indian cricketers from the 1950s to the 1970s depended on using their sporting fame to land jobs with companies or banks that would allow them time off to play cricket and, following retirement, continue to be on the firm's payrolls. Additionally,

India remained an unattractive sporting venue that international teams sought to avoid.

India's unattractiveness as a sporting venue was due to the fact that not only was the country a developing state but it was one that was constrained by the limitations of a socialist-style economy. Ashley Mallett and Ian Chappell, who toured India in the 1960s, point out that, while there was tremendous spectator interest in the game, the infrastructure and accommodations were poor, making a tour of the country an arduous exercise.[9] The revenue potential of cricket was not exploited but, instead, held back by bureaucratic rules and regulations and a lack of vision of the earning potential of the game. One-day cricket, for example, had been introduced in England in the 1960s, but it did not find a market in India until the 1973–1974 season when the Deodhar Trophy was introduced as a tournament.

Coupled with the state of the economy and the lack of vision of the BCCI was the fact that the Indian government was slow to recognize the value of modern communications, particularly the role of television. Jawaharlal Nehru is said to have expressed the view that television was an expensive toy that India could not afford, and this was reflected in state policies toward broadcasting. By 1970, India had issued only 248,300 licenses for television sets; the number had reached 3,632,328 by 1984.[10] This increase occurred due to the development of satellite technology and low power transmitters by India that permitted the broadcast of programming across a greater portion of the country. The decision to expand television transmission was made for political and educational reasons—as the government recognized the value of using television to promote its own message—but it had the unintended impact of helping provide a national audience for competitive sports.

The fact that India started to score a string of successes in the game fueled the synergy between television and Indian cricket in the early 1980s. The country won the 1983 World Cup and followed it up by winning the Australian centenary series in 1985. Cricket, always the most prestigious spectator sport in India, now started to gain more revenues from corporations and businesses who liked the glamour associated with the game.

In 1983, an unrelated event also had an impact on the fortunes of cricket in South Asia in general and India in particular, and it came from the tiny Persian Gulf emirate of Sharjah. A local businessman and cricket enthusiast, Abdul Rehman Bukhatir, organized a series of one-day tournaments that eventually brought in teams from around the world. Bukhatir created the Cricketers Benefit Fund Series that gave $50,000 to current cricketers and over $150,000 to long-retired cricketers who were often facing economic hardship.[11] The India–Pakistan games quickly became huge crowd-drawers because of the large expatriate Indian and Pakistan populations that worked in the Persian Gulf. Further, with the growing willingness of Indian and Pakistani television to show these programs live to domestic audiences, the market for the one-day form of the game grew in South Asia. Cricketers started to receive very attractive salaries for participating in the tournaments that Bukhatir organized, and the old reticence to play games in the non-Western world in arduous conditions melted away. India was initially slow to catch on to the one-day revolution that Bukhatir had brought to Asia, but when the BCCI did, it revolutionized the game.

The third change that facilitated the growth of Indian cricket was the decision in 1991 to undertake economic reforms in India. These economic reforms saw the loosening of India's stifling economic regulations, and more multinational corporations began to enter the country with a range of consumer products (market reforms had started in the 1980s but the economic crisis of 1991 led to a more concerted effort on the part of the Indian government). With the inflow of a new range of consumer products into the country there was a need to advertise these products, and new forms of cricket—with a commercial break every three minutes—provided the perfect setting for doing so.

THE GLOBALIZED SPORTING ARENA

The last factor that shaped modern game of cricket was the technological revolution that created global sports networks and a global sporting audience. As Brian Oliver and Richard Gillis point out, as late as 1987 no satellite television company had been given the license to operate. Moreover, barring 1983, there had never been live coverage of an overseas cricket tour by British television networks.[12] It was only in the late 1980s that British viewers were able to obtain continuous live coverage of overseas Test matches.

The advent of modern technology and the establishment of specialized television networks created a global market for sports and led the marketers of these games to seek an international audience. The American National Basketball Association (NBA) was successful in becoming a global phenomenon because it recruited players internationally and marketed the game around the world—a process that began with the 1989 decision to allow American professional basketball players to play in the 1992 Olympics, followed by the subsequent publicity used to sell the NBA as a global product.

With the creation of global sports networks like ESPN and Star Sports, these companies had to find programming to fill 24 hours/365 days of air time, so a range of sports became available for the hitherto starved sports fan. Fans who had followed their teams often in an expatriate setting through newspapers and radio now found that Australian Rules Football, domestic rugby leagues from Australia, and even second-tier soccer leagues like the Dutch league had become globally available.

Coupled with this phenomenon was the attempt of sports marketers to sell their sport in hitherto uncharted territories. Football and tennis had always had a global reach, but with the advent of global sporting networks there was an attempt to market Formula One racing and golf around the world. Ironically, the fake sport of professional wrestling gained global popularity and air time. Sports, by and large, therefore became characterized by a new imperative of commodification that required an international as opposed to a national audience.

As cricketing power swung toward the non-Western world, the BCCI also sought to commodify the sport, make it more inclusive, and, by creating a domestic league (the

Indian Premier League [IPL]), make it into one that exhibited the best characteristics of "glocalization." The IPL used the technological innovations brought about by globalization, but it succeeds because it is a national cricket league. This is especially important given the place cricket occupies in the international sporting context.

PROMOTING CRICKET IN
A GLOBALIZED WORLD

For cricket to flourish in a globalized environment, the game must be truly global, and it is, instead, a multinational or elite sport. A globalized sport is one that is played by an overwhelming majority of nations, is accessible to the masses, and has developed a fan following that is not based solely on national identity. Football is the one sport that is truly globalized: virtually every nation in the world is a member of FIFA, the game is inexpensive enough that it can be played by anyone, and the fans have developed their allegiances across national boundaries; for example, fans in Africa and Asia support European teams like Manchester United, Real Madrid, and Barcelona. Simon Kuper argues globalized fans are no longer satisfied with the third-rate teams in their own backyards. Instead, they want globalized teams, and with modern technology fans have achieved a "virtual" model of fandom that permits identification with teams and countries that the average fan is unlikely to ever visit.[13]

Multinational sports, on the other hand, are those played in a limited number of nations and do not have a global appeal—rugby is a sport that falls within this category. Within this grouping is the subcategory of elite sports like polo, golf, and yachting that, because of the high costs involved in playing or even watching the game, are restricted to a wealthy subsector of international society. Yet the emergence of Kuper's "virtual fan" may work to cricket's advantage.

Cricket, therefore, is a multinational sport: it is played by a few nations (ten) at the Test match level; it is not popular in the United States (the world's largest sporting market) despite having a long history in the country; and it is unlikely to see an expansion in teams at the highest level since countries like Holland and Namibia have player and fan bases that are too small for the sport to flourish. The limitations of cricket as a multinational sport became apparent in the 2007 Cricket World Cup. Once India was out of the tournament, viewership fell dramatically. On the other hand, the 2011 World Cup was a huge financial success, since it was played in India and the home team won. This situation is unlikely to change in the short to medium term as the ICC has ten Test match playing members and twenty-seven associate members and another fifty-five affiliate members. Realistically speaking, this gives cricket a very small spectator base to operate from and essentially makes it a South Asian sport.

Nor are there any cricketers who have transcended their game and become global icons and advertising brand names in non-cricket playing countries—as David

Beckham, Tiger Woods, and Michael Jordan have done for their sports in countries like China. Kevin Pieterson, Shane Warne, and Sachin Tendulkar remain legendary names in the cricket-playing world, but until cricket takes the unlikely step of becoming a globalized sport, they will remain unknown in two of the largest sporting markets in the world—the United States and China.

Further, regarding the demographics of the sport, India, Pakistan, Nepal, Sri Lanka, and Afghanistan account for 1.6 billion potential cricket fans while South Africa and Zimbabwe (the two other major non-Western Test-playing nations) account for another 72 million-odd fans. In contrast, Australia, New Zealand, and the United Kingdom have a combined fan population of close to 88 million.

Coupled with the demographic advantage of the non-Western countries is the fact that cricket is no longer the premier sport in the Western world. In the United Kingdom, football long ago overtook cricket as the national sport, however much nostalgia cricket may evoke amongst England's political classes. Rob Craddock points out that in a Cricket Australia survey of Australians under the age of thirty, the game came in behind dancing, walking, and tennis as a recreational activity.[14]

Further, unlike football, cricket in most countries does not have a strong domestic league to provide the game with the necessary financial support. Even in England, where the domestic league is stronger, the English county teams have become financially independent from the England and Wales Cricket Board only since the advent of Twenty20 (T20). In the other cricket-playing countries (Australia being a notable exception), domestic leagues are not profitable enough to support the national game. In football, on the other hand, the reverse is true. Even in years when their national teams are not doing well, the English, Italian, and Spanish leagues make large enough profits to help financially sustain the game within these countries. The English Premier League, for example, made a profit of 2.1 billion pounds in 2009–2010 (although, admittedly, sixteen of the top twenty clubs in the league saw a collective loss of 484 million pounds).[15]

In cricketing countries there is a heavy dependence on the international component of the game to survive, hence the critical reliance on the one-day version of the game. With attendance at Test matches generally slipping (again, Australia being a notable exception), it is the one-day or now T20 version of the game that has filled the coffers of the domestic cricket administrations. Even then, cricket associations like that in the West Indies have been chronically affected by the poor finances of the domestic game, and even sponsorship has not helped to move the game to greater financial solvency. The American billionaire Allen Stanford's willingness to put $1 million into a T20 cricket league in the West Indies was dubbed a financial success, but the collapse of the Stanford financial empire placed West Indies cricket's plans for expansion and rejuvenation of the game into doubt. The Stanford scandal also adversely affected England's own plans for financial viability, since the Texas billionaire had agreed to put $20 million for a five- to ten-year period into English cricket for a T20 quadrangular tournament.[16]

In contrast, the BCCI has managed to achieve control of the game because it has drawn on the lessons of successful global sports marketing as well as integrated modern technology to produce what is now a national league with a body of international players. This has removed the limitations of basing its success on a national league with a domestic pool of players—especially in terms of the drawing power of the star players.

THE INDIAN PREMIER LEAGUE

The success of the IPL is due to several factors. The first is India's huge sporting market of over a billion people—a market that is almost three times as large as the United States and over twice as large as the European market. Consequently, the sport, while drawing from a global talent pool, did not require a global television market to become a success. The advertising revenues from domestic sources as well as ticket sales and merchandizing were enough to make the tournament a profitable one in the long run. *The Economist* magazine elaborated this point:

> For advertisers, the IPL's audience is mouth-watering. It is dominated by young, middle-class city-dwellers, who are among India's most free-spending consumers. Remarkably, around 45% of viewers are women. They are attracted not only to the IPL's breathless sort of cricket but also to the glamour that attends it. . . .
>
> In an economy expanding by about 8% a year and with a cable-television market growing at a similar clip, the league's prospects appear gilded. According to Mr. Mallya, "the revenues generated by the league can only go one way, north—and go rapidly north."[17]

Second, the United States is not a factor in the marketing and commodification of the sport. Cricket is, therefore, unique to international sports because a non-Western nation is the largest single market for the game. Third, whereas in other cricket-playing nations the game must compete with a number of sports, in India cricket is the only game that has a huge mass following, television coverage, and corporate sponsorship. Fourth, the IPL brings in the best talent in the world and by creating city-based sides has set the groundwork for true sporting rivalries to emerge, as well as given the league a local character that is so necessary to sell it to the Indian public. In that way, the IPL resembles the football leagues of Italy, Spain, and England (the IPL was in fact modeled on the English Premier League), where international players add talent and glamour to local teams.

ESSENTIAL ISSUES AND QUESTIONS

Three key issues have emerged from the recent history of international cricket: the geographic power shift, the future of Test cricket, and economic pressures on players to make the choice between club and country. The resolution of these issues will shape the sport as it moves into the twenty-first century.

The power shift that took place in the late 1990s witnessed control of the sport moving from the Western nations to South Asia—particularly India and the BCCI. While the shift has led the game to become modernized, financially solvent, and, to an extent commodified, it has brought with it attendant problems of corruption. The question, therefore, emerges: Can modern cricket move away from the corrupt practices that threaten the very future of the game? One way to do this would be to lessen the power of the South Asian nations, particularly India, but that would require massive infusions of capital into the game in the countries that are the traditional powerhouses—Australia and England—since this would bring a financial counterweight to South Asia and help create a more effective monitoring of the game. The latter would be possible because the rest of the Test-playing nations would not be financially beholden to India.

Second, part of the romance of Test cricket lies in the best national players playing at that level of the game. More recently, however, players like Andrew Flintoff and Lasith Malinga have forsaken Test careers to concentrate on shorter versions of the game—a trend that is likely to grow given the more lucrative and less physically taxing nature of T20 and one-day games. If this trend continues, then not only will Test cricket lose its relevance, but the sport's value as an international sporting event is likely to decline because, unlike football, the Test match version of the game remains too long and unwieldy to attract a greater number of viewers.

The third issue comes from the changing nature of the game, the compulsions of modern life, and the emergence of new technologies. In the contemporary world, Test match cricket has lost its attractiveness to fans in most of the cricket-playing nations while shorter versions of the game—T20 and one-day games—remain very popular. For the traditionalists who see Test cricket as being the repository of both the game's true skills and traditions, moving to shorter versions of the game means essentially disassociating the sport from its rich historical past. How cricket administrators are able to package Test cricket to make it attractive to younger viewers and fans will be the key to maintaining the traditions and heritage of the game.

NOTES

1. In 2011 cricket brought in $2.41 billion, about a quarter of the advertising revenue in India. See Shilpa Jamkhandikar, "Cricket-India Advertisers Keep Faith with Struggling Stars," Reuters, http://www.reuters.com/article/2012/01/19/cricket-india-brand-idUSL3E8CI68220120119.
2. Sir Derek Birley, *A Social History of English Cricket* (London: Aurum Press, 1999), 46.
3. Christopher Brookes, *English Cricket: The Game and its Players through the Ages* (London: Weidenfeld and Nicolson, 1978), cited in Keith A. P. Sandiford, "Amateurs and Professionals in Victorian County Cricket," *Albion: A Quarterly Journal Concerned with British Studies* 15.1 (1983): 33.

4. Mike Cronin and Richard Holt, "The Imperial Game in Crisis: English Cricket and Decolonization," in *British Culture and the End of Empire*, ed. Stuart Ward (Manchester, UK, and New York: Manchester University Press, 2001), 115.

5. Cronin and Holt, "The Imperial Game," 118.

6. Brian Stoddart, "Sport, Cultural Imperialism, and Colonial Response in the British Empire," *Comparative Studies in Society and History* 30.4 (1988): 651.

7. Gideon Haigh, *The Cricket War* (Melbourne: Text Publishing, 1993), 16.

8. A recent discussion of the D'Oliveira affair appears in Peter Oborne, *Basil D'Oliveira. Cricket and Conspiracy: The Untold Story* (London: Sphere Books, 2011), 189–207 and 225–228. D'Oliveira had initially been dropped from the 1968–1969 tour of South Africa but was later included, and the South African government decided to refuse D'Oliveira entry into the country. The Maryleborne Cricket Club responded by canceling the tour.

9. Ashley Mallett, with Ian Chappell, *The Ian Chappell Story* (London: Orion, 2006), 35–40.

10. P. C. Chatterji, *Broadcasting in India* (New Delhi: SAGE, 1991), 57.

11. M. Coward, "Bukhatir Has Last Laugh over Cricket in the Gulf," *Courier-Mail*, March 28, 1985.

12. Brian Oliver and Richard Gillis, "Games without Frontiers," *The Observer*, October 28, 2007.

13. Oliver and Gillis, "Games without Frontiers," xiii.

14. Robert Craddock, "Cricket Faces a Gloomy Future," *The Courier Mail*, March 21, 2011.

15. David Conn, "Record Income But Record Losses for Premier League," *The Guardian*, May 19, 2011.

16. Scyld Berry, "Greed Still Rules a Year after the Stanford Debasement; Lessons from Grubby Episode Have Not Been Learned as Cash Remains Major Motivation," *The Sunday Telegraph*, October 25, 2009.

17. "Go Fetch That: The Indian Premier League," *The Economist*, January 15, 2011.

BIBLIOGRAPHY

Beckles, Hilary McD. *The Development of West Indies Cricket: The Age of Nationalism*, Vol. 1. London: Pluto Press, 1998.

Birley, Sir Derek. *A Social History of English Cricket*. London: Aurum Press, 1999.

Bose, Mihir. *A History of Indian Cricket*. London: Andre Deutsch, 2002.

Brookes, Christopher. *English Cricket: The Game and its Players through the Ages*. London: Weidenfeld and Nicolson, 1978.

Chatterji, P. C. *Broadcasting in India*. New Delhi: SAGE, 1991.

Guha, Ramachandra. *A Corner of a Foreign Field: The Indian History of a British Sport*. Basingstoke, UK, and Oxford: Picador, 2002.

Gupta, Amit. "India: The Epicenter of Cricket." In *Cricket and Globalization*, edited by Stephen Wagg and Chris Rumford, 41–59. Newcastle upon Tyne: Cambridge Scholars, 2010.

Haigh, Gideon. *The Cricket War*. Melbourne: Text Publishing, 1993.

Harte, Chris, and Bernard Whimpress. *The History of Australian Cricket*. London: Carlton Books, 2009.

Holt, Richard. "The Imperial Game in Crisis: English Cricket and Decolonization." In *British Culture and the End of Empire*, edited by Stuart Ward, 111–127. Manchester, UK, and New York: Manchester University Press, 2001.

Majumdar, Boria. *Corridors of Uncertainty.* New Delhi: Harper Collins India, 2010.

Majumdar, Boria. *Indian Cricket: An Illustrated History.* Gloucestershire, UK: History Press, 2006.

Mallett, Ashley, with Ian Chappell, *The Ian Chappell Story.* London: Orion, 2006.

Manley, Michael. *The History of West Indies Cricket.* London: Andre Deutsch, 1995.

May, Peter. *The Rebel Tours: Cricket's Crisis of Conscience.* Cheltenham, UK: Sports Books, 2009.

Melville, Tom. *The Tented Field: A History of Cricket in America.* Bowling Green, OH: Bowling Green State University Popular Press, 1998.

Nandy, Ashis. *The Tao of Cricket.* New Delhi: Oxford University Press, 2000.

Oborne, Peter. *Basil D'Oliveira. Cricket and Conspiracy: The Untold Story.* London: Sphere Books, 2011.

Sandiford, Keith A. P. "Amateurs and Professionals in Victorian County Cricket." *Albion: A Quarterly Journal Concerned with British Studies* 15.1 (1983): 32–51.

Stoddart, Brian. "Sport, Cultural Imperialism, and Colonial Response in the British Empire." *Comparative Studies in Society and History* 30.4 (1988): 649–673.

CHAPTER 15

....

SURFING: A GLOBAL
PHENOMENON

....

DOUGLAS BOOTH

TODAY, in the early twenty-first century, surfers glide across, and maneuver around and over, the faces of waves wherever they break. Every ocean and every sea, as well as many rivers and lakes, have been surfed. In the grand narrative of surfing history, the sport began in Hawai'i from where it spread worldwide. The initial diffusion, in the early twentieth century, followed the Hawaiians George Freeth and Duke Kahanamoku, who demonstrated surfing in the United States, Australia, and New Zealand. A second diffusion, in the third quarter of the twentieth century, followed devotees, mainly from California and Australia, in their search for new waves. In the late twentieth century, two processes, codification as a sport and commercialization, homogenized surfing culture. Straightforward and alluring, this story presents a totalizing perspective of surfing that raises historiographical questions about evidence, context, and social memory.

If Hawai'i is the "birthplace" of premodern and modern surfing, historians and anthropologists nevertheless acknowledge that surfing existed throughout Polynesia and elsewhere. They claim Tahitians and Hawaiians were the only people to ride full-length boards and to stand upright, and they identify Hawaiians as uniquely obsessed with the practice. Origin stories invariably refer to the "discovery" of surfing in Hawai'i by Western explorers, disapproval of the practice by American missionaries, its subsequent decline in the mid-nineteenth century, and its revival in the early twentieth century.

Freeth and Kahanamoku were key agents in the revival of surfing at the turn of the twentieth century. Born in Honolulu in 1883 to an Irish father and half-Polynesian mother, Freeth began surfing at Waikīkī in his late teens. He learned to angle his surf-boards, which at the time were made from solid wood. They were heavy and lacked maneuverability across the face of the wave. Tutored by Freeth, Kahanamoku cofounded the Hui Nalu (Club of Waves) at Waikīkī Beach. Freeth and Kahanamoku were also the principal agents of surfing's diffusion. Freeth relocated to California late in 1907 and demonstrated the art at numerous beaches, including Venice and Redondo. In addition to giving wave-riding demonstrations in California, New York, and Atlantic City, as well as Australia and New Zealand, Kahanamoku taught numerous Waikīkī visitors to surf; some, including Nigel Oxendew (Jersey) and Carlos Dogny (Peru), took the pastime home.

Kahanamoku had a profound impact on the development of surfing in Australia through his influence on Claude West and Charles "Snowy" McAlister. Kahanamoku taught West to ride a board, eventually becoming Australia's most accomplished surfer. At eleven, McAlister watched Kahanamoku's demonstrations, and a decade later he succeeded West as Australia's best rider. McAlister contributed to the global diffusion of surfing when, in 1928, he demonstrated the art near Durban in South Africa. Kahanamoku also had a direct influence on Tom Blake, the American swimmer, lifeguard, and surfer who invented the hollow board and fin.

The Wisconsin-born Blake took his first step toward the beach when, as an eighteen-year-old high-school dropout, he went to a Detroit cinema to watch a newsreel of the Antwerp Olympics. In the lobby he met and shook hands with Kahanamoku, who had competed in those games. Blake moved to Santa Monica where he worked as a lifeguard. He took up surfing and developed an interest in the history of the pastime. Blake started visiting Hawai'i beginning in the mid-1920s. Soon thereafter, Blake developed the hollow board based on a box frame covered with plywood. Blake's boards were elongated and attracted appellations such as "pencils" and "toothpicks"; shorter versions were usually designated "surfboards." In 1935 Blake added a fin to the underside tail that enabled surfers to "ride on a tighter angle across the wave."

As well as commercially producing hollow boards, Blake published advice on building them in his book *Hawaiian Surfboard* (1935). The Australian Frank Adler made a hollow board "by carefully following the do-it-yourself instructions from an imported issue of *Modern Mechanix*." In Brazil two teenagers built hollow boards based on Blake's instructions in *Popular Mechanics*. Blake's hollow boards also diffused to the United Kingdom and Europe. English surf pioneer Jimmy Dix tried to build a board based on a picture in an encyclopedia. He failed and wrote to a surf club in Hawai'i for more precise instructions; the club obliged by sending him a hollow board made by Blake. In 1940 Pip Staffieri built a board based on Dix's Blake model, which he saw lying on the beach at Newquay. Lifeguards everywhere prized Blake's boards as rescue equipment. In many places they doubled for wave-riding. In Germany Uwe Drath, a lifeguard at Sylt (near the Danish border) stood on a rescue board in the early 1950s to probably become the first person to surf on his feet in continental Europe.

In the late 1940s, Bob Simmons from California designed the Malibu surfboard, which he built from lightweight balsa and sealed with resin-saturated fiberglass cloth. Simmons' Malibu boards were smaller, lighter, faster, and more controllable than solid or hollow boards. They enabled the rider to choose a more acute angle across the wave face. Most important, they popularized the pastime and quickly diffused to distant shores. Malibus arrived in Australia in late 1956 with a team of American lifeguards who competed in a special international carnival coinciding with the Olympic Games in Melbourne. American surfers Doug McDonald and Dorian "Doc" Paskowitz introduced

Malibu boards to Newquay (England) and Israel, respectively. When Paskowitz headed to Israel in 1956, he took a Malibu "just in case the Mediterranean had waves." Surfing at Frishman Beach, then the Santa Monica of Israel, Paskowitz "awed" local lifeguards Shaul Zinner and Shamai "Topsi" Kanzapolski. "Zinner borrowed Paskowitz's board, paddled out, and stood up on his first wave. Paskowitz left his board with the lifeguards and later sent a further six to seed Israel's surf industry."[1]

Surfboard technology rapidly advanced from the late 1960s. Boards became smaller, lighter, and more maneuverable. Surfer hippies traveling in search of perfect waves contributed to the sport's global diffusion. French surfer Pierre Chalaud pointed some Australians to Morocco and arranged accommodation for them in Mehdiya where they stayed for a couple of years and made the first excursions south for waves. Soon there was a regular trickle of hippie vans up and down the Moroccan coast. Some surfers left behind their boards, which helped the local population to pick up the sport.

A new generation of surf films, notably Paul Witzig's trilogy (*Hot Generation*, 1967; *Evolution*, 1969; *Sea of Joy*, 1971), John Severson's *Pacific Vibrations* (1970), and Alby Falzon and Dave Elfick's *The Morning of the Earth* (1972) inspired many hippie surfers. These films expressed the prevailing *Zeitgeist* of "alternative life styles, . . . psychedelic drugs and letting tomorrow's problems take care of themselves."[2] Sydneysider Peter Neely "discovered Bali" after "a couple of hippy friends . . . returned with bright eyes and wonderful tales of an exotic Asian 'surfer's paradise,' with hippies surfing naked and smoking chillums on the beaches. Then I saw *Morning of the Earth*. . . . The fuse was lit. . . . I quit work and headed over to Bali for two months in April 1975."[3]

Still, Hawai'i, California, and Australia were the epicenters of surfing in the first half of the twentieth century. Distinct cultures in these locales help explain the different ways that these communities received and understood surfing. At Waikīkī, the home of surfing in Hawai'i in the early twentieth century, so-called beachboys built lifestyles around the beach. They earned money as lifeguards and hotel workers. They spent their free time surfing, swimming, fishing, playing music, and engaging in all manner of pranks and buffoonery. While grounded in hedonism, beachboy culture at Waikīkī was also fully integrated into the tourist industry. California surfers established a distinct culture in the 1930s and 1940s.

The American lifeguards/surfers who demonstrated Malibu boards in Australia in 1956 enthralled local surfers and revolutionized the pastime there. The Malibu precipitated a new social movement as young men fled surf lifesaving clubs; some became independent surfers, and some joined the newly formed Australian Surfriders Association that promoted surfing as a sport. In the mid-1960s, a culturally significant debate over surfing style emerged between Australians and Californians. Californian surfers claimed to have forged a distinct riding style over the previous decades. They based this style on tracking along the wall of the wave and changing direction by leaning and shifting their weight, bending their knees and pushing. This style developed into an "American dance" based on enhancing the beauty of a breaking wave and "dueling" with its curl.[4] In 1966, the Australian magazine *Surfing World* boldly announced a "new era" in which "impetuous youth" had swept away the aesthetic grace and poise of the California style and replaced with it aggression, power, and radical (creative) maneuvers. The source of this debate in the grand narrative of surfing lies in a nationalistic Australian culture, to which the surf lifesaving movement contributed, and claims by Australian surfers that their locally designed equipment facilitated radical surfing. Eventually, local variations in surfing style dissolved in the 1970s and 1980s as surfers became "part of a global tribe, sharing the waves and a special brotherhood."[5]

The homogenization of surfing culture accompanied the codification of surfing as a sport (with the formation of a professional circuit) and the commercialization of the production and exchange of surfing's material elements (e.g., surfboards, wetsuits, clothing, magazines, videos). Many surfers have been ambivalent toward competition and suspicious of contests, which they say create jealousies and take the pleasure out of a pastime that should celebrate a communion with nature rather than scoring points. While narratives of competition touch on a range of subjects, including international tensions, personal rivalries, and discrimination against women surfers, two themes dominate: (a) the inevitable growth of professional surfing from 1954 and the inaugural International Surfing Championships held at Makaha (Hawai'i), which marked the formation of an independent sport and (b) the launch of International Professional Surfers, the predecessor of the Association of Surfing Professionals (ASP), as the governing body of professional surfing in 1976.

The second major theme in narratives of competition concerns the relationship between the ASP and the surfing industry and the governing body's reliance on global surfing corporations such as Rip Curl, Billabong, Quiksilver, Hurley, Volcom, and O'Neil to underwrite events as licensees. Given the cultural ambivalence toward surfing contests, the question remains regarding how the surfing industry can maintain credibility while simultaneously advancing elite competition. The answer is benign commercialization.

Surfing became a popular, mass pastime in the late 1950s and early 1960s with the coalescence of the Malibu board, the positive portrayal of surfing by Hollywood beach films such as *Gidget*, and the launch of an organic surfing media that produced films and magazines that spoke to aficionados. While surfing's popular appeal opened commercial opportunities for participants, historians present this process as democratic (by making the practice more accessible) and benign.[6] Bruce Brown, the producer and director of *The Endless Summer* (1966), articulates this perspective:

> Back in the early '50s, when I started surfing, . . . we lived without giving it much thought. We knew we had to live by the ocean and needed to figure out a way to make a living there. Hobie made surfboards, Gordon Clark made foam blanks, John Severson started *Surfer* magazine, I started making movies. Whatever we did, the main focus was how it would affect our surf time. Getting rich wasn't important. What was important was having the freedom to do what we wanted.[7]

The official narratives of the major surfing corporations, notably Rip Curl, Quiksilver, and Billabong, add further authority. Tracing their origins and development from backyard operations in the 1960s and early 1970s, these narratives stress the companies' commitment to surfing culture and lifestyle over profit.

The grand narrative of surfing presents the history of the pastime from its origins in Hawai'i to a contemporary global culture. It is a coherent narrative, the authenticity and truth of which lies in its diverse and rich sources, but, like all narratives, surfing's master narrative is a representation, rather than a reconstruction, of the past, and representations involve tidying complexities and silencing both evidence and alternative interpretations. In fact, a plethora of alternative evidence and interpretations disrupts the grand narrative of surfing and exposes a more complex, disordered, and chaotic past.

The practice of using floating materials to ride waves appears around the world. Fishermen have ridden their craft (of all descriptions) to shore on incoming waves down the ages, while children have long used flat pieces of wood as planning devices that they hold with outstretched arms in front of their bodies The wide dispersal of warm water, waves, and communities interested, and skilled, in water-based activities, along with enormous variations in board shapes and designs, suggest that surfing emerged independently at multiple locations rather than diffusing from a single site. Even as recently as 2000, California surfer Sam George found an "indigenous surf culture" in a fishing village on the south side of São Tomé in the Gulf of Guinea when he went to the island in search of waves; there he "discovered" children riding hand-carved bodyboards and crude wooden surf boats. Australian surfbathers played with homemade boards in the 1890s, twenty years before Duke Kahanamoku's demonstration.

Missionary disapproval was just one factor in the decline of surfing, as was the decimation of the Hawaiian population by Western diseases and the transformation of the economy. The privatization of land and proletarianization of the *maka'ainana* (commoner class) and the restructuring of leisure also contributed. Similarly, the development of the tourist industry by American merchants and commercial interests in the 1890s—coinciding with the overthrow of the Hawaiian monarchy in 1893 and the annexation of Hawaii by the United States in 1898—throws a different light on the revival of surfing. These details channel attention toward structural forces and away from individuals such as Freeth and Kahanamoku.

Polynesians enlisted in the whaling and sealing industries beginning in the late eighteenth century. They roamed widely across the Pacific. Against this background Michael Scott Moore finds that "it is hard to imagine" experienced surfers passing by perfect point breaks in Australia, California, or New Zealand and "not improvising a board" for a surf.[8] Brothers Jonah Kūhiō Kalaniana'ole, David Kawānanakoa, and Edward Keli'iahonui—nephews of Queen Kapi'olani, queen to Hawai'i's King Kalākaua—took surfboards to California when they enrolled at St. Matthew's Military School in San Mateo in the mid-1880s. Evidence shows the trio surfing at the mouth of the San Lorenzo River, Monterey Bay, more than twenty years before George Freeth arrived on the mainland;[9] moreover, Kūhiō was a prominent surfer at Waikīkī in the 1890s.[10]

Similarly, there was a "growing enthusiasm" for Hawaiian surfboards on Sydney beaches nearly a decade before Kahanamoku's visit. Yet, surfing was not always enthusiastically embraced by social establishments. Alex Leonard notes that "the majority of

Kuta residents frowned upon surfing" when it first arrived on Bali in the 1970s, while surfer Peter Rigby recalls local Western Australian farmers in the same period extending "charming salutations" such as "On ya bike, ya farken surfie dickhead."[11] On the other hand, some critics equate surfers to colonizers. "They descend like gods into [a] primitive village in Ghana," writes Joan Ormrod of California surfers Robert August and Mike Hynson in *The Endless Summer* (1966):

> They are the first white men ever seen by many of the villagers, and as the missionaries in Hawaii, they set about spreading the good word, in this case, surfing. They establish a surf school to teach the children how to surf. The children quickly take to this new pastime, making paddleboards for themselves to surf the waves. The wilderness, uncultivated and unshaped is evoked in descriptions of the unknown surf spot. [Producer Bruce] Brown describes, "surf that no one had ever ridden before. . . . This echoes a colonial enterprise as it claims symbolic ownership of the wilderness for surfing and America.[12]

While the grand narrative tends to reify surfing competition and cultural commercialization, criticism of surfing bureaucracies and corporations litter conversations among the grassroots. Stuart Butler and David Shearer echo the concerns of many when they ask how recreational surfers benefit from contests. Butler had just endured a summer in which contests overran his local beaches and seemed to "fuse into one four month long heat" that left "the best sand bars out of bounds to most surfers." "All I gained from surf contests" this year, Butler complained, was "an increasing petrol bill, fewer places to surf, more crowds and more so called surf heroes dropping in on me."[13] Voicing his opposition to a proposed world tour event sponsored by Rip Curl at the northern New South Wales break of Lennox Head and citing a corporate insider who described the annual Rip Curl–sponsored contest at Bells Beach as "a month of total mayhem and disruption," Shearer warned local surfers that they will wake up to find their beaches invaded by "dinky structures selling trinkets, loudspeakers, sirens and flabby music . . ., [and] the water filled with jetskis and cops clearing people out."[14]

Shearer's comments raise questions about the benignity of commercialized surfing culture. Surfer and journalist Derek Rielly finds little amity among Rip Curl, Quiksilver, and Billabong, which he accuses of being "aggressive, conservative and competition-driven global surfing corporations."[15] Indeed, their diversification into fragrances, bedroom accessories, and travel agencies has confirmed that accumulation for the sake of accumulation has penetrated surfing culture. The corporate mindset also extended to protecting their images. After reading Phil Jarratt's draft of their company's history, Quiksilver executives, who commissioned him to write the text, expressed their displeasure at his "warts and all" version, which included details about conflicts within the company as well as tales of "booze, drugs and partying." They offered Jarratt two options, "take a hike" or "start again." Confessing his likes for the money and business-class travel, Jarratt chose to rewrite and produced *The Mountain and the Wave: The Quiksilver Story* (2006). Jarratt subsequently dismissed this text as an "annual report."[16]

In 2012 the ASP sold the elite men's and women's professional circuits to ZoSea Media. ZoSea centralized the management, sponsorship, and broadcasting of the world championship tour and greatly reduced the license fee that surfing corporations, yet to recover from the Great Financial Crisis, pay to host an event. However, the leading surfing companies' names remain etched into the principal sporting events as sponsors, and it is not clear how ZoSea can generate support for the sport among a skeptical surfing community that can access surfing prowess through noncompetition mediums.

Responding to criticisms, the surfing corporations insisted that growth and profits depend on their cultural authenticity. But as the launch of the Hollister surf company by Abercrombie & Fitch in 2000 illustrates, "cultural authenticity" is easily manufactured. According to Abercrombie & Fitch, the merchant J. M. Hollister founded the company in 1922 after discovering "the sun-drenched spirit of California and the surf and soul of the Pacific Ocean"; his goal was to cater for "a laid-back, aspirational lifestyle." In fact, Abercrombie & Fitch launched Hollister as a strategy to reach the mainstream youth market living in the Midwest United States. Hollister surf shops sat at the center of this strategy. On the outside they looked like beach shacks; inside, flat-screen televisions played live feeds of the surf at Huntington Beach, and lounge areas, complete with potted palm trees, offered chairs and surf magazines. The object was to convey a " 'SoCal surf' atmosphere." Tom Holbrook, from rival Quiksilver, gives the stores "A [for] . . . romance" and says Hollister has "packaged the environment better than anybody. 'When you can sit in Michigan and . . . check the surf, they're basically connecting the dots to convey that they are pretty authentic"—even if that authenticity has been, in the words of another retail analyst, "false" and based on "invented" history.[17] The marketing strategies employed by surfing corporations have not escaped grassroots surfers. According to Mark Stranger, many surfers now "shun" the products of Rip Curl, Billabong, and Quiksilver in favor of smaller companies; some "refuse" to wear surf labels.[18]

Stranger's observations introduce the essential role of context in historical narratives. E. P. Thompson labeled history the "discipline of context," which requires historians to establish coherent and consistent relationships between objects, agents, and ideas within their narratives.[19] The sentiments and actions of grassroots surfers provide such critical context in narratives of the homogenization of surfing. Indeed, grassroots culture does manifest in the grand narratives of surfing through themes such as travel (i.e., the "surfari" and its commercialized variant "the search") and localism (a form of territorialism in which surfers who define themselves as locals assume privileges at "their" breaks and display aggression toward outsiders). Commenting that localism has "taken root to one degree or another in virtually all populated surfing areas, from Vancouver Island to the Basque Country to Western Australia to Mauritius," Matt Warshaw puts localism into the context of overcrowding and the commercialization of surfing.[20] In the tradition of searching for origins, Warshaw traces localism to Miki Dora, a legendary outlaw figure in surfing culture, who railed against overcrowding at Malibu in the late 1950s. Dora blamed crowds on commercialization, which he said had led "kooks, fags, finks, ego heroes, Amen groupies and football-punchy Valley swingers" to his playground. According to Warshaw, Dora may not have been the first to direct disdain, abuse, and aggression toward other surfers, but he was the first to render such behavior "fashion-able," and "without him . . . it would never have had the same vogue and cachet."[21]

Others, however, place localism in different contexts or conceptualize it in different ways. Isaiah Walker, Eric Ishiwata, and Alex Leonard explain localism on the North Shore of O'ahu and Bali in the context of anticolonialism against foreign surfers, local governments, tourist industries, and property developers.[22] Many surfers conceptu-alize localism as an issue of respect. Explaining the localism at Padang Padang (Bali), Indonesian professional surfer Rizal Tanjung says:

> We gather in the farthest spot and nobody is allowed to come inside us. We have to be farthest inside. If anybody goes inside us, we let them know it's not right. If I'm surfing in another country, there's no way I'll sit farthest inside. We always have to *respect* the locals. But at Padang Padang we have to control the crowd. In a way, we're like policemen: "You take that wave, I'll take this one. . . ." We have to control the lineup. After all, we were subjugated before, so why should we allow ourselves to be subjugated again now? We have to be the ones to show them how, not they the ones to show us how.[23]

Renowned Burleigh Heads (Australia) local Dwayne Harris and prominent North Shore (Hawai'i) local Makua Rothman echo Rizal. "Wherever I go I *respect* the locals," declares Harris. "I'll sit on the outside and wait my turn. That's what it's all about. That's all the local crew out here want. To get waves . . . without hassling."[24] Rothman similarly comments that Hawaiians do not go to Australia and Tahiti and "drop in" on local surf-ers and then "play dumb" and pretend "we didn't see you." For Rothman, respect for locals who live at a break and surf it irrespective of conditions is paramount: "You *respect* someone, they *respect* you back. It's just like anywhere else in the world. If you don't *respect* us, you're done, see ya, don't come back."[25]

What then do alternative facts and interpretations tell us about such narratives as reconstructions of the past? They are grounded in facts, and the existence of alterna-tive facts and interpretations by no means reduces them to "outright falsehoods."[26] Nonetheless, regardless of the factual content and references, historical narratives remain representations of, or stories about, their subjects rather than precise recon-structions of those subjects.[27] Hence, grand narratives represent the "accentuation of one version of the past over others," usually for "culturally determined reasons." In other words, master narratives reside in social contexts that determine their cultural reso-nance and social memory.[28]

The contrasting cultural resonance of Duke Kahanamoku narratives in Australia and on the Atlantic Coast of the United States is a case in point. In the Australian narra-tive, Kahanamoku introduces Sydneysiders to surfing during the summer of 1914–1915. Despite the fact that Sydneysiders were riding surfboards and had achieved a level of competence well before these exhibitions, the Kahanamoku story endures because, as Gary Osmond observes, it appeals to, and articulates with, prevailing social mem-ories. Elaborating on these conditions, Osmond explains that the story benefits from

Kahanamoku's Hawaiian identity and his role in reviving the pastime in Hawai'i. By contrast, the achievements of Sydney surfers prior to Kahanamoku's appearances were "relatively obscure, less acclaimed and more sparsely documented." The Kahanamoku narrative also benefited from opportunities to remember his 1914–1915 visit. These included Kahanamoku's return to Australia in 1956 and 1963 to attend a surf lifesaving carnival and the ongoing interest in living agents of the narrative such as Isabel Letham who, as a teenager, rode tandem with Kahanamoku on his first visit and who championed his contributions to boardriding until just before her death in 1995. Like all popular narratives, the Kahanamoku story is "simple," "colorful," and "compelling" in that it identifies a "clear origin" moment that was "celebrated and well documented" at the time.

In contradistinction, conditions are less conducive for Kahanamoku stories in New York where he stayed en route to Sweden to compete in the 1912 Olympics. There is debate over whether Kahanamoku surfed, or merely swam, at Rockaway Beach (Queen's) during his stay in New York. Notwithstanding the popularization of surfing in the mid-twentieth century, it was not until the early 1980s that New York City officials dedicated an area to the activity. But the area they sanctioned, around Beach 38th Street (which they also renamed Duke Kahanamoku Way), was "a blighted stretch of burned-out shanties and vacant lots patrolled by ... wild dogs ... [and] crack dealers."[29] In the late 1980s, officials moved the approved surfing area, and Duke Kahanamoku Way, to a safer neighborhood at Beach 91st Street. Even this did not cement Kanahamoku's cultural memory. In 2004 local resident Gail Allen formally requested the City to rename Beach 91st Street in memory of her son Richie, a firefighter who died in the Twin Towers in 2001. Officials approved the request even though some commentators queried Allen's status as a local, claiming the firefighter had grown up in nearby Belle Harbor rather than the Beach 91st Street neighborhood. "The memory of September 11," observes journalist Robert Worth, "proved more powerful than the Duke's legend."[30]

Today, surfing is a truly global pastime. Surfers ride waves wherever they form, and surfing images appear in cities and towns distant from the beach. Like all grand narratives, surfing's version of history is seductive by virtue of its simplicity and its grounding in evidence that justifies belief particularly when that evidence marries with a preponderance of highly visible cultural images of surfing. Both the master and counternarratives presented in this chapter are grounded in reliable evidence. The sources are able and willing to tell the truth, and a multitude of similar accounts add corroborative weight. Yet, the factual content of these narratives cannot disguise the realities that a narrative is a representation and a process of mediation and that historians are authors who, in addition to choosing their evidence, choose the tools of their mediations, including their contexts and concepts. Neither contexts nor concepts produce definitive reconstructions. On the contrary, Frank Ankersmit likens contexts to clouds that obstruct the airline passenger's view of the ground and "prevent us from seeing the past itself or distort our view of it."[31] His analogy applies equally to concepts.[32]

In short, narratives are not forms of presentation designed to privilege truth. Matt Warshaw illustrates this in a discussion of localism: "reputation and notoriety," conveyed through narratives,

> far more than regular doses of violence, made localism an amazingly effective anti-crowd tool. Was there really some lunatic Oxnard dude with a huge galvanized nail resined bayonet-like to the nose of his board, ready to put a hole in any "souther" who dared paddle out at Hollywood-by-the-Sea? Didn't matter. Every day-tripping surfer heading north from L.A. County had heard the *story*, and 99 percent chose to drive right past Oxnard to the less-fraught beaches of North Ventura or Santa Barbara.[33]

The grand narrative of surfing offers a totalizing perspective on the sport's Hawaiian origins and its subsequent diffusion and homogenization. It stresses foundations (revival of surfing), essences (surfboards), and agents (elite surfers). When totalizing narratives disperse beyond their times and places of production and creation, and when they encounter local contexts and new audiences and subjects characterized by different cultural and material locations, they mutate—simultaneously expanding and contracting, and converting and contradicting—and effectively disintegrate.[34] Surfing may have a global presence, but its social meanings reside at the local level.

Questions about origins and diffusion reflect ontological interests concerning the nature of existence; empirical-analytical historians employ a realist positivist epistemology to produce answers (knowledge) to these questions. Although an epistemological skepticism underpins empirical-analytical history and drives historians to search continually for new evidence and new explanations, this skepticism rarely leads historians to question their epistemology even though, ironically, it forestalls consensus.

In the second part of this chapter I drew on, *inter alia*, Osmond and Walker, who emphasize particular and specific knowledge as well as knowledge grounded in social relations to challenge the foundations and essences of the grand narrative of surfing. By privileging epistemology (i.e., what we know about surfing and how we know it) over ontology (i.e., the nature of surfing's existence), Osmond and Walker highlight a key issue in contemporary historiography. Historians know a great deal about surfing. But there is much they do not know, and much they can never know. For example, many surfers consider stoke (*hopupu* in Hawaiian), a "fully embodied feeling of satisfaction, joy and pride,"[35] as an essence of riding waves. "For those time-warped seconds," says big-wave rider Mark Renneker, "life is pure. There is no confusion, anxiety, hot or cold, and no pain; only joy."[36] But what precisely is the evidential basis of stoke in surfing? Neuroscientists and biologists might define it as a vitality affect, a "dynamic, kinetic quality of feeling" that "distinguishes animate from inanimate and . . . involves . . . the organic processes of being alive."[37] How might historians find stoke in the past? Moreover, how might they represent such subjective experiences in their narratives? Surfer journalist Mike McGinty says he needs "elongated vowel sounds and exaggerated hand movements" to portray stoke, not "paper and ink."[38] While most historians of surfing assume that they can find the essences of their subject in its origins and development, the history of modern surfing belies this assumption. Knowing that surfing is a global phenomenon is to know very little. Once we acknowledge this fact, then we must concede the need for a new historiography grounded in epistemology.

NOTES

1. Michael Scott Moore, *Sweetness and Blood: How Surfing Spread from Hawaii and California to the Rest of the World, with Some Unexpected Results* (New York: Rodale, 2010), 154–155 and 177–184.

2. *The History of Australian Surfing*, dir. Nat Young (New York: CBS/Fox, 1986), DVD.

3. Moore, *Sweetness and Blood*, 50.

4. Dave Parmenter, "Epoch-Alypse Now: Postmodern Surfing in the Age of Reason," *The Surfer's Journal* 4.4 (1995): 117–118. For illustrations of the California style, see Don James, *Surfing San Onofre to Point Dume, 1936–1942: Photographs by Don James* (San Francisco: Chronicle Books, 1998).

5. Joan Ormrod, "*Endless Summer* (1964): Consuming Waves and Surfing the Frontier," *Film & History* 35.1 (2005): 49.

6. Frances Bonner, Susan McKay and Alan McKee, "On the Beach," *Continuum* 15.3 (2001): 273.

7. Drew Kampion, *Stoked: A History of Surf Culture* (Los Angeles: General Publishing, 1997), 21.

8. Moore, *Sweetness and Blood*, 3.

9. Ben R. Finney and James D. Houston, *Surfing: A History of the Ancient Hawaiian Sport* (San Francisco: Pomegranate Artbooks, 1996), 82. Likewise the *National Police Gazette* reported a "Sandwich Island girl" surfing at Asbury Park, New Jersey, in August 1888. Timothy Tovar DeLaVega, *Images of America: Surfing in Hawai'i 1788–1930* (Charleston, SC: Arcadia, 2011), 26.

10. Isaiah Walker, *Waves of Resistance: Surfing and History in Twentieth-Century Hawai'i* (Honolulu: University of Hawai'i Press, 2011), 69.

11. Douglas Booth, *Australian Beach Cultures: The History of Sun, Sand and Surf* (London: Frank Cass, 2001), 107–116; Alex Leonard, "Learning to Surf in Kuta," *Review of Indonesian and Malaysian Affairs* 41.1 (2007): 4; Peter Rigby, "Mythical Margs," *Tracks* (December 2011): 32.

12. Ormrod, "*Endless Summer*," 49.

13. Stuart Butler, "The Fear of Shame," *Tracks* (April 2011): 80.

14. David Shearer, "David Versus Rip Curl," *Kurungabaa* 2.2 (2009): 81, 83.

15. Derek Rielly, "Mainlining," in *Surf Rage*, ed. Nat Young (Angourie, NSW: Nymboida Press, 2000), 35.

16. Phil Jarratt, "Totally Unacceptable," *Tracks* (August 2010): 118–119. Jarratt later wrote a critique of the surf industry, *Salts and Suits* (Melbourne: Hardie Grant, 2010).

17. Josh Hunter, "How Hollister Co. Stole Surf," *Transworld Business*, August 13, 2008.http://business.transworld.net/8642/features/how-hollister-co-stole-surf-eight-years-after-abercrombie-fitch-invaded-the-surf-market-what-can-be-done-to-defend-against-them/>

18. Mark Stranger, *Surfing Life: Surface, Substructure and the Commodification of the Sublime* (Farnham, UK: Ashgate, 2011), 203.

19. E. P. Thompson, "Anthropology and the Discipline of Historical Context," *Midland History* 3 (1972): 45.
20. Matt Warshaw, *The Encyclopedia of Surfing* (New York: Houghton Mifflin Harcourt, 2005). 161.
21. Matt Warshaw, *The History of Surfing* (San Francisco: Chronicle Books, 2010), 122.
22. Walker, *Waves of Resistance*, especially 137–148; Eric Ishiwata, "Local Motions: Surfing and the Politics of Wave Sliding," *Cultural Values* 6.3 (2002): 265; Leonard, "Learning to Surf," 4, 27.
23. Emphasis added. Leonard, "Learning to Surf," 24. "Inside" is the position closest to the "curl" of the wave, between the white water and the unbroken wall.
24. Emphasis added. Rielly, "Mainlining," 45.
25. Emphasis added. Brad Melekian, "Interview: Makua Rothman," *Surfer* 43.5 (2008): 88. https://www.icmag.com/ic/archive/index.php/t-70106.html. "Dropping in" refers to interfering with a rider who is on the "inside."
26. Gary Osmond and Murray Phillips, "'Look at That Kid Crawling': Race and the Myth of the 'Crawl' Stroke," *Australian Historical Studies* 37.127 (2006): 44.
27. Alun Munslow, *The Routledge Companion to Historical Studies*, 2nd ed. (London: Routledge, 2006), 223.
28. Gary Osmond, "Myth-Making in Australian Sport History: Re-Evaluating Duke Kahanamoku's Contribution to Surfing," *Australian Historical Studies* 42 (2011): 261.
29. "Clubhouse," *New Yorker* (March 12, 1990): 30.
30. Robert Worth, "Rockaways Journal; Of a Local Legend, Surfing, and How to Honor the Past," *The New York Times*, April 12, 2004. http://www.nytimes.com/2004/04/12/nyregion/rockaways-journal-of-a-local-legend-surfing-and-how-to-honor-the-past.html.
31. Frank Ankersmit, *Sublime Historical Experience* (Stanford, CA: Stanford University Press, 2005), 256.
32. Douglas Booth, *The Field: Truth and Fiction in Sport History* (London: Routledge, 2005).
33. Emphasis added. Warshaw, *History of Surfing*, 264. For a discussion of the essence of form in narrative representation, see Murray Phillips, "A Critical Appraisal of Narrative in Sport History: Reading the Surf Lifesaving Debate," *Journal of Sport History* 29.1 (2002): 25–40.
34. M. G. McDonald and S. Birrell, "Reading Sport Critically: A Methodology for Interrogating Power," *Sociology of Sport Journal* 16.4 (1999): 293. Surfboard technology as a dominant trope in the grand narrative of surfing is an excellent example. The traditional focus on the technological constraints of early boards and subsequent design improvements is currently being revised against eyewitness accounts of skilled riding in the nineteenth century (e.g., Ben Finney, "Whoa, Dude! Surfin's that Old?," in *Surf Culture: The Art History of Surfing*, ed. Cathy Curtis, 87–88 [Corte Madera, CA: Gingko Press, 2002]), "experiments" showing surfers maneuvering finless boards on most types of wave (e.g., *Musica Surfica*, dir. Mick Sowry [Sydney: Screen Australia, 2008], DVD), and a reconceptualization of board design in the twentieth century as a continuous process of experimentation rather than distinct and sharp advances (e.g., Drew Kampion, *Greg Noll: The Art of the Surfboard* [Layton, UT: Gibbs Smith, 2007]).
35. Clif Evers, "How to Surf," *Journal of Sport and Social Issues* 30.3 (2006): 230–231.
36. Matt Warshaw, *Maverick's: The Story of Big-Wave Surfing* (San Francisco: Chronicle Books, 2000), 201.
37. Constantina Papoulias and Felicity Callard, "Biology's Gift: Interrogating the Turn to Affect," *Body & Society* 16.1 (2010): 42–43.

38. Cited in Paul Hersey, *Searching for Groundswell: A New Zealand Surfer's Road Trip* (Auckland: New Holland, 2010), 21.

BIBLIOGRAPHY

Booth, Douglas. *Australian Beach Cultures: The History of Sun, Sand and Surf.* London: Frank Cass, 2001.

Booth, Douglas. "Paradoxes of Material Culture: The Political Economy of Surfing." In *The Political Economy of Sport,* edited by John Nauright and Kim Schimmel, 104–125. Houndmills, UK: Palgrave Macmillan, 2005.

Evers, Clif. "How to Surf." *Journal of Sport and Social Issues* 30.3 (2006): 229–243.

Jarratt, Phil. *Salts and Suits.* Melbourne: Hardie Grant, 2010.

McTavish, Bob. "How Come No One Asked Sooner?" *The Surfer's Journal* 4.3 (1995): 44–55.

Moore, Michael Scott. *Sweetness and Blood: How Surfing Spread from Hawaii and California to the Rest of the World, with Some Unexpected Results.* New York: Rodale, 2010.

Moser, Patrick. *Pacific Passages: An Anthology of Surf Writing.* Honolulu: University of Hawai'i Press, 2008.

Osmond, Gary. "Myth-Making in Australian Sport History: Re-Evaluating Duke Kahanamoku's Contribution to Surfing." *Australian Historical Studies* 42 (2011): 260–276.

Parmenter, Dave. "Epoch-Alypse Now: Postmodern Surfing in the Age of Reason." *The Surfer's Journal* 4.4 (1995): 106–123.

Phillips, Murray. "A Critical Appraisal of Narrative in Sport History: Reading the Surf Lifesaving Debate." *Journal of Sport History* 29.1 (2002): 25–40.

Rielly, Derek. "Mainlining." In *Surf Rage,* edited by Nat Young, 33–53. Angourie, NSW: Nymboida Press, 2000.

Stranger, Mark. *Surfing Life: Surface, Substructure and the Commodification of the Sublime.* Farnham, UK: Ashgate, 2011.

Walker, Isaiah. *Waves of Resistance: Surfing and History in Twentieth-Century Hawai'i.* Honolulu: University of Hawai'i Press, 2011.

Warshaw, Matt. *The History of Surfing.* San Francisco: Chronicle Books, 2010.

Warshaw, Matt. *Maverick's: The Story of Big-Wave Surfing.* San Francisco: Chronicle Books, 2000.

Young, Nat, ed. *Surf Rage.* Angourie, NSW: Nymboida Press, 2000.

PART V

SITES OF SPORT DEVELOPMENT

CHAPTER 16

....

SPORT IN CHINA

....

SUSAN BROWNELL

THE founding of the International Olympic Committee in 1894 was part of a larger process entailing the simultaneous growth of international organizations alongside modern nation-states and nationalism. Like transnational society in general, the global sports system was centered in the developed West, its leadership and membership numerically dominated by men of European descent. One hundred fourteen years later, China hosted the biggest mega-event in human history, the Beijing 2008 Olympic Games, with official rhetoric claiming that the Games would be a "combination of East and West." China had realized its "one hundred year dream" of hosting the Olympic Games and marked its emergence as a superpower, but in all that time, the Western-centric character of global sports had not greatly changed, and the price of playing the game was a growing sense of the loss of a Chinese identity.

The expansion of sports and Olympic participation around the globe were in large part motivated by the desire of nations to write themselves into world history. Perhaps no nation felt this desire as keenly as China did. And so to understand the history of sport in China it is necessary to understand the writing of world history over the past 150 years. During the late nineteenth and early twentieth centuries, when Europe and the United States were dominating the world through colonialism and imperialism, Western scholars writing amidst the rapid social changes wrought by industrialization considered that only Western civilization had a history; to them, the "Orient" seemed to be trapped in perpetual stasis. Scholars such as the German classicist Ernst Curtius (1814–1896), who led the first full-scale archaeological excavations at ancient Olympia in Greece, characterized the East as sonorous and lethargic, by contrast with the dynamic West, which had "chained the course of history to its steps."[1] The academic disciplines of Classicism and Orientalism emerged, in that order, out of this context. The neoclassical revival that had been popular in the West since the late eighteenth century helped to strengthen a common identification with "Western civilization" in Europe, North America, Australia, and New Zealand. Sports played a central role in the formation of this identity: the Olympic Games were considered a hallmark of Western civilization and an embodiment of democratic values.

Because they associated competitive sports with Western civilization and democracy, historians writing about China in the late nineteenth and early twentieth centuries assumed that China lacked sports. China was overpowered not only by the military strength of the Western nations that first pried open its ports to foreign trade in the Opium Wars of the mid-1800s but also by the forcefulness of the new kinds of knowledge generated by new Western sciences such as archaeology and sociology and new theories such as social Darwinism. Western-educated Chinese accepted the Western view that Chinese society lacked dynamism and that this was reflected in the absence of indigenous sporting traditions. There was a near total lack of writings on ancient Chinese sports in any language, including Chinese. It appears that the first academic work on ancient Chinese sports was the 1906 article on "Football and Polo in China" by the prominent British Sinologist Herbert A. Giles. He began the article by wondering "if anyone would take an interest in, or even believe, the fact that football was played by the Chinese several centuries before Julius Caesar landed in Britain."[2] Eight years later, Xu Yibing's (1914) essay on *Tiyu Shi* (History of Physical Education) became the first article on ancient Chinese sports written by a Chinese author. It held the political agenda of correcting Western misperceptions: it acknowledged that China lacked Western sports but argued that China had its own rich traditions. Guo Xifen's *Zhongguo Tiyu Shi* (History of Chinese Physical Culture, 1919) was the first book-length treatment of Chinese sport history; it argued that the lethargy imposed by Confucian culture prevented sports, a superior cultural form, from developing in China.[3] Ever since that time, histories of ancient and indigenous Chinese sports have taken a defensive tone regarding China's purported "lack." Until China was recognized as a superpower after the Beijing Olympics, to simply write the history of traditional Chinese sports was a political act, because it meant writing against the grain of Western-centric sport history in which the West was taken as the desirable standard and everyone else was found lacking.

ANCIENT CHINESE SPORTS

Because the aim of historians for the past 150 years has mainly been to demonstrate differences between China and the West, until recently there has been little scholarship about their similarities and interconnections. Ideology has been particularly able to shape the scholarship on sports due to the paucity of hard evidence. Archaeology came to a near standstill during the Cultural Revolution (1966–1976), and, in any case, sport has not been a focus of archaeologists and ancient historians because it was assumed to be unimportant—an assumption that served the political agendas of both Western and Chinese would-be modernizers. Ren Hai was the first scholar to write a book about ancient Chinese sports after the Cultural Revolution. The book, *Gudai Zhongguo Tiyu* (Ancient Chinese Sports, 1996), was based on the doctoral dissertation in Olympic history that he had written in English at the University of Alberta in Canada. No

Chinese-language works have substantially added to this book since then, and a revised edition was printed in 2011. To promote China's bid for the 2008 Olympics, International Olympic Committee (IOC) member He Zhenliang organized an exhibition of ancient Chinese sport art at the IOC's museum in Lausanne. He first had to overcome the resistance of IOC members who felt that Chinese sport art was not "Olympic,"[4] but afterward the IOC published a large-format album based on the exhibition.[5]

Actually, in the four centuries between 700 and 300 BCE, the ancient Greeks and Chinese lived parallel histories on two sides of the Eurasian continent, characterized by the rise of city-states, the invention of modern mass warfare, and the flourishing of the great foundational thinkers of Western and Eastern civilization. The city-state era ended in both East and West at about the same time with the ultimate incorporation of the city-states into larger empires (the Macedonian Empire followed by the Roman Empire in the West; the Qin dynasty followed by the Han dynasty in the Far East). The incessant warfare in the city-state era led to innovations in interstate diplomacy: the ancient Greeks created the Olympic Games, and the ancient Chinese created a comprehensive political philosophy (Confucianism) and a ritual system (the Zhou rites). The Olympic Games and the Zhou rites became hallmarks of their respective civilizations, human inventions still in use nearly three thousand years later.

During the Eastern Zhou (722–221 BCE), visits of state to the Zhou king by his vassal princes included a hunt from chariots in the king's royal park followed by a banquet with wine, music, dance, and archery contests among the king and the princes. Thus archery, charioteering, music, and ritual protocol were indispensable diplomatic skills, and together with mathematics and writing—necessary skills of government—they formed the six subjects in the education of elite men advocated by Confucius.[6] While the Zhou world was not vastly different from the ancient Greek world described by Homer, changes in warfare beginning in the eighth century BCE finally resulted in different sport histories in Greece and China. In both societies, chariots driven by aristocrats were replaced by infantry recruited from among all farmers, and military service was extended to greater numbers of commoner men. Wooyeal Paik and Daniel A. Bell are two of the rare Sinologists who have turned their attention to sports. They observe that while the Greeks advocated training in the gymnasium for every free-born man as part of their military preparedness, in China a "gentleman" shunned military service, and soldiers were viewed as mindless masses guided by the intellect of the commander, hardly worthy of systematic training. In the foundational text of military science, Sunzi's *Art of War*, the only physical exercise that gains attention is squatting.[7]

Another rare work on ancient Chinese sports is Mark Edward Lewis's treatment of the two most well-attested ancient sports in the Warring States period (450–221 BCE)—wrestling contests that imitated bulls butting horns (*jiaoli* or *juedixi*) and a kind of football called kick-ball (*cuju*). He argues that these games reinforced the covenant between heaven and the king by re-enacting myths about the suppression of violence and the harmony between humans and cosmos in the well-ordered state.[8] Lucas Christopoulos challenged Greek and Chinese exceptionalism by putting forward the provocative proposal that the rulers of the Warring States period were influenced by contact with

Central Asians who had been Hellenized in the easternmost outposts of the former Macedonian Empire. He offered textual evidence that these rulers trained in gymnasiums and entertained audiences of distinguished guests at court with wrestling contests, employing trainers who had learned their craft in Hellenistic gymnasia.[9]

Works such as these only hint at the insights that might be gained when detailed comparative research is finally undertaken into the sports of the civilizations that flourished in East and West.

INTRODUCTION OF WESTERN SPORTS BY THE YMCA

From the turn of the twentieth century on, most of the leading physical educators in East Asia were either educated in Western missionary schools in their home country, were sent to the YMCA's training base in the United States at Springfield College, or studied at a university in Europe or the United States. Perhaps the first book-length history of Chinese sports in English was written in 1926 by Gunsun Hoh, a Springfield College graduate. Sportspeople who received a Western education before 1949 continued to play crucial roles in Chinese sports even up to the Beijing Olympics.

The first YMCA office in China was opened in the port city of Tianjin in 1895, the same year that China had lost the Sino-Japanese War. Tianjin became the most influential YMCA center in China, made possible by the multiple foreign concessions that were located there as a result of the Second Opium War in 1860, in which Britain forcibly opened the port to foreign trade. Japan, which had launched Western-style modernization in 1868, served as a channel for the flow of ideas from the West into China. Like many of the new words that accompanied modernization, the Chinese word for "sport" entered China via Japan. *Tiyu* is the Chinese pronunciation of the Japanese *taiiku*, a literal translation of the English "physical education." In Japan, the first call to host the Olympic Games as a way of standing as an equal among the nations of the world dated to 1897. The concept of physical education, which was just emerging as a professional discipline in the West, fit well with the crisis of confidence caused by the defeat by the Japanese. The defeat initiated a debate about the reasons that China had become the "sick man of East Asia" (*dongya bingfu*). For a century, this phrase has loomed in the Chinese imagination as an insulting label applied to China by Japan and the West. The first published calls for China to host the Olympic Games appeared in two Tianjin YMCA publications: a 1908 essay in the magazine *Tientsin [Tianjin] Young Men* and an item in the 1910 report to the YMCA's International Committee by the director of the Tianjin YMCA.[10] The YMCA report raised three questions, which gained infamy over the next century:

1. When will China be able to send a winning athlete to the Olympic contests?
2. When will China be able to send a winning team to the Olympic contests?

3. When will China be able to invite all the world to Peking for an International Olympic Games?

The first two questions would be answered at the Los Angeles 1984 Olympic Games, and the third would be answered when Beijing hosted the 2008 Olympic Games. Thus the Beijing Games were said to be the fulfillment of China's "one hundred-year dream."

China did not take part in any Olympic Games until 1932, but in 1904 the Qing dynasty's delegation to the Louisiana Purchase Exposition in St. Louis was China's first official delegation to an international exposition. The third modern Olympic Games were held alongside the world's fair in St. Louis and were covered by newspapers in China. In those times, athletic contests were often held together with a major trade exposition; in 1910 China joined the trend with the Nanyang Industrial Exposition in Nanjing, China's first international exposition. The YMCA was invited to organize a sports event in conjunction that was later listed as the first national athletic games of the Republic of China (founded in 1912).

THE FAR EASTERN CHAMPIONSHIP GAMES, 1913–1934

The Philippine Islands had been ceded to the United States at the end of the Spanish-American war in 1898, and the YMCA office established there became the launching pad for an "Oriental Olympic Games." The first "Far Eastern Olympiad" was held in Manila in 1913. The word "Olympic" was removed from the title by 1914 at the request of the IOC, which agreed to support the games because it was argued that regional games could serve as feeder events for the Olympic Games—which were then struggling to establish themselves even in the West and had no grassroots organization in the non-Western world. Although the Philippines, China (including Hong Kong), and Japan were the only participants, invitations were issued to independent states and colonies all over Asia. The games in Shanghai in 1916 were the first international games held in China. China intended to send a team to the 1916 Olympic Games, but they were cancelled due to the outbreak of the war.

Ten installments of the Far Eastern Championships were held up until 1934. All of them took place during the Japanese occupation of Korea and Taiwan, with the accompanying hostile relationships between the Chinese and Japanese governments. After Japan invaded northeast China and set up the puppet state of Manchukuo, it organized a Manchukuo Amateur Athletic Association and prepared to take part in the Far Eastern Games and the Olympic Games. China opposed the move, and IOC approval was not obtained in time for Manchukuo to participate in the Los Angeles 1932 Olympic Games, but the attempt did spur China to send its first Olympic athletes. The Far Eastern Games left a complex legacy in East Asia. They were the product of American imperialism in the Far East, but they had the paradoxical effect of stimulating anti-Western sentiments. They disseminated the ideal of sport as a vehicle for peaceful relations between hostile nations, but they also stimulated nationalism.[11]

China attempted early on to assert its influence within the IOC. The China National Amateur Athletic Federation (CNAAF) was formed in 1921 and was recognized as China's Olympic Committee in 1922. C. T. Wang (Wang Zhengting) became Asia's second IOC member in 1922, after Japan's Kano Jigoro (co-opted in 1909). On the eve of the establishment of the People's Republic of China (PRC) in 1949, there were only eight IOC members from Asia, and three of these were Chinese (three were from Japan and two from India). In 1946, the CNAAF decided to bid for the 1952 Games, but the outbreak of the civil war prevented this.[12]

The establishment of the world's first regional games in East Asia laid the foundation for this part of the world to emerge after World War II as the only region outside the developed West to host Olympic Games and FIFA World Cups. The three non-Western summer games were hosted in Tokyo in 1964, Seoul in 1988, and Beijing in 2008. In addition, Japan hosted two Winter Games in Sapporo in 1972 and Nagano in 1998. Korea will host the 2018 Winter Games in Pyeong Chang, Tokyo will host the 2020 Summer Games, and Beijing and Zhangjiakou will host the 2022 Winter Games. Sports had been established early as a vehicle for international rivalries, and the intense rivalries between China, Japan, and South Korea drove government support of sport thence forward.[13]

THE COMMUNIST REVOLUTION AND THE FOUNDING OF THE PEOPLE'S REPUBLIC OF CHINA, 1949

The Western Orientalist view that sports offered a remedy for the "lethargy" that permeated China and that they would facilitate the inculcation of democratic values—including the equality of women—was internalized by Chinese reformers and revolutionaries. Physical education played a key role in the rapid transformation of the status of women, as the customs of semiseclusion, arranged marriage, and footbinding were attacked by reform-minded intellectuals.[14] The first published article by Mao Zedong, who would later lead the Communist revolution, was "A Study of Physical Education" in 1917. Chinese Communists were known as sports fans: particularly famous was the use of basketball to keep soldiers fit and provide them with recreation in the Yan'an revolutionary base in the 1920s after the retreat from the Nationalists known as the Long March. The founding of the PRC in 1949 was celebrated one year later by the first National Worker's Games. The first Chinese National Games were held in 1959, and these became regular occasions for the promotion of national pride, held quadrennially since 1979.

After the 1917 Revolution, the Soviet Union began developing a government-led model for sports in its search for new social forms to serve the new workers' state. This model was imposed upon other socialist countries between 1948 and 1956, including China after the founding of the PRC in 1949. Large numbers of Soviet sports experts were sent to China to provide the expertise to set up and run the Commission for Physical Culture and Sport established in 1952 (it became the State General Administration for Sport in 1998). Its first minister-in-charge was Marshal He Long, a respected revolutionary general. Experts from the Soviet Union continued to visit China in large numbers even after the Sino-Soviet split in 1960, and it was not until after the reform era that visiting coaches and sport scientists from Europe and North America started to outnumber them.

However, the Chinese system very quickly diverged from the Soviet model as the sports teams administered by units of the government became the backbone of the system, rather than those administered by industries. Top athletes were recruited from some three thousand local sport boarding schools nationwide into the boarding schools administered by the sports commissions of the provincial and municipal governments. The pinnacle of the system was the national training center in Beijing administered by the State Sports Commission. In addition, outside of the Sports Commission system, the People's Liberation Army fielded the nation's strongest sports teams from 1952 to 1983.

SPORT DIPLOMACY AND THE TAIWAN PROBLEM

The Soviet Union rejoined the international sport system after World War II, competing in its first Olympic Games in 1952. Hoping to strengthen the socialist presence, it persuaded China to attend. Chinese foreign policy did not allow official Chinese participation in any event or organization that recognized the Republic of China, the name of the defeated regime that had fled to Taiwan and still claimed to be the legitimate government of mainland China. Because the IOC and most other international sport federations refused to expel Taiwan, the token delegation that made it to Helsinki for the raising of the red five-star flag in the Olympic village was China's last Olympic delegation until the Lake Placid 1980 Winter Games. The International Table Tennis Federation was one of only three international sports federations in which the PRC had membership and Taiwan did not. It was headed by Lord Montagu, a British Communist Party member who favored the PRC and was later revealed to have been a spy for the KGB. China's first medal in any sports world championship was Rong Guotuan's gold medal in men's singles in 1959. The 1961 World Championships held in Beijing were the first world championship event held in China, and China won three gold medals. This would create the foundation for "ping pong diplomacy" in the 1970s.

During the period of its exile from the global sport system between 1958 and 1980, China sought to circumvent the Western-dominated structure by establishing alternative structures. The 1962 Asian Games were held in Indonesia, with which the PRC had established diplomatic relations. The identity cards mailed by the Indonesian organizers to Taiwan mysteriously disappeared in the mail, and the team was unable to enter Indonesia. The IOC withdrew its patronage of the Asian Games and banned all of the athletes from the Tokyo 1964 Olympics. This angered Indonesia's president Sukarno, and he led the establishment of the Games of the New Emerging Forces (GANEFO). The first GANEFO in Djakarta in 1963 attracted forty-eight nations. It also marked China's first full-scale participation in a major, international, multisport event.[15] A coup d'état in Indonesia and the Cultural Revolution in China put an end to GANEFO, but it had emboldened China to act more assertively in the international sports world.

The Sports Commission suffered as much as any other ministry during the Cultural Revolution, as Chairman Mao's wife Jiang Qing seemingly considered it a rival to her plans to create a new revolutionary culture through the fine arts. Marshal He Long was imprisoned and harassed to death. Rong Guotuan hanged himself while in confinement. These two deaths became two of the best-known national tragedies of that era. The Sports Commission was disbanded and put under the control of the military, and the cadres were sent to the countryside to "labor with the peasants." The leaders who suffered so much during this period ensured that it was remembered in official histories as the low point of PRC sport history. However, Dong Jinxia has demonstrated that after the worst period was over in 1969, there was extensive government effort in building up the grassroots-level sport system. The foundation laid during the 1970s enabled the quick emergence of sports stars on the international scene after 1978, particularly sportswomen.

After the worst of the Cultural Revolution was over, Chairman Mao began making small overtures to the United States, which went unnoticed. At the 31st World Cup in Table Tennis in Japan in 1971, the US team expressed interest in visiting China, and Mao decided that this was the opening he was looking for. The US delegation visited China, and the United States reciprocated by inviting a Chinese delegation. Ping-pong diplomacy paved the way for China's admission to the United Nations in October 1971, eight years before the establishment of diplomatic relations with the United States. A series of international table tennis invitationals in Beijing between 1971 and 1973 also served as platforms for the establishment of diplomatic relations with African and Asian countries.[16]

As it returned to normalcy at the end of the Cultural Revolution, China joined an initiative by Third World countries pushing to form an intergovernmental sports organization inside UNESCO to act as a check on the power of the Western-dominated IOC and international sports federations. The Intergovernmental Committee for Physical Education and Sport under UNESCO was established in 1978. Its main activities were in the realm of school sports, sports science, and recreation, but in competitive sports it did not have much effect; the IOC maintained its worldwide influence along with FIFA and other international federations.

By this time the anti-Communist, American president of the IOC, Avery Brundage, had been replaced by the more conciliatory Lord Killanin. He pushed through China's readmittance into the IOC in 1979 under the "Olympic formula," which prohibits the use of the name, flag, and anthem of the Republic of China and requires the name "Chinese Taipei" in all Olympic settings.[17] After supporting the US-led boycott of the Moscow Games, the PRC returned to the summer games in Los Angeles in 1984. No longer on the outside of the global sport system, it soon became one of its most influential members. Chinese sportswomen led the rise to Olympic prominence. The women's volleyball team won five consecutive world events, including Olympic gold in Los Angeles, stimulating the revival of Chinese patriotism. Women achieved world preeminence in gymnastics, swimming, long-distance running, judo, football, softball, and other sports over the next decades, provoking an internal debate about why "the yin waxes and the yang wanes."[18]

Taiwan, forced to accept a subordinate position, engaged in subtle maneuvers to resist the Olympic formula. Nor did it abdicate the writing of Chinese Olympic history to China. Tang Mingxin's 1,100-page, two-volume set *Woguo canjia Aoyun cangsang shi* (History of the Vicissitudes of Our Nation's Participation in the Olympics) claimed prerevolution mainland history as belonging to the Republic of China on Taiwan and told postrevolution history from the Republic of China's point of view.[19]

Sport and the Economic Reforms, 1978–Present

In China, history-making and government have gone hand in hand for millennia; China may well be the most history-obsessed country in the world. After the era of opening up to the outside world began in 1978, government-sponsored publications formed part of the return to normalcy at home and the effort to regain legitimacy internationally.[20] The Sports Commission produced its compendium of the sporting achievements of the first three decades of the "New China," *Dangdai Zhongguo tiyu* (Contemporary Chinese Sports), in 1984.[21]

After the start of the market reforms in 1978, the Sports Commission was one of the first to "break the big pot" (a lifetime job with nothing but seniority-based pay raises) by giving bonuses to coaches and athletes for sports victories. China's return to the Summer Games in Los Angeles was an eye-opener, and the Sports Commission immediately set out to implement sports marketing and corporate sponsorship. The 1987 National Games were the first to have international corporate sponsors such as Pepsi and Fuji Film. The intention was to wean sports off of government funding. However, the initial achievements stalled out over the next two decades even while private enterprise flourished and China's economy grew at unprecedented rates. In 1994 and 1995, men's professional football and basketball leagues were formed, but only the football league became relatively financially independent, and some basketball teams continued to require government subsidies. The sport system remained almost completely government-led and funded. Finally, the sport system came to be viewed as a last bastion of the state-planned economy.

The evolution of the system over the years had made it highly dependent on big, showy events. Championships multiplied across the calendar until there were ten national championships on the Chinese sport calendar, an average of three per year: Winter and Summer National Games, College Games, Middle School Games, Minority Nationalities Games, Worker's Games, Farmer's Games, City Games, and so on. These were in addition to high-profile international events such as the 1990 and 2010 Asian Games, 2010 Combat Games, and 2011 Universiade. The Beijing 2008 Olympic Games, with their total cost of $43 billion, were the pinnacle. The logic of the system required championships because they forced local governments to allocate money for training the teams, sending them to the meets, building the venues, and so on—or risk a very public loss of face. If there were no competition, then the local governments would not invest money into sports. Gold medals were held out as the reward. Thus the whole system was permeated by the pursuit of medals from top to bottom. The system had enabled China to surpass the United States in the gold medal count at the Beijing Olympics, but it went along with an almost total lack of central government investment in recreational and popular sports. The national pride stimulated by international achievements was generally considered a good thing, but the sport system increasingly came to be seen as a symbol of a government that cared only about mega-projects and not about the everyday quality of life of its people. When Beijing won the bid for the Olympic Games, it ensured that the pursuit of medals would remain important so that China would make a good showing in its own Olympics, but after the Games, the discussion continued as to whether the sport system should be reformed. The leaders of the Sport General Administration fought to maintain it as an independent body, while beginning to give more attention to school and popular sport.

Heading into the second decade of the new millennium, few Olympic sports could have survived without government support. Table tennis and badminton attracted enough popular interest that coaches could support themselves giving private lessons; basketball and football were popular recreational sports, but tournaments and leagues were difficult to organize due to the controls on freedom of assembly. University sport and the elite sport system were not seamlessly joined, since university athletes could not take part in competitions organized by the Sport General Administration.

The hosting of the first Chinese Olympic Games in 2008 stimulated the production of a new round of multiple websites and books with limited scholarly value, which could be found in any bookstore. This stopped immediately after the Games. As of 2016, no scholarly analysis of the Beijing Olympics had been published in China. Scholars claimed that everyone was too exhausted and just wanted to put it behind them. On the other hand, because the games were so closely linked with the legitimacy of the Communist Party, any genuine analysis would perhaps be too politically sensitive to pass the censorship system.

Wushu, a "Traditional Chinese" Sport

The Beijing Olympics also brought to the fore another tension that had been simmering for a long time—that between Chinese and Western traditions. Most of the sports on the Olympic program were spread throughout the world through Western colonialism and imperialism. The only Olympic sports of clearly non-Western origin were judo and taekwondo. Judo was a demonstration sport at the Tokyo 1964 Olympics and was included in the official program starting with the Munich 1972 Olympics (women in 1992). Taekwondo was a demonstration sport at the Seoul 1988 Olympics and Barcelona 1992 Olympics and became an official sport in 2000. Most of the Olympic sports are inaccessible to the average Chinese person due to the lack of facilities, the prohibitive cost, the absence of recreational leagues, or general disinterest. Chinese martial arts, wushu, are one of the few sports in China that were well established before the creation of the state-supported sport system and have continued to thrive outside it.

Wushu is the label for the Chinese martial arts that were standardized in the 1950s and included in the state-supported system. Wushu draws on Taoist and Buddhist meditation traditions, which utilize techniques for controlling the flow of vital energy, *qi*. The Mawangdui silk scroll dating to 168 BCE, depicting robed figures doing exercises that imitate animal movements, is often considered one of the earliest pieces of evidence for this tradition. Although Chinese athletes use some *qi*-cultivation techniques in warm-up and cool-down exercises, wushu is different from Olympic sports in the importance assigned to *qi*. Over the past century, wushu has been deemed a quintessential example of authentic Chinese culture, and as a result of this association it has alternated between being a source of national pride and a subject of vilification due to its "feudal" associations.[22]

Today the official version includes two kinds of disciplines: *taolu* ("forms") is judged on a 10-point scale and is divided into twelve subdisciplines contested bare-handed or with various weapons; *sanshou* ("sparring") is scored by a panel of judges like boxing and is divided into eight weight categories. In 1982, shortly after the beginning of the era of reform, the State Sports Commission established the policy of promoting wushu internationally with the eventual goal of seeing it included in the Olympic Games. The International Wushu Federation was formally established in 1990, the same year that wushu was first included in the Asian Games program when China hosted its first Asian Games in Beijing. Internationally, it grew rapidly along with the numbers of practitioners who emigrated from China and started their own schools.

The creation of the state-supported sport system initiated an institutional divide between the state-supported athletes, coaches, and administrators in the government-led system on one side and the "folk" masters and their students who practice in parks and are largely self-funded on the other side. Chinese policy requires a sports group or team to have a "sponsoring unit." Martial arts forms in China fall under the administration of the National Wushu Association, which is under the State Sport General

Administration. One function of the sport system is to suppress the kinds of social movements that have arisen repeatedly in China over the past two centuries as a backlash to modernization. The Boxer Rebellion of 1900, so-called because of the martial arts practices engaged in by adherents who called themselves the "Righteous Fists," was a nationwide uprising that resulted in the perception among both Westerners and progressive Chinese that wushu practitioners were subversive due to their superstitions beliefs.

In the 1980s a craze for *qigong*—meditation and breathing techniques—swept across China. Qigong responded not only to the health-care needs of urbanites who had lost their medical benefits with the dismantling of the welfare state but also to the loss of faith in Communist ideology. In the late 1980s, the government deemed necessary the arrest of some of the most popular masters who had attracted a large following. Falungong, a branch of qigong, was invented by Li Hongzhi in 1992. Initially it benefited from official support, but it began to attract official disapproval, Li fled to the United States, and in 1999 a government crackdown was instituted that has continued ever since that time. Wu Shaozu, the director of the State Sports Commission between 1988 and 2000, was a promoter of qigong and a supporter of Falungong. He was replaced as director in 2000, perhaps due to the Falungong protests.[23]

The fate of Falungong reveals the pressures exerted on a "traditional" sport by a regime committed to wholesale modernization. Wushu had been under pressure to cleanse itself of "feudal superstition" ever since the early part of the twentieth century. After it ran afoul of the government, Falungong was accused of adhering to an overtly antiscience, anti-Party stance, was excluded from the sport system, and became a "heterodox sect" subject to intense persecution. If a sport does not shape itself into a standardized competitive sport form in the Western model and find a home inside the government-led sport system, it runs the danger of being targeted as subversive.

However, despite a century of wushu being pushed into a Western template, the Western leaders of the sports world still did not perceive wushu as an "Olympic" sport. Despite strong lobbying from the Sport General Administration, the IOC Programme Commission failed to even put wushu forward for a vote by the IOC Session. Thus wushu was not on the Beijing Olympic program, nor was it a demonstration sport, since the IOC had eliminated that category. When new program changes were considered in 2009, wushu was again not considered, but the session voted rugby sevens and golf onto the program for the Rio de Janeiro Olympics in 2016.

Chinese sportspeople had always assumed that China would be able to add its sport to the Olympic program when it hosted the Olympic Games, as had Japan and Korea. The Sports General Administration fought the IOC's decision but was only able to wrangle permission to organize an "International Wushu Tournament" during the Games. Wushu's failure sparked a great deal of debate inside China. One position criticized the Western domination of the Olympic system and viewed wushu's rejection as yet one more sign that the West did not want to accept China's rise. China's most radical critic, scholar Lu Yuanzhen, wrote that the addition of judo and tae-kwondo to the Olympic program was "just like slapping two Eastern Band-Aids onto the Olympic Games." He added, "Even at the 2008 Beijing Olympic Games, Eastern sport culture will only be a 'show' that, at most, will be temporarily acknowledged by the West. The time is not yet ripe for the Olympic Movement to realize the integration, coexistence, and equality of Eastern and Western culture, or perhaps this is even impossible."[24]

On the other hand, there were those who started to feel that wushu's inclusion in the Olympic Games would accelerate the loss of its authentic Chinese character. They complained that proper wushu training requires years of the cultivation of *qi*, which cannot be scored by judges, and international wushu had become too similar to gymnastics. A plethora of books and articles dealt with the topic of wushu's future, generally agreeing with the traditionalists.

In the inaugural World Martial Arts and Combat Sports Games held in Beijing in October 2010, wushu combined with a dozen other combat sports, of which eleven originated in East Asia (aikido, judo, ju-jitsu, karate, kendo, kickboxing, muaythai, sambo, sumo, taekwondo, and wushu). The only Olympic sports on the program were boxing and wrestling. They were organized by SportAccord, the umbrella association for all of the international sport federations. Russia won the gold medal count, and China was second. Great Britain placed twenty-sixth and the United States fortieth. The second installment was planned for Russia.

The Combat Games were the latest twist in the century-long dance between China and the Western-dominated global sport system. China attempted to create alternative structures when it was excluded, invested tremendous sums of money and manpower toward assuring sporting success when it was included, and many Chinese people were left feeling that they had lost their Chinese identity in the process.

NOTES

1. Susan Brownell, *Beijing's Games: What the Olympics Mean to China* (Lanham, MD: Rowman & Littlefield, 2008), 25–27.
2. Herbert A. Giles, "Football and Polo in China," *The Nineteenth Century and After* 59 (1906): 508–513, quote on 508.
3. A. Morris, *Marrow of the Nation: A History of Sport and Physical Culture in Republican China* (Berkeley: University of California Press, 2004), 42–44.
4. Liang Lijuan, *He Zhenliang and China's Olympic Dream*, trans. Susan Brownell (Beijing: Foreign Languages Press, 2007), 383.
5. International Olympic Committee, *5000 Years of Sport in China: Art and Tradition* (Lausanne: Olympic Museum, 1999).
6. Mary H. Fong, "The Origin of Chinese Pictorial Representation of the Human Figure," *Artibus Asiae* 49.1–2 (1988–1989): 5–38.
7. Wooyeal Paik and Daniel A. Bell, "Citizenship and Physical Education: Ancient Greece and Ancient China," *The Review of Politics* 66.1(2004): 14.

8. Mark Edward Lewis, *Sanctioned Violence in Early China* (Albany: State University of New York Press, 1990), 149–150.

9. Lucas Christopoulos, "Early Combat Sport Rituals in China and the Rise of Professionalism (475 BC to 220 AD)," *Nikephoros* 23 (2010): 19–41.

10. A. Morris, *Marrow of the Nation: A History of Sport and Physical Culture in Republican China* (Berkeley: University of California Press, 2004), 1–2; Xu Guoqi, *Olympic Dreams: China and Sports, 1895–2008* (Cambridge, MA: Harvard University Press, 2008), 28–30.

11. Ikuo Abe, "Historical Significance of the Far Eastern Championship Games: An International Political Arena," in *Olympic Japan: Ideals and Realities of (Inter)Nationalism*, ed. Andreas Niehaus and Max Seinsch (Würzburg, Germany: Ergon-Verlag, 2007), 69–72, 86.

12. Tan Hua and Dong Erzhi, *Suyuan—Dong Shouyi Zhuan* [Long-Cherished Wish—The Story of Dong Shouyi] (Beijing, People's Sports Publishing House, 1993), 93.

13. Susan Brownell, "The Beijing Olympics as a Turning Point? China's First Olympics in East Asian Perspective," in *The Olympics in East Asia: Nationalism, Regionalism, and Globalism on the Center Stage of World Sports*, ed. William Kelly and Susan Brownell, Yale Council on East Asian Studies Monograph Series (New Haven, CT: Council on East Asian Studies, Yale University, 2011), 199–200.

14. Hong Fan, *Footbinding, Feminism and Freedom: The Liberation of Women's Bodies in Modern China* (London: Frank Cass, 2007).

15. Liang, *He Zhenliang*, 80–90.

16. Xu, *Olympic Dreams*, 117–164.

17. Lord Michael Morris Killanin, *My Olympic Years* (London: Secker and Warburg, 1983); Susan Brownell, "'Sport and Politics Don't Mix': China's Relationship with the IOC during the Cold War," in *East Plays West: Essays on Sport and the Cold War*, ed. Stephen Wagg and David Andrews (New York: Routledge, 2007), 261–278; Xu, *Olympic Dreams*, 104–116.

18. Susan Brownell, *Training the Body for China: Sports in the Moral Order of the People's Republic* (Chicago: University of Chicago Press, 1995), 213–237.

19. Tang Mingxin, *Woguo canjia Aoyun cangsang shi* [History of the Vicissitudes of Our Nation's Participation in the Olympics], 1896–1948, Vol. 1 (Taipei: Chinese Taipei Olympic Committee, 2000); *Woguo canjia Aoyun cangsang shi* [History of the Vicissitudes of Our Nation's Participation in the Olympics], 1949–1996, Vol. 2 (Taipei: Chinese Taipei Olympic Committee, 2001).

20. Brownell, *Beijing's Games*, 37–39.

21. Rong Gaotang et al., eds. *Dangdai Zhongguo tiyu* [Contemporary Chinese Sports] (Beijing: Chinese Academy of Social Sciences Press, 1984).

22. Susan Brownell, "Wushu and the Olympic Games: 'Combination of East and West' or Clash of Body Cultures?" in *Perfect Bodies: Sports, Medicine and Immortality*, ed. Vivienne Lo (London: British Museum, 2012), 61–72.

23. Nancy Chen, *Breathing Spaces: Qigong, Psychiatry, and Healing in China* (New York: Columbia University Press, 2003); David Ownby, *Falun Gong and the Future of China* (Oxford: Oxford University Press, 2008); David Palmer, *Qigong Fever: Body, Science, and Utopia in China* (New York: Columbia University Press, 2007).

24. Lu, Yuanzhen, "Hope Lies in the Revival of Eastern Sport Culture," in *Olympic Studies Reader*, Vol. 1, ed. Hai Ren, Lamartine DaCosta, Ana Miragaya, and Niu Jing (Beijing: Beijing Sport University Press, 2010), 84.

BIBLIOGRAPHY

Abe, Ikuo. "Historical Significance of the Far Eastern Championship Games: An International Political Arena." In *Olympic Japan: Ideals and Realities of (Inter)Nationalism,* edited by Andreas Niehaus and Max Seinsch, 67–87. Würzburg, Germany: Ergon-Verlag, 2007.

Brownell, Susan. *Beijing's Games: What the Olympics Mean to China.* Lanham, MD: Rowman & Littlefield, 2008.

Brownell, Susan. "The Beijing Olympics as a Turning Point? China's First Olympics in East Asian Perspective." In *The Olympics in East Asia: Nationalism, Regionalism, and Globalism on the Center Stage of World Sports,* edited by William Kelly and Susan Brownell, 185–203. Yale Council on East Asian Studies Monograph Series. New Haven, CT: Council on East Asian Studies, Yale University, 2011.

Brownell, Susan. "'Sport and Politics Don't Mix': China's Relationship with the IOC during the Cold War." In *East Plays West: Essays on Sport and the Cold War,* edited by Stephen Wagg and David Andrews, 261–278. New York: Routledge, 2007.

Brownell, Susan. *Training the Body for China: Sports in the Moral Order of the People's Republic.* Chicago: University of Chicago Press, 1995.

Brownell, Susan. "Wushu and the Olympic Games: 'Combination of East and West' or Clash of Body Cultures?" In *Perfect Bodies: Sports, Medicine and Immortality,* edited by Vivienne Lo, 61–72. London: British Museum, 2012.

Chen, Nancy. *Breathing Spaces: Qigong, Psychiatry, and Healing in China.* New York: Columbia University Press, 2003.

Christopoulos, Lucas. "Early Combat Sport Rituals in China and the Rise of Professionalism (475 BC to 220 AD)." *Nikephoros* 23 (2010): 19–41.

Dong Jinxia. *Women, Sport, and Society in Modern China: Holding Up More Than Half the Sky.* London: Frank Cass, 2003.

Fan Hong. *Footbinding, Feminism and Freedom: The Liberation of Women's Bodies in Modern China.* London: Frank Cass, 2007.

Fong, Mary H. "The Origin of Chinese Pictorial Representation of the Human Figure." *Artibus Asiae* 49.1–2 (1988–1989): 5–38.

Giles, Herbert A. "Football and Polo in China." *The Nineteenth Century and After* 59 (1906): 508–513.

Guo Xifen. *Zhongguo Tiyu Shi* [History of Chinese Physical Education]. Shanghai: Shangwu Yinshuguan, 1919.

Hoh, Gunsun. *Physical Education in China.* Shanghai: Commercial Press, 1926.

International Olympic Committee. *5000 Years of Sport in China: Art and Tradition.* Lausanne: Olympic Museum, 1999.

Killanin, Lord Michael Morris. *My Olympic Years.* London: Secker and Warburg, 1983.

Lewis, Mark Edward. *Sanctioned Violence in Early China.* Albany: State University of New York Press, 1990.

Liang Lijuan. *He Zhenliang and China's Olympic Dream.* Translated by Susan Brownell. Beijing: Foreign Languages Press, 2007.

Lu Yuanzhen. "Hope Lies in the Revival of Eastern Sport Culture." In *Olympic Studies Reader,* Vol. 1, edited by Hai Ren, Lamartine DaCosta, Ana Miragaya, and Niu Jing, 83–91. Beijing: Beijing Sport University Press, 2010.

Mao Zedong. "Tiyu zhi yanjiu" [A Study of Physical Education]. *Xin qingnian* [New Youth] 3.2 (1917): 5–12.

Morris, Andrew. *Marrow of the Nation: A History of Sport and Physical Culture in Republican China*. Berkeley: University of California Press, 2004.

Ownby, David. *Falun Gong and the Future of China*. Oxford: Oxford University Press, 2008.

Paik, Wooyeal, and Daniel A. Bell. "Citizenship and State-Sponsored Physical Education: Ancient Greece and Ancient China." *The Review of Politics* 66.1 (2004): 7–34.

Palmer, David. *Qigong Fever: Body, Science, and Utopia in China*. New York: Columbia University Press, 2007.

Ren Hai. *Gudai Zhongguo tiyu* [Ancient Chinese Sports]. Beijing: Shangwu yinshugan, 1996; rev. ed.: Beijing: International Broadcasting Press, 2011.

Rong Gaotang et al., eds. *Dangdai Zhongguo tiyu* [Contemporary Chinese Sports]. Beijing: Chinese Academy of Social Sciences Press, 1984.

Shahar, Meir. *The Shaolin Monastery: History, Religion, and the Chinese Martial Arts*. Honolulu: University of Hawai'i Press, 2004.

Tan Hua and Dong Erzhi. *Suyuan—Dong Shouyi Zhuan* [Long-Cherished Wish—The Story of Dong Shouyi]. Beijing, People's Sports Publishing House, 1993.

Tang Mingxin. *Woguo canjia Aoyun cangsang shi* [History of the Vicissitudes of Our Nation's Participation in the Olympics], 1896–1948, Vol. 1. Taipei: Chinese Taipei Olympic Committee, 2000.

Tang Mingxin. *Woguo canjia Aoyun cangsang shi* [History of the Vicissitudes of Our Nation's Participation in the Olympics], 1949–1996, Vol. 2. Taipei: Chinese Taipei Olympic Committee, 2001.

Xu Guoqi. *Olympic Dreams: China and Sports, 1895–2008*. Cambridge, MA: Harvard University Press, 2008.

Xu Yibing [published under pen name Xu Yibin]. "Tiyu Shi" [History of Physical Education]. *Tiyu zazhi* [Physical Education Magazine] 1 (2014): 1–5, continued in 2 (2014): 7–11.

···

CHAPTER 17

SOUTH ASIAN SPORT

···

BORIA MAJUMDAR

IN his justly celebrated essay on the dynamics of the Balinese notion of cockfighting, anthropologist Clifford Geertz famously noted: "The Balinese cockfight is—or more exactly, deliberately is made to be—a simulation of the social matrix, the involved system of crosscutting, overlapping, highly corporate groups—villages, kin groups, irrigation societies, temple congregations, "castes"—in which its devotees live. And as prestige, the necessity to affirm it, defend it, celebrate it, justify it, and just plain bask in it . . . is perhaps the central driving force in the society."[1]

By transposing the terms "cockfight" with hockey or cricket and "Bali" with India or more broadly South Asia, one may in essence capture the significance of sport in this part of the world. Despite these ground realities, it is important to state at the outset that even today South Asian scholarship on sport inevitably boils down to a handful of perceptive histories of Indian sport. Without ignoring the works of Chris Valiotis and Omar Noman[2] on Pakistan cricket and Michael Roberts on Sri Lankan cricket,[3] it should be acknowledged that these continue to be in a minority when writing about the history of South Asian scholarship on sport, a discipline that is at the margins of mainstream scholarship on South Asia. At the same time, it must be acknowledged that there has been a surge in sports history writing in India/South Asia since the 1990s with the growing realization that India's cricket, hockey, and football teams represent India and not Bengal, Maharashtra, or Tamil Nadu or any other Indian state. Sport is perhaps the most visible site for the playing out of the erotic passions of nationhood, where being "Indian" matters more than anything else. This has become marked in recent years with the passionate display of the flag's tricolors during international sports tournaments. If only for a few weeks every year, Indian sports fans, from home and the diaspora, celebrate the cardinal truth of being "Indian."

For a country obsessed with history and transformed by its well-spread postcolonial diaspora, the need to find a common barometer of "Indian-ness" may seem unlikely, even unnecessary. But looking beneath the surface shows that the central role of sport in fashioning a common national identity is difficult to doubt. Indians across the country, it is known, learn varied versions of their history in school textbooks. While for school kids in the east it is Subhas Chandra Bose who led the nation to freedom, in pockets of the west dominated by lower caste groupings it may be Ambedkar; in the north Indian heartland it is Gandhi.

In stark contrast to this peculiar situation, most discussions of "Indian" hockey/cricket or Olympic sports and issues governing their fortunes are still relatively uniform and are mentioned almost daily in the national/local media. The intersecting vectors of politics and commerce continually influence sport in India, but there is no doubt that sport itself is intrinsically linked to ideas of identity, self, and nationalism. Yet, in the vast literature on Indian and more generally South Asian history, sport, one of the most important cultural practices of the twentieth and twenty-first centuries, finds little mention. The reason behind this absence, not only in the Indian context but for South Asia more generally, as scholars like Dipesh Chakrabarty have pointed out, are varied and complex. For Chakrabarty, the contours of the (British) social history or "history from below" movement, which influenced much of the writing of Indian social history and into which sports scholars wanted to be integrated, had certain built-in intellectual priorities. Sporting events, he argues, were seen as less important than strikes or some other act of overt class conflict or class resistance. Chakrabarty is thus of the opinion that even though the defenders of sports history in the 1970s and 1980s perceived it as central to the business of social history, it "never quite became a mainstream subject to historians who saw themselves as engaged in that trade."[4]

If we advance Chakrabarty's argument to the present, it can be argued that historians can hardly attempt to understand the workings of contemporary Indian societies without bringing sport into their ambit. Cricket, it is widely acknowledged today, is the single most important realm for the articulation of Indian nationalism. It is for this reason that cricket often obscures the importance of other sports, pushing them to the backburner in studies attempting to understand contemporary India's sporting contours. However, as this chapter demonstrates, more recent studies of India's Olympic encounters or a study of Indian football not only enriches our understanding of the Indian present but also enhances the comprehension of India's nationalist past by introducing nuances that conventional historical narratives have tended to gloss over.

It is important to reiterate upfront that the story of Indian cricket cannot pass as the story of Indian sport. Cricket in contemporary South Asia and more so in India is imbued with a frenzied sense of hyper-nationalistic jingoism and is certainly one of the strongest of contemporary Indian allegiances. It is also true that nothing beyond international cricket or a hyper-commercialized spectacle like the Indian Premier League, a more recent domestic competition involving city-based clubs, matters in India. If only India or for that matter Pakistan, Sri Lanka, or Nepal had done well in Olympic sports, as was the case with field hockey until the 1960s for both India and Pakistan, the popularity and commercial currency of international cricket would surely be under threat. Yet, stories of failure on the Olympic stage, often for reasons unconnected to sport, help us understand postcolonial South Asia and more specifically India better, as scholarly studies have very recently brought to light.

This chapter is divided into two parts. The first deals with the histories of South Asian/ Indian cricket, literature that is gradually assuming the size of a substantial corpus. The second part deals with Olympic sporting histories, a very recent addition to South Asian/Indian sports scholarship but that have helped open up new areas of research and avenues of inquiry.

HISTORIES OF CRICKET: THE ARCHITECTS

Historians of cricket in India often complain of the paucity of secondary literature. The truth, however, is that they are more fortunate than most others; they have at their disposal more secondary sources than all the other Olympic sports taken together. The deficiency is in the harnessing of these. The historian has priceless resource in the four classics of Parsi cricket published in the years 1892 to 1905, which give fascinating details about the origins and spread of the game in Western India in the second half of the nineteenth century.

The first, Mankasji Kawasji Patel's *Parsi Cricket* (1892), a lecture delivered on the state of the game to the Parsis before they played Lord Hawke's touring English team in 1892, is invaluable for its detail. It was followed by Shapoorjee Sorabjee's *A Chronicle of Cricket Amongst Parsees* (1897), which tells the story of native aspirants in Mumbai trying to establish their right to cricket-playing space around the city's Esplanade grounds, the use of which was monopolized by the colonial Bombay Gymkhana. Sorabjee had, in fact, organized a concerted campaign to convince the presidency administration to accede. The campaign brought together established Parsi, Hindu, and Muslim families and assumed the form of a genuine nationalist protest. The tussle was over a stretch of ground from which Indians were forcibly ousted so that British army sergeants and corporals could play polo. As Ramachandra Guha puts it, "The Asian game played by Europeans became the emblem of patriotic power and the English sport indulged in by natives the mark of plebeian resistance."[5]

The third Parsi classic is M. E. Pavri's *Parsi Cricket* (1901), which, while drawing much on Sorabjee's work, provides valuable insight into the nature of the game in Mumbai's educational institutions. Finally, J. M. Framjee Patel's *Stray Thoughts on Indian Cricket* (1905) is central to any reconstruction of Indian cricket history. At the forefront of cricket administration in Mumbai, Patel has left exhaustive accounts of Parsi, Hindu, and Muslim cricket of the period and of the early Parsi tours to England in 1886 and 1888.

Social historians of Indian cricket also depend on the accounts penned by contemporary cricket journalists. Books and annuals authored by P. N. Polishwala, Berry Sarbadhikary, and J. C. Maitra not only contain details of clubs, matches, and players but also include anecdotes and stories. These are pointers to the relationship between the players and their princely patrons. Sarbadhikary's *Indian Cricket Uncovered* (1945) describes the communal tensions of the 1930s and 1940s and the emergent patron–player tussles. In 1934 W. D. Begg's *Cricket and Cricketers in India* was published, the first encyclopedia of Indian cricket. This remains the most important repository of information on cricketing traditions in the princely states of Gwalior, Idar, Rajputana, Kathiawar, Wadhwan, and Dungarpur.

Beyond this mass of literature, the historian has at his or her disposal a plethora of twentieth-century accounts, whether national or region-specific. G. A. Cancer's monograph on Karachi (1941), H. D. Darukhanawala's *Parsis and Sports and Kindred Subjects* (1935), Narendranath Ganguly's *Calcutta Cricket Club: Its Origin and Development* (1936), S. M. H. Maqsood's *Who's Who of Indian Cricket* (1940), A. S. De Mello's *Portrait of Indian Sport* (1959), and Sujit Mukherjee's *The Romance of Indian Cricket* (1968) are cases in point. Finally, regional histories like Sandeep Bamzai's *Guts and Glory: The Bombay Cricket Story*, S. Muthiah's *The Spirit of Chepauk*, and V. Ramnarayan's *Mosquitoes and Other Jolly Rovers: The Story of Tamil Nadu Cricket* are valuable resource material.

Foreigners too have attempted to tell the story of Indian cricket. Perhaps the best documented and popular are the histories by Edward Docker and Richard Cashman. Docker's *History of Indian Cricket* (1976) is chronologically correct, beginning with the Marylebone Cricket Club tour of 1926–1927 and the establishment of the Board of Control for Cricket in India in December 1928. Cashman's *Patrons, Players and the Crowd* (1979) takes the story back to the late nineteenth century and describes the relationship between cricket's colonial missionaries and their Indian converts.

Of the recent histories, the two best known are Mihir Bose's *History of Indian Cricket* (1990, revised and updated in 2002) and Ramachandra Guha's *A Corner of a Foreign Field* (2002). Both have their relative merits. Bose provides intricate details of princely rivalries between the Maharajkumar of Vizianagaram (Vizzy) and the Maharaja of Patiala in the 1930s and draws attention to how cricket was a means of self-aggrandizement for cricketers like Ranji (K. S. Ranjitsinhji)—a point made most eloquently by Simon Wilde in his book *Ranji—A Genius Rich and Strange*. On his part, Guha is concerned with establishing the link between cricket, caste, and religion. In the best section of his book, "Caste," Guha traces the career of Palwankar Baloo, the best-known Dalit cricketer of colonial India. Baloo, though the subject of numerous essays in the past, has never before been dealt with in such detail. The tracts from contemporary newspapers and Marathi sources, describing his political career as a Dalit cricketer, are instructive, opening up before the reader an appreciation of the game as a ladder for social mobility in a caste-ridden society. The contest between Baloo and B. R. Ambedkar in the 1930s, again a much dwelt upon narrative in the recent past, is demonstrative of cricket's wider sociopolitical potential.[6]

Ashis Nandy's *Tao of Cricket* (1989, republished 2000) and Arjun Appadurai's article "Playing with Modernity: Decolonisation of Indian Cricket" (1996) also contribute to an understanding of India's cricket history. These are statements on the politics of cultural choices and visions in South Asia using the metaphor of cricket.

CENTRAL ARGUMENTS

The literature mentioned here indicates three major strands of scholarly interest on cricket. The first, illustrated by Parsi cricket histories and Polishwala's works, are more concerned with detailing landmarks. Parsi tours to England in 1886 and 1888, the institution, in 1892, of the presidency matches between the Europeans and the Parsis—this eventually became the Pentangular, with the inclusion of the Hindus in 1907, the Muslims in 1912, and the "Rest," comprising Indian Christians and Anglo-Indians, in 1937—and the inauguration of the Harris Shield school cricket tournament in Mumbai in 1896 are described with meticulous care.

The second, encyclopedic approach is a repository of information on cricketing traditions and histories in specific regions and princely states. It also describes the role played by British administrators in cricket promotion. Whether or not cricket traditions in the princely states were sustained, however, remains beyond the scope of such works. The first two approaches, it is evident, complement each other.

The third approach attempts to map the historical trajectory of cricket across the country. Issues of patronage, crowd behavior, and resistance against colonial rule are central to it. Guided by assumptions about the "gentlemanly" nature of the game, these histories portray cricket in chaste terms—as a social unifier cutting across caste and class. Nationalism and communalism, pillars of Indian history writing, are principal concerns of this school.

Yet, while these works have dealt with princely investment in cricket, the complex reasons behind this have been only partially analyzed. The princely patrons were propelled by a variety of factors. The most common was a quest for social mobility within the colonial framework, to gain "acceptance" as it were. There were exceptions though. The Maharaja of Natore, for example, saw cricket patronage as part of a nationalist enterprise.

In the case of Ranji, love for cricket was rooted in self-aggrandizement, not, as is commonly argued, in an Anglophile's desire to imitate the white man. Also, the way in which Ranji, Duleep (K. S. Duleepsinhji), and Iftikhar Ali Khan, the Nawab of Pataudi (Sr.) were looked upon by Indian masses makes them key players in India's cricket history. Even if they were not nationalists in the way we understand "nationalism," the fact that the masses perceived them as Indians, men who competed on equal terms with the British and captured the imagination of the West, cannot be discounted. The final reason for princely patronage of cricket was, simply put, peer rivalry. The competitive urges of regions and royal families found expression in putting together the better cricket team.

The complexity of princely patronage leads to some unorthodox conclusions. Contrary to the dominant argument that has stressed the historical irreconcilability of the princes and the educated middle classes, the Maharajas often joined hands with the nationalists, if only to fulfill personal ambitions. This alliance has received scant attention in the works mentioned previously.

Second, most histories of cricket in India until my own intervention into the discipline in 2002–2003 were, in effect, histories of cricket in Mumbai. They assumed the Mumbai model was replicated in other parts of the country and so describe early Indian cricket as organized on communal lines. It follows that a desire to prevent communal disharmony inspired the protests against the Pentangular, the most popular tournament in pre-Partition India. A history of cricket in Bengal, Chennai, and parts of north India such as Punjab calls into question such a premise. Cricket in these places was not organized communally, and the problems specific to Mumbai had no impact on these regions.

My own work starting with *Twenty Two Yards to Freedom: A Social History of Indian Cricket* (2004)[7] does not seek to affirm the preeminence of the east, south, or north Indian narrative over that of Mumbai/western India. Rather, it tries to make the point that one cannot claim to write a history of "Indian" cricket by simply looking at the history of the game in one province or region. Further, I have tried to argue that it would be incorrect to understand cricket in purely functionalist terms, in terms of the exigencies of the colonial and postcolonial state. Should that have been the case, the game would not have outlived colonialism to generate the following it has today.

My intention has been to bring to light histories of the game in India that have hitherto remained untold. These "lost" histories tell us why various Indian groups started playing the game, often for reasons more complex than simply trying to emulate the British. By reading this history against the broader cultural life of the nation, I have tried to introduce into the study of Indian history the whole question of the relationship between leisure and national identity, one that continues to animate Indian society to this day. To that extent cricket is a truly postcolonial game—one that has outlived colonialism but also one that originated in the metropolis, was then taken up by the colony and can now be invoked by Indian historians to critique metropolitan practices.

Concerned with overarching themes of nationalism, communalism, and caste, existing histories tended to ignore signs of cricket's early commercialization. This may, in some cases, be traced back to the 1930s and 1940s. Attempts to analyze the anti-Pentangular movement (a movement aimed at abolishing the most popular communally organized tournament in pre-independence India competed for by the Parsis, Europeans, Hindus, Muslims, the Rest comprising Sikhs, Anglo Indians, and so on) in terms of the nationalist-communal equation obscures crucial realities. More than communal antagonism, it was the commercial viability of the Pentangular that irked its opponents. Unable to contend with the successful Pentangular, the Board of Control for Cricket in India, organizer of the Ranji Trophy, India's premier domestic cricket competition, summoned an extraordinary general meeting in January 1942 to put a forcible end to the tournament. While the degree of cricket's commercialization has increased manifold since the 1970s, culminating with the organization of the Indian Premier League in 2008[8]—reaching a point where a cricketer's social worth is judged in terms of earnings and corporate clout—its roots are discernible in colonial India.

Finally, within the constraints of a relatively underresearched field, a neglect of sources in the vernacular contributes to a skewed understanding of Indian cricket history. Episodes depicted by English-language sources as imperialist successes are strikingly appropriated as nationalist triumphs in vernacular writings. The Parsi victory over G. F. Vernon's team in 1889–1890 is a case in point. While noted historians look upon this victory as a fulfillment of the colonial "civilizing mission," vernacular sources see it as a nationalist triumph on the sporting field.

A study of vernacular tracts on cricket is crucial to an understanding of imperialist-nationalist politics in late-nineteenth- and early-twentieth-century India. While scholars like J. A. Mangan have shown concern with what happened to the "games ethic"[9] in subsequent stages, most European histories of South Asian sport continue to be ethnocentric. Turning the colonial ideology on its head, resistance and subversion were often dominant in the second phase of the histories of British games in the colonies, especially cricket and soccer. It is in understanding the process of subversion of the "games ethic" that vernacular literature plays a key role, leading to a more nuanced look at the history of cricket in India.

Most recent works starting with my own have also used the premise that a social history of Indian cricket can only be meaningfully written by looking beyond the cricket field. They aim to show how South Asian history and society have transformed cricket in the region while the game has simultaneously shaped the history and society of India, both before and after India's independence from colonial rule in 1947.

Pakistan and Sri Lanka

Cricket histories of Pakistan and Sri Lanka, which have been published more recently, follow a similar holistic approach. The best work on Pakistan is that by Chris Valiotis, who argues "that Pakistan—like all nation states—is an imagined community of competing national and regional narratives." This, he contends, offers him a framework for understanding and interpreting the central themes of his work: the historical organization and control of cricket in Pakistan being the most important concern. Valitios argues that

> since the 1970s Pakistan cricket has come to be controlled by authoritarian politicians who define what is and what is not Pakistani cricket just as they define what is and what is not Pakistani nationalism. Power in Pakistan is held by a narrow military, bureaucratic and landholding elite, overwhelmingly drawn from the numerically and economically dominant Punjabi regional community. It is they who continue to define the national doctrine, political system, economic approach and cultural framework of the Pakistan nation state. Consequently, other cultural groups in Pakistan have been denied the opportunity to contribute to the structure and organisation of cricket and government in the country at the formal level, but not at an informal, popular level where regional identities and cricket have become multilayered idioms for cultural inclusion.[10]

While Valiotis's work is more analytical, Oman Noman's narrative on Pakistani cricket published by Oxford University Press is also invaluable in reconstructing the history of the game in the country. His work was part of the Oxford effort to document national histories on the occasion of fifty years of Pakistani independence in 1997.

What Valiotis is to Pakistan, Michael Roberts is to Sri Lanka. His corpus of work, starting with his 1981 article "Ethnicity and Riposte in Sri Lankan Cricket," brings to the fore the central tensions in Sri Lankan cricket. Michael documents the impact of the Tamil–Sinhala divide, the importance of class conflict, and the overtly politicized nature of the game in the country.[11] Roberts' journalistic work is also impressive and is of paramount importance in reconstructing any history of cricket in Sri Lanka.

Roberts argues that cricket is the raft that ferries Sri Lankans from profane realities to sacred realities and enables them to rise above the ordinary to the ultimate experience. At almost every instance over the past decade and a half that the small island nation has been faced with an ultimate crisis, cricket has come to its rescue. It is perhaps pertinent to turn back to their cardinal cricketing moment—the World Cup victory in 1996. It was a tournament organized by India, Pakistan, and Sri Lanka. Indeed, a junior partner, this was the first occasion Sri Lanka played host to an international sporting contest of this dimension. But far from being smooth, the experience at organization was harrowing. A bomb blast a few weeks before the tournament, a regular feature of Sri Lankan life, was enough to scare the Australians and the West Indians from stepping onto the island. Forfeiture and having points docked was acceptable, but a trip to Sri Lanka was not. While this was a plain and simple security issue for cricket's two traditional powerhouses, for Sri Lanka far more than prestige was at stake. If the matches scheduled on the island were cancelled or relocated to the other host countries, there was a strong possibility that Sri Lanka would be declared a terrorist state. It was a crisis that went far beyond the boundary. The organizers of the tournament stood up to the task. And, to their credit, the national governments of India and Pakistan backed them to the hilt. Within days, in fact hours, it was decided that a joint India–Pakistan team would travel to Sri Lanka to demonstrate to the world that the island was indeed a secure haven for cricketers. The LTTE, nemesis in chief, too came out in declaration pledging not to cause harm to cricketers or their supporters. However, none of these pledges/ acts proved potent enough to convince the Australians or West Indians to travel to Sri Lanka. Far from that, even Kenya and Zimbabwe seemed reluctant to travel and were only silenced by the joint India–Pakistan visiting team.

Humiliated and troubled, Sri Lanka turned to its multiethnic and multilingual cricket team. And the team, which had a Tamil leading the bowling attack in Muralitharan and an economically underprivileged from Matara taking first strike in Sanath Jayasuriya, more than stood up to the task. Within the team there was no Sinhala–Tamil divide, nor were there differences based on class backgrounds. Cricket was an avenue for both individual and group escape from the tremors of the politically unstable everyday life; it offered an opportunity for aesthetic pleasure, was a source of individual and group psychological uplift, and was a means of ethnic and class cohesion, facts highlighted by Roberts in his work spanning three decades.[12]

OLYMPIC SPORTING HISTORIES

At a time when historians around the world are increasingly recognizing global stories of Olympism as crucial to understanding the working of societies, there was until recently no detailed history of India's or for that matter South Asia's Olympic experience. It was in 2008 that this was finally addressed when I (with Nalin Mehta) published *Olympics: The India Story*, a work that documents India's Olympic history in detail. This was a glaring anomaly for a country that became the first colonized nation to join the Olympic movement, one that dazzled the world with its early field hockey wins and whose Olympic history contains within its folds hitherto unknown chapters of the development of Indian nationalism and identity. Accordingly, until very recently, historians of Indian sport or, more specifically, historians of Olympism, have met an insurmountable barrier as they sought to decipher the Indian Olympic story.

All that existed were memoirs of a few hockey players—Dhyan Chand,[13] Aslam Sher Khan—and books written on the achievements of some rare Indians on the Olympic stage by sports writers. By themselves, these are invaluable, but they were not enough to piece together a comprehensive and complete history of India's Olympic encounter.

It took until 1920 for India to participate in the Olympic Games, and no formal institutional mechanism for supporting Olympic sport was established in the subcontinent until the early 1920s. But by the mid-1920s, driven by nationalist enterprise and princely patronage, India's Olympic structure was well in place. The Indian Olympic Association as we know it today was formed in 1927, and a strong Indian contingent participated in the Amsterdam Games of 1928, winning India her first gold medal in field hockey in the very first year of official participation. A precursor to the Indian Olympic Association had been formed in 1923 with the same name and had served the Olympic cause for three years until 1926 before being shut down.[14]

Our work documents the origins of Olympism in India and what it meant for India, for the British Empire and for the global Olympic movement. As a movement led by nationalist elites and princes, the early story of Indian Olympism is also the story of a global league of upper-class elites, connected through patronage networks in Europe, who passionately pushed the Olympic ideal. Until the 1920s, the Olympics were largely a Euro-centric enterprise, but India's embrace of Olympism in the 1920s was also simultaneously accompanied by a powerful push for diffusing the Olympic ideal in Latin America and Southeast Asia. In all three cases, the same strategy was followed: the use of the global network of the YMCA and the co-option of local elites with enough private resources and European contacts to liaise with the Olympic movement's center. In that sense, the origins of Olympic sport in India is a missing piece in the global story of Olympism. In a Europe divided by war, the International Olympic Committee (IOC) pushed this expansion as a strategy for survival, and in India the ideal was appropriated by elite nationalists as a new avenue for self-respect, modernity, and identity politics in the sporting arena. Olympism came to India as part of the processes of globalization, decades before the term itself became fashionable. But once it was initiated, it was appropriated by and became inseparable from the forces of nationalism to begin with and the centrifugal regional tendencies thereafter.[15]

The Indian Olympic story also helps draw attention to fascinating moments in global Olympic history, interludes that have not been documented in detail in existing histories of the Olympic movement. One such interlude is the story of the Games of the Newly Emerging Forces (GANEFO), which on the one hand is the story of Sukarno's efforts to do a Nehru and become the preeminent leader of the postcolonial countries of Asia and Africa and on the other hand constitutes the single biggest challenge to the IOC in the global history of the Olympic movement.

When Indonesia failed to allow Taiwanese and Israeli athletes to take part in the fourth Asian Games in Jakarta, it was Indian officials who took on Sukarno's regime, and the resultant confrontation led to Indonesia's expulsion from the IOC. Sukarno, with Chinese support, responded with the creation of GANEFO, explicitly linking it to his global leadership aims. Again, it was Indian officials who lobbied the hardest against him at the IOC. China, which had just humiliated India in the border war of 1962, played a crucial role in funding and supporting Sukarno.

The problem arose over Israeli and Taiwanese athletes. Both countries were recognized by the IOC—the People's Republic of China (PRC) did not become an official member of the IOC until 1979—but not by Indonesia. Both Israel and Taiwan were also recognized by the Asian Games Federation under whose aegis the Asian games were organized every four years. Indonesia could not refuse them entry openly, so it resorted to subterfuge. Athletes from these countries were invited, but their packets containing identity cards, it turned out, were full of blank cards! Considerable intrigue surrounded the participation of these two countries even before the Jakarta Asian Games started. There was talk that the participant identity cards could be used as substitutes for official visas and they may be given over on entry at the Jakarta airport. Israel, for instance, had already cabled the Indonesians to keep their cards ready and that a plane was on standby to fly to Jakarta as soon as assent was received. As things turned out, the identity cards were never sent, and things came to a head on August 21, 1962, when a Taiwanese official was returned from the Jakarta airport. His plane was not even allowed to land, and it seemed that Indonesia had finally drawn the line with this refusal.

It was at this point that India took an aggressive stance. On August 24, the day the Games were scheduled to start, G. D. Sondhi, representing India at the Asian Games Federation Congress, also being held in Jakarta, objected strongly to the Indonesian action. Arguing that the exclusion of athletes based on politics was against the Asian Games charter, he proposed that the status of Asiad be withdrawn from the Games. Sondhi wanted Jakarta to be punished by taking away the mantle of the Asian Games and turning the Games into "merely an international athletic and sports meeting." The Games duly opened later that day, but the political question continued to haunt the event. Sondhi would not let go and continued to his agenda.

The IOC responded quickly to the Indonesian decision not to include Taiwan and Israel. On February 7, 1963, the IOC indefinitely suspended Indonesia. The news was greeted with great glee in the Tel Aviv and Taiwanese press, but India's role in this move was crucial. This was the first time in its history that the Lausanne-based IOC had sacked a member. Sondhi played a big hand in this decision. In the mythology of the IOC, devoted as it is to the notion of amateurism, political interference is the one notion that is more of an anathema than any other. Accordingly, soon after his return to Delhi, Sondhi, also a member of the IOC, got busy writing to the president, Avery Brundage, explaining the "governmental" designs in the incidents at Jakarta. As he put it, "it is clear that the Government of Indonesia—under strong pressure from the local Chinese and the Communist Government of China—was determined not to invite the Taiwanese teams. Pressure from Arab states was likewise responsible for non-issuance of Identity cards to Israel. . . . All show of welcoming Taiwan and Israel representatives, prior to the Games was an elaborate hoax. The Government of Indonesia was determined not to invite these countries."

It is no coincidence that Sondhi was among the four members of the IOC executive board who ultimately made the decision to suspend Indonesia. An angry Sukarno saw this as a humiliation and instructed the Indonesian Olympic Association to resign immediately. The Indonesian sports minister denounced the Olympic Games as an "imperial tool" while announcing his president's intentions to organize his own kind of Olympiad. Ironically, what Indonesia saw as imperialism was led by Indian officials. In fact, the Indians were so put off by the events at Jakarta that they upped their demands. As the Indians lobbied opinion against Sukarno, he proceeded with his new GANEFO. Sukarno saw in the Games an opportunity to become the leader of the "New Emerging Forces"—all those countries struggling for a New World Order—but his biggest ally was Beijing. Chinese Prime Minister Zhou Enlai wrote to him expressing full cooperation, and delegations of specially deputed Chinese experts began arriving in Indonesia to put the Games together. The PRC, which was excluded from the Olympic movement, saw GANEFO as an opportunity to gain global legitimacy. Maoist China pulled out all the stops "to persuade Asian and African countries to join the games." In addition, the PRC gifted the Indonesians with $18 million to organize GANEFO.

The rhetoric of GANEFO made it explicit that the Games would be based on the "spirit of Bandung," but it was also a direct challenge to India and the Olympic movement. As many as forty-two countries took part in the first Games at Jakarta that began on November 10, 1963. Most of the participating countries did not send official teams for fear of being barred from the Olympics. Despite this, at the time GANEFO did seem like a major challenger to the Olympic movement. The Indians were the most vocal in their opposition and made common cause with the IOC. In letter after letter to the IOC, which faced its biggest potential crisis since its formation, Indian officials rammed home their opposition to GANEFO and took a hard line against what they saw as "political influence" by Sukarno.

Just as the Indians were scared of losing their hegemony in Asian sports management, the IOC was worried about the prospect of a rival body. When Cambodia hosted a mini "Asian" GANEFO in 1966, thirty-seven countries participated. Again the PRC underwrote the event by building a brand-new stadium. Beijing had successfully turned sport into a tool of influence. As a worried IOC president, Avery Brundage, noted, the PRC was using the Games to strengthen its diplomatic linkages across Asia and Africa, giving, for instance, Congo Brazzaville a $20 million loan for sporting activity. The IOC's immediate priority was to avoid a split engineered by Beijing. The IOC need not have worried. The GANEFO initiative died a natural death with Sukarno's relinquishing of power in 1966. The new Suharto regime was not interested in pursuing sport diplomacy at a time when the Indonesian economy was in grave crisis. Moreover, Chinese and Indonesian diplomatic relations first cooled off and then were broken. GANEFO lost its primary sponsor. Cairo was to host GANEFO II in 1966, but with the Chinese and the Indonesians not interested any more, the lack of financial resources meant that GANEFO died a natural death.

In the end, it must be acknowledged that the GANEFO constituted the greatest breakaway challenge the IOC had ever faced. It threatened to overturn the entire edifice of the Olympic movement. Indian and IOC officials had the most to lose if GANEFO succeeded: India, its Asian hegemony, and the IOC, its global control over international sport.[16]

HISTORIES OF FOOTBALL

Just as the Indian Olympic story is crucial to an improved understanding of the global history of the Olympic movement and also contributes to a better understanding of Indian colonial and postcolonial history, a history of Indian football brings to light important chapters in the evolution of the Indian state.

Among notable scholars who have contributed to scholarship on Indian football are Kausik Bandyopadhyay,[17] James Mills, Paul Dimeo,[18] and Tony Mason.[19] Most early writing on the history of football was concerned with the spread of the game in certain regions or with documenting the impact of particular victories or events on the history of Indian nationalism. Much, for example, has been written on the Mohun Bagan victory against the English East Yorkshire Regiment in the final of the Indian Football Association Shield in 1911 or the particular local history of soccer in Goa in western India (James Mills). My own work, in collaboration with Kausik Bandyopdhyay, has attempted to revise the anomalies of earlier writing on Indian football and is the only effort so far that has tried documenting the history of Indian soccer as a whole. It seeks to explore the relationship between soccer and the imperial order, socialization, and cultural replication or "cloning" in the interests of Pax Britannica. It also explores the role of soccer in the formation of a distinctive, Indian identity in the face of self-assured imperial rule. In trying to document the relationship between soccer and anticolonial nationalism, we have relied heavily on vernacular sources. These sources, largely ignored by earlier analysts like Tony Mason, are fundamental to an understanding of the role soccer played in the formation of an Indian identity. Their use, in conjunction with little-consulted Indian English-language sources, has helped us analyze the relationship between the princes and the middle class; between class, caste, and gender; and between the imperialist and the Indian subject.

As mentioned earlier, Mohun Bagan's epochal Indian Football Association Shield victory of 1911 is one of the most commented-on events in Indian football/history. From scholars to enthusiasts, every Indian takes a legitimate pride in reckoning that this sporting success was a historic milestone not only in the history of Indian sport but in that of Indian nationalism as well. Existing historiography of this event describes it in terms of nationalism, racism, commercialism, and culture. While European scholars seek to analyze its nationalist-racist significance in the context of imperial mission of the "games ethic" and consider it to be a success story of British "cultural imperialism," most Indian historians see it as the culmination of the nationalist celebration of brawn and the cult of physical fitness and hail it as an indigenous nationalist reaction with potential repercussions on society, culture, and economy. There is yet another line of interpretation that looks at the event from purely a footballing angle, stressing the club's professional attitude toward the game. Despite all this, much remains to be explained as far as the true historical significance of this much commented on sporting event in Indian history is concerned. To be more specific, none of the available works seek to analyze the character and pattern of sporting nationalism and specific forms of nationalist sporting culture in the wake of the victory, the story of racist discrimination that followed in its aftermath, the moral impact of the event on Bengali social psyche, or the enduring commercial implications of the success. Our own work is in some sense a corrective to the conventional historical interpretations of the Mohun Bagan victory of 1911 and attempts to reconstruct its nationalist, racist, social, cultural, and economic significance in proper historical perspective.[20]

THE FUTURE

Scholarship on South Asian sport continues to evolve. India's cricket history and Olympic encounter are subjects of considerable scholarly inquiry. Younger scholars like Souvik Naha, who has written on cricket, and Amitava Chatterjee, working on the commercialization of sport in pre- and post-Partition India, have added to the growing corpus of scholarship. Contemporary scholars are concerned with issues of national representation, colonial and postcolonial resistance through sport, women's empowerment, and the fight for the control of sporting organizations. In cricket, the impact of commercialization on the game itself and on the Indian economy at large has been the subject of much scholarly attention of late. Such recognition, it can be surmised, will only help in enriching sports scholarship in the future and will eventually make sport a subject of mainstream historical inquiry in India and South Asia.

NOTES

1. Clifford Geertz, "'Deep Play': Notes on the Balinese Cockfight," in *The Interpretation of Cultures: Selected Essays* (New York: Basic Books, 1973): 436.

2. Valiotis did his doctoral dissertation on Pakistan cricket from Australia and is currently the best-known scholar on Pakistan sport. Noman's work, more narrative in nature, is also a valuable source on the early history of cricket in Pakistan.

3. Michael has written volumes on Sri Lankan cricket; his most recent work is more journalistic in nature. For his more analytical work, see Michael Roberts, "Ethnicity in Riposte at a Cricket Match: The Past for the Present," *Comparative Studies in Society and History* 27 (1985): 401–429.

4. Dipesh Chakrabarty, "Introduction," in *Sport in South Asian Society: Past and Present*, ed. Boria Majumdar and J. A Mangan (Routledge: London, 2005).

5. Ramachandra Guha, *Corner of a Foreign Field: The Indian History of a British Sport* (New Delhi: Pan Macmillan, 2002).

6. Guha, *Corner of a Foreign Field*.

7. The book's genesis was my doctoral dissertation on the social history of Indian cricket at Oxford University conducted in the years 1999 to 2003. It was published by Penguin-Viking in 2004 under the title *Twenty-Two Yards to Freedom: A Social History of Indian Cricket*. Some of my other books on Indian cricket include *The Illustrated History of Indian Cricket* (New Delhi: Roli Books, 2006; revised and updated ed., 2009); *Lost Histories of Indian Cricket: Battles of the Pitch* (London: Routledge, 2005); *Indian Cricket Through the Ages: A Reader* (New Delhi: Oxford University Press, 2005).

8. A franchise based domestic completion currently valued at over US$4 billion.

9. J. A. Mangan, *The Games Ethic and Imperialism* (London: Frank Cass, 2001).

10. Chris Valiotis, "Sporting Nations of the Imagination: Pakistani Cricket and Identity in Pakistan and Anglo-Pakistan" (PhD diss., University of New South Wales, 2006). More recently Osman Samiuddin and Peter Oborne have also published some really interesting work on Pakistan cricket. Osman Samiuddin, *The Unquiet Ones: A History of Pakistan Cricket* (Noida, Uttar Pradesh: Harper Sport, 2014), and Peter Oborne *Wounded Tiger: The History of India in Pakistan* (London: Simon and Schuster, 2014).

11. Roberts, "Ethnicity in Riposte."

12. For Sri Lankan cricket, also see Qadri Ismail, "Batting against the Break: On Cricket, Nationalism, and the Swashbuckling Sri Lankans," *Social Text* 50 (1997): 33–56.

13. Dhyan Chand, "Goal!" *Sport & Pastime* (1952). The book has been digitized and is available at http://www.bharatiyahockey.org/granthalaya/goal/.

14. For details, see Boria Majumdar and Nalin Mehta, *Olympics: The India Story* (New Delhi: HarperCollins, 2008, revised and updated ed., 2012).

15. Majumdar and Mehta, *Olympics*.

16. For the whole story on GANEFO see Majumdar and Mehta, *Olympics*, chapter 7.

17. Boria Majumdar and Kausik Bandyopadhyay, *Goalless: The Story of a Unique Footballing Nation* (New Delhi: Penguin Viking, 2006).

18. James Mills and Paul Dimeo, eds., *Soccer in South Asia: Empire, Nation, Diaspora*, (London: Frank Cass, 2001).

19. Tony Mason, "Football on the Maidan: Cultural Imperialism in Calcutta," in *The Cultural Bond: Sport, Empire, Society*, ed. J. A. Mangan (London: Frank Cass, 1992).

20. Majumdar and Bandyopadhyay, *Goalless*.

Bibliography

Bose, Mihar. *Magic of Indian Cricket: Cricket and Society in India*. London: Routledge, 2006.

Majumdar, Boria. *The Illustrated History of Indian Cricket*. Delhi: Lustre Press, Roli Books, 2009.

Majumdar, Boria. *Indian Cricket Through the Ages: A Reader*. New Delhi: Oxford University Press, 2005a.

Majumdar, Boria. *Lost Histories of Indian Cricket: Battles off the Pitch*. London: Routledge, 2005b.

Majumdar, Boria. *Twenty-Two Yards to Freedom: A Social History of Indian Cricket*. New Delhi: Viking, 2004.

Majumdar, Boria, and J. A. Mangan. *Sport in South Asian Society: Past and Present*. London: Routledge, 2005.

Mangan, J. A. *The Games Ethic and Imperialism: Aspects of the Diffusion of an Ideal*. London: Frank Cass, 2001.

Mills, James, and Paul Dimeo, eds. *Soccer in South Asia: Empire, Nation, Diaspora*. London: Frank Cass, 2001.

Nandy, Ashis. *The Tao of Cricket: On Games Destiny and the Destiny of Games*. New York: Oxford University Press, 2000.

Oborne, Peter. *Wounded Tiger: The History of Pakistan Cricket*. London: Simon and Schuster, 2014.

Samiuddin, Osman. *The Unquiet Ones: A History of Pakistan Cricket*. Noida, Uttar Pradesh: Harper Sport, 2014.

......

CHAPTER 18

DIFFUSION AND TRANSFORMATION OF WESTERN SPORTS IN NORTH ASIA

......

SAYURI GUTHRIE-SHIMIZU

SPORT came to North Asia as a fellow traveler to God and Mammon. In the late nineteenth century, Protestant Christianity and Western capitalist economy began to penetrate this corner of the globe that had been largely shielded from Western influences by local choice aided by geographical distances. The same forces of world history that cracked open China's diplomatic isolation in the mid-century—technological advances, expansionist thrusts of the capitalist world economy, and Christendom's self-assigned civilizing mission—brought to the shores of Japan and Korea Anglo-American merchants, diplomats, Protestant missionaries, advisers, and teachers of various sorts. As these pioneering Westerners took up residency and established community life first in treaty ports and then elsewhere, their social visions and everyday practices were planted in the indigenous soil already fertilized with yearning for reform and experimentation to survive the approaching age of high imperialism.

Like the scientific and technological knowledge learned and the novel social institutions adopted, a new body culture came embedded in the overarching process of Westernization and modernization. This new system of thought and practices imbued positive values in the exertion and strategic deployment of the human body, embracing the Anglo-American notion that physical activity was meaningful in and of itself, conducive to values such as learning and character-building. Modern athletics and competitive sports, avatars of this new body culture, elicited largely willing local receptions in North Asia, though there were no doubt isolated cases of coercive foisting better characterized as cultural imperialism. Sport in North Asia, churned out of this global cultural transmission, also disseminated unevenly. Its benefits were not equally accessible to all denizens of North Asia, especially in its early phases. This asymmetrical development of sport provides another window into the history of North Asia's citizenship regimes stratified along national origin, ethnicity, class, and gender. In this regard, sport development in Japan and Korea paralleled the commensurate processes elsewhere in the world, but it also carried unique features engraved by the regional history of colonialism and decolonization.

DIFFUSION OF WESTERN SPORTS IN JAPAN

After the unwelcome visits by Commodore Perry's naval squadron ushered in Japan's reluctant opening to the outside world (1854), the nation began to play host to foreign nationals spearheaded by diplomats, merchants, Protestant missionaries, and foreign advisers and teachers called *oyatoi* (hired hands). During the reign of Emperor Meiji (1868–1912), the Japanese government and private organizations recruited more than three thousand experts from abroad in a wide range of fields to guide them through the path toward Western-style modernity. Organized sports then becoming popular and increasingly codified in Europe and the United States were introduced to Japan by these Euro-American expatriates, an unintended consequence of the state-driven modernization project. Europeans and Americans formed exclusive clubs and engaged in such recreational activities as horseback riding, rowing, cricket, football, tennis, and golf in the protected sanctuaries of treaty ports and foreign settlements, most importantly Yokohama and Kobe. Young American *oyatoi* teachers who staffed Japan's early elite educational institutions in the 1870s turned their students on to baseball, a sport that was even evolving into commercial business stateside. The Meiji government's attempt to create a modern national military also yielded an unintended result of introducing, through French military advisers and German instructors, more individualized Western athletics, such as gymnastics, fencing, rifle-shooting, and, later, skiing.

American Protestant missionaries, particularly those associated with the Young Men's Christian Association (YMCA), and Japanese youth returning from studies in the United States were instrumental in the introduction and popularization of basketball and volleyball, the two indoor sports invented in the 1890s at the Christian organization's athletic training college in Springfield, Massachusetts. First established in Tokyo in 1880, the YMCA in Japan had opened branches in more than ten key cities by the turn of the century. Their sport enrichment programs included organizing sport meets and dispatching sport instructors to schools upon request. This network of "muscular Christianity" later helped propagate other Western sports such as field hockey, badminton, handball, and table tennis among Japan's youth population. Privileged foreign residents and their Japanese social equals were credited with introducing yachting, ice skating, and mountain climbing to Japan. In 1878, the Japanese government opened a national institute devoted to physical education with the help of George Leland, a sport pedagogue trained in Amherst College.

In the early Meiji period, the opportunity to participate in the imported Western sports was largely limited to the nation's modernizing (male) elite class and well-heeled urbanites. Unique in that regard was baseball, which spread among all classes of Japan's youth like a wildfire as it was adopted into the physical education curriculum of the nation's newly instituted universal primary and secondary education system. Baseball also became the centerpiece of interscholastic sport competition among the first generation of colleges and universities, such as Tokyo Imperial University, Keio, Waseda, and Meiji Gakuin in Tokyo, and Kyoto Imperial University and Doshisha in Kyoto. Outdoor athletic activities also occupied an important place in the pedagogy of William S. Clark, the Amherst-educated scientist and inaugural president of Sapporo Agricultural College (later Hokkaido University).

Besides baseball, both forms of British football, soccer and rugby, became an extramural sport commonly played among Japan's private colleges in the Meiji era. The Japanese collegiate athletes honed their skills in rugby, the more popular of the two, and baseball through occasional challenge matches with foreign expatriates' clubs and US and British navy teams on shore leave. Track and field and light calisthenics became a fixture in Japanese student life through gym class and a school-sponsored athletic event called *undokai* (Field Day). This type of structured day of games and sports was first organized in the 1870s by British naval instructors at Japan's newly established Naval Academy in Tokyo. A young English *oyatoi* teacher Frederick W. Strange, an avid oarsman and player of cricket and baseball, laid the groundwork for institutionalizing *undokai* in the Japanese schools when he organized a day-long track-and-field event in 1883 for students at Ichiko, the prestigious preparatory academy feeding into Tokyo Imperial University. The day's program Strange designed included running, jumping, vaulting, and various throwing events. That year, Strange also penned a manual titled *Outdoor Games,* translated into Japanese two years later. The widely circulated booklet explicated a variety of outdoor sports, such as baseball, football, field hockey, and lawn tennis.

Intercollegiate sport competition became institutionalized and, for baseball in particular, became a spectator sport with entertainment value in Japan in the early twentieth century along the lines similar to the developmental trajectories of intercollegiate sports in the United States. First sporadic, and then periodic, challenge matches evolved over time into a more stable system of regular competition structured around league and tournament championships administered by a standing bureaucracy. The six-team league among Tokyo Imperial University and five private universities in the metropolitan area was organized in 1925 as Tokyo Big-6, modeled after the conference of elite US Northeastern colleagues that would later formalize into the Ivy League. Similar multiteam collegiate baseball leagues were organized elsewhere in Japan in the subsequent decades. With the beginning of play-by-play radio broadcast in 1929, Tokyo Big-6 baseball became a hugely popular form of sport entertainment.

Japan transitioned into a period of heavy industrialization and economic take-off following its relatively easy victory in the first Sino-Japanese War (1894–1895) and acquisition of its first overseas colony (Taiwan). The nascent industrial economy received a further boost induced by World War I in Europe. Thus the economic expansion and urbanization experienced in the early decades of the twentieth century broadened the socioeconomic basis and infrastructure of popular sport participation in Japan. It was during this period of industrial growth that affordably priced sport equipment began to be produced by domestic manufacturers such as Mizuno to replace expensive American imports. Many industrial and commercial sport leagues appeared in this period, and company sport programs for employees, a distinct future of Japan's corporate welfare capitalism, enabled many working men and women to continue to participate in sports after the end of their formal education.

The 1920s also saw the construction of several large-scale public athletic facilities, playing fields, and steel-and-concrete modern baseball parks such as Koshien Stadium (modeled after New York's Polo Grounds) in western Japan and Jingu Stadium, built adjacent to the sacred compound of the shrine honoring the late Emperor Meiji. These modern stadiums provided venues for American Major League off-season exhibition tours in 1931 and 1934, the latter featuring Babe Ruth and Lou Gehrig and later became home grounds for Japan's own professional baseball franchises.

Contemporaneous to this social transformation conducive to sport development in the early twentieth century was Japan's joining the International Olympic Committee (IOC). As the first nation outside of Europe and North America, Japan received formal invitation from Pierre de Coubertin to participate in the Stockholm Olympics. Kano Jigoro, the founding father of Judo as a modern sport, was chosen as the IOC's first member from Asia. The performance of the two athletes sent to the 1912 Olympics, sprinter Mishima Yahiko and long-distance runner Kanaguri Shizo, was nothing but humiliating—with Mishima finishing last in his 100-, 200-, and 400-meter heats and Kanaguri passing out and withdrawing from his marathon race. However, the nation's entry into the multination competitive arena thus far reserved for white Europeans and North Americans uplifted Japan's self-image as a "civilized nation" (*bunmeikoku*) in the world and further fueled the growth of public enthusiasm in sports in the rising Asian empire.

Participation in the Olympic Games and other international athletic competitions initiated the Japanese to other sport forms played in those venues, for example, Western-style wrestling, boxing, and weightlifting. While the Olympic movement went into abeyance during World War I in Europe, Asians continued to deepen their engagement with Western sports at a venue of their own: The Far Eastern Games (initially called the Far Eastern Olympics—the name "Olympics" was dropped from the second meet in Shanghai because the event was not sanctioned by the IOC). Beginning in Manila in 1913, Asia's first multievent athletic meet was the brainchild of an American YMCA official stationed in Manila, Elwood S. Brown. The biennial Far Eastern Games lasted until 1934 when they collapsed under the weight of the controversy over participation by the Manchukuo.

Through this system of regular international competition, Asian athletes and coaches were able to update their knowledge about and learn new techniques and strategies in YMCA-invented team sports as well as Olympic events such as track and field, swimming, and wresting. The Far Eastern Games also helped popularize the notion of sport as distinct from traditional martial arts and folk games in the participating countries. The trination enterprise also contributed to the rise of women's sports in Japan by including women's swimming, tennis, and volleyball as "exhibition events" in the sixth games held in Osaka in 1923. The Far Eastern Games and its variant West Asia Games in India (1934) also left behind learning experiences for Asia's sport administrators in planning and organizing a multination, multievent sport competition, a historical legacy that would emerge relevant when Asians resuscitated the dormant institution as the Asian Games after World War II.

The Olympic Games resumed in 1920, and Japan sent to Antwerp a fifteen-man delegation, organized around the track-and-field team coached by American Franklin Brown, sports director of the YMCA Japan. Kanaguri avenged himself of his ignominious performance in Stockholm, finishing in sixteenth place with a not-so-shabby record of 2 hours 48 minutes. Yet the real bright spot for Japan in the 1920 Olympics was Kumagai Kazuya's unanticipated winning of a silver medal in men's singles tennis. He and partner Kashio Seiichiro duplicated the feat in the doubles. The glory of the first Olympic medals was soon tempered when the cash-strapped Japanese Olympians were unable to go home. Thanks to a $15,000 donation by two industrial giants Mitsui and Mitsubishi, the stranded athletes finally managed to pay for their return travel. After this massive embarrassment, the Japanese government began in 1924 to provide a subsidy of 60,000 yen for sending athletes to the Olympics. Japan won its first gold medal at the 1928 Amsterdam Olympics when Oda Mikio finished first in the triple jump. A second gold medal was brought home by swimmer Tsuruta Yoshiyuki, in the 200-meter breaststroke. In the 1930s, Japan emerged as a major force in the international swimming competition to rival the United States, winning four gold, five silver, and two bronze medals at the Los Angeles Olympics.

ORIGINS OF SPORT IN KOREA

While not sharing common landed borders, Japan and Korea do share a deeply entwined and convoluted history, and sport is one arena in which their historical trajectories have been problematically intertwined. Like China and Japan, no indigenous tradition of organized sports had existed in Korea prior to the arrival of Westerners. After the "Hermit Kingdom" was forced open with a string of unequal treaties (first with Japan in 1876 and then with the United States in 1882), Korea found itself at the brunt of Western and Japanese imperialism. To navigate these perilous geopolitical waters, indigenous reformers came to espouse new directions in military, economy, national education, and public health policies, similar to China's self-strengthening movement and Japan's early Meiji-era reforms. It was during this Kabo reform that the germ of a vision of physical education and sport as integral to the development of the total human being can first be detected. King Kojong's Imperial Rescript (1895) on education included a reference to physical education, but the public school curricula subsequently designed and implemented did not actually entail physical education. The lack of trained teachers, resources, and facilities made physical education in the public schools virtually impossible.

Initially at least, the push for adopting physical education and Western sports had to come from extraneous agents, and here again, American Protestant missionaries, arriving in the beleaguered kingdom after 1882, played a critical role. One of the most notable among them, Presbyterian missionary Horace Allen, came as a physician, and through his modern scientific medical work he gained the confidence of King Kojong and the reform-minded Korean elite. His handiwork included a modern hospital and medical school that would evolve into present-day Yonsei University. The first Western-style school in Korea, Pai Chai Hak Dang, was established in the nation's capital (Hwang Sung, present-day Seoul) in 1885 by American Methodist missionary Henry Appenzeller. The school's curriculum initially emphasized academic subjects, offering physical education only as extracurricular activity. It was mainly through this and other privately funded Protestant mission schools that elite local children gained initial exposure to modern sports such as baseball and football during the waning days of Chosŏn dynastic rule.

The main drive for promotion of Western sports came from the YMCA after its Korean branch was opened in Hwang Sung in 1903. One of the American founding members, Philip Gillett, an alumnus of the YMCA training college in Springfield and a former classmate of James Naismith (the inventor of basketball), is credited with introducing baseball, soccer, and basketball to Koreans between 1904 and 1907. Gillett and his colleague at the Hwang Sung YMCA, Frank Brockman, used Western team sports as a tool of social engineering with which the Americans exhorted young Koreans to steel themselves and their nation against outside intruders by cultivating physical strength and spiritual fortitude. This brand of muscular Christianity gained a dedicated following among young Korean nationalists.

Due in part to baseball's primary association with Japanese intruders, Korean youth initially took to succor more passionately. That soccer required less equipment was also a factor. Just as the enthusiasm for baseball in Meiji Japan was kept replenished by a continual back flow of study-abroad students and businessmen returning from the United States, baseball owed its long-term acceptance to Korean students fresh from their studies in Japan. Led by Yun Ik-hyon, twenty-five former study-abroad Korean students formed a private baseball club in Hwang Sung in 1906. In one of the earliest historic references to baseball play in Korea, the squad walloped a team of American expatriates. Equipment and uniforms, mostly imports from the United States, were also brought back from Japan by these Korean youth elite, thus turning American athletic paraphernalia into an alluring symbol of consumer modernity and an object of envy in the Japanese colonial city.

In the tumultuous post-1910 era of formal Japanese colonial rule of Korea, the Seoul YMCA was inevitably drawn into the Korean nationalist agitation launched out of Christian churches as its key organizational hubs. Several Korean members of the Seoul YMCA were implicated in the trumped-up charge of an assassination attempt on Governor General Terauchi Masatake, resulting, among other things, in Gillett's forced transfer to Shanghai in 1913. To co-opt Korean Christians at the core of anti-Japanese agitation, the governor general's office hand-picked nineteen pro-Japan Seoul YMCA leaders for an all-expenses-paid trip to Japan in the fall of 1911. The delegation's baseball pickup games in Japan were prominently reported and touted as evidence of an insepa-rable binational bond. The Japanese colonial government banned or disbanded Korean civic organizations, including sport groups. Under the new colonial education regime, a two-track system separating Japanese and Korean students was rigidly enforced. Physical education in the primary and vocational schools open to or Korean students was made available only as an elective.

Despite—or perhaps because of—this limited access to sport and physical educa-tion accorded to locals by the colonial state, sport and Korean nationalism fused into a potent composite symbol of anticolonial defiance and pride, provoking suitably repres-sive Japanese reactions. Students at all-Korean elite Bibun and Onsei schools demanded greater access to sport as part of their public protests for greater educational oppor-tunity. They also demanded their baseball and tennis players be allowed to challenge Japanese players in their age cohort. In 1913, the Japanese colonial state intervened to call a closely-contested (4–3) baseball game between the Seoul YMCA and an all-Japanese club after the seventh inning in order to prevent agitated and overflowing spectators on both sides from sparking a riot. This match-up was banned for three years. A year later, the colonial police ordered the goal posts in Appenzeller's Pai Chai School's soccer field be painted black because Korean nationalists organized around Yoon Chi Ho and Yi Sang Jae had painted the goal posts white, the symbolic color of the nation of Korea, in a show of anticolonial defiance. Repression on bicycling, an event where Koreans excelled, was particularly glaring. At the All-Korea bicycling meet in 1913, Gen Fukudo, a Korean national champion and folk hero, was prohibited on dubious eligibility grounds from competing in the finals against three Japanese contenders.

The prolonged nationwide uprising starting on March 1, 1919, however, forced the Japanese government to reassess its colonial policy. As part of new Governor General Saito Makoto's more conciliatory approach, calibrated accommodation of local Korean needs and aspirations was pursued in the 1920s. The publication of vernacular-language newspapers was permitted; restrictions on associations and assemblies were eased, freeing up social space for Korean civic enterprises, including sports. This new orienta-tion in Japanese colonial policy also permitted the establishment in 1920 of the Korean Athletic Association (the institutional forerunner of the Korean Olympic Committee) as an independent sport organization with an all-Korean charter membership. Most important, the era's remodeled education system abolished the two-track formula in public education, making it possible for Korean students to play with and compete against their Japanese peers in intramural and interscholastic sport competitions.

As various national sport championships began in the colonial metropole, a still modest yet growing number of Korean top athletes began to claim their place in the sun in Japan's expanding sportscape. Korean student soccer teams did particularly well in the all-Japan championships in the 1920s and 1930s. Two Korean runners and a boxer represented Japan at the 1932 Olympics in Los Angeles, placing sixth and ninth in the marathon. Four years later, a total of ten Korean nationals competed as Japanese repre-sentatives in the Winter Olympic Games in Germisch-Partenkirchen and the Summer Games in Berlin. Kim Yong Sik, a member of the Japanese national soccer team, con-tributed to Japan's stunning first-round 3–2 victory over gold medal favorite Sweden, an upset valorized as the "Miracle in Berlin" in the European and Japanese press.

Given the tangled nature of Korean anticolonial nationalism and sport, the con-vulsive aftermath of Soon Kee-chung's victory in the marathon at the 1936 Berlin Olympics may seem in retrospect almost preordained. Soon and his Korean teammate Nam Sung-ying finished first and third, but neither medalist could bear to look up to the Japanese national flag rising on the flagpole as Japan's national anthem was played at the medal ceremony. The Korean-language newspaper *Dong-a Ilbo* proudly reported its native sons' athletic feats with a front-page picture of Soon at the center of the medal stand, with the Japanese flag on Soong's uniform blacked out. The colonial government immediately shut down the daily, and the masterminds of the elision were brutally punished. Japanese gold medalists such as triple jumper Tajima Naoto and swimmer it Maehata Hideko, returned to Japan to a hero's and heroine's welcome, but Soong was conspicuously excluded from all festivities. Harassed persistently and placed on the surveillance list of the Japanese public security authorities, Soon gave up competitive running. No one probably imagined then that he would reemerge in the international media fifty-two years later as the penultimate runner in the torch relay for the Seoul Olympics.

Before the 1936 Berlin Games opened, the IOC voted Tokyo as the host of the next Olympics. The IOC's decision vindicated the six years of lobbying by Tokyo, which aspired to be a world-class city on a par with London, Paris, and Berlin. Tokyo's Olympic dream was short-lived, however. Japan resumed military aggression in north China in the summer of 1937. The organizers of the Tokyo Olympics came under mounting pres-sure from the military to refrain from deflecting resources of the nation at war. Once it became clear that the military clash in China would metastasize into a protracted war, the Tokyo realized that the projected scarcity of resources available for civilian projects, such as stadium construction, would make it impossible to carry out the plan. At the IOC meeting in Cairo in July 1938, the city of Tokyo relinquished its right to host the games in 1940.

Japan's substitute for the aborted Olympics was the East Asian Games held in Tokyo and Osaka in June 1940. This sportive event was also built into the nation's year-long cel-ebration of the 2,600th anniversary of the mythical reign of the Imperial Household. The two-thousand-member roster of participants in this nominally international athletic event only included Japan, Manchukuo (fielding an all-ethnic Japanese team), Wang Zhaoming's collaborationist Nationalist China, the Philippines, Hawai'i, and Mongolia. This geographical configuration mirrored the diplomatic isolation into which Japan had painted itself by that time. The highlight of the East Asian Games was the final match of baseball, which pitted the all-Japan team against the Hawai'i team, which was comprised of the all-Nisei Honolulu Asahi. The latter's expedition to Japan was funded through pri-vate donations from the Japanese American community in Hawai'i.

The war mobilization after 1937 put severe strains on sport in Japan and Korea in terms of resource scarcity and state repression. The militarization of physical education that began in the 1930s accelerated across the Japanese Empire. Regular physical education teachers were replaced by martial arts instructors charged with paramilitary training. A new Ministry of Health and Welfare was created in 1938, and its Board of Physical Fitness assumed control of all sports and athletic activities except physical education. After the war with the United States began, all sport governing bodies were merged into a quasi-governmental entity directed by Prime Minister Tojo Hideki. The Ministry of Education suspended all collegiate sports except Japanese archery, kendo (bamboo stick fencing), and judo. Comparable state control (i.e., ban) of sports took place in Korea. After 1943, swimming and water polo were the only athletic meets held in Korea in the name of military training.

New Sport Regimes in North Asia after World War II

With Japan's surrender to the Allied Powers in August 1945, the US Army occupied Japan and Korea south of the 38th parallel. During the US occupation period, sports sprang back to life in Japan and its liberated former colony. The American occupying forces poured their abundant resources into athletic and recreational programs for their soldiers and officers. In Japan, the destruction of the local sport infrastructure and postwar material shortage were severe, but the occupation forces' supreme commander General Douglas MacArthur and his entourage encouraged participation in sports as a way for the local population to cleanse itself of the wartime fanaticism and relearn the spirit of American-style democracy. Baseball was particularly privileged by the occupation authorities; student national championships were resumed, and professional baseball opened for its first postwar season in April 1946, less than a year after Japan's surrender. With the advent of television, professional baseball became a hugely popular form of national entertainment, eclipsing collegiate baseball. Bicycling proved to be an accidental beneficiary of war: to raise revenues for postwar urban reconstruction, the Japanese government enacted a law in 1948 enabling "local public bodies" to hold bicycle races (and generate revenues from betting). Local governments scrambled to organize bicycling races, turning *keirin* into a popular working-class spectator sport.

In the postwar education reform, an American model was adopted in both Japan and Korea where Western sports were reinstated as the core elements of physical education. In occupied Japan, kendo and other traditional martial arts were banned from the school curriculum or even as extracurricular activities as part of the demilitarization program. Only sumo was allowed to resume before the end of 1945. Gender equality in access to sports in the schools was a neglected area of the postwar education reform, a blind spot reflective of the American reformers' own gendered assumptions about girls' sports and female physicality as well as the entrenched local practices. Japan's sport administration was now freed of state control and reestablished as a private enterprise, resulting in a federation of national sport organizations to supervise amateur sports on the model of America's Amateur Athletic Union. In US-occupied Korea, the Korean Athletic Association reconstituted itself. A separate sport organization was created by the local communist authorities north of the 38th parallel.

For both Japan and Korea, a place in the restored international sport community carried significance far beyond securing for their athletes' opportunities to compete and excel on the world stage. For Japan, being readmitted into the IOC and other international sport federations meant the nation's postwar redemption; for Korea membership in these organizations was a shining badge of newly acquired independent nationhood and legitimacy in a world rapidly becoming polarized by the Cold War confrontation. Once the US-occupied southern half of the Korean peninsula became an independent nation in August 1948, followed a month later by the northern communist half, sport competition became one among many battlefields where the divided Koreas would vie for international recognition and claims of superiority of their newly adopted systems of social organization.

South Korea beat its former colonial master to the punch by gaining IOC membership in 1947 and securing an invitation to the first postwar Winter Olympics in St. Moritz and the Summer Games in London even before it was formally established as an independent nation. Forceful championing by IOC Vice President Avery Brundage made this rather unusual accession possible. The five-man delegation from US-occupied Korea inconspicuously sent to St. Moritz was headed by Che Yong-jong, a former "Japanese" national champion speed skater. The costs of a larger delegation of sixty-seven athletes that arrived in London via occupied Japan in July was defrayed with revenues generated from an Olympic lottery held at the sufferance of the US occupation authorities and monetary contributions by resident Koreans in Japan. Since the Soviet Union snubbed the Olympics as a contemptible bourgeois enterprise, the Kim Il-song' regime in the north showed no interest in this locus of international representation at this point.

Although Japanese sport officials began lobbying for their return to the IOC as soon as the war was over, the door to the London Olympics remained tightly shut to Japanese athletes. The exclusion was particularly painful to a group of top-flight Japanese swimmers spearheaded by Furuhashi Hironoshin who, a year earlier, had clocked the first of many world records—4:38 for the 400-meter freestyle—that he would later mark in distances from 400 to 1,500. Japan's sport officials held the 1948 national swimming championships on the same day as the London Olympics swimming events, determined to prove that theirs were the world's fastest swimmers. There Furuhashi and his teammates Hashizume Shiro far outpaced the American Olympic gold medalists in London, but their times were not recognized as world records due to Japan's disbarment from the IOC. But their exploits, buttressed by intercession by head coach Robert Kiputh of the US national swimming team with a history of prewar sport exchange with Japan, persuaded the International Swimming Federation to reinstate Japan to its ranks after the London Olympics. Furuhashi and his domestic rivals' continued dominance in international competition between 1949 and 1951, along with the US occupation authorities' public endorsement, eased the way for Japan's return to the IOC in May 1951. Although still on a path to postwar economic recovery, Japan sent a large contingent of 102 athletes and officials to the 1952 Helsinki Olympics. Freestyle wrestler Ishii Shohachi won Japan's first postwar gold medal.

Despite the legacy of its wartime aggression in Asia, Japan was allowed to be present at the inaugural Asian Games, the quadrennial regional games launched in March 1951 in New Delhi under the leadership of Indian IOC member Guru Dutt Sondhi. The key instigator of the prewar West Asia Games, Sondhi's commitment to a vision of "All Asian Games," coupled with Japan's then overwhelming dominance in sports in Asia only recently released from colonialism, made for its relatively smooth inclusion into this new regional arena of competition. Japan's seventy-seven-member national team returned home triumphant from the Indian capital with twenty-five gold medals out of fifty-five in six events. Japan's reign in the Asian Games would continue until it was dethroned by emergent China in medal count at the eighth games in Bangkok in 1978. Conspicuously absent from the inaugural Asian Games was South Korea. Nearly a year into the internecine war ranging on the divided peninsula, South Korea would only make its debut in the Asian Games at the second meet held in Manila in 1954.

The ravages of war and poverty and the domestic political turmoil and social dislocation wrought by the national bisection placed enormous road blocks before Korea, both South and North, in building domestic sport infrastructure. Regardless, both Koreas had their own reasons for making determined efforts to promote sport. For South Korea, the need for achieving excellence in the global sports arena was twofold, both equally nationalistic: to catch up and overtake its former colonial master Japan and to outshine its northern rival, also contending for international legitimacy. For North Korea, the Soviet Union's sudden change in attitudes toward the Olympics, manifested in the communist superpower's participation in the 1952 Helsinki Olympics, drastically repainted the political topography of international sport. Winning twenty-two gold medals, trailing behind only the United States, the Soviet Union's rise in sports was meteoric. At the next Olympics in Melbourne, the Soviet Union even breezed past its capitalist rival in medal count, and sports clearly became a new major battlefield of the Cold War for the two superpowers.

Reflecting the communist bloc's newfound interest in sport, in 1954 North Korea created a centralized national sport training system directly answerable to the cabinet. Kim Il-song's regime also began aggressively to seek membership in world sport federations in key events such as volleyball (1956), basketball (1957), and soccer (1958), clearly eyeing the IOC as its ultimate target. In 1962, at the IOC meeting held in its capital, the Soviet Union succeeded in having the international governing body adopt a resolution allowing North Korea to compete in the future Olympics as an independent team should South Korea refuse to constitute a unified national team, the gambit that would culminate in North Korea's formal entry to the IOC a year later.

Confronted by these threatening prospects emanating from the north, President Park Chong-hee's military regime enacted a national system of promoting sports in schools and workplaces and subsidizing local governments sponsoring athletic events. Established in October 1962, the program in the south, however, was initially no match for its equivalent in the north in terms of resources actually invested. That changed after 1964 under the leadership of Min Guan-sik, a former parliamentarian who became the president of the Korean Olympic Committee that year. The impetus for gearing up his nation's sport promotion also came from Japan where Min had lived before the war as a student. In 1959, the city of Tokyo was awarded a chance to achieve its long-deferred dream: hosting the Olympics in 1964.

As Tokyo prepared for this historic event with the material and moral support of the national government behind it, Min visited the city to inspect the Olympic facilities and fundraise among Korean nationals in Japan. The trip was an eye-opening experience for the former star tennis player at Kyoto Imperial University. Min was deeply struck by the gap that existed between Olympic-ready Japan and South Korea in terms of facilities, scientific training of athletes, and the use of foreign coaches. The disappointing performance of the South Korean 224-member national team at the Tokyo Games, the fifth largest contingent of all—even its vaunted soccer team ended winless—further hardened Min's determination to steer South Korea's sport administration in a bold new direction.

What became institutionalized in South Korean sports under Min's and his successor Kim Taek-Su's strong leadership was a system of direct state involvement in the recruiting, training, and rewarding of elite athletes, unheard of in a noncommunist country at the time. In 1966, South Korea opened a national training center in Taereung, a small village outside of Seoul. The athletic complex was still relatively modest in the 1970s, but throughout the period of South Korea's spectacular economic expansion known as "miracle on the Han," the facilities were progressively enhanced with state subsidy and private corporate donations to become one of the world's top scientific sport training centers where South Korea's elite athletes trained full time unencumbered by demands of school or work.

Alongside improvements in facilities, two programs were launched in 1973 to accelerate the nation's near-obsessive quest for world-class sport excellence. One was instituting a preferential quota for elite youth athletes in college admissions and exemption of the two-year compulsory draft for male Olympic medalists and winners of the Asian Games and world championship titles. That North Korea won its first Olympic gold medal (in rifle shooting) at the Munich Games eliminated whatever skepticism or opposition that might have existed in South Korea about such unburnished sport elitism. As a powerful incentive program for adult athletes, a new pension fund for Olympic medalists and world champions was also endowed in 1975 with a gift of 20 million won from President Park. The fund was also expanded with a partial gift from the emergent automaker Hyundai Corporation. Among the first group of athletes who became eligible for the athlete pension were Soon Kee-jong and Nam Sung-ying, the two marathon medalists from the 1936 Berlin Olympics. The recruitment of foreign coaches also accelerated and with it South Koreans' willingness to set aside their entrenched anti-Japanese nationalism, as in the case of Daimatsu Hirofumi, the famously spartan coach who brought to Japan a gold medal in women's volleyball over the much taller Soviet Union at the 1964 Tokyo Olympics.

The first tangible effect of these state-driven elite athlete programs came at the 1976 Montreal Olympics. Freestyle wrestler Yan Jong-mo won South Korea's long-awaited first Olympic gold medal. He became an instant national hero and received a 5 million won one-time cash award from the Korean Olympic Committee (and a warning from the still-amateurism-bound IOC as a result) on top of eligibility in the just-instituted athlete pension program. The rise of South Korean elite sport in the subsequent two decades was as spectacular as the nation's contemporary economic growth, capped by the capital's hosting of the Summer Olympics 1988. Among many rapturous moments for South Koreans coming out of the highly successful enterprise was the fact that they won twelve gold medals, beating Japan, which had to content itself with only four gold medals. South Korea's edge over Japan in Olympic medal count continued until the 2004 Games in Athens. Beginning with the 1986 Asian Games, South Korea also outperformed Japan in medal count except for the 1994 Games held in Hiroshima.

Contemporaries and commentators since have drawn many parallels between the two Olympics held in East Asia in 1964 and 1988. Both Olympics were held amid dizzying economic growth analogized as a postwar "miracle" with the full weight of state support behind it. Japan leapt into the ranks of the world's major countries after the Olympics, and so did South Korea after the Seoul Olympics. The hosting of this mega-event ushered in a wholesale alteration in the capitals' transportation infrastructure with lasting implications for their urban landscapes and spatial configurations. After the Olympics, the mass basis of sport participation in Japan and South Korea expanded significantly. In both Olympics, the nations' overseas diaspora community was a major source of private-sector donations to the enterprise and played a critical part in rallying support among the IOC members for their homeland's Olympic bid. Another common denominator between the two East Asian Olympics is that the host city proved its ability to organize a mega sporting event to the IOC by successfully hosting the Asian Games as a kind of a test run two years before the "main event": in Tokyo in 1962 and Seoul in 1986. These similarities across time and space speak to a universal theme of the interconnectiveness of the Olympic Games, national identity, economic development, and local social change, as well as North Asia's staggered historical development and legacies of colonialism. The nationalist passion and mutual jousting that continue to characterize the engagement among Japanese athletes and those representing the two Koreas in the stadiums, playing fields, aquatic centers, and on marathon routes in the new millennium are testimonies to how history is played out and nation is imagined, enacted, and enforced through the medium of sport.

BIBLIOGRAPHY

Bridges, Brian. *The Two Koreas and the Politics of Global Sport*. Leiden: Brill, 2012.
Cha, Victor D. *Beyond the Final Score: Politics of Sport in Asia*. New York: Columbia University Press, 2011.

Gems, Gerald R. *The Athletic Crusade: Sport and American Cultural Imperialism*. Lincoln: University of Nebraska Press, 2006.

Guthrie-Shimizu, Sayuri. *Transpacific Field of Dreams: How Baseball Linked the United States and Japan in Peace and War*. Chapel Hill: University of North Carolina Press, 2012.

Guttmann, Allen, and Lee Thompson. *Japanese Sports: A History*. Honolulu: University of Hawai'i Press, 2001.

Hong, Fan, ed. *Sport, Nationalism and Orientalism*. London and New York: Routledge, 2007.

Kelly, William, and Atsuo Sugimoto, eds. *This Sporting Life: Sport and Body Culture in Modern Japan*. New Haven, CT: Yale University Council on East Asia, 2007.

Kelly, William, and Susan Brownell, eds. *Olympics in East Asia: Nationalism, Regionalism, and Globalism on the Center State of World Sport*. New Haven, CT: Yale University Council on East Asian Studies, 2011.

Kietlinski, Robin. *Japanese Women and Sport: Beyond Baseball and Sumo*. London and New York: Bloomsbury Academic, 2011.

Mangan, A. J., and Fan Hong, eds. *Sport in Asian Society*. London and New York: Routledge, 2004.

Miyung Joo, Rachel. *Transnational Sport: Gender, Media and Global Korea*. Durham, NC: Duke University Press, 2012.

Niehaus, Andreas, and Christian Tagsold, eds. *Sport, Memory, and Nationhood in Japan: Remembering Glory Days*. London and New York: Routledge, 2012.

Park, Sung Jae. "Physical Sport and Sport as an Instrument of Nation Building in the Republic of Korea." PhD diss., Ohio State University, 1974.

Rieves, Joseph A. *Taking in a Game: A History of Baseball in Asia*. Lincoln: University of Nebraska Press, 2004.

Tomlinso, Alan, ed. *National Identity and Global Sports Events: Culture, Politics and Spectacles in the Olympic Games and the Football World Cup*. Albany: State University of New York Press, 2006.

Tutsui, William, and Michael Baskett. *East Asian Olympiads, 1934–2008*. Amsterdam: Brill, 2011.

CHAPTER 19

··

SPORT IN THE MIDDLE EAST

··

ALON K. RAAB

FOR the past five thousand years, sports have been an essential part of Middle East history. With roots in religious ceremonies and royal courts, their birth, life, and development into the twenty-first century have intersected with important cultural and historical processes. Sports activities have been influenced by these processes and have helped shape them as well. While there is a tendency by the media and by fans to focus on professional teams and star players, it is important to pay heed to the broader sweep of sport's influence. As elsewhere, sports, especially football (soccer), have been an important agent of social integration and a major arena in which ethnic and religious identities and conceptions and practices of gender and class are played out. Leaders and regimes have cynically used sports to further their aims. Matches have been a locale where conflicts were manifested and violence has erupted. At the same time, sports have created a place where fraternity and cooperation are common, as a source of pride, joy, independence, and dignity.

Geographical names are important, revealing, like archaeological layers, the complex history of a place. Considering how often the designation "the Middle East" is uttered, it is not surprising that there is argument about its boundaries. The term has aroused criticism and charges of being a reflection of a Eurocentric view.

The first recorded use of the term dates from 1850. Coined by the British India Office, it was only at the beginning of the twentieth century that it came into popular use. An inability to agree on boundaries continues today among geographers, historians, politicians, and the general public, both in the region and in the West. The recent "War on Terror" has added to the confusion as it expanded the conception, at least in the West, of what constitutes the region. In this chapter, the focus is on the countries that are part of the "traditional" Middle East, comprising seventeen countries, from Yemen in the south to Turkey in the north and from Iran in the east to Egypt in the west. There is recognition by many inhabitants of these lands that they are part of a distinct political and cultural entity, one known in Arabic as Al-sharq Al-Awasat, comprised of the Maghreb (the west) and the Mashriq (lands in the east.) It is also a reflection of the way that many in the region perceive a common past and destiny.

This unity does not obscure the many divisions between and within nations, religions, and ethnicities or the many animosities and conflicts or imply that all share the perceived commonality. For a long time, many living outside the Middle East have regarded it as a dangerous monolithic unit, confusing Muslims and Arabs, ignoring the fact that Christians (of many denominations) also live in the region. The way football was introduced and grew in Saudi Arabia differs from the way it appeared in neighboring Yemen. The present-day character of Iranian football is different from that practiced in Cyprus. This is true of other sports as well.

While Ancient Greece and Rome have received well-deserved attention for the essential role sports have played in their societies, only in the past few years have scholars spotlighted the important contributions made by Middle Eastern lands. The works of Wolfgang Decker, Donald G. Kyle, and Nigel B. Crowther have been especially illuminating. The origins of ancient games are shrouded in mystery and often contested, but ample archaeological evidence testifies to the presence of running, archery, horseback riding, and wrestling in the region starting in the third millennium BCE. These activities were connected from their first days to religious ceremonies, rulers' power, and spectacle. Many were an integral part of rituals marking nature's abundance and were performed to honor divinities such as Ishtar, the Babylonian goddess of war and love.

Mesopotamian kings and Egyptian pharaohs used sport to glorify their names and consolidate their power, presenting their sporting skills as evidence of their divine right and embodying the cosmic order. As living representations of the gods, they could not show fatigue or lose to mere mortals. Fortunately, the outcome always favored them. Gradually, commoners too participated in the contests as individuals and as part of teams representing the court or the city. Prizes, at first wine and then monetary, were introduced. Physical fitness and readiness for battle were important for the success of empires, and exercise was encouraged, as noted by Xenophon describing in *The Cyropaedia* the young Persian king Cyrus and his nobles' rigorous regimen of athletic training. Many sport activities were related to hunting or war (archery, javelin throwing, stick fencing, chariot racing, and wrestling,) while swimming, rowing, high jumping, acrobatics, and ball games embodied more peaceful aims. The latter included in Egypt an early form of hockey in which players using sticks made of palm trees and rounded at their end hit a ball of compressed papyrus covered with leather. Many of these games were depicted vividly on the walls of the Beni Hassan monarchs' tombs, where hundreds of drawings from around the twentieth century BCE feature skillful and joyous male and female athletes in action.

After the fourth century BCE Greek conquest, rulers organized regular athletic festivals that were combined with emperor cults. Sporting events served as important symbols of Hellenistic identity and power and were part of a conscious Hellenization of the region. Sports became an integral part of urban life with gymnasia and stadiums serving as social centers for Greeks and for local elites seeking assimilation. Bolstered by an extensive infrastructure that included sport academies, special training, and subsidizing talents, Egyptian athletes competed successfully in Greece.

The Turkish tribes of Asia Minor esteemed athletics as promoting physical health and moral development. In addition to archery and wrestling, Turkish men also favored *cirit,* a fast-paced javelin chase and hurling that was pursued while astride a horse, resulting, unsurprisingly, in many casualties.

The popularity of sporting activities in the land of Israel is indicated by Biblical and Talmudic stories. The patriarch Jacob wrestled with an angel all night, releasing him only after being blessed by the divine messenger and told that his name will now be "Israel" for he struggled as equal with El (God.) Among the swift runners celebrated were Ahimaz and Asahel, described "as light of foot as a wild roe" (2 Samuel 2:18), while the Psalmist described the sun as eager to fulfill its course like a runner.

Greek and Roman conquests introduced a variety of new sports. King Herod built in Caesarea a stadium where, according to the historian Josephus, horse racing and gladiatorial contests took place. Jewish opposition to public displays of nakedness and to the pagan divinities to whom the games were dedicated fanned resentment and revolt.

Games were played widely, and Talmudic literature mentions leading rabbis who prided themselves on their mastery of long jumping, gymnastics, running, and ball handling. The texts also include debates about such matters as the ritual purity of a leather ball and liability when a ball accidently kills a man during a game. Sports continued to be popular during the early days of Christianity as St. Paul's call, urging Christians to strive for eternal salvation with the same dedication and discipline that runners employ, indicates. Later theologians such as Tertullian in *On the Spectacles* warned against sports' pagan origins and dammed spectators and practitioners, but other church leaders extolled the benefits of physical exercise.

In the ancient Middle East, women too participated in sports. Egyptian murals depict them engaged in acrobatics, gymnastics, and ball games. During the Hellenistic period royal and noble women competed. Arsinoe, sister and wife of Ptolemy the Second of Egypt, and Berence, wife of Ptolemy the Third, won chariot races in Egypt and Greece. Female participation flourished also in Anatolia and extended to women of all classes. They competed against men, as did an unnamed servant, who in the *Book of Dede Korkut,* the seminal collection of pre-Islamic tales of adventures and morality, challenges Prince Beyrek, her mistress's suitor, to athletic competitions. With great effort the prince manages to best her in riding, archery, and wrestling. The Islamic conquest of many Middle Eastern lands in the seventh century and of Anatolia in the eleventh century diminished this engagement of women in sports.

As noted earlier, various ball games involving batting and kicking were popular in the ancient Middle East. Other forms, such as Harpastum (in which two teams attempt to move a ball beyond the opponent's line by using hands and feet), were introduced by the triumphant Legions of Rome and adapted by local elites who wished to emulate their masters. Association football made its appearance in the Middle East at the same time that the modern history of the region begins. Most historians consider as the birth of the new era the end of the nineteenth century through the early twentieth century, when major changes, most notably the collapse of the Ottoman Empire and the emergence of nationalist movements, ensued.

While many areas in the world have known conflict and strife, the Middle East's location, as a bridge between the continents of Asia, Africa, and Europe, has guaranteed that since ancient times a continual array of armies and nations would move through it, searching for navigation routes, salt, spices, land, cheap labor, and oil. Military invasions, occupations, and protectorates have been familiar features. At the same time, there has been a steady infusion of trade and commerce, educational institutions, religious practices, as well as new ideas and facets of life and culture. These foreign interventions (militarily, economically, and culturally) as well as conquest by local groups and tribes have continued even after the colonial yoke was broken.

While every locale is unique, a brief examination of the game's history in one country, Egypt, will illuminate the way that some of the larger political and social forces have held sway over football. British sailors, merchants, teachers, and engineers introduced football to Egypt, the region's most populous nation, at the end of the nineteenth century. After Britain conquered the land in 1882 (to guarantee control of the Suez Canal), British officials and military personnel helped the game spread. Soon there were accounts of soldiers playing football in front of curious Egyptians. While the British had economic and military interests, the empire was also a universe of educational institutions, cultural practices, and values, all of which were disseminated and then adapted by the local elites.

Unlike the North African countries under French control where the game was restricted to Europeans, in Egypt the educated local elites were allowed to play. In newly established schools, such as the Victoria Colleges in Cairo and Alexandria, sports were used, as in Victorian England, to teach moral lessons and strengthen a sense of unity among the ethnically and religiously diverse student body. Sports were an essential way of introducing Western civilization to the natives and teaching discipline and respect for authority.

After the First World War, football became an arena where resistance to British rule was manifested. Starting in 1920, a football team representing Egypt participated in the Olympics. Its performance, particularly in the 1928 Games where it reached the semifinals, was viewed by many Egyptians as proof that they were as good as their rulers.

At first, football was played mostly by the members of the educated classes such as Hassan Hegazi who was the first Egyptian to play in England, for Fulham FC, and who went on to study at Cambridge. Soon the game was adapted rapidly by the masses with many of the players coming from the ranks of the urban poor. In many of the clubs they joined, players encountered nationalist and socialist ideas as well as the ideology of the Muslim Brotherhood. The connections to political ideologies were expressed most strongly in the struggle, on and off the pitch, between the two main Cairo teams: Al-Ahly and Zamalek. Al-Ahly, whose name translates as "the National," was formed in 1907 and Zamalek in 1911. Zamalek was initially named Kasr El-Nile Club and in 1940 renamed Farouk, after the (puppet) King Farouk who supported the team generously. After the 1952 revolution it was renamed Al Zamalek for the area where it is based. Al-Ahly was from its inception supported by the nationalist and liberal elements and was seen as standing for national independence while Zamalek was supported by royalists and conservative elements. Other teams, such as Port Said's Al-Masry team, also represented political aspirations. Founded a year after the Egyptian Revolution of 1919, the team, unlike other teams of this Suez Canal's city, included only Egyptian players. It was a symbol of national identity and independence.

The arbitrary drawing of national boundaries by colonial powers had an impact on football. The 1920 French-British Sykes-Pico agreement created the new states of Syria and Lebanon and defined the boundaries of Turkey, Iran, and Iraq but left the Kurdish people without a homeland, resulting in a protracted struggle for independence. This has meant that the game in Kurdistan has been played against a background of war and conflict, limiting its growth. The dispersion of a large number of Kurds and the absence of an independent state has resulted also in the creation of diaspora teams, often representing the towns from which their members came.

Another common feature of the game has been its use by leaders and regimes to advance particular policies, gain legitimacy, increase public support, or pacify the restless masses. In the Middle East, all kinds of regimes—monarchies, state socialism, dictatorships, and democracies—at times of calm as well as during unrest have made political use of football. Leaders have noticed that success by a local team or a national team in the international area or the hosting of an important tournament often raise citizen support and confer authority on the regime. Ataturk harnessed the game in 1920s' Turkey as part of his secular nationalist agenda. The Saudi royal family controlled the national football federation, and various princes ran their own teams, with game results sometimes reflecting the shifting hierarchical power relations in the kingdom. Employing "football diplomacy," the game has also served as a bridge between hostile sides, including the two rival Yemen states in the 1980s and Turkey and Armenia in 2009.

Islam has also impacted the development and character of the game. As with other religions, attitudes toward the game vary. Some adherents have viewed football, since first encountering it, as a dangerous Western import that encourages political reforms, destruction of family life, and abandonment of the faith. This attitude has resulted in fatwas condemning the game. Some Islamic groups have threatened to kill followers of the game and (in Somalia) have bombed public TV-viewing gatherings during the World Cup. The passion for the game is often viewed as being in competition with religious agendas. Unable to compete against its popularity and fearful that fans would abandon their prayer duties during the 2010 World Cup, Saudi authorities brought mobile mosques on trucks to cafés where men, fervently following games, would pray during halftime.

While football is the sport most widely played, others have their following. Among ancient games various forms of wrestling are prominent, including Turkish oil wrestling. This ancient sport has enjoyed great popularity in the Ottoman Empire and continues today with the annual tournament in Edrine, held since 1346. In Iran, the ancient wrestling forms Zurkhaneh and Varzesh-e Bastani are still practiced. Both integrate Sufi spiritual traditions and beliefs, as purity of heart, modesty, and truthfulness are emphasized and expressed in prayer, drum beating, and poetry recitation during contests.

Another traditional Iranian sport is polo. Originally cavalry-training exercises, early matches involved over two hundred riders. Seventh-century Queen Shirin and women of her court also played. The sport was depicted by many artists and praised by the poet Firdowsi in his tenth-century national epic, the *Shahnameh* (The Book of Kings). Its 55,000 verses include, among the legends and history of the land, lyrical descriptions of royal tournaments and the skills of prince Siyâvash, whose name, fittingly, means, "the one with the black horse." After the 1979 revolution, polo and other equestrian sports were associated with the previous regime and viewed with derision.

Among sports introduced by colonial powers in the late nineteenth century, basketball, tennis, and cycling remain popular. Globalization has influenced the way they are played as exemplified by the way professional basketball (enjoying a large following in Turkey, Lebanon, and Israel) has adapted aspects of American National Basketball Association culture and commercial values.

The struggle of Middle Eastern girls and women to participate fully in sport despite familial and religious prohibitions has been long and arduous. Their efforts have received increased public and scholarly attention as they intersect with societal attitudes to sports and the body, notions of modesty and honor, and ideas about a woman's rightful place. Women's participation in physical activities, especially in the public sphere, has been an indication of their general lesser status in society. Women participated in sporting events in the ancient world and through the centuries. The colonizing French and British introduced modern sport activities and expanded women's involvement. Limited at first to the wealthy able to pay the high membership fees in clubs, they adopted such sports as tennis, badminton, and swimming. Their activities were viewed as endorsing individualism, secularism, and rationalization. Emerging national movements heralded sports as uniting people, increasing national awareness, strengthening the body and spirit, and preparing for confrontations with foreign conquerors. The clubs and groups (such as the Egyptian Civil Committee for Physical Education and the Palestinian [Christian] Orthodox club of Jaffa) included both men and women, who also engaged in education and political organizing. With independence, Syria, Iraq, and Egypt, following the Soviet model, established sport centers and encouraged both genders' participation. State-controlled media provided extensive sport coverage featuring female athletes. The Palestinian guerrilla organizations also emphasized the importance of women taking part not only in military training but also in running, swimming, and various ball games.

While secular women have participated in sports, there remains a wide spectrum of attitudes by Muslim religious authorities and adherents. Some hold up the Hadith passage describing Aisha challenging her husband, the Prophet Mohamed, to a race, which she wins as an indication that women's participation is acceptable. The exact nature and proscriptions for clothing and mixing with men are, however, debated. Other religious practitioners have rejected all participation, claiming that sports encourage lax morals. These elements have used laws and physical violence to enforce their theology.

It is important to note that the levels and forms of participation vary from country to country and are in flux. In 1930s' Iran the Women's Awakening Movement was instrumental in the banning of the veil, regarded as an obstacle for women's physical activity and rightful place in society. For over four decades, the participation of women, wearing Western athletic outfits, in local and international sporting events was regarded as a sign of their political progress. Shortly after the 1979 revolution, new laws were enacted. These prohibited females over the age of nine from participating in gymnastic events and all international competitions (except shooting), banned them from stadiums men attended, required the wearing of long coats and head scarves, and eliminated sport facilities in schools. Women resisted these restrictions by exercising at home or in public parks before dawn, attempting to enter stadiums, publishing manifestos, and calling for equal participation in sports and society.

After gaining independence from foreign rule, national sports administrations, like other aspects of society, were rife with corruption and nepotism. Political leaders often took credit for team or national success while using football to distract attention from their regimes' failures. During times of war, stadiums served for detention, torture, and murder, as in Hama, Syria, 1982, by the Assad regime, and in Beirut, by the Christian Phalangists the same year.

Starting in the late 1980s, groups of Egyptian fans organized nationwide, including Cairo's Ultras Ahlawi and Ultras White Knights. At first, they focused on traditional displays of fandom, but they gradually became politicized and resembled the militant nationalist youth groups active between the two world wars. Before the 2011 revolt their ideology was based on an antipolice, antimedia, anticorporate, antistate, and antifootball establishment stance, represented in extensive literature, art, graffiti, and stadium conduct. Though many members were of the antiauthoritarian left, they were disenchanted with the possibilities of political change. Their rise coincided with the emergence of other youth activist groups, such as *Sitah April* (the Sixth of April) and the *Kulina Khalid Said* (All of Us Are Khalid Said), which organized against the regime. While these groups were mostly comprised of middle- and upper-class individuals, the ultras were working- and lower-middle-class youth acutely affected by the economic disaster. Many were arrested for fighting the hated security forces but were quickly released as the regime regarded their behavior as part of general football hooliganism and a safety valve for pent-up tensions. On January 25, 2011, the ultras joined the mass demonstrations and went on to play a critical role in toppling Mubarak. They were especially effective during battles on the Qasr al-Nile bridge that led to the takeover of Tahrir Square by the demonstrators and in "the Camel Battle," when armed supporters of the regime, riding on camels and horses, attacked the demonstrators. The ultras' long history of street battles and experience working together were well employed as they held off their opponents. Several members were killed and scores injured. Hundreds of Middle Eastern athletes joined the revolts. Among them were the fastest Arab sprinter, Egyptian Amr Seoud, Baharani footballers Aal'a and Mohammed Hubail, and Syrian national team goalkeepers Abdelbaset Sarout and Mosab Balhous.

Palestinian cultural scholar and political activist Edward Said showed, in his 1977 book *Orientalism* and in subsequent writings, the way Europeans (and especially the colonizing French and British) related to the region and how ideological biases have shaped their vision. Said's analysis is substantiated by other scholars such as Jonathan Lyons, who in his *Islam Through Western Eyes: From the Crusades to the War on Terror* (2012) posits that for nearly a thousand years there has been an anti-Islamic rhetoric based on the idea that Islam is inherently violent and antiwomen and that its believers have always been irrational and opposed to science, democracy, and modernity. Similarly, Jack Shaheen in his books *Reel Bad Arabs: How Hollywood Vilifies a People* (2001) and *Guilty: Hollywood's Verdict on Arabs after 9/11* (2008) examines the stereotypical portrayals of Arabs and Muslims in thousands of American and European films since the birth of cinema.

If these distorted images of Muslims and Arabs in scholarship, literature, the arts, media, and other political and cultural representations are indeed as prevalent and negative as these and other scholars suggest, what are the implications for Western understanding about sports in the region and for its study? If mainstream media is embedded with these biases, do these extend to its coverage of Middle Eastern sport?

Several studies have examined how local and Western media have reported sporting events in the region. These include portrayals of Palestinian athletes in the Israeli media and a study of US print media coverage of the 1998 World Cup Iran–United States match. The latter analysis concluded that the game was mostly presented in the familiar ideological frames based on the two nations' long and often antagonistic history, but layers related to national identity, fans, and sport were also present in some of the reporting.

The focus on the political dimension when Western sport venues report on the Middle East has been seen in sport stories involving dramatic and negative phenomena: disputes over female Muslims athletes' attire, the violent clashes following the Algerian-Egyptian World Cup qualifying games in 2010, and Qatari officials buying votes to gain the right to host the 2022 World Cup. Occasionally, a more positive story receives attention, such as the success of the Iraqi football team in the 2004 Olympics and its role as a unifying force of a divided nation.

Considering the long and rich history of sports in the region, it is surprising historians and sport scholars long ignored the world of games. Popular works such as those by historians Bernard Lewis and Albert Hourani have left out sports entirely. Even Eugene Rogan, in his well-researched *The Arabs: A History* that includes not only official reports and sources but also many accounts of daily life, does not mention the region's sports.

Similarly, most sport historians have until recently ignored the Middle East in their global histories, giving the impression that the region does not exist. Stephen Wagg included a chapter on the region in his 1984 study of global football and the excellent film series *The Beautiful Game* devoted a section of its "Global Football Cultures" episode to Iran, but, as with many other aspects of the game, it was left to David Goldblatt in his magisterial and comprehensive *The Ball Is Round* (2006) to devote several pages to the way the game was introduced and the larger political forces in play.

For many years the field of sport research, in the West and also in the home countries, was small. There were rare exceptions, such as K. Fisek's 1963 book *Devlet Politikas Ve Toplumsal Yapyla Iliskileri Acsndan Spor Yonetimi: Dunyada-Turkiye'de* (The Administration of Sport in Turkey and in the World). Turkish scholar Cuneyd Okay's

2002 observation applied to his country and to other lands as well: "The history of sports is generally a neglected field in Turkish historiography. Consequently, the history of football has been examined in a superficial and populist way, and has not been the subject of any comprehensive academic study in the real sense. No detailed study has been undertaken to reveal how this sport was introduced into the country, how it became popular and how it developed." This task was then taken up by Okay, who in his study explained how football entered Turkey during the period of modernization (1890–1914). He examined early publications on football, including press coverage, the journal *Futbol*, and books by Selim Sirri Tarcan as well as the Istanbul Futbol Birligi (Istanbul Football Association). Okay's work was followed by other historical studies, including Ceviker Turgut's anthology *Turk Edebiyatinda Futbol* (Football in Turkish Literature, 2002), which included the writings of major Turkish journalists, poets, and novelists starting in 1913, and Gökhan Akçura's comprehensive work on the history and culture of cycling (2003).

Gradually, a number of excellent works—academic studies, essays, fiction, and films about sports in the Middle East—appeared. Academic journals devoted to sports such as *The International Review for the History of Sport, Sport in Society, Soccer and Society,* and *The International Review for the Sociology of Sport,* as well as general sociological journals, began paying attention to sport. Several studies including Houchang Chehabi's writings on the politics of sport in Iran and Abdul Karim Alaug and Thomas B. Stevenson's research on the origins of Yemini football were important contributions.

A high percentage of the studies centered on one of the smallest and least populous lands—Israel/Palestine—with notable work by the likes of Yair Galily, Tamir Sorek, Amir Ben Porat, and Hagai Harif. Many of the Israeli sport historians and sociologists were members of the Israeli political left. In their work, whether about the Arab teams of Hapoel Tayibe FC and Bnei Sakhnin FC or the transformation of Israeli football from "a game to a commodity," they have attempted, in subject and approach, to move beyond narrow nationalistic ideologies. Writings by Palestinian scholars are few. This is due to many factors. Chief among them are the many wars that along with major displacements and expulsions of Palestinians have included the intentional and accidental destruction of archives and valuable primary materials. Of late, Palestinian scholars such as Issam Khalidi have started to spotlight Palestinian sport during the Mandate period, in the Jewish state, and in the Palestinian diaspora. This work has shed light on a vital sports culture and its connection to its people's history. The challenge of writing sport histories in a politically contested land is ongoing, and the important work of bringing to light lost histories will continue to enrich our understanding of Israeli and Palestinian societies.

In the middle of the first decade of the new millennium, several journalistic works have appeared, including James Montague's *When Friday Comes: Football in the War Zone* (2008), a lively travelogue recording his visits among the football faithful, and Simon Freeman's *Baghdad FC* (2005), which describes Iraqi football's' bloody history under repressive regimes and the courage and faith exhibited by players and fans. These works contain useful information but do not aim to provide deeper analysis.

Considering the place sports, and especially football, holds in the lives of many writers, artists, musicians, and filmmakers, it is not surprising that they have expressed this love in their works. In addition to Noble Prize–winner Naguib Mahfouz, some of these creators include fellow Nobel Prize–winner Orham Pamuk of Turkey; Turkish poet and communist activist Nazim Hikmet, who during his long imprisonment wrote an autobiography in which he evoked his childhood games of football; and Palestinian national poet Mahmud Darwish who in the summer of 1982, in the besieged city of Beirut, as bombs rained, wrote in his journal about the World Cup.

Often writers employed a sport setting to examine their societies. In Mohamed El-Bisatie's novel *Drumbeat* (2010), the national team of an "Emirate" qualifies for the World Cup and the country's monarch requires every citizen to go to France and support the team. Those left are the many foreign workers who do all the work but lack basic human rights. Suddenly they are the ones in control, and El-Bisatie imagines what might happen when power relations are turned upside down. Ali, the narrator of Mohamed Al-Mansi Qandil's *Moon Over Samarqand* (2009), is the son of a powerful member of the Egyptian security forces. The boy is sent, against his wishes, to an elite military academy where he encounters the hatred of other recruits, resentful over his class privileges and connection to the regime. In the latter part of the novel, these hatreds are played out on the pitch as another cadet, a member of a banned Islamist group, roughs him up. Khaled al-Berry's autobiographical account *Life Is More Beautiful than Paradise: A Jihadist's Own Story* (2009) also connects politics and football, as the game, played with his comrades, serves to cement their friendships and loyalty to the Islamic militant cause. *The Golden Scales* by Parker Bilal (the pen name of Jamal Mahjoub, 2012) is the story of Somali detective Makana, coming to terms with the murder of his wife and child while earning a meager living in Cairo. He is hired to find Adil Romario, a missing football star. The search takes him through the corrupt and violent worlds of big business, the security forces, and religious fanaticism.

Among films, some are light comedies (including Togo Mizrahi's 1937 Egyptian film *Shalom al-riyadi* [Shalom the Athlete]) about a Jewish football manager. Other works address societal problems, injustices, and hopes through the lens of sport. Noteworthy films include Mohamed Diab's *678*, which centers on sexual violence against Egyptian women, with one of the main characters, a wealthy secular woman, assaulted at a match; *Wahid sifr* (One-Zero), Ilham Shahin's portrait of a group of fans whose joy over Egypt's victory cannot obscure the many problems facing their society and the lack of options in their own lives; and Ugur Yucel's *Yazi Tura*, the story of three demobilized Turkish soldiers and their difficult adjustment to civilian life. Three recent films center on women and bicycles: the Yemeni *A Stranger in Her Own City*, directed by Khadija al-Salaami; Iranian Marziyah Mishkīnī's *Rūzī kih zan shudam* (The Day I Became a Woman); and Saudi Haifaa Al-Mansour's *Wadjda*. The films depict girls and women prevented from riding and extol bicycles as vehicles of profound individual and societal transformation. They join a small but growing body of work, such as the photo projects of Claudia Wiens

(2011) and Karijn Kakebeeke and Brigitte Lacombe's exhibit "Hey'Ya: Arab Women in Sport" (2012).

Sports' growing academic and institutional acceptance is evidenced by the 2009 Arab Women Sport Journalists' Forum held in Qatar, panels on sport during Middle Eastern Studies conferences, and new scholarly works published by the Middle East Institute of Washington, DC (Calabrese 2010) and *The International Journal of the History of Sport*. The Middle East Institute publication included research on female athletes and traditional values, basketball as a peace-building bridge between Arab and Jewish youth in Jerusalem, the struggles of Yemeni football in the midst of challenging economic and political difficulties, and football as the embodiment of the national pride of Syriacs/Assyrians in Sweden and Palestinians in Jordan. *The International Journal of the History of Sport* has presented studies of the Pan-Arab Games, Lebanese sport, women in management and leadership roles of the Olympic movement, cultural barriers to female sports participation in Qatar, and the history of the first physical education teacher's training for women in Oman.

Four recent books containing essential research and suggesting possibilities for future work are a welcome addition to the field. Algerian Mahfoud Amara's *Sport, Politics and Society in the Arab World* (2012) connects sport with the formation of national identity, nation-state building, international relations, the commercialization of sport, and the growth of sport media. Amara also examines how football has been for many years the site of unrest and resistance and a place where people can still win symbolic victories over their difficult socioeconomic and political realities. *Muslim Women and Sport,* edited by Tansin Benn, Haifaa Jawad, and Gertrud Pfister (2010), adds to our understanding of a much-neglected subject. Among its chapters are studies of women's' narratives of sport and war in Iraq, the Palestinian women's national football team, and Syrian women. The anthology *Soccer in the Middle East,* edited by Alon Raab and Issam Khalidi (2013), contains both scholarly studies and literary treatments. The first are about the international arena, the national game, women, media representations, and the Arab Spring. The second includes some of the rich literary works created by regional novelists. An important contribution to the field has been made by James M. Dorsey whose website and book, both titled The Turbulent World of Middle East Soccer, add to our our understanding of sport and society.

Among the important new publications are two by Egyptian journalists. The first, Yasser Thabit's *Ḥurub kurat al-qadam* (Football Wars, 2011), is a study of Egyptian football history from its origins to the recent conflict between Algeria and Egypt on and off the field. *Al-Altirās* (The Ultras Book, 2011) by Mohamed G. Beshir is based on his time, as an observer and participant, with a group of Cairo ultras. Appearing just as these passionate Egyptian fans assumed an important part in the uprising, its lively descriptions and theoretical framework brought the book a wide audience.

As the field of Middle Eastern sport scholarship is in its infancy, practically every area deserves to be explored. This applies to sports with small followings like kayaking and fencing as well as to football. The various individual football cultures, the game of football as part of the fabric of societies, football's importance to individual lives as a source of both conflict and unity, and women overcoming patriarchal barriers are all areas for future work. Sophisticated historical studies that examine various sports in context are especially needed, as well as works done from a comparative perspective. There is a dearth of good research on many lands, especially Yemen, Syria, Lebanon, and the Gulf States. Lebanon is a nation where football has not attained a high level of achievement, despite a large and enthusiastic fan base. The civil war of 1975–1990, Israeli invasions, Syrian occupation, and long-simmering animosities born decades earlier have created a football universe where each team has a distinct political identity. In many lands, teams were born of political organizations, parties, unions, and as representatives of ethnic entities, with a strong fan base reflecting these origins.

Examining national styles of play, incorporating the theoretical speculations of such football historians as Jonathan Wilson in *Inverting the Pyramid* (2009) and Simon Kuper and Stefan Szymanskii in *Soccernomics* (2009) would also add to our knowledge. Works in this vein prompt us to consider whether there are indeed national styles of play and national characteristics influencing them and if a society's opening to political and social changes leads to greater success on the field or to a more free-flowing style of play.

The relationship between football and religion is another important area that needs investigating. Possible avenues might include how the game relates to religious institutions, how it takes on religious dimensions, and its role in the process of secularization. Has it helped undermine levels of attendance and participation in these institutions, or undermined faith? Will religious authorities try to incorporate the game into their political agendas? Comparing the influence and attitudes of Islam with those of the Muscular Christianity movement of an earlier era could also yield insights.

Women's participation in sports is an important area of study. The barriers they face are not new, as evidenced by Turkish scholar Betul Yarar in her study on modernization, women, and sport in the early years of the Turkish Republic. Looking at historical precedents and scholarship that addresses the way obstacles are overcome would be welcome. The recent anthropological studies by Geoff Harkness and Samira Islam of Muslim athletes and the Hijab, of Kurdish women footballers, Kenda R. Stewart on Palestinian footballers in the Galilee, and Petra Gieß-Stüber on the Palestinian national team are all welcome models. They explore women's participation in a sport that is considered a male bastion, the challenges they face, and the ways they navigate between individual and community expectations and demands.

The histories of many teams offer fascinating portraits of their societies. Egypt's Al-Ahly and Zamelek, with their origins in the early days of the twentieth century and the different sides they have represented in the struggle for independence, are obvious choices. In Cyprus, Appolon and APOEL are popular with more politically conservative fans while Omonoia is associated with the left. In the politically turbulent 1940s, APOEL players who refused to align themselves with a right-wing ideology founded Omonoia. This history and the way the teams have interacted over the decades are an unexplored area of research.

In Jordan, the refugee camp team Al-Wihdat has represented the Palestinian community and has created a space for expressing anger at the Hashemite regime's discriminatory policies as well as strengthening a separate identity. Palestinian leader
Yasser Arafat, who exclaimed, "one day when we had no voice, Al-Wihdat was our
voice," has underlined the importance of the team to national life. A study of the team
would add an important dimension to the study of Palestinian society and politics. As
with sport literature elsewhere, there are portraits of Middle Eastern players, coaches,
and managers, but most are of the factual or hagiographic kind while critical explorations of their subject's political commitments and connections to the larger social
issues are rare. Some past football players who challenged their societies' norms and
political structures include the Iraqi player and coach Ammo Baba, whose endurance
and resistance, at great personal risk during the Saddam Hussein era, made him a
national hero.

Turkish Metin Kurt came from a working-class background. While starring for
Galatasaray in the 1970s, Kurt expressed his political opinions and tried to organize a
footballers' union, paying a price for it. His career and politics, as a player and later a
union activist, examined in the context of his era, would provide a fascinating biography. Notable women football pioneers whose lives and careers could shed much light on
their societies include Egyptian Sahar Al-Hawari and Saudi Reem Abdullah, founder
of the Jeddah Kings United Team, Saudi Arabia's first (semiclandestine) women's team.

Similarly, there is a need for more work on the way sports are played by millions of
nonprofessionals in the streets, schools, playgrounds, and improvised settings and
whose devotion to sport is beyond the quest for fame and monetary rewards. How and
why do games matter so much in the daily lives of men and women, during peaceful
times and also during tumultuous periods? Nashaat Hussein's recent study of street
football in Cairo is one such work.

While British sports publishing is rich in fans' autobiographical accounts, few such
works by Middle Easterners have appeared. Among the exceptions is Nader Jahanfard's
Everything I Need to Know in Life I Learned in Football (2009), the story of his football-
enthused youth in pre-Islamic Revolution Iran. There are a growing number of literary,
artistic, and film works where football is the subject or features prominently, and these
could be analyzed, individually, thematically, or cross-culturally. The new forms of fandom expressed, via social media, songs placed on the Web, fanzines, and street art, offer
additional possibilities for analysis such as the blog written under the name suzeeinthe-
city ("In the Midst of Madness" 2012).

Sport has brought together individuals, classes, and nations under its banner in the
Middle East at least since the end of the nineteenth century. Sport has helped usher in
Western ideas and values and served as a political tool for leaders and states to overcome
opposition by conservative elements. At these times of great political and cultural turmoil and change across the Middle East, the future of the region is unclear. What is certain, however, is that sport will continue to influence political and cultural changes and,
most important, will continue to be widely played and loved.

BIBLIOGRAPHY

Amara, Mafoud. *Sport, Politics and Society in the Arab World.* New York: Palgrave MacMillan, 2012.

Benn, Tansin, Gertrude Pfister, and H. A. Jawad, eds. *Soccer in the Middle East.* London: Routledge, 2012.

Dorsey, James M. *The Turbulent World of Middle East Soccer.* London: C. Hurst, 2014.

Khalidi, Issam, and Alon K. Raab, eds. *Soccer in the Middle East.* London: Routledge, 2013.

CHAPTER 20

··

SPORT IN AFRICA

··

PASCAL CHARITAS

In their quest for the legitimacy of the imperial movement, French historians of colonialism sought to develop a set of beliefs about Africa. They denied the historic character of the African continent. The common belief had been that black Africa had no written testimony of its past and therefore no history. The scarcity of written documents on African civilizations supported the idea that, beyond the borders of the Sahara, the glorious past of conquered peoples was more mythical than real. Europeans believed that Africa only entered the realm of history in the eighteenth and nineteenth centuries, when they started colonizing it. Oral traditions were discredited. Colonial knowledge that generated colonial history was based on geography and was soon taught in French colonies. That knowledge developed in close relationship with the imperialism it served, under pressure from the colonial lobby.

In contrast, the indigenous elites of the countries of the former British Commonwealth were offered the opportunity to attend university. Such was not the case in French and Belgian colonies. Some of the best indigenous students of the Commonwealth were encouraged to take courses at the London School of Economics. In the French and Belgian colonies, there had been a policy of "confining" African elites to bureaucratic activities. This state of mind remained unchallenged long after the Second World War. One could arguably claim that the British Empire started being dismantled in 1947 with the independence of India. It was also marked by the establishment of chairs in African British history. The French Empire, on the other hand, lingered on until 1960.

Until the mid-twentieth century, sport in Africa was reserved for European settlers, at least in civil society. Be it competitive or leisurely, sport was then part of the distinctive features of settlers in their logic of the "superiority of the white race." However, school education in the large urban centers of the colonies and the practice of physical education were used as means to "civilize" and improve the economic productive capacity of the natives. In addition to formal education, the Catholic, Protestant, and secular missions participated in the implementation of sport and physical practices among indigenes. The offspring of indigenous elites pursued their studies in the major French (Science-Po, the Sorbonne) and British schools (Oxford, Cambridge). There, they engaged in sports. Some African sports stars then came into being, especially in boxing, athletics, and football. These athletes were sometimes included in British and French national squads, a tribute to their excellent performances. There was a potential reservoir of "black athletes" in the colonies. The colonial nation was then represented on the international sports scene through the logic of the empire.

Elite athletes in the Francophone and Anglophone African colonies were seen as "noble savages." In Francophone African colonies, such sportsmen created the first founding myths of African sport. They were often the children of *Senegalese tirailleurs* or sometimes military men themselves. Battling Siki was the first boxer to be a French, European, and African champion. Raoul Diagne was a football champion. Thierno Sall excelled at cycling, and Taka N'Ganguey was a master of the javelin.[1] In 1932, some of them integrated professional clubs in France. In the United Kingdom, where modern sports were invented, professional football further accelerated this trend. Yet the apartheid regime in some colonies slowed the process of emergence of the first indigenous elite athletes, as some were mestizo. As was true elsewhere, the first sportspeople in the colonial empires were exclusively male.

Among scholars, the original historians of Africa were primarily English speaking. The British, the Americans (specializing in African American studies), and some Africans were the first to rely on oral sources. French historians rediscovered such sources much later, caught in their own contradictions. Consequently, French African history was not recognized as a field until 1961. It took the advent of geography, nineteenth-century ethnology, physical anthropology, the structural anthropology of Claude Lévi-Strauss, and the independence of West African nations for the historical profession to start analyzing colonial and postcolonial ruptures. In the context of the post–World War II decolonization, a renewed outlook on Africa was required in order to rethink power relations, as well as sociocultural and economic transformations. More than twenty years after African independence, "postcolonial studies" saw the light of day in English-speaking academia. Three Australians (Bill Ashcroft, Gareth Griffiths, and Helen Tiffin) laid claim to the postcolonial concept. Later, Edward Said, Gayatri Spivak, and Homi Bhabha would make their mark.[2] Postcolonial studies along with surrounding emerging research became established academic fields in English-speaking universities in the 1980s, questioning the phenomenon of cultural domination.

Postcolonial studies is an approach, a way of posing problems, or a critical stance that looks at the conditions of cultural production of knowledge about the self, the other, and the capacity for agency. It also looks into resistance and the actions of the oppressed by stating the idea of "autonomous action potential." The ambition of postcolonial studies is to go beyond the binary dominant-dominated world, beyond the colonizer–colonized duality, and highlight patterns of autonomous thought, thereby reflecting the realities of the oppressed. When Foucault's hypothesis of constitutive discourse of social reality is taken into account and Saïd's hypothesis of Western discourse as a producer of the conditions of imperialism is acknowledged, one can start deconstructing that discourse, interrupting and undermining its authority. Then the fabric of imperialism can be understood. The themes addressed by postcolonial studies emphasize primarily the deconstruction of colonial discourse.

The authors mentioned previously developed a theory of postcolonial forms that starts with the organization and resistance of the dominated in order to overcome a Eurocentric reading of the history of colonized peoples, whose strongest criticism is echoed in subaltern studies. This approach gives a voice to the dominated and the colonized. It participates in the dialectics of the power relations of former empires and the formation of newly independent nation-states. These studies reinterpret the effects of domination in the guise of mimicry and hybridism. Mimicry is "the desire for a reformed recognizable other, as the subject of a difference that is almost the same, but not quite." Ambivalence, uncertainty, imitation, and mockery but also similarity and threat all come as forms of the "prohibition as otherness." Thus it is necessary to consider the African situations as a whole by taking into account the histories and cultures of both the colonial and the postcolonial worlds in which the present and the past interpenetrate. This field covers the era of empires, the early years of independence, and the period that followed independence.

The French and British colonial administrations were against the internationalization of Africa. They were hoping the "colonial situation"[3] would go on, but gradually the colonial systems of the British and French empires were challenged by the two new superpowers after World War II. International law concerning empire had been based on the Fourteen Points of Woodrow Wilson established after the First World War, the Pan-African Congress of Paris (1919), and the reconstruction of European borders. Faced with these geopolitical changes, the principle that people must have the right to determine their own form of government, regardless of any foreign influence, gradually made its way. This new doctrine led to the creation of the League of Nations, which was accompanied by a commitment from France and Britain to the principles of good government.

The British Empire created a segregationist model (before switching to assimilation) and an indirect administration jointly managed by the Foreign Office and the Colonial Office. Britain chose to maintain local metropolitan authority and traditional structures, albeit without any real autonomy of action. This colonial model was later strengthened by the Commonwealth, which was established as an association of free and equal countries whose membership was based on a common allegiance to the British crown. This new structure came as the successor to the empire and had its origins in the Imperial Conferences of the late 1920s when the former dominions and colonies were gradually accorded sovereignty. It was finally endorsed by the Statute of Westminster of 1931. Already, the United Kingdom had offered the possibility of a first opening to universal sport with the first Games of the British Empire in 1930.

This indirect colonization was accompanied by bilateral technical assistance agreements, concluded within the framework of regional treaties. These included such "humanitarian" initiatives as the Colonial Development Corporation (1948), the Colombo Plan (1950), and mutual aid to a sub-Saharan Africa Foundation. The doctrine followed the political reforms of the colonial ideology of Winston Churchill, which adapted to changes in the international context while providing indigenous elites with more autonomy. Indeed, from 1948, the British wanted a new relationship with their colonies. The same year, the reform of the British Nationality Act granted the status of "citizen of the United Kingdom and Colonies" to any person born in the United Kingdom or in any colony of the empire. In that respect, British colonization differed from its French counterpart in the creation of artificial structures and a mode of peaceful disengagement once a stable and non-Communist government could replace colonial authority.

The French colonial system was an assimilationist utopia. It was still a mode of direct government of the colonies from the mainland, but expatriate indigenous elites were in charge. Each ethnic group was divided into several cantons, gathering several ethnic groups. These cantons were organized into territories and greater territories (West Africa and French Equatorial Africa). The administrative system in the North African states, which were theoretically administered by their own governing bodies, was nonetheless hierarchical and authoritarian. Colonial sports, until independence, followed this pattern. Only indigenous elites who had attended a French school could participate. There was no direct competition with colonists until the 1950s.

French colonial policy is considered by some authors to combine assimilation and autonomy. A gradual political decolonization enabled a gradual transfer of sovereignty and decentralization. This favored the emergence of political elites who were democratically elected by local assemblies and council governments. All such territories could lay claim to the status of Overseas Territories. They were allowed to vote on the referendum of the Fifth Constitution of the French Republic (1958). General Charles de Gaulle wanted these territories to enter the Franco-African Community as autonomous states. Yet the Franco-African Community was dismantled. Its sporting games were called *Jeux de la Communauté*, then *Jeux de l'Amitié*. Former African colonies overwhelmingly voted for independence between 1959 and 1960, through negotiation and cooperation agreements with France. The British and the French each established settlements (South Africa and Algeria) and exploitation colonies (Rhodesia, sub-Saharan Francophone Africa).

The establishment of a new international order after World War II profoundly transformed the relationship between the empires and their colonies. The League of Nations and the African Conference, the creation of the United Nations (UN) in 1945, the Cold War between the Soviet and American systems, and the rise of African nationalism in the wake of the emergence of the Third World all contributed to a strategic use of the international scene to affirm African unity. A new international economic order appeared with the creation of the Marshall Plan meant for the rehabilitation of Europe, and the American liberal economic policy was implemented in the former French and British colonial empires. The Brazzaville Conference, the General States of Colonization (1944), and the conferences in San Francisco (1945) and Bandung (1955) helped redesign the process of globalization in the context of the decolonization of Africa in the Cold War, with new guidelines for relations between the major powers and colonized countries.

Specifically, the creation of the UN was meant to manage and prevent conflict in order to establish peacekeeping forces on the world stage. This was reaffirmed in the UN charter, ratified in 1945. The strengthening of this line of thought within the UN was a reflection of the seeming anticolonialism of the United States. The United States aimed at publicizing its cultural values to new nation-states, just as the Soviets had done for years. Africa was one of the continents that both superpowers courted. The birth of the UN saw a new interest in forms of cooperation in international relations under the banner of racial equality. Development assistance was also sustained and promoted by many international organizations under different initiatives by the United States, the USSR, Britain, and France.

Africa did not take a back seat in this process. In 1955, it took part in a Third World rejection of neocolonial guardianship. In this Africa was supported by the USSR and China. Thus the "non-aligned countries" were at the center of important geopolitical and strategic issues. There were spheres of influence: the "rim land" (the United States, Western Europe, Asia) and the "heartland" (the Soviet Union). "North–South" relations in Africa all too often were seen as the periphery in theories of developmental sociology.[4] With the decline of colonial empires and the advent of the Cold War, this approach was no longer sufficient to examine new places and power relations that had emerged. New transnational and nongovernmental organizations redefined the "law of the jungle" of international relations.

Under these conditions, the internationalization of African sport depended on the decolonization movements, along with integration into the Olympic movement. This Olympic opening led to a competition for the political influence of both the Soviet and American blocs as well as the assertion of an international African politics. Thus the intersection of strategic influences through the internationalization of African sport reveals postcolonial ideological *simulacre*[5] that emerge from the decline of colonial empires. The first was development aid to sport (the Olympics), and the second was the fight against apartheid or racial discrimination through sport as factors of formation and transformation of sports and political Africa.

Before this, universal exhibitions during the colonial period were an opportunity to show the natives of the colonies to metropolitan populations through anthropomorphology. The combination of sport with Anthropological Days at the Olympics in St. Louis (1904) demonstrated this rule, and this stress on anthropomorphology would last throughout the first half of the twentieth century. It was only after World War II that international sporting arenas became new exhibit places of otherness. Gradually, the British Empire Games, the Olympic Games, and the Games of the Community or of Friendship (1960–1963) made these minorities more visible by integrating them progressively in the British and French national squads. In the case of the French Empire, some indigenous elite athletes (mainly from Senegal) had attended colonial schools and participated in the championships of French schools and universities. At this point, sport was becoming a means of emancipation, a claim to autonomy and political independence. African elites seized it as a chance to fight against apartheid, to participate in the development of African sport, and to advance their political demands.

In 1956, football took on a continental dimension in Africa with the establishment of the Confederation of African Football. One of the founders of the confederation was Ethiopian footballer Ydnekatchew Tessema. In comparison, the African Athletics Confederation was founded only in 1979. The establishment of this African sporting organization reflected the Africans' desire to unite against colonialism through the Africa Cup of Nations.[6] This Pan-Africanism expressed through sports was nonetheless conditioned by affiliation with Western sporting federations such as FIFA, which was led by the British from 1955 to 1974. At the same time, the exchanges at the International Association of Athletics Federations, dominated by the British, were not trivial. The gradual recognition for citizenship of the natives of the British Empire opened a door to the sporting representation of African athletes and served as a step in the process of British decolonization based on the Olympic movement and the formation of the Commonwealth.[7] India's membership from 1949 as an independent nation and republic demonstrated that the constitutional link with the British crown was no longer necessary to belong to the Commonwealth of Nations. Consequently, the change of name from the IV British Empire Games in Auckland, New Zealand, in 1950[8] to the British Empire and Commonwealth Games in 1954 in Vancouver, British Columbia, Canada, marked a transformation.

Indirect rule had enabled a dual process of self-government under British influence. This process unfolded with the first participation at the Empire and Commonwealth Games and thus endorsed membership of the geopolitical space of the Commonwealth of Nations (1950–1965). The teams from the English-speaking black African colonies that took part in the British Empire and Commonwealth Games in Vancouver in 1954 were the Gold Coast (Ghana, twelve athletes), Northern Rhodesia (seventeen), Nigeria (fifteen), South Africa (sixty-four), Southern Rhodesia (fifteen), Kenya (thirteen), and Uganda (six). As early as 1948, a team of seven Nigerian athletes entered the London Olympics in the British delegation. Thus the colonial doctrine of indirect rule and the dual mandate by the progressive empowerment of the British colonies in Africa contributed to the creation of the National Olympic Committee (NOC) under the leadership of the Colonial Office, the Foreign Office, and British members of the IOC.[9] More often than not, in the English colonies the sporting ruling elite were white. Sir Reginald Stanley Alexander, for instance, was a member of the IOC and of the NOC for Kenya. In the Olympics in 1956, five new nations of Anglophone Africa were represented alongside the Union of South Africa: Ethiopia, Kenya, Liberia, Nigeria, and Uganda. Thus, with two NOC in 1948 and 121 athletes, newly independent Africa was propelled onto the international sports scene at the Olympics Tokyo (1964) with twenty-one NOC and three hundred African athletes. This era embodied the premises of African Olympic sport for the summer Olympics.

The French Empire became the Franco-African Community in 1958. It launched the internationalization of the sports movement in its former African colonies. Indeed, whereas sporting confrontation between blacks and whites was previously forbidden by the colonial powers, the context of decolonization induced a major change (most African colonies become independent from France in 1960). The Rome Olympics in

1960 may be considered as the point in time in which black Africa entered the Olympic sphere. African sportsmen were very successful during these Olympics: Ghanaian Clement "Ike" Quartey became the first black African to win an Olympic medal by winning the silver medal in boxing. Five days later, in the marathon race, Abebe Bikila (a member of the Ethiopian Imperial Guard) beat Moroccan Rhadi Ben Abdesselem and became the first black African Olympic champion ever. But these games were also an opportunity for the newly independent countries to request their integration in the Olympic movement.

Before the Olympic integration of Francophone Africa, the Games of the Franco-African Community, renamed *Jeux de l'Amitié* (1960, 1961, 1963), had to be organized to prepare the African sports *début* on the international sports scene. The *Coupe des Tropiques*, created in 1962, prepared French-speaking Africa for the games that were to come and laid the groundwork for the future Cup of African Nations. These games, which were first open to new Francophone African states, were later expanded to include English-speaking countries in Africa and Arabic states, as well as women. The French IOC members, French politicians, and IOC president Avery Brundage (from the United States) helped these new Francophone African countries develop their NOCs.[10] This sporting event was extended to the entire African continent. Based on the *Jeux de l'Amitié*, the first African Games were created in Congo-Brazzaville in 1965. The first African Games allowed the creation of the Higher Council of Sports in Africa (Yaoundé, 1966), which was chaired by Congolese Jean-Claude Ganga. The aim was to organize sport on the African continent. This political and governmental institution, attached to the Organization of African Unity, became a counter power to the IOC in the fight against apartheid. It distinguished itself in the boycotts of the 1976 Olympic Games in Montreal, the same year as the riots in Soweto, South Africa, and the 1980 Moscow Olympic Games.

During the first African Games (1965), a new generation of athletes appeared with Kipchoge Keno (Kenya), Henry Elende (high jump, Congo), and Samuel Igun (Nigeria). IOC recognition of the African Games occurred despite hostility from British members, who feared a revolt against South Africa and its apartheid policy. The IOC's decision to grant recognition reflected the growing influence of African nations as new African NOCs emerged in the early 1960s, as well as IOC fears that these African Games would be used for nonsporting purposes by the Third World movement Games of the New Emerging Forces (1963 and 1965) and the Soviets. These games allowed members of the governing bodies of African sports to emerge and evolve in international sports organizations. Meanwhile, in football, the victory of the Douala Oryx (Cameroon) in the first edition of the African Cup of Champions Clubs in 1964 (Kwameh N'Kruma Trophy) prepared the national squad for other victories. The *Lions indomptables* won the Cup of Nations four times in 1984, 1988, 2000, and 2002. They completed a total of seven podiums. Cameroon has also participated in six finals of the World Cup, a record in Africa, and notably reached the quarterfinals in 1990. Among the football players that have marked the history of the squad, some have won several African Golden Ball trophies, as well as African Player of the Year awards: Samuel Eto'o (four times), Roger

Milla, and Thomas N'Kono (twice). In 1982, Cameroon was the second country to be qualified for a World Cup football after Zaire in 1974. Ghana—Cameroon's greatest rival—has won the African Cup of Nations four times (1963, 1975, 1978, 1982). Ghana holds the record for number of finals played (eight), and Egypt is the runner-up. The Black Stars have participated in two World Cups (2006 and 2010), where they reached the quarterfinals. Among Ghanaian football players who have marked the history of the national squad, three have won the African Golden Ball: Abedi Pele (1991, 1992, 1993), Ibrahim Sunday (1971), and Karim Abdul Razak (1978). In 1992, Abedi Pele was the first winner of the African Player of the Year award, which has since replaced the African Golden Ball.

Little by little, the African sports movement took shape in the second half of the twentieth century. Contributing to this was the creation of the Union of African Sports Confederations (1983) and ephemeral initiatives such as the Central African Games (1976–1987), or more political and cultural initiatives, such as the integration of the Francophone sphere with the creation of the Francophone Games (1989). The British Commonwealth Games in 1970 kept only the political aspect. These games have never been held on the African continent. Initially scheduled for the second edition in Johannesburg (1930), they moved to London because of the policy of apartheid. It was not until 1977 that the Commonwealth signed a document called the Gleneagles Agreement to ban South African sport and protest against the policy of apartheid.

The issue of apartheid in sport actually appeared on the international sports scene in 1960 with the global shock of the Sharpeville massacre, denouncing the discriminatory and racial regimes of South Africa, Namibia, and Rhodesia. For this reason, the IOC excluded South Africa from the Tokyo Olympics (1964). The General Assembly of the UN created the International Convention against Apartheid in Sports (1985). In 1976, African nations protested against the New Zealand rugby team's tour of South Africa. Tanzania and twenty-two other African nations participated in a boycott after the IOC did nothing about New Zealand. Following the invasion of Afghanistan by the Soviets, some African nations joined the US boycott of the Olympic Games in Moscow (1980). The following year, in 1981, a nonwhite player, Errol Tobias (followed by Avril Williams in 1984), would wear the green and gold South African jersey.

Africa has unevenly entered the organization of major sporting events. Apart from Egypt (1999) and Tunisia (2005), which both hosted world championships in handball, no other world championship of a sport recognized by the IOC has been held on the African continent. There is one exception: the 1995 rugby World Cup, which symbolically marked the end of apartheid and the birth of a new nation. The trophy was held by black president Nelson Mandela and his victorious Springboks (even though the team was comprised mostly of whites). Fifteen years later, the men's soccer World Cup 2010 was held in post-apartheid South Africa. A page had been turned, strengthening the construction of this African nation. Indeed, South Africa cultivates a seductive and attractive paradox when hosting international sporting events: its liberal economic potential and the application of humanistic values of sport contrast with the long march for the eradication of all forms of discrimination.

There is now a considerable literature on sports in Africa. The works of Anglophone researchers were the first to theorize postcolonialism, stressing the themes of racial segregation and apartheid. Indeed, the English literature had captured these objects through the intellectual/political approaches of cultural studies and postcolonial studies. The English-language literature on colonial and postcolonial sports was the first to invest a field that had long been left fallow.[11] Beginning in the 1980s, British scholars analyzed sport as a model of imperial diffusion and evaluated its implications for the Commonwealth and the United Kingdom.

Ultimately, many of them adopted a descriptive and highly localized perspective in Africa, such as Edward Wagner.[12] Later, the relationship between the empire, the British state, and the geopolitical entity of the Commonwealth was analyzed from social and cultural perspectives. The concept of "race" and ethnicity in the field of cultural studies has been central with regard to sports in Africa and with the understanding that African communities were integrated into the United Kingdom. These were complemented by studies on indigenous populations in India, Australia, America, and New Zealand.[13]

These studies gradually opened up the question of national identities in the postcolonial period.[14] These researchers were influenced by global theory or world village theory, as well as the theory of globalization.[15] Arjun Appadurai later defined cultural movements in globalization by using the notion of "ethnoscape," which refers to a space in between, a liminal or "third space." This movement supported subaltern studies, which has been useful in research on sports postcolonialism in Asia and then in Africa.[16] In these studies, the issue of gender first appeared with the interventions of such authors as Jennifer A. Hargreaves, who worked on the intersection of issues of race, gender, and policy in Africa.[17] Regarding masculinity in African sports, one must read the works of John Nauright and Timothy J. L. Chandler, Laura Fair, and Robert Morell.[18] More recently, some scholars have studied and critically analyzed nongovernmental organizations and their use of sports for development and peace building.[19] The issue of gender and women in the developmental approach to sport shows the tensions at work in understanding the postcolonial.

Finally, some authors approach sports aid to developing countries from a humanist perspective of social development and integrate the Olympic ideology in the process. One may disagree, however, with their appropriation of Western capitalist logic, which is based on Rostow's stages of development theory. For them, there is a worldwide Olympic ideal, in which sports are considered an essential part of the "civilizing process." According to Mansour Al-Tauqi and Allison Lincoln, disseminating an idealistic vision of the Olympics and sports across the globe as a way to develop humanity and human dignity is a "neo-imperialist" tactic, a kind of monoculture Olympics deployed by the IOC.[20] Peter Donnelly calls it "prolympism."[21] This approach relaunches the debate on what strategies are best when disseminating sports in developing countries.

Given the importance of the Asian continent and the opening of China to the world market, other authors question the power of games and sports for dominated nations, as well as for the construction of national identities.[22] The organization of the Olympic Games in Beijing in 2008 renewed the interest in Asian countries and raised awareness in nations at the periphery where geopolitical issues are at stake. The men's football World Cup in South Africa (2010) also produced a magnifying effect in both academic and editorial spheres, especially on the history of African football. Indeed, when it comes to Africa, only one attracts academics, and that is football, but this does not reflect the multitude of practices on the African continent.[23] Nevertheless, these studies are useful when it comes to questioning international sports organizations in football and means of resistance.[24]

However, once again, sub-Saharan Africa is widely understudied. It is true that there has been research on colonial dominions and territories with a large population of white settlers because of the issue of apartheid. Barbados, the Dominican Republic, and of course South Africa have been case studied by Rob Ruck and Peter Alegi.[25] The latter, in a recent book, referred to the colonial period and incorporated the former French colonies in Africa. Through their foundations and theoretical influences, these English works differ somewhat from Francophone studies, which are attached to a more dynamic view of analytical integrations in the historical process. Anglophone works have integrated sport as engines of Western cultural diffusion and even speak of sports globalization.

French historical literature has only very recently chosen to focus on youth movements, sporting practices, and traditional competitive games. In the past fifteen years, four historical schools have gradually emerged at the Universities of Strasbourg, Aix-en-Provence, Bordeaux, Orsay, and Marseilles. Some of these institutions have a historical legacy. Strasbourg was chosen to establish a training school for African professionals in the 1960s. Bordeaux and Marseilles are located next to two major port cities that took part in the slave trade, but, curiously enough, the connecting of sports and Africa did not emerge in these universities, nor did the link between international relations and Olympism.

Contrary to what one might expect, the scholarly study of sports and Africa was quickly linked to the Olympic movement. Economists such as Wladimir Andreff[26] and geographers from the University of Franche-Comté (Besançon) such as Jean Praicheux were involved in the first geopolitical readings of the Olympics and international sporting events in which formerly colonized countries appeared. Around the same time, geographer Jean-Pierre Augustin from the University of Bordeaux combined sport relationships, decolonization, and international relations.[27] This work resonates with British studies that focus on Africa. The French studies are mainly those of sociogeographers. Gradually, African academic elites such as Ly Bocar studied the history of Western French-speaking Africa during the colonial period. François Dikoume focused his study on the structure of the sport system in Cameroon and opened the issue of ethnogeographic questions.[28] Indeed, starting with colonialism and youth movements, physical and sporting activities were later addressed at the University of Provence. Some sport researchers gradually joined the Center of African Studies in Paris. Works by Jean-Marie Mignon, Phyllis M. Martin, Serge Nedelec, and Odile Goerg studied the impact of leisure activities during the colonial period and looked into the conditions of receptions in youth movements in francophone sub-Saharan Africa.[29]

Francophone literature, just as its English counterpart, scrutinized football in the colonial period: Thomas Riot focused on Rwanda, Tshimanga Bakadiababu E. studied the trafficking of African footballers, and Cheik Fantamady Condé analyzed the Haifa soccer team, a club in Guinea, basing his study on the pioneering work of Marc Barreau.[30] The postcolonial period was analyzed by Pierre Lanfranchi with Matthew Taylor and recently Stanislas Frenkiel. Both gradually integrated the notion of migration.[31] Manuel Schotté included athletics, and finally, more recently, Paul Dietschy and David-Claude Kemo-Keimbou compiled a history of African football between the colonial and postcolonial periods, coordinated by FIFA.[32] North–South migrations are now the subject of specific studies, such as the one carried by the International Centre for Sport Studies (Lausanne) and its researcher Raffaele Poli.[33] It explores, among other things, the migration of African footballers in Europe and the recruitment strategies of European clubs in Africa, as does the new book of Michel Pautot on foreign soccer players in France and Europe.[34] However, this vision is still Eurocentric. It would benefit from studying the phenomenon of migration to the United States (for some sports like basketball) and especially South–South migration with the recent overhaul of African professional football leagues.

In the late 1990s and early 2000s, French historical literature developed a keen interest in colonial and postcolonial history. At the time, France wished to show the world it remembered and repented its past "civilizing mission." The fiftieth anniversary of colonial independence in Algeria raised important questions, just as had the celebration of the First World War in which black troops and many natives of the French Empire had participated. France sought to face publicly both its abuses in the former colonies and its own treatment of migrant workers. All this was celebrated in legacies between France and French-speaking African countries. Thus academic social sciences as a whole and those taking sport as their object of study revived painful periods in their histories. In this respect, sports historian Nicolas Bancel sought to transfer these questions, which were present in the fields of history and sociology, to the field of sport. His sociopolitical and cultural analyses focus on youth movements and sports to understand the processes of acculturation and the training of the elites and future leaders of African states.[35]

Thus, from the 1990s to today, the study of the deconstruction of the colonial history of sports has gradually opened to the postcolonial. According to Bernadette Deville-Danthu, the French Empire wanted to benefit from the athletic potential of African athletes. The same could be said of former British colonies. A form of fake continuity with the colonial era was installed through the development of aid policies in sport. This ideology originated in Western countries, mainly France and the United Kingdom. The construction of sports infrastructure, financial and material assistance, as well as many other schemes served to counter the interference of the United States and that of the USSR. This assistance aimed at serving the *grandeur* of France and Britain and preserving their respective areas of influence. The French used Franco-African sports cooperation (run by the Ministry of Cooperation) and *Francophonie* (International Organization of Francophonie), whereas the British based themselves on the British Commonwealth and the Foreign Office. French analyses of the political structures of colonial and postcolonial power can easily be explained by French direct rule. Anglophone studies, because of indirect rule, seek to understand the cultural aspects as well as ethnic communities in the United Kingdom. The postcolonial societies are different since France opted for integration following an assimilationist policy, while the United Kingdom chose multiculturalism. France and the UK have gained a better understanding of the process of integrating people from their former colonies. Focusing on sports can further that understanding.

Finally, new perspectives have been opened up with the study of traditional African games. For if we are to understand the propagation of sport and globalization on the African continent, it is necessary to consider preexisting tangible and physical practices. Charles Béart (1960) did so by paying attention to symbolism, religious cultures, and the social and political power of ethnic groups.[36] Other recent studies mix religion and football.[37] Olivier P. Nguema Akwe studies the link between martial arts and witchcraft in Africa.[38] Even traditional games reveal a logic that derives from postcolonialism. Some of these studies generally emanate from African academic elites. They are recent, due to the late development of structures of social science research with an interest in sport and physical and bodily practices in Africa.[39] Researchers from the world over find it hard to resist this form of essentialism, even if theoretical and methodological choices seem to legitimize it. Some researchers are trying to address dimensions of bodily and physical practices and traditional sports. These include Blaise Ndaki Mboulet, who combines analysis of traditional sports and games as factors of social development. Thierry Terret and Apolline Abena study Pygmies in Southern Cameroon and traditional practices incorporating the gendered dimension.[40] More recently, Joseph Bouzoungoula has analyzed the cultural dimensions of sports in the Congo.[41] In the French literature, there is nothing on the gendered approach in terms of either femininity or masculinity. More recently, studies in English are being conducted on the analysis of self-organized sports in Africa and in sport tourism. Such lines of research were initiated by Hameth Dieng on football practiced in the neighborhoods of Dakar. These practices preceded official football in Senegal and Cameroon and help us to understand the relationship between non official sporting organizations and the state management of space and sports facilities.[42]

Postcolonial studies that deal with sport in Africa should include works on the survival of traditional games that are also undergoing reconstructions. The objects that are studied in the functioning of sports in the West are too often imposed on the African continent. To avoid Westernization and the formation of a North-led history, it is now necessary to open our eyes to other external influences: the Soviets, Americans, Asians, or even Latin Americans. Similarly, it is necessary to examine the internal relations on the African continent. In what ways are African countries structuring their own continental sports field? Finally, the South–North studies question the former colonial empire's approach. Should not the North be taking into account the presence of Africans on its soil, be they migrants or nationalized? New identities and social and cultural relations are studied through sport and are part of the "new new worlds" as defined by Balandier. Africa, according to the capitalist doctrine of social development, needs to catch up socially, economically, and democratically. It is nonetheless culturally rich.

Africa is affected by new technology and information technology (the Internet, social networks, and so on), media (TV, radio), biological science, health (HIV and sport), doping, and disability (Paralympism). All this contributes to the transformation of bodies and redefines new social and cultural corporealities Africa.

Ongoing research in the field of sport in Africa should be expanded through greater collaboration between French-speaking and English-speaking research units. In this respect, there should be more scholarship programs, calls for proposals, and funding research on African sport. This should enable African academics and researchers to integrate into research groups. In Africa, there should be development aid not only in sport but in sport research. Indeed, on the African continent, the very limited number of congresses, conferences, workshops, journals, and publishers forces African researchers to move to the West or publish in foreign venues. This is an issue elsewhere, but it raises the question of equal access to research and training when dealing with sport in Africa.

But, in order to develop research on sport in Africa, there must be sports competitions. In search of visibility and international recognition, Africa focuses its efforts on high performance sport while abandoning grassroots sport. The instrumentation which is made of sport is the marker of some African regimes. The continent is heterogeneous in the development of sport, and the national representation of sports is diverse and often uneven. This area is neglected by private structures, which turn to more lucrative sectors. The implementation of public policies is not proactive in the development of local recreation and sport management training sectors. As such, mimicry of the Western model should be questioned. African policymakers who are responsible for sport should innovate and seek new forms of appropriation of physical culture and sports in line with their country's needs and their social and cultural diversity. The transition from high-level athletes to political positions can be an advantage and a drawback when facing the choice between tradition and modernity.

In conclusion, we should note that the African continent is well represented in the Olympics. When comparing the London Olympics of 1948 and 2012, we can see a major change has occurred. In 1948, there were two African NOCs (out of fifty-one NOCs). In 2012, there were fifty-three African NOCs (out of two hundred four). In line with the celebrations of African political independence in 2010, African countries are celebrating the fiftieth anniversary of the creation of their Olympic committees and the birth of the African Games. This marks the postcolonial passage of the battle of values in African sport. Once, the fight was only against apartheid. The challenge is now economic. In this respect, the ideology of development aid to sport as a feature seems to be an interesting sector in Africa, but it cannot be the only answer. Indeed, sport may be the place where private and public interests can be combined in a common goal under the control of nongovernmental organizations. Today, Africa is the continent that has the largest number of NOCs. It receives more support from international sports organizations, but it holds the fewest international sporting events. But we must remember that Africa as we know it is young. Its fifty-four states and its sports fields, as well as its accession to the international scene, are likely to evolve. At the turn of the century, Africa must be noted for its potential. For African athletes and for researchers (both Western and African), the task is to pursue the long march of African sport.

Notes

1. Timothée Jobert, *Champions noirs, racisme blanc: la métropole et les sportifs noirs en contexte colonial, 1901–1944* (Grenoble: Presses Universitaires de Grenoble, 2006), 155.
2. Neil Lazarus, *The Cambridge Companion to Postcolonial Literary Studies* (Cambridge, UK: Cambridge University Press, 2004).
3. Georges Balandier, "La situation coloniale: approche théorique," *Cahiers internationaux de sociologie* 11 (1951): 44–79.
4. Samir Amin, *L'impérialisme et le développement inégal* (Paris: Les Editions de Minuit, 1976); *La faillite du développement en Afrique et dans le Tiers-Monde: Une analyse politique* (Paris: L'Harmattan, 1989).
5. Achille Mbembé, "Notes provisoires sur la postcolonie," *Politique africaine* 60 (1995): 76–109.
6. Paul Darby, *Africa, Football and FIFA Politics, Colonialism and Resistance* (London: Frank Cass, 2002), 236.
7. Harold Perkin, "Teaching the Nations How to Play: Sport and Society in the British Empire and Commonwealth," *International Journal of the History of Sport* 6.2 (1989): 145–155.
8. With the participation of South African Union, South Rhodesia, and Nigeria.
9. The first English-speaking NOC in Africa was composed of South Rhodesia (Zimbabwe, 1934), Uganda (1950), Nigeria (1951), Ghana (1952), Liberia (1954), Kenya (1955), Sudan (1956), Tanganyika (Tanzania, 1956).
10. The first French-speaking NOC in Africa was composed of Senegal (1961), Ivory Coast (1962), Mali (1962), Dahomey (1962), Mauritania (1962), Malagasy (1963), Chad (1963), Togo (1963), Cameroon (1963), Democratic Republic of Congo (1963), Niger (1963), Congo-Brazzaville (1964), Guinea-Conakry (1964), Central African Republic (1964), Haute-Volta (1965), Gabon (1965).
11. James Riordan, "State and Sport in Developing Countries," *International Review of Sociology of Sport* 21.4 (1986): 287–303; William Baker James ad James Anthony Mangan, *Sport in Africa: Essays in Social History* (London: Holmes & Meier Pub, 1987); Brian Stoddart, "Sport, Cultural Imperialism, and Colonial Response in the British Empire," *Comparative Studies in Society and History* 30.4 (1988): 649–673; and again James Antony Mangan, *The Cultural Bond: Sport, Empire, Society* (London: Routledge, 1993) followed by Ossie Stuart, *Sport in Africa* (London: MacMillan, 1993); and of course Allen Guttmann, *Games and Empires. Modern Sports and Cultural Imperialism* (New York: Columbia University Press, 1994) and Roger Hutchinson, *Empire Games: The British Invention of Twentieth Century Sport* (London: Mainstream Publishing, 1996) began their studies between the 1980s and the 1990s.
12. Eric A. Wagner, *Sport in Asia and Africa: A Comparative Handbook* (New York: Greenwood Press, 1989).
13. Harry Edwards, *The Revolt of the Black Athlete* (New York: The Free Press, 1969); March Krotee, "Apartheid and Sport: South Africa Revisited," *Sociology of Sport Journal* 5.2 (1988): 125–135; and Cheryl C. Roberts, *Sport and Transformation* (Cape Town: 1989) who provided a critique of the South African sports system (Joan Brickhill, *Race against*

Race: South Africa's "multi-national" Sport Fraud [London: International Defence & Aid Fund for South Africa, 1976]); Bruce Kidd, "The Campaign against Sport in South Africa, " *International Journal* 43.4 (1988): 665–682; Richard E. Lapchick, *The Politics of Race and International Sport* (Westport, Connecticut: Greenwood Press, 1975); Tom Oliver Newnham, *A Cry of Treason* (Palmerston North: Dunmoire Press, 1978); Sam Ramsamy, *Apartheid The Real Hurdle: Sport in South African and the International Boycott* (London: International Defence & Aid Fund for South Africa, 1982); Richard Thompson, *Retreat from Apartheid* (Wellington: Oxford University Press, 1975); Donald Woods, *Asking for Trouble: Autobiography of a Banned Journalist* (New York: Atheneum, 1981). Francophone literature, with Antoine Bouillon, Robert Archer (*Le sport et l'apartheid* [Paris: Albatros, 1981]) and Jean-Pierre Bodis (*Le rugby sud-africain, histoire d'un sport en politique* [Paris: Karthala, 1995]) focused on the phenomenon of apartheid in sports but only on rugby. Their English counterparts are Albert M. Grundlingh, Andre Odendaal, and Barridge Spies (*Beyond the Tryline: Rugby and South African Society* [Johannesburg: Ravan Press, 1995]).

14. Adrian Smith and Dylwin Porter, *Sport and National Identity in the Post-War World* (London: Routledge, 2004).

15. Immanuel Wallerstein, *Africa: The Politics of Independence* (New York: Vintage, 1961) and Arjun Appadurai, *Modernity at Large: Cultural Dimensions of Globalization* (Minneapolis: University of Minnesota Press, 1996).

16. Among Subaltern Studies researchers, one finds Robert Chappell and John F. Coghlan, *Developing Countries and Sport for All: Some Thoughts on the Problems and Issues* (Uxbridge, UK: Brunel University Press, 1997); Robert Chapell, *Sport in Developing Countries* (England: Roehampton University, 2007); John J. MacAloon, *Muscular Christianity in Colonial and Post-Colonial* Worlds (London: Routledge, 2008); John Bale and Mike Cronin, *Sport and Postcolonialism* (Oxford: Berg Publishers, 2003); Patrick Ismond, *Black and Asian Athletes in British Sport and Society* (New York: Palgrave MacMillan, 2003); and Allison Lincoln, *The Global Politics of Sport: The Role of Global Institutions in Sport* (London: Routlege, 2005). Marion Keim (*Nation Building at Play. Sport as a Tool for Social Integration in Post-apartheid South Africa* [Oxford: Meyer & Meyer Sport, 2003]) addressed the issue of integration and nation building in a postcolonial or post-apartheid world. John Nauright (*Long Run to Freedom: Sport, Cultures and Identities in South Africa* [Morgantown: Fitness Information Technology, 2010]) focused specifically on South Africa.

17. Jennifer Hargreaves, *Heroines of Sport: The Politics of Difference and Identity* (London: Routledge, 2000).

18. John Nauright and Timothy J. L. Chandler, *Making Men: Rugby and Masculine Identity* (London: Frank Cass Publishers, 1996); Laura Fair, *Pastimes and Politics: Culture, Community, and Identity in Post-abolition Urban Zanzibar, 1890–1945* (Athens: Ohio University Press, 2001); Robert Morrell, *Changing Men in Southern Africa* (Pietermaritzburg/London: University of Natal Press/Zed Books, 2001).

19. Scarlett Cornelissen and Albert Grundlingh's (*Sport Past and Present in South Africa: (trans)forming the Nation* [London: Routledge, 2013]) recent review of the research on the development of sport in Zambia (like Lain Lindsay and Alan Grattan, "An 'International Movement'? Decentring sport-for-development within Zambian Communities," *International Journal of Sport Policy* 4.1 (2012): 91–110) is considered too Eurocentered by Simon C. Darnell and Lindsay Hayhurst ("Hegemony, postcolonialism

and sport-for-development: a response to Lindsey and Grattan," *International Journal of Sport Policy and Politics* 4.1 (2012): 111–124). They claim the analysis is too static and that power relations and hegemony are depoliticized.

20. Mansour S. Al-Tauqi, "Olympic Solidarity: Global Order and the Diffusion of Modern Sport between 1961 and 1980," PhD. Diss., Université de Loughborough, 2003; Lincoln Allison, *The Global Politics of Sport. The Role of Global Institutions in Sport* (London: Routledge, 2005).

21. Peter Donnelly, "Prolympism: Sport Monoculture as Crisis and Opportunity," *Quest* 48 (1996): 25–42.

22. Such authors include Mike Speak, "China in the Modern World," in SPEC, ed. James Riordan and Robin Jones (London: E & FN Spon, 1999), 86; John and Alan Sugden Tomlinson, *Power Games: A Critical Sociology of Sport* (London & New York: Routledge, 2002); Andrew Morris, *Marrow of the Nation: A History of Sport and Physical Culture in Republican China* (Berkeley: University of California Press, 2004); and James Mills, *Subaltern Sports: Politics and Sport in South Asia* (London: Anthem Press, 2005).

23. Ian Hawkey, *Feet of the Chameleon: The Story of African Football* (London: Portico, 2009).

24. Gary Armstrong, "Talking up the Game: Football and the Reconstruction of Liberia, West Africa," *Identities* 9.4 (2002): 471–494; Paul Darby, *Africa, Football and FIFA Politics, Colonialism and Resistance* (New York: Frank Cass Publishers, 2005).

25. Rob Ruck, *The Tropic of Baseball: Baseball in the Dominican Republic* (Westport: Meckler, 1991); Peter Alegi, *African Soccerscapes: How a Continent Changed the World's Game* (Athens: Ohio University Press, 2010).

26. Wladimir Andreff, "Les multinationales et le sport dans les pays en voie de développement," *Tiers-Monde* 29.113 (1988): 73–100; Wladimir Andreff, "Une taxe contre la misère du football africain?" *Afrique contemporaine* 233.1 (2010): 89–98.

27. Jean Praicheux and Daniel Mathieu, "L'espace mondial des grandes manifestations sportives internationales," *Mappemonde* 2 (1989): 7–13; Jean-Pierre Augustin, "Sports en Afrique noire: Développer les recherches sur les institutions, les pratiques et les aménagements sportifs," *Historiens & Géographes: Regards sur l'Afrique* 379 (2002): 103–109.

28. Ly Bocar, *Football. Histoire de la Coupe d'AOF* (Dakar: Nouvelles Editions Africaines, 1980); François Dikoumé, *Le service public du sport en Afrique noire (l'exemple du Cameroun)* (Paris: Dalloz, 1989).

29. Jean-Marie Mignon, *Afrique: jeunesses uniques, jeunesses encadrée. Institutions de jeunesse d'éducation populaire et de sports dans onze pays d'Afrique francophone* (Paris: L'Harmattan, 1984); Phyllis M. Martin, "Colonialism, Youth and Football in French Equatorial Africa," *International Journal of the History of Sport* 1 (1991): 56–71; Phyllis M. Martin, *Loisirs et société à Brazzaville pendant l'ère coloniale* (Paris: Karthala, 2005); Serge Nédélec, "Jeunesses, Etat et Société au Mali au 20ème siècle," PhD diss., Nouveau Régime en Histoire contemporaine, Université Paris VII, 1994; Odile Goerg, "Le mouvement associatif et le processus des indépendances en Afrique occidentale française," in L'Afrique noire française: l'heure des indépendances, (dir.) Charles-Robert Ageron and Marc Michel (Paris: CNRS, 1992).

30. Thomas Riot, "Le football au Rwanda: un simulacre guerrier dans la créolisation d'une société (1900–1950)," *Canadian Journal of African Studies* 44.1 (2010): 35–74; Tshimanga Bakadiababu E., *Le commerce et la traite des footballeurs africains et sud-américains en Europe* (Paris: L'Harmattan, 2001); Cheik Fantamady Condé, *Sport et politique en*

Afrique. Le Hafia Football-Club de Guinée (Paris: L'Harmattan, 2008); Marc Barreau, *Dictionnaire des footballeurs étrangers du championnat professionnel français (1932-1997)* (Paris: L'Harmattan, 1998).

31. Pierre Lanfranchi and Matthew Taylor, *Moving with the Ball: The Migration of Professional Footballers* (Oxford: Berg Publishers, 2001); Stanislas Frenkiel, "Des footballeurs professionnels algériens entre deux rives, travailler en France, jouer pour l'Algérie (1954–2002)," PhD diss., Université Paris-Sud Orsay, 2009.

32. Manuel Schotté, "Destins singuliers. La domination des coureurs marocains dans l'athlétisme français," PhD diss., Université Paris Ouest Nanterre La Défense, 2005; Paul Dietschy and David-Claude Kemo-Keimbou, *Le football et l'Afrique* (Paris: Hachette-Livre-FIFA, 2008).

33. Raffaele Poli, "Le marché des footballeurs africains entre l'Europe et l'Afrique," *Questions internationales* 44 (2010): 73.

34. Michel Pautot, *Sport et nationalités, quelle place pour les joueurs étrangers?* (Paris: L'Harmattan, 2014).

35. Nicolas Bancel, "Entre acculturation et revolution: Mouvements de jeunesse et sports dans l'évolution politique et institutionnelle de l'AOF (1945–1962)" (PhD diss., University Paris I-Sorbonne, 1999).

36. Charles Béart, *Recherche des éléments d'une sociologie des peuples africains à partir de leurs jeux* (Paris: Présence Africaine, 1960).

37. Tado Oumarou et Pierre Chazaud, *Football, religion et politique en Afrique* (Paris: L'Harmattan, 2010).

38. Olivier P. Nguema Akwe, *Sorcellerie et arts martiaux en Afrique: Anthropologie des sports de combats* (Paris: L'Harmattan, 2011).

39. Granted, some Western scholars examined sport from the perspective of African art and African culture in the broader sense (William J. Baker, *Sports in the Western World* (Urbana: University of Illinois Press, 1988); John Blacking, *How Musical is Man?* [Seattle and London: University of Washington Press, 1973]; Alyce Taylor Cheska, *Play As Context* [Champaign: Human Kinetics Publishers, 1987] incorporating dance). Physical practices, often called African "traditional games" have been the object of anthropological and ethnological studies (Kendall Blanchard & Alyce T. Cheska, *The Anthropology of Sport* [Massachussetts: Bergin & Garvey, 1985]; Robert R. Sands, *Anthropology, Sport and Culture* [Westport: Bergin & Garvey, 1999]).

40. Blaise Ndaki Mboulet, "Contribution à la recherche d'un nouvel équilibre culturel au Cameroun. Le cas du sport et des jeux populaires," PhD diss., Université de Paris VII, 1980; Thierry Terret and Appolline Abena, "Bapea, Yende et football chez les Pygmées Bagyeli du Sud-Cameroun. Pratiques sportives et activités physiques traditionnelles," *STAPS* 68.2 (2005): 55–75.

41. Joseph Bouzoungoula, *Sports, identités culturelles et développement en Afrique noire francophone: La sociologie des jeux traditionnels et du sport moderne au Congo-Brazzaville* (Paris: L'Harmattan, 2012).

42. Hameth Dieng, "La formation du champ du football au Sénégal. Enjeux et fonction (1960–2002)," PhD. Diss., Université Paris-Sud Orsay, 1998; Frank Michael Mbida Nana, "De nouvelles articulations entre les politiques publiques et les pratiques sportives auto-organisées: l'exemple des septs communes de Yaoundé (Cameroun)," PhD diss., Université Paris-Sud Orsay, 2016.

BIBLIOGRAPHY

Alegi, Peter C. "Playing to the Gallery? Sport, Cultural Performance, and Social Identity in South Africa, 1920s–1945."*International Journal of African Historical Studies* 35.1 (2002): 17–38.

Auger, Fabrice. "The African Games: An Attempt to Colonial Modernization." *Journal of Olympic History* 14.1 (2006): 15–23.

Baker, James W., and Mangan A. James. *Sport in Africa: Essays in Social History*. London: Holmes & Meier, 1987.

Bale, John, and Mike Cronin. *Sport and Postcolonialism*. Oxford: Berg, 2003.

Bancel, Nicolas. "Sport civil et politique sportive en Afrique Occidentale Française (1944–1958)." *STAPS* 52 (2000): 79–94.

Benson, Peter. *Battling Siki: A Tale of Ring Foxes, Race, and Murder in the 1920s*. Fayetteville: University of Arkansas Press, 2006.

Butchart, Alexander. *The Anatomy of Power: European Constructions of the African Body*. London: Zed Books, 1998.

Chappell, Robert. *Sport in Developing Countries*. London: International Sports Publications, 2007.

Darby, Paul. *Africa, Football and FIFA Politics, Colonialism and Resistance*. London: Frank Cass, 2002.

Desai, Ashwin. *The Race to Transform: Sport in Post-Apartheid South Africa*. Cape Town: HSRC Press, 2010.

Deville-Danthu, Bernadette. *Le sport en noir et blanc, Du sport colonial au sport africain dans les anciens territoires français d'Afrique occidentale (1920–1965)*. Paris: L'Harmattan, 1997.

Dietschy, Paul, and David-Claude Kemo-Keimbou. *Le football et l'Afrique*. Paris: Hachette Livre-FIFA, 2008.

Giulianotti, Richard, and Roland Robertson. *Globalization and Sport*. Malden, MA: Blackwell, 2007.

Guttmann, Allen. *Games and Empires, Modern Sports and Cultural Imperialism*. New York: Columbia University Press, 1994.

Lanfranchi, Pierre, and Matthew Taylor. *Moving with the Ball: Migration of Professional Footballers*. Oxford: Berg, 2001.

Macaloon, John. *Muscular Christianity in Colonial and Post-Colonial Worlds*. London: Taylor & Francis, 2008.

CHAPTER 21

....

SPORT IN RUSSIA
AND EASTERN EUROPE

....

MAURICIO BORRERO

THE history of sport in Russia and eastern Europe is deeply marked by the long period of Communist rule that both regions experienced during the twentieth century. Accordingly, for most observers and scholars, the point of entry into the study of Russian and east European sport has been a narrative that emphasizes the ideological dimension of sport as an extension of Communist politics and as a surrogate arena for superpower competition during the Cold War, particularly through the study of the Olympic Games between 1952 and 1992. This Cold War narrative has worked well for understanding the history of multimedal sports, such as track and field, gymnastics, and swimming, where a running count of medals won by both superpowers (and Soviet bloc countries) was kept. With the exception of the 1980 and 1984 Olympic Games marred by mutual boycotts, the two superpowers went head to head for victory in the total medal count, with a slight edge going to the Soviet Union in terms of Olympic Games "won." It also worked well with the history of Olympic team sports such as basketball or hockey, particularly at times when the United States and the Soviet Union faced each other for crucial matches or gold medal finals. Hence, the controversial 1972 Munich Olympic basketball gold medal match that ended with a Soviet upset of the United States team and the 1980 Winter Olympics, where an underdog American team defeated the highly rated Soviet ice hockey team, are both important landmarks in Cold War sports narratives.

While the Cold War narrative provides a valuable conceptual framework, it has also cast a distorting shadow over the study of Russian and eastern European sport. Coupled with the dearth of historical scholarship in the field, particularly in the English language, this version of events has helped to obscure other important elements in the region's sports history. It has minimized the prewar and postwar traditions of nations such as Hungary, Czechoslovakia, and Yugoslavia, which were important contributors to the burgeoning scene of international sport. It has also minimized the distinctive alternate path that the Soviet Union tried to forge in the world of sports in the years between the 1917 revolution and World War II. Finally, the old master narrative has failed to find a place for soccer, the massively popular sport that has long captured the imagination of Russian and eastern European athletes and spectators. This approach is particularly ill-suited for soccer, where neither superpower was at the pinnacle of the sport. Instead of the bipolar power structure that reduced competitions to Soviet Union versus United States, soccer has featured a multipolar structure where traditional powers such as Brazil, Germany, Italy, and Argentina have held hegemony, joined occasionally for shorter periods by countries such as Uruguay, Spain, the Netherlands, and, as we will see, Hungary in the 1950s.

Based on its initial modest achievements, there was little indication that Russia would become a major sport powerhouse after World War II. Russia sent five athletes to the 1900 Olympics in Paris, where they won no medals, and six to the 1908 London Olympics, where they won their first goal medal in figure skating, along with two other silver medals. A much larger contingent of 159 athletes took part in the 1912 Stockholm Games, but the results were hardly better: two silver and three bronze medals. With the cancelation of the 1916 Games due to World War I and the refusal of the Soviet government to participate in Olympic competitions after the Russian revolution of 1917, it would not be until 1952 that Russian athletes took part in Olympic competitions.

The 1917 revolution disrupted all aspects of Russian life, including sport. The reconstituted Russian Empire, now known as the Soviet Union, entered the interwar period with the same rejectionist attitude toward what it considered "bourgeois" sport that it had toward the capitalist world in general. During the first decades of Communist rule, Soviet sport exhibited two main features: a governmental and ideological preference for sport as a vehicle for developing a healthy Soviet body through physical culture (*fizikul'tura*) and a rejection of existing international sporting competitions, best expressed through the creation of a parallel network of international sporting organizations.

The Red Sport International or Sportintern was part of the broader attempt by early Soviet leaders to create alternative international Communist communities, be they of Communist parties, trade unions, or in this case working-class sports organizations. First founded in 1921, by the late 1920s the Sportintern featured member organizations from Europe, the United States, and South America. Its featured sports such as gymnastics reflected Communism's built-in preference for sport as organized physical culture and its disapproval of the bourgeois sports that were gaining worldwide mass popularity in the 1920s. The Sportintern's main organized event was the Spartakiad, first held in Moscow in 1928. Subsequent Spartakiads were held in Berlin (1931), Antwerp (1937), and a winter version in Oslo (1928). The Spartakiads remained limited in scope. In time, they could not compete with the growing popularity of the Olympic Games, which increasingly gained traction in the interwar period, culminating in the two media-savvy spectacles of the 1932 Los Angeles Olympics and 1936 Berlin Olympics. The Comintern disbanded the Sportintern in 1937, and the international Spartakiad movement came to an end, even though the name later was revived for national sporting competitions across the Soviet Union and eastern Europe during the Cold War era.

The nations of eastern Europe played a more important role in the world of interwar sport than the Soviet Union. British-style modern sports had already made inroads into eastern Europe by the late nineteenth century. At the same time, parts of eastern Europe were also home to indigenous sporting traditions, such as the Sokol movement, initially centered in the Czech lands of the Habsburg Empire but that in time spread across the Slavic lands of east and central Europe. Heavily influenced by the Turner movement that had gained popularity in the German lands in the early nineteenth century, the Sokol movement featured a similar combination of mass gymnastic festivals with strong nationalist overtones. Eastern Europe embraced the Olympic movement, beginning with the first modern Olympics in 1896, where Hungary, competing as a separate team from Austria, won a total of six medals, two of them gold. After World War I, when many eastern European lands formerly ruled by the German, Habsburg, Russian, and Ottoman empires gained independence, Olympic sport provided these new nations with a vehicle for achieving international recognition.

On a different tack, by the 1920s soccer was attaining a massive global popularity that rivaled, and at times exceeded, that of Olympic sport. As with other parts of the world, soccer came to the region through contact with Great Britain. In some cases, British sailors or expatriate workers brought the sport to such cities as Rijeka, Odessa, or St. Petersburg; in others it was brought by eastern European students and individuals returning to the region after exposure to life in Britain. The oldest and most storied clubs in the region, such as Levski in Bulgaria, Sparta Prague and Slavia Prague in the Czech Republic, and Ferencváros and MTK in Hungary, date their origins to the first two decades of the twentieth century. By the 1930s, most countries in the region had established professional leagues. Even the Soviet Union, mired in the relative isolation of the first decade of Stalinist rule and its rejection of global sporting trends, could not ignore the growing popularity of soccer. An All-Union Soviet soccer league was established in 1936. By then, there were several strong rivalries, especially among Moscow-based clubs, such as Spartak and Dinamo Moscow, that were as intense as other rivalries in major cities of the European continent. At the international level, eastern European national squads were active participants in both the Olympic Games for amateurs and the World Cup, first held in 1930, for professionals. Yugoslavia, one of the few European nations to attend, finished fourth in the inaugural cup, hosted by Uruguay. At the next two prewar editions of the World Cup, eastern European teams finished as runners-up to Italy both times: Czechoslovakia in 1934 and Hungary in 1938. Along with Austria, Hungary and Czechoslovakia were leading exponents of the Danubian School of soccer, an innovative and visually appealing style that revolutionized soccer in the 1930s. Hungary's Golden Squad of the 1950s and the Dutch "total football" of the 1970s, both of which emphasized creative passing and the interchangeablity of players, were descendants of the Danubian style that enthralled spectators in the 1930s.

World War II interrupted the hosting of major international sporting competitions for more than a decade. No Olympic games were held between the 1936 Berlin Olympics and the 1948 Olympics, while the 1950 World Cup in Brazil was the first to be held after the 1938 World Cup in France. By the time athletes met in London and Brazil, the international geopolitical situation had changed dramatically, particularly for the nations of eastern Europe, which now found themselves with Communist governments firmly planted in the Soviet orbit of politics and sport.

The Sovietization of eastern European sport was most evident in the growing level of state resources devoted to sporting activities and in the propaganda value assigned to sport. In Czechoslovakia, Hungary, and Yugoslavia this renewed emphasis on sport merely built on significant prewar legacies. The Communist model of sport entailed devoting more state resources, identifying and training of potential athletes at an early age, and integrating athletes into the network of privileged social groups that received preferential treatment in societies where scarcity and shortages of consumer goods were often the norm.

In the area of professional soccer, eastern European countries adopted the Soviet model of individual club sponsorship by major bureaucratic institutions, such as the army, police, or trade unions. In the Soviet Union, the club Dinamo was sponsored by the internal security apparatus, CSKA by the army, and Lokomotiv by the railway work- ers' union. But unlike the Soviet Union, where privately owned teams had not existed before the establishment of a soccer league, across eastern Europe the process was far less organic. Wherever a smooth transition to the new model could not be made, it involved forced takeovers or unwieldy amalgamations of previously existing clubs. There were a few exceptions. Teams with a particularly strong fan base or identity, such as Ferencváros, Slavia Prague, and Sparta Prague, continued to exist, but they were deprived of resources and entered a period of decline.

The first post–World War II decade was one of significant achievement for Soviet and eastern European soccer. The cloak of secrecy with which Soviet soccer had surrounded itself in the interwar period was broken by Dinamo Moscow's impressive goodwill tour of the United Kingdom in 1945. In the mid-1950s, before the rise of Brazilian hegemony, the center of the soccer universe briefly relocated to Budapest, where Hungary wrote one of the most glorious chapters in the history of international soccer. Following its gold medal at the 1952 Helsinki Olympics, the Hungarian national team, known to locals as the *Aranyicsapat* or Golden Squad, enthralled football audiences for almost half a decade. Also dubbed the "Magical Magyars" by the English press, the Hungarian squad announced itself to the world with dazzling 6–3 and 7–1 victories over England at London's iconic Wembley Stadium and in Budapest. Heavily favored to win the 1954 edi- tion of the World Cup, Hungary romped through the tournament's early stages before succumbing to a West German side that was making a history of its own by winning the first major postwar international competition for the partitioned Germany. Despite fail- ing to win soccer's supreme trophy, Hungary's graceful, intelligent style left an indelible mark on world soccer with a team that is still considered among soccer's greatest ever.

The success of the Hungarian national side was indisputably based on the remarkable talents of a group of players such as Ferenc Puskás, Nándor Hidegkuti, and Jószef Bozsi, a "golden generation" much like other nations have produced from time to time. But behind the Hungarian success were several organizational and training principles that, although not exclusive to Communist nations, were more easily implemented within the authoritarian structures of those societies. The national team was based on players from the army club, Honvéd, and its coach, Gusztáv Sebes, was given great power in recruiting the best players, including the option of drafting players into the army. But if the rise of the Golden Squad can be tied to the practices of Communist sport management, then its demise was also the result of Communist politics. The failed 1956 Hungarian revolution found the team traveling abroad in preparation for the Melbourne Olympics to be held in November. Some players returned to Hungary while others did not, resulting in the dispersal of a hugely talented squad. Puskás, for example, landed in Spain, where he continued his stellar career playing for Real Madrid and briefly for the Spanish national team, once he attained Spanish citizenship. Yet, even without its major stars, Hungary's talented generation remained an important player in international soccer until the 1966 World Cup, after which the country lapsed into a half-century of mediocrity that has transcended both the late Communist and post-Communist years.

The performance of Soviet bloc soccer teams in professional international tournaments revealed some problems in competing with established European and South American powers that were less apparent in other sports. By arguing that professional sports as such did not exist under Communism, the Soviet bloc countries were able to field athletes that would elsewhere be considered professionals. Thus the Soviet bloc had a built-in advantage in Olympic competitions. Following a Yugoslav silver medal in 1948, Soviet bloc teams won the soccer gold medal every time between the 1952 Olympics and the 1988 Olympics, with the obvious exception of the boycotted 1984 Olympics. The Soviet bloc's domination of Olympic soccer went beyond the gold medal. In those same years (again not counting the boycotted 1984 Olympics), Soviet bloc teams won twenty-one out of a possible twenty-seven medals. During these years, the Olympic teams were often indistinguishable from the teams that participated in the professional World Cup. With the introduction of a more level playing field for the 1992 Barcelona Olympics, the Soviet bloc's advantage disappeared. With the sole exception of a silver medal for Poland in the 1992 games, no former Soviet bloc nation has since won gold, silver, or bronze at the Olympic Games.

The domination of Cold War–era Olympic soccer did not translate to the World Cup, where all nations fielded professional players. Here, the performance of Soviet bloc teams, while not entirely undistinguished, was nowhere as dominant. Although they never produced a side as dazzling or dominant as the "Magical Magyars," Soviet bloc soccer teams continued to shine intermittently as late as the 1982 World Cup. Czechoslovakia finished second to Brazil in 1962, while Yugoslavia finished fourth. Led by the outstanding goalkeeper, Lev Yashin, the Soviet Union placed fourth in 1966, its best-ever World Cup performance. An entertaining Polish side, led by the striker Grzegorz Lato, finished third in 1974, while a less dynamic version of that team also finished third in 1982. By the end of the Cold War, though, the failure of Soviet and eastern European teams to keep up with more talented Europeans and South Americans was becoming readily apparent.

This emphasis on soccer is not meant to minimize the importance of Olympic sport in the history of Soviet and eastern European sport. Throughout the Cold War era, athletes from the region were crucial contributors to the Olympic Games both in team sports such as water polo and handball, as well in the multimedal sports such as swimming, fencing, track and field, weightlifting, and gymnastics. Not counting the controversial Soviet victory in the 1972 Olympics, the Soviet Union and Yugoslavia made significant inroads into the American-dominated sport of basketball. By 1988, the Soviet Union won the gold in men's basketball, with Yugoslavia obtaining silver and the United States relegated to a bronze medal. This third-place result was instrumental in the rewriting of the rules that allowed the United States to bring National Basketball Association (NBA) players to the next Olympics, the famed "Dream Team" that dominated the 1992 Barcelona Olympics. In the 1950s and 1960s, Hungary was a consistently powerful competitor, shining in such sports as fencing, water polo, canoeing, and wrestling. In the 1970s and 1980s, East Germany emerged as a dominant sporting power in track and field, swimming, and skating, even though widespread suspicions about the systematic use of steroids tainted their achievements.

The Cold War narrative can also be found outside of the framework of Olympic sport. The 1958 Soviet–American track and field meet held in Moscow, a subject that opens David Maraniss's history of the 1960 Rome Olympics, followed by a return meet the following year in Philadelphia, were important landmarks in the brief thawing of superpower relations of the late 1950s. In 1972 the hockey world was treated to the fascinating Summit Series between the Soviet national team and a team of Canadian all-stars, with four matches played in Canada and four in the Soviet Union. With Canada serving as the representative of the West against a Soviet team that had dominated the sport at the international level in recent years, the series was full of Cold War symbolism at a time when tensions between the two superpowers were again on the rise. Even the 1972 competition in Reykjavik for the title of world chess champion between the Soviet Boris Spassky and the American Bobby Fischer fit into the Cold War narrative. By the late 1980s, the thawing of the Cold War sporting rivalry reflected the thawing of the Cold War itself, as traveling NBA and other US teams received a warm reception in the Soviet Union.

The initial impact of the collapse of Communist regimes across the region was mostly negative, primarily because of the removal of financial subsidies and other forms of state support for teams and athletes. The lifting of travel restrictions on athletes contributed to an exodus of the most qualified athletes, which affected the quality of domestic sport. The disintegration of multinational states such as the Soviet Union, Czechoslovakia, and Yugoslavia weakened their ability to compete at the international level. The border changes that accompanied the end of Communism in the region altered the balance of power in international sporting competitions. Most obvious was the disappearance of East Germany, now subsumed into a unified Germany, as a major sporting power. Shorn of the non-Russian Soviet republics, Russia managed to remain a major but somewhat weaker competitor, slipping to third in the total medal count at the 2004 Athens Olympics and 2008 Beijing Olympics, and even fourth at the 2012 London Olympics. The dissolution of Yugoslavia into six independent states removed a powerful international competitor, particularly in major sports such as soccer and basketball as well as lesser known Olympic sports such as handball. The transitional nature of the region's politics in the early 1990s led to temporary anomalies in international competitions such as the Unified Team that represented all but three of the former fifteen republics of the Soviet Union or the disqualification of Yugoslavia from the continental soccer competition, the 1992 European Cup.

The overall picture of post-Communist sport is not solely one of decline. Paradoxically, the exodus of soccer players to the top foreign leagues, where they could compete regularly at a higher level, initially helped eastern European nations in international competitions. A talented Romanian side reached the quarterfinals of the 1994 World Cup, only to be eliminated by penalty kicks, while Bulgaria, led by the magnetic Hristo Stoichkov, finished in fourth place. Although Yugoslavia's "golden generation" was not able to fulfill the promising international potential it had shown in the late 1980s, a skilled Croatian team finished third in the 1998 World Cup. Occasional international success extended to other sports beyond international soccer. At the 1992 Barcelona Olympic Games, an underdog Lithuanian basketball team, competing in its first-ever Olympics and outfitted with distinctive Grateful Dead–designed jerseys, won the bronze medal, led by the twin talents of an NBA-based player, Sarunas Marciulonis, and the magnificent Arvydas Sabonis, who would join the NBA toward the twilight of his career. Whether the successes of these teams in the early post-Communist period represented the maturation of foundations that had been laid during the late Communist period is a question that deserves further attention.

To Western spectators, the impact of the end of Communism on sport was first evident in the influx of top talented athletes, particularly in soccer and hockey, to their leagues. Trained to recognize talented players and a comparatively inexpensive investment, North American hockey clubs and western European soccer clubs snapped up the region's top players. Croatian, Serbian, Czech, and Polish soccer players became common in the English, Italian, German, and Spanish leagues, while Russians joined Czechs and Slovaks in the National Hockey League (NHL). The incorporation of Soviet bloc athletes was perhaps most seamless and successful in the world of hockey. Although hockey fans of the more bruising North American style often decried them as "soft," Russian players brought a combination of speed and style to the NHL that increased the appeal of the game and the league. The moment that perhaps best symbolized the successful integration of Soviet hockey with North American hockey was the Detroit Red Wings' domination of the NHL in the late 1990s with its "Russian Five" of Sergei Fedorov, Slava Fetisov, Igor Larionov, Vladimir Konstantinov, and Vyacheslav Kozlov working together with the hometown icon, Steve Yzerman. The term "Russian Five" itself was a reference to the earlier Green Unit that also featured Fetisov and Larionov, which dominated Soviet and international hockey in the 1980s.

In addition to the large influx of hockey players to the NHL, individual Russian and eastern European athletes have also achieved distinction and popularity in other sports. Relatively knowledgeable basketball fans would recognize the Serbian Vlade Divac or the Croatian Drazen Petrovic, whose NBA career was tragically cut short by a fatal automobile accident, as well as the Lithuanians Marciulonis and Sabonis and the

Russian Andrei Kirilenko. Meanwhile, the Bulgarian Stoichkov, the Ukrainian Andriy Shevchenko, and the Czech goalkeeper Petr Cech have had distinguished careers with leading western European clubs such as FC Barcelona, AC Milan, and Chelsea. In this sense Russian and eastern European athletes have become integral members of the constellation of international sport, transcending the dichotomies that characterized the Cold War era.

Tennis perhaps has been the most consistently successful eastern European and Russian sport in the post-Communist period. Despite its overtly "bourgeois" roots in the country clubs of capitalist countries, there was a tradition of strong tennis play in the Communist years. Players such as Jan Kodes from Czechoslovakia, Alex Metreveli from the USSR, and Ilie Nastase from Romania achieved international success in the 1960s and 1970s, although Nastase arguably became as well known for his antics and tantrums on the court as for his victories. Nevertheless, he led Romania to the finals of the Davis Cup in 1972, where the team lost to the United States in Bucharest in matches that were heavily colored by the Cold War politics of the era. But it was Czechoslovakia that first produced two world-class dominant players in the 1980s, in Martina Navratilova and Ivan Lendl, even though both flourished only after defecting to the West. In the 2000s the Russian Maria Sharapova occasionally broke the stranglehold of the Williams sisters, Serena and Venus, on women's tennis, while the Serb Novak Djokovic successfully climbed to the top echelon of men's tennis, next to Roger Federer and Rafael Nadal. More important, however, is that these two are not isolated successes in the way that the region's tennis stars of the 1960s, 1970s, and 1980s were. At various times since the end of the Communist era, more than a handful of eastern European and Russian tennis players have been ranked in the top levels of the sport.

Finally, the experience of the Kontinental Hockey League (KHL), first established in Russia in 2008, suggests that the region is not entirely limited to serving as a feeder of high-quality athletes to more successful western European or North American leagues. The initial success of the KHL coincided with one of the work stoppages that have punctuated the recent history of the North American NHL. Several prominent hockey players took temporary refuge in the KHL, attracted by competitive salaries and the possibility of keeping their skills sharp. When a new labor pact was signed by the NHL and its players, many of these players returned to the NHL. But the KHL continued and in fact expanded its operations to become a truly international Eurasian league, with franchises in Latvia, Belarus, Ukraine, Croatia, Slovakia, and the Czech Republic complementing a Russian core of teams stretching from St. Petersburg to Vladivostok.

Despite substantial contributions to world sport itself, the history of sport in Russia and eastern Europe remains a vastly understudied field. Existing English-language scholarship boasts a few outstanding works amidst an overall scarcity of published work. The works of James Riordan and Robert Edelman provide the essential introduction to students of Russian and Soviet sport. Although written at the height of the Brezhnev era, Riordan's *Sport in Soviet Society* (1977) remains an authoritative survey of sport in the late imperial Russian period, the early revolutionary years, and the post–World War II decades. Grounded in the literature on popular culture, Edelman opened up the hitherto little-known world of Soviet sporting audiences in his book *Serious Fun: A History of Spectator Sports in the USSR* (1993). The focus on spectator sports popular among the Soviet public, primarily soccer and hockey, brought to the surface an entire area where the government could not always dictate choices to its citizens.

Edelman further explored this area of research in his second book, *Spartak Moscow: A History of the People's Team in the Workers' State* (2009). The first English-language study of a Soviet soccer club, Edelman's history of Spartak Moscow joins a select number of international club histories that not only examine their institutional inner workings but also illuminate those occasions when a soccer club is *más que un club* ("more than a club"), as in the well-known relationship between FC Barcelona and Catalan identity. Drawing from a wide range of primary sources, Edelman recreates an alternative private and public space where Spartak fans sought shelter from the totalizing tendencies of the Soviet regime, particularly during the Stalinist years.

Culture, diplomacy, and the connections between sport and politics are the subjects of other important contributions to the historiography of Soviet and Eastern European sport. In *Sport in the USSR: Physical Culture—Visual Culture* (2006), Mike O'Mahony explores the rich legacy of the Soviet visual arts as it relates to sport as a cultural manifestation. Barbara Keys's *Globalizing Sport: National Rivalry and International Community in the 1930s* (2003) brings a comparative focus to the role of international sport at a time when governments were advancing strong nationalist agendas, including a chapter on Soviet soccer in the 1930s. One of the few Russian-language scholarly contributions to Soviet sport history is Mikhail Prozumenshchikov's *Bol'shoi sport i bol'shaia politika* (Big Sport and Big Politics, 2004), a study that traces the mechanisms by which the Soviet political world influenced and shaped Soviet sport. The terrain of eastern European sport remains even less explored than that of Russian sport. In her book *Training Socialist Citizens: Sport and the State in East Germany* (2008), Molly Wilkinson Johnson investigates the East German government's attempts to create a socialist citizenry through mass-participatory sports.

The publication of *Euphoria and Exhaustion: Modern Sport in Soviet Culture and Society* (2011), an international collaboration edited by four German scholars, represents a major advancement in the expansion and diversification of research on Soviet sport. Focusing on three major themes—sites and media, milieus and memory, and gender and science—the book features a wide range of essays on women swimmers, Baltic wrestlers, Soviet mountaineering, soccer fandom, and images of Soviet female athletes. It also features an intriguing comparison between Soviet sporting cultures and those of the early Turkish Republic and an exploration of Elem Klimov's 1970 documentary, *Sport, Sport, Sport*. Unwieldy yet stimulating, this veritable explosion of Soviet sports research provides the jolt of energy and enthusiasm that the field needs to grow beyond the earlier confines of traditional Cold War historiography.

Its publication bodes well for the future of the field, suggesting that the study of Russian and eastern European sport will begin to catch up with the worldwide field of sports studies. With far fewer obstacles to international scholarly collaborations than during the Cold War era, the possibilities for advancing a research agenda on Russian and eastern European sport are numerous.

The relative scarcity of existing scholarship on Russian and eastern European sport provides a wealth of opportunities for future research. So far, soccer has received the most attention from scholars as shown by a number of ongoing international collaborations, often within the context of the European Community, but other sports and topics also call for attention.

Former Russian president Boris Yeltsin may have brought high visibility by playing the sport, but the popularization of tennis across Russia and eastern Europe and the production of a large cohort of internationally competitive players have deeper roots that deserve further study. The frequent appearance of eastern European coaches in Latin America and Africa, dating back to the 1960s, provides an interesting example of the transfer of sporting knowledge. The influential work of the Romanian gymnastics coach Bela Karolyi with American gymnasts shows that this knowledge transfer was not limited to the Third World locations of the Cold War era. Following in the steps of Edelman's history of Spartak Moscow, there are several storied soccer clubs in the region, such as Red Star Belgrade, Slavia Prague, Sparta Prague, Levski, and Ferencváros that attained the status of "teams of the people" during the Communist era, which could benefit from individual or comparative histories. Students of Russian hockey can build on the authoritative two-volume history by Mathieu Boivin-Chouinard *Chaibou! Histoire de hockey russe* (2011), but there is still room for further research on the success of Cold War–era Soviet hockey, the post-Soviet integration of Russian hockey into North American hockey, and the more recent emergence of the KHL.

There is also room for greater research into an often neglected dimension of the Cold War narrative: internal rivalries within the Communist world and the role of sport as a surrogate for anti-Soviet, nationalist feeling within the Soviet bloc. The fierce water polo semifinal match between Hungary and the Soviet Union at the 1956 Melbourne Olympics almost a month after the suppression of the Hungarian Revolution, colloquially known as the "blood in the water match," is a well-known example of this. The tense hockey matches between Czechoslovakia and the Soviet Union that followed the Warsaw Pact's suppression of the 1968 Prague Spring provide another instance of this important intra-Soviet bloc dynamic. A study of the ways in which the Soviet-era soccer teams Dinamo Kiev and Dinamo Tbilisi served as vehicles for the expression of suppressed Ukrainian and Georgian national identity would provide a finer understanding of nationalist feeling in the last decades of the Soviet Union.

In the field of sport history as a whole, biographies have found a receptive audience beyond the academic world, and there is no shortage of potential biographical subjects among Russian and eastern European athletes. These could include the Czech long-distance runner Emil Zatopek, who dominated his field in the 1948 and 1952 Olympic Games, winning three gold medals in the latter, or the precocious Yugoslav soccer player Dragoslav Sekularac, who after a decade of stardom at his team Red Star Belgrade blazed an international trail playing for teams in Germany, the United States, Colombia, and France from 1966 to 1975, well before it was common for athletes from Communist countries to play outside the region. The case of Martina Navratilova contains several Cold War motifs—early training in Czechoslovakia and a request for political asylum in the United States in 1975, which led to her being stripped of Czechoslovak citizenship, with an additional twist. Her early rivalry with the highly popular Chris Evert and her homosexuality, which she publicly announced in 1981, resulted in an ambivalent reception from the American public at a time when gender and sexual stereotypes were still rather inflexible.

Navratilova's career provides a segue to issues of gender in sport, an issue that has received some attention but like so many others remains understudied in Russian and eastern European sport. Communism provided greater opportunities for female athletes to participate in sport, as it did with the labor force in general, even as patterns of gender bias and stereotypes remained firmly in place. The debate about which sports are suitable for female athletes has been a permanent feature of modern sports, even after competitions such as the Olympic Games reluctantly opened their doors to female athletes. The success of Soviet bloc female athletes in "nontraditional" female sports such as the shot put, discus, javelin, and hammer, as well as weightlifting, helped affirm Western stereotypes about the physicality and lack of traditional femininity that Communism imposed on its women. This physical stereotype is the subject of Stefan Wiederkehr's contribution to the *Euphoria and Exhaustion* collection but deserves further research.

Yet, for all the stereotypes about tractor-driving Communist women, Soviet bloc countries also helped shape another gender-defining trend: the girl-like teenage gymnast. It was first seen at the 1972 Munich Olympics, where the seventeen-year-old Soviet gymnast Olga Korbut took the gymnastics world by storm, winning three gold medals and one silver medal. Although Korbut's domination of the competition was truly remarkable, it is difficult to deny that a big part of the attention she received in the Western press came from the fact that she played against existing stereotypes of women from Communist countries. Korbut found a successor in the Romanian Nadia Comaneci who at age fifteen dominated the gymnastics competitions at the 1976 Montreal Olympics, winning five medals, three of them gold. The trend was continued by the media-friendly American Mary Lou Retton at the 1984 Los Angeles Olympics and has become a permanent feature of gymnastics since.

Race has belatedly emerged as a feature of Russian and eastern European sport, particularly in soccer, where African and South American players have been contracted by numerous regional teams. Such prominent clubs as Shakhter Donetsk in Ukraine and Zenit St. Petersburg in Russia regularly feature players of color, as do smaller teams from provincial cities across the regions. As with the earlier experiences of African students in Soviet universities, they have received a mixed welcome that often taps into deeply ingrained racial prejudices. This is an area where oral histories can make a particularly valuable contribution to our understanding of the experiences of foreign players and the attitudes of local fans.

The field of Russian and eastern European sport is ripe for extensive exploration and research. With these and other projects, Russian and eastern European sport can come to occupy as prominent a place within the landscape of sports history scholarship as its own record of achievement on the playing fields suggests it deserves.

BIBLIOGRAPHY

Boivin-Chouinard, Mathieu. *Chaibou! Histoire de hockey russe.* 2 vols. Montreal: Keruss, 2011.
Edelman, Robert. *Serious Fun: A History of Spectator Sports in the USSR.* New York: Oxford University Press, 1993.
Edelman, Robert. "A Small Way of Saying 'No': Moscow Working Men, Spartak Soccer, and the Communist Party, 1900–1945." *American Historical Review* 107.5 (2002): 1441–1474.
Edelman, Robert. *Spartak Moscow: A History of the People's Team in the Workers' State* Ithaca, NY: Cornell University Press, 2009.
Goldblatt, David. *The Ball Is Round: A Global History of Football.* London: Penguin Books, 2007.
Gounot, André. "Sport or Political Organization? Structures and Characteristics of the Red Sport International, 1921–1937." *Journal of Sport History* 28.1 (2001): 23–39.
Johnson, Molly Wilkinson. *Training Socialist Citizens: Sports and the State in East Germany.* Leiden: Brill, 2008.
Katzer, Nikolaus, Sandra Budy, Alexandra Köhring, and Manfred Zeller, eds. *Euphoria and Exhaustion: Modern Sport in Soviet Culture and Society.* Frankfurt-on-Main: Campus Verlag, 2010.
Keys, Barbara J. *Globalizing Sport: National Rivalry and International Community in the 1930s.* Cambridge, MA: Harvard University Press, 2003.
Maraniss, David. *Rome 1960: The Summer Olympics that Changed the World.* New York: Simon & Schuster, 2008.
O'Mahony, Mike. *Sport in the USSR: Physical Culture—Visual Culture.* London: Reaktion Books, 2006.
Prozumenshchikov, Mikhail. *Bol'shoi sport i bol'shaia politika* [Big Sport and Big Politics]. Moscow: Rosspen, 2004.
Riordan, James. *Sport in Soviet Society: Development of Sport and Physical Education in Russia and the USSR.* Cambridge, UK: Cambridge University Press, 1977.
Wilson, Jonathan. *Behind the Iron Curtain: Travels in Eastern European Football.* London: Orion, 2006.

CHAPTER 22

....

SPORT IN WEST
AND NORTH EUROPE

....

CHRISTOPHER YOUNG

IN relative terms at least, the northwest of Europe is indubitably the most important region in the history of modern sport. The whole of Europe, excluding Russia and Turkey, measures less than two-thirds the area of Brazil, while its three most powerful countries—Britain, France, and Germany—take up a mere 13.5 percent of this space and an eighth of that of the United States. Yet this small corner spawned many of the world's most popular sports. The world's most widely diffused sports include football, athletics, tennis, and table tennis from Britain and gymnastics from Germany but only basketball and volleyball from the United States. In the top thirty, these are joined by boxing, badminton, archery, hockey, bowling and squash (Britain), handball (Germany), and cycling (France).[1] It was in northwest Europe, too, where the most important governing bodies were founded—the International Olympics Committee (IOC, 1894), Fédération Internationale de Football Association (FIFA, 1904), International Association of Athletics Federations (IAAF, 1912), and Union of European Football Associations (UEFA, 1954)—and the world's sporting imagination molded. The quadrennial World Cups and Olympics, unparalleled in their global reach, have folded into the rhythm of passing years, while the more recent Champions League has become the largest club competition worldwide, its final eclipsing the Super Bowl. FIFA began life in 1904 with representatives from France, Belgium, Holland, Denmark, Sweden, Switzerland, and Spain and has been presided over by northern Europeans for all but twenty-four years since. The Olympics were incubated in Athens and, bar two excursions to the United States, grown in the period before the Second World War in Paris, London, Stockholm, Antwerp, Amsterdam, and Berlin. Western Europe has provided all but one IOC president, Belgium two of them.

The move from traditional/folk activities to regulated ones in the physical realm took place in Britain, Europe, and the United States from the mid- to late nineteenth century, although the sports played and watched by Europeans are predominantly European in origin. Football is the most popular everywhere except for Switzerland (shooting) and

Austria (skiing), and handball is the focus of intense international rivalry, save for the United Kingdom where it was barely recognized before the 2012 Olympics. The United States imports of basketball and volleyball have enjoyed greater success on mainland Europe than in Britain, while Britain and the United States share a common love of bat and ball singularly lacking on the continent.

Despite this mottling, Europe is fundamentally different from the United States—and not just in the sports it chose to follow. In the United States, sport thrived in educational establishments, developed at an early stage into a professional business, was organized within closed leagues run by competing franchises, remained national in focus, and largely avoided government interference. In Europe, by contrast, sport flourished in voluntary clubs and associations, persevered (not without hypocrisy and contradiction) with the ideal of amateurism, formed leagues on the principle of promotion and relegation, opened itself to transnational institutions, and was subject to various degrees of political support and control. Europe's sports space is therefore clearly distinct from the American, as it is from those of the less influential continents. But despite its commonalities, it is also perhaps the most heterogeneous region. As Richard Holt aptly remarked, "The British could no more understand [the Tour de France,] a cycle race lasting three weeks[,] than the French could comprehend watching a cricket match for five days."[2] The same could be said of gymnastics and darts, or rugby league and biathlon.

Sport in northwest Europe is therefore both similar and diffuse, and its history is a difficult one to write. The history of sport in the region still awaits its definitive account. The first, and greatest, problem is the dearth of comparative work. While good histories of the economy, society, and politics of Europe have been written, there is far less on music, film, and sport, despite the latter being the most important shared form of popular culture across the continent. Sports history has existed as a discipline for thirty years or more in the major countries, and each of them has now produced a substantial body of research. Britain, France, Germany, and Scandinavia are well accounted for, and there has been considerable industry in the Low Countries as well.[3] However, there is no general account of the modern history of European sport from a comparative and international perspective and until recently no attempt to assemble and examine the various strands of the relevant research emerging.[4] This lack of an up-to-date, or indeed any, historiography of European sport is a gaping hole in the discipline.

Writing a history of sport on a continent of forty-nine national Olympic committees and at least as many sports is, admittedly, an inherently complex undertaking. There is no real substitute for linguistic competence, and the ideal scholar of European sports would need a working knowledge of English, French, and German as well as a Slavonic, Scandinavian, and further Romance language. And this challenge comes at a time when the traditional specialist centers that laid the foundations of the subject are withering away due to funding cuts and national reprioritizations. Sports history as a separate discipline is dwindling in the United Kingdom and France and disappearing in Germany, Austria, and Italy. Only Scandinavia seems to be maintaining its modest equilibrium. The only hope is that researchers from mainstream history departments and beyond who have studied sports in the wake of the cultural and other turns will take up the slack.

They will find that the sports history of Europe has been almost exclusively locked within national borders. Few scholars venture seriously beyond their native lands, even fewer deal with more than one country with any real expertise, no monograph treads there, and virtually nothing has been translated. It is hard to imagine such a situation being tolerated in any other branch of the profession. As Paul Dietschy and Richard Holt lament: "The particular has triumphed over the general, the local and national have overwhelmed the comparative and the European dimensions. With occasional exceptions, writing the national narrative has taken precedence over constructing 'macro' accounts. Instead of looking at how the industrialising nations of Europe created similar sporting forms—which would have provided an account of commonalities—historians of sport instinctively addressed the familiar agenda of their own national histories."[5]

The tendency of those national histories, written largely in ignorance of the intricacies of the others, is to view their own case as exceptional or, to use the loaded German term that has now seeped into Scandinavian historiography, representative of a *Sonderweg* (special path). The British point to their donor role, their splendid isolation at key moments in the institutional history of international federations, and their affection, shared by former colonies but largely spurned elsewhere, for sports such as cricket and rugby. The Germans recount the clash between a conservative nationalist Turnen and modern, international sport that assisted the rise of a new professional middle class of teachers and then the slide of the latter, somehow still in conflict with the former but ultimately in its spirit, into National Socialism. With their peculiar spirit of universalism and mix of *anglomanie*, invented traditions, state intervention, and eclecticism, the French imagine themselves in a special position, halfway between the British and other continental traditions.[6] And the Scandinavians assert a third way based on their own Lingian gymnastics movement and a "balance between freedom and equality," "pragmatism as an organizational principle," and "conformity as an organizational form."[7]

These statements contain more than a modicum of truth but are also a bland overpuffing. Who could deny that Paris by the 1920s was the world capital of transnational sporting federations? How can Scandinavia have a monopoly on the "democratic legitimacy of the body"? And if any country in the region can claim uniqueness, it is Ireland, which "reject[ed] the monotony of mass gymnastics but also refus[ed] to follow the dominant forms of British sport; adopted amateur values but rejected the social distinctions that went with them; embraced spectator sport but refused the American model of sport as commercial entertainment" and in so doing "created a unique blend of the traditional and the modern, which has survived and prospered for 125 years."[8] More important, since the late 1980s the concept of the *Sonderweg* has enjoyed only limited currency in the mainstream German historiography that coined it, the idea of energetic progressivity straining against backward structures and ideologies giving way to a more nuanced understanding of modernity as a contested and contradictory phenomenon. General historians tend not to deny national peculiarities, but they tread the special path with caution.

However, a common strand running through most individual histories of European sport (East and West)—with the exception of Britain—is the presence of an alternative,

native form of physical culture in the respective countries that rivaled and contested sport as it transformed into a pan-continental practice. Turnen, Swedish gymnastics, the Czech form *Sokol*, traditional Turkish disciplines such as Osmanic wrestling, bull-fighting, Alpinism, and Russian *fizkultura* usually make a cameo appearance in general histories of sport. Yet the fact that such alternatives are omnipresent across the continent is rarely emphasized enough. By taking them seriously as a common factor and giving them a more central role, sports history will find itself transported to the heart of debates about contemporaries' aspirations and fears about selfhood, identity and otherness, modernization, tradition and primitiveness. It will also be forced to acknowledge the stubbornness and longevity of some traditional forms, which led to significant overlap with the innovations that eventually replaced them. The similarities and differences in these conflicts and discourses await their full comparative treatment, but they hold great potential to tell us about Europeans' understanding, experience, and expectations of sport.

This is not to say that no comparison has taken place at all. In fact, the most invigorating work in sports history has attempted to capture some sort of bigger picture, but this work, which focuses on the origins and spread of modern sport, has mostly been undertaken by nonhistorians. This brings us to the second problem of sports history in our region: the danger of theory determining or predetermining historical interpretation.

In two germinal books, German theorist Henning Eichberg, too, operated within a configurational framework (based on Norbert Elias, Michel Foucault, and historian August Nitsche) to demonstrate the marked changes in bodily practices that occurred across Europe between 1770 and 1820: in the shift from dressage, epee fencing, court tennis, vaulting, military exercise, and court dancing (minuet) to horse racing, boxing, football, gymnastics, and rapid dances such as the waltz, the period witnessed a distinct increase in tension and emphasis on achievement.[9] Critiquing Elias's civilizing process along the way, he successfully charted the major developments in sport into the industrial era, pointing—as so few scholars since have done—to the possible reasons why modern sports forms held participants' and spectators' fascination. Although sidelined in Germany for perceived political infelicities, Eichberg's insights influenced two leading American historians of world sport, Allen Guttmann and Richard Mandell, and recently underpinned an important section of Peter Borscheid's cultural history of acceleration.[10] Eichberg's work, however, is not without deficiencies. Pulsating with "interconnections at a variety of geographical scales" and "highly imaginative contextual and conceptual leaps,"[11] it is, however, weak on explanation. Eichberg might marvelously map the transformations of modern sport but willfully fails—to adopt the terms Joan Scott employed when launching gender history—to value "meaningful explanation" over "universal, general causality."[12]

Similar, although less conscious, failings mark the other major theses in the field. The British economist Stefan Szymanski has recently proposed that modern sport, in line with the Habermasian notion of the public sphere, developed out of new forms of associativity created during the European Enlightenment. In doing so, his aim was to correct what he saw as two major premises of the literature—that "modern sport evolved in the nineteenth century" and that it "was a simple consequence of the industrial revolution"—and to elevate sport above its usual position as a mere "peripheral manifestation of commercial culture."[13] Szymanski argued that "the variety and intensity of sporting practice in Britain and the United States stemmed precisely from their liberal approach to the formation of voluntary associations, in contrast to Germany and France where such associations tended to be regulated by the state."[14] In the former two countries, sports had no wider meaning and were played for their own sake as an escape from the responsibilities of everyday life, whereas in the latter, they were pressed into the service of the state, predominantly to enhance military preparedness. Despite the plaudits this theory has received, it ultimately fails, like Eichberg, to show *how* independent associativity actually fostered modern sport.[15]

A number of historical facts also undermine key strands of the argument. The role of industrialization is no longer read as simply as Szymanski portrays it, not least because even at the end of the nineteenth century in Britain sport was characterized precisely by its mix of the modern and traditional, and recent interventions have persuasively called for greater, not less, emphasis on the role of commerce.[16] Moreover, the overall thesis could be stretched at both ends. Wolfgang Behringer, for instance, demonstrates not only the importance of Italy, France, and southern parts of Germany (e.g., in racket sports and disciplines such as fencing that retained a high profile well into the twentieth century) from the Renaissance onward but the emergence of a small professional class of athletes, coaches, referees, and groundkeepers.[17] At the other end of the temporal spectrum, Szymanski's account does little to circumvent the fact that modern forms of sport—on both sides of the Atlantic—took shape from the 1860s onward, with even cricket not assuming its modern form until the 1870s. Furthermore, athletic activity in Britain might have developed in an apparently autonomous realm, but notions of sporting amateurism in the nineteenth century were inextricably linked with ideas of nation and empire. Much greater differentiation between is needed within and between the non-British states. Not all German or Swedish gymnastics was driven by military consideration.[18] France, where the urban population did not reach a majority until 1931, had a vibrant associational cycling culture. And athletic activity thrived in nineteenth-century Scandinavia, which took up a distinctive cooperative "third way" between free association and the state.

Dutch sociologist Maarten van Bottenburg must take credit for broadening our understanding of the diffusion of modern sports. Whereas traditional accounts naturally highlighted Britain's role in "giving sport to the world," van Bottenburg recognized that sports from America (basketball and volleyball), Japan (martial arts), and Germany (gymnastics and handball) also had a significant impact across the globe. From these four epicenters he traces the spread of sporting disciplines through societies, using a process and figurational approach to account for the traction each gained at specific points. The underlying explanation that the sports of the most powerful nations in a certain era tended to diffuse to other countries within their sphere hardly extends the explanatory power of traditional accounts, but from a European perspective, the spread of US sports to the continent and the inclusion of a non-British starting point, Germany is particularly innovative. However, Bottenburg's assumption that "the differential popularization of sports . . . is a relatively autonomous, 'blind' and to a certain extent structured process" is problematic because it underestimates the power of individual agency in the early phase of sport and oversimplifies real historical processes that can only be uncovered by extensive empirical work.[19]

His account does scant justice to the phenomenon of secondary diffusion—that is, the spread of sports to countries by nonnatives. The Swiss, for example, took football to southern Europe, with Hans Gamper famously founding FC Barcelona. The Swiss and French spread other sports to the rest of Europe, in particular the east. The Belgian and Italian governments sent emissaries around Europe to garner best practice for burgeoning educational programs at home, and a lively trade in translated books (e.g., Gutsmuth's treatises on gymnastics) carried information beyond the reach of mere political or trading influence. In the case of gymnastics and handball, we are dealing at most with a very soft power, since the harder variant van Bottenburg seems to impute in the nineteenth century to Germany (a country not united until 1871) hardly stands up to historical scrutiny. Gymnastics spread as much to countries that feared as that admired Germany (e.g., France). It was transformed in Czechoslovakia as an expression of resistance to German hegemony and in the so-called *Barrenstreit* was tempered by a gust of blow-back as Germans wrangled over the superior benefits of the Swedish form. Such caveats remind us that although sociological theses often are not supported by empirical historical investigation, they should encourage historians to paint from a broader palette. Van Bottenburg's twin claims, for instance, that the gym halls of Europe provided the infrastructure in which basketball and volleyball would later prosper and that these sports flourished precisely in the southern states of Turkey, Bulgaria, Italy, Spain, and Greece because late industrialization had left their sports space more open to late imports are hugely suggestive and worthy of close investigation.

Less subtle, however, are the politically based master narratives that dominate the big picture of European sports history—and these bring us to the third major issue in the field: its reluctance to give up long-cherished truths. This is particularly acute in Germany, where the moral maze of the two twentieth-century dictatorships continues to keep sports historians busy and much of the discipline's energy has consequently been sucked into political themes and debates. Two decades on from German reunification, details of the German Democratic Republic's (GDR) talent spotting, training methods, drug programs, and ideological manipulation of athletes have now been well established on the basis of a series of large-scale, archive-intense studies financed by central government sources.[20] Yet the recent past is far from over. Fifty percent of schoolchildren living in former East Germany are unaware of the nature of the GDR regime, and in the sporting realm, victims of doping live cheek by jowl with former coaches who deny all blame, while the Federal courts offer risible and undignified sums of victim compensation. Understandably, German sports historians are driven to invest in educational outreach, even to the point of repeating the obvious. More puzzling to the uninitiated is the same cohort's continued "hunt for Nazis." Considerable time is still spent establishing culpability in the National Socialist era—with the acerbic debates about the political colors of Carl Diem, the organizer of the 1936 Olympics a prime example[21]—and there has been little methodological innovation in the area. This strange situation, however, must be viewed in the light of the postwar consensus in the Federal Republic that sport and its functionaries (many of whose careers prospered long after 1945) had been innocent in the Third Reich, a myth that held throughout the Cold War but has now been dismantled. Each new federation that agrees to open its archives to warts-and-all investigation—as the German Football Association did before the 2006 World Cup—is applauded for its long-overdue stab of conscience.

What is morally right does not always make for exhilarating scholarship. And because the major sports history traditions outside Germany are located in Britain, France, and Scandinavia—the few major European states not to have been enveloped by some form of Fascism in the 1930s—there is a lack of motivation to refresh the German scene from without. While the grand span of the nineteenth century into the first half of the twentieth still traces sport's continued "innocence" in the liberal democracies and arcs toward sport's abuse under Fascist and totalitarian regimes, mainstream historians are now much less in thrall to such staid narratives. British historian of France Julian Jackson has recently noted, for instance:

> One certainly does not have to be an extreme post-modernist to be dissatisfied with some of the polarities which once presented themselves as a way of organizing a narrative of twentieth-century history. One such polarity might, for example, be the conflict between liberal democracy, on the one hand, and varieties of fascism, on the other, culminating in the triumph of the humane values of the liberal democratic model in western Europe after 1945. . . . liberal democracy was not always pluralist or tolerant, especially of ethnic and religious difference . . . and fascism could open up opportunities to social groups who had been excluded from traditional liberal politics. The frontiers between democracy and fascism could be blurred.[22]

Indeed, recent work in sports history has shown some promising signs of light and shade, even if these have not always been appreciated or fully acknowledged. The 1936 Olympics, the trusty perennial of Sports History 101, have been subject to careful revisionist assessment: even within national socialist structures, sport initially enjoyed relative autonomy; its functionaries, who had spent the previous decade fighting their cause against the Turner decision achieved considerable gains in finance and prestige and in 1936 were even granted a reprieve from the normal execution of Nazi business. The Berlin Olympics, therefore, mark a complex endpoint in the first phase of modern sport's development in Germany.[23] Swedish gymnastics, German Turnen, and British sport too—normally regarded in strict opposition to each other—are now sometimes portrayed in terms of their similarities: "their rational approach to the body and movement, their systematization of exercises, their claim to be of overall social significance, their connection with national traditions and myths, and their defined goals," which included "making a contribution to education, above all to a nationalist education, promoting a sense of national identity, and improving both public health and the population's ability to fight for its country."[24] While differences between these disciplines, such as nationalism versus internationalism, the collective versus the individual, cannot be ignored, considering their wider function within the societies in which they evolved gives a sense of the "structural narratives" (which extend from the mid-nineteenth to the late twentieth century) that Harvard historian Charles Maier recently championed over reductionist "moral narratives," which focus exclusively on the atrocities of the twentieth.[25]

The British and French cases are also being reevaluated. The untarnished image of British sports—previously set against the militarization and nationalistic agenda of the Fascist states—must now be considered in the light of the British government's own use of sport in the armed forces, its political investment in image projection at the interwar Olympics, and the sculpting of a national physique before the Second World War.[26] Across the channel, the emphasis on physical renewal under Vichy after the military defeat in 1940 can be traced not so much to direct Nazi influence but to similar developments in interwar France, where a sense of the interwoven crises of masculine and national virility led to a surge in physical activity.[27] This is not, of course, to say that Britain and France were pseudo-Fascist states—strikingly in both countries the far right had no monopoly on the discourses surrounding sport and fitness. But it is to suggest that more lateral and comparative thinking will ease sports history away from predictable moral narratives to which it has been so attached. After all, both the emergence of a mass culture of leisure and the increase of state power determine many aspects of European societies and polities in the first half of the twentieth century. Radio, glossy magazines, the daily press, and cinema newsreels made household names of the Finnish runner Paavo Nurmi, French boxer George Carpentier, British tennis player Fred Perry, and a host of other European sportsmen and women and their North American counterparts. And state involvement in health and organized leisure brought benefits, as Jackson notes, in "social democratic Sweden, conservative Britain, Nazi Germany, Fascist Italy, [and] Soviet Russia" alike.[28] Sports history could look very different in ten years' time if it continues to respond to the challenges set for it by the mainstream discipline.

A fundamental hurdle to arriving at a sound understanding of European sports history is the divergent research agendas followed by each national community. National perspectives are a natural phenomenon in the humanities, but the diminutive scale of the discipline denies sports history a critical mass of break-out or bridging scholars. The subject in Britain has been carried largely by social and cultural historians, in France by physical educational departments, and in Germany by specialist institutes anchored in kinesiology. Germany is strong on top-down institutional history, for example the gymnastics movement, workers' sport, and Jewish bodily culture, as well as the aforementioned National Socialist and GDR periods. France has focused with equal intensity on the gymnastics movement,[29] on the relationship between the educational system and the state, and—with a quite different texture—the theories and history of the body. Britain, without a native gymnastics tradition, has underemphasized physical education, overstressed the private schools, and avoided the state. Its historians have ploughed rich furrows, though, through the themes of class, economics, and identity. The finance of sport has been much less treated in France and Germany and identity differently in both. In Germany, this question is almost exclusively mired in National Socialism, although some excellent regional studies are now emerging to complement the general recognition in the historical mainstream of the importance of strong local affinities in the *Länder*; in France, too, regional variety is strongly emphasized alongside sport's role in uniting the nation, with the Tour de France only one example.[30] In Britain, by contrast, regional differences are understood in terms of antagonism, either between different codes of the same game (rugby league in the north of England, union in the south) or between the constituent nations that make up the British state.

Class—with its theoretical underpinnings in Marxism and the writings of Pierre Bourdieu and its innate ability to speak both to social and cultural branches of the profession—is the most important theme in northwest Europe, going by work already published and the potential for further growth. It has been relatively unimportant to date in France but vital to British and German historiographies, although in quite distinctive ways. In Germany, at first, a zealous blast of class critique after the student revolt skewed the field away from theory for a considerable period of time. Theodor Adorno asserted that "modern sports belong to the realm of unfreedom, no matter where they are organized,"[31] and cultural Marxists argued that sport was simply analogous to labor and the values and ideologies of advanced capitalist societies.[32] In England (and North America), by contrast, Marxist approaches to sport broke through a decade later, and this longer maturation process and the bulwark of wider and more sophisticated Marxist-inspired traditions in British social history generally allowed advocates to advance more sophisticated arguments that impacted significantly on the discipline—even if the category is too often reduced to the working class.

The complexities of class, however, are tricky to capture, as British writers have amply demonstrated. Martin Johnes summarizes the positions taken by three seminal mainstream historians thus: Eric Hobsbawm argued that "commercial leisure forms created a mass culture, which in turn fed class consciousness, enabling the rise of the Labour Party. In other words, leisure gave working men similar lives and thus helped them feel similar, thus underpinning the growth of a politicized class consciousness." Gareth Stedman Jones observed that "working men were largely non-political and that commercial leisure was beyond their control. It did, though, create 'a culture of consolation' that compensated for the hardships workers endured and contributed to their lack of radicalism."[33] And Ross McKibbin highlighted "the agency workers had over their free time, leisure and hobbies, but has argued that leisure did detract from political activism by absorbing working-class time and energy."[34] The differing opinions that emerge warn about the difficulty of extrapolating from of the detail of working-class culture but nonetheless collectively underscore the importance of understanding sport's contribution to this vital area of society.

Germany, having sidestepped the turbulence of Marxist revolt, has fallen back on its strengths in institutional history and considered class mainly within the framework of the workers' sports movement. This is understandable for two reasons: first, the economic miracle and social economic model of the Federal Republic rendered class distinctions largely obsolete after 1945; and second, with over 1.2 million and 125,000 members, respectively, Germany accounted for two-thirds of the Socialist Worker Sports International and 45 percent of its smaller Communist counterpart the Red Sport International. In this one area perhaps more than any other, excellent—although mainly top-down—comparative work has been conducted.[35]

As André Gounot has observed, the success of the movement stands in relation to the political and social integration of workers generally in the respective countries.[36] Thus the numbers are sparse in Britain and France (five thousand and six thousand in the census of 1931, equating to only 1 percent of the active sporting nation) because neither country had fostered a strong working-class counter-culture that would gain power or create "a new man." In England and Scotland, for instance, football had become *the* cohesion-building popular attraction, along with the music hall, for the urban working class, as had rugby in the mining towns and villages of the Welsh valleys. In Germany, the sociopolitical configuration was quite different due to the long stand-off between the Social Democratic Party and the establishment from Bismarckian times onward, and workers' sport became a strong third way in the 1920s between the bourgeois Turnen and sports and remained so until its immediate disbanding in 1933. The correlation between low integration and high membership of the movement is replicated by the relatively buoyant numbers in Finland, where a close-knit workers' culture existed at the time of Russian Tsarist rule.

A weakness of the German focus is that while it records the national movement's leaders' fears about the emerging consumer culture and the lure of spectator sport to sloth—concerns, incidentally, voiced with equal conviction by the adherents of bourgeois sport during the Weimar Republic, the National Socialists, and the French Front Populaire government from 1936[37]—it has little to say about the lived experience of working-class men or women. Many—perhaps even the vast majority of these—read tabloid newspapers bursting with sports news alongside the party paper; indulged their fantasies through glossy magazines; marveled at the latest exploits of professional sports men from around the world on the weekly news reels; and, of course, attended events organized in the sporting mainstream. Much work still remains to capture the typical patterns of such patchwork loyalties, identities, and habits of consumption in Germany as in other countries.

This chapter has concentrated on the main concerns of western European sports history from the nineteenth century until the Second World War, since the bulk of research to date engages with developments until that caesura. In each of the major historiographies, the post-1945 period is relatively underexplored, although this is changing over time and with the opening of archives. Sports historians have also been joined in their labors by economists and sociologists seeking to add time-depth to their exploration of contemporary phenomena. Nonetheless, serious desiderata remain. The 1950s, a period when much of the verve of the 1920s boom returned before consumerism set in for good and eroded the primacy of sports as a leisure spectacle, is a lost decade. There is a lack of any serious analysis of mass-participation sport across the continent and an overconcentration on cities over regions, centers over peripheries. A great deal has been written about football, its professionalization, mediatization, and globalization, and about representational aspects of the Olympic Games—to the detriment, in most countries, of in-depth studies on football outside the upper echelons, cycling, motor sports, athletics, and swimming, to name but a few. As Martin Johnes aptly observes, what is currently studied is sadly "a greater reflection of the contemporary popularity of different sports than of their popularity in the past."[38]

The history of postwar Europe can be painted in three broad brush strokes: increasing affluence in the West, the Cold War, and the increasing integration of European states, politically via the European Economic Community and its later iterations and in sport primarily via Europe-wide club football competitions that began with the romance of midweek matches under the floodlights in the late 1950s and wrote itself into the popular imagination via triumph (the multiple title winning Real Madrid) and disaster (the Munich air disaster that devastated Manchester United's Busby Babes). Most major projects have engaged or will have to engage with one or more of these wider themes.

The effects of affluence on sport are the least studied aspect, despite the stunning general statistics and complex patterns in sport. Germany's growth rate measured 7.4 percent in the decade up to 1959, with France averaging a decent 4.5 percent and Britain lagging behind at 2.4 percent. Such was the transformation of everyday lives that general historians have wondered whether the economic boom of the third quarter is actually the twentieth century's most significant feature.[39] Sport and leisure came to be seen as an important feature of the parties of center right and left in the western European democracies, and increased urbanization and the building of new towns offered ready-made opportunities for sports policies to be transformed into infrastructural reality. Participation in team sports declined over the long postwar boom, and individual sports such as tennis, previously the preserve of elites, grew in popularity as the middle class expanded. But at the same time, football, its honeymoon period over, underwent what sociologist Tony King has described as a lengthy phase of Eurosclerosis, particularly in the most affluent nations of the Northwest.[40] The 1970s and 1980s were marked by drastically emptying stadiums and often marred by aggression and violence, both domestically and in the international sphere, in Britain, Holland, and Germany, while a livelier and generally more peaceful fan culture enveloped the nations of the South, including France. While hooliganism has been well researched in individual countries, it could be extended into a comparative dimension and explored in the general context of increasing prosperity and the growth of other sports.

Football, Europe's dominant sport, was to be saved by television—the medium that had helped put it under threat as the purchase of sets spread across the continent in the 1960s and 1970s—with the advent of cable and satellite technology in the late 1980s and the money that subsequently flooded into the game in previously unimaginable sums as the major domestic leagues transformed into global brands. It would be easy to lump these later developments in the Northwest together—but contemporary observers already note how the football systems of the different countries vary, sometimes quite strikingly, in their operational structures and traditions.[41] They have also fed off each other in intriguing ways as sporting bodies looked to neighboring countries for examples of successful sport development programs.

This last point opens up onto some of the more innovative work conducted on sports in the Cold War, a period that ended with the fall of the Iron Curtain in 1989, a year after East Germany, with a population of 17 million, defeated the United States at the Olympics, and thus forms a powerful conjuncture with the revolution in television.[42] Not merely a conflict between the United States and the Soviet Union, or even between capitalism/democracy and communism, the Cold War was a far-reaching combination of negotiations and conflicts in which nations and peoples sought effective ways of promoting their political, social, and economic development. Sport was uniquely positioned between high politics and diplomacy on the one hand and the television screens and back pages of newspapers consumed across the social spectrum in countries around the world on the other. As an endeavor in which results could be easily measured and quickly understood, and in which connections and rivalries flourished across national borders, international sport assumed arguably more significance for governments and societies in this period than at any other stage in its history.[43] This was no more so than in divided Germany, which served as a lightning rod for the tensions of the era and whose serial diplomatic fracas have been well described by scholarship.[44]

The sports systems of this period in the East and West tend to be imagined as photographic negatives of each other. In the West, the story goes, sport was characterized by individual freedoms, political and bureaucratic decentralization, insufficient medical and scientific support, and problems of identifying young talent. In the East, sport was top-down and all-encompassing. Seen as a vital contribution to the intellectual and physical development of the "socialist personality," it was organized according to the principles of the planned economy and regulated via myriad forms of technical and infrastructural support. This black-and-white snapshot presents a certain likeness, but it misrepresents the picture as a whole.

Although both German states approached the issue from different ideological bases, changes in the one led to inevitable catch-up moves in the other: always lagging some way behind, the West was nonetheless dragged up, like a second climber attached to a leader by rope.[45] France provides another striking example of this process of response. De Gaulle's assumption of power in 1958 and the creation of a more powerful and presidential Fifth Republic brought with it a new agenda for national competitiveness—*la France qui gagne*—and led to a government outcry over the poor performance of France at the 1960 Olympics. The subsequent successes of the rival Germans only sharpened the French sense of failure, which led to a new manifestation of a long-standing discourse of decline. This was taken up by the Gaullists who formally legislated in 1975 to provide public funds for the identification and training of elite athletes, both in Olympic sport and football.[46] The successive waves of French footballing excellence in the 1980s and 1990s are in large part due to these measures.

In the post–Cold War era, the GDR system—state-sponsored doping aside—crystallized out as the very model of modern elite sports. At the same time, direct lines of influence can also be drawn: Australia explicitly drew on East German expertise after

1989 to fuel its academies in preparation for the Sydney Olympics, and Britain looked to its Commonwealth cousins as it in turn geared up for London 2012. By this stage, Britain's greatest Olympian, Sir Steve Redgrave, was already being coached by an East German.

Structurally, the story of sport in northwest Europe, therefore, ends where it began: with the free flow of talent and expertise across the continent. If sports history can rethink "Europe's age of fascism" in less obviously moralistic ways and continue to break down the binaries of the Cold War, this transnational dimension could become the defining feature of the subject.

NOTES

1. Maarten van Bottenburg, *Global Games* (Urbana and Chicago: University of Illinois Press, 2001), 10–45.
2. Richard Holt, "Ireland and the Birth of Modern Sport," in *The Gaelic Athletic Association, 1884–2009*, ed. Mike Cronin, William Murphy and Paul Rouse (Dublin: Irish Academic Press, 2009), 33–46, quote on 41.
3. Overviews of this extensive literature are given in S. W. Pope and John Nauright, eds., *Routledge Companion to Sports History* (London: Routledge, 2010); the forum section of *Journal of Sport History* 38.2 (2011); Kay Schiller and Christopher Young, "The History and Historiography of Sport in Germany: Social, Cultural and Political Perspectives," *German History* 27.3 (2009): 313–330.
4. See the Sport in Modern Europe Project, sponsored by the UK's Arts and Humanities Research Council: htpp://www.sport-in-europe.group.cam.ac.uk.
5. Paul Dietschy and Richard Holt, "Sports History in France and Britain: National Agendas and European Perspectives," *Journal of Sport History* 37.1 (2010): 83–98, quote on 93.
6. Paul Dietschy, "French Sport: Caught between Universalism and Exceptionalism," *European Review* 19.4 (2011): 509–525.
7. Niels Kayser Nielsen and John Bale, "Scandinavia," *Journal of Sport History* 38.2 (2011): 223–236, quote on 233–234.
8. Holt, "Ireland and the Birth of Modern Sport," 45.
9. Henning Eichberg, *Der Weg des Sports in die industrielle Civilisation* (Baden-Baden: Nomos, 1973); *Leistung Sport, Geschwindigkeit: Sport und Tanz im gesellschaftlichen Wandel des 18./19. Jahrhunderts* (Stuttgart: Klett-Cotta, 1978).
10. Peter Borscheid, *Das Tempo-Virus: Eine Kulturgeschichte der Beschleunigung* (Frankfurt and New York: Campus, 2004), 176–192.
11. John Bale and Chris Philo, "Introduction," in *Henning Eichberg—Body Cultures: Essays on Sport, Space and Identity* (London and New York: Routledge, 1998), 3–21, quote on 4.
12. Joan W. Scott, "Gender: A Useful Category of Historical Knowledge," *The American Historical Review* 91 (1986): 1053–1075, quote on 1055.
13. Stefan Szymanski, "A Theory of the Evolution of Modern Sport," *Journal of Sport History* 35.1 (2008): 1–32, quote on 3.
14. Szymanski, "A Theory," 3.
15. See, for instance, the articles in *Journal of Sport History* 35.1 (2008).
16. Jonathan Morris, "Europe Versus America?" *European Review* 19.4 (2011): 611–616.

17. Wolfgang Behringer, "Arena and Pall Mall: Sport in the Early Modern Period," *German History* 27.3 (2009): 331–357.

18. Heikki Lempa, *Beyond the Gymnasium: Educating the Middle-Class Bodies in Classical Germany* (Lanham, MD: Lexington Books, 2007), esp. 67–111.

19. van Bottenburg, *Global Games*, 42.

20. This body of work is considerable. The key scholars are Hans-Joachim Teichler, Lorenz Peiffer, and Giselher Spitzer; English-language syntheses are given by Christopher Young, "East Versus West: Sport as a German Cold War Phenomenon," in *Divided But Not Disconnected: German Experiences of the Cold War*, ed. Tobias Hochscherf, Christoph Laucht, and Andrew Plowman (New York and Oxford: Berghahn, 2010), 148–162; Mike Dennis and Jonathan Grix, *Sport Under Communism: Behind the East German "Miracle"* (London: Palgrave, 2012).

21. See the special issue on Carl Diem: *Zeitschrift für Geschichtswissenschaft* 59.3 (2011).

22. Julian Jackson, "Introduction," in *Europe 1900–1945*, ed. Julian Jackson (Oxford: Oxford University Press, 2002), 1–15, quote on 4.

23. Christopher Young, "A Victory for the Olympic Idea: Berlin 1936 in its Sporting and Socio-Cultural Contexts," *Stadion: Internationale Zeitschrift für Geschichte des Sports* 33 (2007): 1–27.

24. Gertrud Pfister, "Cultural Confrontations: German *Turnen*, Swedish Gymnastics and English Sport—European Diversity in Physical Activities from a Historical Perspective," *Culture, Sport, Society* 6.1 (2006): 61–91, quote on 73; Alan Tomlinson and Christopher Young, "Towards a New History of European Sport," *European Review* 19.4 (2011): 487–507. For the retention of the opposite view, see Christiane Eisenberg, "Towards a New History of European Sport," *European Review* 19.4 (2011): 617–622.

25. Charles S. Maier, "Consigning the Twentieth Century to History: Alternative Narratives for the Modern Era," *The American Historical Review* 105.3 (2000): 807–831.

26. Tony Mason and Eliza Riedi, *Sport and the Military: The British Armed Forces 1880–1960* (Cambridge, UK: Cambridge University Press, 2010); Ina Zweiniger-Bargielowska, *Managing the Body: Beauty, Health, and Fitness in Britain 1880–1939* (Oxford: Oxford University Press, 2010).

27. Joan Tumblety, *Remaking the Male Body: Masculinity and the Uses of Physical Culture in Interwar and Vichy France* (Oxford: Oxford University Press, 2012).

28. Jackson, "Introduction," 11.

29. For a classic account, see Eugen Weber, "Gymnastics and Sports in Fin-de-Siècle France: Opium of the Classes?" *The American Historical Review* 76 (1971): 70–98.

30. Christopher S. Thompson, *The Tour de France: A Cultural History* (Los Angeles and Berkeley: University of California Press, 2006).

31. Theodor Adorno, *Prisms*, trans. Samuel and Shierry Weber (London: Spearman, 1967), 81.

32. See, for instance, Bero Rigauer, *Sport und Arbeit* (Frankfurt: Suhrkamp, 1969).

33. Johnes, "Great Britain," 447.

34. Johnes, "Great Britain," 447.

35. Eike Stiller, ed., *Literatur zur Geschichte des Arbeitersports in Deutschland von 1892 bis 2005: Eine Bibliographie* (Berlin: Trafo, 2006).

36. André Gounot, *Die Rote Sportinternationale, 1921–1937: Kommunistische Massenpolitik im europäischen Arbeitersport* (Münster: LIT Verlag, 2002).

37. Nicholas Hewitt, "Introduction: Popular Culture and Mass Culture," *Contemporary European History* 8.3 (1999): 351–358.

38. Martin Johnes, "Putting the History into Sport: On Sport History and Sport Studies in the U.K." *Journal of Sport History* 31.2 (2004): 153.
39. Rosemary Wakeman, ed., *Themes in Modern European History since 1945* (London: Routledge, 2003).
40. Anthony King, *The European Ritual* (Aldershot, UK: Ashgate, 2003).
41. Arne Niemann, Borja Garcia, and Wyn Grant, eds., *The Transformation of European Football: Towards the Europeanisation of the National Game* (Manchester: Manchester University Press, 2011).
42. Richard Holt, Alan Tomlinson, and Christopher Young, "Sport in Europe 1950–2010: Transformation and Trends," in *Sport and the Transformation of Modern Europe* (London: Routledge, 2011), 1–17.
43. See in general Stephen Wagg and David Andrews, eds., *East Plays West: Sport and the Cold War* (London: Routledge, 2007).
44. Summarized in Kay Schiller and Christopher Young, *The 1972 Munich Olympics and the Making of Modern Germany* (Los Angeles and Berkeley: University of California Press, 2010), 157–186.
45. Uta Balbier, *Kalter Krieg auf der Aschenbahn: der deutsch-deutsche Sport 1950–1972* (Paderborn: Schöning, 2007).
46. Lindsay Krasnoff, *The Making of Les Bleus: Sport in France, 1958–2010* (New York: Lexington Books, 2012).

BIBLIOGRAPHY

Dietschy, Paul, and Patrick Clastres. *Sport, Société et Culture en France du XIXème Siècle à Nos Jours*. Paris: Hachette, 2006.
Eisenberg, Christiane. *"English Sports" und Deutsche Bürger: Eine Gesellschaftsgeschichte 1800–1939*. Paderborn: Schöningh, 1999.
Holt, Richard. *Sport and Society in Modern France*. London: Macmillan, 1981.
Holt, Richard. *Sport and the British: A Modern History*. Oxford: Oxford University Press, 1989.
Holt, Richard, and Tony Mason. *Sport in Britain 1945–2000*. Oxford: Blackwell, 2000.
Nielsen, Niels Kayser. *Body, Sport and Society in Norden: Essays in Cultural History*. Aarhus, Denmark: Aarhus University Press, 2005.
Schiller, Kay, and Christopher Young, eds. *Special Issue: German Sport. German History* 27.3 (2009).

CHAPTER 23

SPORT IN SOUTHERN EUROPE

ANDREW McFARLAND

SINCE the nineteenth century, sport in Southern Europe has become intertwined with identity, politics, consumerism, and culture. It is difficult to imagine Spain, Italy, Portugal, or Greece without the whole range of competitive athletic endeavors and football in particular. The region houses some of the world's most legendary football clubs, such as A. C. Milan, Juventus, F. C. Barcelona, and Real Madrid, and prominent leagues, such as Serie A and the Primera Liga, which have deep-rooted connections to the political, economic, and social histories of their cities, regions, and nations. Beyond football, Southern Europe has hosted six Olympic Games and boasts several unique connections to sport, most notably Greece's Olympic heritage and the influence of fascism.

This chapter explores these themes to draw a broad outline of sport's development in the region and set out the most important issues this growth has faced. Geographically, Italy and Spain receive the most attention as Southern Europe's largest nations and dominant sporting cultures, but examples are occasionally drawn from Greece, Portugal, and the former Yugoslavia when they provide examples of common regional experiences or exceptional cases. The first portion of the chapter looks at the introduction of modern sport to the region, particularly some of the initial challenges it faced as a new foreign activity forging an audience within well-established cultures. The second section shifts attention to the connections between sport and identity throughout the twentieth century with special attention to political regimes; national, regional, and civic identities; as well as the development of strong sporting clubs that served larger roles in their communities. Last, some changes in the later third of the twentieth century are discussed, namely the rise of Spanish sport and the growth of basketball in the region.

As elsewhere in the world, the countries of Southern Europe were introduced to most modern sports by foreigners during the mid- to late nineteenth century through trade and educational connections. By the period from the 1880s through the start of World War I, a few sports had gained significant traction by establishing numerous clubs, along with national competitions and federations. Sections of the urban upper and middle classes comprised the most common pioneers in these ventures because of their connections to other European countries, particularly Great Britain, France, Switzerland, and Germany. These early sportsmen combined the affluence necessary to engage in new forms of conspicuous consumption with a desire to display their rising importance in the community as both individuals and as an emergent social class. They became actively engaged in football, cycling, and gymnastics and to a lesser degree in swimming, hiking, track and field, tennis, and other activities. In the process, these activities gradually expanded their influence into each nation's daily life.

In the Spanish case, a few writers have discussed the introduction of non-native sports primarily by British, French, and Swiss nationals, often through business and educational connections. A classic example is the first football club established in the nation, Recreativo de Huelva, which was founded in 1889 by British employees of the Rio Tinto copper mines in southwestern Spain for which Huelva was the point of embarkation of their shipments.[1] Similarly, the iron and coal trade between the Basque Country and Britain (and the educational connections that fostered) introduced football to that region, while French nationals connected to an international oil company brought gymnastics to Madrid, leading to the creation of the Federacíon Gimnástica Española in 1902. On the educational side, the liberal and pro-European Institución Libre de Enseñanza in Madrid imported modern pedagogy into Spain, bringing with it football and other sports. The school's educators and graduates then founded Real Madrid, helped send Spain's observing representatives to the Olympic Congress at the Sorbonne, and played other key roles in establishing sport in the country. The new activities initially drew interest primarily in Madrid, Barcelona, and the Basque Country because of a combination of urban concerns, the national desire for "regeneration," and the growth of the urban middle classes who used sport to create new identities.

Italy experienced similar, albeit earlier, development. Its strongest foreign influences came from Britain and central Europe. Instead of coal or copper interests, the British had connections to the emerging cities of Northern Italy as an ideal stopping point during trips through the Mediterranean to India.[2] As a result, British nationals established Italy's first football club in 1893—Genoa Cricket and Football Club. This was followed by another pair of British nationals who founded A. C. Milan in 1899, and locals gradually nationalized both. Gymnastics was introduced in Italy even earlier when King Carlo Alberto of Piedmont brought in a Swiss educator to teach a version of Turnen to his army in 1831. This led to the establishment of the Turin Gymnastic Society in 1844. It became an organization that actively supported Piedmont's successful push for national unification through the 1870s, echoing the role Turnen played in Germany.

One of the key hurdles modern sport had to surmount in each case, therefore, was the inherently foreign nature of the new activity. This was doubly true because the region's nations were sensitive to the correct perception that they had fallen behind and become weaker than their northern neighbors. In Spain, such fears dated to the loss of much of their empire after the Napoleonic Wars, an old wound reopened humiliatingly for the world to see during the Spanish-American War of 1898. Italy had similar issues rooted in their newness as a nation and a desire to construct an empire with the ghosts of the

Roman past at their back. The region's nations were also conscious of their industrial weakness having attained only regional industrial development in Northern Italy, Catalonia, and the Basque Country and barely even that in Portugal and Greece. Even the cases of regional industrialization produced problems as those areas developed a more international or "European" outlook that differentiated them from the rest of their nations, including the less industrial national capitals of Madrid and Rome. This recognition of their imperial, military, and industrial weaknesses made the idea of national "regeneration" a common theme in Spain and Italy. Arguments for how to achieve such regeneration ranged widely from conservatives who reasserted traditional moral and religious values to liberals who advocated opening the national floodgates to the sciences, democratic government, and more flexible social mores. All of these changes made the nations of Southern Europe sensitive to accepting such new ideas as modern sport into their national cultures.

A balance was struck that included claiming their own authorship over some of the new activities, asserting unique connections to international sports, and simply nationalizing the new activities as quickly as possible. One example comes from Spain, which had an authentic, century-old, mass entertainment activity of its own, the *corrida* or bullfight. The historian Adrian Shubert has effectively argued that, by the end of the eighteenth century, bullfighting had become an established activity that then took off as a mass spectacle in the nineteenth with a dramatic rise in the number of annual *corridas*, bullfighters' fees, and purpose-built bullrings.[3] In the 1910s and 1920s, bullfighting reached new heights of popularity, led by the *toreros* Joselito and Juan Belmonte. However, while the institutions surrounding bullfighting were certainly those of a modern sport, the on-field event itself only debatably fell into that category. Instead, because of the bloody nature of the spectacle and its traditional roots, bullfighting became a symbol of the nation's backwardness and antiquarianism instead of the modernity that underlay its bureaucratic organization.

Greece also has a claim to a unique role in the sporting world through the Olympic Games. Not only had the Games been a tradition in the classical world, but Greek attempts to revive them predated the efforts of Pierre de Coubertin. The wealthy Greek patriot Evanghelos Zappas first sought their revival and managed to organize in Athens an event of debatable success in 1859.[4] When he died, Zappas left his estate to these games, leading to subsequent competitions in 1870, 1875, and 1889 and the construction of a meeting hall and gymnasium. The events lapsed at this point for a want of local organization and funding but not interest. When Coubertin launched his revival of the games, he appointed Demetrios Bikelas as the first president of the International Olympic Committee (IOC). Bikelas had connections to Zappas's revival games and enabled Coubertin to ally this local enthusiasm with the money, organization, and international stature he provided. Coubertin's 1896 revival of the games in Athens proved a great success, not least of which for King George I of Greece and his son Constantine, who used the event's success to shore up their control over the country. During his speech at the banquet closing the 1896 Games, George argued that Athens should host the next games, but the combination of military defeat by the Ottoman Empire, bankruptcy, and Courbertin's preference for the now-familiar rotation of cites thwarted this desire. Nonetheless, the Greeks maintained their interest and convinced the IOC to let them host another event in 1906, now referred to as the Intercalated Games because of their placement in between two regular events. Though later removed from official Olympic history, the Intercalated Games were a surprising success partially because they focused exclusively on sport over only a few weeks. This helped them avoid getting subsumed within the larger World's Fairs that enveloped the 1900 and 1904 Olympics. As a result of these events, Greece's unique Olympic connection has a mixed legacy. On one hand, it has hosted several events and received significant international attention. On the other, the nation's athletes and infrastructure have often struggled to live up to this special position in the sports world. Regardless, the Games clearly play a significant role in the nation's political and cultural history, yet there is little academic literature that focuses on these internal effects instead of the importance of the Greek games to Olympic history.

The most common response to the foreign nature of modern sport in Southern Europe, especially Spain and Italy, was to nationalize it as swiftly and thoroughly as possible. As discussed previously, the Italians adopted Turnen gymnastics as part of their nineteenth-century movement toward unification, directly adopting the sporting activity and transposing its message of national strength through physical fitness from Germany to their own cause. The Italians also appropriated football by rebranding their version of the English sport as *calico* or *calico Fiorentino*. The process of nationalizing football reached a first crescendo in 1909 when the Italian national football association replaced the word "football" with *calico* in its name.[5] Later, the Mussolini government embraced this process in the 1920s, typified by the journalist Amerigo Bresci's lengthy argument in 1925 that Italian football originated from a medieval game played in Florence. With this justification in place, Bresci and other Italians launched into a much more common means of nationalizing a foreign sport: asserting the use of their own language within the game. As Simon Martin has effectively detailed, "To educate the readership and reinforce the modern game's Italian identity, Bresci assembled a glossary of foreign words and their 'correct' Italian counterparts. These ranged from standard terms such as a goal kick (*calico di rinvio*), forward (*attacante*) and 'kich-off' [sic] (*calico d'inizio*) to the more bizarre or specialized plungeon (*tuffo: uno dei caratteristici movimenti del portiere per impedire che la palla entri in porta*) and daisy-cutter (*tiro radente, o raso terra*)."[6] Those who preferred the English words were criticized in the press and generally pressured to use the Italian terms. Niccolo Carosio, Italy's foremost football radio announcer, reinforced their use during his broadcasts in the 1920s and 1930s.

Linguistic nationalization occurred in Spain as well, but it was more contested than in Italy because of Spain's weaker national identity. On a basic level most clubs gradually migrated from the English phrase "football club" to the hispanized *club de fútbol* to emphasize the Castilian version of the English words; however, as cognates such changes were quite superficial. Starting in 1907, the journalist Mariano de Cavia organized a newspaper campaign against the use of English football terms.[7] He supported the direct invention of a Castilian vocabulary for football including terms like *saque de esquina* (corner), *fuera de juego* (offsides), and *balompié* (a literal translation of foot/*pié* and ball/*balón*) that were adopted to varying degrees. *Balompié* became something of a touchstone for the issue when clubs like Real Betis in Sevilla used it to replace "football" in their names as a way to assert their Spanish identity in the 1910s. Nonetheless, other groups resisted using the Castilian terms, sometimes as a form of regional resistance and other times simply because they found it awkward. Ricardo Ruíz Ferry, a leading Spanish sports journalist of the period, argued that with good or bad pronunciations most Spaniards used "offside" or "corner" instead of their equivalents because translating everything was simply impractical. Alexandre Barba echoed this in his 1910s sports manual that included a vocabulary section, of which forty-three terms were either English words or cognates ranging from "back" and "kick" to "goal keeper" and "*triangulación.*" In the 1950s, the Franco government again promoted the translation of football language into Castilian but also failed to change the national culture, leaving the modern usage a thorough mix. As these conclusions suggest, in both Italy and Spain solid studies have been done into the use of language in sport though more remains to provide a nuanced view that considers differences in region, sport, and time period. Fortunately, such work continues through projects such as the online Spanish journal *Idioma y Deporte.*

By the end of World War I, sport had become an increasingly popular activity in Southern Europe. It played an ever larger role in national cultures from the 1920s onward. During this time, a number of common issues shaped the region's sports cultures, most notably the involvement of strong central (usually Fascist) governments, tensions between each nation's core and periphery, and the large size and influence that clubs and stadia attained. Easily the aspect of sport in the region most discussed by academics has been the involvement of governments and in particular the connection between Fascism and sport. With a few exceptions, these studies focus primarily on football and bolster sports history's credibility in the larger field because of the insights they provide into how political movements used social and entertainment activities to shape their societies.

On the most basic level, all the centralizing, conservative dictators throughout the region, either overtly or tacitly, connected themselves to football clubs in their national capitals. Francisco Franco and Real Madrid FC are the most famous iteration of this, and many have suggested that the club became an important piece of Spanish diplomacy during the 1950s and 1960s. During that period, many of Spain's regular diplomatic and cultural connections with its neighbors were severed because of the conservative Franco government's survival after its ideological allies were defeated in World War II. However, similar identifications of ruler to club existed between Lisbon's Benfica and António Salazar in Portugal and Athens' Panathinaikos and the Colonels government in Greece.[8] The Italian case even reveals direct involvement when in 1927 the National Fascist Party ordered Rome's older teams to combine and form AS Roma with the explicit goal of creating a club capable of challenging those of Northern Italy in the name of the national capital.

Beyond the association of certain clubs with political leaders, Fascist governments used sport as a means to shape and control their nations in numerous ways. In Spain, such discussions focus on the Franco Regime from the Spanish Civil War through the 1970s where, as noted earlier, Real Madrid became a symbol of Spanish nationalism internally and internationally through a combination of official support and fantastic on-field success. Duncan Shaw opened this topic for academic study with *Fútbol y franquismo* in which he confronted the regime's use of football as a distraction from Spain's economic depression and political repression.[9] More recent authors like Carlos Fernández Santander have addressed similar themes, again emphasizing the sport's role as a distraction from political life. He detailed the Spanish government's reorganization of Atlético de Madrid and other clubs after the Civil War to mitigate their role as focal points of resistance to the central government.[10] Most writers since have agreed that Franco used sport primarily as a distraction and focus for Spanish nationalism, not as a means to reshape Spanish society. This more limited goal reflected the Franco government's general aim of reasserting traditional, Catholic culture and societal norms that have led historians to debate how Fascist the Franco regime actually was. It also resulted from Spain's exceptionally weak economic position after 1945 because the country simply lacked the finances for comprehensive goals.

The situation was significantly different in Italy where Mussolini's Fascist government held sway from 1922 through World War II and overtly used sport as a means to mold the Italian people. Most generally, Victoria de Grazia's work focuses on the Fascist government's larger reorganization of leisure, which included the promotion of recreational sports and competitions.[11] Other writers focus directly on Fascism and sport. Through several works, Simon Martin discusses the Italian government's reorganization of *calico* from Serie A through recreational play starting in 1926, the planning and building for the 1934 World Cup,[12] and the role of athletes as "soldiers of sport."[13] Similarly, Gigliola Gori focuses on how the Fascist movement specifically targeted women when reshaping Italian physical culture,[14] and Alessio Ponzio investigates the establishment of a sport university in Rome whose graduates were expected to create a Fascist generation.[15] The project's success is debatable, but it provides a valuable avenue through which to explore the Regime's goals. Overall, these works show that Italian Fascism strove aggressively to use sport more than its counterparts in Spain.

While centralizing governments certainly influenced Southern European sports communities, regional forces did so as well. Sports clubs offered a powerful public medium for establishing regional and civic identities, often in resistance to the national core as embodied most famously by the role of FC Barcelona as an outlet for Catalan nationalism. Since 1908, the club has recruited local political leaders, chosen colors, and used many other tactics to affiliate itself with *catalanismo*.[16] Then, during the 1950s, it became a focus for anti-Franco Catalan resistance, as discussed in depth by Carles Santacana. By the end of the twentieth century, Barça epitomized its slogan *més que un club* (more than a club) because of its prominence in the city and region.[17] Much the same can be said for Athletic de Bilbao, which has also received the attention of academic writers as a flagship institution for Basque nationalism. Authors have chronicled Athletic's history, its persistence in fielding exclusively ethnic Basque players, and its connection to the city of Bilbao itself.[18] Yet these are only the two most famous of numerous examples of this phenomenon. Real Sociedad de San Sebastian also represents Basque identity, while SSC Napoli is a standard bearer for Neapolitan identity, especially after the success it achieved with Diego Maradona in the 1980s. Northern Italy's cities also have a long history of independence and well-established civic identities that the arrival of football helped sustain. Clubs like Juventus of Turin, AC and Inter Milan, and Genoa CFC swiftly became centers for civic identity within each city through consistent success against Italian and European competition.[19] In the region's smaller nations, FC Porto garnered significant support as the only one of Portugal's *tres grandes* not based in Lisbon, while clubs from Thessalonika played a similar role in Greece as the most successful opposition to the dominant Athenian organizations. With significant attention to Southern Europe, Christos Kassimeris has delved into the myriad of European club crests, slogans, and other symbols revealing dozens of examples that illustrate how clubs embedded themselves into their respective civic cultures and histories, yet many opportunities remain.[20]

The strong connection between clubs and civic identities is rooted in their foundation by the merchant elite and business bourgeoisie of their respective cities. These groups were the first to cleave to foreign sport, and they had the business acumen to recognize the potential profitability and use for political mobilization that a sports organization represented. Many of these sports clubs in Spain, Italy, and other areas around the Mediterranean swiftly became multisport organizations that dominated athletic competition of all sorts in their localities. For example, the founders of Club Gimnàstic de Tarragona established it in 1898 as a gymnastics organization, but by 1922 they had developed sections dedicated to ten different sports ranging from football to Basque pelota and fencing.[21] Today the largest football clubs often dominate competition in numerous in other sports, notably FC Barcelona, Real Madrid, Panathinaikos, and Olympiacos, who lead their respective nations' professional basketball leagues as well.

These organizations own their own massive, multisport complexes, usually on either one or two sites, including three of Europe's largest stadia, Real Madrid's Santiago Bernabeu (completed in 1947), FC Barceloan's Nou Camp (dedicated in 1957), and SL Benfica's Estádio da Luz in Lisbon (the original stadium was completed in 1954 and then replaced with a larger version in 2003).[22] As of 2017, the grounds at Camp Nou contain a gigantic stadium, secondary stadium, museum and archive, indoor arena for basketball and other sports, dorms for youth players, tourist shops, and practice fields. Real Madrid has developed a similar complex, establishing Ciudad Deportiva in 1963 in northern Madrid complete with training facilities, indoor stadium, and member facilities like tennis courts and a pool. Other clubs around the region have similar facilities, including Benfica's Caixa Futebol Campus and AC Milan's Milanello Sport Center.

Southern European clubs also commonly work with city, regional, and national governments to construct shared, multipurpose facilities that provide a common focus for their city's sporting and entertainment life. Fascist Italy epitomized this approach, having supported the construction of monumental stadia in Florence, Bologna, and Rome for the 1934 World Cup along with Rome's multisport Foro Italico complex.[23] In other cases, multiple clubs share common facilities as with Estadio Olympico (1932) in Rome, San Siro (1926) in Milan, and Olympic Stadium in Athens (1982). As the names suggest, many of these were constructed as part of Olympic building projects, a tradition that includes Barcelona's Estadi Olímpic Lluís Companys (originally built in 1927). Clearly, then, Southern Europe has a wealth of large-scale sports facilities, representing millions of euros in investment and going back as far as the 1920s. Simon Martin has written about the role this stadium building played in Italy's national and political culture, and Pierre Lanfranchi has done so more generally for the entire region, but there remains much to explain on the topic.

In the last decades of the twentieth and first decade of the twenty-first century, the Southern European sports world changed yet again with the fading of the last authoritarian governments, conclusion of the Cold War, and growing influence of US consumerism. This period witnessed a period of competitive success for Spain that reflected its economic rise and reintegration into the European mainstream. The region also embraced basketball as much as any other part of Europe and indeed the world, developing and sustaining important leagues in Spain, Italy, and Greece.

Since the late 1970s, Spain has blossomed as a powerful force in an array of sports. This rise largely correlates with the nation's economic growth over the past quarter century and the democratic constitution's allocation of significant powers to regional governments that have used sport to promote their local identities. Naturally, the 1992 Barcelona Olympics that ended the Olympic Cold War era, crowned Juan Antonio Samaranch's reign as president of the IOC, and spurred a new generation of Spanish athletes were of vital significance for this change. Those Games have received significant scholarly attention through support from the Barcelona Olympic Foundation itself, often in conjuction with the city's universities like the Centre d'Estudis Olímpics at the Universitat Autònoma de Barcelona. As a result, Miquel de Moragas, the Centre, and others like John Hargreaves have produced numerous books and conference anthologies on the organization and effects of the 1992 Games, their connection to television and the Internet, regional and national symbolism, economic impact, and urban planning.[24]

Beyond the Olympics, Spanish football has also experienced a great deal of success. The country hosted the 1982 World Cup, and the sport has since moved into a new golden age in the 1990s and 2000s. The Primera Liga has become one of the most respected football leagues in the world, Real Madrid CF and FC Barcelona have cemented their position as two of the world's most influential and successful club teams, and the national side has won international acclaim with consecutive victories in Euro 2008, the 2010 World Cup, and Euro 2012. Not surprisingly, Spain's football success has quickly drawn academic attention, most notably Alejandro Quiroga's recent investigation into the changes success brings to discussions of the national team's identity as well as many of the studies on earlier time periods previously discussed.[25]

Beyond football, the country has developed strong traditions in a variety of sports. In tennis, Manuel Santana was the first Spaniard to become successful in the 1960s, and by the early 1990s the country had produced so many competitive players that some announcers regularly referred to them as the "Spanish Armada." This group consisted mostly of clay-court specialists, but since the foundation of Barcelona's Academia Sánchez-Casal in 1998 Spanish players have increasingly found success on all surfaces. This growth yielded competitors of the highest quality and profile like Arantxa Sánchez Vicario on the women's side and Rafael Nadal on the men's side. Spain has also produced numerous internationally competitive cyclists and hosts the Vuelta de España, one of cycling's three Grand Tours along with the Tour de France and Giro d'Italia. As with tennis, Spanish cyclists have included competitors of the highest caliber since the 1980s such as Tour de France champions Miguel Indurain and Alberto Contador. In golf there was again a successful pioneer, Seve Ballasteros in the late 1970s, who brought the sport to prominence within the country and inspired later generations of internationally successful golfers like José María Olazábal and Sergio García. Ballasteros also helped bring the first Ryder Cup to continental Europe at Valderrama Golf Club in 1997, establishing Spain's ability to host events in the sport, not only produce athletes. This role as a host for high-profile sporting events can also be seen in sailing, where America's Cup defender Alighi selected Valencia to host their 2007 and 2010 cup defenses. All of these achievements demonstrate that Spain has risen significantly in the sports world in a variety of sports since the 1980s.

Perhaps the most important change throughout the region has been the growth of basketball into a significant sport. After basketball's invention in 1891, YMCA connections quickly introduced it to Europe, and then US soldiers during both World War I and World War II sparked further interest. When eight European nations founded the Fédération Internationale de Basketball in 1932 Italy, Greece, and Portugal from Southern Europe were included and interest throughout the region grew from there. The sport blossomed around the Mediterranean during the 1980s and 1990s, and today every major nation sustains a professional league. If we include the Adriatic League that represents the former Yugoslavia, they comprise four of the five most important leagues on the continent, the fifth being Russia. Further, clubs from Italy, Spain, Greece, and the former Yugoslavia have won a total of forty of the fifty-seven Euroleague championships held. Southern European nations have even found success on the international stage with Spain, Greece, Turkey, and teams representing the former Yugoslavia winning the International Basketball Federation (FIBA) World Championships twice, reaching the title game five times, and hosting the event three times since 1998. Players from the region have also found success in the National Basketball Association (NBA), including the Spaniards Pau and Marc Gasol, the Croatian Toni Kukoc, and the Turk Hedo Türkoğlu. In fact, as of 2017 Spain, Croatia, Serbia, Italy, Greece, and Turkey had each produced at least six NBA players and several of those nations more than twice that many.

Clearly, then, Southern Europe now supports thriving basketball communities that invest thousands of euros into the sport and produce top-level athletes and teams. Nonetheless, very little academic research even attempts to explain basketball's growth in the region and its effects. Certainly the US military played a role as locals were taught the sport on military bases in Spain, Italy, and Turkey during the Cold War, though the

US Army bases of West Germany provide the clearest example of such diffusion. On the other side of the Iron Curtain, the sport's growth in Yugoslavia likely originated from connections to the Soviet Union. Expansion in the 1990s was part of the general growth of basketball internationally during that period as a television-friendly sport in an age when media connections grew at an astounding rate. Historian Walter LeFeber has discussed how the combination of transnational corporations like Nike, digital broadcast satellites that sent images around the world rapidly, and aggressive advertising campaigns turned Michael Jordan into an international superstar and thrust the sport he played into the spotlight as well.[26] From a regional perspective, the peak of that fame came at the 1992 Barcelona Olympics where basketball enthusiasts throughout Southern Europe watched the Dream Team perform on their own soil. This brought basketball to prominence in a region that already had ties to it, and the NBA has since regularly organized outreach campaigns and sent scouts, coaches, and teams to Europe to nurture that interest. A few Spanish academics have even begun to consider the topic, with Xavier Ginesta and Jordi Sopena discussing the role of Spain's 2006 FIBA world championship in reinforcing national identity across the nation[27] and Juan Antonio Simón Sanjurjo writing about the Franco government's mid-century promotion of the sport and the role played by Raimundo Saporta.[28] Yet these first forays remain just that until the topic has been fully investigated.

As this chapter demonstrates, Southern Europe has a long and complex relationship with sport that is one of the richest in the world. Academics have done significant work to expand our understanding of this history, yet many avenues remain for new projects. The region's nations can claim their own sporting activities like bullfighting and their own relationship to international sports through Italian *calico* and Greece's unique role within the Olympic movement. Most of these topics, however, require consideration from more perspectives to be fully understood. For example, few scholars have looked at bullfighting as a modern activity and connected it to sports history or studied the early Olympic movement from the perspective of Greek history. Nonetheless, foreign sports successfully forged an audience within the cultures of Italy, Spain, and Greece as they modernized in the nineteenth and early twentieth centuries. In particular, football became thoroughly intertwined with national, regional, and civic identities as centralizing political regimes and regional groups resisting them used football clubs as foci for popular identities and a means of socialization. This has resulted in football clubs across Southern Europe becoming powerful organizations that are imbued with cultural symbols, own some of the largest facilities on the continent, and often dominating sports beyond football. Future scholars can add to this literature by considering the smaller football clubs of Spain and Italy as well as those of other countries as foils to their more famous neighbors. It will also be valuable to learn how the Salazar and Colonel governments in Portugal and Greece sought to use sport in comparison to Franco and Mussolini. Such studies will produce a more complete picture of sport's development in the region and enable more comparative studies. The region also has a long history in cycling, tennis, alpine sports, sailing, and many other activities whose surface has only been scratched. The Southern Europe sports world has also changed in the last third of the twentieth century, reflecting larger socioeconomic developments. Spain has emerged as a sporting power in parallel with its reintegration in the European mainstream politically and economically since the 1980s, and basketball has grown into the second most popular team sport across most of the northern Mediterranean. The latter raises interesting questions about what influences have spurred it other than basketball's general international growth. All of these topics promise decades of productive and interesting research on sport in Southern Europe that will benefit our understanding of both the region itself and the role sport plays in the larger world.

NOTES

1. Andrew McFarland, "The Importance of Reception: Explaining Sport's Success in Early Twentieth-Century Spain," *European Review* 19.4 (2011a): 527–543.
2. Simon Martin, *Sport Italia: The Italian Love Affair with Sport* (London: I. B. Tauris, 2011); "Italian Sport and the Challenges of Its Recent Historiography," *Journal of Sport History* 2 (2011): 199–209.
3. Adrian Shubert, *Death and Money in the Afternoon: A History of the Spanish Bullfight* (Oxford: Oxford University Press, 1999).
4. John MacAloon, *This Great Symbol* (Chicago: University of Chicago Press, 1981), 151–153.
5. Simon Martin, *Football and Fascism* (Oxford: Berg, 2004), 65–67.
6. Martin, *Football and Fascism*, 66.
7. Andrew McFarland, "Building a Mass Activity: Fandom, Class, and Early Spanish Football," in *Football Fans Around the World*, ed. Boria Majumdar and Sean Brown (London: Routledge, 2008), 205–220.
8. Pierre Lanfranchi and Stephen Wagg, "Cathedrals in Concrete: Football in the Southern European Society," in *Giving the Game Away*, ed. Stephen Wagg (Leicester, UK: Leicester University Press, 1995), 129.
9. Duncan Shaw, *Fútbol y franquismo* (Madrid: Alianza, 1987).
10. Carlos Fernández Santander, *El fútbol durante la guerra civil y el franquismo* (Madrid: San Martín, 1990).
11. Victoria De Grazia, *The Culture of Consent: Mass Organization of Leisure in Fascist Italy* (Cambridge, UK: Cambridge University Press, 1981).
12. Martin, *Football and Fascism*.
13. Martin, *Sport Italia*, primarily chapter 3.
14. Giglioa Gori, *Female Bodies, Sport, and Italian Fascism* (London: Frank Cass, 2004).
15. Alessio Ponzio, *La Palestra del Littorio: L'Accademia della Farnesina. Un'esperimento di pedagogia totalitarian nell'Italia Fascista* (Milan: Franco Angeli, 2009).
16. Andrew McFarland, "Founders, Foundations and Early Identities: Football's Early Growth in Barcelona," *Soccer & Society* 14.1 (2013): 95.
17. Carles Santacana, *El Barça y el franquismo: Crónica de unos años decisivos para Cataluña, 1968–1978* (Barcelona: Apóstrofe, 2006).
18. Jeremy MacClancy, "Nationalism at Play: The Basques of Vizcaya and Athletic Bilbao," in *Sport, Identity and Ethnicity*, ed. Jeremy MacClancy (Oxford: Berg, 1996), 181–200; Simone Bertelegni, *L'ultimo baluardo: Il calico schietto dell'Athletic Bilbao* (Trieste, Italy: Limina, 2006); Juan Carlos Castillo, "Play Fresh, Play Local," *Soccer in Society* 10 (2007): 680–697.

19. John Foot, *Calcio: A History of Italian Football* (London: Fourth Estate, 2006), 40.
20. Christos Kassimeris, *Football Comes Homes: Symbolic Identities in European Football* (Lanham, MD: Lexington, 2010).
21. Andrew McFarland, "Sport's Growth in Barcelona and Catalonia from the 1890s to 1920: A Case Study," *Soccer & Society* 13.4 (2012): 586.
22. Lanfranchi, "Cathedrals in Concrete," 126–127.
23. Martin, *Football and Fascism*, chapters 4 through 6 focus on stadium construction specifically.
24. John Hargreaves, *Freedom for Catalonia? Catalan Nationalism, Spanish Identity, and the Barcelona Olympic Games* (Cambridge, UK: Cambridge University Press, 2000); Ferran Brunet, *Economy of the 1992 Barcelona Olympic Games* (Lausanne, Switzerland: Centre d'Estudis Olímpics, 1993); Miquel de Moragas and Miquel Botella, eds., *The Keys to Success: The Social, Sporting, Economic and Communications Impact of Barcelona '92* (Bellaterra, Spain: Servei de Publicacions de la Universitat Autònoma de Barcelona, 1995).
25. Alejandro Quiroga, *Football and National Identities in Spain: The Strange Death of Don Quixote* (Basingstoke, UK: Palgrave Macmillan, 2013).
26. Walter LeFeber, *Michael Jordan and the New Global Capitalism* (New York: Norton, 1999).
27. Xavier Ginesta and Jordi Sopena, "Building the Nation: Contributions from the Mainstream Spanish Sports Press in 2006," *Esporte e Sociedade* 3 (2008): 1–29.
28. Juan Antonio Simón Sanjurjo, "Playing Against the Enemy: Raimundo Saporta and the First Trip of Real Madrid CF's Basketball Team to the Soviet Union," *Revista Internacional de Ciencias del Deporte* 8.28 (2012): 109–126.

BIBLIOGRAPHY

Bahamonde Magro, Ángel. *El Real Madrid en la historia de España*. Madrid: Taurus, 2002.
Bertelegni, Simone. *L'ultimo baluardo: Il calico schietto dell'Athletic Bilbao*. Trieste, Italy: Limina, 2006.
Brunet, Ferran. *Economy of the 1992 Barcelona Olympic Games*. Lausanne, Switzerland: Centre d'Estudis Olímpics, 1993.
Castillo, Juan Carlos Castillo. "Play Fresh, Play Local." *Soccer in Society* 10 (2007): 680–697.
De Grazia, Victoria. *The Culture of Consent: Mass Organization of Leisure in Fascist Italy*. Cambridge, UK: Cambridge University Press, 1981.
Fernández Santander, Carlos. *El fútbol durante la guerra civil y el franquismo*. Madrid: San Martín, 1990.
Foot, John. *Calcio: A History of Italian Football*. London: Fourth Estate, 2006.
Ginesta, Xavier, and Jordi Sopena. "Building the Nation: Contributions from the Mainstream Spanish Sports Press in 2006." *Esporte e Sociedade* 3 (2008): 1–29.
Gori, Giglioa. *Female Bodies, Sport, and Italian Fascism*. London: Frank Cass, 2004.
Hargreaves, John. *Freedom for Catalonia? Catalan Nationalism, Spanish Identity, and the Barcelona Olympic Games*. Cambridge, UK: Cambridge University Press, 2000.
Kassimeris, Christos. *Football Comes Homes: Symbolic Identities in European Football*. Lanham, MD: Lexington, 2010.
Lanfranchi, Pierre, and Stephen Wagg. "Cathedrals in Concrete: Football in the Southern European Society." In *Giving the Game Away: Football Politics and Culture on Five Continents*, ed. Stephen Wagg. Leicester, UK: Leicester University Press, 1995.

LeFeber, Walter. *Michael Jordan and the New Global Capitalism.* New York: Norton, 1999.

MacAloon, John. *This Great Symbol.* Chicago: University of Chicago Press, 1981.

MacClancy, Jeremy. "Nationalism at Play: The Basques of Vizcaya and Athletic Bilbao." In *Sport, Identity and Ethnicity,* edited by Jeremy MacClancy, 181–200. Oxford: Berg, 1996.

Martin, Simon. *Football and Fascism.* Oxford: Berg, 2004.

Martin, Simon. "Italian Sport and the Challenges of Its Recent Historiography." *Journal of Sport History* 2 (2011a): 199–209.

Martin, Simon. *Sport Italia: The Italian Love Affair with Sport.* London: I. B. Tauris, 2011b.

McFarland, Andrew. "Building a Mass Activity: Fandom, Class, and Early Spanish Football." In *Football Fans Around the World: From Supporters to Fanatics,* edited by Boria Majumdar and Sean Brown, 205–220. London: Routledge, 2008.

McFarland, Andrew. "Founders, Foundations and Early Identities: Football's Early Growth in Barcelona." *Soccer and Society* 14.1 (2013): 93–107.

McFarland, Andrew. "The Importance of Reception: Explaining Sport's Success in Early Twentieth Century Spain." *European Review* 19.4 (2011a): 527–543.

McFarland, Andrew. "Spanish Sport and the Challenges of Its Recent Historiography." *Journal of Sport History* 2 (2011b): 211–221.

McFarland, Andrew. "Sport's Growth in Barcelona and Catalonia from the 1890s to 1920: A Case Study." *Soccer and Society* 13.4 (2012): 584–598.

Moragas, Miquel de, and Miquel Botella, eds. *The Keys to Success: The Social, Sporting, Economic and Communications Impact of Barcelona '92.* Bellaterra, Spain: Servei de Publicacions de la Universitat Autònoma de Barcelona, 1995.

Ponzio, Alessio. *La Palestra del Littorio: L'Accademia della Farnesina: Un'esperimento di pedagogia totalitarian nell'Italia Fascista.* Milan: Franco Angeli, 2009.

Quiroga, Alejandro. *Football and National Identities in Spain: The Strange Death of Don Quixote* Basingstoke, UK: Palgrave Macmillan, 2013.

Santacana, Carles. *El Barça y el franquismo: Crónica de unos años decisivos para Cataluña, 1968–1978.* Barcelona: Apóstrofe, 2006.

Shaw, Duncan. *Fútbol y franquismo.* Madrid: Alianza, 1987.

Shubert, Adrian. *Death and Money in the Afternoon: A History of the Spanish Bullfight.* Oxford: Oxford University Press, 1999.

Simón Sanjurjo, Juan Antonio. "Playing Against the Enemy: Raimundo Saporta and the First Trip of Real Madrid CF's Basketball Team to the Soviet Union," *Revista Internacional de Ciencias del Deporte* 8.28 (2012): 109–126.

Wagg, Stephen, ed. *Giving the Game Away: Football Politics and Culture on Five Continents.* Leicester, UK: Leicester University Press, 1995.

CHAPTER 24

SPORT IN LATIN AMERICA[1]

BRENDA ELSEY

AT the end of the twentieth century, when the idea of "Latin America" underwent great scrutiny, Eduardo Galeano wrote *Soccer in Sun and Shadow*. Galeano placed soccer, or football, at the center of a common regional identity. According to Galeano, "The history of soccer is a sad voyage from beauty to duty. When the sport became an industry, the beauty that blossoms from the joy of play got torn out by its very roots. In this *fin-de-siècle* world, professional soccer condemns all that is useless, and useless means not profitable."[2] This mix of hopelessness and nostalgia reflected an historical juncture on the continent. After a century of political experimentation, modernization projects, and social reform movements, the region's inequalities remained deeply entrenched.[3] Following transitions to democracy in the 1980s, many countries experienced a decline in civic engagement. While human rights organizations achieved important milestones, some argued that the new democracies provided legitimacy for the neoliberal policies implemented during the authoritarian regimes. Against this backdrop, scholars of Latin America have criticized the role of sports in state propaganda, consumerism, and social inequalities. Yet millions of fans experience sports as freedom.

Research on Latin American sports has clustered around themes of enduring consequence, such as the Cuban Revolution, Brazilian racial hierarchies, and Argentine national identity.[4] Scholars have taken an interest in sports as a lens through which to understand class formation, national identity, civil society, and gender in the region. Interest in sports came out of social history in the academies of North America and Europe during the 1970s. Historians working within Latin American research institutions continued to pursue questions of political economy and state-building.[5] Thus early histories appeared in English, from academics based in the United States and Europe.[6] This began to change in the early twenty-first century, as academics working within Latin America founded interdisciplinary research centers. Research of sports history tended to be adjacent to larger research agendas.[7] As a result, anthologies figured importantly in the literature.[8] Scholars of Latin American sports interact with journalists and fans entranced with the past. Sports communities engage in memory-making, statistical studies, historical comparisons, and analysis. As with other cultural practices, such as samba, sports embody local histories outside of formal narratives. Much of the work on sports history has focused on creating the first histories and "filling in the blanks."[9] Despite the transnational trends in the profession, most historians have focused on national case studies.[10] While football dominates the historiography of Latin American sports, baseball, boxing, cricket, and basketball have also attracted the attention of scholars.[11]

The bulk of research on sports focuses on the modern period and usually urban areas.[12] However, there are important forays into earlier periods. In pre-Columbian Mesoamerica, historians hoped that understanding leisure would shed light onto the cosmology and political structure of indigenous groups. Evidence of Mayan ball games intrigued scholars. Ball courts, dating back to 1400 BCE, and ceramic figures of players have been found throughout the region.[13] Arenas belied the game's importance, yet their size indicates that the Mayan ball game was not a mass-spectator sport.[14] Apparently, its significance rested with the participants' re-enactment of the myth that provided the backbone to the socioreligious order, the story of the Hero Twins from the Popul Vuh. Gambling seems to have saturated the sport and heightened its importance.[15] Some speculated that wagers served to reconcile political differences. In addition, the elaborate pageantry of the ball games enlivened the marketplaces surrounding the arenas in which they were held.

As with the pre-Columbian period, there are precious few studies of sports in colonial Latin America. European empires proscribed, adopted, and modified Native American cultural practices as they colonized the Americas. New forms of leisure emerged from the interaction between African, European, and indigenous traditions. In Spanish America, contests of horsemanship provided an arena to establish one's masculinity, status, and talent. Colonial officials limited indigenous and poor people's access to horses, but this proved difficult given the labor needs of landowners. One of the most popular colonial sports was the *charreada,* or the Mexican rodeo, which consisted of events that tested one's prowess in riding and herding.[16] Later, such performances commemorated Mexican military events. Likewise, equestrian sport thrived in the colonial pampas, the plains of what became Argentina and Uruguay. Ranch hands developed games as a show of skill and honor.[17] Perhaps because of the lower cost of horses, by the nineteenth century, the rural poor participated in horse games. The urban elite looked upon these practices with consternation. The roaming *gaucho* presented an obstacle to assembling a reliable labor force. Eurocentric elites encouraged gauchos to embrace more genteel leisure activities.

The transition from pastimes with the danger of death and dismemberment to less violent sports constituted part of the modernizing process in Latin America.[18] Furthermore, the distinction between work and play proved central in establishing a capitalist economy. Sports with greater physical contact, such as boxing and stick games, demarcated the line between play and violence that the state could regulate.[19] In order to extract labor from rural men, the elite limited their freedom of mobility, particularly important to hunting. Meanwhile, in the cities, sports clubs became exclusive sites of sociability. Jockey clubs institutionalized gambling and horse racing.[20] By 1900, the Jockey Club of Argentina held gaucho games, with riders dressed in costume, thus rendering "real" *gauchos* anachronistic and silly.[21] In Mexico, horse racing, cycling, and cricket became part of the elite's class identity.[22] This new elite was far from cohesive, however. Historian William Beezley has researched the Jockey Club to understand cleavages among the traditional elite and the new rich of the Porfiriato.[23]

The rise in nationalism facilitated the diffusion of sport in Latin America. Associations frequently formed in response to invitations sent by sportsmen from abroad seeking competitors. International sports events constituted spaces where participants constructed and reflected upon national identity. In the press, stadiums, and clubhouses, enthusiasts interpreted sports teams' performances as national allegories. Given that sports traversed classes, it offers a counterpoint to a cultural history of elite nationalism. In the West Indies, cricket players created a national community within the empire's dominant cultural practice.[24] This transpired in spite of elite hopes that baseball and cricket would distract workers from politics during the *tiempo muerte* of the sugar harvest. Hinging the weighty political project of nationalism upon games with uncontrollable outcomes proved risky. Regionalism, gender, and ethnicity are just a few of the cleavages that complicate sport as a tool of nationalists. In other words, sports can manifest a thin nationalism, in tension with other forms of identification.

FOOTBALL IN SOUTH AMERICA

In the nineteenth century, British bankers and engineers brought their love of football to mainland South America. At the same time, young men from elite families discovered the sport during their studies in Europe, such as the "father" of Brazilian football, Charles Miller. By the 1890s, football clubs were forming rapidly in the Southern Cone.[25] Although its British origins may have lent football legitimacy among the elite, it did not remain an exclusive practice for long.[26] Within a generation, enthusiasts from across the social classes founded clubs. South American clubs adhered to amateurism through the 1930s, long after the British adopted professionalism. Amateurs modeled themselves after the dispassionate and restrained British sportsmen. Club structure borrowed from the statutes of other civic associations, including labor unions and mutual aid societies. Even after professionalization, most clubs were nonprofit organizations owned collectively by their members. Club participants gained valuable political skills, including public speaking, writing petitions, and lobbying.[27]

Football became part of reform movements that emerged in the early twentieth century in response to industrialization and labor agitation. Company-sponsored teams placed working-class players in relationships with their bosses, conceived of as voluntary. Middle- and upper-class reformers hoped that sports could encourage workers to develop respect for their managers. Reform leaders, among them many sports journalists, worried about the enervating effects of the city on the male body. The public health campaigns of the 1910s, wrapped up in the "social question," tied ideas of eugenics and race to football. The professions emerging around sports claimed sports could repair the racial deficiencies that stemmed from the African and indigenous ancestry of the working class. Increased immigration from Italy and Spain furthered football's popularity and complicated its association with British culture. In Chile and Argentina these immigrants integrated easily into football organizations, but Uruguayan clubs, such as Nacional, expressed a "Creole" resentment of them.[28] Players of Middle-Eastern descent, on the other hand, faced overt discrimination.[29]

Despite the hopes of elites and industrialists, sports clubs created spaces that generated working-class solidarity. For example, as early as 1906, the Chilean Workers Football Association formed in response to discrimination players faced in public parks. Talented football stars from working-class backgrounds constructed alternative masculinities that posited the strength, rather than the decadence, of the working-class male body. Labor unions drew upon the athletic prowess of poor players to challenge the shame associated with poverty. By the 1920s, semiprofessionalism had already begun in factories, like Bangú, in Brazil.[30] The team was a publicity tool for the factory, which afforded players special privileges. For the textile workers of Bangú, however, the football club bolstered workers' identification with one another, their community, and manual labor. In the 1940s and 1950s, amateur football clubs connected members to leftist political parties. In turn, political parties recognized the power of football to mobilize enthusiasts. For example, in 1945 the Brazilian Communist Party organized a tournament, "Tribute to the Unity of the Worker's Movement," featuring two of the country's leading professional clubs, Palmeiras and Corinthians.[31] The Party used this match to raise funds for two of their electoral candidates.

The relationship between racial hierarchies and football has preoccupied historians of Brazil. Early football directors assumed the superiority of whiteness and Anglo heritage. In the 1910s, for example, Club Fluminense sponsored a tour of Oxford players to educate Brazilians in proper sportsmanship.[32] However, fans often preferred talent to European-ness, disregarding journalists' warnings against black players and celebrating their abilities.[33] According to scholar José Leite Lopes, professionalism led to the inclusion of working-class and Afro-Brazilian players.[34] The club of the Portuguese community, Vasco da Gama, was among the first large clubs to integrate Afro-Brazilian players. The color line in Europe meant that Brazil lost fewer star players than neighboring Argentina.[35] Intellectuals of the 1930s, including Gilberto Freyre, claimed that football proved the positive outcomes of racial mixing.[36] Whereas European football reflected discipline and science, it was banal compared with the artistry of Brazilians. In the 1940s, the populist government of Getulio Vargas invested in football, boosting its popularity.[37] Given these developments, many scholars have characterized this period as the "democratization" of football.[38] Scholarly research has yet to prove that this democratization of football did not merely obfuscate socioeconomic inequalities in other spheres.

For historians of Argentina and Chile, football contributed to a vibrant civic culture in the first half of the twentieth century.[39] An economic boom, the regulation of hours for the working class, and the bourgeoning of a consumer culture fueled remarkable growth of clubs and stadiums in the 1920s. Along with dance halls, movie theatres, and department stores, football defined the urban experience.[40] Politicians, mostly conservatives, involved the largest football clubs in vote-buying schemes in the 1930s.[41] Thus leftist parties in Argentina expressed greater skepticism of football and did not develop lasting connections to clubs. The rise of Peronism in the 1940s profoundly affected Argentine sports. Juan Perón viewed sports as essential to shaping bodies for the New Argentina. Moreover, sports offered a vehicle to strengthen community within the Peronist Party. Perón subsidized sports facilities, youth clubs, professional leagues, and *barras bravas,* or fan organizations.[42] The political turbulence that followed Perón's departure meant a drop-off in state support for sports programs.

A renewed state interest in Argentine sport occurred during the military dictatorship, in the preparation for the 1978 World Cup. The junta recognized a unique opportunity to mobilize consent during the event.[43] General Jorge Rafael Videla, head of the military junta, emphasized that the orderly planning of the event reflected the success of the military's victory over Communist "subversion." The junta hoped to improve its reputation among international investors, and the event prompted even greater infiltration of opposition groups. Moreover, the tournament afforded the dictatorship an opportunity to invest millions in stadiums and update tourist facilities. Figures within football, such as the left-leaning national coach César Menotti, countered efforts to turn the event into a pro-junta spectacle. Menotti emphasized the tradition of Argentine football, rather than the recent nature of its success, which drew credit away from the junta. According to Pablo Alabarces, the festivities surrounding the Cup prompted the Argentine public, terrorized by mass arrests and disappearances, to reoccupy public space.[44] As the junta retained its power following the Cup, however, barras bravas became more deeply entrenched in extortion rackets and organized violence.[45]

In Chile, amateur clubs contributed to the democratization of the public sphere. Clubs introduced members to local politics and offered sites for political critique.[46] Campaigns to access public space, for example, educated members in requesting permits and writing petitions. The close relationship between amateur clubs, labor unions, and leftist political parties created a new ideal footballer, unique in his social commitment and political militancy. By the 1950s, clubs participated in land occupations and mobilized in support of leftist politicians. These actions brought amateurs into conflict with professionals, who denounced their programs as violations of the free market. Tensions within football reached an acute antagonism before the military coup of 1973, led by General Augusto Pinochet. Pinochet recognized the importance of football clubs as civic associations and targeted them for repression. The junta turned stadiums into torture centers, raided local fields, and severely restricted club activity. At the 1974 World Cup in West Germany, the opposition movement to Augusto Pinochet staged protests during matches and held teach-ins throughout the country.[47] Thus international football served as a site of struggle between authoritarian and democratic factions.

PHYSICAL EDUCATION, GENDER, AND RACE

Sports represent one of the most fluid and powerful means of constructing models of gender and sexuality. Historical research into sport and masculinity has been a fruitful line of inquiry, yet it remains incomplete without a robust scholarship on women and femininity.[48] Debates in Latin America over women's participation in sports began in the late nineteenth century. Promoters of women's athletics pointed to female athletes in Europe as evidence that women's sports were important to modernity. Detractors claimed that the exertion of sports harmed women's fertility and beauty. Before the institutionalization of sports in associations, women participated in a variety of sports. For example, in the 1890s women baseball teams traveled between Cuba and the United States.[49] Women's early attendance at baseball games provided avenues for their participation in the public sphere.[50] International competition spurred Latin American countries to form women's delegations, though later than their counterparts in Europe. Women competed in the Olympics beginning in 1900, but it was not until 1932 that Latin America fielded its first woman, Brazilian swimmer Maria Hulga Lenk.[51]

Given the scarcity of working-class women's leisure time, physical education provided a unique opportunity for them to practice sports. The gymnastics movement, inspired by Swedish therapist Henrik Ling, was popular among educators in Latin America. Ling's students promoted women's gymnastics and wrote manuals of intricate exercise regimens. Physical education fit the policies implemented by Liberal governments at the turn of the twentieth century. As governments devised national curricula, they hosted advisors from Ling's Stockholm Institute to create mixed-sex physical education. Bolivia, Chile, and Argentina hoped Ling's methods for women's fitness would improve the racial health of their youth.[52] According to these physical education professionals, women could acquire the strength and vigor of Europeans through properly guided exercise. While football was deemed unacceptably violent, tennis, golf, and basketball were encouraged among female students.[53] Women athletes frequently met with hostile reactions to their participation in sports. Most notably, in 1941 Brazil banned women from playing football, rugby, polo, boxing, and water polo.[54] This decree remained in place for forty years to the great detriment of women's athletics.

The development of physical education brought together state agencies, sports organizations, educators, and students. State interest in producing bodies habituated for industry and military service tied physical education to eugenics in the first half of the twentieth century. Physical education curriculum was designed for women as future child-bearing vessels. As such, women's bodies were crucial in racial engineering. In Bolivia, Liberals considered the indigenous to be the primary obstacle to the country's modernization. In 1904, they modeled their curriculum on that of Argentina, which they viewed as having successfully dealt with its "Indian problem."[55] The

Liberals' focus on physical education diverged from Conservatives, who envisioned an exclusively spiritual regeneration. Liberals hoped that discipline and physical control promoted in physical education would adapt students to a future industrialized society. In the early years of the twentieth century, acceptance of physical education increased across state agencies. Peruvian prison officials reversed their ban on sports and came to see football and boxing as efficient instruments of rehabilitation.[56] If politicians in the Andes focused on Indians, their counterparts in the Caribbean worried about their population of African descent. In Puerto Rico, the United States imposed physical education on the island. Although imbued with sexism and racism, these programs were more inclusive than private initiatives, such as the San Juan YMCA, which excluded nonwhites.[57]

International tournaments, particularly the Pan-American Games, encouraged Latin American women's participation in sports.[58] Beginning with the first tournament, held in Buenos Aires in 1951, women's delegations represented about a third of the athletes. First Lady Eva Perón took a special interest in organizing the tournament. Eva had supported Juan Perón's efforts to enact women's suffrage. The games coincided with the first year women could stand for election. Furthermore, Eva hoped to be included as a vice-presidential candidate on the upcoming ballot. In her opening speech, Eva emphasized women's contributions to peace in Latin America.[59] In other speeches, she connected athletics to women's progress. At her insistence, a female athlete recited the Olympic oath alongside a male counterpart in the opening ceremonies. Furthermore, Eva Perón arranged housing for female delegations adjacent to the presidential residence. These gestures endeared Eva to women's delegations.

Images of female athletes differed radically from the commonplace photographs in fashion magazines. Their bodies, sweating, struggling, and performing, displayed ambition rarely featured in mainstream media. Female athletics confounded traditional sports writing, which disparaged femininity as weakness and ineptitude. In response to news of the Pan-American women's track and field team's formation, one fan observed that, "Women foot racers ... are interesting to watch until they move. Then their ungraceful waddles destroy all illusions and make men turn to the dainty gals who walk, and do not run, to the nearest beauty parlor."[60] Despite such scorn, women athletes increased their numbers in subsequent games and celebrated one another's accomplishments.[61] Benefitting from two generations of physical education and association activity, volleyball, basketball, track and field, and football disseminated rapidly among Latin American women in the 1960s. The expansion of higher education to women opened doors to female athletes. Leftist governments, in particular, found a role for sports in integrating women into new socialist societies. Cuban sports programs were very influential in this regard. Physical education teachers and sports trainers were sent to Cuba to study their curriculum, national teams, and spectatorship.[62] Military dictatorships of the 1970s and 1980s curtailed support for women's athletics as part of the promise to reestablish traditional gender roles.

BÉISBOL IN THE CARIBBEAN

The extended period of slavery and colonialism, followed by US intervention, distinguished the Caribbean from South America. The Cuban Revolution of 1959 and the success of its sports program intensified scholarly interest in the subject of baseball.[63] In the late nineteenth century, independence from Spain demanded the development of national cultures. Historian Louis Pérez Jr. argued that the popularity of baseball in nineteenth-century Cuba was a rejection of the Spanish pastimes, especially "barbaric" bullfighting. The circulation of elite Cuban students in the United States helped disseminate baseball throughout the Caribbean. For example, Fordham University became one of the "birthplaces" of Cuban baseball when "Steve" Bellán learned the game while studying there. After professional success in the United States, Bellán founded the Cuban professional league in 1878, which fielded integrated teams.[64] Fans and sportswriters described the Cuban game as faster, with better showmanship. The political potential of baseball was not lost on the Spanish, who banned it in 1895 during the final war for Cuban independence.[65] Baseball club leaders were frequently supporters of the independence movement and suffered Spanish repression.

Along with US military personnel, migrant Cuban players introduced baseball to the Dominican Republic, Mexico, Nicaragua, Puerto Rico, and Venezuela.[66] The US business community encouraged workers to form baseball clubs as a way to develop discipline.[67] By the early 1900s, Havana had become the capital of a regional baseball craze. Players from around the Caribbean played in the Cuban professional league. Spalding produced a Spanish-language guide to baseball as early as 1911 in response to enthusiastic Caribbean fans.[68] Before the integration of baseball in the United States, players from the Negro League found opportunities in Cuba. Integration in the Cuban leagues enriched its baseball leagues. Working-class and black players came to view baseball as a vehicle to overcome social barriers.[69] The emergence of the Cuban tourist industry further supported the development of professional baseball. However, the involvement of gambling rings frustrated managers and reformers who touted the moral value of sports.[70] The political turmoil during the dictatorship of Gerardo Machado in the early 1930s displaced many players. The career of Cuban Manuel "Cocaína" García is representative. "Cocaína," named for his stunning pitching and perhaps his high-spirited lifestyle, played professionally from 1926 until 1949.[71] García played in Cuba, the Dominican Republic, Mexico, Puerto Rico, and Venezuela. In addition, he completed ten seasons in the US Negro Leagues.

The revolution's deprofessionalization of Cuban baseball had the unintended consequence of moving the center of baseball in the Caribbean to the Dominican Republic. Popular wisdom cites the US occupation of the Dominican Republic, from 1916 to 1924 with an explosion in baseball's popularity. However, Cuban immigrant laborers organized clubs in the Dominican Republic in the 1890s.[72] Although the Great Depression slowed the progress of Dominicans' professional league, it rebounded in the late 1930s when Dictator Rafael Trujillo noticed its political potential. Dominican agents took advantage of the segregation in the United States to sign important players from the Negro League, including Satchel Paige.[73] Although Rafael Trujillo associated himself with Spanish cultural practices, his family members enmeshed themselves in baseball. The Trujillo clan supported Club Escogido and used their influence to ensure the club's success. Some historians have suggested that baseball constituted one of the few outlets for conflict among the elite during Trujillo.[74] However, baseball did not merely reproduce power relations. The success of clubs from San Pedro de Macorís, made up of refinery and sugar-cane workers, became a source of pride for the community. Politicians pointed to these clubs as evidence of working-class potential for citizenship. The severe limits on political participation during the Trujillato diminished the value of this cultural capital.

Although Cuban sports had a long trajectory, Fidel Castro and the revolutionary government placed sports at the center of building a Socialist society. State investment in sports programs produced impressive results. The diffusion of physical education was part of the government's massive health programs. The success of Cuban sport integrated women and people of color into government projects and projected a strong image of Cuba abroad. However, it also acted as a site for Cubans to debate politics and even criticize state projects.[75] Since the 1960s, the example of Cuban sports, both as a revolutionizing and a diplomatic tool, inspired similar programs throughout Latin America.[76] Following the Cuban Revolution, scouts from the Major League Baseball (MLB) concentrated on young Dominican and Puerto Rican players. Cuban baseball officials that supported the revolution argued that the MLB practices were yet another example of imperialism, but Dominican players and fans felt they validated the quality of their baseball. The ballplayer who migrated to the United States and returned home a wealthy man became a popular icon. By the 1980s, MLB decided it was cost effective to open baseball academies in the Dominican Republic, strengthening the relationship between personnel on the island and the United States.

Looking Ahead

Thematically and methodologically, histories of sport have enriched our understanding of Latin America. Further scholarship should connect physical education, sports clubs, and body politics with broader questions in the historical field.[77] A few obvious areas of research would strengthen the historiography considerably. The scarcity of research on Mexican sports is surprising, and much of it has focused on the Olympics of 1968.[78] Historians found that the ruling government utilized this event as an opportunity to orchestrate popular spectacles.[79] However, sports fans criticized state corruption laid bare in the infrastructural projects in preparation for the tournament.[80] The possibilities of local case studies are exemplified in Heather Levi's work on Mexican professional wrestling. Levi found that wrestlers and their fans mocked the Partido Revolucionario Institucional government, demystifying it for the working class.[81] In the case of Central America, there are even fewer histories of sport.[82] Pioneering studies of Costa Rican sport signal the potential of such research to understand the country's stability, its relationship to the Catholic Church, and globalization's effects in the countryside.[83] Moreover, an examination of sexuality would make a major contribution to our understanding of the lived experience of sexuality and the persistence of violent homophobia in sport.

Sports serve as an arena where participants perform citizenship and create understandings of civil rights. In a provocative essay, Carlos Forment analyzed the municipal elections of 2003 in Buenos Aires, in which football clubs played an important role.[84] Club members imagined football clubs as a micro-model of how to implement neoliberal policies of privatization. Furthermore, mayoral candidate Mauricio Macri, one-time president of club Boca Juniors, represented the conservative manifestation of a shift away from state-centered rights to local democracy. Corporate influence in sports, particularly in the International Federation of Association Football (FIFA), promoted a model of global consumer-citizens. As Leite Lopes explained, "Marketing thus aestheticizes poverty, while the large multinational companies express their concern about it—a very paradoxical concern, since it comes from the same enormously wealthy, powerful, and profitable companies."[85] Sponsorship urges athletes and clubs to remain "apolitical" lest they lower their value. The privatization of clubs in Latin America will no doubt change their role in civil society. Historians face the task of analyzing this process, with a subject saturated with nostalgia. Without rigorous research, an important stage for the performance of everyday politics will remain shrouded in romanticism.

NOTES

1. This essay was written prior to the 2014 World Cup in Brazil, which is inspiring a rich academic and popular literature that will inform future historians. Among the best works are Paulo Fontes and Bernardo Buarque, eds., The Country of Football: Politics, Popular Culture, and the Beautiful Game in Brazil (London: Hurst, 2014); Roger Kittleson, The Country of Football: Soccer and the Making of Modern Brazil (Berkeley: University of California Press, 2014), Josh Nadel, Fútbol!: Why Soccer Matters in Latin America (Gainesville: University of Florida Press, 2014).
2. Eduardo Galeano, Soccer in Sun and Shadows (New York and London: Verso, 1998), 2.
3. Paul Gootenberg and Luis Reygadas, eds., Indelible Inequalities in Latin America (Durham, NC: Duke University Press, 2010).
4. Sportsmen wrote histories of sport early in the twentieth century: Fernando Azevedo, A Evolução do Esporte no Brasil (Sao Paulo: Weiszflog Irmãos, 1930). For a comprehensive bibliography, see Joseph Arbena, Sport in Latin America: An Annotated Bibliography, 1988–1998 (Westport, CT: Greenview Press, 1999) and Joseph Arbena, An Annotated Bibliography of Latin American Sport: Pre-Conquest to the Present (Westport, CT: Greenview Press, 1999). On Latin American football, see Carlos Aguirre, Bibliography on Soccer in Latin America, http://uoregon.academia.edu/CarlosAguirre/Teaching/22828/Bibliography_on_Soccer_in_Latin_America; Laurent Dubois, "Football in Latin America: A Field and its Challenges," Journal of Latin American and Caribbean Anthropology 3.2 (2008): 486–494.
5. Latin American cultural studies did not develop a parallel to Britain's "Birmingham school," which promoted a consideration of popular culture in relation to socioeconomic structures,

Ana del Sarto, Alicia Ríos, and Abril Trigo, eds., *Latin American Cultural Studies Reader* (Durham, NC: Duke University Press, 2004).

6. The Centro de Estudios del Deporte, in the Universidad Nacional de San Martín in Argentina, began in 2004 and has deepened the historical dimension of sports studies. See Julio Frydenberg and Rodrigo Daskal, eds. *Fútbol, Historia y Política* (Buenos Aires: Aurelia, 2010).

7. Important exceptions come mostly from anthropologists and sociologists, such as Roberto González Echevarría, *The Pride of Havana: A History of Cuban Baseball* (New York: Oxford University Press, 2001); Janet Lever, *Soccer Madness: Brazil's Passion for the World's Most Popular Sport* (Chicago: University of Chicago Press, 1983); Heather Levi, *The World of Lucha Libre: Secrets, Revelations, and Mexican National Identity* (Durham, NC: Duke University Press, 2008); Roger Magazine, *Golden and Blue Like My Heart: Masculinity, Youth, and Power among Soccer Fans in Mexico City* (Austin: University of Arizona Press, 2007); Tony Mason, *Passion of the People? Football in South America* (New York: Verso, 1995); Eduardo Santa Cruz, *Crónica de un encuentro: fútbol y cultura popular* (Santiago de Chile: Ediciones Instituto Arcos, 1991); and Christopher Gaffney, *Temple of the Earthbound Gods* (Austin: University of Texas Press, 2010).

8. Pablo Alabarces, *Peligro de gol: Estudios sobre deporte y sociedad en América Latina* (Buenos Aires: CLACSO, 2000); Joseph Arbena and David LaFrance, eds., *Sport in Latin America and the Caribbean* (Wilmington, DE: Scholarly Resources, 2002); Gary Armstrong and Richard Giulianotti, eds., *Fear and Loathing in World Football* (Oxford: Berg, 2001); Rory Miller and Liz Crolley, eds., *Football in the Americas: Fútbol, Futebol, Soccer* (London: Institute for the Study of the Americas, 2007); Aldo Panfichi, ed., *Ese Gol Existe: Una Mirada al Perú a través del Fútbol* (Lima: Fondo Editorial Pontificia Universidad Católica del Perú, 2008); Francisco Teixeira da Silva and Ricardo Pinto dos Santos, eds., *Memória Social dos Esportes* (Rio de Janeiro: Mauad, 2006).

9. Pablo Ramírez, "Los que entraron en la historia del deporte," *Todo es historia* 22.254 (1988): 38–59.

10. An important exception includes Mason, *Passion of the People?*

11. On distinctions between sport, martial arts, and dance, see Joshua Rosenthal, "Recently Scholarly and Popular Works on Capoeira," *Latin American Research Review* 42.2 (2007): 262–272. On boxing, see Daniel Fridman and David Sheinin, "Wild Bulls, Discarded Foreigners, and Brash Champions: U.S. Empire and the Cultural Constructions of Argentine Boxers," *Left History* 12.1 (2007): 52–77.

12. The study of rural sports is sorely lacking; see Bernardo Guerrero Jiménez, *El Libro de los Campeones: Deporte e Identidad Cultural en Iquique* (Iquique, Chile: El Jote Errante, 1992) and Franco Reyna, *Cuando éramos footballers: Una historia sociocultural del surgimiento y difusión del fútbol en Córdoba (1900–1920)* (Córdoba, Argentina: Centro de Estudios Históricos, 2011).

13. Susanna Ekholm, "Ceramic Figurines and the Mesoamerican Ballgame," in *The Mesoamerican Ballgame*, ed. Vernon Scarborough and David R. Wilcox (Tucson: University of Arizona Press, 1991), 241–249.

14. Thomas Guderjan, *The Nature of an Ancient Maya City: Resources, Interaction, and Power at Blue Creek, Belize* (Tuscaloosa: University of Alabama Press, 2007).

15. Barbara Fash and William Fash, "Religion, Politics and Plenty of Betting: The Old Ball Game in Mesoamerica," *Revista* (Spring 2012), http://www.drclas.harvard.edu/publications/revistaonline/spring-2012/religion-politics-and-plenty-betting.

16. Kathleen Sands, *Charrería Mexicana: An Equestrian Folk Tradition* (Tucson: University of Arizona Press, 1993).

17. Richard Slatta, "The Demise of the Gaucho and the Rise of Equestrian Sport in Argentina," *Journal of Sport History* 13.2 (1986): 97–110.

18. Norbert Elías and Eric Dunning, *Quest for Excitement: Sport and Leisure in the Civilizing Process* (Oxford: Blackwell, 1986).

19. Matthias Röhrig Assunção, "Juegos de palo en Lara: elementos para la historia social de un arte marcial venezolano," *Revista de Indias* 59.215 (1999): 55–89.

20. William Beezley, *Judas at the Jockey Club and Other Episodes of Porfirian Mexico* (Lincoln: University of Nebraska Press, 1987); Leandro Losada, "Sociabilidad, distinción y alta sociedad en Buenos Aires: los clubes sociales de la elite porteña (1880–1930)," *Desarrollo Económico* 45.180 (2006): 547–572.

21. Losada, "Sociabilidad."

22. Michael Costeloe, "To Bowl a Mexican Maid Over: Cricket in Mexico 1827–1900," *Bulletin of Latin American Research* 26.1 (2007): 112–124.

23. Beezley, *Judas at the Jockey Club*.

24. C. L. R. James, *Beyond a Boundary* (Durham, NC: Duke University Press, 1963).

25. Juan Carlos Luzuriaga, *El football del novecientos: orígenes y desarrollo del fútbol en el Uruguay (1875–1915)* (Montevideo: Uruguay: Fundación Itaú, 2009).

26. Eduardo Archetti, *Masculinities: Football, Polo and the Tango in Argentina* (London: Berg, 1999); Mason, *Passion of the People?*

27. Brenda Elsey, *Citizens and Sportsmen: Fútbol and Politics in Twentieth-Century Chile* (Austin: University of Texas Press, 2011).

28. Luzuriaga, *El football*, 125.

29. Elsey, *Citizens and Sportsmen*.

30. José Sergio Leite Lopes, "Class, Ethnicity, and Color in the Making of Brazilian Football," *Daedalus* 129 (2000): 239–270.

31. Aldo Rebelo, *Palmeiras e Corinthians 1945: o jogo vermelho* (São Paulo, Brazil: UNESP, 2010).

32. Gregg Bocketti, "Brazil in International Football," in *Negotiating Identities in Modern Latin America*, ed. Hendrik Kraay (Calgary: University of Calgary Press, 2011), 71–92.

33. Bocketti, "Brazil in International Football," 82, and Leonardo Affonso de Miranda Pereira, *Footballmania: Uma história social do futebol no Rio de Janeiro, 1902–1938* (Rio de Janeiro: Nova Fronteira, 2000).

34. Leite Lopes, "Class, Ethnicity, and Color."

35. Leite Lopes, "Class, Ethnicity, and Color."

36. Bernardo Borges Buarque de Hollanda, *O descobrimento do futebol: modernismo, regionalismo e paixão esportiva em José Lins do Rego* (Rio de Janeiro: Edições Biblioteca Nacional, 2004).

37. Francisco Carlos Teixeira da Silva makes a similar point in "Futebol: Uma Paixão Coletiva," in *Memória Social dos Esportes*, ed. Francisco Carlos Teixeira da Silva and Ricardo Pinto dos Santos (Rio de Janeiro: Mauad, 2006), 15–32, esp. 28.

38. Teixeira da Silva, "Futebol."

39. Vic Duke and Liz Crolley, "Fútbol, Politicians and the People: Populism and Politics in Argentina," in *Sport in Latin American Society: Past and Present*, ed. J. A. Mangan and Lamartine Pereira DaCosta (London: Frank Cass, 2002), 93–116; Elsey, *Citizens and Sportsmen*; Julio Frydenberg, *Historia social del fútbol: Del amateurismo a la profesionalización* (Buenos Aires: Siglo XXI, 2011).

40. Julio Frydenberg, "Los clubes de fútbol de Buenos Aires en los años veintes," in *Fútbol, Historia y Política*, éd. Julio Frydenberg and Rodrigo (Buenos Aires: Aurelia, 2010), 23–81.

41. Frydenberg, "Los clubes," 68–69.

42. Duke and Crolley, "*Fútbol*, Politicians and the People," 93.

43. Pablo Alabarces, *Fútbol y Patria: El Fútbol y Las Narrativas de la Nación en la Argentina* (Buenos Aires: Prometeo, 2002); Eduardo Archetti, "Argentina 1978: Military Nationalism, Football Essentialism, and Moral Ambivalence," in *National Identity and Global Sports Events*, ed. Alan Tomlinson and Christopher Young (Albany: State University of New York Press, 2006), 133–147; Efraim Davidi and Raanan Rein, "Sport, Politics and Exile: Protests in Israel during the World Cup (Argentina, 1978)," *The International Journal of the History of Sport* 26:5 (2009): 673–692; Marina Franco, "Solidaridad internacional, exilio y dictadura en torno al Mundial de 1978," in *Exilios: Destinos y experiencias bajo la dictadura militar*, ed. Pablo Yankelevich and Silvina Jensen (Buenos Aires: Libros de Zorzal, 2007), 147–186.

44. Alabarces, *Fútbol y Patria*.

45. Duke and Crolley, "*Fútbol*, Politicians and the People," 112.

46. Elsey, *Citizens and Sportsmen*.

47. Brenda Elsey, "'As the World Is My Witness': Chilean Solidarity and Popular Culture, 1973–1987," in *Human Rights and Transnational Solidarity in Cold War Latin America*, ed. Jessica Stites Mor (Madison: University of Wisconsin Press, 2013), 177–208. The solidarity movement prepared and organized a boycott movement in advance of the Argentine Cup, see Davidi and Rein, "Sport, Politics, and Exile."

48. "Exceptions include the work of Silvana Goellner, see for example, "A construção/estruturação do género na Educação Física," *EX Aequo (Oeiras)*, v. 17, p. 169-173, 2008.

49. Louis Pérez Jr., "Between Baseball and Bullfighting: The Quest for Nationality in Cuba, 1868–1898," *Journal of American History* 81 (1994): 493–517.

50. Pérez, "Between Baseball and Bullfighting," 507.

51. X Olympiad Committee, *Official Report: 1932 Los Angeles* (Los Angeles: Wolfer, 1933).

52. François Martinez, "¡Que nuestros indios se conviertan en pequeños suecos! La introducción de la gymnasia en las escuelas bolivianas," *Bulletin de l'Institut Francais d'Etudes Andines* 28.3 (1999): 361–386, esp. 372.

53. Claudia Guedes, "Empowering Women through Sport: Women's Basketball in Brazil and the Significant Role of Maria Helena Cardoso," *The International Journal of the History of Sport* 27.7 (2010): 1237–1249.

54. Silvana Goellner, "Imagens da mulher no esporte," in *História do Esporte no Brasil*, ed. Mary del Priore and Victor Andrade de Melo (São Paulo: UNESP, 2009), 269–292.

55. Martinez, "¡Que nuestros indios," 364.

56. Carlos Aguirre, "Los usos del fútbol en las prisiones de Lima (1900–1940)," in *Ese Gol Existe: Una Mirada al Perú a través del Fútbol*, ed. Aldo Panfichi (Lima: Fondo Editorial Pontificia Universidad Católica del Perú, 2008), 155–176.

57. Roberta J. Park, "From la Bomba to Béisbol: Sport and the Americanisation of Puerto Rico, 1898–1950," *The International Journal of the History of Sport* 28.17 (2011): 2575–2593.

58. Raanan Rein, "'El Primer Deportista': The Political Use and Abuse of Sport in Peronist Argentina," *The International Journal of the History of Sport* 15.2 (1998): 54–76; César Torres, "The Limits of Pan-Americanism: The Case of the Failed 1942 Pan-American Games," *The International Journal of the History of Sport* 28.17 (2011): 2547–2574.

59. Comité Olímpico Argentino, *Primeros Juegos Deportivos Panamericanos* (Buenos Aires: N.p., 1951).

60. "Proposal for Patagonia," *The New York Times*, March 8, 1941, p. 13.

61. One Chilean runner confessed that she stole the glasses of Mexican javelin-thrower Hortensia García López as a souvenir of the star, whom she greatly admired. "Mexico en Buenos Aires," *El Universal*, March 2, 1951, p. 19. See also Abelardo Sanchez-Leon, "The History of Peruvian Women's Volleyball," *Studies in Latin American Popular Culture* 13 (1994): 143–153.

62. Elsey, *Citizens and Sportsmen*, 232.

63. Echeverría González, *Pride of Havana*; Pérez, "Between Baseball and Bullfighting"; Geralyn Pye, "The Ideology of Cuban Sports," *Journal of Sport History* 13 (1986): 119–127; Eric A. Wagner, "Sport in Revolutionary Societies: Cuba and Nicaragua," in *Sport and Society in Latin America*, ed. Joseph Arbena (New York: Greenwood Press, 1988), 113–136.

64. Echeverría González, *Pride of Havana*.

65. Pérez, "Between Baseball and Bullfighting."

66. Rob Ruck, *Tropic of Baseball: Baseball in the Dominican Republic* (Lincoln: University of Nebraska, 1998).

67. Orlando Arrieta, *Crónicas del Deporte Regional* (Venezuela: Ed. De la Academia de Historia del Estado Zulia Maracaibo, 2001).

68. "Jugadores del Habana," in *Spalding's Official Base Ball Guide*, Spanish-American ed. (New York: American Sports Publishing Company, 1911), 18.

69. Arrieta, *Crónicas del Deporte Regional*.

70. Adrian Burgos, "The Latins from Manhattan," in *Mambo Montage: The Latinization of New York*, ed. Agusín Lao-Montes and Arlene Dávila (New York: Columbia University Press, 2001), 71–93.

71. Echeverría González, *Pride of Havana*.

72. Ruck, *Tropic of Baseball*.

73. Alan Klein, *Sugarball: The American Game, the Dominican Dream* (New Haven, CT: Yale University Press, 1993).

74. Ruck, *Tropic of Baseball*, 32.

75. Thomas Carter, *The Quality of Home Runs: The Passion, Politics, and Language of Cuban Baseball* (Durham, NC: Duke University Press, 2008).

76. Wagner, "Sport in Revolutionary Societies."

77. Joseph Arbena, "Sport, Development, and Mexican Nationalism, 1920–1970," *Journal of Sport History* 18.3 (1991): 350–364.

78. One journal has dedicated an entire issue to the event, see Claire Brewster and Keith Brewster, "Representing the Nation: Sport, Control, Contestation, and the Mexican Olympics," *The International History of Sport* 26.6 (2009): 711–866; see also Joseph Arbena, "Hosting the Summer Olympic Games: Mexico City, 1968," in *Sport in Latin America and the Caribbean*, ed. Joseph Arbena and David G. LaFrance (Wilmington, DE: Scholarly Resources, 2002), 133–144; and Eric Zolov, "Showcasing the 'Land of Tomorrow': Mexico and the 1968 Olympics," *Americas* 61.2 (2004): 159–188.

79. Zolov, "Showcasing the 'Land of Tomorrow.'"

80. Zolov, "Showcasing the 'Land of Tomorrow.'"

81. Levi, *World of Lucha Libre*.

82. Jorge Eduardo Arellano, *El Béisbol en Nicaragua: Rescate Histórico y Cultural, 1889–1948* (Managua: Academia de Geografía e Historia de Nicaragua, 2007).

83. Chester Urbina Gaitán, "The Catholic Church and the Origins of Soccer in Costa Rica in the Early 1900s," in *Sport in Latin America and the Caribbean*, 1–8; Sergio Villena, *Golbalización: siete ensayos heréticos sobre fútbol, identidad y cultura* (Buenos Aires: Norma, 2006).

84. Carlos Forment, "The Democratic Dribbler: Football Clubs, Neoliberal Globalization, and Buenos Aires' Municipal Election of 2003," *Public Culture* 19.1 (2007): 85–116.

85. Leite Lopes, "Class, Ethnicity, and Color," 240.

BIBLIOGRAPHY

Alabarces, Pablo. *Peligro de gol: Estudios sobre deporte y sociedad en América Latina*. Buenos Aires: CLACSO, 2000.

Arbena, Joseph, and David LaFrance, eds. *Sport in Latin America and the Caribbean*. Wilmington, DE: Scholarly Resources, 2002.

Brewster, Claire, and Keith Brewster, "Representing the Nation: Sport, Control, Contestation, and the Mexican Olympics." *The International History of Sport* 26.6 (2009): 711–866.

Carter, Thomas. *The Quality of Home Runs: The Passion, Politics, and Language of Cuban Baseball*. Durham, NC, and London: Duke University Press, 2008.

Davidi, Efraim, and Raanan Rein, "Sport, Politics and Exile: Protests in Israel during the World Cup (Argentina, 1978)." *The International Journal of the History of Sport* 26.5 (2009): 673–692.

Elsey, Brenda. *Citizens and Sportsmen: Fútbol and Politics in Twentieth-Century Chile*. Austin: University of Texas Press, 2011.

Frydenberg, Julio, and Rodrigo Daskal, eds. *Fútbol, Historia y Política*. Buenos Aires: Aurelia, 2010.

González Echevarría, Roberto. *The Pride of Havana: A History of Cuban Baseball*. New York: Oxford University Press, 2001.

Leite Lopes, José Sergio, "Class, Ethnicity, and Color in the Making of Brazilian Football." *Daedalus* 129 (2000): 239–270.

Levi, Heather, Mangan, J. A. and Lamartine da Costa, eds. *Sport and Society in Latin America: Past and Present*. London: Frank Cass, 2002.

Teixeira da Silva, Francisco, and Ricardo Pinto dos Santos, eds. *Memória Social dos Esportes*. Rio de Janeiro: Mauad, 2006.

Tomlinson, Alan, and Christopher Young, eds. *National Identity and Global Sports Events*. Albany: State University of New York Press, 2006.

CHAPTER 25

....

THE CHANGING FIELD
OF SPORTS HISTORY
IN AUSTRALASIA

....

GARY OSMOND

SPORT holds a mythical place in Australia and New Zealand—Australasia, for the purposes of this chapter—where it is a popular activity, a passionate obsession, and a commemorated practice. Sports history-making results from this popularity, passion, and commemorative impulse and from a conviction that sporting traditions can offer up profound insight into social and cultural history. At a popular level, sports history is expounded, displayed, and celebrated in museums like the National Sport Museum in Melbourne and the New Zealand Olympic Museum in Wellington; on Internet sites like the Sport Australia Hall of Fame and "New Zealand History Online" sports pages; in movies, video documentaries, and radio programs; in books, magazines, and newspapers; and in a staggering variety of other material, visual, audio, and digital forms. At a scholarly level, where sports history has emerged over the past four decades as a legitimate subdiscipline with deep tendrils in universities, a scholarly association, and published forums, interest in popular culture forms of narrative-making and representation is growing.

This chapter focuses on sport historiography in Australasia and has three broad aims. The first is to survey historic and historiographic developments. The intent is not to chart or summarize comprehensively the very broad literature but to indicate something of the trajectories of sports historiography in Australia and New Zealand. One facet of this that becomes quickly apparent is the "mnemonic density"[1] of particular sports, especially cricket and some football codes, in the sports histories of both countries—the way these sports dominate the historiography both topically and as case studies of broader social themes. The second aim, therefore, is to consider this preferential treatment for what it reveals about the field of sports history as it has developed. The final aim is to consider recent and emerging directions. As I have alluded already, popular sports history and popular sports culture increasingly bleed into scholarly sports history. Few sports historians are attempting to staunch this flow and quarantine sports history as an entirely separate field. Instead, responses range from skeptical but grudging acceptance to deep curiosity. In some cases, sports historians are leaping in with scalpels brandished to open the flow. This development is consistent with scholarly evolution as old paths become too well-trodden but is also partially a response to wider intellectual trends, particularly postmodernism, and to cultural and technological shifts that permit new ways of conceptualizing, exploring, and discussing the sporting past.

Defining "Australasia"

The term "Australasia" requires elucidation and comment. Geographically, Australasia has multiple meanings, from Australia and New Zealand combined to broader Oceanic configurations including New Guinea and other Pacific islands. Historically, and in terms of sports history, however, Australasia refers specifically to Australia and New Zealand. It is in this combined sense that the term "Australasia" is used in this chapter. Usage of the term in this way harks back to the colonial era, before Australian federation as a united country in 1901 and New Zealand's attainment of dominion status in 1907, when the continental colonial entities of New South Wales, Queensland, South Australia, Victoria, and Western Australia and the island colonies of New Zealand and Tasmania were seven British settler outposts with more in common than their present political status might suggest. Combined Australasian teams competed in the 1908 and 1912 Olympic Games and in Davis Cup tennis championships until the 1920s, and Australasian athletic and swimming championships alternated between the various colonies from the 1890s until well after Australian federation.

The emphasis on historic similarity and commonalities that is evoked by "Australasia" is both advantageous and disadvantageous. Editorially, it is a convenient grouping for two countries that are geographically proximate (separated by the Tasman Sea), bonded in colonial history to the British Empire, and culturally similar with overlapping sporting pasts. This merging of identities is also the chief drawback of the label, ignoring as it does both the decline of a trans-Tasman sporting cooperation over the past century and the intense sporting rivalry that now exists between the two countries. In this chapter, however, the term is appropriate because of the frequent convergence of researchers, approaches, and topical focus in the scholarly creation of sports histories.

Broad Trajectories

While it is not the intention of this chapter to survey comprehensively all works and historiographical tangents, a brief directional overview is necessary in order to steer discussion of key trends and emerging directions. Inevitably, this will omit many works whose contribution to the field is not deliberately diminished by their elision here. Sports history and historiography have developed along similar trajectories in Australia and New Zealand. A great deal of historical writing on sport has occurred in the long histories of both countries, but sport remained on the periphery of what was a predominantly political history focus. A growing "fugitive enthusiasm"[2] for understanding the contributions of sport to Australian society and culture led to the formation of the Australian Society for Sports History (ASSH) in 1983. ASSH has nurtured sports history through the facilitation of communication, conferences, awards, and publications. Among the latter is the biannual refereed academic journal *Sporting Traditions*, the encyclopedic *Oxford Companion to Australian Sport*, and a successful ASSH Studies thematic series. While nominally Australian, ASSH effectively includes New Zealand. The first issue in the ASSH Studies series, published in 1986, was titled "Sport and Colonialism in Nineteenth Century Australasia," for example, and a 2005 special edition of *Sporting Traditions* was guest-edited by New Zealand sports historian Clare Simpson and titled "Fresh Perspectives on New Zealand's Sporting Past." Stuart Macintyre and Daryl Adair, along with Rob Hess and Matthew Klugman, offer extended discussions of the development of Australasian sports history.

The thirtieth ASSH *Sporting Traditions* conference, held in 2007 in Canberra, prompted the president, Tara Magdalinski, to riff on the pathways taken by Australian sports history using indicative book titles to ponder whether the organization was "simply a *Paradise of Sport* (1995) or merely *One-Eyed* (2000) and to establish whether we, as scholars, perceive the *Saturday Afternoon Fever* (1986) to be *More than a Game* (1998) or had really only understood *Half the Race* (1991)." Magdalinski argued that if ordered chronologically, these titles reflect the evolution of Australian sports historiography. She was astute in the thrust of this observation, and her witty concoction serves well to guide a summative overview of the major contributions.

Brian Stoddart's *Saturday Afternoon Fever* was the first of several global Australian academic sports histories to be published and reflected the field's emergence from subaltern to legitimate status. As a social history, it created a template for future works by its chapter focus on analytical categories such as class, gender, multiculturalism and race, politics, media, and commercialism. Marion Stell's *Half the Race*, which examines the history of Australian women in sport, is indicative of several major social histories with a specific thematic focus that emerged in this period. Notable among these were Colin Tatz's *Aborigines in Sport* and other works by the same author (e.g., *Obstacle Race: Aborigines in Sport* and, with Paul Tatz, *Black Gold: The Aboriginal and Islander Sports Hall of Fame*) that critically examined the discrimination, injustice, and struggles of Indigenous Australians in sport. Other important social histories on specific themes included a book on ethnicity and the contribution of migrants to Australian sport edited by Phillip Mosely and colleagues, while issues such as class and religion await systematic book-length analysis.

Richard Cashman's *Paradise of Sport* was the second general academic sports history. This important and influential book, which was later revised and expanded, represents a wider effort to encapsulate global Australian sports history covering the two centuries since the arrival of the First Fleet in 1788 and colonization of continental Australia and Tasmania. Other works that attempted this in various ways included Reet Howell and Maxwell Howell's largely pictorial overview *A History of Australian Sport*, Daryl Adair and Wray Vamplew's *Sport in Australian History*, Wray Vamplew and Brian Stoddart's edited social history organized around specific sports, *Sport in Australia*, and, more recently, Richard Cashman and Rob Hess's edited work revising, reprinting, and extending their earlier publications, *Sport, History and Australian Culture*. A particularly significant work in the genre of general Australian sports history broadly considered over time is the *Oxford Companion to Australian Sport*, first published by ASSH in 1992 and edited by five eminent sports historians, led by Wray Vamplew. This single-volume tome offered entries on individual sports, biographies, and thematic essays. In addition to general histories, works also appeared that concentrated on specific time frames, such as the period around the federation of the Australian colonies in 1901, and the role of sport in identity formation.

Rob Hess and Bob Stewart's *More than a Game*, which addresses Australian Rules football, represents the wide array of works that focus on single sports that augment the general histories of sport and broad histories covering specific time frames. While Vamplew and Stoddart's *Sport in Australia* devoted a chapter each to fourteen separate sports, the majority of sport-specific books have been on a narrower range of sporting pursuits—in particular cricket, rugby, and Australian Rules football. Notable exceptions to this trend appeared, of course, but a concentration around particular sports is discernible, as is argued later in this chapter.

Douglas Booth and Colin Tatz's *One-Eyed*, self-consciously titled in metaphoric opposition to the notion of athletic nirvana suggested by *Paradise of Sport*, posed challenges to some of the earlier works by drawing upon Australia's sports history to critique sporting cultures. The significance of Booth and Tatz's work for this overview is its reflexive departure from the then-dominant trends in narrating sports history. As is discussed in greater detail later, more recent developments in Australian sport historiography have been decidedly not "one-eyed" but rather multifocal and refractory in their approach.

As in Australia, New Zealand sport had long formed part of a popular discourse, but it was not until the 1980s that historians began to analyze sport comprehensively as part of the constitutive fabric of New Zealand society. One broad impetus for reflection on the place of sport was the anti-apartheid movement and protests against the 1981 South African Springboks rugby tour of New Zealand. Academic interest in sports history grew from the 1980s, resulting in the development of monographs, journal articles, and edited collections; conferences on the history and sociology of sport; and new university courses and departments. Notable, generative histories from this period that addressed sport included Keith Sinclair's book *A Destiny Apart*, which considered sport as historically integral to national identity, and Jock Phillips' *A Man's Country?*, which viewed rugby as central to the construction of New Zealand masculinity. John Nauright, Douglas Booth, and Malcolm MacLean each offer useful overviews of these general developments in New Zealand historiography.

Unlike in Australia, no general, national New Zealand sports history has yet been published.[3] Rather than suggest that sports history is in an embryonic form in that country, this situation belies an active scholarly interest in New Zealand sports history.[4] A number of works assume historical as well as contemporary or sociological perspectives on sport, including John Nauright's *Sport, Power and Society in New Zealand*; Brad Patterson's *Sport, Society and Culture in New Zealand*; and Chris Collins' *Sport in New Zealand Society*. Greg Ryan's *The Making of New Zealand Cricket* and *Tackling Rugby Myths: Rugby and New Zealand Society* are examples of histories of single sports notable for challenging accepted narratives and interpretations. While not addressing sport per se but rather related issues of leisure, recreation, and fitness, Caroline Daley's *Leisure and Pleasure* and Charlotte Macdonald's internationally comparative *Strong, Beautiful and Modern* represent the take-up by sports historians of the body as a site of cultural enquiry. The 'fanning out' of topical, structural, and epistemological approaches represented by these few examples indicates something of the broader range of research presentations, book chapters, and journal articles within New Zealand sports historiography, a rich domain that is outside the ambit of this chapter but that is well surveyed and critiqued elsewhere.[5]

Apart from examples that specifically but separately address Australian or New Zealand sports history, very few works deliberately address *Australasian* sports history as an attempt to link themes, approaches, and scholarship in the two countries. One notable exception is J. A. Mangan and John Nauright's edited collection *Sport in Australasian Society*, which united nearly twenty scholars of sports history from both sides of the Tasman. While individual chapters are laudable, the editors do not conceptualize Australasia, there is little comparative analysis, and the geographic balance is heavily slanted toward Australia. Malcolm MacLean and Daryl Adair both offer insightful critiques of this situation and discuss the merits and problems of a combined Australasian approach.

MNEMONIC DENSITY: BALL SPORTS

Various critiques have emerged of Australian and New Zealand sports history as a field, including its focus on male-dominated sports,[6] unduly inward-focused national perspectives,[7] narrow epistemologies,[8] and particular sports at the expense of others. Many of these critiques are not unique to Australasia, of course, but they manifest in particular ways that cast light on sports historiography as it has developed in these two countries. Rather than review all of these areas of critique, the intention here is to address the domination of certain sports in order to survey how these historiographical emphases have provided staging grounds for various important intellectual debates.

In his examination of the social construction of time, Eviatar Zerubavel argues that historical narratives vary in their "mnemonic density," or the way that certain periods, events, or subjects are favored over others and dominate historiographically.[9] In

Australasian sports historiography, various such densities are readily discernible. Little published research exists on Māori or Indigenous Australian sporting activities prior to European colonization, for example. This particular example may be partly attributed to the lack of written sources, but new research efforts by scholars like Ken Edwards and Brendan Hokowhitu are adding to knowledge. Other critiques, such as male sports domination, have already been noted. These, and other lacunae, are increasingly being remedied, yet certain densities tenaciously remain.

An exaggerated focus on certain sports, especially cricket, rugby, and Australian Rules football, constitutes a major mnemonic density. Research on football codes has been seminal to the subdiscipline in both countries. As noted, anti-apartheid protests that coalesced around the South African Springboks rugby tour in 1981 helped generate academic interest in sports history in New Zealand, and rugby featured prominently in the influential 1980s books by Sinclair and Phillips. In Australia, sports historians credit a public lecture by social and labor historian Ian Turner in 1965 with instigating a prolific scholarly research into Australian Rules football.

The prevalence of these "big boys' ball sports" is clearly manifest in scholarly writing of all types.[10] The extensive bibliography contained in the 1997 second revised edition of the *Oxford Companion to Australian Sport* exemplifies this preoccupation. Cricket has the most entries, which occupy eight pages, followed by tennis (seven pages), rugby league (five pages), Australian Rules football (four pages), horse racing (four pages), golf (three pages), rugby union (two pages), and boxing (two pages). Taken together, the three major football codes comprise over eleven pages. A glance at more recent book titles, book chapters, and journal articles reveals no significant shift in overall emphasis, although several key works on other individual sports and wider-ranging themes have been published in that period as well.

The existence of mnemonic densities in any history should not be surprising, as historiographical layering is not a finite, exhaustible process of amassing factual research but a malleable product of its time; its economic, political, and cultural circumstances; and the intellectual positions and predispositions of its practitioners. A number of related factors help to explain the domination of cricket, rugby, and Australian Rules football in Australasian historiography. Culturally, these sports have had an enduring popularity in both countries, and their perceived paramountcy in national, state, and regional identities in both Australia and New Zealand has promoted their study as vehicles for social and cultural critique.[11] The personal sporting predilections, genders, and class backgrounds of sports historians also play a role. Written sources, too, are significant; the domination of contemporary newspaper sports pages by cricket and some football codes echoes historic patterns.

There is little doubt that the density of cricket and football-focused sports histories is problematic in terms of its exclusivity of other sports and in terms of its contribution to the narrowing of the definition of sporting practices, but the trend has helped facilitate many important scholarly discussions and debates. Two of these serve to illustrate the generative potential of these sometimes frustrating mnemonic densities and evolving scholarship: rugby union in New Zealand sports historiography and emergent arguments about the Aboriginal origins of Australian Rules football.

The influence of both Sinclair and Phillips on New Zealand sport historiography cannot be underestimated. Both historians address the 1905 rugby union All Blacks' tour of the United Kingdom, a key mythical fixture in New Zealand national identity. In *A Man's Country?*, Phillips critiques the constructed success of that tour as measured empirically by games won and assesses the team within his analysis of New Zealand masculinity. While highly influential, the work has evoked scholarly responses that represent high-water marks in the development of New Zealand sports history. Caroline Daley has problematized masculinity and gender, for example, and Greg Ryan has engaged directly with Phillips both empirically and conceptually by challenging his rural-roots construction of New Zealand rugby. The dynamism of these intellectual discourses can also be seen in other recent rugby historiography, such as Brendan Hokuwhitu's work on Māori masculinities and colonialism and Malcolm MacLean's writing on *Pakeha* (white) masculinities.

In Australia, amongst the broad scholarship about Australian Rules football covering facets as far-ranging as club histories, biographies, social dimensions, and cultural analyses, an intriguing and increasingly culturally significant debate percolates over origins. At the heart of this contentious discussion is the claim that the game emerged from, or at the very least was significantly influenced by, a precolonial Aboriginal game called Marngrook. The debate is perhaps less interesting for the empirical evidence behind the claim but for the manner in which the issue exposes cultural fault lines between Indigenous and non-Indigenous Australia.

Considered by some writers and historians to be a derivation from Gaelic football, introduced by Irish migrants in the nineteenth century, Australian Rules football was first played in 1858 in Victoria and codified in 1859.[12] Tom Wills, who grew up in western Victoria and learned the local Aboriginal language as a child, was instrumental in the development and codification of the game. His link with Aboriginal culture, and presumed familiarity with the football-style game called Marngrook, led to claims that he was influenced by this body-cultural practice. The Marngrook claim for Aboriginal provenance, expounded by Jim Poulter in 1993, was predicated on family oral histories and by Wills's life story. The claim coincided with a growing Indigenous rights movement in Australia demanding a number of reparatory measures for injustices committed against Aborigines and Torres Strait Islanders and at a time when racial issues in the football code, and in Australian sport more generally, were capturing national attention.

These contemporary sociopolitical factors amplified the power of the Marngrook claim, especially amongst Aboriginal Australians and Aboriginal football players, who today constitute 10 percent of players in the national professional body, the Australian Football League, while comprising roughly 2 percent of the national population. Despite its appeal, the Marngrook claim was strongly rebutted by sports historian Gillian Hibbins as a "seductive myth."[13] Her empirically based argument has been widely accepted and supported by other scholars, including Wills's award-winning biographer Greg de Moore. Academic analysis favors neither the Irish nor Aboriginal creation stories and instead attributes the genesis of Australian Rules football to English football traditions.[14] Marngrook has its staunch defenders, however, including a number of scholars who contend that historians' insistence on verifiable written evidence overlooks inherited oral evidence and other non-Western epistemological systems.[15] The debate thus not only highlights the particulars of this subject but illuminates larger issues of cultural relations, systems of knowledge production, and interpretation of evidence and, in the process, signals shifts in the ways sports history is increasingly understood, approached, and practiced.

New Directions

Pleas for attention to overlooked areas of sports history are commonplace, and all Australasian sports historians are aware of gaps and opportunities in their own and others' fields of research. It is standard authorial practice to note these in conclusions of published academic work, and new research efforts continually extend our knowledge. The histories of particular sports offer one example. In their hybrid book revising their earlier works and offering further reflections, Richard Cashman and Rob Hess consciously included new research on lesser studied sports, including cycling and swimming. Drivers for new research on particular sports can include significant anniversaries, such as occurred after 2001 with Australian and New Zealand swimming, surfing, and related aquatic sports that formed or formalized in the early twentieth century.[16] Other sports have also benefitted from expanding scholarship.

New research also furnishes well-established analytical categories with new examples. Caroline Symons's *The Gay Games: A History* broke ground for historical treatment of sexuality in sport that incorporated Antipodean as well as international perspectives. Brendan Hokowhitu's work on Māori masculinity offers important new perspectives on both gender and race in a specific Australasian context. And research into race and sport in Australasia historically has benefitted from a geographical expansion to include previously neglected regions, such as Matthew Stephen's book *Contact Zones*, which focuses on the Northern Territory, as well as from new insights on the redemptive power of sport in Aboriginal communities.[17]

Calls for new research directions are also frequently heard. For example, Richard Cashman has appealed for a shift from general sports histories to more works on specific time periods and challenged colleagues to pay greater attention to modes of representation.[18] Perhaps the most challenging intellectual appeal to new directions, of thinking as well as practice, came a few years later from Douglas Booth and Murray G. Phillips, writing almost simultaneously from both sides of the Tasman.

Booth's book *The Field* and Phillips's *Deconstructing Sport History* encouraged sports historians to acknowledge, consider, and engage with the cultural turn in history and, in the process, grapple with often-neglected methodological, epistemological, and ontological issues in their craft. Utilizing Alun Munslow's epistemological typology of reconstructionism, constructionism, and deconstructionism and David Hackett Fischer's paradigmatic framework for analysis, Booth surveyed and critiqued the titular field of sports history, including New Zealand and Australia, to argue for a greater engagement with the cultural turn. In his edited collection, Phillips and contributors applied the precepts of deconstructionism to sports history, in effect suggesting how Booth's appeal might be applied. The impact of these complementary works was major. Booth won the North American Society for Sport History (NASSH) book award for *The Field* in 2006, which also received the ASSH Special Commendation in 2007, while Phillips took the inaugural NASSH edited book award for *Deconstructing Sport History* in 2007. Further indicating their impact, the ideas and approaches espoused in these two works were also heavily critiqued.[19] More significant to sports history than the immediate gongs and brickbats, however, has been the encouragement these works have provided some sports historians to experiment with new approaches.

Methodologically and epistemologically, the cultural turn has helped direct growing research into the fields of visuality, materiality, affect, bodies, and other areas new or rare in sports history. Visual images have always been important to sports history, providing information on sporting arenas, facilities, and equipment; capturing dramatic and memorable moments in sport; and creating iconic referents. Used as illustrative material, such images tended to escape rigorous analysis. The visual turn has increased awareness of the untapped potential of images to yield more than simply factual or descriptive information about the sporting past. Increasingly, images are understood to offer insight into the multiple possible cultural meanings of sport, and their reproduction and continued use can offer a perspective on how the past circulates in the present and how images can influence interpretations of past events. The theme has been taken up in Australasia by several sports historians.[20]

Likewise, the cultural turn has contributed to a growing awareness of the potential importance of material artifacts in sports history, including objects such as trophies, statues, monuments of various types, sports equipment, and memorabilia, and built physical structures such as stadia, gymnasia, sporting grounds, and grandstands. There is, of course, a great deal of overlap between visuality and materiality. Such commonalities are important considerations in the cultural turn; both visuality and materiality are concerned less with images and objects as sources of factual information about the past and more as keys to understanding cultural practices and meanings. Where materiality differs from visuality as an approach is its appreciation of the physical qualities of objects and how these dimensions can influence understandings of the sporting past through physical presence, form, and, potentially, human interaction. In proposing a typology of sporting material culture and an analytical framework based on systems of values and practices, Stephen Hardy, John Loy, and Douglas Booth argue that "analysis of material culture shines a light on the meaning of sport as bright as that emanating from archives or deep theory."[21] This tantalizing claim has yet to be properly tested in the Australasian context in the way it has elsewhere.[22]

The influence of the cultural turn on Australasian sports history is reflected in the special issue of the ASSH journal *Sporting Traditions*, guest-edited by Douglas Booth and Murray Phillips, titled "Sport History and the Cultural Turn." In addition to contributions that address visuality and materiality, the collection highlights a third emergent area of research—the emotional or "affectual" turn. Affect requires a repositioning of the body as the locus of inquiry in sports history and addresses the emotional, physical, and visceral reactions of sporting participants. This is an embryonic field in sports history, with many epistemological, methodological, and ontological questions yet to be framed. Matthew Klugman's book *Passion Play*, which addresses seasonal cycles of passion, love, and suffering amongst fans of Australian Rules football, is an important and ASSH-commended case study. John Cash and Joy Damousi's 2010 book *Footy Passions*, together with Douglas Booth's work on affect in surfing, also explores these questions in useful ways that will help influence future research in this area.

Bodies are important not only to the study of affect, emotion, and passion but also in other ways. The cultural turn acknowledges the cultural creation and control of human bodies, questions around which have informed the aforementioned works of Caroline Daley, Charlotte Macdonald, and Brendan Hokowhitu's Foucauldian analyses of Māori masculinity. Bodies, pleasure, and discipline are also central to much of Douglas Booth's work and constitute an important focus in his book *Australian Beach Cultures*.

The influence of social theory, as evidenced in the general repositioning of the body in sports history, reflects a growing cross-fertilization between sports history and other disciplines. Sports historians are increasingly willing to borrow approaches, concepts, and theoretical perspectives from sociology, cultural studies, and other fields. Holly Thorpe's book *Snowboarding Bodies in Theory and Practice*, while not a work of sports history per se, indicates the potential of cross-fertilization. Murray G. Phillips's edited book, *Representing the Sporting Past in Museums and Halls of Fame*, similarly borrows from another field and conceptual approach—museum studies and the "new museology"—to comprehensively extend the remit of sports history to examine international sports museums. In addition, sports historians are increasingly willing to collaborate with scholars in these other fields. New Zealand sociologist Richard Pringle and Australian Murray G. Phillips's edited collection on postmodernism and sports history, *Critical Sport Histories*, exemplifies this interdisciplinary, and intra-Australasian, cooperation. The theme of the 2011 ASSH Sporting Traditions XVIII conference—"The Past in the Present: Sport History and Popular Culture"—along with individual published output from that meeting, offers a further example of cross-fertilization and the influence of the cultural turn.

Other new directions can also be charted. Of these, attention to globalization and to transnational perspectives are particularly evident. Barbara J. Keys's examination of these themes in the context of 1930s international sporting competitions, *Globalizing Sport*, which won both the NASSH and ASSH book awards in 2007, is an exemplar of this approach in sports history. A movement away from nationalist frameworks for analysis can be discerned in several works. Caroline Daley calls for a decentering of New

Zealand identity in favor of non-nationalistic frameworks for analysis. Sean Brawley and Nick Guoth's edited book, *Australia's Asian Sporting Context, 1920s–30s*, while not decentering Australia in Daley's sense, does extend the nation's sports history beyond sovereign borders and into untapped territory. The involvement of Australian sports historians and their universities in two recent emerging international sports studies conferences, each of which has enjoyed multiple iterations—"Sport and the Pacific Region" and "Sport, Race and Ethnicity"—further reflects this global refocusing as well as the trend toward interdisciplinarity.

Conclusion

The breadth of Australasian sports history contributes to understandings of Australasian history in two fundamental ways. First, topics, themes, and time frames extend critical understandings of Australia and New Zealand culture and society, and Australasian sports historians increasingly present and publish in "mainstream" history-related forums. Second, through this dissemination, and through increased interdisciplinarity, emerging methodological, epistemological, and ontological approaches in sports history also reach wider academic audiences and have the potential at least to influence Australasian history more broadly. Certainly, sports history no longer sits on the fringe, and it contributes intellectually to Australasian history in the same manner as other fields such as cultural studies and gender studies.

A limitation to the impact of sports history on Australasian history more broadly is the number and dispositions of its practitioners. While the preponderance of references to certain authors indicates something of their concentration and contributions, what is not immediately obvious is the relatively small field of players that exists. Australia and New Zealand are, after all, not densely populated, with 22 million and 4.4 million residents, respectively. Scholarly circles are small, and the involvement of independent and non-academic scholars in the creation of sports history is vital. While this amalgamated group has produced a continuous and prolific output over the brief decades in which sports history has emerged, the potential for internecine dispute is high, as sometimes erupts in conferences, publications, and other communication. Disagreement is evident in any grouping, can be constructive, and therefore is not a problem in itself, but it can stymie productive debate and development. Sports history in Australasia, like everywhere, is a dynamic process involving interpretation, mediation, reworking, and injection of new and challenging ideas. All ideas and works should be subject to critical but genuinely open reception, and even canonical works should be sacrificial. Scholarly work demands this. Viewed in this way, the Australasian historiography surveyed in this chapter has not been critiqued with a view to hierarchies of importance but rather as contributions to a field that does not, and cannot, remain static in its obsessions, approaches, and methodologies.

NOTES

1. Eviatar Zerubavel, *Time Maps: Collective Memory and the Social Shape of the Past* (Chicago: University of Chicago Press, 2003), 26.
2. Stuart Macintyre, "Sport and Past Australasian Culture," in *Sport in Australasian Society: Past and Present*, ed. J. A. Mangan and John Nauright (London: Frank Cass, 2000), 1.
3. At the time of writing, historians Greg Ryan and Geoff Watson are completing the first, with the working title *Sport and the New Zealanders*.
4. Malcolm MacLean, "Reading Sport in Aotearoa/New Zealand: Where's the History?" *Sporting Traditions* 17.2 (2001): 65–71; Clare Simpson, ed. *Special Issue: Fresh Perspectives on New Zealand's Sporting Past, Sporting Traditions* 21.2 (2005).
5. Clare Simpson, *Women and Recreation in Aotearoa/New Zealand: An Annotated Bibliography* (Canterbury, New Zealand: Department of Parks, Recreation & Tourism, Lincoln University College, 1991); Douglas Booth, "Searching for the Past: Sport Historiography in New Zealand," *Sporting Traditions* 21.2 (2005b): 1–28; Malcolm MacLean, "New Zealand (Aotearoa)," in *Routledge Companion to Sports History*, ed. S. W. Pope and John Nauright (London: Routledge, 2010), 510–525.
6. Marion K. Stell, *Half the Race: A History of Australian Women in Sport* (Sydney: Angus & Robertson, 1991); MacLean, "Reading Sport."
7. Caroline Daley, "Women Endurance Swimmers: Dissolving Grease Suits and Decentring New Zealand History," *Sporting Traditions* 21.2 (2005): 29–55.
8. Murray G. Phillips, ed. *Deconstructing Sport History: A Postmodern Analysis* (Albany: State University of New York Press, 2006); Douglas Booth, *The Field: Truth and Fiction in Sport History* (London: Routledge, 2005a).
9. Zerubavel, *Time Maps*, 26.
10. MacLean, "Reading Sport," 70.
11. Malcolm MacLean, "Football as Social Critique: Protest Movements, Rugby and History in Aotearoa, New Zealand," in *Sport in Australasian Society*, 255–277.
12. Geoffrey Blainey, *A Game of Our Own: The Origins of Australian Football* (Melbourne: National Australian Football Council, 1990), ch. 9.
13. Gillian Hibbins, "A Seductive Myth," in *The Australian Game of Football: Since 1858*, ed. Geoff Slattery (Melbourne: Geoff Slattery Publishing, 2008), 45.
14. Blainey, *A Game of Our Own*; Greg de Moore, *Tom Wills: His Spectacular Rise and Tragic Fall* (Sydney: Allen & Unwin, 2010), 283–286.
15. Barry Judd, "Australian Rules Football as Aboriginal Cultural Artifact," *The Canadian Journal of Native Studies* 25.1 (2005): 215–237; *On the Boundary Line: Colonial Identity in Football* (Melbourne: Australian Scholarly Publishing, 2008); Ciannon Cazaly, "Off the Ball: Football's History Wars," *Meanjin Quarterly* 67.4 (2008): 82–87.
16. Ed Jaggard, ed., *Between the Flags: One Hundred Summers of Australian Surf Lifesaving* (Sydney: University of New South Wales Press, 2006); Sean Brawley, *Bondi Lifesaver: A History of an Australian Icon* (Sydney: ABC Books, 2007); Tracy Rockwell, *Water Warriors: Chronicle of Australian Water Polo* (Sydney: Pegasus, 2008); MacLean, "New Zealand (Aotearoa)."
17. Sean Gorman, *Legends: The AFL Indigenous Team of the Century* (Canberra: Aboriginal Studies Press, 2011); Judd, *On the Boundary Line*.
18. Richard Cashman, *Sport in the National Imagination: Australian Sport in the Federation Decades* (Sydney: Walla Walla Press, 2002), 7.

19. Allen Guttmann, "Review Essay: The Ludic and the Ludicrous," *The International Journal of the History of Sport* 25.1 (2007): 100–112.
20. Mike Huggins and Mike O'Mahony, eds., *The Visual in Sport* (London: Routledge, 2012).
21. Stephen Hardy, John Loy, and Douglas Booth, "The Material Culture of Sport: Toward a Typology," *Journal of Sport History* 36.1 (2009): 129.
22. Patricia Vertinsky and Sherry McKay, eds., *Disciplining Bodies in the Gymnasium: Memory, Monument, Modernism* (London: Routledge, 2004).

BIBLIOGRAPHY

Adair, Daryl. "Australia." In *Routledge Companion to Sports History*, edited by S. W. Pope and John Nauright, 330–349. London: Routledge, 2010.

Adair, Daryl. "Australian Sport History: From the Founding Years to Today." *Sport in History* 29.3 (2009): 405–436.

Adair, Daryl. "Sports History in the 'Antipodes' and 'Australasia.'" *Sporting Traditions* 19.1 (2002): 65–74.

Adair, Daryl, and Wray Vamplew. *Sport in Australian History*. Melbourne: Oxford University Press, 1997.

Australian Society for Sports History. *Sport and Colonialism in Nineteenth Century Australasia*. ASSH Studies in Sports History 1. Sydney: Australian Society for Sports History, 1986.

Blainey, Geoffrey. *A Game of Our Own: The Origins of Australian Football*. Melbourne: National Australian Football Council, 1990.

Booth, Douglas. "Ambiguities in Pleasure and Discipline: The Development of Competitive Surfing." *Journal of Sport History* 22.3 (1995): 189–206.

Booth, Douglas. *Australian Beach Cultures: The History of Sun, Sand and Surf*. London: Frank Cass, 2001.

Booth, Douglas. *The Field: Truth and Fiction in Sport History*. London: Routledge, 2005a.

Booth, Douglas. "(Re)Reading *The Surfers' Bible*: The Affects of *Tracks*." *Journal of Media & Cultural Studies* 22.1 (2008): 17–35.

Booth, Douglas. "Searching for the Past: Sport Historiography in New Zealand." *Sporting Traditions* 21.2 (2005b): 1–28.

Booth, Douglas. "Surfing '60s: A Case Study in the History of Pleasure and Discipline." *Australian Historical Studies* 26.103 (1994): 262–279.

Booth, Douglas, and Colin Tatz. *One-Eyed: A View of Australian Sport*. Sydney: Allen & Unwin, 2000.

Booth, Douglas, and Murray Phillips, eds. *Special Issue: Sport History and the Cultural Turn*. *Sporting Traditions* 27.2 (2010): iv–vi.

Brawley, Sean. *Bondi Lifesaver: A History of an Australian Icon*. Sydney: ABC Books, 2007.

Brawley, Sean, and Nick Guoth, eds. *Australia's Asian Sporting Context, 1920s–30s*. London: Routledge, 2013.

Cash, John, and Joy Damousi. *Footy Passions*. Sydney: University of New South Wales Press, 2010.

Cashman, Richard. *Paradise of Sport: A History of Australian Sport*. Sydney: Walla Walla Press, 2010.

Cashman, Richard. *Paradise of Sport: The Rise of Organised Sport in Australia*. Melbourne: Oxford University Press, 1995.

Cashman, Richard. *Sport in the National Imagination: Australian Sport in the Federation Decades*. Sydney: Walla Walla Press, 2002.

Cashman, Richard, and Rob Hess, eds. *Sport, History and Australian Culture: Passionate Pursuits*. Sydney: Walla Walla Press, 2011.

Cashman, Richard, John O'Hara, and Andrew Honey, eds. *Sport, Federation, Nation*. Sydney: Walla Walla Press, 2001.

Cazaly, Ciannon. "Off the Ball: Football's History Wars." *Meanjin Quarterly* 67.4 (2008): 82–87.

Collins, Chris, ed. *Sport in New Zealand Society*. Palmerston North, New Zealand: Dunmore Press, 2000.

Daley, Caroline. *Leisure and Pleasure: Reshaping and Revealing the New Zealand Body 1900–1960*. Auckland: Auckland University Press, 2003.

Daley, Caroline. "Women Endurance Swimmers: Dissolving Grease Suits and Decentring New Zealand History." *Sporting Traditions* 21.2 (2005): 29–55.

de Moore, Greg. *Tom Wills: His Spectacular Rise and Tragic Fall*. Sydney: Allen & Unwin, 2010.

Edwards, Ken, with Troy Meston. *Yulunga: Traditional Indigenous Games*. Canberra: Australian Sports Commission, 2008.

Fischer, David Hackett. *Historians' Fallacies: Toward a Logic of Historical Thought*. New York: Harper & Row, 1970.

Gorman, Sean. *Legends: The AFL Indigenous Team of the Century*. Canberra: Aboriginal Studies Press, 2011.

Guttmann, Allen. "Review Essay: The Ludic and the Ludicrous." *The International Journal of the History of Sport* 25.1 (2007): 100–112.

Hardy, Stephen, John Loy, and Douglas Booth. "The Material Culture of Sport: Toward a Typology." *Journal of Sport History* 36.1 (2009): 129–152.

Hess, Rob, and Bob Stewart, eds. *More than a Game: An Unauthorised History of Australian Rules Football*. Melbourne: Melbourne University Press, 1998.

Hess, Rob, and Matthew Klugman. "Australian Sporting Culture: Bibliographical Perspectives." In *Sport, History and Australian Culture*, edited by Richard Cashman and Rob Hess, 165–172. Sydney: Walla Walla Press, 2011.

Hibbins, Gillian. "A Seductive Myth." In *The Australian Game of Football: Since 1858*, edited by Geoff Slattery, 45. Melbourne: Geoff Slattery Publishing, 2008.

Hokowhitu, Brendan. "Authenticating Māori Physicality: Translations of 'Games' and 'Pastimes' by Early Travellers and Missionaries to New Zealand." *International Journal of the History of Sport* 25.10 (2008): 1355–1373.

Hokowhitu, Brendan. "Māori Rugby and Subversion: Creativity, Domestication, Oppression and Decolonization." *International Journal of the History of Sport* 26.16 (2009): 2314–2334.

Hokowhitu, Brendan. "Rugby and *Tino Rangatiratanga*: Early Māori Rugby and the Formation of 'Traditional' Māori Masculinity." *Sporting Traditions* 21.2 (2005): 75–95.

Howell, Reet, and Maxwell Howell. *A History of Australian Sport*. Sydney: Shakespeare Head Press, 1987.

Huggins, Mike, and Mike O'Mahony, eds. *The Visual in Sport*. London: Routledge, 2012.

Jaggard, Ed, ed. *Between the Flags: One Hundred Summers of Australian Surf Lifesaving*. Sydney: University of New South Wales Press, 2006.

Judd, Barry. "Australian Rules Football as Aboriginal Cultural Artifact." *The Canadian Journal of Native Studies* 25.1 (2005): 215–237.

Judd, Barry. *On the Boundary Line: Colonial Identity in Football*. Melbourne: Australian Scholarly Publishing, 2008.

Keys, Barbara J. *Globalizing Sport: National Rivalry and International Community in the 1930s*. Cambridge, MA: Harvard University Press, 2006.

Klugman, Matthew. *Passion Play: Love, Hope, and Heartbreak at the Footy*. Melbourne: Hunter, 2010.

Macdonald, Charlotte. *Strong, Beautiful and Modern: National Fitness in Britain, New Zealand, Australia and Canada, 1935–1960*. Wellington, New Zealand: Bridget Williams Books, 2011.

Macintyre, Stuart. "Sport and Past Australasian Culture." In *Sport in Australasian Society: Past and Present*, edited by J. A. Mangan and John Nauright, 1–8. London: Frank Cass, 2000.

MacLean, Malcolm. "Football as Social Critique: Protest Movements, Rugby and History in Aotearoa, New Zealand." In *Sport in Australasian Society: Past and Present*, edited by J. A. Mangan and John Nauright, 255–277. London: Frank Cass, 2000.

MacLean, Malcolm. "New Zealand (Aotearoa)." In *Routledge Companion to Sports History*, edited by S. W. Pope and John Nauright, 510–525. London: Routledge, 2010.

MacLean, Malcolm. "Of Warriors and Blokes: The Problem of Maori Rugby for Pakeha Masculinity in New Zealand." In *Making the Rugby World: Race, Gender, Commerce*, edited by Timothy J. L. Chandler and John Nauright, 1–26. London: Frank Cass, 1999.

MacLean, Malcolm. "Reading Sport in Aotearoa/New Zealand: Where's the History?" *Sporting Traditions* 17.2 (2001): 65–71.

Magdalinski, Tara. "Sport History in Australia: Past Achievements, Future Challenges." *Journal of Sport History* 36.1 (2009): 123–128.

Mangan, J. A., and John Nauright, eds. *Sport in Australasian Society: Past and Present*. London: Frank Cass, 2000.

McLean, Gavin. *Blue, White and Dynamite: 100 Years of the Lyall Bay Surf & Life Saving Club*. Wellington, New Zealand: Lyall Bay Surf & Life Saving Club, 2010.

Mosely, Philip A., Richard Cashman, John O'Hara, and Hilary Weatherburn, eds. *Sporting Immigrants: Sport and Ethnicity in Australia*. Sydney: Walla Walla Press, 1997.

Munslow, Alun. *Deconstructing History*. London: Routledge, 1997.

Nauright, John. "Sport History in Aotearoa/New Zealand." *ASSH Bulletin* 18 (1993): 43–47.

Nauright, John, ed. *Sport, Power and Society in New Zealand: Historical and Contemporary Perspectives*. ASSH Studies in Sports History 11. Sydney: Australian Society for Sports History, 1995.

Patterson, Brad, ed. *Sport, Society and Culture in New Zealand*. Wellington, New Zealand: University of Wellington, 1999.

Phillips, Jock. *A Man's Country?: The Image of the Pakeha Male—A History*. Auckland: Penguin, 1987.

Phillips, Murray G. *Swimming Australia: One Hundred Years*. Sydney: University of New South Wales Press, 2008.

Phillips, Murray G., ed. *Deconstructing Sport History: A Postmodern Analysis*. Albany: State University of New York Press, 2006.

Phillips, Murray G., ed. *Representing the Sporting Past in Museums and Halls of Fame*. London: Routledge, 2012.

Poulter, Jim. "Marn-Grook—Original Australian Rules." In *This Game of Ours: Supporters' Tales of the People's Game*, edited by Peter Burke and Leo Grogan, 64–67. Melbourne: EATWARFLEMSD, 1993.

Pringle, Richard, and Murray G. Phillips, eds. *Critical Sport Histories: Paradigms, Power and the Postmodern Turn*, Morgantown, WV: FiT, University of West Virginia, 2013.

Rockwell, Tracy. *Water Warriors: Chronicle of Australian Water Polo*. Sydney: Pegasus, 2008.

Ryan, Greg. *The Making of New Zealand Cricket 1832–1914*. London: Frank Cass, 2003.

Ryan, Greg, ed. *Tackling Rugby Myths: Rugby and New Zealand Society 1854–2004*. Dunedin, New Zealand: University of Otago Press, 2005.

Simpson, Clare. *Women and Recreation in Aotearoa/New Zealand: An Annotated Bibliography*. Canterbury, New Zealand: Department of Parks, Recreation & Tourism, Lincoln University College, 1991.

Simpson, Clare, ed. *Special Issue: Fresh Perspectives on New Zealand's Sporting Past. Sporting Traditions* 21.2 (2005).

Sinclair, Keith. *A Destiny Apart: New Zealand's Search for National Identity*. Wellington, New Zealand: Allen & Unwin/Port Nicholson Press, 1986.

Stell, Marion K. *Half the Race: A History of Australian Women in Sport*. Sydney: Angus & Robertson, 1991.

Stephen, Matthew. *Contact Zones: Sport and Race in the Northern Territory 1869–1953*. Darwin, Australia: Charles Darwin University Press, 2010.

Stoddart, Brian. *Saturday Afternoon Fever: Sport in the Australian Culture*. Sydney: Angus & Robertson, 1986.

Symons, Caroline. *The Gay Games: A History*. London: Routledge, 2010.

Tatz, Colin. *Aborigines in Sport*. ASSH Studies in Sport 3. Bedford Park: Australian Society for Sports History, 1987.

Tatz, Colin. *Obstacle Race: Aborigines in Sport*. Sydney: University of New South Wales Press, 1995.

Tatz, Colin, and Paul Tatz. *Black Gold: The Aboriginal and Islander Sports Hall of Fame*. Canberra: Aboriginal Studies Press, 2000.

Thorpe, Holly. *Snowboarding Bodies in Theory and Practice*. Basingstoke, UK: Palgrave Macmillan, 2011.

Vamplew, Wray, and Brian Stoddart, eds. *Sport in Australia: A Social History*. Cambridge, UK: Cambridge University Press, 1994.

Vamplew, Wray, Katherine Moore, John O'Hara, Richard Cashman, and Ian Jobling, eds. *The Oxford Companion to Australian Sport*. 2nd rev. ed. Melbourne: Oxford University Press, 1997.

Vertinsky, Patricia, and Sherry McKay, eds. *Disciplining Bodies in the Gymnasium: Memory, Monument, Modernism*. London: Routledge, 2004.

Zerubavel, Eviatar. *Time Maps: Collective Memory and the Social Shape of the Past*. Chicago: University of Chicago Press, 2003.

PART VI

NEW GLOBALIZATIONS AND THEIR DISCONTENTS

....

CHAPTER 26

CONTEMPORARY GLOBALIZATION AND RECENT OLYMPIC LEADERSHIP

....

STEPHEN R. WENN AND ROBERT K. BARNEY

INTRODUCTION

....

IN July 2001, far from shamed by the fallout from the Salt Lake City bid scandal, Juan Antonio Samaranch stepped aside as president of the International Olympic Committee (IOC) amidst much pomp and circumstance in the Hall of Columns at Moscow's famed House of Trade Unions. As much as Samaranch carefully scripted his pursuit of the IOC presidency in the 1970s,[1] so too did he fastidiously choreograph his exit. The Hall, renowned for its twenty-eight faux marble columns, stunning chandeliers, and a visual fusion of white and gold, also served as the site of state funerals for the likes of Vladimir Lenin (1924) and Joseph Stalin (1953), the show trials of Stalin's rival Nikolai Bukharin (1938), and US U2 pilot Francis Gary Powers (1960), the first of a series of highly anticipated clashes between Soviet chess grand masters Anatoly Karpov and Garry Kasparov in the 1980s, numerous classical music concerts, and Samaranch's own election to the IOC's highest office twenty-one years earlier. Its selection as the setting for the closing session of his presidential tenure was no coincidence. The circle was complete for the man who brought much change to the Olympic movement. Celebrated by some for his vision in rescuing a failing enterprise beset by problems tied to its poor financial status and the intrusion of world geopolitics but harshly criticized by others who railed at the commodification of the Olympics on his presidential watch, there is no denying his imprint on the IOC and the Olympic world in the late twentieth century and beyond.[2] Samaranch, more than anyone else in in the Olympic movement, established the IOC as an organization fully engaged in the process of contemporary globalization.

Much has been written about the challenges faced by Juan Antonio Samaranch when he ascended to the IOC presidency in 1980 and the manner in which he vaulted the IOC to a position of financial wealth, expanded the place of women on the Olympic event program, and tackled the problems associated with the boycott era of the 1970s and early 1980s. Far less research and commentary has been accorded to the array of challenges that Jacques Rogge inherited from his predecessor, the manner in which he confronted them, and his effort to consolidate gains made under Samaranch with respect to the IOC's revenue generation capabilities. This chapter examines their recent leadership amidst an era of global economic change.

GLOBALIZATION: A NEW ECONOMIC TERRAIN FOR SPORT LEADERS

In "Modern Sport and Olympic Games: The Problematic Complexities Raised by the Dynamics of Globalization," Deane Neubauer highlights the pervasive nature of globalization within everyday discourse. As well, he explains the varying connotations of the term. For some, globalization denotes the closeness of people in the world resulting from technological advances over time in communications (telegraph, telephone, fax machine, Internet) and transportation (sea and air travel). For others, globalization is a reflection of the realities of our consumption of goods as they are produced in locations often far distant from our place of residence.[3] Kate Galbraith reduced globalization to a central element, the crossing of borders, whether one identifies, capital, goods, ideas, individuals, diseases, or governments.[4] Giving substance to this notion, Frank J. Lechner and John Boli identified the spread of Japanese sushi; the passion for, and prevalence of, soccer, an English game, all around the world; and the parental acceptance of immunization on a global basis as tangible evidence of globalization in the twentieth century.[5] Some researchers involved in the study of globalization have expounded on the process as one involving "the greater integration of peoples and places,"[6] or "border flattening,"[7] that has unfolded over centuries. As a transnational organization, the IOC has long operated across borders. John Hoberman pointed to the IOC's global outlook through this longer historical lens in his comparative analysis of the IOC, the Scouting and Esperanto movements, all global movements that established their roots in the late nineteenth or early twentieth century. The longer term political, cultural, and economic ties of globalization to the emergence of mega-events such as World's Fairs and Olympic Games served as the central focus for Maurice Roche.[8] Others, notes Neubauer, isolated distinct events in the past half century that have altered and accelerated the globalization process in ways deserving of unique classification—*contemporary globalization*. Our focus as a backdrop for the examination of the Samaranch and Rogge presidencies is on this latter concept, contemporary globalization.

Evidence of the influences of an increasingly globalized world on sport over the latter half of the twentieth century surrounds us. Franchises such as the New York Yankees, Manchester United, and Los Angeles Lakers possess international brand recognition prompting youth in all corners of the world to purchase and wear team apparel. Major professional leagues in North America extended the reach of their product to Europe and Asia, not merely through the peddling of apparel or the sale of television rights but also by establishing development leagues or by encouraging teams to undertake international tours. Similarly, European soccer teams routinely visit North America on preseason tours to capitalize financially on the stature of the likes of Paul Pogba and Cristiano Ronaldo. The National Hockey League, the premier ice hockey league in the world, boasts players from a multitude of countries. Once exclusively American in terms of its participant base, the National Basketball Association has welcomed many European athletes in recent years. Athletes stymied in their efforts to represent the nation of their birth in international sport, whether as a result of their inability to qualify or their dissatisfaction with the level of financial support available to them, have taken their talents abroad.[9] Today's sporting world hardly resembles its appearance in the middle of the twentieth century.

In his effort to capture the essence of contemporary globalization, Neubauer isolated six key drivers involved in altering the foundation of the world marketplace in the latter half of the twentieth century: (a) the collapse of time and space, (b) migration and urbanization, (c) wealth creation and distribution, (d) transformation of global media, (e) trade and consumption, and (f) transformation of value.[10] The shipping and airline industries, through the container ship and the Boeing 747, move goods and people around the world more efficiently, while the advent of satellite technology and the development of the Internet advanced our ability to share ideas across flattened borders. These innovations furthered the process launched much earlier by the invention of the automobile, radio, and telephone.[11] Contemporary globalization has been marked by a discernible movement of people from rural to urban environments, resulting in the growth of mega cities with large populations that serve as cauldrons for more rapid social and cultural change. While global wealth experienced a significant rise in individual income, it has been skewed, creating income inequality within and between countries. However, globalization's effect on this process remains fodder for debate amongst the world's economists. Neubauer highlighted the emergence of global media firms such as Time Warner, Walt Disney Corporation, News Corp, and Bertelsmann AG intent on dominating the mediascape through their subsidiary companies. This process raised concerns about how particular points of view might dominate various media platforms. Companies such as Google and Yahoo, whose business encompasses nontraditional media, burst onto the scene.[12] Despite the evidence of the extent of global trade, Neubauer notes that the preponderance of trade still occurs on an intraregional, as opposed to interregional, basis and that the enhanced degree of interdependence within the global economy can have both positive and negative consequences. A global economy, adds Neubauer, relies on people's willingness to engage in consumption of goods and/or services and demonstrates the inclination of people in regions all over the world to set aside social and cultural traditions in their decision-making concerning the consumption of goods, largely as a result of the power and influence of a new global marketplace.

CONTEMPORARY GLOBALIZATION AND THE OLYMPIC MOVEMENT

The emergence of the Olympic movement's place within a globalized economy relied substantially on three factors: (a) the evolution of satellite technology that permitted the instantaneous transmission of Olympic events on a global basis and the concomitant increase in exposure for the Olympic enterprise via the medium, which, of course, greatly raised the monetary value of Olympic television rights; (b) the emergence of multinational corporations conducting business on a global scale that desired a worldwide advertising platform coupled with the business guile of Adidas's boss, Horst Dassler,[13] who envisioned the Olympics as just such a promotional vehicle; and (c) Juan Antonio Samaranch's relationship with Dassler, their shared vision of the way in which the IOC could capitalize on the shifting basis of the world's economy, and Samaranch's ability to convince his IOC colleagues of the benefits of a much closer articulation between the IOC and commercial firms.

In early 1964, the Syncom III satellite, the first to be placed in a high-altitude, synchronous orbit, some 22,000 miles above the earth, altered the television and communications landscape. "At that altitude," wrote *The New York Times'* Richard Witkin, "a satellite just keeps pace with the west-to-east rotation of the earth below. It is like a miler in the outside lane who keeps even with the man on the inside by running somewhat faster."[14] The National Broadcast Company (NBC), the US Olympic rights holder, now had the capacity to televise the 1964 Tokyo Olympics as Syncom III maintained simultaneous contact with the US and Japanese coastlines. However, NBC chose to televise only the opening ceremonies live on the East Coast and made no further use of the live technology for the duration of the Games. NBC pinned its hopes for recouping its $1.5 million rights investment on commercials sold to advertisers for premium prices during US prime-time (delayed) broadcasts.[15] Despite the bitter disappointment of Tokyo organizers with NBC's programming decisions,[16] the event augured well for the IOC in terms of future revenue and the "reach" of the Olympic Games (see Table 26.1).

In *Selling the Five Rings: The International Olympic Committee and the Rise of Olympic Commercialism*, we (Robert K. Barney and Stephen R. Wenn), along with Scott G. Martyn, examined developments regarding the IOC's pursuit of television revenue during the Avery Brundage (1952–1972) and Lord Killanin (1972–1980) presidencies. Brundage struggled philosophically with the immense profit potential posed by the IOC becoming more closely articulated with the television industry, largely due to his devotion to Pierre de Coubertin's vision of the Games. But, as a career businessman, he was unable to walk away from the money. Satellite technology accelerated revenue

Table 26.1 Summer Olympic Broadcast Revenue and Number of Broadcasting Countries, 1964–1980

Year	Location	Total Television Revenue (US$, millions)	Broadcasting Countries
1964	Tokyo	1.6	40
1968	Mexico City	9.8	n/a
1972	Munich	17.8	98
1976	Montreal	34.9	124
1980	Moscow	88	111

prospects and heightened the level of interest in the psyches of the IOC's Olympic partners, the International Sport Federations (ISFs), the National Olympic Committees (NOCs), and the Organizing Committees (OCOGs), each of which demanded greater shares of Olympic television revenue to be directed to their coffers. Brundage ushered the IOC into the television era. He was largely responsible for the drafting of its initial television policies, including those that dealt with how the money would be distributed. However, with respect to the generation of sums of money for the IOC, ISFs, NOCs, and OCOGs, Brundage and his closest IOC colleague, David Cecil, the Marquess of Exeter, were "reluctant revolutionaries."[17] The IOC, decreed Brundage, would not be involved in negotiating the television contracts, leaving the job to the OCOGs. Involvement in such potentially messy commercial transactions might sully the IOC's image. Nevertheless, the IOC retained the right to distribute the money. Both Brundage and Exeter fretted over the manner in which commercial revenue would alter the foundation of the Olympic movement. They soon had good reason for such concern. OCOGs rapidly discovered ways to circumvent existing distribution policies in favor of their own financial agendas, to the detriment of the Olympic Tripartite.[18]

Brundage's successor, Lord Killanin, understood that television money might very well serve as the adhesive necessary to keep the Olympic Tripartite functioning in collaborative fashion after years of Brundage's autocratic leadership.[19] He authorized the establishment of a working committee tasked with improving the IOC's knowledge base concerning the television industry and negotiating practices with an eye to becoming more involved in the negotiation of television contracts in future years. Eventually, Killanin established the IOC as a participant in negotiations for Olympic television contracts. His precise intent was to protect the IOC's financial interests. Killanin can be considered a transitional figure who took deliberative steps to advance the IOC's ability to generate commercial revenue.[20]

Despite the availability of increasing sums of television revenue in the 1960s and 1970s, Samaranch inherited an organization that was far from affluent and lacked stability, especially when one considers the litany of problems stemming from world geopolitics that buffeted the Olympic movement in the 1970s.[21] Richard Pound observed: "In

1980, the Olympic Movement was under sustained attack from political powers and was, indeed a virtual hostage to world tensions. It was disunited, well short of universal, and had no financial resources to give it the autonomy and independence to resist political pressures."[22] A worrying feature of the IOC's fiscal foundation remained that its budget was driven in excess of 90 percent by television revenue, and therefore, fragile in nature given the pervading threat of Olympic boycotts and fears that festivals would be cancelled. Greater discipline with respect to its financial practices was also required. Peter Ueberroth, president of the Los Angeles OCOG, recounts the time when he held back transfer of a $25 million check to an IOC official for one day in 1979 as a means of retaining $9,000 in interest payments. Ueberroth could hardly contain his amazement when that same IOC representative[23] did not cash it for twenty days, thereby sacrificing a substantial sum of money in interest payments.

Samaranch was both focused and productive during the first twelve years of his presidency that culminated with the successful Barcelona Olympics, one of the Olympic movement's signal successes in terms of post-Olympic legacy for a host city.[24] He traveled the world, reportedly some 1.86 million miles, seeking audiences with political leaders and espousing the virtues of Olympism, the ill-advised nature of Olympic boycotts that stifled the dreams of the world's athletes, and the potential of the Olympic movement as an instrument of world peace.[25] While little could have been done to dissuade the Soviets from launching their boycott of the 1984 Los Angeles Olympics, Richard Pound provided an insider's view of the masterful job Samaranch did in averting a large-scale boycott of the 1988 Seoul Olympics.[26] His diplomatic acumen displayed over these years explains his success in nullifying the threat of Olympic boycotts. Samaranch also believed that the Olympic movement could be strengthened by increasing its reach, especially within the developing world. The community of NOCs experienced notable and steady growth under his stewardship (see Table 26.2).

But, for Samaranch, the IOC's dependency on television revenue remained a central component of his managerial agenda. His approach to this dependency revealed much concerning his vision for the Olympic Games. At the 1981 Baden Baden Olympic

Table 26.2 National Olympic Committees Growth by Region, 1980–2010

Year	NOCs	Africa	Asia	Europe	Oceania	The Americas
2010	204	53	43	49	17	42
2005	202	53	44	48	15	42
2000	199	53	42	48	14	42
1995	197	52	43	48	12	42
1990	165	45	36	34	7	39
1985	161	45	37	35	7	37
1980	147	42	31	35	4	35

Congress, Samaranch tackled the thorny issue of amateurism and its hypocrisy that favored the participation of paid athletes who participated in state-funded athletic programs such as those operating in the Soviet Union and East Germany, against the exclusion of those who parlayed their athletic talents into a career in professional sport in North America, Europe, and Oceania. Samaranch wanted the best athletes present at Olympic festivals. The best athletes would attract the biggest sums of television revenue, especially from the United States. They would drive further interest in the Olympics around the world as the contests would be seen as the pinnacle of sport competition. Yet Samaranch understood the dynamics of his conservative, tradition-laden organization, and rather than moving headlong into the process and forcing a vote on the declaration of the Games being open to professional athletes, a move that would have provoked much criticism from both inside and outside the organization, he coolly maneuvered his colleagues into granting the ISFs more autonomy in determining eligibility requirements for Olympic athletes within their respective sports. He fully comprehended the desire of these same federations to have the best athletes present in Olympic competition to garner the volume of media attention necessary to spur the growth and continued development of their sport on a global scale. The path to a (near) open Olympics had been established.

While the move to open the Olympics to professional athletes enhanced the amount of television revenue flowing to the IOC, OCOGs, NOCs, and ISFs (see Table 26.3), it did little to address the issue of dependency on television money. Samaranch's increasing discomfort with the IOC's fiscal status stimulated him to seek alternative sources of revenue. Would the best athletes also stimulate a core group of corporate investors that might be courted—major multinational corporations seeking a global marketing platform for their products and services in an increasingly globalized economy? In the early 1980s, preliminary discussions between Samaranch and Horst Dassler, Adidas's boss, who had recently founded International Sports and Leisure Marketing (ISL), a sport marketing agency that swiftly carved out a relationship with the Fédération International de Football Association (FIFA), as well, encouraged Samaranch to explore means of capitalizing commercially on the Olympic logo.

Table 26.3 Summer Olympic Broadcast Revenue and Number of Broadcasting Countries, 1984–2008

Year	Location	Total Television Revenue (US$)	Broadcasting Countries
1984	Los Angeles	286.9 millions	156
1988	Seoul	402.6 millions	160
1992	Barcelona	636.1 millions	193
1996	Atlanta	893.3 millions	214
2000	Sydney	1,331.6 billions	220
2004	Athens	1,494.0 billions	220
2008	Beijing	1,739.0 billions	220

Ultimately, Samaranch and the IOC Executive Board convinced the General IOC Session to embrace the establishment of a worldwide corporate sponsor program (The Olympic Program, now The Olympic Partners [TOP]), emphasizing the need for the IOC to diversify its revenue base while structuring a commercial marketing program that protected the image of the Olympic movement and prevented the wanton exploitation of its logo, one of the perceived distasteful trends of professional sport. Samaranch envisioned that ISL's involvement would streamline the IOC's marketing efforts, benefit all NOCs, and negate the need for sponsor companies to negotiate a series of individual contracts with multiple NOCs—a single sponsorship contract granted marketing access to all the territories embracing an NOC. It required prolonged negotiations to obtain the agreement of the British Olympic Association and the US Olympic Committee to support the ISL initiative. Corporate sponsors, too, were slow in buying into the IOC's new marketing program prior to its launch in conjunction with the staging of the 1988 Calgary Olympic Winter Games and Seoul's Olympic Summer Games.[27] However, TOP has provided a steadily increasing and lucrative source of revenue for the Olympic movement since its inception (see Table 26.4) and, in the process, accomplished Samaranch's goal of reducing the Olympic movement's dependency on television money.

Samaranch's success in revolutionizing the IOC's and the Olympic movement's revenue base, however, aroused criticism. Despite the clear need to address the IOC's ability to generate revenue, Samaranch was assailed for having tainted the Olympic image by furthering a marriage to commercialism. In the eyes of many, a sharp relationship with the corporate world somehow compromised the Olympic movement's long and hallowed traditions of incorruptible fair play and noble amateurism. This debate will continue for the foreseeable future, and we certainly do not propose to settle it at this time; however, given the increasing size of the Games and the cost in staging them, as well as the growing unwillingness of governments to foot the entire bill for a city to host the Olympics, private-sector money is necessary. We judge Samaranch's course of action as wise and prudent. The *clear venue* policy is an important distinguishing feature of Olympic broadcasts that should be maintained in our view and provides a needed

Table 26.4 The Olympic Program/The Olympic Partners Revenue, 1985–2012

Quadrennium	Games	Partners	NOCs	Revenue US$, millions
1985–1988	Calgary/Seoul	9	159	96
1989–1992	Albertville/Barcelona	12	169	172
1993–1996	Lillehammer/Atlanta	10	197	279
1997–2000	Nagano/Sydney	11	199	579
2001–2004	Salt Lake /Athens	11	202	663
2005–2008	Turin/Beijing	12	205	866
2009–2012	Vancouver/London	11	205	957

bulwark against the overcommercialization of the Olympic Games. The bottom line is this: Olympic festivals of the size and scope we witness today would not be possible without private-sector money, and those who decry the involvement of the corporate world might well harken back to a time long past, a time no longer remotely recoverable in our new globalized circumstances.

Similarly, Samaranch's decision to open the Games to professional athletes resulted in much contemporary criticism and even today sparks discussion; for instance, when a US men's basketball team, stacked with National Basketball Association star players, mauled an opposing team that was woefully mismatched, such as the case in London, when the United States defeated Nigeria 156–73. Samaranch systematically dismantled amateurism and its built-in hypocrisy to extend an opportunity for the best athletes from the far corners of the world to compete. To avoid situations as noted previously, the IOC would have to reduce the size of the basketball tournament and in the process reduce the extent to which participating teams represent certain regions. Our sense is that the IOC is willing to accept such mismatches in order to maintain its position on universality that governs its approach to the entry list for all other sports, and it is likely that the Nigerians, while not content with the score line, relished the opportunity to compete in the Olympic Games. The participation of National Hockey League players has produced storied Olympic tournaments since Nagano. Soccer's governing body, FIFA, appears content with providing access to professional players under the age of twenty-three (with the exception of two overage players), which has resulted in greatly enhanced soccer on the Olympic stage minus the threat to FIFA's World Cup in terms of relative prestige. Professional tennis players, too, have produced top-flight entertainment, and most surely the London and Rio organizers appreciated the opportunity for the Andy Murray storyline. While figure skating has provided its share of controversy with respect to judging practices, there is no questioning the entertainment value of the competitions involving professional skaters.

Samaranch's success in growing the financial foundation of the Olympic movement and his move to welcome the best athletes to Olympic precincts also resulted in unintended consequences. The IOC's demonstrated ability to "sell" the Olympics for burgeoning television rights fees and market the Games to the CEOs of a select number of multinational corporations, in part, spurred a hyper-competitive Olympic bid city process. Peter Ueberroth's lesson in securing private-sector dollars in support of the efforts of an OCOG (Los Angeles, 1984) also contributed mightily to the awakening of renewed interest in cities around the world to pursue hosting distinction. This renewed interest was welcomed, nurtured, and highlighted as but one measure of the global popularity of the Olympics under Samaranch. However, when Samaranch failed to establish any meaningful oversight or monitoring of IOC members' interaction with officials from bid committees eager to win their support by both legitimate and illegitimate means, and his reticence to pursue rumors of misconduct by a number of IOC members not in keeping with that which would be expected of them, the stage was set for a simmering crisis that bubbled to the surface in light of revelations concerning the Salt Lake City bid for the 2002 Olympic Winter Games.[28]

Jacques Rogge succeeded Samaranch as president of the IOC in July 2001. The task before him was substantial and multifaceted. He needed to restore and safeguard the Olympic brand that had been badly damaged by the Salt Lake City bid scandal, engage the recent establishment of the World Anti-Doping Agency as a springboard to aggressively combat doping in sport, oversee the 2004 Athens Olympics in the face of slow progress in preparations and rising costs, and restrain the growth of the size and cost of the Summer Olympics. His challenge also entailed leading the IOC through the preparations for an Olympic festival to be staged for the first time in China despite concern in many quarters about that nation's commitment to human rights and media access. In managing these tasks, there is little to criticize. He succeeded in steering clear of major controversies, continued the fight against doping, managed to see Athens across the finish line, albeit with a substantial debt, and maneuvered the IOC and the Olympic movement with little serious backlash through the preparations for, and execution of, the Beijing Olympics. He was an effective caretaker, but not a visionary. To be fair, it could be argued that the IOC required just such an individual to stabilize the organizational environment in the wake of the turbulence experienced in the latter years of Samaranch's tenure.

For Rogge, the growth of the Olympic Games, and the associated rise in costs of staging them, was a more nettlesome problem, and it remains a major issue confronting the Olympic movement, especially in light of the economic downturn of 2007 and 2008. In 1999, the IOC decreed that future Summer festivals would be limited to 280 events, but this target was exceeded in Sydney (300), Athens (301), Beijing (302), and London (300). Similarly, at its 2002 Session, the IOC failed in its efforts to limit the number of participants to 10,000. In a decision prompted by expediency, the number of participants was elevated to 10,500. Yet, even that adjusted limit was exceeded in Athens (10,560) and Beijing (10,906). Bill Mallon and Jeroen Heijmans asserted that the problem for Jacques Rogge rested, in part, on the success of the Olympic Games as a global spectacle.[29] As recently as April 2012, at a meeting of the IOC Executive Board with the Association of National Olympic Committees, Rogge reiterated his concerns about the challenge confronting host cities. "We have to be reasonable and the price of the Games must be affordable," he said, and added, "We are not going to propose something radical."[30] Perhaps, he offered, the IOC needed to reassert its commitment to the guidelines established in 2002. The Executive Board discussed the issue at some length at its subsequent meetings in Quebec City.

There is little sign that costs can be reined in by OCOGs without definitive action and imposition by the IOC. First, the cost of construction materials and the bills inherent in providing the venue infrastructure for an Olympic festival will not decline in the future. As noted by J. A. Mangan and the cadre of colleagues recruited to contribute to a special issue (2008) of the *International Journal of the History of Sport* focusing on Olympic legacies, we have witnessed a proliferation of "white elephant" sport facilities in recent host cities.[31] Second, security is an alarmingly expensive portfolio for OCOGs. Given the realities of global terrorism in the early twenty-first century, this too will demand increasing fiscal resources from those entrusted to host the Olympics in the years ahead.

Third, the massive infrastructure costs associated with nonsport facilities that cities feel compelled to construct in order to host the Summer Olympics are very rarely paid for by the time that the Olympians and Paralympians leave town. Local taxpayers foot bills outstanding, in many cases, for lengthy periods of time. Fourth, we do not subscribe to the belief that the continuance of the ambulatory mission of the Olympics Games depends on significantly scaling down the size of all venues that would, in the end, create a mere "made for television" or "in studio" spectacle. The Olympics can and should remain a gathering place for thousands of people from all over the world, not simply the athletes who come to compete. And, while the IOC will need to address this matter going forward, it should be noted that Xiaowei Yu's extensive study of the post-Olympics use of Beijing's Olympic facilities[32] demonstrates two important lessons for future organizers independent of any effort on the part of the IOC to alter the demands placed on a host city: (a) post-Olympic use of facilities is enhanced if those facilities are situated on university campuses, and (b) there is much wisdom in emphasizing temporary facilities that can be dismantled at the close of the Games as opposed to incurring ongoing maintenance, security, and operation costs, especially if the sports supported by those facilities lack cultural tradition in the host city (and country).

While the easiest, and previously suggested means of dealing with these issues is to seek a permanent host site for both the Summer and Olympic Games, the IOC has no interest in such a plan.[33] It would betray Coubertin's expressed desire for an ambulatory tradition for Olympic festivals and challenge a fundamental desire to advance Olympism and the practice of sport in different regions of the world. It perpetually falls on deaf ears in Lausanne despite its economic merits. We offer two possible alternate approaches for consideration: (a) host the Summer Olympics in two cities at the same time, on the same or different continents, or (b) when awarding the Games to a host city, grant the city the opportunity to host two successive Games.[34] Both options would be seen by most, including Rogge, as "radical." But if one is not willing to pare down the number of athletes through more rigorous qualifying procedures and recognize the accelerating costs of facility and infrastructure construction, then maybe, just maybe, "radical" is the prescribed tonic.

As one can see, the Games remain ambulatory with both plans, thereby leaving Coubertin's wishes intact. The first proposal permits the distribution of construction, accommodation, infrastructure, and facility costs across two cities. If the two cities are on different continents, then the athletic facilities that service particular sports can be distributed to the two cities after factoring their relative popularity in the regions, thereby limiting the likelihood that white elephant, underused facilities result. It is difficult to judge how corporate sponsors and television partners might react. The former would have access to two markets, while the latter would be forced to divide a portion of their broadcast personnel teams across two locations. However, if the Games occur in two different locations, the schedules of the sports contested can be adjusted to provide more rest for the athletes in a good number of the disciplines, perhaps aiding their performance and enhancing their Olympic experience. Costly opening and closing ceremonies could be scaled down at both locations.

With the second option, the city chosen would have maintenance costs of the facilities for a four-year period but would also have two sets of television contracts, as well as two sponsorship (TOP and domestic) and ticket-selling cycles to recoup its investment. Television partners might not like the need to "tell the Olympic story" from the same location four years later, and corporate sponsors might not appreciate the slowing down of their access to new markets, but in the final consideration more concern needs to be demonstrated with respect to the economic landscape of the host city when the Olympic Games (and Paralympics) conclude and the Olympic phenomenon departs. Then, too, host cities could aggressively pursue world and regional championships in select sports over the four-year interval between festivals to assist in maintaining their use and/or open the facilities to serve as athlete training centers staffed with expert coaches (and apprentice coaches) from around the world (the latter being paid by the IOC through its solidarity fund). NOCs would be responsible for transporting their athletes to the site and accommodation costs incurred, but if planned effectively, especially in team sports, visits could be coordinated in such a way so as to provide training opportunities, exhibition games, tournaments, or regattas with other visiting contingents. Athletes from around the world could meet and train together, and learn from each other. It might very well afford athletes from developing nations a better opportunity to access world-class training facilities than they currently experience. Cities gain a steady stream of sport-related revenue for the years in advance of the second hosting opportunity, as well as the second opportunity to stage the Olympics, thereby accruing revenue without the burden of massive capital costs to clear their debt. Security protocols would merely have to be revised, as opposed to generated from scratch; however, we concede that the increasingly sophisticated methods employed by those who harbor ill intention, and the necessary advances in technology required to thwart their efforts, provides less in the way of a retardant on expenses than is the case with the venues or structures themselves. At the close of the second hosting opportunity, having had additional time available to fully contemplate the desired legacy use of facilities, more informed decisions might be facilitated as venues experience their transformation into their post-Olympic existence. The Games remain ambulatory, as Coubertin would have wished, albeit in a more restricted sense, and yet they do so in a judicious economic manner considering the size of the festivals and the rising cost of staging them.

Two other initiatives supported by Jacques Rogge during his presidency merit attention in any discussion linked to globalization. First, there is little doubt that Rogge supported Rio's efforts to convince IOC members that a South American city was prepared to host the Olympics. Some viewed the IOC's decision favorably because it extended the Olympic brand to a continent that had not yet hosted an Olympic festival.[35] Others saw the decision as risk-laden and expressed concern about security problems for athletes and visitors given Rio's well-reported crime, violence, poverty, and environmental problems. The final report of the IOC Evaluation Commission, a body chaired by Nawal El Moutawakel, downplayed Brazil's security issues.[36] By all accounts the energy and passion of the Rio bidders were exemplary, and they sold IOC members on the central premise that it was "South America's time."[37] The decision of IOC voters to abandon

Chicago, Rio's perceived major rival, leaving it in the rather embarrassing position of being the first city removed from the ballot, served notice to the USOC that its long-standing dispute with IOC officials over the USOC's share of TOP and global television dollars required resolution before any US city was likely to be granted host city privileges.[38] Second, the Youth Olympics were Rogge's brainchild.[39] He envisioned the Youth Games as a means of connecting with the world's youth on a global scale, delivering a message about fitness and physical activity and establishing a testing ground for events that might eventually find their way onto the Olympic program. It is one definitive legacy that he left when he departed office in 2013; however, it is too early to discern their longer term influence. They have unfolded with little media interest.

CONCLUSIONS

Globalization and its pervasive effects on the world's economy and industry of sport were central considerations for both Samaranch and Rogge during their presidencies. The IOC, an organization with barely $2 million in total assets and approximately $200,000 in its bank accounts in 1980, shed its cloak of aversion to an overtly commercial model of revenue generation to become an economic juggernaut.[40] Samaranch grasped the commercial value of the Olympic five-ring logo, and the movement's attractiveness as an advertising platform for multinational firms that conducted their business across borders in an increasingly globalized economy. He also unleashed Richard Pound to pursue maximum dollars for Olympic television rights.[41] Further, by tossing the hypocrisy of amateurism into the dustbin of history and welcoming professional athletes into Olympic competition,[42] Samaranch sought to expand the cachet of the Olympic product.

Rogge and his team of television rights negotiators, led by Richard Carrion, enjoyed success too.[43] The US market, in part due to NBC's continuing commitment to the Olympics as an element of its sport property pursuits, continued to bear fruit. Not to be overlooked in regard to Rogge's effort to expand the value of global television rights was his decision to abandon the IOC's past relationship with the European Broadcasting Union (EBU). Samaranch, despite Pound's counsel to aggressively explore possible relationships with private European networks, had been unwilling to take this step, often voicing his belief that the collection of public broadcasters was the only entity capable of blanket coverage in the European market. EBU used this to its negotiating advantage. In 2009, Rogge and chief European television rights negotiator Thomas Bach took the bold step of signing a $316 million contract with Sportfive, a sport marketing agency, for the television rights in forty European countries for the 2014 Olympic Winter Games and the 2016 Summer Olympics, excluding France, Germany, Spain, Italy, Britain, and Turkey.[44]

Toward the close of Rogge's presidency, specifically within the 2009–2012 quadrennium, the IOC generated in excess of $4.8 billion in marketing revenue from the sale of television rights and TOP sponsor contracts covering two Olympic festivals.[45] Neubauer mused whether Juan Antonio Samaranch, who "arrived at the takeoff stage of corporate globalism [should be] given credit either for steering the Olympics along a bountiful course in this flood tide or simply having been fortunate to garner a benefit that came with the massive increase in global corporate wealth during his tenure."[46] We believe Samaranch deserves much credit for moving an organization largely skeptical and fearful of commercial revenue to a necessary position of welcoming such money, given the geopolitical pressures on the organization, its need for greater financial autonomy, and the imperative to find additional money to aid the mission of OCOGs burdened with costs only destined to rise given the growth trajectory of Olympic festivals.

The Salt Lake City scandal rocked the Samaranch presidency. And Samaranch bears much responsibility for its occurrence given his demonstrated unwillingness to rein in rumored questionable practices emerging within the Olympic bid process. Yet the strength and resilience of the Olympic brand was indelibly confirmed as the IOC and the Olympic movement emerged from the wreckage of the Salt Lake City bid scandal near the close of his presidency. Jacques Rogge then placed a steady hand on the tiller and assisted the IOC in further recovering the luster of the Olympic brand during the course of his term. In his quest to extend the global reach of the Olympics, a *sine qua non* of the Samaranch presidency, Rogge championed the establishment of the Youth Olympics and successfully nurtured Rio's bid for the 2016 Olympics, thereby extending the Olympic brand to that continent. Importantly, too, he brought resolution to the dispute between the IOC and the USOC over the distribution of television and corporate sponsorship dollars[47] and competently managed the oversight process leading up to the 2008 Beijing Olympics, amidst much continuing media scrutiny of the award of the Games to China given its human rights record, its relationship with Tibet, and its record of impassiveness in relation to the Darfur crisis. Massive television audiences also consumed events from Salt Lake City, Athens, Turin, Vancouver, and London, lending credence to the belief that the Olympic enterprise had not only survived the Salt Lake City scandal but also thrived as the twenty-first century opened. While Rogge slowed the growth of the Summer Olympics, he did not find a method to abate the tendency of host cities being saddled with white elephant facilities. Success in this regard will require creative planning and a willingness to embrace change, a fact not lost on Rogge's successor, Germany's Thomas Bach. Still, for Rogge, it is all too early to discuss his personal legacy. "I'm not a legacy man," observed Rogge. "People speak about legacy when you're dead—I'm not in a hurry."[48]

Thomas Bach wasted little time in placing his imprint on the organization.[49] The expenses accrued by the OCOGs in Beijing ($43 million) and Sochi ($51 billion) made those bid committees chasing the right to host the 2022 Olympic Winter Games skittish. Four of the finalist candidates withdrew from the process, leaving the IOC with only two options: Beijing, China, and Almaty, Kazakhstan. Bach understood the need for the IOC to revisit its bidding procedures, in terms of the costs as well as its expectations of host cities with respect to infrastructure, and did so through his Olympic Agenda 2020 think-tank exercise. While not as "revolutionary" or "radical" as our suggested alternatives, the recommendations dealing with host cities flowing from this process included

(a) placing more emphasis on preexisting facilities in assessing bids; (b) permitting cities to place a sport on the Olympic program that has deep cultural connection to the host country; (c) reducing the cost of bidding by limiting the required number of presentations and authorizing the production of the bid books in electronic format only; and (d) permitting joint city bids, with the possibility that the two cities might be in different countries, however with the intent that they be located close to one another. The early returns are mixed as a competitive field of three cities (Budapest, Los Angeles, Paris) exists, but two withdrew.[50] Bach championed "new blood" in the leadership ranks of various IOC Commissions, such as Tsunekazu Takeda (Marketing), Gerardo Werthein (Radio and Television), Larry Probst (Press), and Egur Erdener (Medical), and he leaned further on Australia's John Coates, already head of the Court of Arbitration and Sport and the Coordination Commission for Tokyo 2020, whom he asked to pilot the Juridical and Sport and Law Commissions.[51]. Bach's energy and industry have been noteworthy. The manner in which he navigates the revelations related to the doping scandal in Russia will be heavily scrutinized.

Thomas Bach is the organization's ninth president and the eighth who has hailed from Europe. The only deviation from the tradition of a European president was American Avery Brundage's presidency between 1952 and 1972. In that regard, the IOC treats the presidency of the organization in much the same fashion as the World Bank and the International Monetary Fund. In the former, only Americans have served as president[52]; in the latter, only Europeans have guided the organization, save for American John Lipsky who served as acting managing director for less than two months in 2011. The IOC should not aspire to this model where the leadership of an organization is so firmly rooted in any one of the world's regions. If the Vatican can see its way to electing a non-European to papal office in 2013, so too can the IOC dispense with its traditional approach, especially if it claims to be a global organization. We are not sure exactly what characteristics and skills form a list describing those required to serve as president of the IOC—no doubt this exercise merits considered reflection—but we are confident that they are possessed by a number of members of the organization whose birth certificate does not bear the name of a European country. Its membership must understand in future years that in order to more effectively assert the IOC's global identity, it is imperative to loosen Europe's iron grip on the organization's presidency.

Notes

1. Dick Pound, *Inside the Olympics: A Behind-the-Scenes Look at the Politics, the Scandals, and the Glory of the Games* (Toronto: John Wiley, 2004), 230–235.
2. For treatment of Samaranch, see Robert K. Barney, Stephen R. Wenn, and Scott G. Martyn, *Selling the Five Rings: The IOC and the Rise of Olympic Commercialism*, rev. ed. (Salt Lake City: University of Utah Press, 2004); John E. Findling, "Juan Antonio Samaranch," in *Encyclopedia of the Modern Olympic Movement*, ed. John E. Findling and Kimberly D. Pelle (Westport, CT, and London, Greenwood Press, 2004), 487–494; David Miller, *Olympic Revolution: The Biography of Juan Antonio Samaranch* (London: Pavilion Books, 1992);

The Official History of the Olympic Games and the IOC (London: Mainstream Publishing, 2008), 236–243; Michael Payne, *Olympic Turnaround* (London: London Business Press, 2005); Pound, *Inside the Olympics*; Vyv Simson and Andrew Jennings, *The Lords of the Rings: Power, Money and Drugs in the Modern Olympics* (Toronto: Stoddart, 1992); Stephen R. Wenn and Scott G. Martyn, "Juan Antonio Samaranch's Scoresheet: Revenue Generation and the Olympic Movement, 1980–2001," in *Onward to the Olympics*, ed. Gerald P. Schaus and Stephen R. Wenn (Waterloo, ON: Wilfrid Laurier University Press, 2007), 309–323; and Stephen Wenn, Robert Barney, and Scott Martyn, *Tarnished Rings: The International Olympic Committee and the Salt Lake City Bid Scandal* (Syracuse, NY: Syracuse University Press, 2011).

3. Deane Neubauer, "Modern Sport and Olympic Games," *Olympika: The International Journal of Olympic Studies* 17 (2008): 1–3.

4. Kate Galbraith, "Introduction," in *The Economist: Globalisation*, ed. Kate Galbraith (London: The Economist/Profile Books, 2001), ix.

5. Frank J. Lechner and John Boli, "General Introduction," in *The Globalization Reader*, 3rd ed., ed. Frank J. Lechner and John Boli (Oxford: Blackwell, 2008), 2.

6. Neubauer, "Modern Sport," 2.

7. This is a central concept noted by Thomas L. Friedman. See Friedman, *The World Is Flat: A History of the Twenty-First Century*, updated and expanded ed. (New York: Farrar, Straus and Giroux, 2007).

8. John Hoberman, "Toward a Theory of Olympic Internationalism," *Journal of Sport History* 22 (1995): 1–37; and Maurice Roche, *Mega-Events Modernity: Olympics and Expos in the Growth of Global Culture* (London and New York: Routledge, 2000).

9. For athlete migration in the sporting world, see, for instance, *Sport and Migration: Borders, Boundaries and Crossings*, ed. Joseph Maguire and Marc Falcous (New York: Routledge, 2011).

10. Neubauer, "Modern Sport," 2–3.

11. Neubauer, "Modern Sport, 3.

12. Neubauer, "Modern Sport," 4–8.

13. For Dassler's background, see Barbara Smit, *Sneaker Wars: The Enemy Brothers Who Founded Adidas and Puma and the Family Feud that Changed the Business of Sports* (New York: Harper Perennial, 2009).

14. "Use of Syncom Satellite Weighed for Televising Tokyo to N. America; Japan Hopeful," *The New York Times*, January 26, 1964, Section V, 3.

15. "Syncom III Satellite to Be Tested in October in Attempt to Relay Pictures to US and Canada: TV Satellite Test to Show Olympics," *The New York Times*, July 23, 1964, 24.

16. *The New York Times*, October 11, 1964, 1.

17. Stephen Wenn, "Rivals and Revolutionaries: Avery Brundage, the Marquess of Exeter and Olympic Television Revenue," *Sport in History* 32 (2012): 257–278.

18. See, for instance, Stephen R. Wenn, "Television Rights and the 1976 Montreal Olympics," *Sport History Review* 27 (1996): 111–138.

19. Lord Killanin, *My Olympic Years* (London: Secker & Warburg, 1983), 21–22.

20. Scott G. Martyn and Stephen R. Wenn, "A Prelude to Samaranch: Lord Killanin's Path to Olympic Commercialism," *Journal of Olympic History* 16 (2008): 40–48.

21. Payne, *Olympic Turnaround*, 9.

22. David Miller, "Evolution of the Olympic Movement," in *From Moscow to Lausanne* (Lausanne: International Olympic Committee, 1990), 9.

23. Peter Ueberroth, with Richard Levin and Amy Quinn, *Made in America: His Own Story* (New York: William Morrow, 1985), 69.

24. See, for instance, Francisco-Javier Monclús, "Barcelona 1992," in *Olympic Cities: City Agendas, Planning, and the World's Games, 1896–2012*, ed. John R. Gold and Margaret Gold (Abington, UK: Routledge, 2007), 218–236.

25. Miller, *Olympic Revolution*, 4; and Payne, *Olympic Turnaround*, 15.

26. Richard Pound, *Five Rings over Korea: The Secret Negotiations Behind the 1988 Olympic Games in Seoul* (Boston: Little, Brown, 1994).

27. Barney, Wenn, and Martyn, *Selling the Five Rings*, 153–180. In the first six months of operation, the IOC secured TOP agreements with a mere three multinationals—Coca-Cola, Kodak, and FedEx. Visa's decision to pursue a TOP sponsorship when American Express balked was a turning point in this process. Visa Senior Vice President of Marketing John Bennett implored Visa's board of directors to approve the $14.5 million investment as it would "stick the blade into the ribs of American Express." 3M soon followed, as did Philips, Time-Sports Illustrated, Panasonic, and Brother Industries. See Kristine E. Etu, "A Competitive Spirit," *Canisius College Magazine* (Winter 2006), 16, http://www.canisius.edu/alumni/magazine/win06/alumni_profile.pdf; and, Scott G. Martyn and Stephen R. Wenn, "Ambushing Olympic Sponsors: The Case of Visa and American Express, 1992," paper presented at the North American Society for Sport History Conference, Texas Tech University, May 2007; and Payne, *Olympic Turnaround*, 84–87.

28. In addition to Wenn, Barney, and Martyn, *Tarnished Rings*, see also Douglas Booth, "Olympic City Bidding: An Exegesis of Power," *International Review for the Sociology of Sport* 46.4 (2011): 367–386.

29. Bill Mallon and Jeroen Heijmans, *Historical Dictionary of the Olympic Movement*, 4th ed. (Lanham, MD: Scarecrow Press, 2011), 12–13.

30. "On the Scene in Moscow—Rogge Calls for Limits on Olympics," *Around the Rings*, April 15, 2012, http://www.aroundtherings.com/articles/view.aspx?pv=xqv&id=39780.

31. See J. A. Mangan and Mark Dyreson, eds., *Special Issue: Olympic Legacies: Intended and Unintended, Political, Cultural, Economic, Educational, The International Journal of the History of Sport* 25.14 (2008).

32. Xiaowei Yu, "The Question of Legacy and the 2008 Olympic Games: An Exploration of Post-Games Utilization of Olympic Sport Venues in Beijing" (PhD diss., Western University, 2012), http://ir.lib.uwo.ca/etd/739.

33. The best-known and most detailed debate on this issue relates to an attempt by Greece to provide a permanent site for the Games in the face of rising world tensions in the 1970s. For further enlightenment on this, see Evangelis Albinidis and Robert K. Barney, "In Search of an Olympic Sanctuary: The Quest to Permanently Host the Olympic Games in Greece," *Journal of Olympic History* 15.2 (2007): 28–39.

34. For related thoughts, see Stephen R. Wenn, "Peter Ueberroth's Legacy: How the 1984 Los Angeles Olympics Changed the Trajectory of the Olympic Movement," *The International Journal of the History of Sport* 32.1 (2015): 165–166.

35. As North Americans, we consider North America and South America to be separate continents. IOC members, however, view North and South America as one continent, simply "the Americas."

36. *Report of the 2016 IOC Evaluation Commission: Games of the XXXI Olympiad*, September 2009, 81–82, esp. 85, http://www.turin2006.com/Documents/Reports/EN/en_report_1469.pdf.

37. Michael R. Payne, "The Race for 2016—How Rio Won" [Blog post], November 2009, http://www.michaelrpayne.com/how_rio_won.html; and "Rogge Says Economics Should

Not Drive 2016 Vote," *USAToday.com*, June 16, 2009, http://www.usatoday.com/sports/olympics/2009-06-16-ioc-meetings-rogge_N.htm.

38. Rogge invested significant IOC resources in negotiations with USOC officials on this very matter in the years leading up to the 2009 IOC session, with most of the heavy lifting provided by the IOC's chief negotiator, Gerhard Heiberg, but with no success. Following Chicago's collapse in Copenhagen, USOC and IOC officials returned to the table, ultimately reaching agreement on these matters in mid-2012. Chicago's plight is detailed in Stephen R. Wenn, "IOC/USOC Relations and the 2009 IOC Session in Copenhagen," *Rethinking Matters Olympic: Investigations into the Socio-Cultural Study of the Modern Olympic Movement*, ed. in Robert K. Barney, Janice Forsyth, and Michael K. Heine (London: University of Western Ontario, 2010), 60–75.

39. Geoffrey A. Fowler and Matthew Futterman, "Rogge's IOC Presidency Was a Study in Details," *The Wall Street Journal*, August 12, 2012, http://online.wsj.com/article/SB10000872396390444772404577585452344701454.html; and Sonali Shah, "Winter Youth Olympics: Jacques Rogge on the Dream behind the Games," *BBC Sport*, January 17, 2012, http://www.bbc.co.uk/sport/0/winter-sports/16595001.

40. Michael Payne, "Reinventing the Rings," *Business Strategy Review*, Spring 2008, http://bsr.london.edu/lbs-article/251/index.html.

41. For the depth of Samaranch's labors, see Barney, Wenn, and Martyn, *Selling the Five Rings*; and Wenn and Martyn, "Juan Antonio Samaranch's Scoresheet."

42. For the changes to the IOC's eligibility policies, see, for instance, John A. Lucas, "From Coubertin to Samaranch: The Unsettling Transformation of the Olympic Ideology of Amateurism," *Stadion* 14.1 (1988): 65–84.

43. Perhaps most reflective of this success were the negotiations staged in Lausanne, in June 2003 for the US television rights to the 2010 Olympic Winter Games and the 2012 Summer Olympics. This set of negotiations yielded not only an offer of $2.001 billion for the television rights, but a linked proposal from its parent company, General Electric, to become a TOP sponsor through 2012. Payne, *Olympic Turnaround*, 59–65.

44. "IOC Awards European Broadcast Rights to Sportfive," *The New York Times*, November 8, 2009, http://www.nytimes.com/2009/02/18/sports/18iht-olytv18.20285494.html?_r=0. More recently, US-based media corporation Discovery Communications, the parent company of Eurosport, a major European sport network, purchased the European rights for the 2018, 2020, 2022, and 2024 Olympic festivals (fifty countries) for $1.45 billion. "Discovery Wins European Olympic TV rights," *CBSNews.com*, June 29, 2015, http://www.cbsnews.com/news/discovery-wins-european-olympic-tv-rights/.

45. *IOC Marketing: Media Guide, London 2012* (Lausanne: IOC, 2011), 6. When revenue from ticket sales, licensing, and domestic corporate sponsorship generated by OCOGs is added, the dollar figure reached $8 billion in relation to 2009–2012. See *Olympic Marketing Fact File* (Lausanne: International Olympic Committee, 2014), 6. http://www.olympic.org/Documents/IOC_Marketing/OLYMPIC_MARKETING_FACT_%20FILE_2014.pdf.

46. Neubauer, "Modern Sport and Olympic Games," 19–20.

47. The new agreement runs from 2020 to 2040. The USOC, which currently receives 20 percent of TOP revenue and 12.75 percent of US television contracts, maintains these percentages going forward for total revenue (adjusted for inflation) accumulated from the 2009–2012 quadrennium. For revenue beyond these levels, the USOC percentage share is reduced. See Amy Shipley, "USOC, IOC on Verge of Deal that Will Pave the Way for Future Olympics in the United States," *The Washington Post*, May 23, 2012, http://www.washingtonpost.com/sports/olympics/usoc-ioc-reach-deal-that-will-pave-the-way-for-future-olympics-in-united-states/2012/05/23/gJQAddXelU_story.html.

48. Shah, "Winter Youth Olympics."

49. Bach spearheaded negotiations on a six-festival (2022, 2024, 2026, 2028, 2030, and 2032) contract for US television rights with NBC Universal. A $7.75 billion deal was reached in May 2014. Tripp Mickle, "Improved IOC-USOC Relationship on Display," *Street & Smith's Sport Business Journal*, May 12, 2014, http://www.sportsbusinessdaily.com/ Journal/Issues/2014/05/12/Olympics/.

50. "Olympic Agenda 2020: 20 + 20 Recommendations," Olympic.org, http://www. olympic.org/Documents/Olympic_Agenda_2020/Olympic_Agenda_2020-20-20_ Recommendations-ENG.pdf; and Philip Hersh, "IOC Allows Summer or Winter Olympics in Two Countries; Baseball, Softball Get Second Life," *Chicago Tribune*, December 8, 2014, http://www.chicagotribune.com/sports/breaking/chi-ioc-will-allow-summer-or-winter-olympics-in-two-countries-20141208-story.html. Hamburg withdrew its bid in November 2015. Rome withdrew in September 2016.

51. David Owen, "This Week's Extensive Reshuffle of IOC Commission Personnel Will See New Blood Rise to Olympic Prominence," *Inside the Games*, April 4, 2014,<http://www. insidethegames.biz/blogs/1019276-david-owen-this-week-s-extensive-reshuffle-of-ioc-commission-personnel-will-see-new-blood-rise-to-olympic-prominence.

52. James Wolfensohn (1995–2005) was born in Australia but was an American citizen at the time of his appointment. Its most recent appointee, Jim Yong Kim, while born in South Korea, is an American citizen and a former president of Dartmouth College. "Current President," World Bank.org, http://www.worldbank.org/en/about/president/about-the-office/bio.

BIBLIOGRAPHY

Albinidis, Evangelis, and Robert K. Barney. "In Search of an Olympic Sanctuary: The Quest to Permanently Host the Olympic Games in Greece." *Journal of Olympic History* 15.2 (2007): 28–39.

Barney, Robert K., Janice Forsyth, and Michael K. Heine, eds. *Rethinking Matters Olympic: Investigations into the Socio-Cultural Study of the Modern Olympic Movement*. London: University of Western Ontario, 2010.

Barney, Robert K., Stephen R. Wenn, and Scott G. Martyn. *Selling the Five Rings: The IOC and the Rise of Olympic Commercialism*. Rev. ed. Salt Lake City: University of Utah Press, 2004.

Chappelet, Jean-Loup, and Brenda Kübler-Mabbott. *The International Olympic Committee and the Olympic System: The Governance of World Sport*. New York: Routledge, 2008.

Gold, John R., and Margaret M. Gold, eds. *Olympic Cities: City Agendas, Planning, and the World's Games, 1896–2012*. New York: Routledge, 2007.

Findling, John E., and Kimberly D. Pelle, eds. *Encyclopaedia of the Modern Olympic Movement*. Westport, CT, and London: Greenwood Press, 2004.

Friedman, Thomas L. *The World Is Flat: A History of the Twenty-First Century*. Further updated and expanded. New York: Farrar, Straus and Giroux, 2007.

Galbraith, Kate, ed. *The Economist: Globalisation*. London: The Economist/Profile Books, 2001.

Gold, John R., and Margaret M. Gold, eds. *Olympic Cities: City Agendas, Planning, and the World's Games, 1896–2012*. New York: Routledge, 2007.

Guttmann, Allen. *The Olympics: A History of the Modern Games*. Champaign: University of Illinois Press, 1992.

Hoberman, John. "Toward a Theory of Olympic Internationalism." *Journal of Sport History* 22 (1995): 1–37.

Killanin, Lord. *My Olympic Years*. London: Secker & Warburg, 1983.

Lechner, Frank J., and John Boli, eds. *The Globalization Reader*. 3rd ed. Oxford: Blackwell, 2008.

Lucas, John A. "From Coubertin to Samaranch: The Unsettling Transformation of the Olympic Ideology of Amateurism." *Stadion* XIV.1 (1988): 65–84.

Maguire, Joseph, and Marc Falcous, eds. *Sport and Migration: Borders, Boundaries and Crossings*. New York: Routledge, 2011.

Mallon, Bill, and Jeroen Heijmans. *Historical Dictionary of the Olympic Movement*. 4th ed. Lanham, MD: Scarecrow Press, 2011.

Martyn, Scott G., and Stephen R. Wenn. "A Prelude to Samaranch: Lord Killanin's Path to Olympic Commercialism. *Journal of Olympic History* 16 (2008): 40–48.

Miller, David. *From Moscow to Lausanne*. Lausanne: International Olympic Committee, 1990.

Miller, David. *Olympic Revolution: The Biography of Juan Antonio Samaranch*. London: Pavilion Books, 1992.

Miller, David. *The Official History of the Olympic Games and the IOC*. Edinburgh, UK, and London: Mainstream Publishing, 2008.

Neubauer, Deane. "Modern Sport and Olympic Games." *Olympika: The International Journal of Olympic Studies* 17 (2008): 1–3.

Payne, Michael. *Olympic Turnaround*. London: London Business Press, 2005.

Pound, Dick. *Inside the Olympics: A Behind-the-Scenes Look at the Politics, the Scandals, and the Glory of the Games*. Toronto: John Wiley, 2004.

Pound, Richard. *Five Rings over Korea: The Secret Negotiations Behind the 1988 Olympic Games in Seoul*. Boston, New York, Toronto, and London: Little, Brown, 1994.

Roche, Maurice. *Mega-Events Modernity: Olympics and Expos in the Growth of Global Culture*. New York: Routledge, 2000.

Schaus, Gerald P., and Stephen R. Wenn, eds. *Onward to the Olympics*. Waterloo, Ont.: Wilfrid Laurier University Press, 2007.

Simson, Vyv, and Andrew Jennings. *The Lords of the Rings: Power, Money, and Drugs in the Modern Olympics*. Toronto: Stoddart, 1992.

Smit, Barbara. *Sneaker Wars: The Enemy Brothers Who Founded Adidas and Puma and the Family Feud that Changed the Business of Sports*. New York: Harper Perennial, 2009.

Ueberroth, Peter (with Richard Levin and Amy Quinn). *Made in America: His Own Story*. New York: William Morrow, 1985.

Wenn, Stephen R. "Peter Ueberroth's Legacy: How the 1984 Los Angeles Olympics Changed the Trajectory of the Olympic Movement." *The International Journal of the History of Sport* 32.1 (2015): 157–171.

Wenn, Stephen. "Rivals and Revolutionaries: Avery Brundage, the Marquess of Exeter and Olympic Television Revenue." *Sport in History* 32 (2012): 257–268.

Wenn, Stephen R. "Television Rights and the 1976 Montreal Olympics." *Sport History Review* 27 (1996): 111–138.

Wenn, Stephen, Robert Barney, and Scott Martyn. *Tarnished Rings: The International Olympic Committee and the Salt Lake City Bid Scandal*. Syracuse, NY: Syracuse University Press, 2011.

Young, Kevin, and Kevin B. Wamsley, eds. *Global Olympics: Historical and Sociological Studies of the Modern Games. Research in the Sociology of Sport*, Vol. 3. Boston, Elsevier, 2005.

Yu, Xiaowei. "The Question of Legacy and the 2008 Olympic Games: An Exploration of Post-Games Utilization of Olympic Sport Venues in Beijing." PhD diss., Western University, 2012.

CHAPTER 27

···

WADA AND DOPING
IN WORLD SPORT

···

THOMAS M. HUNT

FROM ANCIENT GREECE TO
THE TWENTIETH CENTURY

···

THE use of performance-enhancing substances by athletes has a long history. Indeed, evidence of the practice can be traced as far back as the Greek sporting competitions of antiquity.[1] It was not until the late 1800s, however, that doping became a matter of any controversy. Even then, such attention to the subject remained confined mostly to the sport of horse racing—a development that John Gleaves attributes to worries among gamblers that chemically altered performances might negatively affect their betting odds. In response to those concerns, racing organizations and thoroughbred tracks adopted, over the next decade, the first set of anti-doping prohibitions in the modern history of sport.[2] Human sportspersons, on the other hand, faced no such official restrictions, at the time, regarding the employment of performance-enhancing agents to improve their physical functioning.

Over the next several decades, however, the social elite increasingly worried that the lower classes could not be trusted to use drugs appropriately. The aristocratics in charge of international athletics convinced themselves that doping contravened the amateur ideals upon which they hoped to build their competitions. In 1928, the International Association of Athletics Federations made the decision to prohibit doping at its events. The International Olympic Committee (IOC) followed suit a few years later. The ideological roots of these early efforts have only very recently received detailed treatment.[3]

THE SECOND WORLD WAR AND
THE COLD WAR

From 1939 to 1945, the international sports movement was sidelined by the cataclysmic upheavals of the Second World War. Historians have to a large degree failed to note, however, that those years had a profound (if indirect) impact on the relationship of drugs to sport. This significance lay in the war's catalyzing effect on pharmaceutical research and production.[4] Those who served among the military forces of the various national combatants (and especially those of the United States) gained access to—and familiarity with—a theretofore unprecedented number of drug treatments.[5] These events set the stage for a rapid integration of pharmaceutical products into Western consumer culture during the postwar period.[6] Indeed, the application of new marketing methods during this period alongside a sweeping campaign to convince physicians as to the benefits of the new therapies led to an explosion on drug usage in the United States and Europe.[7]

Given this situation in the wider society, the fact that elite athletes turned to pharmacology in their efforts to find competitive advantages should not surprise. For many years, the primary drugs available to them were amphetamines and other stimulants.[8] In 1958 they gained access to a revolutionary performance-enhancing agent when CIBA Pharmaceuticals released an anabolic steroid that it had developed for Western markets under the trade name Dianabol. As Terry Todd has written, the drug was adopted in short order by American weightlifters. Given the dramatic strength increases enjoyed by weightlifters as a result, it was only a matter of time before anabolic steroids spread to the broader world of sport.[9]

For the leaders of international sport, however, doping became increasingly perceived as contrary to their conception of sport as an ethical and physical salve to the problems of modern society—a concept they had worked hard to cultivate among Western audiences.[10] Even so, the costs of taking policy action subject seemed to them to outweigh the benefits of the status quo. The situation changed rapidly when a Danish cyclist named Knud Enemark Jensen died during the 1960 Rome Olympic Games due, it was thought, to amphetamines (an incorrect belief as it turns out, as Danish scholar Verner Möller has shown).[11] In the aftermath of the tragedy, the leadership of the IOC engaged in lengthy policy debates on the subject. With the allegedly drug-related death of British cyclist Tom Simpson in the 1967 Tour de France, these discussions became even more urgent. According to legal anthropologist Katherine Henne, the set of moral and technological beliefs held by the IOC's medical leaders at the time resulted in a "technocratic" anti-doping framework based on prohibition and testing—one that the committee put into effect in the year that followed the Simpson tragedy.[12]

International sport leaders have received considerable criticism for the failure of this system to diminish the use of drugs by athletes in the following decades. John Hoberman has been particularly scathing in his criticisms of IOC president Juan Antonio Samaranch and Olympic medical official Alexandre de Merode for their neglect of the issue.[13] Even a cursory review of the historical record reveals that Hoberman was quite right in stating that the IOC's anti-doping initiatives were so inadequate in both design and funding as to have little chance of success. Even so, the challenges of creating an effective anti-doping system were perhaps greater than he appreciated.[14] Indeed, the growing presence of drugs in sport was to a large degree the result of forces outside the ability of Olympic officials to control.

The political dynamics of the Cold War have received considerable attention from scholars interested in the history of doping. Studies by Paul Dimeo, Rob Beamish, and Ian Ritchie have argued that by giving anti-doping advocates a set of descriptions based on the rhetoric of a "Free World" and an "Evil Empire," the superpower conflict ensured that many in the West would see doping as an issue of "Good versus Evil."[15] I have argued in *Drug Games* that this did not lead Western sports authorities to take aggressive action on their side of the Iron Curtain. To the contrary, the unprecedented stakes of the superpower conflict made those officials reluctant to do anything that might place their athletes at a disadvantage.[16]

Although easy to criticize in hindsight, the absence of aggressive action by these officials should be appreciated as the result of a policy dilemma without a satisfactory solution. It was strongly suspected, after all, that athletes on the other side of the Iron Curtain were using performance-enhancing drugs in wide numbers. The most notorious confirmation of this reality in the historical record was the systemic doping program initiated during the 1970s by the East German state under the umbrella of its *Ministerium für Staatssicherheit* (the *Stasi*).[17] Intended as a mechanism by which to impress foreign audiences and promote a domestic sense of East German identity, this effort allowed the Soviet satellite to obtain incredible successes at the Olympic Games.[18] Indeed, until the collapse of the country in 1989, the German Democratic Republic (GDR) remained on a per capita basis the most successful sporting nation in history.[19]

Yet our understanding of Cold War doping remains imperfect. Several recent studies have pointed out flaws in the preceding literature on the *Stasi* doping program. Some of the most trenchant criticisms concern Steven Ungerleider's influential 2001 book *Faust's Gold: Inside the East German Doping Machine*—a work that helped to entrench Western notions of the GDR doping program as the epitome of Cold War sporting evil.[20] During post–Cold War legal proceedings, a number of former East German athletes gave testimonies about the health problems they faced due, they believed, to their participation in the GDR program. Sadly, as a work of history, *Faust's Gold* possessed a number of shortcomings. In addition to grossly overgeneralizing the experiences of East German athletes, the book made a number of dubious claims regarding the decision-making processes of the officials who oversaw their training. At one point, Ungerleider even analogized the East German doping program to Nazi medical experimentation during the Second World War.[21] Happily, with the 2012 publication of *Sport under Communism: Behind the East German "Miracle"* by British scholars Mike Dennis and Jonathan Grix, the historiography of the subject improved dramatically.[22]

In addition, the scholarship on communist-bloc doping remains surprisingly underdeveloped on nations other than the GDR. It has long been assumed that the Soviet

Union ran a state-sponsored doping program similar to that of the *Stasi's* during the Cold War.[23] Michael I. Kalinski, a Soviet-bloc sports scientist who relocated to the West in 1990, has served as a rare source of credible information on the subject.[24] His most notable evidential disclosure took place in the form of a summary report that he co-wrote for a German academic journal regarding the contents of a secret 1972 Soviet document titled "Anabolic Steroids and Sport Capacity."[25] The fact that no English-language work has yet cited that report in a peer-reviewed setting says something about the need for additional research on Eastern-bloc doping. The same can be said for the absence of scholarly attention to the testimony of a Czech sports physician named Jan Hnizdil on the existence of doping program in Czechoslovakia during the Cold War.[26]

The Final Drive to WADA

The winding down of the Cold War during the late 1980s finally made anti-doping reform possible.[27] It is noteworthy that in the waning stages of the conflict, the United States and the Soviet Union pledged to cooperate in an aggressive anti-doping program.[28] The Soviet state disintegrated before the partnership could make much progress, however. Advocates of reform received an important boost when Canadian sprinter Ben Johnson tested positive for anabolic steroids at the 1988 Seoul Olympic Games after setting a new world record in the 100-meter sprint.[29] The event was in essence so prominent and so shocking that it focused governmental attention on the ineffectiveness of the existing system. In the aftermath of the scandal, state authorities came to believe that meaningful change was unlikely to happen within the existing sport governance structure.

Policy analyst Barrie Houlihan has shown that the fragmented way in which the various organizations in the international sport system handled the issue resulted in a reform process that centered on regulatory harmonization.[30] This, in turn, led to the proposal of a new, independent body to take charge of the issue. The idea came to fruition with the establishment of the World Anti-Doping Agency (WADA) in February 1999 and the subsequent adoption of an international set of standards in the form of the World Anti-Doping Code.[31] In the years that followed, WADA consolidated its powers on the issue of performance enhancement in sport.[32] Today, the agency serves as the centerpiece of a truly global anti-doping network.[33]

Evolution of Contemporary Ideas on Doping

Tracing the history of doping in modern world sport in terms of ideas rather than events is no easy task given the fact that an extensive body of literature exists on the subject.

Moreover, each of the traditions within this body of work reflects a considerable diversity of opinion, and so one must be careful to avoid overstating their uniformity.

Although secondary works written by scholars on a particular subject constitute the traditional subjects of historical analysis, texts written by actual participants in the history of doping in world sport constitute a key source of information regarding the events that led to today's international anti-doping system. In his 1983 memoir *My Olympic Years*, former IOC president Lord Michael Killanin asserted that "the most obnoxious aspect of sport . . . is the abuse of drugs to aid performance. . . . Not only does the use of drugs put the put the individual's welfare at risk, but it also jeopardises the whole future spirit of sport."[34] Although he suggested a certain degree of culpability on the part of national and international sports leaders, Killanin did so without going into much detail. The 1991 publication of the sinisterly titled *Drugs, Sport, and Politics* by American sports physician Robert Voy made a compelling case that the international sport system was indeed corrupt on the subject of doping.[35] The fact that Voy was a former long-standing chief medical officer of the US Olympic Committee gave the book instant credibility.

Dick Pound, a former vice president of the IOC and the first director of WADA, has argued passionately on behalf of WADA's mission.[36] Two passages in his 2006 *Inside Dope* merit special consideration. The first (found in the book's introduction) provided a justification for policy action on doping that is representative of the official narrative on the subject:

> Many believe that drug use simply does not matter. . . .
> This attitude is wrong. For one thing, sporting heroes are role models to kids, and do we want our little moppets doing what they see their heroes doing? Not only is it also dangerous to the health of athletes who use drugs—and not just in mild terms but sometimes fatally—it's most importantly dangerous to the ethics of sport. This attitude is like a disease that can spread beyond the playing fields and have an impact on the entire lives of athletes, those close to them and our society as a whole.[37]

In the second passage, Pound described the policy structure that he and other anti-doping leaders had created to deal with the issue:

> I do not think you have to tiptoe around the fact that people are cheating. I believe that they should be caught, identified, and taken out of the competitions. It is also important to identify those who help athletes to cheat, and those who force them to cheat, and those who allow them to cheat.
> In my view, nothing can justify such behavior, and I will do everything in my power to make sure that the enablers, along with the guilty athletes, are exposed and punished. We will enlist the public in our fight. This is a war that we simply cannot afford to lose. The future of sport and of our children depend [*sic*] on it.[38]

The first wave of scholarly literature on doping in world sport featured similar claims regarding the detrimental impact of performance-enhancing drugs on the health of athletes as well on the negative effects of those substances on the fairness of athletic competition. Bob Goldman's chillingly titled 1984 book *Death in the Locker Room* serves as a representative example.[39] The far more sophisticated works of John Hoberman can also be described as possessing a rather purist tone. Published some two decades ago, his seminal *Mortal Engines: The Science of Performance and the Dehumanization of Sport* argued that doping should be understood as the regrettable product of a sporting ethos that values high performance above all else.[40] Moreover, it is perhaps noteworthy that Hoberman remains today—just as he has for many years—the single most influential scholar on the subject of doping.[41]

In recent years, a revisionist school of interpretation has called the central tenants of the modern anti-doping movement into question. A small number of its most extreme members have even argued that performance enhancement should be wholeheartedly embraced by humanity.[42] Most of the works in the revisionist vein are based on one or the other of two more limited critiques, however. The first pertains to the jurisprudential morality of the steps taken by WADA to combat the use of performance-enhancing drugs in athletic competitions. In doing so, the texts under this school point to the fact that athletes are deprived of legal rights taken for granted in other aspects of life.[43] The fact that WADA officials have over the past ten years established close ties to state law enforcement actors makes this especially concerning, say the revisionists.

A parallel set of scholars argues that the contemporary anti-doping system was founded upon exaggerated medical claims as to the harmfulness of doping. The rigid policy positions adopted in reaction to such claims, the revisionists argue, reduce the medical risks of doping. Without access to medical oversight and forced to obtain their drugs from the black market rather than by means of legitimate suppliers, athletes are more likely to overdose or take tainted pharmacological products. A more rational system given the realities of modern sport, the revisionists claim, would be to allow for doping in a controlled manner with strict medical oversight. These arguments have been strengthened by the publication in recent years of several historical studies that have overturned long-held beliefs regarding cases in which athletes were thought to have suffered medical harm from doping. Inspired by Möller's efforts to demonstrate absence of evidence connecting the death of Knud Jensen to drugs (discussed earlier), Bernat López later debunked a myth that some eighteen Belgian and Dutch cyclists died during the 1980s and 1990s due to their usage of the blood-boosting hormone erythropoietin.[44]

It seems unlikely that a paradigm shift on the subject of doping will occur anytime soon, however. After all, IOC president Juan Antonio Samaranch barely survived a public scandal that ensued after he expressed an opinion that "for me, everything that does not injure the health of the athlete is not doping."[45] On the other hand, it is quite possible that the ineffectiveness of the current testing system at actually catching doping transgressors will result in the adoption of protocols even more repressive than those currently in place.[46] Such has been the pattern for over fifty years.

Notes

1. See Panayiotis J. Papagelopoulos, Andreas F. Mavrogenis, and Panayotis N. Soucacos, "Doping in Ancient and Modern Olympic Games," *Orthopedics* 27.12 (2004): 1226, 1231; A. J. Higgins, "From Ancient Greece to Modern Athens: 3000 Years of Doping in Competition Horses," *Journal of Veterinary Pharmacology and Therapeutics* 29 (2006): 4–8.
2. John Gleaves, "Enhancing the Odds: Horse Racing, Gambling and the First Anti-Doping Movement in Sport, 1889–1911," *Sport in History* 32.1 (2012): 26–52.
3. John Gleaves and Matthew Llewellyn, "Sport, Drugs, and Amateurism: Tracing the Cultural Origins of Anti-Doping Rules in International Sport," *The International Journal of the History of Sport* 31.8 (2014): 839–853; Rob Beamish and Ian Ritchie, "From Chivalrous 'Brothers-in-Arms' to the Eligible Athlete: Changed Principles and the IOC's Banned Substance List," *International Review for the Sociology of Sport* 39 (2004): 355–371; and John Gleaves, "Doped Professionals and Clean Amateurs: Amateurism's Influence on the Modern Philosophy of Anti-Doping," *Journal of Sport History* 38.2 (2011): 237–254; Erkki Vettenniemi, "Runners, Rumors, and Reams of Representations: An Inquiry into Drug Use by Athletes in the 1920s," *Journal of Sport History* 37.3 (2010): 415–430.
4. See Nicolas Rasmussen, "Of 'Small Men,' Big Science and Bigger Business: The Second World War and Biomedical Research in the United States," *Minerva* 40.2 (2002): 115–146; and Dennis B. Worthen, *Pharmacy in World War II*, Pharmaceutical Heritage series (New York: CRC Press, 2004).
5. Peter Steinkamp, "Pervitin (Metamphetamine) Tests, Use and Misuse in the German Wehrmach," in *Man, Medicine, and the State: The Human Body as an Object of Government Sponsored Medical Research in the Twentieth Century*, ed. Wolfgang U. Eckart (Stuttgart: Franz Steiner Verlag, 2006), 61–71; and Stephen Snelders and Toine Pieters, "Speed in the Third Reich: Metamphetamine (Pervitin) Use and a Drug History from Below," *Social History of Medicine* 24.3 (2011): 686–699. See also Nicolas Rasmussen, "Medical Science and the Military: The Allies' Use of Amphetamine during World War II," *Journal of Interdisciplinary History* 42.2 (2011): 205–233; and Marcel Reinold and John Hoberman, "The Myth of the Nazi Steroid," *The International Journal of the History of Sport* 31.8 (2014): 871–883.
6. See Robert Bud, "Antibiotics, Big Business, and Consumers: The Context of Government Investigations into the Postwar American Drug Industry," *Technology and Culture* 46.2 (2005): 329–349; Dominique A. Tobbell, "'Who's Winning the Human Race?' Cold War as Pharmaceutical Political Strategy," *Journal of the History of Medicine and Allied Sciences* 64.4 (2009): 429–473.
7. See Jeremy A. Greene, "Attention to 'Details': Etiquette and the Pharmaceutical Salesman in Postwar American," *Social Studies of Science* 34.2 (2004): 271–292; and Jeremy A. Greene and Scott H. Podolsky, "Keeping Modern in Medicine: Pharmaceutical Promotion and Physician Education in Postwar America," *Bulletin of the History of Medicine* 83.2 (2009): 331–377.
8. See Charles E. Yesalis and Michael S. Bahrke, "Anabolic Steroid and Stimulant Use in North American Sport between 1850 and 1980," *Sport in History* 25.3 (2005): 434–451; and John Hoberman, "Amphetamine and the Four-Minute Mile," *Sport in History* 26.2 (2006): 289–304.

9. See Terry Todd, "Anabolic Steroids: The Gremlins of Sport," *Journal of Sport History* 14.1 (1987): 94–95; and John Fair, "Isometrics or Steroids? Exploring New Frontiers of Strength in the Early 1960s," *Journal of Sport History* 20.1 (1993): 1–24.

10. Ian Ritchie. "Pierre de Coubertin, Doped 'Amateurs' and the 'Spirit of Sport': The Role of Mythology in Olympic Anti-Doping Policies," *The International Journal of the History of Sport* 31.8 (2014): 820–838.

11. Thomas M. Hunt, *Drug Games: The International Olympic Committee and the Politics of Doping, 1960–2008* (Austin: University of Texas Press, 2011), 11; and Verner Möller, "Knud Enemark Jensen's Death During the 1960 Rome Olympics: A Search for Truth?" *Sport in History* 25.3 (2005): 452–471.

12. Kathryn Henne, "The Emergence of Moral Technopreneurialism in Sport: Techniques in Anti-Doping Regulation, 1966–1976," *The International Journal of the History of Sport* 31.8 (2014): 884–901; Alison Wrynn, "The Human Factor: Science, Medicine and the International Olympic Committee, 1900–70," *Sport in Society* 7.2 (2004): 211–231.

13. John Hoberman, "How Drug Testing Fails: The Politics of Doping Control," in *Doping in Elite Sport: The Politics of Drugs in the Olympic Movement*, ed. Wayne Wilson and Edward Derse (Champaign, IL: Human Kinetics, 2001), 241–274; "Sports Physicians and the Doping Crisis in Elite Sport," *Clinical Journal of Sport Medicine* 12.4 (2002): 203–208.

14. Paul Dimeo, Thomas M. Hunt, and Matthew T. Bowers, "Saint or Sinner? A Reconsideration of the Career of Prince Alexandre de Merode, Chair of the International Olympic Committee's Medical Commission, 1967–2002," *The International Journal of the History of Sport* 28.6 (2011): 925–940.

15. Paul Dimeo, "Good versus Evil: Drugs, Sport and the Cold War," in *East Plays West: Sport and the Cold War*, ed. Stephen Wagg and David L. Andrews (New York: Routledge, 2006), 149–162; Rob Beamish and Ian Ritchie, "The Spectre of Steroids: Nazi Propaganda, Cold War Anxiety and Patriarchal Paternalism," *The International Journal of the History of Sport* 22.5 (2005): 777–795; Rob Beamish and Ian Ritchie, "Totalitarian Regimes and Cold War Sport: Steroid 'Übermenschen' and 'Ball-Bearing Females,'" in *East Plays West: Sport and the Cold War* (New York: Routledge, 2007), 11–26.

16. Thomas M. Hunt, *Drug Games: The International Olympic Committee and the Politics of Doping, 1960–2008*, Terry and Jan Todd Series on Physical Culture and Sports (Austin: University of Texas Press, 2011).

17. See Werner W. Franke and Brigitte Berendonk, "Hormonal Doping and Androgenization of Athletes: A Secret Program of the German Democratic Republic Government," *Clinical Chemistry* 43.7 (1997): 1262–1279; Brigitte Berendonk, *Doping Dokumente: Von Der Forschung Zum Betrug* (Berlin: Springer, 1991); Giselher Spitzer, *Doping in der DDR: Ein historischer Überblick zu einer konspirativen Praxis* (Cologne: Sport und Buch Strauss, 1998); Mike Dennis, "Securing the Sports 'Miracle': The Stasi and East German Elite Sport," *The International Journal of the History of Sport* 29.18 (2012): 2551–2574.

18. Thomas M. Hunt et al., "The Diplomatic Context of Doping in the Former German Democratic Republic: A Revisionist Examination," *International Journal of the History of Sport* 29.18 (2012): 2486–2499; Sheldon Anderson "Soccer and the Failure of East German Sports Policy," *Soccer & Society* 12.5 (2011): 652–663; Mike Dennis and Jonathan Grix, "Behind the Iron Curtain: Football as a Site of Contestation in the East German Sports 'Miracle,'" *Sport in History* 30.3 (2010): 447–474.

19. Medals Per Capita, June 29, 2013, http://www.medalspercapita.com/.

20. Steven Ungerleider, *Faust's Gold: Inside the East German Doping Machine* (New York: Macmillan, 2001). Paul Dimeo, Thomas M. Hunt, and Richard Horbury, "The Individual and the State: A Social Historical Analysis of the East German 'Doping System,'" *Sport in History* 31.2 (2011): 218–237; Paul Dimeo and Thomas M. Hunt, "The Doping of Athletes in the Former East Germany: A Critical Assessment of Comparisons with Nazi Medical Experiments," *International Review for the Sociology of Sport* 47.5 (2012): 581–593. In making their cases, it is perhaps notable that Dimeo and Hunt drew from a collection of documents that Ungerleider had himself compiled on the GDR doping program. Mike Dennis and Jonathan Grix, *Sport Under Communism East German "Miracle"* (Basingstoke, UK: Palgrave Macmillan, 2012).

21. Paul Dimeo, Thomas M. Hunt, and Richard Horbury, "The Individual and the State: A Social Historical Analysis of the East German 'Doping System,'" *Sport in History* 31.2 (2011): 218–237; Paul Dimeo and Thomas M. Hunt, "The Doping of Athletes in the Former East Germany: A Critical Assessment of Comparisons with Nazi Medical Experiments," *International Review for the Sociology of Sport* 47.5 (2012): 581–593.

22. Dennis and Grix, *Sport Under Communism*.

23. Jim Riordan, "The Rise and Fall of Soviet Olympic Champions," *Olympika: The International Journal of Olympic Studies* 2 (1993): 38–39; Jim Riordan, "Rewriting Soviet Sports History," *Journal of Sport History* 20.3 (1993): 253–257.

24. Andrew Nynka, "Ukrainian Scientist Details Secret Soviet Research Project on Steroids," *Ukranian Weekly*, November 9, 2003.

25. M. I. Kalinski and M. S. Kerner, "Empfehlungen zum Einsatz von anabolen Steroiden im Sport aus der ehemaligen Sowjetunion" [Recommendations for Androgenic-Anabolic Steroid Use by Athletes in the Former Soviet Union: Revelations from a Secret Document], *Deutsche Zeitschrift für Sportmedizin* 53.11 (2002): 317–324; Michael I. Kalinski, "State-Sponsored Research on Creatine Supplements and Blood Doping in Elite Soviet Sport," *Perspectives in Biology and Medicine* 46.3 (2003): 445–451.

26. See Jan Sliva, "Czechs Admit to State-run Doping in Past: Drug Program Abruptly Halted after Ben Johnson Caught at Tokyo Olympics," *Ottawa Citizen*, February 11, 2000; "Documents Describe Czechoslovakia Doping Program," ESPN.com, August 16, 2006, http://sports.espn.go.com/oly/news/story?id=2551078.

27. Hunt, *Drug Games*, 87–99. Maria Tai Wolff, "Playing by the Rules? A Legal Analysis of the United States Olympic Committee—Soviet Olympic Committee Doping Control Agreement," *Stanford Journal of International Law* 25 (1989): 611.

28. See Wolff, "Playing by the Rules?"

29. Richard Moore, *The Dirtiest Race in History: Ben Johnson, Carl Lewis and the 1988 Olympic 100m Final* (London: Wisden, 2012). See also Judith Blackwell, "Discourses on Drug Use: The Social Construction of a Steroid Scandal," *Journal of Drug Issues* 21.1 (1991): 147–164; and Bruce Kidd, Robert Edelman, and Susan Brownell, "Comparative Analysis of Doping Scandals: Canada, Russia, and China," in *Doping in Elite Sport*, 155–161. Charlie Francis and Jeff Coplon, *Speed Trap: Inside the Biggest Scandal in Olympic History* (New York: St. Martin's Press, 1990).

30. Barrie Houlihan, "Anti-Doping Policy in Sport: The Politics of International Policy Co-ordination," *Public Administration* 77.2 (1999): 311–334.

31. Barrie Houlihan and John Hoberman, "Harmonising Anti-Doping Policy: The Role of the World Anti-Doping Agency," in *Doping and Public Policy*, ed. John Hoberman and

Verner Møller (Odense: University Press of Southern Denmark, 2004), 19–30; Dag Vidar Hanstad, Andy Smith, and Ivan Waddington, "The Establishment of the World Anti-Doping Agency A Study of the Management of Organizational Change and Unplanned Outcomes," *International Review for the Sociology of Sport* 43.3 (2008): 227–249; Ulrik Wagner, "The World Anti-Doping Agency: Constructing a Hybrid Organisation in Permanent Stress (Dis)order?" *International Journal of Sport Policy and Politics* 1.2 (2009): 183–201; and Ulrik Wagner, "Towards the Construction of the World Anti-Doping Agency: Analyzing the Approaches of FIFA and the IAAF to Doping in Sport," *European Sport Management Quarterly* 11.5 (2011): 445–470.

32. Barrie Houlihan, "Policy Harmonization: The Example of Global Antidoping Policy," *Journal of Sport Management* 13.3 (1999): 197–215.

33. Dag Vidar Hanstad, Eivind Å. Skille, and Sigmund Loland, "Harmonization of Anti-Doping Work: Myth or Reality?" *Sport in Society* 13.3 (2010): 418–430.

34. Michael Morris Killanin, *My Olympic Years* (London: Secker & Warburg, 1983), 155.

35. Robert Voy and Kirk D. Deeter, *Drugs, Sport, and Politics: The Inside Story about Drug Use in Sport and Its Political Cover-Up, with a Prescription for Reform* (Champaign, IL: Leisure Press, 1991).

36. Dick Pound, *Inside Dope: How Drugs Are the Biggest Threat to Sports, Why You Should Care, and What Can Be Done About Them* (Mississauga, ONT: John Wiley, 2006); Dick Pound, *Inside the Olympics: A Behind-the-Scenes Look at the Politics, the Scandals and the Glory of the Games* (Mississauga, Ontario: John Wiley, 2004), 49–86.

37. Pound, *Inside Dope*, 1–2.

38. Pound, *Inside Dope*, 228. David Millar, *Racing Through the Dark: Crash. Burn. Coming Clean. Coming Back*, reprint ed. (New York: Touchstone, 2012).

39. Bob Goldman, *Death in the Locker Room: Steroids and Sports* (South Bend, IN: Icarus Press, 1984); Bob Goldman, *Death in the Locker Room II: Drugs & Sports* (Chicago: Elite Sports Medicine, 1992).

40. John Hoberman, *Mortal Engines: The Science of Performance and the Dehumanization of Sport* (New York: Free Press, 1992); *Testosterone Dreams: Rejuvenation, Aphrodisia, Doping* (Berkeley: University of California Press, 2005).

41. Paul Dimeo, "A Critical Assessment of John Hoberman's Histories of Drugs in Sport," *Sport in History* 27.2 (2007): 318–342.

42. Andy Miah, *Genetically Modified Athletes: Biomedical Ethics, Gene Doping and Sport* (London: Routledge, 2004).

43. Angela J. Schneider, "Privacy, Confidentiality and Human Rights in Sport," *Sport in Society* 7.3 (2004): 438–456; Barrie Houlihan, "Civil Rights, Doping Control and the World Anti-Doping Code," *Sport in Society* 7.3 (2004): 420–437; Dionne L. Koller, "How the United States Government Sacrifices Athletes' Constitutional Rights in the Pursuit of National Prestige," *Brigham Young University Law Review* 5 (2008): 1465–1544; Hunt. *Drug Games*.

44. Bernat López, "The Invention of a 'Drug of Mass Destruction': Deconstructing the EPO Myth," *Sport in History* 31.1 (2011): 84–109; Bernat López, "Creating Fear: The Social Construction of Human Growth Hormone as a Dangerous Doping Drug," *International Review for the Sociology of Sport* 48.2 (2013): 220–237.

45. Hoberman, "How Drug Testing Fails," 266.

46. Paul Dimeo and John Taylor, "Monitoring Drug Use in Sport: The Contrast between Official Statistics and Other Evidence," *Drugs: Education, Prevention, and Policy* 20.1 (2013): 40–47.

BIBLIOGRAPHY

Dimeo, Paul. *A History of Drug Use in Sport: 1876–1976: Beyond Good and Evil.* New York: Routledge, 2007.

Hoberman, John. *Mortal Engines: The Science of Performance and the Dehumanization of Sport.* New York: Free Press, 1992.

Hoberman, John. *Testosterone Dreams: Rejuvenation, Aphrodisia, Doping.* Berkeley: University of California Press, 2005.

Hunt, Thomas M. *Drug Games: The International Olympic Committee and the Politics of Doping, 1960–2008.* Terry and Jan Todd Series on Physical Culture and Sports. Austin: University of Texas Press, 2011.

Möller, Verner. *The Ethics of Doping and Anti-Doping: Redeeming the Soul of Sport?* 1st ed. New York: Routledge, 2009.

Möller, Verner. "Knud Enemark Jensen's Death During the 1960 Rome Olympics: A Search for Truth?" *Sport in History* 25.3 (2005): 452–471.

Pound, Dick. *Inside Dope: How Drugs Are the Biggest Threat to Sports, Why You Should Care, and What Can Be Done about Them.* Mississauga, ONT: John Wiley, 2006.

Ungerleider, Steven. *Faust's Gold: Inside The East German Doping Machine.* New York: Macmillan, 2001.

Waddington, Ivan. *Sport, Health and Drugs: A Critical Sociological Perspective.* London and New York: E & FN Spon, 2000.

Wilson, Wayne, and Edward Derse, eds. *Doping in Elite Sport: The Politics of Drugs in the Olympic Movement.* Champaign, IL: Human Kinetics, 2001.

PART VII

RECONSIDERING
ESTABLISHED
CATEGORIES AND
CONTEMPLATING
NEW ONES

CHAPTER 28

··

CLASS AND SPORT

··

LEWIS H. SIEGELBAUM AND SASU SIEGELBAUM

CLASS, once the dominant category among social scientists, has fallen on hard times. The combination of the near universal collapse of political regimes inspired by Marxism, the assertion of the importance of a whole range of alternative categories, and the emergence of postmodern sensibilities have doomed class as the key organizing principle of scholarly inquiry. Class increasingly has been subsumed under other identities—race, gender, and ethnicity in particular. If twenty or thirty years ago it would have been inconceivable to write about sport without addressing class, these days it is quite common.

Yet one need not retreat to nostalgia or genuflect before the idols of Communism to assert the importance of class. Intellectual fashions may come and go, but capitalism, which gave birth to modern class society, has developed further and faster in recent decades than at any other time in its existence. But while deepening the economic gulf separating one class from another, the very dynamism of capitalism that Marx and Engels lauded in *The Communist Manifesto* may be blurring class identities and blunting our ability to identify them. Even if class has retained its importance as an analytical tool, how we think about classes may be stuck in a previous phase. If previously class categories worked within national political structures, those structures have given way to increasingly globalized flows of capital and labor. Consequently, the battles over rights and opportunities have been deflected away from nationally defined class struggles and onto larger and more individualistic terrains.

Richard Gruneau's observation that "The definition of the concept of class, like the definition of sport, is in itself an 'object' of struggle" written during the heyday of Marxist class analysis, retains its pertinence. All definitions are exclusionary. They also contain implicit or explicit antitheses. In the case of class, the main parameters have been "in itself" versus "for itself," objective versus subjective, structure versus agency, consciousness and the lack thereof. Social theorists from Marx onward have tried to synthesize or surmount the antinomies. Anthony Giddens' definition "a large-scale aggregate of individuals comprised of impersonally defined relationships and nominally open in form"—is unusual for its brevity. Gruneau's own definition characteristically empha-sizes the element of struggle:

> I have accepted a view of social classes as social formations whose particular shape is defined on the basis of struggles over "ways of doing things"—struggles which can only be studied as they work themselves out over a given historical period. That the issues which surround these "ways of doing things" are generally tied in some way to opposing "interests" and to the productive relations into which humans beings are born I take to be self-evident.[1]

In this light, the history of sport can be considered an arena in which struggles over ways of doing things have worked themselves out, sometimes to the advantage of one class as against another but occasionally to the benefit—or detriment—of more than one class. Like class, sport too has its antitheses—amateur versus professional, competi-tive versus noncompetitive, the individual versus the team. In what follows, collective actors—players, fans, owners, governing bodies, the media—are treated as representa-tives, projections, or embodiments of classes and class fractions, struggling amongst themselves and occasionally against each other.

THE BRITISH MODEL

In writing, "Many have worked so that few could play," Richard Holt may have been referring specifically to the social conditions of Victorian-era British society. Yet his apothegm could be applied far beyond the empire on which the sun never set. If British culture served as a model for colonial elites throughout the empire, the way sport was organized in Britain became a paragon for imitation throughout the world. Reproduction of the British model of sport entailed adoption or adaptation of its rules of play, imitation of its organization of leagues and schedules, and repetition of the class implications of its distinction between professional and amateur status. By surveying the social conditions from which organized sport sprang in Britain, it is possible to con-sider other dimensions of class and sport as they played themselves out elsewhere.

The Industrial Revolution eroded the social dominance of Britain's old landed elites in favor of the new banking and commercial elites. Adapting the aristocratic ideal of "gentlemanly behavior" to their own needs, the moneyed class solidified its social pres-tige by conspicuous displays of leisure. Social differentiation had everything to do with such conspicuous leisure, which most often took the form of exclusive recreational prac-tices like hunting, golf, and angling.[2] Mid-nineteenth-century English social elites also sought to control the leisure activities of the laboring masses by banning certain sports involving animals such as cockfighting, bear-baiting, and dogfighting in the Cruelty to Animals Act (1835) and by suppressing folk football via the Highway Act (1835), respec-tively. Football, rugby, and animal fighting, however, persisted in the face of such legal measures, mostly because local authorities loosely enforced them and because Britain's new business class also had an interest in those forms of play.

But what about the workers? In the preindustrial era work and play were alternating pursuits, tending to occur in the same place. The imposition of time discipline, associated with burgeoning factory labor, physically expelled leisure to other sites and put a premium on its pursuit.[3] Emphasizing continuity, Holt argues that the "preference of traditional [sic] workers for free time rather than increased income was not simply a reaction against industrial forms of production"[4] The Industrial Revolution may have engendered the raw conditions under which organized sport was to thrive, but British workers had long preferred play to longer working hours. It was precisely this inclination toward physical recreation that oriented the working class toward the "absorption of gentry values," defining in the process the sporting culture of the Victorian era.[5]

Nowhere were such gentry values more apparent than in Britain's elite public schools. It was there that, as Pierre Bourdieu noted, "the sons of aristocratic or upper bourgeois families took over a number of popular—i.e. vulgar—games, simultaneously changing their meaning and function in exactly the same way as the field of learned music transformed the folk dances—bourrées, sarabands, gavottes etc. which it introduced into high-art forms such as the suite."[6]

The process was not as simple as Bourdieu claims, for the games that had long been "a central component of the boys' culture" at schools like Eton, Winchester, and Marlborough, were not those shared by the popular masses.[7] Those games were objectionable to headmasters determined to sublimate young males' sexual energy, imbibe bourgeois codes of restraint, and promote teamwork.[8] Football, or rather the modified/codified version that emerged from the public schools of the mid-nineteenth century, fit the bill.

Public school education served as a crucial mark of one's social standing, but no less significantly it forged, through prescribed athletic activity, critical social networks that extended beyond one's years in the ivy-covered buildings. In an effort to maintain both social ties and physical fitness, public school graduates, along with their former headmasters, organized exclusive sporting clubs that helped bridge the gap between their school days and adult lives. Centered in Britain's towns and cities, the new football clubs quickly attracted popular followings, especially from the new urban working class, which catapulted the sport to the mainstream. The football that emerged with the founding of the Football Association (1863) became the game that "for most of [the late nineteenth and early twentieth] century . . . has been the working man's game."[9]

Most other sports in Britain would repeat this "diffusionist" trajectory with minor variations. Rugby, detached from Association football, became divided between a northern proletarian-based (Rugby League) version, and a southern (Rugby Union) game that had a more socially elite following. Country cricket was aristocratic in its origins, but, as Holt points out, it "reached a peculiarly English accommodation between the upper classes that ruled it and the mixture of middle- and working-class people who watched it." Thanks to its county-organized structure, much of its fan base came from a new suburban middle class. Class divisions between "gentlemen" and "players," however, would remain an important dimension of the sport until the 1960s.

Tennis, golf, and rowing exhibited a more attenuated diffusion mainly because of their spatial requirements and associated costs. Horse racing, long a "favorite pastime of the English aristocracy," was also limited to a largely upper-class live audience but via newspaper reporting of starting prices and runners, televised races, and the lifting of the ban on off-track betting in 1960, became accessible to middle- and especially working-class people.[10] Well before off-track betting became legal, its practice had been an essential part of pub culture. Boxing, a once predominantly publican-organized activity, continued to attract significant betting. The exceptionality of boxing lay in the fact that it was "the most proletarian of sports" already in the late nineteenth century because "by definition gentleman could not box for money."[11]

Gambling was one noteworthy feature of British sports that reinforced class differences even while sinuously tying the classes together. Football, boxing, horse and dog racing, and even angling attracted betting and eventually offered legalized betting pools. While much of Britain's middle class found gambling dishonorable and distasteful, this was not the case with working-class people, who, as Holt points out, "did not believe it was possible to save enough to really improve their lives" and thus looked on the chance for a great windfall as a source of hope and entertainment. For many, filling in a football coupon was as much a part of everyday life as a pint and a game of darts at the local. While "the traditions of the gentry and the common people met [in gambling] in joint recognition of the middle-class sporting morality," the financially secure gambled for other reasons. For the upper class, betting took the form of conspicuous leisure, in which high wagering in its legal form represented a tangible method of social differentiation.[12]

Such then was the British model that expatriate elites and stewards of the empire carried with them to the colonies or absorbed during the nineteenth century and that exercised an enormous influence elsewhere. Many countries, particularly those that had been part of the British Empire, needed to establish their own sporting identities in connection with their national projects and thus abjured association football in favor of other kinds of kicking and passing games. With minor variations, however, the same social trajectory of education and sport (from the elites to the masses and from the amateur ideal to the professionalization and commercialization of sports) held its course from the West to the East Indies. As C. L. R. James explains of his native Trinidad, "It [education] came doctrinally from the masters, who for two generations from the founding of the school, had been Oxford and Cambridge men."[13] The popularity of cricket had the same origination. Similarly, high-caste Indians, who were taught to play sports at fee-paying secondary schools during the Raj, made cricket India's national game.

One can discern analogous processes on the other side of the Channel. As in Britain, sports in France originated from popular town games (via the *fête*), received the gentile values of the Lycée, and were then diffused among wider audiences. Likewise, "Barriers between the upper and middle classes . . . were broken down on the playing fields in imitation of the achievements of the English public schools." However, the more dispersed nature of France's population attenuated the popularization of nonequestrian/venatic sports, as it did the nation's industrial development. The masses did take up rugby and football, albeit later than in Britain, but it was cycling that captivated French audiences, cut across class divisions, and "brought commercial sport to impoverished and remote parts" of the country.[14]

Everywhere, as Gruneau points out in connection with the "dominant moment" in Canada's institutional structuring of sport, residual, contradictory, and even oppositional sporting practices have abounded. Sometimes these have been expressed in a different approach to the game derived from the influx of players from the slums, the "pibe" from the barrio, or their equivalents from the favela; sometimes in the raucous behavior of the crowd (part of what Gruneau refers to as sport's inherent "disorderly or 'profane' side"), and occasionally in direct challenges to the authority of governing bodies.[15] These "possibilities" remind us that no matter how united a nation may seem around "its" national team or favorite sport, sport contains within itself class differences and also that the vast majority of professional athletes are, after all, workers.

PLAYERS AS WORKERS

The 1963 film *This Sporting Life* tells the grim story of Frank Machin, an English Rugby League star who is never truly able to escape his working-class roots.[16] The film captures the bonds among Rugby League players on and off the pitch, but, set in grey, soot-covered northern England of the early 1960s, it also depicts the limits of sport as a vehicle for upward social mobility. Frank's rapid rise from the coal mines to the local rugby club's first team represented the dream of countless working-class Yorkshire youths to become a professional athlete. But through his failure to maintain stable personal relationships and the constant reminders from the club owners, Frank learns the hard lesson that despite his fleeting success on the pitch and the material rewards it brings, he will always be an uneducated, provincial laborer in the eyes of his social betters.

The birthplace of organized sport also gave rise to professional sport. Professionalism was the product of the conflict between the middle-class "democratic" principle of amateur competition and the money-making potential of organized sport. In addition to the codification of select games, late-nineteenth-century Britain witnessed the completion of a national railroad network, new lines of communication and news reporting, and an improvement in labor conditions, all of which facilitated the popularization of sport. These same developments along with the gradual shortening of the working day were crucial in providing an opportunity for male workers elsewhere to indulge their interest in following professional athletics.

As team owners, administrators, league organizers, and investors realized that the economic potential of sport justified making it a full-time commercial enterprise with full-time employees, the burgeoning working-class participants were often forced to choose between manual labor and "an all-together more splendid life" as professional athletes.[17] For working men in late-nineteenth-century Britain, organized athletic participation initially supplemented but eventually came to equal or even exceed their "day job" earnings. Even so, with the exception of the most outstanding performers, players were little different from many assembly-line workers who were treated as interchangeable parts. Players' dispensability, however, does not discount the struggles in which many have engaged in attempting to make a living from playing and the steps they have taken to overcome, or at least reduce, their individual vulnerability.

Many of history's greatest sports teams succeeded because of an intimate understanding and positive energy among teammates. This "team chemistry" is a potent expression of collective identity that has the potential to transcend class affinities and antagonisms. Team chemistry can be derived from a common class background, such as in the case of the University of Michigan's "Fab Five," the mostly Detroit- and Flint-born 1989 National Collegiate Athletic Association basketball finalists, whose mutual understanding on the court was strengthened by a camaraderie stemming from similar "rust-belt" working-class upbringings sometimes mistaken for common racial identities. But beyond individual teams lies the possibility of recognizing common interests that have as much to do with succeeding off the playing field as on it and beyond one's career as well as during it. This recognition has been bound up with the collective representation of players in relation to owners, namely by labor unions.

Labor unions are teams unto themselves whose priority is to collectively improve working conditions for their members. The relationship between unions and professional athletes was not apparent at the outset of professional sports. Trade unionism predated organized sport by at least fifty years, and, indeed, as Holt points out, most trade union leaders along with other socialist activists disapproved of commercialized sport because they feared it would distract workers from both "the historic mission of the proletariat" and from partaking in healthier activities.[18] Nevertheless, by the middle of the twentieth century many "sportsworkers" found it advantageous to be represented by unions, a development that can be explained in two ways.[19]

The geographic and cultural proximity of industrial workers to professional sport paved the way for its permeation by unions. Working-class neighborhoods located within the vicinity of professional teams' home fields and stadiums typically provided their most fervent supporters. Early national figures in the British labor movement, such as Herbert Smith, "the flat-capped miner's leader" whose dedication to labor reforms was only matched by his devotion to cricket and the Barnsley Football Club, were crucial in strengthening the associations between sport and organized labor.[20] Smith and others are illustrative of "the centrality of modern sport in [male] working-class culture."[21] In addition to a general cultural affiliation, many early professionals either doubled as manual laborers or had familial connections to organized labor. When unions began to represent players in the early twentieth century (in Britain first but subsequently elsewhere in the empire and in North America as well), they echoed the relationship that already existed between trade unions and players' familial antecedents. Concerning the Professional Footballer's Association's assertion of the applicability of the Workmen's Compensation Act of 1906 up to and including strike activity, Holt notes that "the widening class-consciousness of militant trade unionism within the Edwardian working class, especially considering the number of players from mining origins, may ... have helped encourage the flurry of industrial action."[22] Whether or not the parents of the talented working-class youths on whom professional teams came to depend were union members, the players at the very least were familiar with the potential of collective bargaining to produce improvements in the workplace.

The very position of professional athletes as people hired to perform for a given period of contracted time makes unionization no less conceivable than for other workers. Whether by negotiating standards for drug-testing, minimum salaries, season lengths, or transfer policies, unions have provided a level of predictability, standardization, and job security that have transcended the issue of pay and that professional athletes have found beneficial. In these respects, they are no different from other skilled workers for whom, as Eric Hobsbawm has noted, unions are about "more than asking for wage-rises."[23]

Still, the majority of professional sports league strikes have concerned wages. The 1948 Fútbolistas Argentinos Agremiados strike may be the sole case of such union action precipitating—or at least being followed by—an expansion of fan interest and revenue for owners.[24] Disputes over salary arrears resulted in disruptions to schedules in Spain's La Liga in 1981, 1984, and 2011. Other cases such as Major League Baseball's impasse between owners and players in 1994, the 2004–2005 National Hockey League lockout, and the 2011 National Basketball Association (NBA) lockout delayed, shortened, or resulted in the cancellation of entire seasons. Anti-union propaganda by team owners, league administrators, and some commentators proved effective. They did this at the risk of eroding the sport's fan base. In the case of baseball, it took more than a decade to match prestrike attendance figures.[25] As with unions outside of sports, owners sometimes have been fiercely hostile to their very existence.

Unions across nearly every skilled trade since the mid-twentieth century have been stigmatized, attacked, and blamed for a host of problems and, as a result, have lost much of their potency. Further detracting from union solidarity is the inflation of top earners' wages. The individualism that has been heightened by neoliberal capitalism obviates the need for union membership for the top performers who can negotiate their own terms of employment. Though noted athletes such as New York Yankees third-baseman Alex Rodriguez and Barcelona's mercurial forward Lionel Messi earn more than US $18 million per year, it is important to remember that such gargantuan salaries are atypical, and, most important, professional athletes are contract workers, hired to perform. Considering their outsized average salaries, one could hardly dispute their place in the "labor aristocracy," but when all is said and done, they remain workers, seasonal and temporary though their work may be.

Or are they? Because of their visibility and commercial potential, elite athletes are both laborers and commodities, occupying what Erik Olin Wright has called "contradictory class locations."[26] "In common with working-class people," wrote John Hargreaves, "they are employees selling their labour, experiencing insecurity and are subject to the authority of employers and officials. But in terms of levels of earnings, work satisfaction, autonomy in the work task and future prospects, most are clearly closer to the middle and upper levels of society."[27] In these respects, they are among a rare group of workers who, like actors and other entertainers, are often in the public eye. But their exalted pay and status should not blind us to two important facts about professional athletes as sportsworkers. First, no less so than the hierarchy separating local repertory company actors from TV and movie stars, baseball's semiprofessional and minor leagues; soccer's second, third, and fourth divisions; and basketball's plethora of regional leagues are a long way from the "big leagues" in terms of visibility, commercial emoluments, salaries, and benefits. Second, even the most successful professionals remain subject to the demands of the owners, who profit not only from gate receipts but indirectly from their players' endorsements, paraphernalia, and media appearances.

Many of the dimensions of players as workers that have been discussed here presuppose a capitalist economy. But what about in the Second World of Communist-dominated state socialism? On the one hand, these countries had both workers and players; on the other, Communists long proclaimed that the former ruled (and therefore were not "proletarians" in the sense they were/are under capitalism) and the latter were nonprofessional. Few regarded these claims as anything but fictions. Yet at least in one respect, a curious reversal of workers as players could be observed. Beginning in the Soviet Union in 1929, "socialist competition" emerged as the dominant mode of agitation for higher productivity. The language of socialist competition was shot through with the military metaphors of "storming," "fronts," and the like, but sports, still genuinely in its preprofessional phase, also provided rhetorical inspiration. The Stakhanovite movement of the mid-1930s, with its emphasis on pace and mania for individual records (*rekordmenstvo*), brought virtual sports celebrity to a select group of production heroes.[28] And, like not a few sports heroes in the capitalist world, some of the leading Stakhanovites—including Aleksei Stakhanov himself—incapable of handling their celebrity, succumbed to alcoholism and hooliganism.

You "Da" Fan: Class, Fandom, and the Practice of Sport

In discussing class thus far, terms such as "working class," "middle class," "elite," "gentry," and "upper class" have been used. It is important to remember that such terms are not indelible or universal. Class, like the rules of a particular sport, is a historically bound concept that in its simplest form can be defined as a measure of the power relations between people. If, in Gruneau's view, "sport is a form of institutionalized social practice that simply mirrors the social conditions which surround it," then we must acknowledge that preferences for particular sports and the ways those preferences are expressed vary over time in relation to both cultural norms and socioeconomic conditions.[29]

That some sports remain more exclusive than others is indisputable. Generally speaking, a linear correlation exists between class hierarchies and the amount and cost of equipment and space required for a sport. It is easy to see why sports with minimal spatial and equipment requirements (soccer in most of the world; basketball in the United States) have attracted such popular followings, especially in urban areas. Correspondingly, those sports that require considerable investments in real estate, equipment, and training such as polo, golf, and tennis remain exclusive. In discussing the dearth of American youth talent on the pro tennis circuit, Martin Blackman, a senior official of the United States Tennis Association, blamed the costs of development, stating that "without a system, you're at the mercy of prodigies and private programs . . . the expense of developing a world-class player from age 10 to 20 is astronomical."[30]

One need not have played a particular sport to be a fan, but the relationship is not hard to fathom. Those who have felt the thrill of crushing a pitch, making a bucket from "downtown," or netting a slapshot could be excused for imagining themselves as the Mick, Mike, or the Great One. They are thus predisposed to following the sport as fans not only while they are playing but also in later years. If this is the case, then given the availability of balls and a modicum of space in which to kick them, the mass following of soccer throughout the world becomes readily understandable. Whereas in the United States it has been largely middle-class kids who have been encouraged to take up the game (hence the stereotype of the soccer mom driving them to and from practices), in much of the rest of the world, soccer is the sport of preference of children—boys in particular—of the working class. Most of the great ones—from Pele to Maradona and Messi—have hailed from working-class backgrounds, and so have their most boisterous fans.

The association of soccer with unruly crowd behavior, and such behavior with the working class, dates from the latter part of the nineteenth century. The full-scale riot occasioned by the 1909 "Old Firm" Scottish Cup Final (Rangers–Celtic) caused "horror" among middle-class Glaswegians, for it appeared "that the once pacific and cowed working-classes were sensing their power and flexing their muscles."[31] Football grounds became favored sites for working-class males to act up, which, if not intended to frighten the middle class, flouted the middle-class values of self-control and restraint. What middle-class adults tended to regard as loutish behavior was precisely what attracted working-class people—and eventually their youthful middle-class imitators—to congregate and behave in such a manner. They congregated typically on the cheaper terraces, giving a geographic specificity within sports venues to class identities. This was not particular to Britain, or even to capitalist societies. In post–Second World War Moscow Dinamo Stadium contained a north stand, which was the "roosting place for party leaders, NKVD officers, and assorted other big shots;" a "semi-aristocratic" south stand with a posh restaurant; and a west stand that was heavily patrolled by the police because of its proximity to the metro, leaving the east end as the home of the "real fans."[32]

Huddled together for warmth as much as for collective mayhem, these fans enacted a sense of community that reproduced the dominant culture of their neighborhoods. Indeed, the association of sporting venues with class-based neighborhoods could be very close—as it once was with Buenos Aires' rival football clubs, Boca Juniors and River Plate. For decades after it opened in 1940, "La Bombonera," Boca's home ground, was also home to the "Xeneize" ("Genovese," referring to the city of origin of many of the immigrants who settled in La Boca) who inhabited the colorful, tightly packed working-class blocks in the stadium's immediate vicinity; by contrast, River's "Monumental" sits among the upscale high-rises of the quiet, leafy districts of Belgrano and Nuñez. In recent times, however, Boca, River, and other premier professional teams throughout Latin America have expanded their fan base to global proportions thanks in part to the investments and marketing campaigns of Petrobras, Budweiser, Telemex, Total S.A., and other international business giants. Yet elsewhere in Buenos Aires and throughout Latin America, second- and third-division teams are still financially dependent on shirt sponsors, team donors, and local ownership. Magallanes of Santiago (Chile), for example, or Vitoria of Salvador (Brazil) retain more intimate neighborhood followings and working-class identities. They and teams like them often function as "feeders" for the first division, a relationship that mimics class hierarchies outside of sport.

But even where team support does not correlate with a particular residentially based class orientation, it can reflect power relations that possess the force of class. In Stalin's Russia of the 1930s, for example, Moscow's Dinamo, "supported by the secret police, was inextricably part of the state sector." Spartak, with origins in the consumer sector, was more the "people's team." This division of fan loyalty was reflected in differing behaviors, with Spartak's "Soviet version of . . . rough British working-class masculinity" opposed to Dinamo fans' "more respectable middle-class manliness."[33]

A third dynamic between class and fan affinities is exemplified by the National Football League's Oakland Raiders. The emblem of the pirate is proudly flown on flags appended to motor vehicles and houses, worn on t-shirts, and tattooed on bodies. These manifestations of Silver and Black pride speak to a working-class rootedness in Oakland that contrasts with the more cosmopolitan character of San Francisco across the bay. Middle-class interest in American football is more apt to manifest itself in season ticket holding, membership in official supporters clubs, identification with one's alma mater at the college level, and fantasy league participation, the latter indicative of managerial aspirations, statistical prowess, and networking know-how. Both soccer and American football, then, have socially eclectic followings, but the class lines among the followers are distinct. These sports are quite unlike yachting and polo, for example, which are accessible almost exclusively to the extremely wealthy. NASCAR, the quintessentially (white) working-class based American sport, may be at the opposite end of the class spectrum.

Supporting professional teams and athletes does not exhaust how nonathletes have experienced sport in class ways. As Richard Holt emphasizes, older sporting activities rooted in the working class such as dog racing, pigeon-flying, darts, and bowls persisted (at least in Britain) well beyond when one might have imagined their abandonment in favor of spectatorship at mass sporting events. He attributes their survival to "a kind of submerged tradition, sustaining skills and providing satisfactions, which the hurly-burly of the playing fields did not."[34] One might extend Holt's point beyond Britain and the mid-twentieth century to include such popular rural pastimes as hunting and fishing, both of which have been inflected by class, to say nothing of bowling, bocce, and other community-based pursuits.[35]

First radio then television played a huge role in expanding sports spectatorship and solidifying identification with local teams, but cable access, streaming via the Internet, and other recent technological innovations that have made a panoply of events accessible to the viewer no matter where he or she happens to be have eroded the close geographic connection between teams and their supporters. It is now possible for followers of "Man U" from as far afield as Austria, Russia, and Malaysia to enter into the debate about ownership of the team and keep abreast of other developments simply by going online. At the same time, the cost of attending many sporting events has become prohibitive to a substantial proportion of working-class youth and even their parents, eroding the traditional spatial-demographic divisions within venues (i.e., the "ends" in football stadiums and the bleacher seats in baseball parks for those of little means as opposed to the luxury boxes and midfield seats).

Apropos of ownership, what as recently as the 1980s would have seemed unimaginable—English Premier League clubs purchased like baubles by fantastically wealthy investors from the United States, Russia, India, and Abu Dhabi—came to pass in the first decade of the twenty-first century.[36] The globalization of capital has facilitated the buying and selling not only of teams but of players, stadium naming rights, and just about anything else subject to commodification. The hire to the tune of US$30 million per season of Cameroon's star forward Samuel Eto'o to play for a team called Anzhi in the relative obscurity of Makahachkala, Dagestan; the purchase of the NBA's New Jersey Nets by Russian billionaire Mikhail Prokhorov (reportedly the third richest individual in Russia); the to-ing and fro-ing between North America and Europe of professional hockey and basketball players; and, for that matter, the accelerated turnover of all professional athletes have complicated the identification of fans with a particular team and its character, whether class-based or not.[37] Teams and their personnel have become the playthings of immensely wealthy corporations and individuals, who in their exclusivity form a class unto themselves. Their global reach is enhanced by what Samuel Martinez refers to as the "sportification" of society, that is, sport's penetration of fashion, literature, film, music, and language even while sport itself is subjected to ever greater degrees of commercialism.[38]

CONCLUSION: DOES CLASS MATTER ANYMORE?

In its multidimensionality, sport can both contribute to working-class solidarity and promote the commercial and political ends of the bourgeoisie, sometimes even within the same country and at the same time. Yet we should not be under any illusion that sport by itself could compose, decompose, or recompose classes. Much evidence points to sport reflecting the larger social and cultural shift of the late twentieth and early twenty-first centuries away from class toward other collective identities. Marx's poetical rendering of capitalism's dynamism—that "all fixed, fast frozen relations, with their train of ancient and venerable prejudices and opinions, are swept away. . . . All that is solid melts into air"—has never resonated so much as it does today.[39] Ironically, class, the principal category that Marx and, after him, Marxists used for analyzing nineteenth- and twentieth-century capitalism, seems to have succumbed to this very dynamic. Massive global flows of migrants, refugees, guest workers, and other itinerants have vastly complicated the possibility of class happening in the sense that E. P. Thompson once celebrated.[40] Collective representation of workers—historically situated in trade unions and leftist political parties—has shrunk while explicitly nonclass affiliations and identities based on race, gender, and (at least implicitly) ethnicity and nationality have attracted greater political energy and media attention.

Social theorists correspondingly have lost much of the interest they previously devoted to class. This is unfortunate, for class can still serve as a powerful tool of analysis. As for sport—one of the principal sites for the production and consumption of popular culture—ignoring it would be foolish. Yet it is ignored. A case in point is the controversy sparked by a statement made by Jalen Rose in the ESPN documentary about the University of Michigan's Fab Five basketball team of the early 1990s, which aired in March 2011. Rose, a member of the team and the program's executive producer, said he hated Duke and everything it stood for because "Schools like Duke don't recruit players like me. I felt like they only recruited black players that were Uncle Toms." The comment so offended former NBA and Duke star forward Grant Hill that he responded on a *New York Times* blog by proudly asserting that "My teammates at Duke—all of them, black and white—were a band of brothers who came together to play at the highest level for the best coach in basketball."[41]

It would seem that this was all about race and that, in the eyes of Rose, Duke was for white boys with the occasional black recruit tolerated if he behaved himself, while Hill claimed that the brotherhood of teammates transcended race. That is largely how the sports commentariat interpreted the flap.[42] Yet Hill himself had noted Rose's resentment of "blacks from two-parent, middle-class families" such as Hill's. Moreover, the in-state tuition at the University of Michigan, although hardly a pittance, is nowhere near what it costs to send someone to Duke, a private school. Evidently, more than race was involved. Rare is the documentary that emphasizes class no less than race—*Hoop Dreams* (1994), about two Chicago youths seeking to "make it" to the NBA like their idol Isaiah Thomas, is an atypical exception.

Gender, like race, intersects with class in important but often underappreciated ways. In 2007 the highly successful Rutgers women's basketball team was subjected to taunts by radio host Don Imus that were not only racist ("nappy headed") and sexist ("hos") but had obvious though seldom noted class connotations ("That's some rough girls from Rutgers. Man, they got tattoos.").[43] Nancy Kerrigan, the victim of an assault at the 1994 US Figure Skating Championships, was no less a working-class girl than Tonya Harding, her rival on whose behalf Kerrigan was attacked. But the media tended to portray Kerrigan, the victim, as more wholesomely middle class, more what a figure skater should be—the "ice princess"—than the eternally notorious Harding.[44] Likewise, Serena Williams' outbursts at the 2009 US Open semifinal and 2011 final tennis matches clearly violated the long-standing association of "ladies' tennis" with gentility and in the latter incident was judged by the on-air commentator to be "bad form."[45]

And so, we turn back to the question posed by the title of this conclusion—does class matter anymore?—to which the answer is: it should more than is generally acknowledged, but neither as an isolated category nor one given a priori explanatory preference. If class used to happen more obviously than it does at present—within sport as well as in the larger social realm to which sport is connected—it is incumbent on social science to explain why that was so and to seek it out still amidst the panoply of power relations, none of which is going away soon.

Notes

1. Richard Gruneau, *Class, Sports, and Social Development* (Amherst, MA: University of Massachusetts Press, 1983), 169.
2. Thorstein Veblen, *The Theory of the Leisure Class: an Economic Study of Institutions* (New York: Modern Library, 1934), 38–40.
3. E. P. Thompson, "Time, Work-Discipline, and Industrial Capitalism," *Past and Present* 38.1 (1967): 56–97.
4. Richard Holt, *Sport and the British: A Modern History* (Oxford: Oxford University Press, 1989), 37.
5. Holt, *Sport and the British*, 95.
6. Pierre Bourdieu, "How Can One Be a Sports Fan?" in *The Cultural Studies Reader*, ed. Simon During (London: Routledge, 1999), 429.
7. David Goldblatt, *The Ball Is Round: A Global History of Soccer* (New York: Riverhead Books, 2006), 24.
8. Gruneau, *Class, Sports, and Social Development*, 103.
9. Tony Mason, "Football," *Sport in Britain: A Social History*, ed. Tony Mason (Cambridge, UK: Cambridge University Press, 1989), 146.
10. Allen Guttmann, *Sports Spectators* (New York: Columbia University Press, 1986), 64.
11. Stan Shipley, "Boxing," in *Sport in Britain*, 78.
12. Holt, *Sport and the British*, 182, 354–355.
13. C. L. R James, *Beyond a Boundary* (London: Yellow Jersey Press, 1963), 32.
14. Richard Holt, *Sport and Society in Modern France* (London: Macmillan, 1981), 48–49, 176.
15. Gruneau, *Class, Sports, and Social Development*, 148–153. Gruneau is obviously indebted to Antonio Gramsci here. For an acute analysis of the implications of Gramsci's understanding of the conditionality of hegemony—national and otherwise—for sport, see David Rowe, "Antonio Gramsci: Sport, Hegemony and the National-Popular," in *Sport and Modern Social Theorists*, ed. Richard Giulianotti (Basingstoke, UK: Palgrave Macmillan, 2004), 97–110. For analysis of how football has been represented hegemonically as an ally of the "underclass," see Fernando Segura M. Trejo, "El Futbol Como Forma De Integracion E Insercion Social: El Campeonato Inersociativo de La *Homeless World Cup*," in *Futbol-espectaculo Cultura y Sociedad*, ed. Samuel Martinez Lopez (Mexico City: Universidad Iberoamericana, 2010), 241–265.

16. The film is based on David Storey, *This Sporting Life* (New York: Macmillan, 1960), a fictionalized version of Storey's own brief career as a rugby player.

17. J.B. Priestley, *The Good Companions* (New York: Harper Brothers, 1929), 56.

18. Holt, *Sport and the British*, 148.

19. We borrow the term "sportsworkers" from John Hargreaves, *Sport, Power and Culture: A Social and Historical Analysis of Popular Sports in Britain* (Cambridge, UK: Polity Press, 1986).

20. Eric Hobsbawm, *Workers: Worlds of Labor* (New York: Pantheon Books, 1984), 212.

21. Gruneau, *Class Sports, and Social Development*, 150.

22. Holt, *Sport and the British*, 298.

23. Hobsbawm, *Workers*, 281.

24. We thank Alex Galarza for this point. The fact that the strike occurred during the heyday of Peronism in Argentina may explain the anomaly.

25. "1994 Was a Low Point for Baseball," ESPN-MLB, August 10, 2004, http://sports.espn.go.com/mlb/news/story?id=1856626.

26. Erik Olin Wright, *Classes* (London: Verso, 1985), 19–63.

27. Hargreaves, *Sport, Power and Culture*, 126.

28. Lewis H. Siegelbaum, *Stakhanovism and the Politics of Productivity in the USSR, 1935–1941* (Cambridge, UK: Cambridge University Press, 1988).

29. Gruneau, *Class Sports, and Social Development*, 35.

30. "Critics See Drop in Talent as U.S.T.A. Grapples With Player Development," *The New York Times*, September 12, 2011, p. D7.

31. Goldblatt, *The Ball Is Round*, 74.

32. Robert Edelman, *Spartak Moscow: A History of the People's Team in the Workers' State* (Ithaca, NY: Cornell University Press, 2009), 144. For an alternative explanation of soccer hooliganism emphasizing the globalization of an "ethos of gangsterism," see Franklin Foer, *How Soccer Explains the World: An Unlikely Theory of Globalization* (New York: HarperCollins, 2004), 14–15.

33. Edelman, *Spartak Moscow*, 103.

34. Holt, *Sport and the British*, 193.

35. See Scott E. Giltner, *Hunting and Fishing in the New South: Black Labor and White Leisure after the Civil War* (Baltimore, MD: Johns Hopkins University Press, 2008). In some parts of Europe, hunting remained an upper-class, even aristocratic, pursuit. See, for example, Gyorgy Péteri, "*Nomenklatura* with Smoking Guns: Hunting in Communist Hungary's Party-State Elite," in *Pleasures in Socialism: Leisure and Luxury in the Eastern Bloc*, ed. David Crowley and Susan E. Reid (Evanston, IL: Northwestern University Press, 2010), 311–343.

36. "Reuters Factbox on Foreign Owners of Premier League Soccer Clubs," Reuters, April 11, 2011, http://uk.reuters.com/article/2011/04/11/uk-soccer-england-owners-idUKTRE73A3TR20110411, lists ten of the twenty teams, including the top three (Manchester United, Manchester City, and Chelsea) as foreign-owned.

37. *The New York Times*, September 12, 2011, p. A10.

38. Martinez Lopez, *Fútbol-espectáculo, Cultura, y Sociedad*, 3.

39. Trejo, "El Futbol," 70.

40. E. P. Thompson, *The Making of the English Working Class* (New York: Pantheon, 1964), 9: "And class happens when some men, as a result of common experiences (inherited or shared), feel and articulate the identity of their interests as between themselves, and as against other men."

41. "Grant Hill's Response to Jalen Rose," http://thequad.blogs.nytimes.com/2011/03/16/grant-hills-response-to-jalen-rose/

42. See for example "Jalen Rose-Grant Hill Discussion," http://sports.espn.go.com/espn/commentary/news/story?id=6226919. Of the six commentators, only one, Jemele Hill (who, like Rose, hailed from inner-city Detroit) mentioned class.

43. "Imus Called Women's Basketball Team 'Nappy-Headed Hos,'" MediaMATTERS for America, April 4, 2007, http://mediamatters.org/research/200704040011

44. See Jane Feuer, "Nancy and Tonya and Sonja: The Figure of the Figure Skater in American Entertainment," in *Women on Ice: Feminist Essays on the Tonya Harding/Nancy Kerrigan Spectacle*, ed. Cynthia Baughman (New York: Routledge, 1995), 16–17.

45. "Serena Williams' US Open Outbursts: An Uncharacteristic Ticking Timebomb," foot fault!, September 13, 2011, http://footfault.net/2011/09/13/serena-williams-us-open-outbursts-an-uncharacteristic-ticking-timebomb/

BIBLIOGRAPHY

Bourdieu, Pierre. "How Can One Be a Sports Fan?" In *The Cultural Studies Reader*, edited by Simon During, 427–440. London: Routledge, 1999.

Edelman, Robert. *Spartak Moscow: A History of the People's Team in the Workers' State*. Ithaca, NY: Cornell University Press, 2009.

Feuer, Jane. "Nancy and Tonya and Sonja: The Figure of the Figure Skater in American Entertainment." In *Women on Ice: Feminist Essays on the Tonya Harding/Nancy Kerrigan Spectacle*, edited by Cynthia Baughman, 3–21. New York: Routledge, 1995.

Foer, Franklin. *How Soccer Explains the World: An Unlikely Theory of Globalization*. New York: HarperCollins, 2004.

Goldblatt, David. *The Ball Is Round: A Global History of Soccer*. New York: Riverhead Books, 2006.

Gruneau, Richard. *Class, Sports, and Social Development*. Amherst: University of Massachusetts Press, 1983.

Guttmann, Alan. *Sports Spectators*. New York: Columbia University Press, 1986.

Hargreaves, John. *Sport, Power and Culture: A Social and Historical Analysis of Popular Sports in Britain*. Cambridge, UK: Polity Press, 1986.

Holt, Richard. *Sport and Society in Modern France*. London: Macmillan, 1981.

Holt, Richard. *Sport and the British: A Modern History*. Oxford: Oxford University Press, 1989.

Mason, Tony, ed., *Sport in Britain: A Social History*. Cambridge, UK: Cambridge University Press, 1989.

Péteri, Gyorgy. "*Nomenklatura* with Smoking Guns: Hunting in Communist Hungary's Party-State Elite." In *Pleasures in Socialism: Leisure and Luxury in the Eastern Bloc*, edited by David Crowley and Susan E. Reid, 311–343. Evanston, IL: Northwestern University Press, 2010.

Rowe, David. "Antonio Gramsci: Sport, Hegemony and the National-Popular." In *Sport and Modern Social Theorists*, edited by Richard Giulianotti, 97–110. Basingstoke, UK: Palgrave Macmillan, 2004.

Segura M. Trejo, Fernando. "El Futbol Como Forma De Integracion E Insercion Social: El Campeonato Inersociativo de La *Homeless World Cup*." In *Futbol-espectaculo Cultura y Sociedad*, edited by Samuel Martinez Lopez, 241–265. Mexico City: Universidad Iberoamericana, 2010.

CHAPTER 29

GENDER MATTERS IN SPORT HISTORY

PATRICIA VERTINSKY

INTRODUCTION

Sport was traditionally thought of as a gender factory—a site where men made themselves into men and women fought to overcome the consequences of that historically constructed "male bastion." This assumption informed popular narratives around histories of sport and underscored the reality that gender matters in sport history. After all, everyone knows that there is a distinct advantage to being "in" history rather than "outside it" and that among those people and groups that are "in" history it is better to be an agent (maker) of history than a participant or commodity thereof.[1]

Feminist sport historians have worked hard to bring women in from outside the accumulated (and imagined) history of sport. In 2012, the *Journal of Sport History* dedicated a forum to a group of young feminist sport historians who claimed to be renewing and reinventing feminism continuously in their work, refusing labels and thinking through the ways in which old scripts need to be rethought and rewritten. They pointed out how the historical analysis of women and gender in sport has undergone radical change in the past two to three decades such that the valuable contributions of feminist approaches to the discipline mean that it is now virtually unthinkable to ignore women when analyzing sport.[2] Quoting Alun Munslow in *The Future of History*, they declared that "we use the past for the kind of history we intend to create, and the history we create inflects our engagement with the present as much as it might the past."[3] They were also careful to point out in their discussion how this new generation of scholars is building their scholarship on the roots and shoots of earlier generations of female sport historians who had to work through and at times against a resolutely gendered profession. Susan Cahn, for example, has long been credited for helping rip sports history out of its overly masculine nature with her provocative book *Coming on Strong: Gender and Sexuality in Twentieth Century Women's Sport* published in 1994. In a 2015 second edition, she rued that the identification of sports with masculine prowess remained firmly in place and that women still faced far too many barriers to breach before "coming on strong."

In this chapter I follow the paths of these generations of scholars in order to illustrate the slow and gradual (and at times unsteady) inclusion within sport history of a focus upon gender, albeit marked by soft essentialism in much of the sport history literature. Michael Messner argues convincingly that once it had become a seriously contested terrain of gender relations and meaning, sport could no longer remain a "masculinist" site where "hard essentialism" could be produced unambiguously. Yet his work shows how there remains a belief system that negotiates the current tensions between beliefs in equal opportunity with stubbornly persistent commitments to the idea of natural difference. Soft essentialism frames sport as a realm in which girls are empowered to exercise individual (albeit continuing gender-appropriate) choices while continuing to view boys as naturally wired to play sport.[4] Indeed, despite the revolutionary changes brought about by second-wave feminism and Title IX in the United States during the 1970s and their impact on opening multiple doors to sport for women and girls, historians such as Kay Schiller and Christopher Young maintain that sport history is still forced by dint of its material to be framed by and to talk predominantly about men.[5]

Despite their gloomy view, I argue that an appreciation within sport history of a focus upon gender during the past two to three decades, which in turn has pressed the academy to pay attention to a wider and deeper version of the history of sport and physical culture, is to be celebrated. In particular the conflation of feminism and certain elements of postmodernism has stimulated new approaches to sport history that have generated greater interest in the construction of the gendered subject and opened up broader, comparative examinations of representations and performances of the active and sporting gendered body. I discuss how postmodernist contributions to sport history have posed useful challenges to the long-standing notion of science and society as a patriarchal hierarchy with a claim to truth while admitting that even here soft essentialism is hard to shake.[6]

I also suggest that an important strategy to avoid the naturalizing of gender asymmetries in sport history has been to encourage a broadening of the sport historian's gaze from the making of men through the (his) story of (his) sport in its many guises to the wider, transnational (and transgendered and transdisciplinary) world of leisure, physical or body culture, gesture, dance, and expressive movement. Wide-ranging historical studies of the extraordinary modernist preoccupation with physical culture that developed in the late nineteenth and early twentieth centuries are demonstrating how gender was caught up in its global tentacles of commodification and institutionalization in schools, gymnastics, dance, and keep-fit organizations generating an unparalleled and lasting transnational interest in sport, recreation, and the moving body.[7] Henning Eichberg has been particularly instrumental in pressing sport historians to move away from an ignorance of other than dominant Western epistemes and intellectual traditions in order to examine the interlacement between Western histories of sport and physical culture and non-Western histories with attention to the political and gendered dimensions of physical/body culture.[8] Indeed, an entire subdiscipline has cohered around the study of physical culture. *Physical cultural studies'* scholars, by token of their critical interest and broad insights into the history of embodiment and movement practices, have begun to develop a range of theoretical and methodological tools to investigate the historical evolution of complex physical culture activities and patterns in a rapidly globalizing world.[9]

WOMEN HISTORIANS AND THE PRACTICE OF HISTORY THROUGH A MALE LENS

While admitting that women's and gender histories are now reverberating with a sense of progress,[10] feminist historian Bonnie Smith has been forthright about how the practices of history have traditionally been negatively affected by gender. Looking back into the profession of history she says, "the profession's unacknowledged libidinal work—the social ideology that draws us to value male plenitude, power and self—presentation is but rarely glimpsed in the mirror of history."[11] As part of her challenge, she shows how the very definition, as well as the practices of history, have been shaped by gender and demonstrates the degree to which the profession defined itself in opposition to amateurism, femininity, and alternative ways of writing history. She documents how the male historians of the archive and the seminar claimed to be searching for "genderless universal truths," which in reality prioritized men's history over women's, white history over nonwhite, and the political history of Western governments over others. Until today, she believes, "we inhabit a gendered profession in which the higher status of the male historian and his topics—considered the loci of universal value—fosters much bad 'acting out' of this obviously fraught role, yet the more sophisticated stage of 'working through,' which accompanies issues of power, abuse and trauma is never reached."[12]

Smith might well have been talking about the subdiscipline of sport history and the play of gender within it. Female sport historians were well aware of the obstacles they faced in gaining acceptance to the domain of sport history that, during the 1970s and 1980s, was carving out a niche within the general field of history as part of history's rapprochement with the social sciences. At the time, sport history took its philosophical, theoretical, and methodological cues largely from social history, which, according to Eric Hobsbawm, was powerfully shaped and stimulated not only by the professional structure of other social sciences and by their methods and techniques, as well as by their questions. Social history required a commitment to understand all facets of human existence in terms of their social determination, and sport and gender relations clearly had an important role. Yet even as social history flourished, women's history—along with women's sport history—was slow to find acceptance.[13] Looking back at his survey of the development of social history during the 1970s, Hobsbawm wrote of his astonished embarrassment that he made no reference whatsoever to women's history. Nor, he added, did most of the distinguished males in the profession notice their blindness to this aspect of their work.[14] Certainly sport historians of the time, who increasingly found their place within the intellectual home of social history and adopted its methodological innovations, typically wrote through a male lens—and largely about men's sporting and athletic achievements. Sport, after all, has been one of the ways in which the male body is constantly represented, examined, worshipped—all too often to the exclusion of the female body as active.[15]

Jack Berryman, editor of *The Journal of Sport History*, admitted in 1983, some nine years after the foundation of that journal, that, overall, sport history remained the history of men's involvement in sport. "Despite the fact that sport has been embedded in, and contoured by patriarchal relationships," he said, "we have still to see an adequate analysis of women and sport."[16] In the same vein, sport historian Mel Adelman complained that what limited historical literature there was on women and sport was largely descriptive, at once elevating analytical studies of sporting culture by men who were considered free from gender constructs and diminishing the role of narrative, experience, and story-telling when it came to women (who it seems could not transcend their gender in their work and were therefore not part of mainstream sporting culture).[17] At the time, feminist-oriented sport historians were working to reveal heroines, evidence women's contextual agency, and provide explanations of oppression and inspiration for action by writing "her-stories" and focusing upon changes in the way history was written (including articulating why and how the "whole story" was not being told).[18] Their work reflected a desire to restore women to history, to focus upon their existence as a meaningful category of analysis, and to counter the dominance of traditional male-centered approaches to sport history.

American sport historian Nancy Struna was among the first to ask prescient questions about women's sport history and its intersection with women's history in 1984. "Has our literature moved beyond the parochial to the universal questions which historians ask; has it begun to suggest what ultimate difference woman's sporting experience makes in our total understanding of the human experience; is it contributing to theoretical debate and methodological innovation?"[19] She attributed the slow development of the field to restrictive assumptions derived from uncritically applying contemporary characterizations of sport as male, modern, and athletic to the past. Noting that women's sporting experience could neither be understood apart from other behaviors and attitudes redolent in society nor adequately addressed through a male prism on sport, Struna called upon scholars to move beyond compensatory "her-story" measures such as mapping particular women's experiences and to explore such themes as identity, conflict, and the relativity of equality.[20] It was a call to move beyond the "add women and stir" approach that had begun to integrate women's history into other histories, and it demanded further questioning around the most basic foundations of historical study.[21] From an initial preoccupation with the need to rediscover and render visible the contributions of women reformers and sporting women from the past, sport historians began to embrace revisionist interpretations to explore and document the diverse nature of women's historical experience.[22]

GENDER AS A WAY OF THINKING ABOUT SPORT HISTORY

Among the many theoretical and methodological issues emerging in women's history and women's sport history during this decade was a critical debate around the use of postmodern theory to reshape women's history in place of more traditional methods of determining historical reality from archival material and other data. Caught up in this continuing debate was the contentious concept of gender history articulated by Joan Scott in "Gender: A Useful Category of Historical Analysis."[23] In her 1986 landmark study, Scott, to the utter disdain of her male historian colleagues in Princeton, underscored how gender offered a good way of thinking about history.[24] Her aim was to bridge the gap between feminist social scientists who critiqued gender and gender roles and the feminist literary critics who deconstructed textual representations of sex difference, an arena soon joined by Judith Butler in *Gender Trouble: Feminism and the Subversion of Identity* where she developed the germinal notion of gender performativity.[25] Scott usefully outlined two key propositions for gender history: gender is a constitutive element of social relationships based on perceived differences between the sexes, and gender is a primary way of signifying relationships of power. Indeed, she insisted, gender needed to be viewed as constitutive of society, deeply affected by culture and indispensable for analyzing not only sexual politics but also politics more generally.

Scott's views on gender history were taken up in J. A. Mangan and Roberta Park's collection of gender-focused sport history essays, *From Fair Sex to Feminism: Sport and the Socialization of Women in the Industrial and Post-Industrial Eras.*[26] The historical studies in this collection marked a discernible shift from women-centered investigations and analyses of sex roles to the study of gender roles involving both men and women, and it began from the poststructural premise that identities are made in relationships. It was a barometer of an emerging trend in the application of feminist analysis to the sporting arena. The changing inquiry in women's sport history and gender relations highlighted the emerging shift from scientific to literary paradigms among social scientists, from an emphasis on cause to one on meaning. Clearly gender was a determining factor in cultural production and was also so in relation to its interpretations. Reclaiming sporting experience was a significant task, but it was equally important to recognize how the forging of experience was itself an outcome of social processes. Experience was now understood to be formed through discourses that must be analyzed in order to view the workings of power.[27] In the end, concluded Scott, there is no way to detach the relations of power, systems of belief, and practices from knowledge and the processes that produce them.[28]

Once sport historians began to scrutinize ways in which the concept of gender legitimized and constructed social relationships, they were able to develop clearer insights into the reciprocal nature of gender and society. Even historians who persisted in treating sport predominantly as a male domain no longer winced at the possibility that it was and is a gendered domain.[29] Male feminist scholars such as Michael Messner, Jim McKay, and Don Sabo provided support by building on the framework developed by feminist analyses of women and sport to demonstrate the fundamental importance of gender in men's sports.[30] Historical sporting studies of men and masculinity began to flourish.[31] It was ironic, noted Shari Dworkin and Michael Messner, that the institution of sport that had contributed to the reconstitution of hegemonic masculinity throughout the twentieth century had become a key site for the development of a critical feminist scholarship on gender.[32]

In 1991, Roberta Park edited a special issue of *The Journal of Sport History* that was a compilation of the growing maturity of scholarship in the area of gender relations and sport history. Her ambition was to include both male and female constructions, interests, and sporting issues and to extend gender analyses to intersect with race, ethnicity, class, location, and aging. In line with the work of R. W. Connell and others, she aimed to show that it was not enough to juxtapose social categories of gender, class, and race and apply them to sport.[33] They needed to be woven together by an inductive analysis, beginning with the most basic element of sport, the human body, and an investigation of its social meanings. Sport is such a diverse phenomenon, or cluster of phenomena, and sporting contexts so varied that the body became seen as a particularly useful way into the topic. Bodies, Park insisted, "are used to convey a host of deep-seated cultural beliefs and values," hence there was a need to explore how views of the body affected the forms of sport that people constructed; how these perceptions and constructions affected notions of manliness, femininity, and gender relations; and how biological thought affected athletics and vice versa.[34] Pointing to the emergence of a new and increasingly popular genre of body history, she underscored how a version of historiography that paid attention to the gendered body might encourage new perspectives on the sporting practices of the past.[35]

Over the years, Scott's article on gender as a useful category of historical analysis has become canonical, and in a recent forum of the *American Historical Review* a group of historians from different chronological and geographical orientations commented upon the staying power of her argument that the history of gender could and must inhabit much more of the historical turf than the history of women. They highlighted the ways in which her work has continued to impact historical thinking through the use of poststructuralist and psychoanalytical theories for thinking about gender and by warning against the fixed or essentialist views that the term has often implied.[36] They also showed how a focus on gender could enter and remap the most resistant domains such as the history of war, politics, and foreign relations—even sport with its traditional focus on men and masculinities.[37]

To be sure, there are those who continue to worry that this "Scottian," "Derridian," "Foucauldian" study of gender ignores women qua women and tends to intellectualize and abstract the inequality of the sexes by emphasizing differences, exclusion, and anti-essentialism and diverting feminist academics from the fundamental transformation of social relations.[38] Critiques of Scott's work have come from both left and right and from different geographical arenas, especially an anxiety over the need to engage more closely with historical women—women who once lived and breathed. Will we not still need women's history, wrote Alice Kessler-Harris in the *Chronicle of Higher Education*?[39] Catriona Parratt warned sport historians that where gender becomes the focus of their analysis they might be in danger of obscuring, marginalizing, or even erasing women. She noted it was possible to focus on gender in sport history and ignore women completely, since the history of sport could be said to be centrally a history of gender, of masculinity, in which women have hardly figured at all. And, she continued, while attention to theory about gender offered a powerful way of exposing and attacking the oppositions and hierarchies on which gender relations are based, it also posed the danger of abandoning concern with the lives of "real women."[40] Sporting women of color and ethnicity, working women, lesbian women, aging women, and those with disabilities were among those who had remained hidden from history and whose voices needed to be heard as authentic and legitimate. If the turn to theory, like the turn to gender with which it is connected, entailed the possibility of abandoning the study of all of these women's experiences, she said, then historians of women's sport and leisure should be warned to make it with caution.[41] Bonnie Smith has tried to quell this anxiety by showing how, over time, twenty-first-century women's history has begun to approximate the fullness of men's historical portrait in a number of ways. "Just as men's political economic and social portrait has thickened, becoming more detailed, complex and colorful with the development of historical professionalism, so too has the portrait of women."[42] Indeed fears of the undermining of women's history by gender studies have remained largely unfounded.[43]

Feminism, Sport History, and Gender Relations

Feminism itself has broadened out in multiple, transnational directions. Chandra Talpade Mohanty calls it "feminism without borders," where it is seen to function as one of the many "ideascapes" that characterize contemporary transcultural global flows.[44] Yet not surprisingly there remain vast differences in approaches to women's and gender sport history geographically as well as ongoing criticism of the inordinate attention paid to US women's history and Western feminist historiography to the detriment of more nuanced perspectives. Although feminist history was an international phenomenon from the outset, there was criticism of a continued focus in debates upon Anglo-American scholarship. Across Europe, for example, a broad spectrum of positions on feminisms' usefulness in understanding central and eastern European societies includes a slippery east/west divide.[45] For example, there is a broad spectrum of positions on feminism's usefulness ranging from sympathetic to the hostile equation of feminism with communist totalitarianism.[46] For China scholars, say Gail Hershatter and Wang Zheng, the scholarly trajectory of gender in Euro-American historical scholarship differs from that in the People's Republic of China, and Joan Scott's work has been a less a roadmap than a working guide on how to trace partially obscured tracks. Viewing women's and gender history as a feminist project is not an automatic move for Chinese historians of women's sport and physical culture, which has developed its own contours.[47] Indeed, scholars of non-Western women's history have successfully attempted to interrogate and dismiss Western paradigms while creating their own approaches.[48] An excellent example is the contrast between Fan Hong's *Footbinding, Feminism and Freedom: The Liberation of Women's Bodies in Modern China*,[49] which approvingly recounts Western missionaries' beneficial influence on Chinese women's bodies, and Dorothy Ko's artful confounding of Western feminist paradigms in *Cinderella's Sisters: A Revisionist History of Footbinding.*

Despite Douglas Booth's acknowledgment in *The Field: Truth and Fiction in Sport History* that "feminists have added to the common treasury of knowledge and interpretation in the field [of sport history] to the extent that it is now virtually unthinkable to ignore women when analyzing sport,"[50] there are sport historians of gender who are pessimistic. Carol Osborne and Fiona Skillen complain that in Britain the dedicated study of women and gender relations in sport history remains a neglected area of academic research. They express disappointment that, in the area of gender relations, women's history and sport history has not fulfilled its promise in the British context. Furthermore, they conclude that its marginality remains partly due to the "maleness of universality"—the continuing view of the nature of sport itself as a male activity, the apparent rigidity of gender identities, and the way that sport in itself perpetuates associated discourses.[51] Such a view is certainly apparent in Mike Cronin's article reviewing "the serious business of sport history" in which he provides a list of contemporary sport historians who are almost without exception males writing about traditional male sporting subjects. Furthermore, he throws doubt upon the utility of sustaining the subdiscipline of sport history altogether, viewing the parent discipline of history as a better home for the production of serious sport history.[52] A similar view was highlighted by Mark Dyreson in his discussion of recent revisionist approaches to the history of sport in Europe.[53] Dyreson pointed to two recent surveys of modern European sport history by Christopher Young and his co-editors, who queried the relationship of sport history to "legitimate history." Their claim "that the absence of a usable historiography of European sport represents 'a glaring hole' that threatens to suck the field (of sport history) into oblivion" suggests that they have largely overlooked vast numbers of studies by established sport historians, male or female, in favor of ma(i)nstream historians who have shown only recent interest in producing studies of sport and physical culture.[54] The relationships between "mainstream" historians interested in sport and sport historians who work in fields related to kinesiology, physical education, and coaching remain strained for a wide variety of reasons, though the role of gender is often the elephant in the room.[55]

Meanwhile, Scott herself has moved in new directions, questioning the ongoing vitality of the term gender once it had lost its ability to startle and provoke. Twenty-four years after the publication of *Gender: A Useful Category of Historical Analysis,* her view is that gender is most usefully viewed as a question. Gender is not a programmatic or methodological treatise, she now says; it is an invitation to continue to think critically about how the meanings of sexed bodies are produced, deployed, and changed. Furthermore, she reminds, questions about gender must always be asked and answered in specific contexts because "for all its corporeality the body is not an originating point nor yet a terminus; it is a result or an effect conceived in a specific time and place."[56]

Judith Butler has similarly enriched our understanding of the ways in which sport historians might approach the precarious performance of gender and the ever-shifting politics of the body in time and space. Feminist historiography has abundantly shown how gender orders are formed and reformed over time.[57] Butler, however, underscores how it is not possible to know what gender is apart from the way that it is produced and mobilized. Nor can we really know whether gender is a useful category of analysis unless we understand the precise purposes for which it is deployed, the broader politics it supports and helps to produce, and the geopolitical repercussions of its circulation. We make a mistake, she says, if we expect that gender or the categories of women and men are either culturally established in fixed form or timeless kinds of being.[58] It is important, therefore, that we continue to ask, in increasingly precarious times, how new forms of gender might affect the ways we live, play, and think about our sporting present as well as our past.

As more sophisticated theories of gender, its performativity and plasticity, have been developed along these lines, a number of feminist sport historians are focusing upon collective radical politics and nonheterosexual sporting lifestyles. An emerging queer agenda of breaking down, rather than mobilizing around, conventional gender categories is leading to a paradigmatic shift in transgender politics and discussions of human rights that is being played out in everyday life, including the sporting arena.[59] This new gender politics is combining movements concerned with transgender, transsexuality, intersex, and their complex relations with feminist and queer theory. Indeed, the significance of gender plurality has become a topic of keen interest (and contestation) in elite competitive sport where sex testing practices, which began decades ago, have historically relied on the idea of sex as a natural, universal, and stable binary while demonstrating, with each new method and technology, the very complexity, mutability, and fluidity of human sexuality.

Claire Hemmings recently warned of the danger of making the story about the past four decades of feminist theory too reproducible and reproductive.[60] Her recommendation that historians experiment with alternative ways of telling feminist stories is one that sport historians of gender are finding increasingly useful to deepen and sharpen their critiques on physical culture and the sporting body. As Elizabeth Grosz points out, "the better we understand the past, the more well-armed we are to welcome the surprise of the future as it makes clear the specificities and particularities—the events of history."[61] If, as she hopes, the future is the domain that endures, with the past enduring only in its capacity to become something other, always open to future rewritings and a radical refusal to settle down, then there is indeed hope for the continuance of a gender sensitive sport history—a sport history that one might describe as "beyond patriarchy," alert and open to new forms of gender and to multiple forms of historical expression. Passion, argues Scott, thrives on the pursuit of the not yet known.[62] With this in mind, sport historians of gender are encouraged to continue to reimagine, refine, and reinvent feminist sport history's future; to foster new feminist coalitions and multigenerational dialogue wherever possible; to expand the feminist sport history toolbox, sources of inspiration, and new paradigms around the sporting gendered body; and to continue to question how feminism relates to itself across time and in relation to race, class, sexuality, and generation.

Notes

1. Hayden White, "Politics, History and the Practical Past," *The New York Times*, January 14, 2008.
2. Holly Thorpe and Rebecca Olive, quoting Douglas Booth, in "Introduction: Feminist Sport History in the Past, Present and Future," *Journal of Sport History* 39.3 (2012): 373–377.
3. Alun Munslow, *The Future of History* (Hampshire, UK: Palgrave Macmillan, 2010), 70.
4. Michael A. Messner and Suzel Bosada-Deas, "Separating the Boys from the Moms: The Making of Adult Gender Segregation in Youth Sports," in *Sociology: Exploring the Architecture of Everyday Life*, ed. David A. Newman and Jody O'Brien (Thousand Oaks, CA: Pine Forge Press, 2009), 232.
5. Kay Schiller and Christopher Young, "The History and Historiography of Sport in Germany: Social, Cultural and Political Perspectives," *German History* 27.3 (2009): 313.
6. See, for example, Patricia Vertinsky, "Time Gentlemen Please: The Space and Place of Gender in Sport History," in *Deconstructing Sport History: A Postmodern Analysis*, ed. Murray G. Phillips (Albany: State University of New York Press, 2006), 227–244. See also Douglas Booth, *The Field. Truth and Fiction in Sport History* (London and New York: Routledge, 2005).
7. See, for example, Helen Thomas, "Physical Culture, Bodily Practices and Dance in Late 19th and Early 20th Centuries," *Dance Research: The Journal of the Society for Dance Research* 22.2 (2004): 135–204; Patricia Vertinsky, "Transatlantic Traffic in Expressive Movement: From Delsarte to Dalcroze to Margaret H'Doubler and Rudolf Laban," *The International Journal of the History of Sport* 26.12 (2009): 1922–1942.
8. Henning Eichberg, "A Revolution in Body Culture," in *Body Cultures. Essays on Sport, Space and Identity*, ed. John Bale and Chris Philo (London: Routledge, 1997).
9. Patricia Vertinsky, "Shadow Disciplines, or a Place for Post-Disciplinary Liaisons in the North American Research University: What Can We Do with Physical Cultural Studies?" in *Playing for Change: The Continuing Struggle for Sport and Recreation*, ed. Russell Field (Toronto: University of Toronto Press, 2015), 389–406. See also David L. Andrews, "Kinesiology's Inconvenient Truth: The Physical Cultural Studies Imperative," *Quest* 60.1 (2008): 46–63. Long before sport sociologists "invented" the subdiscipline of physical cultural studies, Roberta Park as well as others helped stimulate this broadening of sport history's focus by pressing sport historians to constantly expand the kinds of questions they asked about the sporting and physically active male and female body. "I want to make it clear," she said, "that I consider sport history to be a category term that includes, at least, agonistic athletics, vigorous recreational pursuits, and physical education, and intersects with aspects of medicine, biology, social reform and a host of other topics." She was particularly interested in opening up new questions about the historical origins of health education, approaches to fitness, and training regimens for sport, exercise, and physical culture that might borrow models from exercise physiology, sports medicine, and allied fields. Roberta J. Park, *Sport History in the 1990s: Prospects and Problems*, American Academy of Physical Education Papers 20 (Champaign, IL: Human Kinetics Press, 1986), 97.
10. Bonnie G. Smith, "Women's History: A Retrospective from the United States," *Signs: Journal of Women in Culture and Society* 35.3 (2010): 723–747.
11. Bonnie G. Smith, *The Gender of History: Men, Women and Historical Practice* (Cambridge, MA: Harvard University Press, 1998), 235.

12. Smith, *Gender of History*, 240.
13. Geoff Eley, "Playing It Safe, Or, How Is Social History Represented?" *History Workshop Journal* 35 (1993): 206–220.
14. Eric Hobsbawm, *On History* (London: Weiderfield & Nicholson, 1997), 71.
15. Andrew Blake, *The Body Language: The Meaning of Modern Sports* (London: Lawrence and Wishart, 1996), 161.
16. Jack Berryman, "Preface," *Journal of Sport History* 10.1 (1983): 5.
17. Melvin L. Adelman, "Academicians and American Athletics: A Decade of Progress," *Journal of Sport History* 10.1 (1983): 96–97.
18. Reet Howell, ed., *Her Story in Sport: A Historical Anthology of Women in Sport* (New York: Leisure Press, 1982).
19. Nancy Struna, "Beyond Mapping Experience: The Need for Understanding the History of American Sporting Women," *Journal of Sport History* 11.1 (1984): 121.
20. Struna, "Beyond Mapping," 129.
21. See, for example, Mary Hartman and Lois Banner, eds., *Clio's Consciousness Raised: New Perspectives on the History of Women* (New York: Harper & Row, 1974); Nancy Cott and Elizabeth Pleck, eds., *A Heritage of Her Own: Toward a New Social History of American Women* (New York: Simon & Schuster, 1979).
22. Catriona Parratt, for example, called for a more radical agenda in women's sport history that proceeded from women's experiences and that placed women at its center. Catriona M. Parratt, "Women's History and Women's Sport History: Exploring the Connections," paper presented at the annual meeting of North America Society for Sport History, Clemson, South Carolina, May 1989.
23. Joan W. Scott, "Gender: A Useful Category of Historical Analysis," *American Historical Review* 91.5 (1986): 1053–1075.
24. Patricia Vertinsky, "Gender Relations, Women's History and Sport History: A Decade of Changing Enquiry, 1983–1993," *Journal of Sport History* 21.3 (1994): 1–24.
25. Judith Butler, *Gender Trouble: Feminism and the Subversion of Identity* (New York: Routledge, 2006).
26. James A. Mangan and Roberta J. Park, eds., *From Fair Sex to Feminism: Sport and the Socialization of Women in the Industrial and Post-Industrial Eras* (London: Frank Cass, 1987).
27. This did leave questions about the difficulty of disentangling the discursive aspects from the moments of experience and agency in the shaping of identity. Kathleen Canning, "German Particularities in Women's History/Gender History," *Journal of Women's History* 5.1 (1993): 106.
28. Joan Scott, "Women's History," in *New Perspectives on Historical Writing*, ed. Peter Burke (Cambridge, UK: Polity Press, 1991), 65.
29. Nancy Struna, "Social History," in *Handbook of Sport and Society*, ed. Jay Coakley and Eric Dunning (London: SAGE, 2000), 19.
30. Michael A. Messner and Don Sabo, eds., *Sport, Men and the Gender Order: Critical Feminist Perspectives* (Champaign, IL: Human Kinetics, 1990), 2.
31. See, for example, J. A. Mangan, *Athleticism in the Victorian and Edwardian Public School: The Emergence and Consolidation of an Educational Ideology* (Cambridge, UK: Cambridge University Press, 1981); *The Games Ethic and Imperialism: Aspects of the Diffusion of an Ideal* (Harmonsdworth, UK: Viking Press, 1986); John Nauright, ed. *Making Men: Rugby and Masculine Identity* (London and New York: Routledge, 1996);

Greg Ryan, *Tackling Rugby Myths: Rugby and New Zealand Society* (Otago, NZ: University of Otago Press, 2005).

32. Shari L. Dworkin and Michael A. Messner, "Just Do . . . What? Bodies and Gender," in *Revisioning Gender*, ed. Myra Marx Ferree, Judith Lorber, and Beth B. Hess (Thousand Oaks, CA: SAGE, 1999), 341–362.

33. Connell's theory of the gender order as a dynamic system of power relations in which multiple masculinities and femininities were constructed, contested, and altered continually was fundamental to this analysis. R. W. Connell, *Gender and Power: Society, the Person and Sexual Politics* (Stanford, CA: Stanford University Press, 1987).

34. Roberta J. Park, "Physiology and Anatomy Are Destiny: Brains, Bodies and Exercise in Nineteenth Century American Thought," *Journal of Sport History* 18.1 (1991): 63.

35. See, for example, Kathleen Canning, "The Body as Method? Reflections on the Place of Body in Gender History," *Gender and History* 11.3 (1999): 499; see also Joy Parr, "Gender History and Historical Practice," *Canadian Historical Review* 76.3 (1995): 355–356.

36. AHR Forum, "'Revisiting Gender': A Useful Category of Historical Analysis: Introduction," *American Historical Review* 133.5 (2008):1344–1345.

37. There was agreement in the forum that Scott had usefully summarized explanations of gender inequality, captured an emerging historiographical trend, and imported theory to a discipline of committed empiricists. Joanne Meyerowitz, "AHR Forum: A History of Gender," *American Historical Review* 113.5 (2008): 1347, 1356.

38. See, for example, as discussed by Nancy Fraser, *From Redistribution to Recognition? Dilemmas of Justice in a Postsocialist Age* (New York: Routledge, 1997).

39. Alice Kessler-Harris, "Do We Still Need Women's History?" *Chronicle of Higher Education* 54.15 (2007): B6.

40. Catriona Parratt, "About Turns: Reflections on Sport History in the 1990s," *Sport History Review* 29 (1998): 8.

41. Parratt, "About Turns," 8–9. This was also the message of M. Ann Hall, *The Girl and the Game: A History of Women's Sport in Canada* (Toronto: Broadview Press, 2002).

42. Smith, "Women's History," 730.

43. Sue Morgan, "Theorising Feminist History: A Thirty Year Retrospective," *Women's History Review* 18.3 (2009): 381–407.

44. Chandra Talpade Mohanty, *Feminism without Borders. Decolonizing Theory, Practicing Solidarity* (Durham, NC: Duke University Press, 2003); Arjun Appadurai, "Disjuncture and Difference in the Global Cultural Economy," in *Modernity at Large: Cultural Dimensions of Globalization* (Minneapolis: University of Minnesota Press, 1996), 27–47.

45. See, for example, Maria Bucur, "AHR Forum: An Archipelago of Stories: Gender History in Eastern Europe," *American Historical Review* 113.5 (2008): 1375–1389.

46. Allaine Cerwonka, "Travelling Feminist Thought: Difference and Transculturalism in Central and Eastern European Feminism," *Signs: Journal of Women in Culture and Society* 33.4 (2008): 809–832.

47. Gail Hershatter and Wang Zheng, "AHR Forum: Chinese History: A Useful Category of Gender Analysis," *American Historical Review* 113.5 (2008): 1404.

48. Smith, "Women's History."

49. Fan Hong, *Footbinding, Feminism and Freedom: The Liberation of Women's Bodies in Modern China* (London and New York: Routledge, 1997); Dorothy Ko, *Cinderella's Sisters: A Revisionist History of Footbinding* (Berkeley: University of California Press, 2005).

50. Booth, *The Field*, 19.
51. Carol Osborne and Fiona Skillen, "Introduction: The State of Play: Women in British Sport History," *Sport in History* 30.2 (2010): 189–190. See also Fiona Skillen, *Women, Sport and Modernity in Interwar Britain* (Bern: Peter Lang, 2013) and Jean Williams, *A Contemporary History of Women's Sport: Part One: Sporting Women 1850–1960* (London and New York: Routledge, 2014).
52. Mike Cronin, "Review: Playing Games? The Serious Business of Sports History," *Journal of Contemporary History* 38.3 (2003): 495–503.
53. Mark Dyreson, "Mapping Sport History and the History of Sport in Europe," *Journal of Sport History* 38.3 (2011): 397–405; Paul Dietschy and Richard Holt, "Sport History in France and Britain: National Agendas and European Perspectives," *Journal of Sport History* 37.1 (2010): 83–98.
54. Christopher Young, Anke Hilbrenner, and Alan Tomlinson, "European Sport Historiography: Challenges and Opportunities," *Journal of Sport History* 38.2 (2011): 181–188.
55. See, for example, Amy Bass, "State of the Field: Sports History and the 'Cultural Turn,'" *Journal of American History* 101 (June 2014): 148–283.
56. Joan Wallach Scott, "Unanswered Questions, AHR Forum," *American Historical Review* 113.5 (2008): 1423.
57. Sonya O. Rose, *What Is Gender History?* (Cambridge, UK: Polity Press, 2010).
58. Judith Butler, *Undoing Gender* (London and New York: Routledge, 2004). See also J. Jack Halberstam, *Gaga Feminism: Sex, Gender and the End of Normal* (New York: Random House, 2012) for a lashing critique of the fixity of roles for males and females and the role of popular culture in promoting an improvisational feminism that keeps pace with the winds of political change.
59. R. W. Connell, "Transsexual Women and Feminist Thought: Toward New Understanding and New Politics," *Signs: Journal of Women in Culture and Society* 37.4 (2012): 857–881.
60. Claire Hemmings, *Why Stories Matter: The Political Grammar of Feminist Theory* (Durham, NC: Duke University Press, 2011).
61. Elizabeth Grosz, "Histories of a Feminist Future," *Signs: Journal of Women in Culture and Society* 25 (2000): 1018.
62. Joan Scott, "Feminism's History," *Journal of Women's History* 16.2 (2004): 24.

BIBLIOGRAPHY

Adelman, Melvin L. "Academicians and American Athletics: A Decade of Progress." *Journal of Sport History* 10.1 (1983): 80–106.
AHR Forum. "'Revisiting Gender': A Useful Category of Historical Analysis: Introduction." *American Historical Review* 133.5 (2008): 1344–1345.
Appadurai, Arjun. "Disjuncture and Difference in the Global Cultural Economy." In *Modernity at Large: Cultural Dimensions of Globalization*, 27–47. Minneapolis: University of Minnesota Press, 1996.
Berryman, Jack. "Preface." *Journal of Sport History* 10.1 (1983): 5.
Blake, Andrew. *The Body Language: The Meaning of Modern Sports*. London: Lawrence and Wishart, 1996.
Booth, Douglas. *The Field. Truth and Fiction in Sport History*. London and New York: Routledge, 2005.

Bucur, Maria. "AHR Forum: An Archipelago of Stories: Gender History in Eastern Europe." *American Historical Review* 113.5 (2008): 1375–1389.

Butler, Judith. *Gender Trouble. Feminism and the Subversion of Identity*. New York: Routledge, 2006.

Butler, Judith. *Undoing Gender*. London and New York: Routledge, 2004.

Cahn, Susan. *Coming on Strong: Gender and Sexuality in Women's Sport*. New York: Free Press, 1994; 2nd ed., Urbana: University of Illinois Press, 2015.

Canning, Kathleen. "German Particularities in Women's History/Gender History." *Journal of Women's History* 5.1 (1993): 102–114.

Canning, Kathleen. "The Body as Method? Reflections on the Place of Body in Gender History." *Gender and History* 11.3 (1999): 499–513.

Cerwonka, Allaine. "Travelling Feminist Thought: Difference and Transculturalism in Central and Eastern European Feminism." *Signs: Journal of Women in Culture and Society* 33.4 (2008): 809–832.

Connell, R. W. *Gender and Power: Society, the Person and Sexual Politics*. Stanford, CA: Stanford University Press, 1987.

Connell, R. W. "Transsexual Women and Feminist Thought: Toward New Understanding and New Politics." *Signs: Journal of Women in Culture and Society* 37.4 (2012): 857–881.

Cott, Nancy, and Elizabeth Pleck, eds. *A Heritage of Her Own: Toward a New Social History of American Women*. New York: Simon & Schuster, 1979.

Cronin, Mike. "Review: Playing Games? The Serious Business of Sports History." *Journal of Contemporary History* 38.3 (2003): 495–503.

Dietschy, Paul, and Richard Holt. "Sport History in France and Britain: National Agendas and European Perspectives." *Journal of Sport History* 37.1 (2010): 83–98.

Dworkin, Shari L., and Michael A. Messner. " Just Do ... What? Bodies and Gender." In *Revisioning Gender*, edited by Myra Marx Ferree, Judith Lorber, and Beth B. Hess, 341–362. Thousand Oaks, CA: SAGE, 1999.

Dyreson, Mark. "Mapping Sport History and the History of Sport in Europe." *Journal of Sport History* 38.3 (2011): 397–405.

Eichberg, Henning. "A Revolution in Body Culture." In *Body Cultures: Essays on Sport, Space and Identity*, edited by John Bale and Chris Philo, 128–148. London: Routledge, 1997.

Eley, Geoff. "Playing It Safe, Or, How Is Social History Represented?" *History Workshop Journal* 35 (1993): 206–220.

Fraser, Nancy. *From Redistribution to Recognition? Dilemmas of Justice in a Postsocialist Age*. New York: Routledge, 1997.

Grosz, Elizabeth. "Histories of a Feminist Future." *Signs: Journal of Women in Culture and Society* 25 (2000): 1017–1021.

Halberstam, J. Jack. *Gaga Feminism: Sex, Gender and the End of Normal*. New York: Random House, 2012.

Hall, M. Ann. *The Girl and the Game: A History of Women's Sport in Canada*. Toronto: Broadview Press, 2002.

Hartman, Mary, and Lois Banner, eds. *Clio's Consciousness Raised: New Perspectives on the History of Women*. New York: Harper & Row, 1974.

Hemmings, Claire. *Why Stories Matter: The Political Grammar of Feminist Theory*. Durham, NC: Duke University Press, 2011.

Hershatter, Gail, and Wang Zheng, "AHR Forum: Chinese History: A Useful Category of Gender Analysis." *American Historical Review* 113.5 (2008): 1404–1420.

Hobsbawm, Eric. *On History.* London: Weiderfield & Nicholson, 1997.

Hong, Fan. *Footbinding, Feminism and Freedom: The Liberation of Women's Bodies in Modern China.* London and New York: Routledge, 1997.

Howell, Reet, ed. *Her Story in Sport: A Historical Anthology of Women in Sport.* New York: Leisure Press, 1982.

Kessler-Harris, Alice. "Do We Still Need Women's History?" *Chronicle of Higher Education* 54.15 (2007): B6.

Ko, Dorothy. *Cinderella's Sisters: A Revisionist History of Footbinding.* Berkeley: University of California Press, 2005.

Mangan, James A. *Athleticism in the Victorian and Edwardian Public School: The Emergence and Consolidation of an Educational Ideology.* Cambridge, UK: Cambridge University Press, 1981.

Mangan, James A. *The Games Ethic and Imperialism: Aspects of the Diffusion of an Ideal.* Harmondsworth, UK: Viking Press, 1986.

Mangan, James A., and Roberta J. Park, eds., *From Fair Sex to Feminism: Sport and the Socialization of Women in the Industrial and Post-Industrial Eras.* London: Frank Cass, 1987.

Messner, Michael A., and Suzel Bosada-Deas. "Separating the Boys from the Moms: The Making of Adult Gender Segregation in Youth Sports." In *Sociology: Exploring the Architecture of Everyday Life,* edited by David A. Newman and Jody O'Brien, 225–234. Thousand Oaks, CA: Pine Forge Press, 2009.

Messner, Michael A., and Don Sabo, eds. *Sport, Men and the Gender Order: Critical Feminist Perspectives.* Champaign, IL: Human Kinetics, 1990.

Meyerowitz, Joanne. "AHR Forum: A History of Gender." *American Historical Review* 113.5 (2008):1346–1356.

Mohanty, Chandra Talpade. *Feminism without Borders. Decolonizing Theory, Practicing Solidarity.* Durham, NC: Duke University Press, 2003.

Morgan, Sue. "Theorising Feminist History: A Thirty Year Retrospective." *Women's History Review* 18.3 (2009): 381–407.

Munslow, Alun. *The Future of History.* Hampshire, UK: Palgrave Macmillan, 2010.

Nauright, John, ed. *Making Men: Rugby and Masculine Identity.* London and New York: Routledge, 1996.

Osborne, Carol, and Fiona Skillen. "Introduction: The State of Play: Women in British Sport History." *Sport in History* 30.2 (2010): 189–195.

Park, Roberta J. "Physiology and Anatomy Are Destiny: Brains, Bodies and Exercise in Nineteenth Century American Thought," *Journal of Sport History* 18.1 (1991): 31–63.

Park, Roberta J. *Sport History in the 1990s: Prospects and Problems.* American Academy of Physical Education Papers 20. Champaign, IL: Human Kinetics Press, 1986.

Parr, Joy. "Gender History and Historical Practice." *Canadian Historical Review* 76.3 (1995): 354–376.

Parratt, Catriona M. "About Turns: Reflections on Sport History in the 1990s." *Sport History Review* 29 (1998): 4–17.

Parratt, Catriona M. "Women's History and Women's Sport History: Exploring the Connections." Paper presented at the annual meeting of North America Society for Sport History, Clemson, South Carolina, May 1989.

Rose, Sonya O. *What Is Gender History?* Cambridge, UK: Polity Press, 2010.

Ryan, Greg. *Tackling Rugby Myths: Rugby and New Zealand Society.* Otago, NZ: University of Otago Press, 2005.

Scott, Joan W. "Feminism's History." *Journal of Women's History* 16.2 (2004): 10–29.

Scott, Joan W. "Gender: A Useful Category of Historical Analysis." *American Historical Review* 91.5 (1986): 1053–1075.

Scott, Joan W. "Unanswered Questions: AHR Forum." *American Historical Review* 113.5 (2008): 1422–1430.

Scott, Joan W. "Women's History." In *New Perspectives on Historical Writing*, edited by Peter Burke. Cambridge, UK: Polity Press, 1991.

Schiller, Kay, and Christopher Young. "The History and Historiography of Sport in Germany: Social, Cultural and Political Perspectives." *German History* 27.3 (2009): 313–330.

Smith, Bonnie G. *The Gender of History: Men, Women and Historical Practice* Cambridge, MA: Harvard University Press, 1998.

Smith, Bonnie G. "Women's History: A Retrospective from the United States." *Signs: Journal of Women in Culture and Society* 35.3 (2010): 723–747.

Struna, Nancy. "Beyond Mapping Experience: The Need for Understanding the History of American Sporting Women." *Journal of Sport History* 11.1 (1984): 120–133.

Struna, Nancy. "Social History." In *Handbook of Sport and Society*, edited by Jay Coakley and Eric Dunning, 147–203. London: SAGE, 2000.

Thomas, Helen. "Physical Culture, Bodily Practices and Dance in Late 19th and Early 20th Centuries." *Dance Research: The Journal of the Society for Dance Research* 22.2 (2004): 135–204.

Thorpe, Holly, and Rebecca Olive. "Introduction: Feminist Sport History in the Past, Present and Future." *Journal of Sport History* 39.3 (2012): 373–377.

Vertinsky, Patricia. "Gender Relations, Women's History and Sport History: A Decade of Changing Enquiry, 1983–1993." *Journal of Sport History* 21.3 (1994): 1–24.

Vertinsky, Patricia. "Shadow Disciplines, or a Place for Post-Disciplinary Liaisons in the North American Research University: What Can We Do with Physical Cultural Studies?" In *Playing for Change: The Continuing Struggle for Sport and Recreation*, edited by Russell Field, 103–126. Toronto: University of Toronto Press, 2015.

Vertinsky, Patricia. "Time Gentlemen Please: The Space and Place of Gender in Sport History." In *Deconstructing Sport History: A Postmodern Analysis*, edited by Murray G. Phillips, 227–244. Albany: State University of New York Press, 2006.

Vertinsky, Patricia. "Transatlantic Traffic in Expressive Movement: From Delsarte to Dalcroze to Margaret H'Doubler and Rudolf Laban." *International Journal of the History of Sport* 26.12 (2009): 1922–1942.

White, Hayden. "Politics, History and the Practical Past." *The New York Times*, January 14, 2008.

Young, Christopher, Anke Hilbrenner, and Alan Tomlinson. "European Sport Historiography: Challenges and Opportunities." *Journal of Sport History* 38.2 (2011): 181–188.

CHAPTER 30

....

RACE AND SPORT

....

DANIEL WIDENER

SPORT and race belong equally to the world of modern global capitalism that developed during the nineteenth century. To be sure, patterns of play trace back to ancient times. So, too, do patterns of classifying others on the basis of observable and supposedly immutable characteristics. Despite these antecedents, contemporary notions of sport, tracing distinctions between amateur and professional, adhering to commonly understood rules, and engaging questions of spectatorship, are quintessentially modern. Equally recent in origin are the two general and competing understandings of race, the biological and the social. Yet as observers as distinct as Ron Takaki, Amy Kaplan, Elliot Gorn, and Gail Bederman make clear, the late nineteenth century stands apart.[1] For with its conjoined processes of industrial expansion, overseas imperialism, scientific racism, and ideologies of manliness and vigor, the years on either side of the Gilded Age illustrate the extent to which one must speak of race and sport at the same time.

At times, racemaking and the modernization of sport proceeded along parallel, if disconnected, tracks. During the 1840s and 1850s, editorials urged Victorian citizens to take outdoor exercise. New regulations governing sporting contests came into being, and magazines—crucial to building the audiences that would financially underpin professional sport—circulated in ever-greater numbers. These, too, were crucial years for the global history of race, as emancipation and free labor brought about such new, ostensibly "scientific" conceptions of biological differences and as the Indian Removal, war with Mexico, and the transpacific "coolie" trade brought about a polyethnic republic through which, as Melville famously wrote, "the blood of the whole world" flowed. Thus one can see a temporal link between the Yale–Harvard Regatta (1852), commonly understood as America's first collegiate sporting event, and the appearance, between 1853 and 1855, of Arthur de Gobineau's *Essai sur l'inégalité des races humaines*.

This chapter takes up the shifting relationship between race and sport from the late nineteenth through the early twenty-first centuries. The discussion divides roughly into three periods. The first, lasting up until the Second World War, is characterized principally by racial exclusion. The second runs from the 1940s through the 1970s. Confrontation is the crucial byword for this period. The final segment concerns our so-called post-racial era. In each case, the world of sport offers a crucial terrain for understanding unfolding patterns of racial formation and race relations.[2]

Writing in 1903, W. E. B. Dubois argued "the problem of the twentieth century is the problem of the color-line—the relation of the darker to the lighter races of men in Asia and Africa, in America and the islands of the sea."[3] His comment illustrates the value of viewing European and American colonialism alongside domestic patterns of racial exclusion. Although Ben Finney cautions against repeating melancholy generalizations about the decline of "traditional" sports under the colonial onslaught, native Hawaiians had by 1900 almost entirely ceased practicing the traditional sports of *ulu maika* (disk-rolling), *kukini* (foot-racing), and *holua* (landsledding). *He'e nalu*, which would in time be resurrected as modern-day surfing, had also reached a nadir.[4] Across the Pacific, Monroe Wooley noted that "how best to manage the Philippines is one of our gravest national problems," before proposing baseball as a civilizing remedy. In Cuba, baseball took hold with such fervor that many denied it as a colonial import at all. In the British Empire, cricket would serve as a crucial carrier of Victorian values, while football would spread through military and commercial circuits into Africa, South America, Asia, and the Middle East.[5]

If overseas colonial sport seemed concerned principally with a kind of highly super-vised cultural instruction, domestic sport in the late-nineteenth-century United States grew increasingly fixated with the removal of nonwhite participants. In 1875, federal law backed by Union Army bayonets explicitly forbade racial segregation in public accom-modations. Twenty-one years later, *Plessy v. Ferguson* upheld the constitutionality of racial segregation under the "separate but equal" clause. By 1900, uneven patterns of racial exclusion had taken hold. Professional baseball, golf, tennis, and heavyweight boxing would each promote racial exclusion with varying degrees of success. College football was mixed, with segregated Southern universities retaining white teams until the 1960s, while Northeastern universities allowed integrated competitions throughout the Jim Crow era. It is crucial, however, to resist the temptation to view the American dilemma as a purely Southern problem. Charles Martin notes that Fritz Pollard, who played football for Brown University during World War I, was taunted with cries of "catch that nigger" and serenaded by Yalies singing "Bye Blackbird."[6]

In this era, a few prominent black sportsman rose to the fore. Marshall "Major" Taylor became a championship cyclist despite his formal exclusion from the League of American Wheelmen; in 1901, jockey James Winkfield won 220 races, including his second consecutive Kentucky Derby. The case of Jack Johnson, heavyweight champion between 1908 and 1915, is of course well known. For the era of segregation as a whole, there is a strong literature in what African American scholars call the "vindicationist" tradition that extols these and other figures.[7]

For the pre–World War II period, the most extensive research into race and sport concerns racial segregation in baseball. The most celebrated response to exclusion was the development of Negro League Baseball. Bolstered by legendary players like Satchel Paige, Josh Gibson, and James "Cool Papa" Bell, as well as teams like the Homestead Grays, Kansas City Monarchs, and Pittsburgh Crawfords, black professional baseball represented a proud, if financially precarious, form of "race" business during the Jim Crow era.[8]

Baseball proved exceptionally popular among other nonwhite Americans as well. Jeffrey Powers-Beck details "the dozens of American Indians who played Major League Baseball between 1897 and 1945, the hundreds who played Minor League ball, and the thousands who played collegiate and semipro ball."[9] The bibliography on Japanese American baseball is substantial, aided by the efforts of the nonprofit Nisei Baseball Research Project.[10] The case of Mexican American baseball is likewise complex, as it contains both a transnational dimension (given the established Mexican professional leagues) and the contradiction between the reality of racial subjugation in the Southwest and constantly shifting definitions applied to "Hispanic" people in the United States.[11] In the case of Cuban and Puerto Rican baseball, Adrian Burgos' work stands out for its attention to the particular ways in which Caribbean Latinos complicated and challenged the color line, both by their proximity and their interaction with African Americans and through the difficulty their own racial mentalities posed for whites eager to maintain the color line.[12]

As this history makes clear, it is crucial to avoid limiting discussions of race and sport to African Americans and whites. Indeed, there is growing attention to Asian Americans, Native Americans, Mexican Americans, Cubans, and Puerto Ricans in sport. During the era of segregation, each of these communities developed distinct sporting traditions as well as intriguing "interethnic" links across racial boundaries. Baseball furnishes numerous examples of these, from exhibitions in California between Nisei and barnstorming Negro League teams, the presence of Spanish-Caribbean players on "Negro" teams like the Cuban Giants, the presence of African Americans in the Mexican professional leagues, and the widespread practice of African American winter baseball in Puerto Rico, Cuba, and the Dominican Republic. Each of these phenomena is slightly different, but the overarching narrative is one of contact among marginalized minority populations.

If baseball furnishes contrasting examples of exclusion and episodic contact, boxing highlights evolving patterns of racial conflict. Writing in 1938, Ring magazine publisher Nat Fleischer unearthed a hidden history of black champions dating back to the Early Republic.[13] These men were the forebears of Jack Johnson, whose 1910 victory over legendary heavyweight Jim Jeffries ranks only a little bit behind Little Bighorn, Pearl Harbor, and the Tet Offensive on the list of world historical defeats of the American white man. With his riches, white wives, and irresistible talent, Johnson was among the most visible and controversial of sportsmen. Johnson was eventually forced to earn his living outside the borders of the United States, foreshadowing the career of Muhammad Ali. Johnson would also serve as a crucial example for subsequent sportsmen like Joe Louis and Jesse Owens, whose success required they match Johnson's achievements while comporting themselves in ways that whites found less objectionable.

Although the United States, the European colonial powers, and racist democracies like Brazil preferred to view their problems as internal, questions of race and sport received an international airing in the interwar years. Theresa Runstedtler traces Jack

Johnson's antiracist itineraries across Cape Town, Paris, Havana, Mexico City, London, and Sydney.[14] The confrontations between Joe Louis and Jesse Owens and the Nazi regime is better known. Ironically enough, European fascism helped usher in the age of the *jogo bonito*, as Mussolini's search for South American talent (of suitably Italian ancestry) helped end the amateurism and exclusion that had characterized the first epoch of Brazilian football.[15]

In the case of Brazilian domestic football, the opening of space for Afro-Brazilians came as part of a process that was simultaneously about the introduction of working-class participation and professionalism as well. With social relations shaped by the lateness of abolition (1888), fears of popular participation, and the tendency of elites to import fashions, practices, and ideas from Europe, it comes as little wonder that the blacks would initially find themselves barred from football pitches. In contrast to that other marker of Brazilian national identity, Samba, football was linked to sporting clubs that generally excluded nonwhites, and the gradual democratization of the sport was uneven and slow. Despite this, football became an active part of debates about national identity during the middle of the twentieth century, attracting the attention of Rogério Daflon and Teo Ballvé, two of Brazil's most celebrated public intellectuals. In general, exclusionist racism gave way to a shifting pattern of partial inclusion that regarded some form of "racial admixture" as a positive good. Profound problems remain.[16]

As a number of observers, C. L. R James foremost among them, have observed, no game provided so precise a means for delineating the intricacies of caste, class, and color during the colonial epoch as did cricket. Writing of the implications of his decision to choose between a club comprising members of the brown-skinned middle class and a one composed of darker-skinned, lower-middle-class islanders, James argued that "Cricket had plunged me into politics long before I was aware of it. When I did turn to politics, I did not have much to learn." In the fifty years since *Beyond a Boundary* appeared, many excellent studies have appeared that track the interplay between Victorian culture, colonialism, anticolonial resistance, and the problems of postcolonial identity on and off the cricket pitch in South Asia, the West Indies, Australia, and Africa.

Crucial changes affected the entire globe during the last half of the nineteenth century. The spread of modern sport and the emergence of truly global patterns of white supremacy were two of these. New ideas regarding recreation and leisure grew alongside, and indeed shaped, new restrictions on the social and physical mobility of nonwhites. Thus in the United States, among the colonial powers, and within the racially stratified societies of Latin America, race and sport combined in fundamentally similar ways. The principal dynamics that shaped this era were those of exclusion and diffusion, with new sports spreading to new places even as provision was made to avoid embarrassing incidents across the color line. In this context, resistance was delimited by the proliferation of separate traditions like negro baseball and "colonial" cricket; highly charged if symbolic contests, such as the Louis–Schmelling fights and the lives of pioneering individuals like the cricketer Krom Hendricks, the footballer Walter Tull, or the cyclist "Major" Taylor.

A permanent alteration of race relations was one global legacy of the world historical changes wrought by the confrontations between fascism, communism, and liberal democracy between 1939 and 1945. In the United States, blacks who had a generation earlier been urged by their leaders to "close ranks" in the hope of a post-Armistice seat at the table now pushed for a "double victory" over fascism abroad and racism at home. Between 1941 and 1944, tens of thousands of black industrial workers took jobs and struck for better conditions and pay; thousands more pledged to join A. Phillip Randolph's March on Washington Movement. Under legal pressure from Latinos, African Americans, Jews, and Asian Americans, the edifice of segregation showed its first cracks, as the courts declared restrictions like the Texas all-white primary elections unconstitutional.

Other victories would come forth in a gradual and uneven way. By 1948, military segregation and racial restrictions in home sales would go, well in advance of school segregation (1954) or antimiscegenation laws (1967). For some, this progress was not enough, and wartime incidents of draft resistance on the part of urban hipsters (Detroit Red), musicians (Charlie Parker), and political activists (Elijah Muhammad) foreshadowed the black power critiques of American society during Vietnam. Small wonder, then, that one historian would term the Second World War the "forgotten years of the Negro revolution."[17]

As with all revolutions, cultural changes both shaped and reflected the altered landscape. In 1946, activists who noted that the Los Angeles Rams played their home games in a stadium supported by public funds forced the franchise to offer a professional contract to Kenny Washington. This brought about the beginning of the end of segregation in professional football, although the Washington Redskins retained Jim Crow until 1962. The first nonwhite player in the National Basketball Association, Japanese American guard Wataru Misaka, joined in 1947, following a stretch as part of the American occupation Army in Japan. Three years would pass before a trio of African Americans would join the league. Integration of college basketball and football, as well as minor league baseball, accelerated during this period as well.[18]

During the middle of the twentieth century, however, basketball and professional football were little more than footnotes in an American sporting scene dominated by baseball. As noted earlier, baseball's racial landscape was rich and complex, with barnstorming Negro League outfits, local Asian American and Native American clubs, interracial exhibitions held outside the United States, integrated Mexican Leagues, and Latinos whose shifting places along the color line repeatedly exposed the idea of Jim Crow as impossible, in practice, to maintain.

All of this, however, was different than the existence of a formally integrated, and professional, major league. Despite the favorable context promised by a world war against the singularly white supremacist Nazi regime, it is unlikely that the integration of sports would have come when and how it did without the intercession of two factors that have disappeared from the landscape of American life, an independent black-owned press and an organized radical left. Between 1933 and 1947, the Pittsburgh *Courier*'s circulation grew from 40,000 to more than 260,000, making the paper the largest black periodical in the United States. David Wiggins argues that this growth came about in part as a result of the attention the paper gave its campaign to force the integration of baseball. The Communist press, particular the *Daily Worker*, was unceasing as well, with sports editor Lester Rodney among the most vocal white critics of racial segregation to be found in the United States.[19]

Given the extensive extant biography of Robinson, only the briefest of recapitulations is necessary. A children of Georgia sharecroppers who had brought him to California as a child, Robinson was carefully selected by Branch Rickey, a baseball official whose other reforms would include the development of the minor league "farm" system and the introduction of the batting helmet. After searching for two years for a candidate with, as he put it, "guts enough not to fight back," Rickey offered Robinson a minor league contract. Robinson's inclusion would set in motion the rapid desegregation of professional baseball.

Much as Joe Louis had, Robinson rapidly found himself lionized by blacks and marshaled as a racial spokesman by whites. In the context of rising Cold War tensions, this meant entry into debates concerning the relationship between America's racial problems and its international aims.[20] As the global confrontation between the United States and the Soviet Union shifted from Europe and the Far East to the rapidly decolonizing regions of Africa, South Asia, and the Arab world, the persistence of domestic racial troubles proved an embarrassing vulnerability for the United States. Efforts to find a counterweight to international depictions of American racism drew African American entertainers and athletes into the orbit of the US Department of State and other federal agencies. International touring exhibitions were duly organized, and visual artists, jazz musicians, dancers, and athletes were all part of a process meant to highlight an American culture defined by supposedly "free market" values of exuberance, innovation, and spontaneity.[21] As a result, black athletes found themselves cast as actors on a larger and more important stage.

Take, for example, the Harlem Globetrotters. Founded in the 1920s as a kind of touring comedy basketball troupe, the Cold War transformed the team from minstrels to diplomats. In 1951, the American embassy in Berlin wired Secretary of State Dean Acheson asking that he bring the Globetrotters to West Berlin as a counterweight to a massive Third World Festival of Youth and Students being held in East Berlin. By decade's end, the "splendid propaganda stunt" of touring black athletes would culminate in a visit to the Soviet Union, where the team met Soviet Premier Nikita Kruschev and received the USSR's top athletic honors.[22]

As part of what a number of scholars term "Cold War civil rights," the dual opening provided Robinson (as racial spokesman) and the Globetrotters (as representative of core American capitalist values) should not be understated. By the middle of the 1960s, older forms of exclusionist racism were on their way out. In 1956, Althea Gibson won the first of her eleven major tournaments, having already integrated enough tournaments to receive the sobriquet "the female Jackie Robinson." Soon after, Arthur Ashe would become, one supposes, "the male Althea Gibson." Between 1956 and 1963, Gibson and Ann Gregory would integrate women's professional and amateur golf, and by 1961, the PGA would remove "Caucasian-only" restrictions, allowing black participation at many, though certainly not all, PGA-sponsored events.

By the end of the decade, however, minority participation in formerly restricted venues was increasingly beside the point. In a world of black power, black panthers, and the Year of the Heroic Guerilla, what came to be termed the "revolt of the black athlete" was inevitable and inescapable. Even before Harry Edwards, then a twenty-five-year-old assistant professor, sought to organize black athletes into a boycott of the 1968 Olympiad, shifting attitudes were finding their way into the world of sport.[23] Arguably no figure better captured black power's mix of affective and materialist elements than Muhammad Ali. Ali's complex persona and extensive itinerary allow him to be approached from numerous angles, from Jeffrey Sammons' historicist placement within black history, Sohail Daulatzai's framing as part of a global anticolonial Muslim international, Grant Farred's depiction of Ali as a postcolonial vernacular intellectual, or Mike Marqusee's portrayal as simultaneously a global icon of resistance and a "flawed" hero. Ali's embrace of Islam; unilateral revocation of his "slave name," Cassius Clay; and refusal of induction into the Vietnam War–era armed forces cost him popularity and wealth even as these sacrifices endeared him to Third World and domestic minorities alike.[24]

In the former lands of the British Empire, cricket provided a crucial terrain for athletic resistance to racism. How to negotiate the politics surrounding the racist South African regime constituted one of the great questions of cricket and race during the 1970s and 1980s. What to make of the dominant West Indies test side was the other. Led by a quartet of fast bowlers derided as "assassins" and worse, the West Indies lost only 13 of 112 test matches over a fifteen-year period. During this time, the "Windies" won all five test matches against the British and beat the Australians, considered the strongest side in the world, five times out of six. In the era of Michael Manley and the Cuban Revolution, the West Indies Test side stood as a powerful symbol of anticolonialism for Caribbean communities in Britain and the islands. In his foreword to *Liberation Cricket*, Sir Viv Richards claimed "In my own way, I would like to think that I carried my bat for the liberation of African and other oppressed people everywhere."[25] In the postwar period, cricket's anticolonial and antiracist elements attracted the attention of writers and observers based in India, South Africa, and the Kiriwina Islands.[26]

In ways distinct from cricket, the postwar landscape of football (soccer) likewise illustrates the crucial role of race. Numbers rose steadily during the 1970s and 1980s, and by the end of the twentieth century, black footballers constituted around 15 percent of the total population. The conditions faced by players and black spectators, first in England and later across Europe, have led to a variety of research projects, educational campaigns, and minor sanctions. Events from the most recent seasons of European football indicate a continuing problem that highlights the inability of many Europeans to imagine a truly multiethnic continent, or even constituent nations, in which nonwhite populations are "insiders and agents" as opposed to permanent, irreducible, and inassimilable others.[27]

This pattern of conceptual exclusion, so familiar to American historians of slavery and empire, requires a Europe that is profoundly inattentive to its colonialist past. Yet this past is a constant presence, on and off the playing field. Midway through the Algerian War of Independence (1954–1962), FLN operative Mohamed Boumezrag persuaded a group of footballers to leave France and form a football team dedicated to publicizing Algerian independence. Despite threats from soccer's governing body, FIFA, the team played ninety-one competitive matches between 1958 and 1961. The symbolic and material value of the FLN team set the stage for an ongoing dynamic in which the complicated relationship between the two Mediterranean nations would find partial negotiation on the soccer field.[28]

One month after French acknowledgement of Algerian independence, South African police captured Nelson Mandela on the road between Durban and Johannesburg. Mandela's subsequent captivity was not his first, but it was fated to be his longest, and he spent the next twenty-seven years in prison. The year of Mandela's arrest coincided with calls for a boycott of segregated sports competitions by African National Congress president Albert Luthuli and the formation of the South African Non-Racial Olympic Committee by poet Dennis Brutus and others. Questions of sport would remain at the heart of antiapartheid activity until 1994.

South Africa was excluded from the 1964 Olympiad. Ostracism accelerated in the 1970s with the apartheid regime's formal expulsion from the IOC; the spiraling cancellation of cricket, hockey, track and field, and football tournaments and exhibitions; and unprecedented efforts to isolate South African cricket and rugby on the world stage.[29] By the time of the Gleneagles Agreement (1977) and the 1985 United Nations International Convention against Apartheid in Sports, the effort to exclude South Africa from international sport had become one of the most visible dimensions of the broader move to place external pressure on the regime.

Yet it would be a great error to reduce the story of South African sport to its external dimension. Indeed, with the exception of the United States, in no other case is there as developed a bibliography concerning race and sport as in South Africa. Beyond those studies of global efforts to exclude the apartheid regime, the domestic context contains at least three distinct types of studies. The first of these are books that seek to illustrate the racial elements of apartheid era sport as a whole. These generally include the terms "race," "sport," and "apartheid" in some combination in their titles and can be found in a sufficient number to confirm Archer and Bouillon's claim that "South Africa, sport, apartheid: together these three words compose a political know which has fascinated the media and tormented the sporting world."[30] These works are distinct from studies that illustrate particular dimensions of domestic sport history such as the football played by prisoners on Robben Island; *Laduma!*, Peter Alegi's history of South Africa football; and *Blacks in Whites: A Century of Cricket Struggles in KwaZulu-Natal*. For the most part, these works tend to operate within the basic division of South African sport into the efforts to produce nonracialism in those major traditions favored by the black majority (football), the Afrikaner community (rugby), and among Anglophone whites (cricket).

Finally, the period since 1994 has seen the generation of a body of scholarship dedicated to examining South African sport after apartheid. Ashwin Desai's *The Race to Transform: Sport in Post-Apartheid South Africa* is a prime example of this latest tendency. These works generally afford greater attention to minor sports, thus providing a more nuanced depiction of racial conditions in the democratic era. They also serve as an antidote to the idea that events such as winning the 1995 Rugby World Cup (which famously featured Nelson Mandela donning the Springbok jersey reviled as a symbol of Afrikaner nationalism) or hosting the 2010 FIFA World Cup Finals illustrate a playing field that is no longer unequal.

As the sight of Nelson Mandela in a Springbok jersey illustrates, the contemporary landscape of race and sport seems quite different from that of a generation ago. The notion that the rugby and football World Cups combined to serve as the final drama in the elimination of apartheid creates an evocative narrative about the power of sport to play a concrete role in social transformation. And while even the most Pollyannaish understand that South African society is a far cry from that envisioned by the masses who made up the liberation movement, for many it seems that class, rather than race, is the crucial question. If one sets the film *Invictus* alongside the recent protests that surrounded the FIFA Confederations' Cup in Brazil, or the lawsuit by Ed O'Bannon and other college athletes demanding compensation for the use of their images during their time as amateurs, there is a temptation to argue for global confirmation of William Julius Wilson's contention regarding the declining significance of race in favor of more class-based approaches.

In part, this complexity is a function of the increasingly global nature of sport in the context of the larger neoliberal era. Michael Dyson has discussed the process by which Michael Jordan became a "crossover" icon of widespread appeal to white spectators and consumers.[31] As the NBA expanded in popularity beyond the United States, Jordan's mantle seemingly passed to Los Angeles Laker guard Kobe Bryant, whose jersey remained the top selling one in China between 2007 and 2012. Unsurprisingly, golfer Tiger Woods led Forbes' list of the 100 highest paid athletes, while Serena Williams, one of only three women to make the list, and the only woman tennis player to have won more than $40 million in total prize money, landed at #68.

The visibility and wealth of athletes like Bryant, Woods, and the Williams sisters offers one aspect of the changed racial landscape produced by the era of globalized sport. The sight of athletes of African descent representing the national football teams of ostensibly "white" nations, as in the case of Mario Balotelli (Italy) or Theodore Gebre Selassie (Czech Republic), suggests another. Patterns of talent scouting and labor migration have produced professional soccer teams across the European continent with significant numbers of black players. The manager of Tottenham Hotspur could, if he chose, field a team with ten outfield players of black British descent, while the first team at Manchester United features black players from France (Patrice Evra), Ecuador (Antonio Valencia), Brazil (Anderson), England, (Rio Ferdinand), and Portugal (Nani).

Far below these men are the vast masses of black youth desperate for a career in professional athletics. Henry Louis Gates writes of the challenge of getting black audiences to accept the fact that the United States has far more black lawyers and black doctors than black professional athletes. Less than 2 percent of all college students receive athletic scholarships, suggesting that even that goal remains out of reach for most. Earl Smith notes that of the fifty-six colleges that sent teams to postseason bowl games during the 2005 season, forty-one (73 percent) had graduation rates less than 50 percent among their black players. The problem is transatlantic. In France alone, there are more than seven thousand young Africans living on the streets following failed attempts at making it as professional footballers. Without work or immigration papers, nearly all were lured to Europe under false pretense, leaving Jean Claude Mbvoumin to speak of a modern form of slavery in which unscrupulous agents lure children into a life of poverty and loneliness.[32]

Taking the crucial contexts noted here as a point of departure, contemporary works explore the continuing centrality of racial questions within the world of American and global amateur and professional sport. These range from popular titles like Thabiti Lewis' *Ballers of the New School: Race and Sports in America* to Joseph Price's peer-reviewed economics research, which holds that "more personal fouls are called against players when they are officiated by an opposite-race refereeing crew than when officiated by an own-race crew" and that "these biases are sufficiently large" to affect the likelihood of victory or defeat on the basis of the racial composition of a given professional basketball team.[33] Moreover, there is an evolving body of scholarship that connects two crucial facts of contemporary black life in America: the mass incarceration of African American men and the hypervisibility of the black male athlete. Titles in this trend include Billy Hawkins' *The New Plantation*, David Leonard and C. Richard King's *Commodified and Criminalized: New Racism and African Americans in Contemporary Sports*, and William Rhoden's *Forty Million Dollar Slaves*.[34]

Cultural theorists increasingly note how the world of sport serves as a redoubt of biologistic racism at a time when many have come to otherwise accept race as a "social" construct.[35] Brett St. Louis, for example, notes how "suggestions of a racially distributed genetic basis for athletic ability and performance are strategically posited as a resounding critique of the 'politically correct' meta-narratives of . . . that emphasize the social and cultural construction of race."[36] Gamel Abdel-Shehid has written of the need to develop a black queer theory of sport and masculinity to move beyond the supposedly masculinist limitations implied by Edwards and James. Broadly speaking, these projects draw attention to the crucial role advanced research has to play in explicating the precise contours of race within the evermore lucrative world of sport.[37]

Europe provides examples as well. In Italy, football appears to reflect Italian society's general inability to reconcile itself to demographic reality. Thus striker Mario Balotelli regularly faces crowds waving swastikas, throwing bananas, and chanting, "there are no black Italians." In France, the 1998 World Cup victory by a team led in part by footballers of Algerian (Zinedine Zidane) and Caribbean (Lilian Thuram) descent birthed a short-lived conversation about the possibility of harmonious integration in France before giving way to recriminations concerning unofficial quotas aimed at limiting the number of nonwhite players in the national team pipeline as well as controversy over "nonwhite" members of the national team not singing the national anthem.[38]

In the United Kingdom, where mass demonstrations of racist behavior were common a generation ago, black footballers are seemingly integrated enough that Tottenham Hotspur fullback Benoit Assou-Ekotto, of French and African descent, can say, "I have no feeling for the France national team; it just doesn't exist. When people ask of my generation in France, 'Where are you from?', they will reply Morocco, Algeria, Cameroon or wherever. But what has amazed me in England is that when I ask the same question of people like Lennon and Defoe, they'll say: 'I'm English.' That's one of the things that I love about life here."[39]

As these interventions make clear, the ostensibly "postracial" moment is one in which neither exclusion nor resistance encompasses the entirety of events. Indeed, it is probably the case that as yet we lack a vocabulary for determining what the central "problem" of the twenty-first century is to be. Perhaps issues of economic inequality will provide enough common ground that "class" will come be the modality in which class is lived. Or perhaps the contributions of the new social movements, including issues of sexuality, intersectionality, and debates about ableism, for example, will prove sufficient to ignite truly mass movements that echo in the world of sport. Perhaps something else will take us from Marvin Gaye to Lenin—that is, from what's going on to what is to be done. Certainly, as long as sport retains its unique ability to generate dramatic narratives, to counterpoise nations, and to set individuals within a realm pregnant with symbolic meaning, the matrix of race and sport will continue to call attention to the problems and possibilities of our modern world.

Notes

1. Ron Takaki, *Iron Cages: Race and Culture in 19th-Century America* (New York: Oxford University Press, 1990); Amy Kaplan, *The Anarchy of Empire in the Making of U.S. Culture* (Cambridge, MA: Harvard University Press, 2002); Elliot Gorn and Warren Goldstein, *A Brief History of American Sports* (New York: Hill & Wang, 1993); Gail Bederman, *Manliness and Civilization: A Cultural History of Gender and Race in the United States, 1880–1917* (Chicago: University of Chicago Press, 1995).
2. After C. L. R. James, the following mix a commitment to black liberation with an interest in the study of sport. Jeffrey Sammons, "'Race' and Sport: A Critical and *Historical* Examination," *Journal of Sport History* 21.3 (1994): 203–278; Brett St. Louis, "The Vocation of Sport Sociology," *Sociology of Sport Journal* 24.1 (2007): 119–122; Ben Carrington, *Race, Sport and Politics: The Sporting Black Diaspora* (London: SAGE, 2010); Grant Farred, *Re-Thinking C. L. R. James* (Oxford: Blackwell, 1996), 165–186. Dave Zirin, *A People's History of Sports in the United States* (New York: New Press, 2009). For an excellent bibliographic overview, see David K. Wiggins and Patrick Miller, eds., *The Unlevel Playing Field: A Documentary History of the African American Experience in Sport* (Urbana: University of Illinois Press, 2003), 447–477.
3. W. E. B. DuBois, *The Souls of Black Folk* (New York: New American Library, 1903), 19.

4. Ben Finney, "The Development and Diffusion of Modern Hawaiian Surfing," *The Journal of the Polynesian Society* 69.4 (1960): 315–331.

5. Gerald R. Gems, "Sport, Colonialism, and United States Imperialism," *Journal of Sport History* 33.1 (2006): 3–25; Louis A. Perez Jr., "Between Baseball and Bullfighting: The Quest for Nationality in Cuba, 1868–1898," *The Journal of American History* 81.2 (1994): 493–517. The bibliography on cricket is extensive. See Hilary McD. Beckles and Brian Stoddart, eds., *Liberation Cricket: West Indies Cricket Culture* (New York: Manchester University Press, 1995); J. A. Mangan, ed., *Pleasure, Profit and Proselytism: British Culture and Sport at Home and Abroad, 1700–1914* (London: Frank Cass, 1988); Ashis Nandy, *The Tao of Cricket: On Games of Destiny and the Destiny of Games* (New York: Viking, 1989); Bruce Marray and Goolam Vahed, eds., *Empire and Cricket: The South African Experience, 1884–1914* (Pretoria: University of South Africa Press, 2009).

6. Charles Martin, *Benching Jim Crow: The Rise and Fall of the Color Line in Southern College Sports, 1890–1980* (Urbana: University of Illinois Press, 2010), 12.

7. Andrew Ritchie, *Major Taylor: The Extraordinary Career of a Champion Bicycle Racer* (Baltimore, MD: Johns Hopkins University Press, 1996); Edward Hotaling, *The Great Black Jockeys* (Rocklin, CA: Forum, 1999); Marvin Dawkins and Graham Kinloch, *African American Golfers during the Jim Crow Era* (Westport, CT: Praeger, 2000); Sundiata Djata, *Blacks at the Net: Black Achievement in the History of Tennis* (Syracuse, NY: Syracuse University Press, 2006). This list is not exhaustive.

8. For an introduction to the Negro Leagues, see Robert Peterson, *Only the Ball Was White: A History of Legendary Black Players and All-Black Professional Teams* (Englewood Cliffs, NJ: Prentice-Hall, 1970).

9. Joseph Powers-Beck, *The American Indian Integration of Baseball* (Lincoln: University of Nebraska Press, 2004), 1.

10. For an overview of Japanese-American baseball, see Samuel Regalado, *Nikkei Baseball: Japanese American Players from Immigration and Interment to the Major Leagues* (Urbana: University of Illinois Press, 2013).

11. José M. Alamillo, "*Peloteros* in Paradise: Mexican American Baseball and Oppositional Politics in Southern California, 1930–1950," in *Mexican Americans and Sports: A Reader on Athletics and Barrio Life*, ed. Jorge Iber and Samuel Regalado, 51 (College Station: Texas A&M University Press, 2007).

12. Adrian Burgos, *Playing America's Game: Baseball, Latinos and the Color Line* (Berkeley: University of California Press, 2007). See also Rob Ruck, *Raceball: How the Major Leagues Colonized the Black and Latin Game* (Boston: Beacon Press, 2011).

13. Nat Fleischer, *Black Dynamite: The Story of the Negro in the Prize Ring from 1782 to 1938*, 5 vols. (New York: C. J. O'Brien, 1938–1947).

14. Theresa Runstedtler, *Jack Johnson, Rebel Sojourner: Boxing in the Shadow of the Global Color Line* (Berkeley: University of California Press, 2012).

15. Sergio Leite Lopes, Class, Ethnicity, and Color in the Making of Brazilian Football *Daedalus* 129 (2010): 239–270.

16. Mario Rodrigues, *O Negro No Futebol Brasileiro*, 2nd ed. (Rio de Janeiro: Editôra Civilização Brasileira, 1964); Rogerio Daflon and Teo Ballvé, "The Beautiful Game? Race and Class in Brazilian Soccer," *NACLA Report on the Americas* 37.5 (2004): 23–26.

17. Richard M. Dalfiume, "The 'Forgotten Years' of the Negro Revolution," *The Journal of American History* 55.1 (1968): 90–106.

18. Bruce Adelson, *Brushing Back Jim Crow: The Integration of Minor-League Baseball in the American South* (Charlottesville: University Press of Virginia, 1999); Martin, *Benching Jim Crow*.

19. Mark Naison, "Lefties and Righties: The Communist Party and Sports during the Great Depression," *Radical America* (July-August 1979): 47–59; Henry D. Fetter, "The Party Line and the Color Line: The American Communist Party, the Daily Worker, and Jackie Robinson," *Journal of Sport History* 28 (2001): 375–402.

20. Mary Dudziak, *Cold War Civil Rights: Race and the Image of American Democracy* (Princeton, NJ: Princeton University Press, 2001).

21. On the "cultural front" of the Cold War, see Eva Cockcroft, "Abstract Expressionism: Weapon of the Cold War," *Artforum* (June 1974): 39–41; Penny Von Eschen, *Satchmo Blows Up the World: Jazz Ambassadors Play the Cold War* (Cambridge, MA: Harvard University Press, 2004).

22. Damion Thomas, *Globetrotting: African American Athletes and Cold War Politics* (Urbana: University of Illinois Press, 2012), 41–102 (passim).

23. The starting point for any discussion of the "revolt of the black athlete" must be Harry Edwards, *The Revolt of the Black Athlete* (New York: New Press, 1969); Amy Bass, *Not the Triumph But the Struggle: The 1968 Olympics and the Making of the Black Athlete* (Minneapolis: University of Minnesota Press, 2002).

24. Jeffrey Sammons, *Beyond the Ring: The Role of Boxing in American Society* (Urbana: University of Illinois Press, 1988); Sohail Daulatzai, *Black Star, Crescent Moon: The Muslim International and Black Freedom beyond America* (Minneapolis: University of Minnesota Press, 2012); Grant Farred, *What's My Name? Black Vernacular Intellectuals* (Minneapolis: University of Minnesota Press, 2003); Mike Marqusee, *Redemption Song: Muhammad Ali and the Spirit of the Sixties* (London: Verso, 1999).

25. Beckles, *Liberation Cricket*, vii.

26. In addition to C. L. R. James, *Beyond a Boundary* (Durham, NC: Duke University Press, 1993); Nandy, *Tao of Cricket* see Jack Williams, *Cricket and Race* (Oxford: Berg, 2001); Ashwin Desai, Vishnu Padayachee, Krish Reddy, and Goolam Vahed, eds., *Blacks in Whites: A Century of Cricket Struggles in Kwa-Zulu-Natal* (Pietermaritzburg: University of Natal Press, 2002).

27. Fatima El-Tayeb, *European Others: Queering Ethnicity in Postnational Europe* (Minneapolis: University of Minnesota Press, 2011), xxxix.

28. Laurent DuBois, *Soccer Empire: The World Cup and the Future of France* (Berkeley: University of California Press, 2010), esp. 161–206.

29. Robert Archer and Antoine Bouillon, *The South African Game: Sport and Racism* (London: Zed, 1982), 1; Ashwin Desai, ed., *The Race to Transform: Sport in Post-Apartheid South Africa* (Cape Town: HSRC Press, 2010); Christopher Merrett, *Sport, Space and Segregation: Politics and Society in Pietermaitzburg* (Scotsville, South Africa: University of KwaZulu-Natal Press, 2009); Richard Thompson, *Race and Sport* (London: Oxford University Press, 1964).

30. Archer and Bouillon, *South African Game*, 1.

31. Michael Eric Dyson, "Be Like Mike? Michael Jordan and the Pedagogy of Desire," *Cultural Studies* 7.1 (1993): 64–72. See also David L. Andrews, ed., *Michael Jordan Inc.: Corporate Sport, Media Culture, and Late Modern America* (Albany: State University of New York Press, 2001).

32. Henry Louis Gates Jr., "Delusions of Grandeur," *Sports Illustrated*, August 19, 1991, p. 78, http://www.footsolidaire.org; Earl Smith, *Race, Sport and the American Dream* (Durham, NC: Carolina Academic Press, 2009), 101, http://www.footsolidaire.org.

33. Thabiti Lewis, *Ballers of the New School: Race and Sports in America* (Chicago: Third World Press, 2010); Joseph Price and Justin Wolfers, "Racial Discrimination Among NBA Referees," *Quarterly Journal of Economics* 125.4 (2010): 1859–1887.

34. Billy Hawkins, *The New Plantation: Black Athletes, College Sports, and Predominantly White NCAA Institutions* (New York: Palgrave Macmillan, 2010); David J. Leonard and C. Richard King, eds., *Commodified and Criminalized: New Racism and African Americans in Contemporary Sports* (Lanham, MD: Rowman & Littlefield, 2010); William Rhoden, *$40 Million Slaves: The Rise, Fall, and Redemption of the Black Athlete* (New York: Crown, 2006).

35. John Hoberman, *Darwin's Athletes: How Sport Has damaged Black America and Preserved the Myth of Race* (Boston: Houghton Mifflin, 1997).

36. Brett St. Louis, "Sport, Genetics and the Natural Athlete": The Resurgence of Racial Science," *Body & Society* 9.2 (2003): 75–95.

37. Gamal Abdel-Shehid, *Who Da Man? Black Masculinities and Sporting Cultures* (Toronto: Canadian Scholars' Press, 2005), 139–149.

38. Christos Kassimerris, ed., *Anti-Racism in European Football* (Lanham, MD: Lexington Books, 2009); Phil Vasili, *Colouring over the White Line: The History of Black Footballers in Britain* (London: Mainstream, 2000).

39. David Hytner, "Benoît Assou-Ekotto: 'I Play for the Money: Football Is Not My Passion.'" *Guardian*, April 30, 2010.

BIBLIOGRAPHY

Bass, Amy. *Not the Triumph But the Struggle: The 1968 Olympics and the Making of the Black Athlete*. Minneapolis: University of Minnesota Press, 2002.

Burgos, Adrian. *Playing America's Game: Baseball, Latinos and the Color Line*. Berkeley: University of California Press, 2007.

DuBois, Laurent. *Soccer Empire: The World Cup and the Future of France*. Berkeley: University of California Press, 2010.

DuBois, W. E. B. *The Souls of Black Folk*. New York: New American Library, 1903.

Dudziak, Mary. *Cold War Civil Rights: Race and the Image of American Democracy*. Princeton, NJ: Princeton University Press, 2001.

Edwards, Harry. *The Revolt of the Black Athlete*. New York: New Press, 1969.

Gorn, Elliot, and Warren Goldstein. *A Brief History of American Sports*. New York: Hill & Wang, 1993.

James, C. L. R. *Beyond a Boundary*. Durham, NC: Duke University Press, 1993.

Martin, Charles. *Benching Jim Crow: The Rise and Fall of the Color Line in Southern College Sports, 1890–1980*. Urbana: University of Illinois Press, 2010.

Peterson, Robert. *Only the Ball Was White: A History of Legendary Black Players and All-Black Professional Teams*. Englewood Cliffs, NJ: Prentice Hall, 1970.

Regalado, Samuel. *Nikkei Baseball: Japanese American Players from Immigration and Interment to the Major Leagues*. Urbana: University of Illinois Press, 2013.

Rhoden, William. *$40 million slaves: The Rise, Fall, and Redemption of the Black Athlete.* New York: Crown, 2006.

Ritchie, Andrew. *Major Taylor: The Extraordinary Career of a Champion Bicycle Racer.* Baltimore, MD: Johns Hopkins University Press, 1996.

Ruck, Rob. *Raceball: How the Major Leagues Colonized the Black and Latin Game.* Boston: Beacon Press, 2011.

Runstedtler, Theresa. *Jack Johnson, Rebel Sojourner: Boxing in the Shadow of the Global Color Line.* Berkeley: University of California Press, 2012.

Takaki, Ron. *Iron Cages: Race and Culture in 19th-Century America.* New York: Oxford University Press, 1990.

Thomas, Damion. *Globetrotting: African American Athletes and Cold War Politics.* Urbana: University of Illinois Press, 2012.

Zirin, Dave. *A Peoples History of Sports in the United States.* New York: New Press, 2009.

CHAPTER 31

···

SPORT AND NATIONAL
IDENTITY

···

DILWYN PORTER

At half-past two, the men who would soon contend for victory appeared;
eleven white lads and eleven orange. The music played, first the German
national anthem and then the *Wilhelmus* (the Dutch national anthem).
And suddenly your heart really pulsated, as you were now on the cusp of
it; no longer just two teams, but two nations stood opposite each other. It
still says something in our time of increasing internationalism. No train,
bicycle or car, no international congresses and world organisations of any
kind, no *alle Menschen werden Brueder*, and no socialism can erase this—
the sense that our young boys go into the field, flesh from our flesh, blood
from our blood.[1]

IT is not difficult to find evidence of a relationship between sport and national identity.
The Dutch journalist whose report on the soccer international between the Netherlands
and Germany in 1914 is reproduced here clearly saw it with his own eyes, heard it with
his own ears, and sensed its elemental force. For historians, however, it is important to
understand how the relationship has come about and to identify the various ways in
which it has manifested itself. This chapter seeks to address these problems in turn.

It does not help that sport and national identity are slippery concepts, instantly recognizable but hard to grasp in their entirety.[2] It is the sports that have diffused globally
that have proven most effective in constructing and asserting national identities, though
traditional practices have also played a part. This helps to explain why some feature
more prominently than others in any discussion of sport's relationship with national
identity—universal rather than indigenous, modern rather than traditional, Olympic
rather than non-Olympic, elite rather than recreational, professional rather than amateur, men's rather than women's. Team sports rather than individual pursuits also tend
to predominate, possibly because they facilitate the imaginative leap necessary to make
the connection between the private and the public, the singular and the collective. "The

imagined community of millions," as Eric Hobsbawm famously observed, "seems more real as a team of eleven named people." In international events, the various individuals comprising national teams become "highly visible embodiments" of the nations they represent.[3] Yet, though we are accustomed to seeing national identities on display in the world's sporting arenas, it is important to remember that the link between sport and national identity is dependent on contingency and context. It exists but is not characteristic of all sports and all nations in all situations.

As a concept, national identity is even more difficult to pin down than sport. This difficulty is rooted in the problem of defining a nation. A nation-state is instantly recognizable on a map, its outward shape determined by the lines marking its geographical limits, its block coloring suggestive of homogeneity. We might assume that all who regard it as their homeland live within its borders and that all who live within its borders regard it as their homeland, but this would be misleading. Mass movements of population have ensured that the borders of nation-states and the nations they represent seldom coincide. Most of the world's nation-states are polyethnic; many are characterized by significant ethnic divisions. This explains why, when it comes to cricket, British Asians "face the dilemma of where to place their loyalties": Pakistan or England; ancestral or adopted homeland?[4] It also means that when determining the identity of a nation, other factors are likely to be at least as important as territory and/or ethnicity. "Germany," concludes Arndt Krüger, "is a fluid concept."[5] The existence of a national territory (or territories) labeled "Germany" is a component of German national identity, but ethnicity, language, culture, and history also shape the nation's idea of itself. Moreover, as globalization enhances the trend toward ethnic diversity within modern nation-states, cultural signifiers, such as sport, become even more important in defining ethnicity. It has been argued, for example, that sport "represents a particularly helpful vehicle for the integration of immigrants into Swedish society," though this way of "becoming Swedish" is not entirely unproblematic.[6]

It is partly because borders are so often invisible that historians, political scientists, and sociologists often refer to nations as "imagined communities." A nation exists primarily in the minds of those who feel that they are a part of it and who have an innate sense of what they have in common with others who feel the same way. It comprises a group of people with a common stock of knowledge and experience on which they draw in order to function effectively as members of the society in which they live. As Benedict Anderson has explained, "In the minds of each lives the image of communion."[7] Shared cultural practices—of which sport is one of the most important—play a part in generating this state of mind, sometimes referred to as *habitus*, a term used by Pierre Bourdieu to describe what comes to us as "second nature" in our everyday lives.[8] The idea, for example, that Australia is a sporting nation may or may not stand up to academic scrutiny, but believing it and acting it out every year on Melbourne Cup day becomes one of the ways in which Australian national identity finds expression—this day of "the race that stops a nation."[9] At one time, much the same could have been said about the English and the annual ritual of the FA Cup Final at Wembley. In the 1950s, historian Asa Briggs was delighted to find that the US-born poet T. S. Eliot, in searching for authentic

"English culture," had discovered it in nineteenth-century Gothic churches, boiled cabbage, and cup finals. Of these the last was the most important.[10]

Shared experiences are also important in shaping the *habitus* out of which an individual's sense of national identity grows. A nation has been usefully described as "a body of people who are conscious of having 'gone through something' together." War, occupation, liberation, oppression, and revolution are all experiences that might have such an effect; so too might "great *shared* events."[11] It is not necessary to experience them directly; it is enough that they are remembered collectively and recognized as part of the story that a nation likes to tell about itself. "The Fields of Athenry," a song written in the 1970s and the favored anthem of fans following the Irish Republic's soccer team since the 1990s, references the Irish famine of the 1840s, a folk memory hard-wired into the national psyche. But it does not have to be so serious. Modern sport, especially when assisted by the media, has the capacity to deliver high drama to mass audiences. It plays a part in the process by which national identity is generated simply because it supplies so many "great shared events"—occasions experienced communally and remembered collectively. Germany's victory over Hungary in the final of FIFA's 1954 World Cup, *Das Wunder von Bern*, was one such occasion, experienced by most Germans at the time and remembered since through Herbert Zimmerman's radio commentary, which conveyed a sense of "once again having the right to feel good about belonging to a wider entity—a nation."[12]

Over the long run, memory holds the key. "The core meaning of any individual or group identity," it has been argued, "namely a sense of sameness over time and space, is sustained by remembering, and what is remembered is defined by the assumed identity."[13] Remembering enables all who live within the borders of a nation-state and those who constitute its diaspora to unlock the vault in which the nation's culture and history are stored. It thus allows individuals, both singly and collectively, to construct an identity for the nation to which they belong. This process has been neatly encapsulated in a recent study of post-socialist Slovenia that defines national identity as "a shared sense of nationhood grounded in the images and stories associated with an identifiable nation-state or long-standing ethnic population."[14] There are, of course, powerful agencies on hand to assist the individual in making these connections, notably the institutions of the state, aided and abetted by the media. Sport, with its limitless capacity for generating images and stories or, as a Marxist might say, for inventing traditions, has been enormously important in facilitating this process, "providing a medium for national identification and factitious community."[15]

The role of the nation-state in the process of constructing national identity through sport has to be considered here. As Anthony Smith has argued, states have an interest in promoting a distinctive national identity, not least because it underpins internal social cohesion, increasingly important as governments address political tensions arising from ethnic diversity within their borders. "A state that cannot boast some kind of national identity for its citizens is deemed to have failed in one of its primary functions, the creation of a distinctive loyalty based on consent."[16] In Europe and North America especially, the process of inventing traditions in the nineteenth and early twentieth century provided governments of nation-states and the class interests that they represented with new ways of legitimizing their position via sport at a time when its popularity was growing. It became *de rigeur* for state dignitaries to appear at sporting events deemed important to the nation, where national anthems were sung, national flags paraded, and athletes competed in distinctive national uniforms. The opening ceremony of the London Olympic Games of 1908 had all these elements in abundance.[17] Proving that the nation-state possessed the capacity to deliver such an event successfully was increasingly seen as important in itself. For Greece, staging the Olympic Games in Athens provided an opportunity to reaffirm links with classical civilization, thus highlighting a distinctive aspect of the nation's identity while simultaneously demonstrating that it was a modern nation-state. It has been argued that these were challenges that could not be refused, either in 1896 or 2004, "whatever the cost to the taxpayer."[18]

It is also important to remember that the experience of sport for most people is one that has been mediated via newspapers, newsreels, radio, and television. Michael Billig has highlighted the role of the press in underpinning banal nationalism. "There are always sports pages," he observes, "and they are never left empty." They introduce their readers, men in particular, to a world of sport in which the national flag is waved daily for "us," "our heroes," and "our victories."[19] At times, especially in totalitarian regimes where the media was effectively an extension of the state, sport has been used to promote particular versions of national identity in a blatant fashion. In Fascist Italy, as Simon Martin has argued, "sport was a propaganda opportunity," not least because it had such a wide appeal and could carry the Fascist message into so many homes.[20] The government of Gétulio Vargas enabled Brazilians to follow the progress of the national soccer team in the 1938 World Cup by installing loudspeakers on street corners through which radio commentary could be relayed. It has been argued that this initiative helped to popularize a more inclusive conception of Brazilian national identity.[21] Even in more democratic nation-states, sport and the media often combined powerfully to promote a sense of belonging. Public interest in the 1930 Tour de France was raised when national teams were entered for the first time and was further enhanced by the advent of live radio coverage, especially after the sustained excitement of the sixteenth stage when the French nation's favorite, André Leducq, having crashed early in the race, chased down the rest of the field to win. Thereafter, listening to the commentary at home or with friends in a bar or café became a habit as the Tour helped radio to anchor itself both "in the media landscape and in the daily cultural practices of the French."[22]

The World Cup Final of 1966 demonstrated television's immense capacity to translate a great sporting occasion into one of the "great shared events" that shape a nation's collective consciousness. It delivered a total television audience in the UK of 30.5 million, exceeding by 5 million the number of viewers who had watched live coverage of Sir Winston Churchill's state funeral two years earlier. A further 2 million people tuned in to the radio commentary. One fan who was at Wembley Stadium later recalled "the overwhelming feeling that you really had seen history being made"; live television coverage ensured that this feeling was widespread. English memories of the day that their team won the World Cup tend to convey a sense of participating in an extraordinary event that occurred at home in the company of family and friends. The words with which BBC television match commentator Kenneth Wolstenholme described England's fourth goal ("They think it's all over; it is now!") have continued to resonate in English popular culture over the years, often repeated, sometimes parodied, but never forgotten, like an old joke shared and understood within a family.[23] This great shared event has been consigned to a peculiarly English realm of memory—along with Winston Churchill's wartime speeches, the Coronation of Elizabeth II, and the death of Princess Diana—part of a nation-defining cultural heritage to be drawn on as occasion demands.

All sports originate somewhere, though their origins are often contested. It seems appropriate, therefore, when considering the various ways in which the relationship between sport and national identity is made visible, to begin with indigenous sports. As practices unique to particular nations these serve a number of useful purposes, not least as signifiers of cultural difference. "The 'otherness' of the collective," as Aaron Beacon has argued, "may be articulated through sport, as it is through certain forms of art or literature."[24] What could demonstrate Australian "otherness" more effectively than Australian Rules football, or Japanese more than *sumo*, or that of the Basques more than *pelota*? Indigenous sports have a particular importance for nations that have yet to achieve recognition as nation-states. One way of proving that they have an identity is through nurturing—or even reinventing—distinctive cultural practices. In Cornwall, England's most southwesterly county, a significant minority self-identifies as "Cornish" rather than "English" or "British." Those who believe that the Cornish are a Celtic nation have often cited their indigenous version of wrestling as a way of proving that they have a history and culture of their own. "Ever since the first Cornish Wrestler, CORINAEUS, the Cornish hero-chief, threw GOG-MAGOG, the British giant (18 feet tall) into the Sound off Plymouth Hoe, three thousand years ago, there has always been Wrestling in Cornwall," explained the president of the Cornish Wrestling Association in 1972.[25] The implication here was that the Cornish were different and that they had been around for a very long time.

For stateless nations indigenous sports have provided a way of resisting cultural imperialism. Accepting an invitation to become a patron of the Gaelic Athletic Association (GAA) when it was founded in 1884, Archbishop Thomas Croke regretted that British rule in Ireland had seen the demise of native sports including hurling and "football-kicking according to Irish rules." He asked: "And what have we got in their stead? We have got such foreign and fantastic field sports as lawn tennis, polo, croquet, cricket, and the like—very excellent, I believe, and health-giving in their way, still not racy of the soil, but rather alien, on the contrary, to it, as are, indeed, for the most part, the men and women who first imported and still continue to patronise them."[26] The GAA was part of a wider Gaelic cultural revival in Ireland, but it made a particularly important contribution. In revitalizing a heritage that might have otherwise been lost, the GAA and the indigenous sports it promoted to the exclusion of all others helped to ensure that nationalism was securely embedded in Irish popular culture. As Mike Cronin has observed, "While literature is high culture and the preserve of the few, sport is low culture and the preserve of the many."[27] By the time of the War of Independence that preceded the advent of the Irish Free State in 1922, Gaelic sports had become a popular signifier of Irish identity. The GAA had flourished, it was noted many years later, because its members regarded it "as a means of being Irish."[28] The British, it could be argued, made the mistake of confronting Ireland's sporting identity head on, not least in 1920 when police auxiliaries fired on players and spectators at a Dublin–Kildare football match at Croke Park. Other regimes have been more subtle. Allowing some leeway for "indigenous cultures and traditions," including sports such as *goresh* (wrestling) in Turkmenistan, was one strategy used in the Soviet Union to accommodate ethnic diversity.[29]

Over the years since independence, Ireland, despite the GAA's antipathy toward anyone who played "foreign sports," has developed a rich sporting culture embracing indigenous and non-indigenous activities. This reflects trends in other countries where there was cultural resistance to "foreign" sport. In Germany, for example, the strength of the *Turnen* movement dating from the early nineteenth century, with its preference for gymnastics and body culture rather than athletic competition, erected a formidable barrier to the diffusion of sports considered *unduetsch*. After the failed revolutions of 1848, its activities were increasingly underpinned by spiritual attachment to a German identity "born of the mystic unity of *Volk* and *Vaterland*." The *Deutsche Turnenschaft*, it has been observed, "created a public arena in which the invented traditions of a new German nationalism could be displayed." It also provided a forum in which foreign sports were routinely denounced; an anti-soccer polemic, subtitled "The English disease," published in 1898, was indicative of the movement's stance.[30] Its influence, which inhibited the development of non-German sports generally, remained undiminished until Germany became an integral part of the international sports system as it prepared for the 1936 Berlin Olympic Games. There were echoes of this clash of sporting cultures in France where the Ligue National d'Éducation Physique (1888) sought in vain to turn the enveloping tide of *sports anglais*, partly through reinventing ancient traditions such as *lendit*, a sports tournament for students. However, as Richard Holt has noted, a rival organization, the Union des Sociétés Francais des Sports Athlétiques (1889), proved more successful "in spreading a particularly British ideal of amateur sport in France."[31] By the 1930s, unless they were well established, as in Ireland, it was becoming increasingly difficult for indigenous sports to survive and flourish. In Italy, an attempt by Mussolini's regime to promote *volata*, a distinctively Italian, or "Roman" version of football considered a more suitable pastime for *Homo Fascistus* than soccer, was a notable policy failure.[32] This suggests that the value of indigenous sports as cultural signifiers has progressively diminished, even for stateless nations. In 1972, just a year after the GAA had lifted its ban on those who had been contaminated by contact with non-Gaelic sports, it was reported that some members of the Celtic League remained of the view "that each Celtic country should concentrate on its own national sport, such as wrestling in Cornwall and Brittany, shinty in Scotland (and presumably such feats of strength in the Highland Games as tossing the caber) while Ireland has its Gaelic athletes."[33]

By this time, however, it seemed more realistic to accept that indigenous sports had fulfilled a historic role in underpinning "the persistence of difference" but that their capacity for asserting national identity was depleted. In Brittany the local version of hurling (*soule*) had not been played since 1912 and wrestling (*gouren*) reached only a minority audience, despite the efforts of the International Celtic Wrestling Federation, founded in 1985. It was difficult to see how Bretons could "resist the overwhelming hegemony of modern sport, especially that of football."[34] Their identity was now more likely to be made visible both inside and outside Brittany by FC Nantes and Stade Rennais competing in the French League, paralleling the role fulfilled for Catalonia by FC Barcelona and for Corsica by SC Bastia and AC Ajaccio, clubs that "share an openness to the contemporary world shaped by the forces of globalization."[35]

The sporting context in which national identity has most often been constructed and expressed since the late nineteenth century has been that of international or multinational competition. At first, and especially in the United Kingdom, international matches, while allowing space for local rivalries, mainly demonstrated "the links which bound all inhabitants of the national state together, irrespective of local and regional differences." The first England–Scotland soccer "internationals" in the early 1870s certainly fit this pattern with the respective teams drawn from a relatively small circle of young, middle-class males, many of whom knew each other from their time together at school or university. At the first England–Wales rugby match in 1881, the fifteen Welsh players "were socially indistinguishable from their opponents."[36] Matches played in the annual four-nation soccer and rugby championships, both initiated in the 1880s, were known as "home internationals." They served the same function for the British nation-state as the Tour de France (1903) and the Giro d'Italia (1909) did for France and Italy. The Tour was "far more than a race"; it was "a heroic celebration of ancient territories and peoples," locating them within the context of the French state as reconstituted under the Third Republic in 1871. As for the Giro, it "began to shrink the country's perceived size while marking history, local traditions, dialects, values and reference points, all within a nationally shared event."[37]

From 1896 the Olympic movement provided a multinational arena in which national identities could be made visible through sport on a regular basis. Until 1908, competitors were individual entrants rather than national team members, but it soon became clear that nationality mattered in this context. For the host nation in 1896, the marathon was an event of particular cultural significance. The wild enthusiasm that accompanied the victorious Greek athlete as he entered the stadium prompted French writer and right-wing nationalist Charles Maurras to comment with wry satisfaction that "internationalism" appeared only to strengthen "national spirit."[38] Within a few years, Olympic rhetoric relating to sport promoting harmony between nations notwithstanding, the places that competitors called home were increasingly important. When John Pius Boland, the first Irish-born Olympic gold medalist, won the tennis singles and doubles in 1896, he did not actively resist being labeled "English." Like all Irish people at the time, he was a British national. Ten years later, after embarking on a political career as a moderate Irish nationalist, he cheerfully applied "some retrospective greenery to his exploits," recalling that he had won "for Ireland" and that, when awarded his medals, he had complained about the absence of an Irish flag.[39] Flags, symbols of national identity everywhere, were beginning to wrap themselves around Olympic history. At the "inter-calated" games of 1906, two Irish athletes, who had finished first and second in the triple jump and objected to being identified as British, celebrated by asserting their Irishness. "As the Union flag rose to honour their triumphs," Mark Dyreson records, "one of the Irish athletes clambered up the flag pole and unfurled a green Hibernian banner while his teammate guarded the base and fought off officials who tried to prevent their display of Irish patriotism."[40] The opening ceremony at London 1908 was beset with controversies about flags. Athletes from Finland, yet to achieve its independence, intended to march behind their national flag but were thwarted after a Russian protest was upheld. Shot-putter Ralph Rose, the US standard-bearer, refused to dip the stars and stripes to acknowledge King Edward VII, an incident that gave birth to one of the most durable of America's sporting legends, "the flag dipping fable" having been resurrected many times over the years "in a variety of fashions for a variety of purposes."[41]

Thus, within a few years of the first modern Olympic Games, it was clear that they provided an unparalleled opportunity for both established and aspiring nation-states to assert their identities. Indigenous sports, by their very nature, could not guarantee international recognition; participation in the Olympic Games, FIFA's World Cup after 1930, and the various world championships that proliferated in all major sports over the course of the twentieth century signified admittance to the family of nations. In symbolic terms it has become as important to nations as having their own postage stamps and a flag-carrying airline. The growth of competition at this level had important implications for the construction of national identities, not least because it unleashed a wave of sportive nationalism based on the premise that "triumphant athletes promote national prestige."[42] It also created an explicit link between participation in international sport and propaganda. Given the ideological affinities between National Socialism and the Turner movement, the organizers of the Olympic Games scheduled for Berlin in 1936 feared the worst when Hitler came to power but were encouraged to continue their preparations, Goebbels having convinced Der Führer that it would be unwise to miss a unique opportunity to create and disseminate positive images of the new Germany.[43] When Italy's footballers became world champions in 1934, they sealed the fate of *volata*; the rationale for promoting a sport conceived of as an alternative to soccer evaporated overnight. The *Azzurri* offered a more effective way of demonstrating an idealized version of Italian national identity and projecting it worldwide while achieving symbolic victories over teams from other nations.[44] After 1945 even the Soviet Union, which stood apart from the international sporting system that developed so rapidly in the interwar years, began—tentatively at first—to pursue its own policy of sportive nationalism, as evidenced primarily by its appearance at the Olympic Games at Helsinki in 1952. Its debut in this arena indicated that Soviet sports diplomacy was evolving "from an instrument of policy designed in part to achieve the Marxist goal of international worker solidarity to one intended primarily for the advancement of the causes of the Soviet Union as a nation-state."[45]

Ironically, given that policies driven by sportive nationalism demanded sporting success, other manifestations of sport and national identity became increasingly important.

It was in the nature of regulated competition between nations that victory could not be guaranteed, even for the big battalions, and there were always going to be more losers than winners. The special relationships of some nations with certain sports once indigenous to them were an important source of cultural consolation. Cricket seemed to define a certain kind of Englishness and, for some, signified national identity itself. "It is far more than a game, this cricket," observed Neville Cardus of the *Manchester Guardian* in 1945. "It somehow holds the mirror up to English nature."[46] In the United States, baseball played a similar part in the construction of identity. It was, as A. G. Spalding had claimed in 1911, "the American game *par excellence*, because its playing demands Brain and Brawn, and American manhood supplies these ingredients in quantity sufficient to spread over the entire continent."[47] Baseball, like cricket, benefitted from a creation myth that located its origins in a fictionalized version of semirural antiquity quite different from the urban lives that most Americans actually knew, but it connected them to a past that they wanted to remember. In this respect, Cooperstown, where Abner Doubleday "invented" baseball, served essentially the same purpose as "the pretty and sequestered village of Hambledon," where cricket had been played since the eighteenth century and the Bat and Ball Inn could still be found.[48] The shock when other nations, in search of their own identities, turned to baseball and cricket and took on the Americans and English at their own games was profound. Cubans and Mexicans, for example, "embraced baseball as a means of resisting American imperialism"; in the West Indies, India, Pakistan, and Sri Lanka, cricket helped the subject nations of the old British Empire to strike back.[49]

There was also a growing awareness of style as a signifier of identity. Judgments here were subjective, but how games were played seemed to be important for stateless nations and nation-states alike. "The Corsicans," it has been suggested, "are convinced that their football is just as markedly *theirs* as their language and their culture."[50] Even before their national team had won FIFA's World Cup, Brazilians were convinced that *futebol* was different. It reminded Gilberto Freyre in the 1930s "of dancing and *capoeira*, making the Brazilian way of playing football a trademark, which sophisticates and often sweetens the game invented by the English and played so stiffly by them." Gilka Machado, a poet, writing at the same time, underlined the idea that the heroes of the 1938 World Cup squad represented "The miraculous reality/That is the Brazilian Man."[51] Later, the idea that key aspects of national identity could be expressed on the field of play was very evident in ideologically loaded press reports of soccer matches between teams from East and West during the Cold War. Both sides agreed that east European teams played in a collective style whereas their Western counterparts allowed the individual a bigger role. These identity signifiers could be given a positive or negative spin as required. *Der Spiegel* once berated the "system-immanent dogmatism" of East German soccer.[52] Arguably, one reason why the idea of distinctive national sporting styles is so prevalent is that it represents a subtle variation of the well-observed "glocal" response to globalization as nations find ways of expressing their identities without retreating behind the cultural barricade of indigenous sport.

National identity is constructed in the hearts and minds of individuals by drawing on cultural resources they share with the unknown millions with whom they live their everyday lives. The state and the media assist in this process also, increasingly, transnational corporations that "have realized the need to accommodate and negotiate local and national conditions, cultures and sensibilities."[53] For the individual it is largely an unconscious process, one they become aware of only when circumstances force them to think, or perhaps to choose one identity over another. Whereas Northern Ireland and the Irish Republic each have their own soccer teams, players from both sides of the border form a united Irish team for rugby union internationals, with home games played in Dublin. Rugby player David Tweed, from Northern Ireland (Ulster), after making his first appearance for Ireland in 1995, claimed that he sang "God Save the Queen" when "Amhran na bhFiann" (the Republic's national anthem) was played before the match.[54] In the increasingly pragmatic world of international track and field, steeplechaser Saif Saeed Shaheen made his choice for quite different reasons when abandoning his native Kenya for Quatar and a lucrative contract in 2003, competing against his brother who continued to represent his homeland.[55] For most people, however, there is a degree of inevitability in embracing a particular national identity; they may not be elite athletes but they know instinctively which side they are on. Eric Hobsbawm related how, in 1929, at the home of friends in Vienna, he had listened to a radio commentary on an international soccer match between England and Austria. "As the only English boy present," he recalled, "I was England, as they were Austria . . . in this manner did twelve-year-old children extend the concept of team loyalty to the nation."[56]

As they complete the process of constructing their own national identity, individuals surrender to the collective. They may be only "ninety-minute patriots"—the term invented by Scottish Nationalist Jim Sillars in 1992 as he castigated fellow Scots for channeling their nationalist sentiment into sport rather than politics—but they are patriots all the same.[57] Novelist Alan Sillitoe, no sports lover, nevertheless understood how this process worked. In an essay on "Sport and Nationalism," written under the dark shadow of the 1972 Munich Olympics when Palestinian terrorists asserted their national identity by killing Israeli athletes, he observed bleakly: "As soon as a man participates, either in body or spirit, either at the actual place or vicariously through the medium of the television set, or the radio, or the newspapers, he loses his individuality, and becomes part of his nation—with unreasonable yearnings in his heart."[58] But it is also possible to put a more positive spin on the relationship between sport and national identity. Jimmy Burns, reporting for television on the Spain that was emerging after the death of Franco, attended a match at Camp Nou where FC Barcelona was playing Athletic Bilbao. There he found Catalans and Basques waving their national flags and singing songs that had been banned since the end of the Spanish Civil War. "This," he decided, "was not the opium of the masses, but pure adrenalin, passion deeply held and defiant—the kind that makes one happy to be alive."[59] Perhaps, in our search for belonging through sport, we gain as much as we lose.

Notes

1. "Nederland-Duitschland: een leekpratje," *Nieuwe Rotterdamsche Courant*, April 6, 1914, p. 1, cited in Nicholas Piercey, "Football Culture in Two Dutch Cities: Amsterdam and Rotterdam between 1910 and 1920" (PhD diss., University College London, 2011), 162.

2. See Allen Guttmann, *From Ritual to Record: The Nature of Modern Sports* (New York: Columbia University Press, 2004), 162; also Sébastien Darbon, "An Anthropological Approach to the Diffusion of Sports: From European Models to Global Diversity," in *Sport, Representation and Evolving Identities in Europe*, ed. Philip Dine and Seán Crosson (Bern: Peter Lang, 2010), 15–20.

3. Eric Hobbawm, *Nations and Nationalism since 1780: Programme, Myth, Reality* (Cambridge, UK: Cambridge University Press, 1990), 143; Joseph Maguire and Jason Tuck, "Making Sense of Global Patriot Games: Rugby Players' Perceptions of National Identity Politics," *Football Studies* 2.1 (1999): 27.

4. Anthony D. Smith, *Nationalism: Theory, Ideology, History* (Cambridge, UK: Polity Press, 2001), 17; Thomas Fletcher, "Who Do 'They' Cheer For? Cricket, Diaspora, Hybridity and Divided Loyalties among British Asians," *International Review of the Sociology of Sport* 47.5 (2012): 627.

5. Arndt Krüger, "Sport and Identity in Germany since Reunification," in *Sport, Representation and Evolving Identities*, 291–293.

6. Alan Bairner, *Sport, Nationalism, and Globalization: European and North American Perspectives* (Albany: State University of New York Press, 2001), 156–157.

7. Benedict Anderson, *Imagined Communities: Reflections on the Origin and the Spread of Nationalism*, rev. ed. (London: Verso, 1991), 5–7.

8. Pierre Bourdieu, *Pascalian Meditations* (Stanford, CA; Stanford University Press, 2000), 138.

9. Tony Ward, *Sports in Australian National Identity: Kicking Goals* (Abingdon, UK: Routledge, 2010), 18.

10. Asa Briggs, "Football and Culture," *Encounter* 16 (January 1955): 69.

11. John Bowman, *De Valera and the Ulster Question* (Oxford: Oxford University Press, 1982), 18.

12. Ulrich Hesse-Lichtenberger, *Tor! The Story of German Football* (London: WSC Books, 2003), 124–126.

13. John R. Gillis, "Memory and Identity: The History of a Relationship," in *Commemorations: The Politics of National Identity*, ed. John R. Gillis (Princeton, NJ: Princeton University Press, 1994), 3.

14. Mojca Doupona Topič and Jay Coakley, "Complicating the Relationship between Sport and National Identity: The Case of Post-Socialist Slovenia," *Sociology of Sport Journal* 27 (2010): 372–373.

15. Eric Hobsbawn, "Mass-Producing Traditions: Europe, 1870–1914," in *The Invention of Tradition*, ed. Eric Hobsbawm and Terence Ranger (Cambridge, UK: Cambridge University Press, 1983), 300.

16. Anthony D. Smith, *Myths and Memories of the Nation* (Oxford: Oxford University Press, 1999), 257.

17. See Rebecca Jenkins, *The First London Olympics 1908* (London: Piatkus Books, 2008), 105–125.

18. Eleni Theodoraki, "Expressions of National Identity through Impact Assessments of the Athens 2004 Olympic Games," in *Sport, Representation and Evolving Identities*, 62.

19. Michael Billig, *Banal Nationalism* (London: SAGE, 1995), 119–122.

20. See Simon Martin, *Sport Italia: The Italian Love Affair with Sport* (London: I. B. Tauris, 2011), 55–58.

21. Tiago Maranhão, "*Appolonians and Dyonisians*: The Role of Football in Gilberto Freyre's Vision of Brazilian People," *Soccer & Society* 8.4 (2007): 515.

22. Keiran J. Dunne, "Sport and Media as Nexus of Cultural Practices: Live Radio and the Tour de France, 1929–39," *International Journal of Sport and Society* 2.2 (2011): 67–78.

23. See Dilwyn Porter: "Egg and Chips with the Connellys: Remembering 1966," *Sport in History* 29.3 (2009): 519–522, 534–536.

24. Aaron Beacom, "Indigenous Sport and the Search for Belonging," *The Sports Historian* 18.2 (1998): 50.

25. *Omma yn Kernow* 3 (1972): 13.

26. Croke to Michael Cusack (GAA secretary), December 18, 1884, multitext.ucc.ie/d/Archbishop_Croke_the_GAA_November_1884

27. Mike Cronin, *Sport and Nationalism in Ireland: Gaelic Games, Soccer and Irish Identity since 1884* (Dublin: Four Courts Press, 1999), 19.

28. Alf Ó Muirí (GAA president), cited in Brendan Mac Lua, *The Steadfast Rule: A History of the GAA Ban* (Dublin: Press Cuchulainn, 1967), 109.

29. Beacom, "Indigenous Sport," 59.

30. Guttmann, *From Ritual to Record*, 87–89; David Goldblatt, *The Ball Is Round: A Global History of Football* (London: Viking, 2006), 160–161.

31. Richard Holt, "Sport, the French, and the Third Republic," *Modern & Contemporary France* 6.3 (1998): 292.

32. Beacom, "Indigenous Sport," 62–64.

33. Iain Macnair, "Celtic Sports Specialities," in *The Celtic Experience Past and Present*, ed. F. G. Thompson (Dublin: Annual Book of the Celtic League, 1972), 137–138.

34. Michel Lagreé, "Brittany, between Ireland, Scotland and France," in *Sport and the Making of Celtic Cultures*, ed. Grant Jarvie (Leicester, UK: Leicester University Press, 1999), 44–45.

35. Róbert Győri Szabó, "Identity and Soccer in Corsica," *Soccer & Society* 13.1 (2012): 52.

36. Hobsbawm, "Mass Producing Traditions," 301–302; Huw Richards, *The Red and the White: The Story of England v Wales Rugby* (London: Aurum Press, 2009), 16.

37. Holt, "Sport, the French," 290; Martin, *Sport Italia*, 35–36.

38. John Hoberman, "Sportive Nationalism and Globalization," in *Post-Olympism: Questioning Sport in the Twenty-First Century*, ed. John Bale and Mette Krogh Christensen (Oxford: Berg, 2004), 179–180.

39. Kevin McCarthy, *Gold, Silver and Green: The Irish Olympic Journey, 1896–1924* (Cork, Ireland: Cork University Press, 2010), 26–37.

40. Mark Dyreson, *Crafting Patriotism for Global Dominance: America at the Olympics* (London: Routledge, 2009), 14; McCarthy, *Gold, Silver and Green*, 153–154.

41. Jenkins, *First London Olympics*, 121; Dyreson, *Crafting Patriotism*, 9.

42. Hoberman, 'Sportive Nationalism," 184–185.

43. Allen Guttmann, *The Olympics: A History of the Modern Games*, 2nd ed. (Champaign: University of Illinois Press, 2002), 54–55.

44. Beacom, "Indigenous Sport," 64; Martin, *Sport Italia*, 67–71.

45. Victor Peppard and James Riordan, *Playing Politics: Soviet Sport Diplomacy to 1992* (Greenwich, CT: JAI Press, 1993), 50.
46. Neville Cardus, *English Cricket* (London: Collins, 1945), 9.
47. Spalding, cited in Frank Cogliano, "Baseball and American Exceptionalism," in *Sport and National Identity in the Post-War World*, ed. Adrian Smith and Dilwyn Porter (London: Routledge, 2004), 145.
48. Cogliano, "Baseball and Exceptionalism," 149; Derek Birley, *A Social History of English Cricket* (London: Aurum Press, 1999), 33–34.
49. Cogliano, "Baseball and Exceptionalism," 156–160.
50. Szabó, "Identity and Soccer in Corsica," 47.
51. Freyre, cited in Maranhão, *Appolonians and Dyonisians*, 514; Machado, cited in Alex Bellos, *Futebol: The Brazilian Way of Life* (London: Bloomsbury, 2002), 40.
52. *Der Spiegel*, August 14, 1972, cited in John Hoberman, *Sport and Political Ideology* (London: Heinemann, 1984), 15–16.
53. Koji Kobayashi, "Corporate Nationalism and Glocalization of Nike Advertising in Asia: Production and Representation Practices of Cultural Intermediaries," *Sociology of Sport Journal* 29 (2012): 43–44.
54. *Irish Independent*, November 29, 2012, 11.
55. See John H. Hunter, "Flying the Flag: Identities, the Nation and Sport," *Identities: Global Studies in Culture and Power* 10.4 (2003): 409.
56. Hobsbawm, *Nations and Nationalism*, 143.
57. See Bairner, *Sport, Nationalism, and Globalization*, 47–48.
58. Alan Sillitoe, *Mountains and Caverns: Selected Essays* (London: W. H. Allen, 1975), 87.
59. Jimmy Burns, *Barça: A People's Passion* (London: Bloomsbury, 1999), xii.

BIBLIOGRAPHY

Bairner, Alan. *Sport, Nationalism, and Globalization: European and North American Perspectives*. Albany: State University of New York Press, 2001.
Dyreson, Mark. *Crafting Patriotism for Global Dominance: America at the Olympics*. London and New York: Routledge, 2009.
Hoberman, John. "Sportive Nationalism and Globalization." In *Post Olympism? Questioning Sport in the Twenty-First Century*, edited by John Bale and Mette Krogh Christensen, 177–188. Oxford: Berg, 2004.
Martin, Simon. *Sport Italia: The Italian Love Affair with Sport*. London and New York: I. B. Tauris, 2011.
Smith, Adrian, and Dilwyn Porter, eds. *Sport and National Identity in the Post-War World*. London: Routledge, 2004.
Tomlinson, Alan, Christopher Young, and Richard Holt, eds. *Sport and the Transformation of Modern Europe: State, Media and Markets 1950–2010*. London and New York: Routledge, 2011.

CHAPTER 32

HISTORY OF SPORT AND RELIGION IN THE UNITED STATES AND BRITAIN

AMY KOEHLINGER

WHILE historians have analyzed the relationship between sport and religion in all regions of the world, sport historiography has focused primarily on the United States and Britain. Historians of sport in the United States and Britain have long paid attention to the ways that religious attitudes toward games, sporting, leisure, and physical activity have variously expanded or limited the public status of sport on both sides of the Atlantic. More recently, historians of religion in the United States have begun to attend to the ways that sports and attention to physical fitness intersected with important religious trends in piety, revivalism, regionalism, urbanization, gender, ethnicity, and nationalism in the religious history of the United States. As a result, a piecemeal but increasingly comprehensive literature is emerging to document the relationship of sport and religion, especially in American and British history. The diversity of disciplinary assumptions and subfields represented in scholarly literature on sport and religion means that the historiography can be uneven and at times contradictory in its interpretations and conclusions, but a recent proliferation of work on the theory and history of embodiment as cultural process opens exciting new horizons of possibility for studying the intersections of physical performances, sporting activities, and religious experience.

When religion appeared in early narratives about the history of sport in Britain and its colonies, the main question asked of religion was whether adherents of various religious sects approved of or dismissed the sporting life. This meant that the relationship of religion and sport originally was read through the interpretive lens of Christian Reformation history that traced the theological development of diffuse branches of established, dissenting, and revivalist Protestantism to see how changes in religious ideology affected Christian ideas about the value of physical activity, competition, and play. In this initial telling of the history of sport and religion, the Roman Catholic inclination toward feast days and religious celebrations extended into a general tolerance for games, sport, and merry-making, both before and after the Reformation. Because the English reformation in the sixteenth century preserved both many of the theological principles it inherited from the Roman Catholic Church and the imprimatur of the British monarchy, the Anglican Church retained the positive view of sport and amusements long held by the English aristocracy, especially horse-related sports like hunting and racing. When Puritans and other dissenting reformers emerged in England, their central criticism of the Anglican Church was that it had failed to differentiate itself sufficiently from Catholicism. Dissenting Protestants on both sides of the Atlantic restructured worship services to remove liturgical and sacramental elements and discarded the Anglican model of priesthood, among other reforms. And though they rejected religious holidays and celebrations associated with the Catholic liturgical calendar, Puritans generally exhibited a benign tolerance toward sporting amusements so long as such games were detached from the religious calendar. In the seventeenth century, the integration of Calvinist principles into dissenting traditions reoriented Puritans and other reforming Protestants toward more rigorous notions of divine majesty, human depravity, and disciplined asceticism. As a result, dissenting Protestants increasingly limited games and recreation, tolerating only those sporting activities (like military maneuvers) done for sober, practical purposes. The evangelical revolution that gave rise to Methodist and Baptist sects deepened this tendency so that by the late eighteenth century many Protestants—possibly a majority in the United States—rejected sport as frivolous and irreligious. This trend toward religious prohibitionism reversed in the late nineteenth century when evangelical Protestants rediscovered the spiritual and moral value of sport through parareligious organizations like the Young Men's Christian Association (YMCA). By the twentieth century, most Protestant denominations had fully embraced the idea that athletics instilled positive moral virtues like discipline, perseverance, fairness, and teamwork. As a result, sports programming became a regular feature of education and youth ministry in churches and religious schools and colleges by the 1930s. When religious groups expressed concerns about the moral status of athletics in the latter half of the twentieth century, they directed their criticism toward professional sports, arguing that gambling, cheating, and the use performance-enhancing drugs corrupted the otherwise exemplary contribution of sport to godly society.

This initial historiographical narrative, which focused on religious proscription of recreational activities, framed the relationship between religion and sport in negative terms, presenting religion as either neutral or actively hostile to sports and athletic amusements. There are several problems with this approach. One methodological limitation of this approach is that it framed religion as a set of doctrinal principles enforced by clerical or moral elites, failing to acknowledge that religious believers always negotiated unique identities and practices within religious traditions. In all historical periods, devout sport enthusiasts often found ways for games and sport to be integrated into lived religion in ways that were not seen or acknowledged by the official arbiters of the tradition. For example, William Bradford, the Puritan governor of Plymouth Plantation, was firmly opposed to both Catholic festivals and the English leisure tradition—so much so that in 1620 he disbanded a group of settlers who had raised a maypole, sending their leader back to England in chains. Though Bradford personally dismissed the Catholic sanctification of Christmas, in 1621 he allowed some newcomers to the colony who believed that working on Christmas violated their conscience to rest from labor for the day. When Bradford returned from work Christmas evening, he was dismayed and angered to find the newcomers not in prayer and devotion but rather "in the street at play, openly; some pitching the bar, and some at stool-ball, and such-like sports."[1] In Massachusetts Bay, colonists voluntarily honored Sabbatarian prohibitions by integrating informal recreation like cards or ninepins into the daily pattern of weekday agrarian labor and scheduled special community events like football games or bull baits (an illegal but widespread sport) for Tuesdays, the day set aside by English parliamentary legislation for recreation.[2] Moreover, the strict separation of religion from sport in the descriptive categories applied to historical activities in this historiography distorted the way that piety and play, the physical and the spiritual, religion and sport were intertwined and mingled in customs and culture. For example, in the late eighteenth century, "Pinkster" was an important holiday in places of concentrated Dutch migration, like lower New York and upper New Jersey. The holiday commemorated the religious holiday Pentecost ("Pinkster" from *Pfingsten*, the Dutch word for Pentecost) but celebrations primarily consisted of outdoor games, competitive dancing, displays of physical prowess, and general merry-making.[3]

Beyond the methodological problem of viewing religion in terms of its theological support (or not) for athletics, subsequent historians have demonstrated that this historical narrative was inaccurately selective in the specific sports, regions, time periods, and religious traditions it included. Viewing sport and religion through the lens of the sports that were considered licit by the most rigorous of Protestant clergy narrowed the broad spectrum of American sporting practices down to a relatively small selection that included "lawful recreation" of Puritan militia training days, nineteenth-century football, YMCA basketball, Knute Rockne and Notre Dame football, born-again professional baseball players, and evangelical passion for NASCAR racing.[4] This narrative arc occluded important elements of the history of sport that are widely recognized by sport historians and that surely affected how religion intersected with traditional athletics and games. Chief among the sporting traditions censored out of narratives about religion and sport were longstanding customs of bloodsport in American society, including bear- and bull-baiting, cockfighting, ratting and dogfighting, wrestling and bareknuckle brawling, and, depending on one's view of the sport, modern-day professional boxing. The narrative of religious proscription also privileged New England over other regions of the country, ignoring the Chesapeake region, where sport was an essential component of antebellum culture. It attended to the South usually in terms of twentieth-century evangelical affection for football and NASCAR and ignored the West entirely. Women were absent (except for a few brief remarks about gender nonconformists like Billy Jean King) as were enslaved and indigenous persons. Nonwhites and non-Protestants appeared mainly as illustrations of emerging pluralism in twentieth-century American society rather than as members and participants in religious and sporting society from the colonial period onward. Taken together, these omissions from the narrative of religion and sport profoundly limited the ability of the historiography to account for the robust and complex nature human life, where sport and religion alike were found in streets and barns, pool halls and factories, at derby tracks, in ethnic clubs, and at religious sodalities, in slave quarters and bourgeois parlors and town taverns, in Puritan town squares, Jewish enclaves, and conjure circles.

The prominent exception to the historiographical mode that considered religion mainly in terms of its tolerance or intolerance for sport is scholarship about Victorian era "muscular Christianity." The first major work to explore the phenomenon was a collection of literary essays titled *Muscular Christianity: Embodying the Victorian Era*, which documented associations of Christianity with masculine "healthy animalism" in English literature in the mid-nineteenth century.[5] Social, religious, and gender historians quickly followed suit, documenting myriad ways this ideal of Protestant manliness appeared in theology, religious institutions, voluntary associations, cultural movements, and physical aesthetics in Britain and the United States at the time.[6] The most prominent of these historical monographs, Clifford Putney's *Muscular Christianity: Manhood and Sports in Protestant America, 1880–1920*, linked the emergence of Protestant concern with health and manliness to a general cultural anxiety that American men were becoming physically enfeebled and socially emasculated by immersion in domesticated spaces. In response, Putney argued, Protestants developed a range of organizations (the Men and Religion Forward Movement, the YMCA, the Student Volunteer Movement) to introduce outdoor activity, competitive sports, and "the heroic and aggressive in Christianity" back into men's daily lives.[7] In the narrative arc about religion and sport in the dominant historiography, the muscular Christianity documented by Hall, Putney, and others appeared as a moment of détente in the ongoing tension between Protestant prohibitionism and the Anglo tradition of sport, but the significance of this scholarship lies beyond its having captured an apparent historical exception. Rather, the main contribution made by historiography on muscular religion (for, indeed, eventually religious historians would discover corresponding versions of muscular Protestantism within Catholicism, Mormonism, and Judaism) is that it reframed the terms of the relationship of religion and society and by extension the relationship of religion and sport. In place of models that located religion outside of cultural habits as an observer and critic, historians of muscular Christianity placed religion alongside and in full engagement with cultural institutions and social processes that converged to create a cultural appetite for vigorous manhood in the late Victorian and early Progressive eras. This means that religion is implicated in both the positive aspects of muscular Christianity, its affirmation of physical health, and its desire to offer men alternatives to the confining environments of industrialized work in urban paces, as well as in the problematic legacies of masculine violence and white supremacist nationalism that emerged from the confluence of religion, Anglo-capitalism, and Victorian urbanism in muscular Christianity.[8]

In scholarly work on muscular Christianity, religion bends close to human experience, mingling with other arenas of knowledge and activity, including work, family, and play. Religion's interactions with sport appears as bodily practice rather than as abstract theological ideas, shifting the lens of historical inquiry from religious elites who prohibited physical recreation to the religious individuals who engaged in athletics and then, only by extension, to the religious institutions that encouraged them by building physical spaces like gymnasiums and ball parks. The bodies that appear in this historical genre are real, historical, flesh-and-blood bodies—bodies that were trained and disciplined, that sweated and stretched and got strong and also got injured, bodies that were the object (and, according to some scholars, the victims) of religious discourse that equated bodily perfection with moral purity, bodies that had possibilities and limits, bodies that were vehicles of identity and pleasure and pain and religious meaning for the men who inhabited them—not merely the abstract idea of the body that often appears in religious literature as the antithesis of the spirit of soul. By reframing religion as a grounded and embodied cultural process, the historiography on late-nineteenth-century muscular Christianity mapped a richer and more nuanced model for approaching the historical intersection of religion and sport.

More recently, scholars have built on this foundation to craft solid case studies that explore the intersection of specific religious traditions with particular sports. The best works in this genre interrogate the points where religious and athletic cultures intersect, asking how religious devout inhabited and experienced the interplay of religious and athletic discourses about the human body, its essence, purpose, limits, and potential. Julie Byrne's *O God of the Players* is an ethnographically informed history of the Immaculata College "Might Macs," the basketball team from a small Catholic women's college outside of Philadelphia who won the first three national college basketball championships in the early 1970s, capturing the imagination of fans and especially young Catholic girls across the nation. Byrne's subtle analysis reveals that while Might Mac players did not overtly challenge the limited gender roles assigned to them by the Catholic Church (nor did they challenge the unwieldy dress-length uniforms and hot woolen stockings they were required to wear to preserve Mary-like modesty on the court), basketball provided young Catholic women with religiously sanctioned, empowering, and subversive bodily experiences as they reached and ran, jumped, and bumped into each other, fought for loose balls, sweated and got dirty, and simply enjoyed physical proficiency and the ability to dominate opponents.[9] Other works in this genre employ sport as a lens through which to interrogate the ways that abstract theological principles are implemented on the ground by religious groups. In this vein, Richard Ian Kimball's *Sports in Zion: Mormon Recreation, 1890–1940* provides detailed documentation of the recreation programs of the Church of Jesus Christ of Latter Days Saints during the Progressive era. Kimball's attention to the rhetoric Mormons used in publications about recreation suggests that the strong Latter-Day Saints institutional commitment to recreation in the early twentieth century grew from a profound fear among Mormon leaders that urbanization, industrialization, spiritual drift, and generational decline would weaken the religious commitment of Mormon youth. In other words, Mormon leaders may have publicly proclaimed the spiritual value of recreation using overtly religious language, but behind the scenes they also drew on secular experts in sociology, play theory, leadership development, and social reform to craft a comprehensive recreation ideology for the church.[10] On other fronts, in the introduction to his edited collection *Jews, Sports, and the Rites of Citizenship*, Jack Kugelmass argues that the popularity of sports like boxing and baseball among Jews provides a "unique window" of insight into the processes of religious identity and ethnic assimilation among modern Jews, arguing that athletics in the nineteenth and twentieth centuries were not just about muscularity and competition but rather touched on "the observation, establishment, maintenance, transgression, dismantling and redefining of boundaries of boundaries between Jews and the coterritorial populations among whom they reside."[11] Case studies that explore sport in specific historical moments in religious traditions add a rich layer to the historiography of "lived religion," introducing issues of embodiment, health, competition, gender, and play through the lens of athletics and moving scholarship from the discipline of sport history toward the discipline of religious studies.

APPROACHES TO RELIGION IN THE FIELDS OF RELIGIOUS STUDIES

In contrast to the work written by historians, a significant portion of the scholarly literature about religion and sport written within the field of religious studies presents a normative reading of the value of the intersection of religion and sport. In other words, scholars in religious studies often make clear declarations about the moral or religious value of sport. Some scholars find sport to be one of the highest articulations of religious ideals. Others find the close association of sport and religion (especially in contemporary American society) to be a polluting influence that degrades religious ideals and religious institutions. The most common tendency among scholars of religion and sport is to positively appraise athletics by equating the experience of passionate fandom with religious encounters with transcendence.

The study of sport and religion in the American context found its first articulation among scholars of religious studies in Michael Novak's ebullient *The Joy of Sports*. Though Novak's work served as a central foundation for many of the studies of religious elements of sport that came after it, Novak also provided the field with a less than ideal intellectual foundation. Writing alongside other influential early works of sport analysis in the mid-1970s, Novak characterized sport as a "natural religion," arguing that "sports flow outward into action from a deep natural impulse that is radically religious: an impulse for freedom, respect for individual limits, a zest for symbolic meaning, and a longing for perfection."[12] Novak collapsed sport and religion into a single entity by mapping the isomorphic similarities in the anatomies and functions of both areas of human activity. First, Novak identified elements in sport that resemble categories scholars use to describe components of religious traditions (ritual, myth, institution, sacrament, ceremony, martyr). Second, Novak argued that sport performed the same function as religion in human culture—both sport and religion mark special spaces and times that are separate from the ordinary, they explore questions of ultimate meaning, they provide dramas through which human beings interpret large frame questions about meaning—or, in Novak's words, sports "recreate symbols of cosmic struggle, in which human survival and moral courage are not assured."[13] Novak argued that sport, like other forms of religion, satisfied the deepest perennial needs of the human spirit. "They satisfy the most persistent hungers of the human heart—for repetition and for solemn ritual, for pageantry and for uncertain outcomes. For centuries, human beings have gathered so."[14] For Novak, sport can be considered a religion because it has the same anatomy as religion and it performs the same social functions as other recognized forms of religion.

Scholars studying the sociology of sport have made similar arguments. Maurice Roche proposed that Marx's legendary dictum "religion is the opium of the people" should be amended in the late twentieth century to observe that "sport is the religion of the people." Sport can claim this mantle, Roche argues, because it offers apparently secular but "quasi-religious experiences such as those of sacredness and transcendence, communal ritual and symbolism, and collective drama and emotionality." [15] Like religion, he continues, sport also provides arenas for the development, symbolic formation, display, and emotional expression of collective social identities.

Allen Guttmann's influential *From Ritual to Record: The Nature of Modern Sports*, published two years after Novak's *Joy of Sports*, presented a contrary interpretation of the spiritual meaning of contemporary sports. Guttmann's descriptive narrative traced the evolution of sport from sacred games (the "ritual" part of his title) like ancient Mayan ball games and the sacred festivals of Athens through time to the specialized, rationalized, statistics-driven professional athletics of today (the "record" part of his title). In short, Guttmann offered a secularization thesis of sport, arguing that since sports reflect the dominant values and assumptions of the cultures of which they are a part, early sports, like primitive cultures, were religious, and modern sports, like the societies in which they are practiced, are secular.[16] Though the resurgence of religious fundamentalisms worldwide in recent years has largely delegitimated secularization as an explanatory mode, at the time Guttmann was writing the secularization thesis was widely accepted among historians and social scientists, yet Guttmann's interpretation of contemporary sport as profoundly secular was generally rejected by a generation of writers who would follow after who would embrace Novak's more romantic vision of sport as a "natural religion." In fact, a significant portion of the existing scholarship on sport and religion has utilized some variation on the equation of sport and religion that Novak initially proposed.[17] In countless monographs, articles, and edited collections, authors evoke the "church of baseball," compare the Super Bowl to a religious festival, and muse on the Buddhist practice of NASCAR driving. At their strongest, works in this genre take seriously the passion that athletes and especially fans and spectators bring to their encounters with athletics, and they capture something of the uniqueness of sport as a respected social institution in modern society. Though there are scholars who are able to manage the comparison of sport and religion in a way that complicates academic categories and opens new questions rather than simply flattening phenomena to easily equate them to each other, one-dimensional scholarship continues to emerge in this interpretive vein.

Though Novak's formulation was emotionally satisfying to many of his readers, it also was deeply problematic as an intellectual exercise. Novak's argument rested on universalist claims about human nature and human desires that were blind to the specificity of time period, gender, and culture. It generalized all sport based on his favorite sports (baseball, football, basketball). It lumped all religious traditions into one undifferentiated category. In short, Novak offered a deeply flawed foundation for scholarly work on religion and sport. Unfortunately, many of the current intellectual problems in the field of sport and religion reflect the extent to which work after Novak has adopted Novak's problematic conflation of sport with religion.

Fortunately, many works on sport and religion in the past twenty years have stepped back from Novak's most reductive oversimplifications, qualifying the term "religion" in reference to sports by adding prefaces like "cultural" (Catherine Albanese) "civil" (Joseph Price, Charles Prebish, Christopher Evans, William Herzog, Cornish Rogers, William J. Morgan, Eric Forney), and "folk" (James Mathisen) before the term "religion" to describe spiritual dimensions of sport.[18] Though this model of sport as cultural/civil/folk religion is more nuanced than Novak's original formulation, these works often approach the conflation of sport and religion as a reality that can be observed and explained rather than as a constructed and situated interpretive scholarly mode that is laden with embedded with assumptions and ideology. Or, as Steve Bruce put it, "Examining the parallels between football and religion can be interesting and illuminating but it is not helped at all by defining football as a religion. To do so is to establish by definitional fiat what should be demonstrated factually."[19] The strongest works in this interpretive genre—Eric Bain-Selbo's recent book on football in the American South and Anthony Santoro's current work on fan culture of the Oakland Raiders—present the sport-as-civil-religion model as something to be proven through case studies grounded in specific cultures and time periods, rather than as an explanatory trope that is sufficient unto itself.[20] So while the "civil religion" approach is increasingly careful to provide explanatory and theoretical foundations for the isomorphism between certain religions and certain sports, its evolution solves only one of the major problems with Novak's influential approach to sport as a form of religion.

There are two significant flaws in Novak's approach that have been uncritically imported into much of the existing literature on religion and sport. First, the equation of sport and religion often draws from antiquated theories of religion that have been roundly critiqued and largely abandoned by the field of religious studies as the field has become more reflexive about its own origin and history. Second, this scholarship overwhelmingly examines the role sports play in the lives of people in the stands and stadiums rather than its meaning for the players on the field, court, track, ring, and ice.

The two problems are interrelated. Novak, and many of the sport-as-religion scholars who wrote after him, drew on and occasionally explicitly evoked theories of religion that emerged from the early origins of the study of religion in Protestant theological circles, particularly the work of Rudolph Otto and later Mircea Eliade, both of whom approach religion as an absolute reality (or, "the numinous" in Otto's terms) that humans briefly access in moments of hierophany (in Eliade's formulation). Since the 1980s the collective works of Talal Asad, Jonathan Z. Smith, Bruce Lincoln, and Russell McCutcheon, to name just a few, have effectively intellectually delegitimated this approach to the study of religion, replacing it with models that recognize the constructedness of the category of "religion," the colonialist legacies embedded in its deployment, and the situated interpretive perspective of the scholar. The reliance on Otto and Eliade in studies of religion and sport orients analysis toward revelation, symbolism, and meaning-making (the view from the stands) rather than practice, experience, and embodiment (the perspective of the athlete). The result is scholarship that is quite good at using metaphor to argue that sporting fans encounter a form of transcendent meaning in their devotion to sport but that has no theoretical capacity to consider sport as a system of production and consumption (David Chidester), a discipline of the body (Michel Foucault), a somatic form of discourse (Aihwa Ong), or embodied experience (Thomas Csordas)—precisely the kinds of analysis that are at the center of scholarly conversation in the field of religious studies in the present moment.[21] Said another way, the sport-as-religion scholars offer a model for explaining the kind of dedicated fandom Warren St. John documents among RVers who follow the Alabama Crimson Tide across the country their season in *Rammer Jammer Yellow Hammer*, but they offer little to help understand the embodied experiences of pain and transcendence that runners experience that John L. Parker Jr. describes so richly in his famous novel *Once a Runner*.[22]

Some observers responded to Novak's claim that sport is a form of religion by rejecting the conflation as religious heresy. In *God in the Stadium: Sports and Religion in America*, Robert J. Higgs claims to offer a reading of American religious history that traces the complex relationship of religion, sport, and manhood from the colonial period to the present moment. Higgs contrasts two tropes within Christianity: the knight, representing violence and domination, and the shepherd, a religious model of service, peacefulness, and nurturance. Higgs argues that American religion has privileged the dominating and violent knight over the gentle shepherd, inappropriately "muscularizing and militarizing" Jesus, in the process creating a national culture that is dangerously violent. Higgs blames athletics, specifically the religious romanticization of competitive sport that occurred in nineteenth-century muscular Christianity, for the emergence of violent Christology and, with it, a false religion Higgs calls "Sportianity." Though *God in the Stadium* is more a *cri de coeur* for the languishing Christianity of the gentle shepherd than a work of historical scholarship, Higgs does offer a solid historical narrative of developments, events, individuals, and institutions that contributed to the conflation of sports, war, and Christianity in American culture. In doing so he highlights the unique role that the military and higher education have played in the evolution of martial culture and spectator sports in America.[23] Less than decade later, Higgs partnered with psychologist Michael C. Braswell to produce *An Unholy Alliance: The Sacred in Modern Sports*, a more moderate and scholarly challenge to claims that sport is a religion than Higgs' previous volume offered. Braswell and Higgs use theology but also the theory of religion, sociology, sport history, anthropology, and social theory to argue that, though sport does not meet the criteria to qualify as a religion, it does occupy an important, even unique, category of human activity and so merits serious scholarly consideration of the role it plays in human culture and history.[24]

Other scholars acknowledge the close association of religion and sport but reject simple equivalency between them in favor of comparative analysis or functional analysis of the ways the two institutions interact. In *With God on Their Side: Sport in the Service of Religion*, Tara Magladinski and Timothy J. L. Chandler argue that assuming that sport is a religion obscures the complexities of the relationship between them. Instead, the authors collected essays that explore how religions have capitalized on the resemblances between sport and religion to expand the power, range, or depth of theological authority. Using case studies that range from rugby in Cape Town South Africa to Shinto sumo wrestlers in Japan to young female Jewish swimmers in turn-of-the-century New York, the authors in *With God on Their Side* demonstrate that the elements that make religion and sport look alike also make sport a malleable, powerful, and easily deployed tool that religious hierarchies can use to pursue religious agendas.[25] So the fact that churches and stadiums alike function as hybrid public/private space where people gather to experience and express a collective identity means that when the Bad Blue Boys, devoted Croatian fans of Sydney United, gather on soccer terraces and chant "we are red, white and blue, we are Catholic, why aren't you?" they are consolidating religious allegiance as much as they are performing ethnic fandom.[26] In *Muscular Christianity*, evangelical scholars Tony Ladd and James Mathiesen are more direct, arguing that Protestantism and sport have "developed symbiotic relationships around their shared meanings and shifting boundaries" in the United States such that the strong contemporary alignment of sports and evangelical Protestantism in organizations like the Fellowship of Christian Athletes and Athletes in Action emphasizes sports as a way of evangelizing young people.[27] Interestingly, other observers have noted that sport also sometimes exceeds religion's coercive ability, possessing even the ability to rouse people against religious regimes of power. Franklin Foer observed that in 1997 when the Iranian national team qualified for the 1998 World Cup, thousands of Iranian women defied religious laws banning them from attending public soccer events, ignored a steady stream of public broadcasts urging them to stay home, braved a chilling rain, and stood against the heavy presence of paramilitary police to demand admission to the stadium to celebrate the team's return from the match in Melbourne. Shouting, "Aren't we part of this nation? We want to celebrate too. We aren't ants," the women of Tehran "broke through the police glass and muscled their way into the stadium." This striking moment of mass resistance to Islamic authority is but one episode in the Iranian regime's longstanding and overwhelmingly unsuccessful attempt to suppress soccer, Foer argues, and the resilience of public passion for the game in Iran suggests that sport can serve as an important limit on the influence religious discourse wields over both mass culture and individual consciousness.[28]

SPORT AND RELIGION
THROUGH EMBODIMENT

The subfield of religion and sport remains somewhat marginalized in the field of religious studies, isolated from larger disciplinary conversations by an unfortunate perception that individuals working on topics related to sport are simply fans pursuing an academic hobby rather than a serious research questions and by the awareness that many people working in the field are not engaging with the most current, critically informed approach to the category of religion. In order to remedy this intellectual marginalization, scholars working on religion and sport need to take seriously the theoretical developments in that field that problematize some of the central, established analytical modes for writing about religion, engaging critically with the category "religion," and turning its gaze from the spectator to the athlete, from abstract meaning to concrete human bodies. If scholarship on sport and religion reorients itself in this way, it will contribute to a vibrant conversation that is emerging among religion scholars representing diverse subfields about materiality in the study of religion.

In his 2011 study *More than Belief: A Materialist Theory of Religion*, Manuel A. Vasquez challenges scholars to move beyond models that approach religion as social, ideological (or actual) texts and instead employ a "non-reductive materialist" paradigm that studies "how embodiment and embeddedness in time and place enable and constrain diverse, flexible, yet patterned subjective experiences that come to be understood as religious."[29] Vasquez's book is the capstone of a more general shift toward engagement with material and somatic facets of religion, best exemplified by Tom Tweed's work on spatial theory, David Morgan's recent work on visuality, Ann Taves' foray into the neuroscience of religious experience, Martha Finch's surprising examination of the corporeality in Puritan New England, Jennifer Hughes' revolutionary approach to material culture, Thomas Csordas's studies of religious embodiment, and Ariel Glucklich's work on *Sacred Pain*.[30] One effect of the materialist renaissance in the study of religion is that the body is reframed as a concrete biological entity or the simultaneous object/agent of social processes, in contrast to previous models that presented the human body as a passive repository of ideologies or the byproduct of cultural discourse. As religious studies recenters human bodies—addressing their composition, processes, and perceptions, their dynamism and their vulnerabilities—there is an exciting opportunity for scholars working on sport to bring their work directly to bear on how we understand somatic components of religion. Bringing athletic religiosity to the conversation about religious embodiment significantly enriches the intellectual project. In addition to observing religious bodies bent in supplication, extended in dances of spirit possession, disciplined against worldly pleasures, we can add bodies sweating on the basketball court, feeling the ecstatic percussion when the practiced swing of a bat connects with a fastball, and even rising from the canvas after a knockdown punch.

Two different horizons of inquiry emerge from considering the bodies of athletes as the locus where sport and religion converge. The first approach takes the already robust scholarly work on the discursive processes that determine the social values, cultural meanings, and valences of identity that athletes embody and perform in specific historical contexts and considers the influence of religion in the larger significations that are impressed on bodies in athletic discipline.[31] For example, the Christianization of the Roman Empire dramatically altered the meaning attached to the sexual and reproductive capacity of bodies, but it also transformed the value attached to bodies trained for feats of physical prowess, devaluing athletic bodies. Roman sports and gladiatorial games were shut down in Christianized Constantinople because of Christian opposition to the sensualism of bodies displayed in the games. "No longer were the body's taut musculature and its refine poise, signs of the athlete and the potential warrior, put on display . . . as marks of upper class status," Peter Brown observed of the ban. "Egyptian Christians now believed that the shriveled, sterile bodies of monks and virgins caused the valley to turn green every year."[32] The strongest scholarship in this vein attends to the dynamic nature of the religious associations with athletic training while also recognizing the intersectionality of features like gender, race, class, ethnicity, sexuality, and work. The intersection of boxing and Roman Catholicism in the early twentieth century offers a particularly vivid example of this dynamic. Prewar American Catholicism was oriented around a "culture of suffering" that valorized experiences of physical distress as conduits to spiritual transcendence. According to his logic, religion cemented the affection of Catholics for boxing because the sport visually and viscerally engaged a distinctively Catholic constellation of religious ideas about the nature of violence and the experience of the body in pain that permeated Catholic culture at the turn of the century. By the 1950s, Catholic culture had largely moved away from its embrace of bodily morbidity as a sign of grace toward an appreciation of robust physical health as an indication that a Catholic was prepared to do battle against deleterious forces of communism and secularism in society. In this religious context, Catholics still embraced the sport of boxing, but they viewed the bodies of fighters through a very different interpretive lens than their coreligionists a half-century prior, focusing less on the physical punishment and bloodshed of a hard fight and more on the physical prowess exhibited by dominating boxers.

Finally, scholarly attentiveness to the body as the site where sport and religion intersect naturally leads to a closer appraisal of the embodied experience of athletes themselves, a facet that is surprisingly understudied. After all, both religious ritual and athletic training are forms of bodily practice that embed specific somatic knowledge in muscles, reflexes, and memory. Both often are described as modes of bodily discipline. Attending to the athlete's experience of his or her own body presents historians with specific research challenges, the most insistent being that of documenting and/or translating somatic experience into descriptive and interpretive text. Thus this approach would require historians to pay close attention to narratives and descriptions offered by athletes in which they describe experiences of embodiment. Findings may also be supplemented by data gained through research methods from ethnography and sociology and enriched by social theorists and phenomenologists like Michel Foucault, Marcel Mauss, Maurice Merleau-Ponty, Judith Butler, and Michel De Certeau.[33] For all the challenges this angle of investigation and analysis presents to researchers, it offers the possibility of reframing the history of sport in a way that places athletes at the center of the story, and it opens critical analytical space for studying how religious cultures were made real— were achieved and challenged, affirmed, or remade—in the physical bodies of religious athletes. As demonstrated by the championship Immaculata College women's basketball team in Julie Byrne's *O God of the Players*, Catholicism was never more real to the Mighty Macs than when they were having fun, sweating, and dominating the court in their Mary-like modest Catholic uniforms.

Notes

1. Elliott J. Gorn and Warren Goldstein, *A Brief History of American Sports* (New York: Hill and Wang, 1993), 31.
2. Nancy L. Sturna, *People of Prowess: Sport, Leisure, and Labor in Early Anglo-America* (Urbana: University of Illinois Press, 1996), 87–89.
3. Sturna, *People of Prowess*, 192–193.
4. One surprising work that revisits this largely discredited narrative is William J. Baker, *Playing with God: Religion and Modern Sport* (Cambridge, MA: Harvard University Press, 2007).
5. Donald R. Hall, ed., *Muscular Christianity: Embodying the Victorian Age* (Cambridge, UK: Cambridge University Press, 1994).
6. Examples of works exploring muscular Christianity are Gail Bederman, *Manliness and Civilization: A Cultural History of Gender and Race in the United States, 1880–1917* (Chicago: University of Chicago Press, 1995); Mark C. Carnes, *Secret Ritual and Manhood in Victorian America* (New Haven, CT: Yale University Press, 1989); John Corrigan, *Business of the Heart: Religion and Emotion in the Nineteenth Century* (Berkeley: University of California Press, 2002); R. Marie Griffith, *Born Again Bodies: Flesh and Spirit in American Christianity* (Berkeley: University of California Press, 2004); J. A. Mangan and James Walvin, *Manliness and Morality: Middle-Class Masculinity in Britain and America, 1800–1940* (Manchester, UK: Manchester University Press, 1987); Norman Vance, *The Sinews of the Spirit: The Ideal of Christian Manliness in Victorian Literature and Religious Thought* (New York: Cambridge University Press, 1985); James C. Whorton, *Crusaders for Fitness: the History of American Health Reformers* (Princeton, NJ: Princeton University Press, 1982).
7. Clifford Putney, *Muscular Christianity: Manhood and Sports in Protestant America, 1880–1920* (Cambridge, MA: Harvard University Press, 2001), 137.
8. Jack Kugelmass, ed., *Jews, Sports, and Rites of Citizenship* (Urbana: University of Illinois Press, 2007); Moshe Zimmerman, "Muscle Jews versus Nervous Jews," in *Emancipation through Muscles: Jews and Sports in Europe*, ed. Michael Brenner and Gideon Reuveni (Lincoln: University of Nebraska Press, 2006), 13–26; Richard Ian Kimball, *Sports in Zion: Mormon Recreation, 1890–1940* (Urbana: University of Illinois Press, 2003).
9. Julie Byrne, *O God of the Players: The Story of the Immaculata Mighty Macs* (New York: Columbia University Press, 2003).

10. Kimball, *Sports in Zion.*

11. Jack Kugelmass, "Why Sports?" in *Jews, Sports,* ed. Kugelmass, 6.

12. Michael Novak, *The Joy of Sports: Endzones, Bases, Baskets, Balls, and the Consecration of the American Spirit* (Lanham, MD: Rowman & Littlefield, 1976), 19.

13. Novak, *Joy of Sports,* 21.

14. Novak, *Joy of Sports,* 31.

15. Maurice Roche, "Mega-Events and Media Culture: Sport and the Olympics," in *Critical Readings: Sport, Culture, and the Media,* ed. David Rowe (Berkshire, UK: Open University Press, 2004), 160.

16. Allen Guttmann, *From Ritual to Record: The Nature of Modern Sports* (New York: Columbia University Press, 1978).

17. Even books outside the field of religion evoke this equation. A popular sports studies textbook, *Sport Fans: The Psychology and Social Impact of Spectators* (ed. Daniel L. Mann, Merrill Melnick, Gordon W. Russell, Dale G. Pease [New York: Routledge, 2001], 198–199), observes: "The similarities between sport fandom and organized religion are striking. Consider the vocabulary associated with both: faith, devotion, worship, ritual, dedication, sacrifice, commitment, spirit, prayer, suffering, festival, and celebration."

18. Catherine L Albanese, *America: Religions and Religion* (Belmont, CA: Wadsworth, 1981); Joseph Price, *From Season to Season: Sports and American Religion* (Macon, GA: Mercer University Press, 2001); Christopher H. Evans and William R. Herzog, eds., *The Faith of Fifty Million: Baseball, Religion, and American Culture* (Louisville, KY: Westminster John Knox Press, 2002); Cornish Rogers, "Sports, Religion and Politics: The Renewal of an Alliance," *The Christian Century,* April 5, 1972; William J. Morgan, "Baseball and the Search for an American Moral Identity," in *Baseball and Philosophy: Thinking Outside the Batter's Box,* ed. Eric Bronson (Chicago and LaSalle, IL: Open Court, 2004), 157–168; Craig Forney, *The Holy Trinity of American Sports: Civil Religion in Football, Baseball, and Basketball* (Macon, GA: Mercer University Press, 2010); James A. Mathisen, "From Civil Religion to Folk Religion: The Case of American Sport," in *Sport and Religion,* ed. Shirl J. Hoffman (Champaign, IL: Human Kinetics, 1992), 17–33.

19. Steve Bruce, *Religion in the Modern World: From Cathedrals to Cults* (Oxford: Oxford University Press, 1996), 39.

20. Eric Bain-Selbo, *Game Day and God: Football, Faith, and Politics in the American South* (Macon, GA: Mercer University Press, 2009).

21. David Chidester, *Authentic Fakes: Religion and American Popular Culture* (Berkeley: University of California Press, 2005), Michel Foucault, *Discipline and Punish: The Birth of the Prison* (New York: Vintage), Aihwa Ong, "The Production of Possession: Spirits and the Multinational Corporation in Malaysia," in *Beyond the Body Proper: Reading the Anthropology of Material Life,* ed. Margaret Lock and Judith Farquhar (Durham, NC: Duke University Press, 2007), 512–549; and Thomas J. Csordas, *The Sacred Self: A Cultural Phenomenology of Charismatic Healing* (Berkeley: University of California Press, 1997).

22. Warren St. John, *Rammer Jammer Yellow Hammer: A Road Trip into the Heart of Fan Mania* (New York: Three Rivers Press, 2004), John L. Parker Jr., *Once a Runner: A Novel* (New York: Scribner, 1978).

23. Robert J. Higgs, *God in the Stadium: Sports and Religion in America* (Lexington: University of Kentucky Press, 1995).

24. Robert J. Higgs and Michael C. Braswell, *An Unholy Alliance: The Sacred and Modern Sports* (Macon, GA: Mercer University Press, 2004).

25. Tara Magladinski and Timothy J. L. Chandler, eds. *With God on Their Side: Sport in the Service of Religion* (New York: Routledge, 2002).

26. John Hughson, "'We Are Red, White and Blue, We Are Catholic, Why Aren't You?': Religion and Soccer Subculture Symbolism," in *With God on Their Side*, 63.

27. Tony Ladd and James A. Mathiesen, *Muscular Christianity: Evangelical Protestants and the Development of American Sport* (Grand Rapids, MI: Baker Books, 1999).

28. Franklin Foer, *How Soccer Explains the World* (New York: Harper Perennial, 2004), 21.

29. Manuel A. Vasquez, *More Than Belief: A Materialist Theory of Religion* (New York: Oxford University Press, 2011), 7.

30. Thomas Tweed, *Crossing and Dwelling: A Theory of Religion* (Cambridge, MA: Harvard University Press, 2006); David Morgan, *The Sacred Gaze: Religious Visual Culture in Theory and Practice* (Berkeley: University of California Press, 2005); Ann Taves, *Religious Experience Reconsidered* (Princeton, NJ: Princeton University Press, 2009); Martha Finch, *Dissenting Bodies: Corporealities in Early New England* (New York: Columbia University Press, 2009); Jennifer Hughes, *Biography of a Mexican Crucifix: Lived Religion and Local Faith from the Conquest to the Present* (New York: Oxford University Press, 2010); Thomas J. Csordas, "Embodiment and Cultural Phenomenology," in *Perspectives on Embodiment: The Intersections of Nature and Culture*, ed. Gail Weiss and Honi Fern Haber (New York: Routledge, 2004), 143–162; Ariel Glucklich, *Sacred Pain: Hurting the Body for the Sake of the Soul* (New York: Oxford University Press, 2001).

31. For excellent examples of work on the discursive discipline of athlete's bodies, see Pirkko Markula and Richard Pringle, *Foucault, Sport and Exercise: Power, Knowledge and Transforming the Self* (New York: Routledge, 2006), and Allen Guttmann, *The Erotic in Sports* (New York: Columbia University Press, 1996).

32. Peter Brown, *The Body and Society: Men, Women, and Sexual Renunciation in Early Christianity* (New York: Columbia University Press, 1998), 437–438.

33. Michel Foucault, *The Birth of the Clinic: An Archaeology of Medical Perception* (New York: Pantheon, 1973); Marcel Mauss, "Techniques of the Body," *Economy and Society* 2 (1973): 70–80, Maurice Merleau-Ponty, *The Phenomenology of Perception* (London: Routledge, 1962); Judith Butler, *Bodies that Matter* (New York: Routledge, 1993); Michel de Certeau, *The Practice of Everyday Life* (Berkeley: University of California Press, 1984).

BIBLIOGRAPHY

Byrne, Julie. *O God of the Players: The Story of the Immaculata Mighty Macs*. New York: Columbia University Press, 2003.

Griffith, R. Marie. *Born Again Bodies: Flesh and Spirit in American Christianity*. Berkeley: University of California Press, 2004.

Guttmann, Allen. *From Ritual to Record: The Nature of Modern Sports*. New York: Columbia University Press, 1978.

Kimball, Richard Ian. *Sports in Zion: Mormon Recreation, 1890–1940*. Urbana: University of Illinois Press, 2003.

Kugelmass, Jack, ed. *Jews, Sports, and Rites of Citizenship*. Urbana: University of Illinois Press, 2007.

Magladinski, Tara, and Timothy J. L. Chandler, eds. *With God on Their Side: Sport in the Service of Religion*. New York: Routledge, 2002.

Novak, Michael. *The Joy of Sports: Endzones, Bases, Baskets, Balls, and the Consecration of the American Spirit*. Lanham, MD: Rowman & Littlefield, 1976.

Price, Joseph. *From Season to Season: Sports and American Religion*. Macon, GA: Mercer University Press, 2001.

Putney, Clifford. *Muscular Christianity: Manhood and Sports in Protestant America, 1880–1920*. Cambridge, MA: Harvard University Press, 2001.

Sturna, Nancy L. *People of Prowess: Sport, Leisure, and Labor in Early Anglo-America*. Urbana: University of Illinois Press, 1996.

Vasquez, Manuel A. *More than Belief: A Materialist Theory of Religion*. New York: Oxford University Press, 2011.

PART VIII

··

EMERGING AREAS
OF INTEREST

··

CHAPTER 33

....

THE VISUAL TURN
IN SPORT HISTORY

....

MIKE O'MAHONY

In December 1952, British soccer star Stanley Matthews made an unlikely appearance in the pages of the low-budget, popular magazine *Picturegoer*, featuring in two photographs as part of an advertisement for Craven "A" cigarettes.[1] The first of these shows the sports star in action for Blackpool, leaving a defender standing as he demonstrates the skills that led to him being dubbed "the wizard of the dribble." The second presents a smiling Matthews, now wearing an England shirt and puffing contentedly on what he describes in an accompanying caption as "the cigarette for me." This image of a popular sports celebrity at the apex of his career, a renowned non-smoker, teetotaller and vegetarian, not only smoking but also explicitly promoting the practice seems, at the very least, jarring to modern sensibilities. The fact that the advertisement appeared at the same time that connections between smoking and its detrimental impact upon health were first being publicized does little to diminish the sense of incongruity implicit within this visual representation. However, the image is included here not to highlight the historical significance of nicotine for sportsmen of an earlier age, as intriguing an issue as that may be. Rather it is intended to place a spotlight on the intrinsic relationship between sport as a social practice and its wider representation and exploitation within the field of visual culture. The image of an active Matthews in full flight, strategically placed alongside a more passive Matthews, enjoying a leisurely moment notionally enhanced by his consumption of cigarettes, was clearly designed to invoke a connection between the two practices in the minds of the reader. The efficacy of this visual analogy may well be doubted, and it seems unlikely, even at a time when smoking was so widely practiced, that viewers of this advertisement seriously considered the possibility that smoking Craven "A"s was likely to improve soccer skills. Nonetheless, an affinity between sporting ability and the consumption of a specific product is here overtly claimed, and, notably, it is the use of images that most effectively reinforces this unlikely pairing.

This exploitation of Matthews' identity, quite literally of his "image" as a popular sportsman and celebrity, is of course hardly a modern phenomenon. At the ancient

Olympic Games, for example, monuments dedicated to victors adorned the sanctuary at Olympia, erected as evidence not just of the status of individual sporting heroes but also of the regions from which they came.[2] Here long-term sporting reputation, and its civic associations, was dependent as much on the presence of these public expressions of visual culture as on the existence of textual documents recording such victories. Indeed, wherever and whenever sport has been practiced, it has simultaneously attracted the attention of artists. Yet despite the plethora of visual and material culture artifacts inspired by, or dedicated to, sporting practice, the detailed study of this extraordinary range of documentary evidence has, until recently, played a relatively minor role in sport history.

WHY DO IMAGES OF SPORT MATTER?

Sport, as a cultural manifestation, might be regarded as primarily a visual experience. This is not to ignore the fact that sport, from both the participatory and the spectatorial perspective, has its own sounds, smells, and even tastes. Nor is it to overlook the tactile dimension of sporting engagement. The skillful physical manipulation of specialist sports equipment or, in contact sports, the direct encounter with an opponent, highlight the more haptic nature of sporting experience. Rather it is to acknowledge that the specifically visual qualities of sport have marked a major contribution to its appeal and its capacity to communicate so effectively across national and linguistic borders, making sport one of the truly transnational cultural expressions of the modern era. And it is this appeal that has facilitated the generation of a huge body of sporting evidence in visual form. From painting, drawing, and sculpture to film and photography, from architecture to animation, from trophy to costume design, and from public spectacle to staged performance, the material legacy of sport's visual culture provides an extensive and highly valuable resource for research. Equally important, an engagement with the mediated products of visual culture has increasingly come not only to characterize the way in which we, as consumers, experience sport but also to modify it. Today, even at live events, mediated imagery, in the form of programs and advertisements, impacts upon our engagement with the sporting performance whilst the ubiquitous big screen dominates our visual and conceptual field, offering alternative viewpoints, slow-motion replays, and even mirror images of ourselves as spectators. In this way, the visual culture that surrounds sporting action contributes toward shaping our very subjectivity and behavior.

In one sense, visual representations have not so much been absent from historical analyses of sport as undertheorized. Countless sport histories, recognizing sport's visual appeal, have included copious illustrations, most frequently in the form of photographs presented as notional testimony to affirm the story being recounted in text. Thus, as Douglas Booth has pointed out, "Photographic portraits of players, athletes and administrators, and photographs of sporting equipment, uniforms, spectators, and settings for events and incidents, regularly appear in monographs *as visual facts*."[3] Booth's intention here is to problematize this dominant convention, to highlight that visual "evidence" should rather be regarded as contingent and mediated. Murray Phillips reinforces this view when he states that "photographic representations are neither copies of the original text nor transparent replicas of reality nor accurate and unambiguous."[4] Rather, he argues, readers engaging with such visual material should adopt critical and analytical tools, much as would be applied for text or indeed any other form of evidence.

This call for a more critical approach to visual materials within the history of sport essentially stems from developments within other academic disciplines, not least those that foreground visual material, such as art history, film, and media studies. Drawing upon W. J. T. Mitchell's insightful essays of the early 1990s and the focus on developing methods for engaging with visual culture, as explored in the work of Gillian Rose and Peter Burke, this trend has been widely dubbed "the visual turn."[5] Rose, in particular, has proposed "three criteria for a critical methodology" when engaging with visual materials, arguing that images need to be (a) taken seriously, (b) analyzed within the context of the social conditions and effects such artifacts have, and (c) engaged with self-reflexively.[6] In this context, the visual turn in sport history might serve two key purposes; first as a warning against the simplistic and unproblematic deployment of images as incontrovertible evidence of an uncontested history and second to facilitate a more critical and analytical approach to the deployment of such material, enabling a more nuanced engagement with the visual and material culture of sport as a rich and valuable resource both to facilitate and to problematize explorations into sport's many pasts.

When Marshall McLuhan first introduced his oft-quoted, enigmatic phrase "the medium is the message" in 1964, he was specifically drawing attention to the fact that it has often proven all too easy to underestimate the significance of the technological means through which ideas are communicated in modern society. More important, he highlighted how these means can subtly impact upon, even transform, the ideas themselves.[7] From the perspective of the visual turn in sport history, this has much significance for an engagement not only with the "what" of visual representation but also with the "how." Thus in terms of the production of an image, analysis needs to consider what visual conventions, techniques, and devices are deployed, in what medium, and how these factors combine to contribute toward shaping readings of the image. Further, this analysis needs also to be extended beyond production factors to consider an image's potential receptions according to where and how it is displayed, reproduced, and visually contextualized in both spatial and temporal terms. In essence, content needs to be considered alongside medium, execution or style, and reception. This might be demonstrated by reference to one specific example.

In 1960, Mark Kauffman, a staff photographer for *Life* magazine, produced a number of images of sporting action at the Olympic Games in Rome. Amongst these is a photograph of the twenty-one-year old Soviet athlete, Irina Press, competing in the 80-meter hurdles final. In terms of content alone—the "what" of representation—this image might be read as a straightforward visual document recording a specific sporting moment, namely Press's victory in this specific race at the Rome Olympics. But the "how" is also vitally important here in communicating ideas beyond this simple factual information. For example, by adopting many of the conventions of contemporary sport photography, Kauffman not only documents this event but also adds a specific sense of drama to his visual account, shaping, though not ultimately determining, the viewer's engagement with it. At a basic level, the positioning of Press at the very center of the image immediately elevates her status within the compositional structure of the image, reinforcing the notion that the main focus of our attention should be on the ultimately victorious athlete. Moreover, by judiciously editing out most other competitors, the photograph effectively reconstructs the race as one between two Soviet athletes, with Galina Bystrova shown just inches behind her compatriot. However, records show that Bystrova finished only fifth out of six competitors, with British hurdler Carole Quinton securing the silver and Gisela Birkemeyer of West Germany the bronze. Thus Kauffman's exclusive focus on the Soviet athletes might be construed as constructing a rather partial narrative in terms of the final outcome of the race. The viewpoint adopted by Kauffman also contributes toward shaping the viewer's reading of the image. The low-angle, trackside position, up close to the action, emphasizes the privileged access of the professional sport photographer, one indeed that surpasses that not only that of "unofficial" photographers but also of the stadium spectators themselves. This specialist viewpoint not only invokes a sense of authority, lending authenticity to the image, but also further determines that, in essence, the photograph is about the race and its outcome far more than an evocation of the wider event as a purely visual spectacle. This emphasis on visual conventions deployed in a manner to emphasize the potential result of sporting competitions has become so embedded in our visual consciousness that alternative modes of representation have a tendency to disturb or to fail to satisfy. A classic example of this practice can be seen in Leni Riefenstahl's infamous account of the Berlin Games of 1936, *Olympia*. When focusing on the gymnastic and diving events, Riefenstahl studiously ignored the outcome of the events, dwelling instead on the aesthetic values of graceful, harmonious movement. Here, sport is translated into choreographed movement to be appreciated in its own terms, without recourse to result or outcome. And it is, perhaps, this aspect of Riefenstahl's film that has allowed both spectators and commentators with relatively little concern for the competitive dimensions of sport to find interest in the aesthetic qualities of sporting performance, whilst those with more conventional sporting tastes have struggled to find satisfaction with this dimension of the movie.

To return to Kauffman's image, it is also noteworthy that the photographer uses a shallow depth of field to blur the spectators in the background, thus ensuring that the viewer's attention is firmly focused on the athletes alone. The spectators, clearly, are of little interest to Kauffman. The fact that the image is captured on grainy, high-speed, black-and-white film also references the familiar conventions of news reportage photography, and thus even the specific medium deployed reinforces a sense of firsthand authenticity to the image. Kauffman has also selected his moment carefully. By focusing on the latter stages of the race, his image foregrounds the extreme physical demands of the event, as Press's physique and physiognomy reveal the full strain and effort demanded of high-level sporting achievement. Even the slight tilt of the camera from left to right serves to accentuate this physical effort, implying metaphorically an uphill struggle and, simultaneously, a sense of destabilized equilibrium and consciousness reflective of a moment of deep concentration, when the athlete might be described as "in the zone." All these compositional devices should not be considered accidental. Rather they are reflective of a skilled practitioner who, in all probability, is fully aware not only of how to capture a moment on celluloid but also how to facilitate specific interpretative possibilities, to construct a narrative, for the image. In this way, the photograph potentially communicates much more than a straightforward account of a race won by a particular athlete. Rather, it elaborates the drama, emphasizing the effort and the significance of attainment expressed within Press's Olympic victory.

There is, however, another important aspect to reading this image that needs to be considered. Whilst Kauffman's craft in provoking potential interpretations may not be doubted, the probability that an audience will concur with this reading may well be. As has long been argued, the personal experiences, interests, and ideological agendas of those viewing cultural products such as photographs will likely generate disparate responses resulting, as Roland Barthes has argued, not so much in the death of the author as the birth of the reader.[8] Whatever Kauffman's intentions in generating this image may have been, whatever narrative he may have sought to communicate, once this image, like any other constructed "text," entered the public domain it opened itself to as many alternative readings as there are readers. And it is the potential for this plurality of interpretative possibilities that also needs to be considered in any engagement with visual materials as evidence.

Here it may be helpful to cite just one example of how this particular image was subsequently deployed to invoke a different reading to the one likely intended by the author. In September 1966, gender verification tests were conducted at an athletics event for the first time at the European Track and Field Championships in Budapest. Later that year the International Olympic Committee announced that similar tests would be introduced at the Mexico City Games to be held two years later. In the United States, *Life* magazine responded to this development by publishing a controversial article titled "Are Girl Athletes Really Girls?"[9] Significantly, Kauffman's photograph of Irina Press, taken six years earlier, was included alongside photographs of her sister, shot-putter Tamara, and Soviet long-jumper Tatyana Shchelkanova, none of whom had appeared at the Budapest event. The accompanying headline, "Three muscular stars from Russia elected to stay at home" was clearly designed to prompt suspicions concerning the gender identity of these athletes.[10] This objective was further reinforced by the accompanying text describing Irina and her sister as "known to their competitors as 'the Press brothers.'"[11] It is, however, the redeployment of Kauffman's image that is of particular significance here. In the article, the photograph was cropped to isolate Press from her fellow competitor. More important, it was also juxtaposed on the page with a photograph of British athlete Mary Rand, represented wearing a national athletics costume while passively standing by a river and holding aloft her four-year-old daughter. Edited, and placed in this new and heavily loaded context, the physical effort etched on Press's face now foregrounds an alternative interpretation, one in which these marks of physical endurance imply an ambiguous gender identity, especially when contrasted with the dominant Western stereotypical notion of a passive, maternal femininity epitomized in the demure image of Rand. Here the potential significance of Kauffman's original photograph is transformed by its redeployment in this new context. As claims that Soviet and eastern European women might not actually be women were voiced, though significantly unproven, visual materials such as Kauffman's photograph of Irina Press in full flight were redeployed in the West as implied "evidence" of wrongdoing and deviancy amongst the ideological enemy in the Cold War.[12]

What this example goes some way toward demonstrating is the malleability of interpretation of visual culture and the significance of context, presentation, and display in shaping the potential reading of such material. Taking into account the interpretative possibilities as outlined in the previous example, it will hopefully be clear that any engagement with the visual culture of sport needs not only to recognize the contingent nature of the imagery generated but also the particular conventions of the medium in which it is produced. From this perspective it will be useful to outline some of the strengths, limitations, and individual qualities of a variety of visual media in order to suggest some of the ways that visual materials can simultaneously prove meaningful and problematic as research resources for sport history.

Sport and Photography

The most extensively deployed medium for the representation of sporting practices in still images is, without doubt, photography. From humble photographs of children playing sports, taken by enthusiastic parents, to the official sporting portraits of "high art" photographers, such as Annie Leibowitz's images of Olympians, photography has, for over a century and a half, generated a vast visual archive. This has not only documented sport practices but also shaped conceptions of how sport might be represented in visual form.[13] Notably, photographers embraced the sport theme from the earliest days of the new medium. Thus in the early 1840s, just a few years after Jacques-Louis-Mandé Daguerre publicly announced and patented his new photographic image-making process, two of the pioneers of photography in Britain, David Octavius Hill and Robert Adamson, produced images representing tennis players and golfers.[14] The technical limitations of the time—in particular the need for exposures of several seconds—clearly restricted the possibility to represent sport in action and thus Hill and Adamson posed their sitters, effectively using sport's associations with leisure as a theme for the portraiture of the great and the good of Edinburgh society. However, within a relatively short period of time technical advances meant not only that sporting action could be captured on film but also that the medium could produce images not previously available to close visual scrutiny. By the 1880s, both Eadweard Muybridge and Étienne-Jules Marey, in their early experiments with high-speed photography, turned to sporting action as a means not only to test the limits of the technology but also to develop knowledge of sporting movement.[15] Whilst Muybridge's famous photographs, providing definitive proof that the feet of a racehorse at full gallop only left the ground when tucked beneath its body, may have had relatively little potential application, Marey's images of athletes in action, captured at the Paris Olympic Games of 1900, provided an invaluable blueprint for training programs.[16] Marey's claims that his work was undertaken simply to enhance greater understanding of the physiology of humans in motion might be qualified by the fact that he specifically pointed his camera at high-performance US athletes, thus constituting one of the early examples of photography being used as a technical aid in bolstering the future performances of less successful athletes, not least Marey's own compatriots. Later, these early experiments would also form the foundation for the development and widespread adoption of the photo-finish at races of all kinds, thus deploying photography as a key aid in making judgments of victory and defeat and diminishing, in some fields at least, antagonistic claims of sporting injustice.

As the possibility for the mass reproduction of photographs was developed towards the end of the nineteenth century, sport photography began to emerge as a new and significant genre in its own right, not least in response to an enthusiastic public's insatiable appetite for all forms of reporting on sporting activities. The expansion of local, national, and international sporting competitions in the twentieth century further bolstered this ever-expanding market, establishing a symbiotic relationship between live sport action and its representation in the mass media. In this context, the specialist sport photographer gradually became an integral element within an ever-expanding sporting press. In Britain, for example, photographs of sport increasingly played an important role in generalist journals such as the *Illustrated London News* as well as more specialist periodicals such as the *Illustrated Sporting and Dramatic News*. In the United States, coverage of sport in popular illustrated journals such as *The Century* and *Scribner's Magazine* led to more specialist publications such as *Sporting Life* and *Spalding's Official Athletic Almanac*, both of which included photographs from early on. Other European-based sporting journals, such as *La vie au grand air* (France) and *Sport im Bild* (Germany), notably specialized in creative photography and innovative design layouts and thus introduced and established some of the fundamental conventions within the presentation of sport photographs still deployed to this day.

Photography representing sport has also been exploited as a significant medium to document, expose, and critique social issues. Images of children playing soccer and cricket on the streets and in the slum areas of postwar London, or basketball in the housing projects of urban America, have been widely deployed to signify, variously, social integration and exclusion whilst images of conventionally approved and transgressive behavior amongst sport fans has fulfilled a similar role. More recently, the advent of affordable digital cameras and smartphones, aligned with the emergence of social media sites has begun to transform the visual landscape, allowing official and unofficial images of sporting events, from local park games to global Olympic festivals, to be circulated around the globe in seconds. The extent to which this more widespread ownership of sport imagery, and legal attempts by major corporations to resist this, might impact upon the ways that sport is conventionally presented in visual form is yet to be determined.

SPORT ON FILM

If the birth of photography in the late 1830s largely coincided with the initial wave of organization and codification of sporting practices in Britain, the invention of cinematography in 1895 paralleled the broader internationalization of sport as epitomized in the staging of the first modern Olympic Games just one year later. However, whilst the movie camera had early been deployed to record such sporting events as the Epsom Derby in 1896, it would be another decade before the Olympics themselves would be captured in moving images.[17] As with the still camera, technological limitations determined many of the early conventions for filming sport. Heavy cameras, mounted on sturdy tripods, coupled with the need for bright light, largely restricted early sport cinematography to outdoor sports that could be captured from a single, static viewpoint. While this allowed for relatively minimal intervention on the part of the filmmaker, it should not be overlooked, of course, that where the camera was set up, what it chose to focus upon, or indeed what to overlook, as well as subsequent editing processes, were still key factors in shaping the presentation of sport to audiences beyond the stadium. Moreover, one of the most striking innovations here was the compilation of sporting highlights—scoring of goals, tries, touchdowns, home runs, knock-outs, match points, boundaries, and wickets—all compressed into a few seconds of newsreel. Displayed in the warm, dry atmosphere of a cinema with accompanying, and explanatory, commentary, this new visual presentation doubtless impacted upon the perception of sport for wider audiences. For those who had not previously attended such events, sport perhaps now seemed to promise a level of constant excitement that attendance at a live event was less likely to deliver, while for those preferring the more protracted outdoor experience, close-up views and replays offered a new level of visual engagement previously denied them.

The sport film, and more specifically the sport documentary, has raised particular problems for sport historians. Claims of a notional neutrality implicit within the conventional mode of newsreel or documentary presentation need to be tempered by a critical engagement with the editing in both spatial (where the camera points) and temporal (what periods of a competition are included and excluded from the final presentation) terms, thus recognizing, and making subject to analytical and interpretative engagement, the very particularized notion of how sport can be viewed and assessed from positions of both production and consumption. The violent tackle, the deliberate flouting of rules for personal or team gain, and disputes with officialdom were all well-documented aspects of emerging professional sport, and the extent to which live spectators celebrated or condemned such actions is far from clear-cut. However, the relative absence of the representation of such incidents in popular newsreel presentations of sport suggests how ownership of these visual reconstructions also conferred the power to mediate the potential interpretation of a secondary audience. Thus, far from offering straightforward documentary accounts of specific sporting events, newsreels, and sport documentaries, from their very earliest days, presented visual accounts of sport subjectively, seeking to predetermine how audiences might consume the product on offer, even if this uniform reception could never effectively be guaranteed.

Reifenstahl's aforementioned cinematic record of the 1936 Berlin Olympic Games, *Olympia*, offers something of a case in point. This production has inevitably been seen as a landmark event not only for the sport film but also for the study of visual culture within sport history. Yet, whilst its direct and problematic associations with the German National Socialist regime have inevitably shaped the film's political, ideological, and aesthetic reception, leading some to dismiss the film out-of-hand, Riefenstahl's innovative and creative cinematic presentation of sporting theater has also had its supporters and has left its influential mark on sport cinematography in the second half of the twentieth century. Even those later filmic interventions that sought to challenge the ideology underpinning Riefenstahl's film, such as Kon Ichikawa's official documentary of the 1964 Games, *Tokyo Olympiad*, have nonetheless relied upon, and replicated, much of the visual power of the earlier production.[18] Thus where Ichikawa's film effectively replaced Riefenstahl's sporting *übermensch* with the more human, frail, and fallible image of the sportsman and woman, it did so by adopting many of the same visual conventions and editing strategies that made, and continue to make, *Olympia* such a powerful and compelling example of sporting visual culture.

All this might best serve as a reminder that while visual interventions such as the sport documentary are, to a significant extent, shaped and underpinned by the ideological contexts of their production, the particular representational techniques and conventions originally deployed can signify ways that reflect the particular conditions not only of production but also of spectatorship and reception.

More recent interventions into the sport documentary genre have also attracted the attention of sport historians. Most notable, and perhaps controversial, amongst these is Ken Burns's Emmy-award winning, 1994 series *Baseball*. For the series, Burns's production team gathered a wide range of visual material, enhancing the conventionally deployed official film footage and newspaper photographs, with examples of painting, sculpture, and popular or mass culture. Combined with extensive voice-overs presenting recollection and reminiscence, Burns's film thus combined traditional and oral history with examples of what might be construed to be their equivalents in visual terms. It was this combination of narrative with visual material, and not least the artistic license Burns deployed here, that attracted most criticism from his detractors. For example, right-handed Dennis Eckersley is presented as left-handed as a consequence of a reversed negative, whilst several examples of photographs representing either individuals or locations, are used as a backdrop to commentary that is not directly related.[19] Thus, for example, Burns' inclusion of a photograph showing Dodger's president Branch Rickey signing African American baseball star Jackie Robinson has been criticized because the actual signing ceremony represented visually was not the precise one being discussed in the voice-over.[20] The factual basis of such criticism is incontestable. However, the corollary of such criticism is that if the use of a loosely related image presents an untruth, the use of the "correct" photograph would simply and straightforwardly convey the truth. Yet this, of course, is predicated on the assumption that images such as photographs are unproblematic conveyors of historical actuality. Thus whilst Burns' willingness to use imagery creatively to convey an idea certainly ought to be recognized as such, and any claims to the contrary disputed, the notion that this "error" might be corrected by use of a more "authentic" image might be construed as an oversimplistic claim.[21]

This concern that visual representation should somehow carry the burden of authenticity is perhaps held to be most problematic in the dramatic sport film. The litany of factual errors in such cinematic classics as Hugh Hudson's *Chariots of Fire* (1981), Norman Jewison's *The Hurricane* (1999), and Jerry Bruckheimer's *Remember the Titans* (2000) have frequently been the major concerns of sport historians. Yet perhaps all this misses the fundamental point not only that such products of visual culture are essentially produced and consumed as constructed narratives but also that all histories are inevitably constructed and mediate particular ideological and political points of view. Thus both narrative and visual presentations of the past might best be seen as provisional and contested terrain. Perhaps the fault here lies less in the self-evident manipulation of visual material to convey a narrative idea than in an excessive belief in the fundamental veracity of the image. In this context it might be more beneficial to embrace filmic sport dramas as a significant form of intervention within the history of sport, foregrounding and accepting their constructed nature, rather than simply challenging their notional veracity.

THE ART OF SPORT: FROM CANVAS AND PAPER TO BRONZE

Unlike film and photography, representations of sport in the so-called fine arts have attracted considerably less attention from within sport history. Yet sport has frequently provided a key subject matter for artists in a variety of media. Major examples of this would include the horse-racing sketches and paintings of George Stubbs and Edgar Degas; the boxing images of Thomas Eakins and George Bellows; and the rowing works of Eakins, Gustave Caillebotte, and Alfred Sisley.[22] Sport was also a specialist subject matter for some groups of artists, such as the printmakers associated with the Grosvenor School of Modern Art, established in London in 1929.[23] Yet, as Allen Guttmann has recently pointed out, sport historians and art historians "tend to shun intellectual interaction" and "aesthetes and athletes are often ill at ease with each other's company."[24] Guttmann rightly describes this as problematic and sets out to effect a change in this "sorry state of affairs."[25] It is clear, however, that such interdisciplinary collaborations are already taking place and bearing fruit, suggesting a positive way forward.[26] Fear of art amongst sport historians has too often been accompanied by fear of sport amongst art historians. Yet it is the shared expertise of those trained in each field that will enhance a broader understanding of, and engagement with, the visual materials of sport.

The past quarter-century has witnessed a dramatic increase in the number of monuments erected to honor sportsmen and women throughout the world. The commissioning processes, stylistic conventions adopted, and siting strategies deployed in both the production and consumption of these artifacts also provides an opportunity for further research engaging with the visual turn in sport history. Famous examples, such as Paul DiPasquale's statue of African American tennis star Arthur Ashe, controversially erected on Monument Avenue in Richmond, Virginia, in 1996 and the Monument to Tommie Smith and John Carlos, designed by Ricardo Gouveia (Rigo 23) and unveiled at San José State University in 2005, have begun to attract critical attention amongst sport historians.[27] Here, however, there is ample scope for more detailed visual engagement with such works and an opportunity to develop further projects that seek to analyze not only the extent and stylistic conventions of these works but also their function for contemporary society. Here, for example, the concept of pilgrimage and the physical interaction established between these cultural products and their audiences is worthy of further consideration. Moreover, this can extend beyond the predictable swathing of statues in the hats, scarves, and other paraphernalia of fandom, though this is of interest in its own right. For example in 1998, shortly before Newcastle United football club was due to appear in the FA Cup final, local supporters produced a giant team shirt adorned with a number nine and the name of local soccer hero, Alan Shearer. By skillful use of sling shots and fishing wire, this was then mounted onto Antony Gormley's colossal and controversial statue, *The Angel of the North,* recently unveiled in Gateshead. This action, effectively transforming a local monument not previously associated with sport into a sport statue, if only for a brief period, marked a major contribution in turning the tide of local support for the monument. Photographs and film footage recording this transgressive act for posterity might also be read as a kind of surrogate monument in its own right, preserving this modification in visual form, not least through display on the Internet.[28]

Sport and Mass Culture

The popularity and commercial potential of sport has also led to the generation of a vast array of sporting paraphernalia, representing events, teams, and individuals. These range from posters and stamps to souvenirs and collectibles such as cigarette cards and commemorative coins. The sheer scope and ephemeral nature of such material has meant that much of this has been overlooked as potential research material, yet such artifacts can reveal a great deal about how sport was popularly presented, perceived, and economically consumed at different historical moments.[29] To offer just one example, the shift of spectator costumes witnessed on the terraces of British soccer stadia—from the scarves, bobble hats, and rosettes of the mid- to late twentieth century, to the replica shirt adorned with the name of a specific player, from the 1980s to the present day—bespeaks a significant alteration in fan identity. While potentially reflecting a growing level of disposable income on behalf of sport spectators, this shift also foregrounds more commercial interests in controlling the image and visual identity of a team, as business enterprise, as well as assuring the wider dissemination of sponsors' names and logos. Also of significance here is the symbiotic relationship between the players, the fans watching, the stadium environment in which all are situated, and the overall visual spectacle generated. In this broad context, studies into the shifting styles and fashions of sporting costumes, for both players and spectators, can provide valuable insights into the changing meanings and values of sport, whilst analyses of the developing visual and technical vocabularies deployed in the design and social function of stadia and other spaces for sport provide rich opportunities for future historical research.[30]

The Rise of the Sport Museum

If sport historians are to mine this rich vein of visual material as a research resource to exploit fully the visual turn in sport history, they must establish close relationships with the organizations and institutions that conventionally collect, classify, and make available for scrutiny such artifacts. Whilst traditional libraries and archives remain invaluable sites for research, the unprecedented expansion of specialist museums dedicated to sport in the past few decades provides an ideal opportunity for sport historians to develop further research into the visual in sport. In Great Britain, the MCC Cricket Museum claims to be the oldest sport museum in the world, having begun gathering objects and artwork related to the sport as early as 1864.[31] It did not, however, officially open its doors to the public until 1953. The Norwegian Holmenkollen Ski Museum, founded in 1923, also reflects early interests in the display of the visual and material culture of sport, while Baron Pierre de Coubertin, founder of the modern Olympic Games, displayed the International Olympic Committee's collection of artwork, trophies, medals, diplomas, and other sporting paraphernalia at the Villa Mon Repos in Lausanne, opened to the public on Sunday afternoons since 1924. In the United States, too, the National Baseball Hall of Fame and Museum in Cooperstown, New York, has been accepting visitors since the late 1930s. It has mostly been since the 1990s, however, that significant institutions such as the Olympic and Sports Museum and Archive in Lausanne, the Joan Antoni Samaranch Olympic Museum in Barcelona, the Musée National du Sport in Nice, the National Sports Museum in Melbourne, the World Rugby Museum at Twickenham, and the National Football Museum in Manchester have been established and now offer an ideal opportunity to transform the relationship between sport historians, the cultural heritage sector, and the wider public.[32] As custodians of a diverse and ever-expanding range of cultural artifacts, these institutions provide opportunities for sport historians to engage directly with the visual and material culture of sport. The development of collaborative projects between academic institutions and the museum sector may also facilitate a way to link sport history more directly to a wider public, thus enabling the further growth of the sports heritage industry and drawing greater attention to the importance of sport's global legacy for the modern age. And, who knows, half a century from now images showing current sport stars promoting fizzy drinks, fast food or, indeed, any other product may look as incongruous to future eyes as the image of Matthews smoking Craven "A"s does to ours. What matters, fundamentally, is that such images are preserved as vital historical traces to provide insights into current attitudes toward sport and its visual presentation to future generations.

NOTES

1. *Picturegoer*, December 13, 1952, p. 23.
2. Judith Swaddling, *The Ancient Olympic Games* (London: British Museum Publications, 1980), 93.
3. Douglas Booth, *The Field: Truth and Fiction in Sport History* (London: Routledge, 2005), 103; italics added.
4. Murray G. Phillips, ed., *Deconstructing Sport History: A Postmodern Analysis* (New York: State University of New York Press, 2006), 12.
5. W. J. T. Mitchell, *Picture Theory* (Chicago: University of Chicago Press, 1994); Peter Burke, *Eyewitnessing: The Use of Images as Historical Evidence* (Ithaca, NY: Cornell University Press, 2001); and Gillian Rose, *Visual Methodologies: An Introduction to Researching with Visual Materials* (London: SAGE, 2007).
6. Rose, *Visual Methodologies*, 16–17.
7. Marshall McLuhan, *Understanding Media: The Extensions of Man* (London: Routledge and Kegan Paul, 1964).
8. Roland Barthes, "The Death of the Author," in *Image-Music-Text* (London: Fontana, 1977), 142–148.
9. "Are Girl Athletes Really Girls?" *Life Magazine*, October 7, 1966, pp. 63–63.
10. "Are Girl Athletes Really Girls?" p. 66.
11. "Are Girl Athletes Really Girls?" p. 66.
12. See also Stefan Wiederkehr, "'. . . If Jarmila Kratochvilova Is the Future of Women's Sport, I'm Not Sure I'm Ready for It': Media, Gender and the Cold War," in *Euphoria and Exhaustion: Modern Sport in Soviet Culture and Society*, ed. Nikolaus Katzer, Sandra Budy, Alexandra Köhring, and Manfred Zeller (Frankfurt: Campus, 2011), 315–335.
13. Annie Leibowitz, *Olympic Portraits* (Boston: Bullfinch Press, 1996).
14. Sara Stevenson, *Facing the Light: The Photography of Hill and Adamson* (Edinburgh, UK: Scottish National Portrait Gallery, 2002), 88. Hill and Adamson's photograph also inspired Charles Lees' 1847 painting *The Golfers*. Peter N. Lewis and Angela D. Howe, *The Golfers: The Story Behind the Painting* (Edinburgh, UK: National Galleries of Scotland, 2004), 27–28.
15. Marta Braun, *Picturing Time: The Work of Étienne-Jules Marey* (Chicago: University of Chicago Press, 1992), 67.

16. *Concours internationaux d'exercices physiques et de sports* (Official Report of the Olympic Games of Paris, 1900) (Paris: Imprimerie Nationale, 1901), 384–404.

17. "The Derby," www.britishpathe.com/video/the-derby-1/query/Epsom.

18. Ian McDonald, "Critiquing the Olympic Documentary: Kon Ichikawa's *Tokyo Olympiad*," in *Sport in Films*, ed. Emma Poulton and Martin Roderick (London: Routledge, 2008), 182–194.

19. Larry Gerlach, "The Final Three Innings," *Journal of Sport History* 23.1 (1996): 73.

20. Jules Tygiel, "Ken Burns Meets Jackie Robinson," *Journal of Sport History* 23.1 (1996): 70.

21. For a further analysis of the debates surrounding Ken Burns' *Baseball* (Hollywood: PBS Home Video, 2004 [DVD]), see Murray G. Phillips, Mark E. O'Neil, and Gary Osmond, "Broadening Horizons in Sport History: Films, Photographs and Monuments," *Journal of Sport History* 34.2 (2007), 274–276.

22. See, for example, Donna Landry, *Noble Brutes: How Eastern Horses Transformed English Culture* (Baltimore, MD: John Hopkins University Press, 2008), 44–48, 146–163; Jean Sutherland Boggs, *Degas at the Races* (Washington, DC: National Gallery of Art, 1998); Helen A. Cooper, *Thomas Eakins: The Rowing Pictures* (New Haven, CT: Yale University Press, 1996); Kasia Boddy, *Boxing: A Cultural History* (London: Reaktion Books, 2008).

23. Mike O'Mahony, "Imaging Sport at the Grosvenor School of Modern Art (1929–37)," in *The Visual in Sport*, ed. Mike Huggins and Mike O'Mahony (London: Routledge, 2012), 19–34.

24. Allen Guttmann, *Sports and American Art from Benjamin West to Andy Warhol* (Amherst: University of Massachusetts Press, 2011), 3.

25. Guttmann, *Sports and American Art*, 3.

26. See, for example, Huggins and O'Mahony, eds., *The Visual in Sport*, a collaborative venture that explicitly sought to bring together sport and art historians.

27. For an analysis of the Arthur Ashe monument, see Jaime Schultz, "Contesting the Master Narrative: The Arthur Ashe Statue and Monument Avenue in Richmond, Virginia," in *The Visual in Sport*, 149–165. For the monument to Tommie Smith and John Carlos, see Maureen Smith, "Mapping America's Sporting Landscape: A Case Study of Three Statues," in *The Visual in Sport*, 173–174; Gary Osmond, "Photographs, Materiality and Sport History: Peter Norman and the 1968 Mexico City Black Power Salute," *Journal of Sport History* 37.1 (2010): 132–133; Mike O'Mahony, *Olympic Visions: Images of the Games through History* (London: Reaktion Books, 2012), 114–118.

28. This act acquired local cult status and footage of the event has been preserved online, www.youtube.com/watch?v=Mns1MPw6SBs.

29. For Olympic posters, see Margaret Timmers, *A Century of Olympic Posters* (London: V&A Publishing, 2008), and O'Mahony, *Olympic Visions*, 123–140. For stamps, see Gary Osmond and Murray G. Phillips, "Enveloping the Past: Sport Stamps, Visuality and Museums," in *The Visual in Sport*, 52–87.

30. Recent studies into the architecture, sociology, and gender significance of sport spaces include Patricia Vertinsky and Sherry McKay, *Disciplining Bodies in the Gymnasium: Memory, Monument, Modernism* (London: Routledge, 2004), and Mark Dyreson, ed., *The Rise of Stadiums in the Modern United States: Cathedrals of Sport* (London: Routledge, 2009).

31. *Lord's: The Guide* (London: Scala, 2009), 17.

32. This represents only a handful of the sport museums around the world. These include museums dedicated to baseball, bowling, boxing, cricket, golf, hockey, horse racing, motor racing, rowing, rugby, skiing, soccer, surfing, tennis, and wrestling.

BIBLIOGRAPHY

Booth, Douglas. *The Field: Truth and Fiction in Sport History*. London: Routledge, 2005.

Burke, Peter. *Eyewitnessing: The Use of Images as Historical Evidence*. Ithaca, NY: Cornell University Press, 2001.

Huggins, Mike, and Mike O'Mahony, eds. *The Visual in Sport*. London: Routledge, 2012.

Mitchell, W. J. T. *Picture Theory*. Chicago: University of Chicago Press, 1994.

O'Mahony, Mike. *Olympic Visions: Images of the Games through History*. London: Reaktion Books, 2012.

Phillips, Murray G., ed. *Deconstructing Sport History: A Postmodern Analysis*. New York: State University of New York Press, 2006.

Phillips, Murray G., Mark E. O'Neil, and Gary Osmond. "Broadening Horizons in Sport History: Films, Photographs and Monuments." *Journal of Sport History* 34.2 (2007): 271–293.

Poulton, Emma, and Martin Roderick, eds., *Sport in Films*. London: Routledge, 2008.

Rose, Gillian. *Visual Methodologies: An Introduction to Researching with Visual Materials*. London: SAGE, 2007.

Timmers, Margaret. *A Century of Olympic Posters*. London: V&A Publishing, 2008.

CHAPTER 34

···

SPORTS AND SEXUALITY

···

ERIK N. JENSEN

SOCIETIES throughout history have seen athletic practices as means of expressing, taming, celebrating, or rechanneling sexual expression. This should not surprise, considering that both sports and sex, including abstinence from it, involve the physical body in narratives of performance and release. The sports historian Allen Guttmann has pointed to the universal erotic element in sports for both athletes and spectators, across time and space, and he has suggested physiological reasons for this. Humans register both sexuality and aggressiveness, heightened during athletic competition, in proximate parts of the brain. Pheromones in perspiration, after a hard workout or race, act as mild aphrodisiacs. There is also, moreover, the fact that, as Guttmann writes, "some sports involve the body in muscular exertions similar to those of sexual intercourse."[1] Despite this close and perhaps even inherent connection between sports and sexuality, however, historians have only begun since the 1990s to pay much attention to it and how it has evolved over time. This chapter offers an overview of that connection, concentrating on the European and North American experiences from classical antiquity to the present day.[2]

Ancient Greeks famously celebrated the harmoniously proportioned athletic body, and they viewed gymnasia as places to admire and desire such bodies as well as to develop them. Men trained and competed in the nude—a feature unique to Greece in the ancient world—in order to appreciate and glorify their physical development. Indeed, the vision of nude, toned athletes had inspired Greek artists and poets since at least the time of Theognis of Megara, whose rapturous odes in the sixth century BCE expressed the pleasure of spending a day at the gymnasium in the company of a naked boy.

Theognis's ode also speaks to a second important feature of Greek sports: homosexuality—or, perhaps more accurately, pederasty—often accompanied athletic training. In his foundational 1978 text on Greek homosexuality, K. J. Dover described the gymnasium in ancient Greece as a place that "provided opportunities for looking at naked boys, bringing oneself discreetly to a boy's notice in the hope of eventually speaking to him . . . and even touching a boy in a suggestive way, as if by accident, while wrestling with him."[3] Such initial contact between an older and a younger athlete often led to a relationship, in which the older man played the active role, both sexually and pedagogically. In addition to providing sexual pleasure, these relationships formed an important part of the overall education of Greek youth, with the older man engaged in coaching, mentoring, and cultivating his younger charge for adulthood, at which point the latter might take a young lover of his own at the gymnasium.

This linkage of sports and same-sex eroticism in the Greek world seems to have emerged first in Crete and Sparta during the seventh century BCE, perhaps, as the classicist Thomas Scanlon argues, to counteract the significant population expansion of the previous century by facilitating nonprocreative sexual outlets. Athletic nudity and gymnasium-centered pederasty then spread to other city-states, becoming a central component of youth formation (*paideia*) throughout the Greek world by 600 BCE. Practices continued to evolve over time, however, and notable differences emerged between city-states. Not all of them accepted or encouraged pederasty within the gymnasia at all times, and some officials attempted to regulate or curtail the practice. Solon, the chief magistrate (*archon*) in Athens in the late sixth century BCE, for example, introduced two pieces of legislation that had the apparent intent of restricting homosexual practices in the gymnasium. One measure barred slaves from gymnasia in order to prevent them from taking freeborn men as lovers and thus upsetting the social hierarchy, and the second one regulated opening and closing hours for gymnasia to ensure adequate supervision, a move that may, as Scanlon suggests, "also show concern over the possibility of the trainer's sexual harassment of his young charges."[4]

The sexual practices of individual athletes obviously varied as well. Not every athlete took a male lover, and, even when he did, the lover may have been just one of several passive partners in the athlete's life, along with a wife and perhaps even a courtesan. Regardless of the number or the sex of the partners, though, Greeks placed a premium on sexual moderation. Self-control remained the ideal, but this did not necessarily mean outright abstinence. Greeks may well have praised athletic chastity in certain contexts, but they did not require it, even during preparation for important athletic competitions. Some athletes did visibly seek to contain their sexual impulses through the practice of infibulation, referred to as "leashing the dog" (*kynodesme*), in which one would draw the foreskin up, tie it closed, and secure it to one side. Rather than viewing this as a conspicuous sign of chastity, however, Greek spectators may have seen infibulation as an admission of weakness, a sign that the athlete did not have *enough* willpower to control his urges without mechanical intervention. Athletic abstinence attracted increasing admiration from philosophers in the late fifth century BCE, and Plato, for one, praised the Olympic victor Ikkos of Tarentum as an exemplary athlete who "never touched a woman, or a boy either, in the entire course of his training."[5] Still, the lavishness of Plato's praise for Ikkos suggests that chastity was the exception in the Greek world, rather than the rule.

Unmarried women participated in athletic contests too, and their practices similarly expressed an erotic sensibility. Spartan women and girls, in particular, engaged extensively in sports, a difference from other Greek city-states that stemmed from the greater public role that Sparta accorded to its women in general and from that city-state's particularly determined focus on cultivating the body as an aspect of military preparation.

Physical training produced healthy mothers, the Spartans reasoned, and those mothers, in turn, would bear healthy future soldiers. Women's sports may have become more sexually suggestive during the fifth century BCE, as officials took anxious notice of a declining population. In an effort to encourage heterosexual coupling, girls competed in various athletic contests almost entirely in the nude and in front of audiences of single young men. Unmarried women in Olympia similarly tempted young men via a series of running races, and the rhetorician Athenaios referred to an even more explicitly seductive, if not outright sexual, athletic practice on the island of Chios, where adolescents of both sexes wrestled with one another.[6]

Once married, however, women in the Greek world generally stopped participating in sports, in stark contrast to the men. Here, too, though, Sparta offers an interesting exception. Beginning in the late seventh century BCE, married women in that city-state started mentoring younger girls in a manner that, like that of the boys, combined athletic training in a same-sex environment with homoerotic relations. This culture of female pederasty may not have been as formalized as it was for males, but it adopted more or less the same arrangement. It perhaps arose in Sparta because of that society's expectation that adult men spend most of their time in the company of their male peers. Women lived in an almost entirely separate world, an environment that may have fostered the formation of homosexual relationships between adult women and adolescent girls in the context of the latter's overall physical and spiritual cultivation. In contrast to male pederasty, which arose in a couple of city-states and then spread throughout the Greek world, there is no indication that the practice of female pederasty existed beyond Sparta.

Whereas athletic nudity for men and, more rarely, women enjoyed a roughly 800-year tradition in Greece, the Romans deliberately clothed their athletes, in part to reduce temptation and in part simply to distinguish themselves from the Greeks. The Romans also placed less stock in gymnasium training and far more in athletic practices with direct military application, such as sword fighting and chariot racing, which they often packaged as entertainment for a mass public. The intersection of sports and sexuality in the Roman world, therefore, lay not in the intimate same-sex spaces of the gymnasia but instead in the very public mixed-sex spaces of the stadiums. Such a mingling of men and women—opportunities for which scarcely existed in the Greek world—afforded Romans an ideal setting for flirtations, trysts, and engagements. The dictator Sulla, for example, met his last wife, Valeria, after exchanging flirtatious glances during a chariot race around the year 82 BCE.

Sulla and Valeria may well have responded to the heightened erotic charge that many Romans experienced while watching the muscular forms and passionate exertions of the competing athletes. Roman officials, alert to the possibility of illicit liaisons, made some attempts to lower the sexual temperature. Already at the turn of the first century CE, Emperor Augustus ordered the segregation of male and female spectators at gladiatorial contests. His efforts apparently met with little success, though, since Ovid continued to describe sporting events in those same years as the perfect place for women and men to meet one another. Apart from occasional efforts to impose moral and social order, however, most Romans seem to have accepted, if not embraced, the sexually charged atmosphere of sporting contests. Compared to the Greeks, moreover, Romans expressed little regard for the quality of self-control. Pliny the Elder even advised in 77 CE that "athletes when sluggish are revitalized by love-making."[7] The Roman satirist Juvenal, meanwhile, described a senator's wife in the first century CE who fell so madly in love with a gladiator that she ran off with him. Although this man had countless battle scars from years of competing, and no one would have described him as beautiful, Juvenal nevertheless emphasized that he was extremely sexy. He was a gladiator, after all.

A few texts indicate that Roman men may have found sportswomen similarly attractive, even though Roman society allowed women far fewer opportunities for athletic self-development. Women did compete in footraces at several Roman festivals, which would have afforded occasions for men and women alike to admire female athletes in motion, and a very small number of women also competed in gladiatorial competitions, which may have inspired a similar devotion in their fans as the male gladiators inspired in theirs. Sources offer scant insight into these contests, however. Writing in the last decades of the first century BCE, the poet Propertius, in fact, had to travel back in his own imagination to earlier Sparta in order to indulge his lyrical fantasies of women who "put boxing gloves on hands so soft and fair, and whirl the heavy discus through the air."[8] In a similar vein, Ovid, in seeking to persuade his own lover to reveal more of her body, turned to a fleet-footed female athlete of Greek mythology and wrote lovingly of Atalanta's beautiful legs, those swift limbs that Milanion, her successful suitor, "wanted to raise up in his hands."[9]

Such exuberant celebrations of athletic desirability were in decline by the fourth century CE. In the wake of Christianization, European elites reassessed their relationship with the human body. They seemed less openly enamored of physically trained bodies and less accepting of sexual expression, in general, than the ancient Greeks and Romans. The written records of Church-based elites, upon which historians of late antiquity and the medieval period necessarily rely, however, may well not have reflected how people behaved in their daily lives, especially during festivals of social inversion, when such events as footraces between townswomen and prostitutes might be the order of the day. Medieval tournaments, moreover, institutionalized flirtation, with male jousters seeking to impress, and often to win, their female spectators. Apart from an altered class structure, these jousters differed from their athletic predecessors in the Roman coliseum only in their choice of the lance to replace the sword as their phallic weapon of choice. The phallic lance met its yonic counterpart in the opposing knight's shield, which led the twelfth-century writer Étienne de Fougères to employ a jousting metaphor to describe female homosexual relations as well, which he presented as two shields bumping against one another.[10] Horsemanship, swordplay, and other athletic pursuits almost certainly played a role in courtship rituals in early modern Europe as well, but the scholarship on athletic practices during this period still remains thin. Turning to artistic representations at the time, although Michelangelo was lavishing attention on muscular physiques in the sixteenth century, his fellow artists seemed far less interested in celebrating athletic builds, which may offer some barometer of attitudes during the Renaissance.

If European societies had generally neglected physical culture after the fall of the Roman Empire, they began making up for lost time in the nineteenth century. In contrast to the practices of classical antiquity, however, nineteenth-century sports initially promoted a moral asceticism that understood exercise as a redirection of sexual energy, rather than an expression of it. This was certainly true of the form of collective gymnastics known as *Turnen*, which emerged in the context of budding German nationalism during the Napoleonic Wars. "Sexual intercourse with women," writes historian Petr Roubal, with regard to the movement's somatic philosophy, was "regarded as a moral weakness and a danger to the gymnast's body."[11] A similar attitude prevailed a short time later in Victorian Britain, where pedagogues such as Edward Thring promoted the sport of soccer as a beneficial release of pent-up energy that might otherwise find its outlet in sexual intercourse or masturbation. Soccer, in particular, promised an effective means of combating that latter vice because the game so thoroughly redirected the player's attention from his hands to his feet.

This ascetic approach to sports, which viewed piety and physical fitness in a mutually constitutive relationship, took the name "muscular Christianity" in the late 1850s. It found early promoters in the United States, too, such as the Unitarian minister and abolitionist Thomas Wentworth Higginson, but muscular Christianity only gained widespread support in the United States after the Civil War. By the 1860s, institutions across Europe and North America, such as the Young Men's Christian Association, were promoting sports as a means of stiffening men's moral fiber. Professional sports, still in their infancy, also helped to set the tone. American baseball pioneer A. G. Spalding, for example, hired detectives to make sure that his Chicago Cubs did not violate the team's prohibitions on gambling, womanizing, and onanism. The rival Brooklyn Bridegrooms, meanwhile, made celibacy into the *leitmotif* of their 1889 season, ascribing their success in capturing that year's pennant to the strict policy of sexual abstinence, with even the newlywed players reportedly avoiding their wives until after the play-offs. Although proponents of muscular Christianity focused primarily on men, a few advocated it for women as well, including Christine Herrick, who argued in 1902 that athletics would teach women to control their urges, just as it had taught the men.[12] Most physical education experts at the time countered, however, that sports, because they directed attention onto the physical body, would have exactly the opposite effect on female passions than that which the moralists had intended.

Regardless, muscular Christianity had already started to lose ground by the early twentieth century due to the voyeurism and exhibitionism that had reemerged in certain sports—especially bodybuilding and boxing—and to the increasing media coverage of athletes' love lives, which many athletes themselves conducted in very public ways. Strongmen drew packed crowds of swooning female and male fans by the turn of the century for their displays of skill, physical strength, and rippling biceps. Often appearing in nothing but a posing strap, these men capitalized on the public demand for images of muscled bodies by marketing postcards and photographs of themselves, as well as by appearing in physique and naturalist magazines in Europe and North America. Even the sport of baseball, whose athletes dressed positively monkishly in comparison, produced its share of heartthrobs at the time. Win Mercer, a turn-of-the-century pitcher, drew so many adoring female fans when he arrived in Washington to play for the Senators at age nineteen that the owners began to feature him on Tuesdays and Fridays, which they designated as Ladies' Days. Mercer enjoyed such popularity that an 1897 Ladies' Day game ended in a riot after the umpire ejected Mercer, which then prompted women to storm the field in protest.

By the eve of the First World War, elite society was starting to talk about what body-builders, sideshow barkers, and sports promoters had already figured out a decade or two earlier: sports were sexy. Freud first described the erotic element in sports in 1910, in the second edition of his *Three Essays on Sexuality*, when he noted that athletic activity represented a physical and sensual pleasure in its own right. Just two years later, Arthur Mallwitz dedicated his closing address at the first Congress for the Scientific Study of Sports and Physical Exercise in the German town of Oberhof to the subject of "Sports and Sexuality." The following year, in 1913, Pierre de Coubertin, founder of the modern Olympic Games, published an essay titled "On Athletic Voluptuousness," in which he praised the sexual enjoyment of sports and blamed early Christianity for having suppressed "the fleshly satisfaction which sport represented."[13] In the context of greater social mobility, Christianity's declining moral influence, increasing female independence, and the boom in visual media, sports and sex once again intertwined in the public imagination.

This intertwining became particularly visible in the heated discourse that surrounded the prospect of black male athletes having sex with white women, especially in the United States. The strengthening of American antimiscegenation laws in the 1890s coincided with tightened restrictions on black athletes competing in white sports, a timing that sociologist Erica Childs sees as anything but coincidental. It stemmed, she argues, at least in part from "whites' collective fear of black sexuality and the occurrence of inter-racial sex."[14] That collective fear was fueled in the first two decades of the twentieth century by the American boxer Jack Johnson, the first black heavyweight champion and the central figure in the first sex scandal in modern sports. Before Johnson had even won his title, the press had already started to focus on his relationships with white women, beginning with Alma Adelaide Toy, whom he had met in Australia in 1908 while preparing for the bout that would secure him the heavyweight crown in the first place. Four years and several relationships later, in a widely publicized 1912 trial, Johnson became the first man to be convicted of violating the Mann Act, a 1910 US law intended to combat organized prostitution but that was used in its debut application to harass a black boxer whose very public consorting with white women offended the federal authorities' sense of sexual propriety and racial hierarchy. With his global fame, boxer's body, and athletic charisma, the figure of Jack Johnson magnified not only white America's anxiety about interracial relationships but also white men's insecurities about themselves.

The scandalizing headlines and legal proceedings that surrounded Johnson's career shaped the way in which black athletes conducted themselves for decades to come, especially Joe Louis, who followed in Johnson's footsteps to become the second black heavyweight champion in 1937. Louis's managers worked hard to distance him from

Johnson's flashy persona and visible relationships with white women, encouraging Louis, at the very least, to maintain discretion, lest he alienate the white public. Over the course of the 1950s and 1960s, American tolerance of interracial relationships gradually increased, a trend that coincided with the integration of professional and university athletic teams, revealing once again the intersection between race and sexuality within the realm of sports. Concern over black athletes dating white women has not disappeared in the United States entirely, however, as a number of recent studies have pointed out. Meanwhile, scholars have highlighted the intersection of sports and interracial/interethnic dating in other national and cultural contexts as well. Rachael Miyung Joo, for example, has shown how the South Korean media's increasing sexualization of Korean male athletes has sought to promote intraethnic sexual reproduction in an era of official concern about the endangered status of the "pure" Korean family.

If the public attacks on Johnson's lifestyle compelled subsequent black athletes to be more circumspect in their behavior and self-presentation, that very same public attention to his lifestyle ironically empowered many white boxers to cultivate sexualized images for themselves. Prizefighters in 1920s Germany, for instance, promoted the desirability of their bodies just as aggressively as they promoted their fighting skills, an appearance-conscious marketing that Johnson himself had helped to pioneer. Indeed, the figure of the boxer had emerged as a sex symbol by the interwar years, something that American heavyweight Jack Dempsey acknowledged in a 1921 interview when he said, "It's no longer enough to have speed and a good right arm to be the favorite. You have to be good-looking, too, now that ladies go to the fights."[15]

Other sports experienced a sexual awakening in the 1920s too, especially tennis, which rapidly developed the reputation for stoking the libidinal impulses of its male and female players alike. It was no accident that the playwright Vicki Baum chose to make the dapper casanova in her 1930 stage comedy *Pariser Platz 13* both a clothing model and a tennis player. Female athletes, meanwhile, competing in a wide array of sports for the first time in the 1920s, and in a wide array of revealing outfits, both scandalized and titillated the interwar public. A number of officials continued nevertheless to insist upon sports as a useful distraction *from* sexual temptation, especially in youth sports. Vladimir Lenin, for instance, encouraged swimming and gymnastics as a means of diverting Communist youth from sexual experimentation.[16] In the bleachers, locker rooms, and magazines of interwar Europe and North America, however, athletes' sexual attractions and attractiveness drew increasing amounts of attention. Leni Riefenstahl's widely acclaimed documentary of the 1936 Olympic Games, *Olympia*, for instance, eroticized the competing sportsmen and women every bit as much as it chronicled their athletic achievements.

If this increasingly open sexual attitude did not extend equally to all areas of athletic participation, especially to youth sports, it also did not extend equally to all aspects of sexuality. Sexual relationships across socially constructed racial divides, as we have already seen, remained taboo throughout much of the twentieth century, and sports emerged as a key site of both concern and enforcement. Same-sex sexual attraction, which became a subject of scientific attention and public scandal in Europe and North

America at around the same time as organized sports began its rapid expansion in the last decades of the nineteenth century, remained at least as taboo within the world of sports throughout almost the entirety of the twentieth century. Both male and female athletes felt intense pressure from sports institutions throughout this period to keep their same-sex attractions a secret, but sociologist Brian Pronger points out a key difference between the experiences of sportsmen who were attracted to men and sportswomen who were attracted to women: "Women athletes are often expected to be lesbians; men athletes are seldom expected to be gay."[17]

Indeed, gay and bisexual women have, throughout the past century, often sought and found community within the world of sports in a way that gay and bisexual men rarely have, at least not until the advent of gay sports associations in the 1970s. Women's softball teams in 1950s America, for example, provided focal points for the formation of local lesbian subcultures as well as opportunities for women to meet one another. Historian Susan Cahn insists that, for many women in the middle of the twentieth century, "athletic life facilitated the individual process of coming to terms with homosexual desires," which made sports a central part of many women's experience of being gay.[18] Not until the 1970s, as the nascent gay rights movement empowered gay women and men to organize their own local sports teams where they could train and compete in an accepting environment, did significant numbers of gay men find a similar sense of community and support in the world of sports.

As both gay rights and women's sports gained broader acceptance in the United States over the course of the 1980s and 1990s, however, Cahn argues that concerns about lesbianism in women's sports actually increased rather decreased. Precisely because women's sports had such a strong—and, to many, worrisome—reputation for attracting lesbians, women's sports often amplified the pressure on their athletes and coaches to remain silent about their sexuality. The Ladies Professional Golf Association had grown so concerned about the ongoing rumors of widespread lesbianism among its players and spectators that it launched a flashy marketing campaign in 1989 to counteract them. Officials within American women's college sports proved similarly anxious about the public perception that athletics attracted lesbians in disproportionate numbers, perhaps because these officials feared losing recruits, fans, and funding, or perhaps simply because of their own ingrained homophobia. Penn State basketball coach Rene Portland, for example, enforced a "no lesbians" rule on her teams throughout her twenty-seven-year career from 1980 to 2007. Even the sport of tennis, which had pioneered athletic opportunities for women in the late nineteenth century and had fostered a reputation for sexual openness in the 1920s, proved unsympathetic to former champion Billie Jean King's revelation in 1981 that she had, while married to husband Larry King, had an affair with a woman. King resigned as president of the Women's Tennis Association, which she herself had founded in 1973, because of the negative publicity, and she lost a number of sponsorships and endorsements as well.[19]

In the same year as the King scandal, however, tennis player Martina Navratilova came out as a lesbian and faced less immediate backlash. *World Tennis* magazine actually reported receiving twice as many letters applauding Navratilova's courage and honesty as they did letters condemning her sexuality.[20] If Navratilova remained an isolated example in the 1980s, an increasing number of elite female athletes have come out as lesbian since the mid-1990s, most of them to little negative publicity. The golfer Muffin Spencer-Devlin came out in 1996, and the tennis player Amélie Mauresmo did so in 1999, losing none of her sponsors as a consequence. More recently, several female soccer players have revealed that they are gay, also to no significant negative reaction, including the German goalie Ursula Holl and the 2012 FIFA World Coach of the Year winner, Pia Sundhage. At the same time, though, female athletes and coaches clearly still feel pressure to remain circumspect about their sexuality. Of the 350 women's Division I basketball teams in the National Collegiate Athletic Association in 2011, only one had an openly lesbian coach, and the pressure magnifies on women who coach at the high school and youth sports levels. Moreover, the recent examples do not necessarily reflect a universal pattern, as the statements of the Nigerian national women's soccer coach, Eucharia Uche, illustrate. She told *The New York Times* just before the start of the 2011 women's World Cup that she had attempted to rid her players of lesbian behaviors.[21]

Men's sports have proven less hospitable throughout the twentieth century to athletes who express same-sex sexual attraction than women's sports have. Prior to the 1970s, historians can point to only a few cases, and "cases" is the operative word, since researchers have based their assumptions about these athletes' sexuality primarily on the arrest records, court proceedings, or violent incidents in which the athletes' sexual behavior was the central issue. American tennis player Bill Tilden, for example, who redefined the game in the 1920s, served two sentences in the late 1940s for having sex with teenage males. Both the tennis player Gottfried von Cramm, a three-time Wimbledon finalist in the 1930s, and the middle-distance runner Otto Peltzer, who held several world records in the 1920s, were arrested by Nazi authorities in the late 1930s for having violated the regime's strict prohibitions against homosexual actions or intimations. Cramm's family secured his release after seven months, but Peltzer served three different prison terms, spending the last four years of the war in the Mauthausen concentration camp. Although the American boxer Emile Griffith was never arrested, his sexuality was at the center of the notorious world welterweight championship bout in 1962 at which his opponent, Benny "the Kid" Paret, sustained fatal injuries. Griffith delivered twenty-nine consecutive unanswered punches to Paret in the twelfth round, a violent fury that press reports the next day attributed to fact that Paret had called Griffith a *maricón* ("faggot") at the weigh-in. All four cases illustrate the risks—or, in Griffith's case, the shame—that have attended even the suspicion of same-sex sexual attraction in German and American society in the twentieth century in general, let alone within these men's respective sports. Historians should exercise caution, however, in ascribing contemporary identities to these athletes, as gay or bisexual, which the athletes themselves might not have claimed.

As the notion of a gay identity has established itself in Europe and North America since the late 1960s, though, a number of male athletes have come out at the local, regional, and collegiate levels of sports, including youth leagues and high school teams. At the professional and elite levels, however, only a very few have come out, and they have almost always done so only after first retiring from the sport, as the former American football player Dave Kopay did in the mid-1970s and the former baseball player Glenn Burke did in 1980. With a very few notable exceptions, including the Welsh rugby player Gareth Thomas, the Australian rugby player Ian Roberts, and the British soccer player Justin Fashanu, however, almost no professional team athlete at the elite level in a major sport had come out during his career. In a September 2012 press conference, German Chancellor Angela Merkel even took the extraordinary action of encouraging gay male professional soccer players to come out in response to an earlier published interview with an anonymous Bundesliga player who spoke of his fear of publicly acknowledging his sexuality.[22] Even in men's figure skating, which one openly gay skating judge called "the gayest sport in America," most competitors wait until retirement before speaking openly about their sexuality, and not a single openly gay man competed in the 2006 Winter Olympics—not in singles, pairs, or ice dancing.[23]

One might possibly ascribe the historical absence of openly gay professional athletes to a reluctance on the part of sportsmen to discuss their sexuality in general, if it were not for the large number of male athletes who have explicitly proclaimed their heterosexuality in press conferences and interviews since the early 1990s. In one of the first such examples, basketball legend Earvin "Magic" Johnson, after announcing that he had contracted HIV in 1991, went out of his way to squelch potential gay rumors by emphasizing that he had contracted the virus through *heterosexual* promiscuity and noted that he had had sexual relations with around twenty-five hundred women. Other athletes have also publicly outed themselves as straight, including National Football League quarterbacks Troy Aikman, Kordell Stewart, and Jeff Garcia; the British heavyweight boxer Lennox Lewis; the Australian swimmer Ian Thorpe; and the Duke University basketball center and later National Basketball Association pro Christian Laettner. In one of the more remarkable instances, baseball player Mike Piazza announced in a 2002 press conference, "I'm not gay. I'm heterosexual," a statement apparently prompted by a *New York Post* report that a member of the Mets was about to announce his coming out. Indeed, elite athletes in recent years have also talked openly about their sexual escapades during the Olympic Games and about the fact that they do not have sex at all, as the public announcements by hurdler Lolo Jones and New York Jets quarterback Tim Tebow that they were virgins have demonstrated. Same-sex sexual attraction, with only a few exceptions, seems to have been the one topic that has not come up.

Brian Pronger, writing in 1990, ascribed this closeting pressure on elite male athletes, especially in team sports, to the homoerotic nature of the sports themselves. Because sports teams foster intense camaraderie and the enthusiastic appreciation of male physicality, the players' identities as both straight and masculine depends upon a universally enforced heterosexuality. Just as lesbian athletes often feel compelled to maintain a heterosexual facade so that the public will not see women's sports as too homosexual, Pronger suggests a similar dynamic at work in men's sports. Notwithstanding the decreasing levels of homophobia within men's professional team sports in the early 2000s, most male athletes still fear being publicly perceived as homosexual, as shown by the large numbers who out themselves as straight and the remarkably small numbers who do so as gay. Financial considerations have clearly played a role as well. As the National Football League agent Leigh Steinberg suggested in the late 1990s, it was "easier to win endorsement deals for an athlete who has committed a felony than for one who has committed fellatio."[24] As in women's sports, though, some recent examples in men's sports point to a gradually increasing tolerance of diverse sexual identities. Welsh rugby player Jed Hooper came out in 2011, and, in 2012, Puerto Rican featherweight Orlando Cruz became the first active prizefighter to do the same. Neither player received significant negative reaction from colleagues, fans, or sponsors.

The tentativeness toward homosexuality since the 1990s has contrasted with the dramatically sexual self-presentation of elite athletes in general during that very same time span. A brief survey of the sports scholarship between the mid-1990s and the mid-2000s has reflected the incredible pace of this change. Whereas Allen Guttmann complained in 1996 that society denied the erotic element in sports, Toby Miller was already, by 2001, cataloging the examples of individuals, teams, and entire sports leagues that had begun to market the sex appeal of athletic bodies. The following year, journalist Mark Simpson identified English soccer player David Beckham as the quintessential "metrosexual," Simpson's 1994 neologism for men who love to be looked at and therefore devote commensurate attention to their physical appearance. One could draw up an entire roster of elite male athletes who fell into that category, in fact, gracing the covers of fashion magazines, posing in underwear ads, and stripping for gay publications, including over half a dozen professional Brazilian soccer players who have posed nude for G Magazine. Financial incentives certainly explain this trend to some extent, but it also illustrates a change in cultural attitudes that have made it acceptable for men to want to be desired, with sportsmen leading the way. Referring to the eroticization of male athletes in 2006 as "sporno"—a portmanteau of "sports" and "pornography"—Simpson described the new generation of sports stars as "equal opportunity flirts," who "want to turn everyone on."[25]

A similar shift has occurred in women's sports in the same span of time. A long list of elite sportswomen have posed nude for Playboy since the late 1990s, for example, from figure skater Katarina Witt to boxer Mia St. John to swimmer Amanda Beard, and top female athletes began posing for Sports Illustrated's annual swimsuit issues in the 2000s. Moreover, nearly a dozen female athletes, along with a similar number of male ones, have posed annually in ESPN Magazine's "Body Issue." In many ways, this simply reflects a magnification of the pervading attitudes that have always existed toward sportswomen. Male fans and commentators, after all, have objectified female athletes since women first began competing in modern sports in the nineteenth century, making it all the more difficult for women to gain consideration and respect as serious competitors. Furthermore, as sociologist Jennifer Hargreaves has pointed out, what constitutes a sexualized display has varied over time and from culture to culture. Algerian heptathlete Yasmina Azzizi, for instance, had to endure shouts of "Whore" during her training sessions in the 1990s because her athletic uniforms violated the local norms of modesty.

Beginning in the 1990s, though, many female athletes seem to have become more comfortable marketing themselves in a sexualized manner similar to that of some of their male contemporaries. This might be due in part to the fact that women's sports had finally started in the 1990s to gain the respect in many parts of the world that it had long deserved. In addition, and perhaps more so than for the men, financial considerations have certainly fed this trend, since professional female athletes still earn much less than their male counterparts in nearly every sport. Furthermore, sportswomen have always had a more difficult time than men in attracting attention to themselves in the first place, a fact that has contributed to decisions like that of high jumper Amy Acuff to produce and market a calendar of seminude women's track and field athletes in 2000.

Given this increasingly open and exuberant eroticization of athletes in recent decades, one might be tempted to see the history of sports and sexuality as having come full circle over the past three thousand years. Indeed, scholars such as David Coad have pointed to similarities between the sexual atmosphere of sports today and that of classical antiquity.[26] Thomas Scanlon sees these similarities too, but he also cautions against carrying the comparison too far. Our modern categories of sexuality differ markedly from those of the Greeks, for instance, and today's athletics are also almost entirely secular. "The openly institutionalized Greek nexus of upbringing, athletics, religion, and Eros is alien to modern culture," Scanlon writes, "even though scholars of today's phenomena can usefully uncover less explicit and less formalized interconnections."[27] Moreover, female athletes and women's sports play a much more prominent and public role in today's world than they seem to have in ancient Greece, including Sparta.

The limited resemblances between our contemporary age and the ancient past do, however, suggest a deep-seated, possibly inherent connection between sports and sexual expression over time and possibly even space. Athletic practices that seek to deny sexuality altogether, such as Indian wrestling, with its strict demands of celibacy in thought and deed, are, in the act of articulating that denial, making human sexuality the very centerpiece of those sports. Viewed in this light, Edward Thring and Thomas Wentworth Higginson, in their vocal, Victorian-era promotion of athletics as an antidote to sexual activity, may have done more to sexualize sports than female Jell-O wrestling and David Beckham combined. Abstinence too—whether during training, competition, or as a central element of the athletic practice—has a long history in sports, but it is still an aspect of sexuality.

NOTES

1. Allen Guttmann, *The Erotic in Sports* (New York: Columbia University Press, 1996), 10.
2. I extend my heartfelt thanks to the following people for their generous advice and assistance in helping me to complete this article: Stephen Kidd, Ron Becker, Mark Sedway, Aaron Miller, Jean Williams, Veronika Springmann, Denise McCoskey, and Jeff Bowman.
3. K. J. Dover, *Greek Homosexuality* (Cambridge, MA: Harvard University Press, 1978), 54–55; quoted in Guttmann, *The Erotic in Sports*, 18.
4. Thomas Scanlon, *Eros and Greek Athletics* (New York: Oxford University Press, 2002), 214.
5. Quoted in Elizabeth Abbott, *A History of Celibacy* (New York: Scribner, 2000), 209.

6. Athenaios, (XIII. 566E), quoted in Paul Cartledge, "Spartan Wives: Liberation or License?" *The Classical Quarterly* 31.1 (1981): 91, n.43.

7. Quoted in Mary Carmichael, "No Sex, Please, We're Soccer Players," Thedailybeast.com, June 11, 2010.

8. Propertius, *The Poems of Propertius*, trans. John Warden (Indianapolis: Bobbs-Merrill, 1972), 166–167; quoted in Guttmann, *The Erotic in Sports*, 30.

9. Ovid, *Amores* 3.2, 29–30.

10. Étienne de Fougères, *Livre des Manières*. Saher Amer (*Crossing Borders: Love Between Women in Medieval French and Arabic Literature* [Philadelphia: University of Pennsylvania Press, 2008]) argues that Fougères may have drawn his ideas on female homosexuality from earlier Arabic texts.

11. Petr Roubal, "Politics of Gymnastics: Mass Gymnastic Displays under Communism in Central and Eastern Europe," *Body & Society* 9.2 (2003): 5.

12. Christine Herrick, "Women in Athletics: The Athletic Girl Not Unfeminine," *Outing* 40 (September 1902): 714–720; quoted in Susan Cahn, *Coming on Strong: Gender and Sexuality in Twentieth-Century Women's Sport* (New York: Free Press, 1994), 288, n.53.

13. Pierre de Coubertin, "De la volupté sportive" (1913); quoted in Guttmann, *The Erotic in Sports*, 6.

14. Erica Childs, "Images of the Black Athlete: Intersection of Race, Sexuality, and Sports," *Journal of African American Men* 4.2 (1999): 24.

15. Jack Dempsey, a 1921 interview by Djuna Barnes, in *I Could Never Be Lonely Without a Husband: Interviews by Djuna Barnes*, ed. Alyce Barry (London: Virago, 1987), 284.

16. Atina Grossmann, *Reforming Sex: The German Movement for Birth Control and Abortion Reform, 1920–1950* (New York: Oxford University Press, 1997), 127–128.

17. Brian Pronger, *The Arena of Masculinity: Sports, Homosexuality, and the Meaning of Sex* (New York: St. Martin's Press, 1990), xi.

18. Cahn, *Coming on Strong*, 185.

19. Jennifer Hargreaves (*Heroines of Sport: The Politics of Difference and Identity* [New York: Routledge, 2000], 147) estimates that King lost $1.5 million in endorsements and sponsorships over the subsequent three years.

20. Hargreaves, *Heroines*, 148.

21. Jeré Longman, "In African Women's Soccer, Homophobia Remains an Obstacle," *The New York Times*, June 21, 2011.

22. For the interview with the anonymous player, see Adrian Bechtold, "Ein Mann, den es Eigentlich nicht gibt: Gespräch mit einem Schwulen Fussballbundesligaspieler," *Fluter: Magazin der Bundeszentrale für Politische Bildung*, September 11, 2012.

23. Lorrie Kim, "Gayest Sport in America: So How Come No Figure Skaters Are Out?" Outsports.com, February 9, 2006.

24. Quoted in Toby Miller, *Sportsex* (Philadelphia: Temple University Press, 2001), 68.

25. Mark Simpson, "Sporno," *Out* (July 2006): 46.

26. Coad points to the contrast that Guttmann drew in his 1996 book, *The Erotic in Sports*, between the open celebration of erotics in ancient Greek sports and its denial in contemporary sports and then states that he will extend "the research of Guttmann by demonstrating how metrosexuality is contributing toward making sports erotics normal again." David Coad, *The Metrosexual: Gender, Sexuality, and Sport* (Albany: State University of New York Press, 2008), 143.

27. Scanlon, *Eros and Greek Athletics*, 333.

BIBLIOGRAPHY

Abbott, Elizabeth. *A History of Celibacy*. New York: Scribner, 2000.

Alipour, Sam. "Will You Still Medal in the Morning?" *ESPN the Magazine*, July 23, 2012.

Alter, Joseph S. *The Wrestler's Body: Identity and Ideology in North India*. Berkeley: University of California Press, 1992.

Anderson, Eric. "Masculinities and Sexualities in Sport and Physical Cultures: Three Decades of Evolving Research." *Journal of Homosexuality* 58.5 (2011): 565–578.

Anderson, Eric, and Jenny Hargreaves, eds. *Routledge Handbook of Sport, Gender and Sexuality*. New York: Routledge, 2013.

Cahn, Susan. *Coming on Strong: Gender and Sexuality in Twentieth-Century Women's Sport*. New York: Free Press, 1994.

Cartledge, Paul. "Spartan Wives: Liberation or License?" *The Classical Quarterly* 31.1 (1981): 84–105.

Childs, Erica. "Images of the Black Athlete: Intersection of Race, Sexuality, and Sports." *Journal of African American Men* 4.2 (1999): 19–38.

Christesen, Paul. *Sport and Democracy in the Ancient and Modern Worlds*. New York: Cambridge University Press, 2012.

Coad, David. *The Metrosexual: Gender, Sexuality, and Sport*. Albany: State University of New York Press, 2008.

Deford, Frank. *Big Bill Tilden: The Triumphs and the Tragedy*. New York: Simon & Schuster, 1976.

Enke, Anne. *Finding the Movement: Sexuality, Contested Space, and Feminist Activism*. Durham, NC: Duke University Press, 2007.

Faderman, Lillian. *Odd Girls and Twilight Lovers: A History of Lesbian Life in Twentieth-Century*. New York: Columbia University Press, 1991.

Fisher, Marshall Jon. *Terrible Splendor: Three Extraordinary Men, a World Poised for War, and the Greatest Tennis Match Ever Played*. New York: Crown, 2009.

Fredrick, David, ed. *The Roman Gaze: Vision, Power and the Body*. Baltimore, MD: Johns Hopkins University Press, 2002.

Gumbrecht, Hans Ulrich. *In Praise of Athletic Beauty*. Cambridge, MA: Belknap Press, 2006.

Guttmann, Allen. *The Erotic in Sports*. New York: Columbia University Press, 1996.

Hargreaves, Jennifer. *Heroines of Sport: The Politics of Difference and Identity*. New York: Routledge, 2000.

Jensen, Erik N. *Body by Weimar: Athletes, Gender, and German Modernity*. New York: Oxford University Press, 2010.

Joo, Rachael Miyung. *Transnational Sport: Gender, Media, and Global Korea*. Durham, NC: Duke University Press, 2012.

Kasson, John. *Houdini, Tarzan, and the Perfect Man: The White Male Body and the Challenge of Modernity*. New York: Hill and Wang, 2002.

Kim, Lorrie. "Gayest Sport in America: So How Come No Figure Skaters Are Out?" Outsports. com, February 9, 2006.

Kopay, David. *The David Kopay Story: The Coming-Out Story that Made Football History*. Los Angeles: Advocate Books, 2001.

McCullough, Anna. "Female Gladiators in Imperial Rome: Literary Context and Historical Fact." *The Classical World* 101.2 (2008): 197–209.

Messner, Michael. "AIDS, Homophobia, and Sports." In *Sex, Violence and Power in Sports: Rethinking Masculinity*, edited by Michael Messner and Donald Sabo. Freedom, CA: Crossing Press, 1994.

Messner, Michael. *Power at Play: Sports and the Problem of Masculinity*. Boston: Beacon Press, 1992.

Miller, Toby. *Sportsex*. Philadelphia: Temple University Press, 2001.

Nash, Bruce, and Allan Zullo. *The Baseball Hall of Shame*. New York: Pocket Books, 1985.

Pears, Tim. "Otto the Strange: The Champion Who Defied the Nazis." *The Observer*, June 29, 2008.

Pronger, Brian. *The Arena of Masculinity: Sports, Homosexuality, and the Meaning of Sex*. New York: St. Martin's Press, 1990.

Putney, Clifford. *Muscular Christianity: Manhood and Sports in Protestant America, 1880–1920*. Cambridge, MA: Harvard University Press, 2001.

Runstedtler, Theresa. *Jack Johnson, Rebel Sojourner: Boxing in the Shadow of the Global Color Line*. Berkeley: University of California Press, 2012.

Scanlon, Thomas. *Eros and Greek Athletics*. New York: Oxford University Press, 2002.

Scullard, Howard Hayes. *From Gracchi to Nero: A History of Rome from 133 b.c. to a.d. 68*. London: Methuen, 1959.

Simpson, Mark. "Meet the Metrosexual." Salon.com, July 22, 2002.

Simpson, Mark. "Sporno." *Out* (July 2006): 44–49.

Smith, Earl, and Angela J. Hattery. "Hey Stud: Race, Sex, and Sports." *Sexuality & Culture* 10.2 (2006): 3–32.

Smith, Gary. "The Shadow Boxer." SI.com, April 18, 2005.

Wedemeyer, Bernd. *Starke Männer, starke Frauen. Eine Kulturgeschichte des Bodybuildings*. Munich: C. H. Beck, 1996.

Winner, David. *Those Feet: A Sensual History of English Football*. London: Bloomsbury, 2005.

Wolf, Sherry. "America's Deepest Closet." *The Nation*, July 27, 2011.

INDEX

Qandil, Mohamed Al-Mansi, 296
qigong, 252
queer studies, 453
Quiksilver, 230

Raab, Alon, 297
race and racism, 461–71. *See also* ethnicity, and
    ancient sport
  in Australasia, 384
  in baseball, 200, 201–2, 203
  and Berlin Olympic Games, 31–32
  class and, 440
  and competitive success, 71
  and Cuban baseball, 368
  and eastern European sport, 329
  and football in Latin America, 364
  and history of sport and religion, 493–94
  and sexuality in sport, 530–31
  and sport in Latin America, 364, 366–67
Racing Calendar, 159
radio, 165, 167–68, 439, 480
Rail, Geneviève, 53
railroads, 162
Rand, Mary, 513
Ranji, 260, 261
Ranjitsinhji, K. S., 260, 261
Ranjitsinhji, Prince, 174
rationality and rationalization, 16–17, 47,
    48, 134
Real Madrid, 351, 352, 353
records, mania for, 134, 135
Recreativo de Huelva, 348
Red Sport International, 320
reformers, urban, 148
Reform Movement, 152–53
religion
  approaches to, in religious studies, 496–500
  and early modern sport, 115–16
  and football in Middle East, 298
  and sport in United States and Britain,
    491–503
  and sport through embodiment, 501–3
Renaissance, 113–14, 117, 121–22
Ren Hai, 242–43
Renneker, Mark, 234

*Representing the Sporting Past in Museums and
    Halls of Fame* (Phillips), 386
Revue des deux mondes (Jusserand), 107
Richards, Sir Viv, 467
Rickard, Tex, 165–66
Rickey, Branch, 466, 517–18
Riefenstahl, Leni, 68, 168, 512, 517, 531
Rielly, Derek, 230
Riess, Steven, 147, 148, 150, 151
Rigby, Peter, 230
Rio de Janeiro, Brazil, 406
Riordan, James, 326–27
riots, 437
Ritual to Record (Guttmann), 79
River Plate, 437–38
Roberts, Michael, 264
Robinson, Jackie, 466, 517–18
Roche, Maurice, 497
Rodriguez, Luis Orlando, 204
Rogan, Eugene, 294
Rogge, Jacques, 403–4, 406, 407–8
Rolph-Trouillot, Michel, 56
Roman Catholic Church, 491–92, 502
Roman Empire
  ancient sport and ethnicity in, 83
  breakdown of, 102–3
  Christianization of, 502
  as cradle of sport, 6
  gladiators, 89, 90–91, 103, 528
  Greek sport at, 91–92
  mass spectatorship in, 92
  Olympia under, 92–93
  and sexuality in sport, 527–28
  spectacles in, 88–89, 103
  sport facilities in, 89–90
  sport scholarship on, 80
Romania, 326
Rong Guotuan, 247, 248
Roosevelt, Theodore, 165
Rose, Gillian, 511
Rose, Jalen, 440
Rose, Ralph, 484
Rothman, Makua, 232
Roubal, Petr, 529
Ruck, Rob, 176, 177, 310
rugby, 72, 275, 308, 382, 431

CPSIA information can be obtained
at www.ICGtesting.com
Printed in the USA
BVHW082226200520
579770BV00004BA/6

9 780197 520956